The Grammar of Modern Hebrew

The grammar of Modern Hebrew

LEWIS GLINERT
Department of the Near and Middle East
School of Oriental and African Studies,
University of London

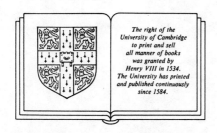

The right of the
University of Cambridge
to print and sell
all manner of books
was granted by
Henry VIII in 1534.
The University has printed
and published continuously
since 1584.

CAMBRIDGE UNIVERSITY PRESS

CAMBRIDGE

NEW YORK   PORT CHESTER   MELBOURNE   SYDNEY

Published by the Press Syndicate of the University of Cambridge
The Pitt Building, Trumpington Street, Cambridge CB2 1RP
32 East 57th Street, New York, NY 10022, USA
10 Stamford Road, Oakleigh, Melbourne 3166, Australia

First published 1989

Printed in the United States of America

Library of Congress Cataloging in Publication Data
Glinert, Lewis.
The grammar of Modern Hebrew.
Bibliography:
1. Hebrew language – Grammar – 1950–
I. Title
PJ4564.G68   1989   492.4'5   87-10265

British Library Cataloging in Publication Data
Glinert, Lewis
The grammar of Modern Hebrew.
I. Hebrew language – Grammar
I. Title
492.4'82421   PJ4564

ISBN 0-521-25611-9 hard covers

FOR
YOSIF B., YULY E. and ROALD Z.

'Thine is not to finish the work, but neither art thou free to desist from it.'

Talmud, Avot

Contents

Preface

This volume was written with two kinds of reader in mind: the advanced student of Modern (and, specifically, Israeli) Hebrew who knows next to no linguistics, and the general linguist who knows no Hebrew. No contradiction this: by use of notes and word-for-word glosses, and by infinite effort at avoiding needless abstraction, I hope to have made it possible for each to use this book without tripping over the other's feet.

This is a work of reference. It is tightly packed and arranged to be digested a little at a time rather than read through rapidly.

Anyone attempting an 'objective' and comprehensive description of contemporary Hebrew (and there have been too few) is liable to be accused of debasing the purity of the language and even of distorting reality. 'It is newly reborn', one is informed, 'It has not yet settled down'. But ten years' fieldwork and theorizing tell me that is just not so. Infinite sociolinguistic and personal variation there is in any language; but that still leaves a wealth of sharp features to describe and explain. And in my love for the Hebrew language as medium of a people's life-force, rooted in revered sources but never ceasing to change through sheer vitality and use, I have wished to see it set out in all its new glory – the only known case of a mother tongue reborn.

My thanks go to Professors Moshe Chayen, Robert Hetzron and Chaim Rabin for their painstaking comments and criticisms; to Penny Carter of Cambridge University Press for the wondrous gift of patience; to the School of Oriental and African Studies for the typing services of Denise Long and her colleagues; and to the irrepressible candour of my beloved informants: Avraham Beeri, Amram Ben-Sher, Dorit Ben-Dror, Yaakov Carmel, Eliezer Don-Yehiya, Avi Felber, Michael and Rachel Gruenzweig, Uri Karmazin, Batsheva Koren, Liora Koppelman, Meir and Rachel Lifshitz, Mordechai Omer, Shula Papkin, Orli Pen, Merav Raviv, Yosef Shilhav, Orli Taffel, Hila Yehieli and Esther Zucker.

But, above all, I thank my wife Joannie.

Abbreviations and conventions

The following abbreviations are used:

ADJ	adjective	N	noun
ADV	adverb	NEG	negator
C	casual usage	OBJ	object
CONJ	conjunction	OM	object marker
COP	copula	PART	participle
DEF	definite	pl.	plural
DET	determiner	PRED	predicate
DIR	direct	PREP	preposition
EMPH	emphatic particle	PRES	present
F	formal usage	Q	question
f.	feminine	QUANT	quantifier
FUT	future	REL	relative
IMP	imperative	s.	singular
IND	indirect	SUBJ	subject
INDEF	indefinite	SUBORD	subordinate
INF	infinitive, infinitival	SUFF	suffix
INTERROG	interrogative	V	verb
m.	masculine		

*   before an example indicates 'unacceptable'
?   before an example indicates 'questionable'
( ) within an example indicates an optional item, e.g.:

         (ha-)baaya (ha-)zot   (ה)בעיה (ה)זאת

A hyphen in a transcription indicates that in the Hebrew the corresponding word is written as one word (as in the preceding example).
The format indicating optional alternatives is:

      baaya   zo   'problem this'   בעיה זו
             zot   זאת

Certain conventions reduce the need for a separate translation and word-by-word gloss: [= . . .] helps elucidate the real meaning of a word-by-word gloss, as in example (1) below; ⟨   ⟩ in a translation indicates words not present in the Hebrew that must be supplied in the English, as in (2); and bold face in a

Hebrew example and in its translation or gloss is frequently employed to draw attention to the point of the example, as in (3).

(1) ha-baaya ha-zot...   הבעיה הזאת...
     the problem the this [= this problem]...

(2) ha-baaya kasha   הבעיה קשה
                                                   'The problem ⟨is⟩ difficult'

(3) ha-baaya **kasha**   הבעיה **קשה**
                                                   'The problem ⟨is⟩ **difficult**'

1. About Israeli Hebrew

1.1 The status of Israeli Hebrew

This volume deals with Israeli Hebrew, commonly known today as 'Modern Hebrew'. Hebrew ('Ivrit') is the national spoken and written tongue of the Jewish majority in the State of Israel.

Of a total population of more than four million as of 1986, the Jewish population is some three-and-a-half million, of whom the two million Israeli-born Jews ('Sabras'), and probably many more, have Hebrew as their mother tongue Indeed, according to 1983 figures, 42% of Israeli Jews aged 15+ know *only* Hebrew and 83% use it as their main language (such census figures, of course, report what people *say* that they do). Israel's Arab citizens use Hebrew for day-to-day contact with Hebrew speakers (32% of non-Jews aged 15+ can speak it), but otherwise employ Arabic. Literary Arabic is itself an official language in Israel. In addition, at least 380,000 Israelis are conservatively estimated to be residing abroad. Although it is true that of some 10-11 million other Jews around the world few could claim mastery of spoken or written Hebrew, whether actively or passively, it is studied widely, in either its modern or its older form.

Hebrew functions in all realms and levels of usage - from small talk to poetry, in science and in sport. Nearly all Israeli Jews can read and write Hebrew; indeed, in 1972 70% reported that the last book they read was in Hebrew, while 75% of conversations recorded in a Jerusalem street were in Hebrew. Several Israeli authors have been widely translated.

Equally important, since the 1890s Hebrew has been, and remains, a main plank in Zionist and Israeli ideology and society - both symbol and agent of the Ingathering of the Exiles and 'normalization' of Jewish national life, echo of the Biblical past, substitute for the Yiddish, Judeo-Arabic, Judeo-Spanish and other Jewish and non-Jewish languages of the Diaspora, and vehicle of modernism.

FURTHER READING
Bachi & Schmelz 1974; Bentolila 1983; Cooper 1984; Hofman & Fisherman 1972; Nadel & Fishman 1975; Rabin 1983; Schmelz 1984; Schmelz 1987: 57-60; Statistical Abstracts of Israel 1984.

1.2 Classical, Modern, and Israeli Hebrew

Israeli Hebrew is the latest stage in Hebrew's 3000 and more years of attested evolution - through all its Biblical, post-Biblical and diaspora varieties, though it ceased to be spoken by the second or third century. There ensued some 1700 years during which it was in many periods and places the educated Jew's main written language (but apparently never a mother tongue) - in poetry, religious and profane, in philosophy, in popular scriptural commentaries, business, law, medicine and science, evolving variously while forever harking back to ancient texts. All of this was largely in the framework of Judaism, but of course Judaism is bound up with the technicalities and language of everyday living.

Eastern Europe in the mid-nineteenth century witnessed the secularization of Hebrew and the emergence of such genres as newspapers, novels and educational non-fiction, with diametric trends in Hebrew semantics, grammar and style - towards a scriptural purism or towards Europeanization and mass coinage This, already, was *Modern Hebrew*, a new set of variations on the ancient tongue, rather than a different language as in Modern vs. Old English.

The end of the century saw the rapid eclipse of written Hebrew by European languages, yet by a supreme irony it re-emerged as a spoken native tongue in Ottoman Palestine - a form of popular written Hebrew used on schoolchildren as a chaotically experimental language of instruction, then picked up by their parents and siblings in the space of one generation, born of revolutionary nationalism and traditionalist love of Zion.

The Balfour Declaration (1917) and Britain's award of official status to Hebrew secured its place as a spoken vernacular and as an all-purpose written medium. By high-pressure innovation and historical restoration (here the lexicographer Ben Yehuda should be mentioned), by the prescriptive efforts of individuals and organizations such as the Israel Defence Forces and the Hebrew Language Academy, and above all by popular conformity and sheer intensive use, Hebrew has now evolved into a cohesive, standardized Israeli Hebrew, with its own distinctive pronunciation, grammar, syntax, and lexicon, at all levels of usage - but still recognizably a direct outgrowth of the previous stage of Hebrew. Moreover, with the destruction of Jewish traditional culture in Europe and Moslem lands, and Israel's new centrality to world Jewish life, Israeli Hebrew now stands alone as virtually the only actively written Hebrew and has outstripped traditional pronunciations in prayer and study (though in Israel some 10% of schools uphold these traditions).

FURTHER READING
Bar-Adon 1975; Fellman 1973; Fishman & Fisherman 1975; Glinert 1983; Rabin 1974a; Rosén 1977.

1.3   Varieties

Given the multitude of mother tongues spoken by preceding generations, the Hebrew of native, and many non-native, Israelis is strikingly uniform within its dialects and other varieties of usage - and even across them.

1.3.1 Ethnolects and sociolects

Israeli Jews, even native-born, are commonly classed as being of Afro-Asian (dubbed 'Sephardi' or 'Oriental') and European-American ('Ashkenazi') background, the former probably in a slight and increasing majority - though considerable intermarriage makes the picture unclear. Many Sephardim are distinct in two or three consonants (indeed, very prominently so), in intonation, vocabulary and in some casual constructions (eg. ?מחר אבוא *avo maHar?* vs. ?מחר לבוא *lavo maHar?* 'Shall I come tomorrow?'); but *how* many Sephardim are involved is a matter for sorely needed research. 'Oriental' pronunciation, though widely considered historically more correct and used by many educated Sephardim, has in practice been generally stigmatized because it is typically spoken by the less-educated, lower-income Sephardim of Israel's 'development towns' and poor urban neighbourhoods; and where the two communities mix, this ethnolect has been publicly on the wane (though not necessarily so in private usage, despite the impression given by many Israeli linguists). However, in the development towns, which contain some 20% of the Jewish population and which are predominantly (75%) Sephardi, the picture is uncertain: their recent emergence as political power bases, coupled with general Sephardi self-assertion, could conceivably have significant consequences for the 'Oriental' ethnolect as a whole

Of any other sociolects or dialects that may exist, little has been established beyond the morphological differences in young children and lexical peculiarities in, for example, Jerusalem and Haifa; the substantial differences in, say, kibbutz or army vocabulary are largely a matter of 'register' (subject matter) - see 1.3.2.

FURTHER READING
Ben Zadok & Goldberg 1984; Bentolila 1983; Devens 1981.

1.3.2 Mediums, levels and registers

Israeli Hebrew as a whole has many (intersecting) varieties, involving pronunciation, lexis and grammar:

1. Speech and writing, the latter intrinsically more careful and explicit.
2. A scale of formality: elevated → formal ('cautious') → casual, in both speech and writing - though it is common to switch back and forth in the same discourse
3. A scale of education and status: university graduates → high school graduates → early school-leavers.
4. A multitude of 'registers' for various activities and roles, eg. law, religious study, sports commentaries, soldiering, bureaucracy, press reports, novels, children's poetry (in these, casual-level ephemeral jargon is to be termed 'slang'). Here a difference in grammar is often more one of stylistic preponderance than a simple presence or absence of a feature

1.4   Norms and normativism

In both written and spoken Hebrew there are *in practice* formal and casual educated 'norms', varieties that the broad public seeks to use For formal writing, this can be represented by business letters, newspaper features, technical articles; for formal speech, by media reports, lectures; for casual writing, by educated personal letters; for casual speech, by educated conversation on serious topics (the usage of humanities graduates may be particularly close to 'normative' Hebrew).

Examples: 'No one knows that you have this school here'

Formal writing:
ish eno yodéa ki   איש אינו יודע כי
yesh laHem kan bet-séfer ze   יש לכם כאן בית-ספר זה

Formal writing or speech:
ish eno yodéa she-yesh   איש אינו יודע שיש
laHem kan bet-séfer ze   לכם כאן בית-ספר זה

Casual writing or speech:
af eHad lo yodéa she-yesh   אף אחד לא יודע שיש
laHem kan et bet-ha-séfer ha-ze   לכם כאן את בית-הספר הזה

Casual speech:
af eHad lo yodéa she-yesh   אף אחד לא יודע שיש
laHem kan ta bet-séfer a-ze   לכם כאן ת' בית־ספר הזה

Be it noted that by 'educated norms' we mean the general usage of educated people, rather than what is designated 'educated' by educators.

Certain other varieties, eg. poetry and artistic prose, though admired, are beyond the active capability of the general public, and if used prosaically are deemed 'affected'. Others are considered uneducated ('substandard'), as in **השכונה הזאתי** *ha-shHuna ha-zóti* 'this' neighbourhood'.

Neither the gap between written and spoken, nor that between formal and casual usage, is anything approaching a diglossia; indeed, the usages shade into one another. The public tends to be only dimly aware of the norms it is using (see ch.2), but uses them quite confidently and uniformly, though keenly conscious, from its schooldays, of there being a somewhat different, quasi-official 'correct Hebrew' - normativists' Hebrew.

The rulings of Israeli purists ('normativists') on pronunciation, spelling, grammar, syntax and lexis are of some significance Invoking ancient sources and certain medieval and modern authors (rather than the usage of a present-day elite), the legally authoritative, if self-effacing, Hebrew Language Academy - and a number of vocal private grammarians, lexicographers and coinage committees - seek a 'compromise' revision of present-day norms, a kind of 'damage limitation'. The method is largely one of unsystematic tinkering, with scant consensus or even debate and little explanation of goals and criteria: much on pronunciation and spelling, less on lexis and morphology, and precious little on syntax.

The linguistic effect is mixed: pervasive in school-teaching, broadcasting (particularly news and advertising), *belles-lettres* and bureaucracy, moderate in general public and journalistic writing habits, and negligible in casual speech - although the educated tend to pay lip-service to normativism. But the net psychological effect is an insecure coyness about one's actual usage, felt notably among Hebrew teachers, and a dearth of hard research data, let alone any codification of actual norms - once the necessary resources are forthcoming.

FURTHER READING
Bahat & Ron 1960; Ben-Asher 1969; Blanc 1957a, 1968; Donag-Kinnarot 1978; Goshen-Gottstein 1969: 189ff; Landau 1970; Nahir 1978; Nir 1981; Rabin 1958, 1977, 1978, 1983; Rosén 1977; Sivan 1974.

2. The data

This is primarily a description of *educated Israeli Hebrew* grammar, with the emphasis on syntax. It is intended both for linguists and for Hebrew students, and should not be taken as a normative statement of how Hebrew ought to remain.

The description is based on acceptability judgments by a team of half-a-dozen informants, varying somewhat over the ten years of research. All were native-born Israelis, aged 16 to 50 (largely in their twenties and thirties), mostly with Ashkenazi pronunciation, mostly university-educated, and with equal numbers of men and women. All had to undergo gradual attunement to the task of sincerely stating their personal norms. The emphasis in choice of informants and test material was on educated norms (see 1.4, 3.3).

Through interviews (not questionnaires), informants heard or read utterances and had to judge acceptability in casual and formal speech and writing. Among equally acceptable forms, scales of preference were sometimes established. Elevated or uneducated usage too was noted, if it occurred. The utterances tested were sometimes prefabricated, sometimes elicited, and sometimes - particularly with formal constructions - derived from actual writings and speech. The small amount of linguistic research already available was also generally tested.

While a large stratified sample is highly desirable, the remarkable uniformity of informant judgments (in a multitude of matters never rote-taught in schools) gives hope that this study is representative of educated Israeli Hebrew. At the very least, it may yield a framework for detailed trial and refutation - and the funding cum manpower that such work would require. In any event, the drawbacks of relying on a corpus have been shown by Svartvik: the million-word Brown University corpus of American Printed English yielded just 32 cases of *need+not* and eleven of *dare+not*. Nor can a linguistic's introspection as native speaker suffice: over-exposure and prejudice in favour of one's own hypotheses are the dangers here. Questionnaires too, as Greenbaum has argued, are primarily of use for resolving difficult cases.

FURTHER READING
Greenbaum 1984: Svartvik 1968.

3. The description

3.1 Introduction

This book is first and foremost a syntax: it covers as much of sentence structure as space allows (though, regretfully, little of paragraph structure). If the impression is given that 'minor' constructions are crowding out all else, it is because traditional Hebrew syntax has chosen to focus on a very few phenomena and make them appear 'major'. Note that a truly comprehensive syntax would be very much larger.

Morphology is presented in brief and for convenience sake Much fuller (normative) lists of inflections are available in most Hebrew grammars.

3.2 Theoretical basis

The collection of data for this book is predicated on a generative theory of linguistic 'competence'. The description itself is set in a conventional generative mould but with transformational assumptions kept to a minimum. Overall, though, considerations of space have prevented us spelling out the detailed theoretical workings by which we arrived at our analyses; their rightful place is in learned journals. On the other hand, where they are of direct relevance as data, relatively technical phenomena are supplied in notes to each chapter, which are collected at the end of the volume

3.3 Describing varieties of Hebrew

Of the many varieties of Hebrew distinguished in 1.3, this study addresses itself to the standard varieties in most general use, i.e the speech and writing, formal and casual, of educated speakers of the 'prestige' sociolect, namely those with a non-Oriental pronunciation.

Formal and casual will be labelled as such; what is unlabelled is 'neutral', i.e what is in all-round use However, speakers frequently mix formal and casual; further research about, for example, כי *ki* in the sense of ש *she* 'that' (higher formal) and יש את *yesh et* 'there's' (lower-formal, casual) may justify further subdivisions.

Examples (from 'degree words'):

Formal:

ko 'so'   כה   kim'a 'a trifle'   קמעא

7

Casual:
nora 'very'   נורא   tip-tipa 'a bit'   טיפ-טיפה

Neutral:
me'od 'very'   מאד   yoter 'more'   יותר

We make little reference to poetry and other elevated writing, army or school usage, 'substandard' Hebrew and so on (elevated uses would include: interrogative -ה *ha-*, omission of את *et*, conversive -ו *va-*).

3.4 Format

All examples are given in (a) unpointed Hebrew, as in standard Israeli usage, (b) transcription, (c) usually, an English gloss, and (d), where helpful, a morpheme-by-morpheme gloss. The transcription is adjacent to the Hebrew, thus:

(b) ha-yéled ha-ze	(a) הילד הזה
(d) the boy the this	(c) 'this boy'

Within the running text, examples are given in the order: Hebrew, transcription, gloss, as in "Hebrew repeats the determiner הזה *ha-ze* 'this'."

3.5 References

References with each chapter are a guide to further reading or alternative analyses. Full details of the title of each reference are given in the final bibliography. Though frequently in disagreement with the works referred to (details of where and how are beyond the scope of this book), we cite them in acknowledgement of the stimulus they have given us.

4. Pronunciation and spelling

4.1 Pronunciation

The transcription reflects Israeli Hebrew slow speech. This has the sounds set out in the following tables (for convenience, the transcription is a compromise between phonemic and phonetic transcription).

4.1.1 Consonants

Letter	Usual transcription	Usual phonetic value[1]
א	'	[ʔ][2] (catch in the throat), zero
ב	b,v	[b] or [v], depending on the word
ג	g	[g]
ג׳	j	[ǧ]
ד	d	[d]
ה	h	[ʔ], [h],[3] zero
ו	v	[v]
ז	z	[z]
ז׳	zh	[ž]
ח	H	[x] (as in 'Bach'), [ḥ][4]
ט	t	[t]
י	y	[y][5]
כ	k,H	[k] or [x], depending on the word
ך	H	[x]
ל	l	[l] (clear, as in 'leaf')
מ,ם	m	[m]
נ,ן	n	[n]
ס	s	[s]
ע	'	[ʔ], zero, [ʕ][6]
פ	p,f	[p] or [f], depending on the word
ף	f	[f]
צ,ץ	ts	[c]
צ׳,ץ׳	tsh	[č]
ק	k	[k]
ר	r	[ʁ] (uvular, like German 'r'), [r][7]
ש	sh,s	[š], in some words [s]
ת	t	[t]

9

Notes:
1 Syllable-initial stops are moderately aspirated.
   Often there is regressive voicing assimilation in consonant sequences, as in דפוס [tfus], משדר [miždar].
2 Most commonly [ʔ] before a stressed vowel, hence ארעי *ara'i*. Elsewhere, it is commonly zero and is then not transcribed.
3 [ʔ] and [h], or a mix of both, may be equally common pronunciations. [ʔ] becomes zero as in note 2.
4 Pharyngal [ḥ] is a distinctive characteristic of many Sephardim, especially of Yemenite or Moroccan background. In mixed communities it is generally used intermittently or not at all.
5 [yi] is commonly pronounced [i].
6 The pharyngal glide [ʕ] has the same social features as [ḥ], but is further restricted: it generally only comes before a stressed vowel. It often has an *a*-like quality, so עי sounds much like [aɛc].
7 The tongue-tip [r] is common only among Israelis of Yemenite descent.

4.1.2 Vowels

Letter	Usual transcription	Usual phonetic values
י	i ('beat, bit')	[i], sometimes [ɪ] if unstressed
-	e ('bet')	[ɛ]
-	a (American 'car')	[a]¹, sometimes [ʌ] if unstressed
ו	o (between British 'not' and 'nought')	[o], sometimes [ɔ] if unstressed
ו	u ('pull')	[u]
-	e (between 'bet' and 'bit')	[ᵉ]²
In combination with [y] to form diphthongs:		
י	ey ('bay')	[ɛy]
י	ay ('buy')	[ay]
וי	oy ('boy')	[oy]
וי	uy	[uy]

Notes:
1 Some speakers have [α] to replace an adjoining [ʕ], e.g. טעם [taám], מעיין [mayan].
2 Vowel length: vowels are shorter when unstressed or in closed syllables. [ᵉ] is especially short. In homorganic consonant clusters or those beginning with a sonorant, [ᵉ] is generally audible, e.g. מלאה, שזיפים [šᵉzifim], [mᵉlea]; in others it is barely audible, e.g. זוועה [zvaʔa], not [zᵉvaʔa].

4.1.3 Prosody

Word stress is on the last syllable, unless specifically transcribed with an acute accent. It is occasionally phonemic, e.g. טעם ~ טעם *taám* ~ *táam* 'tasted ~ taste'.

Sentence stress and intonation are not generally indicated ('Ashkenazi' and 'Oriental' intonation differ somewhat).

4.1.4 Fast speech

Fast speech is not reflected in the transcription. It is characterized by shift and weakening of stress, and consequent weakening or loss of vowels, notably: (1) laxing and centralization of all vowels but [u], e.g. בשביל, עכשיו [bɪšvɪl, ʌxšav]; sometimes leading to (2) neutralization as [ə], e.g. לעבוד עם [laavodəm], אבל [əval]; or (3) its loss, e.g. של, ששים [šḷ, ššim]. The whole syllable may even drop, especially (4) in affixes, e.g. נותנת, הוא מלמד [notent, humlamed]; and (5) in unstressed words such as עכשיו [xšav]; and (6) with consecutive vowels, e.g. להם [laɛm → lɛm], מישהו [míšu].

In fast speech, (7) the palatals [y, š] can raise [ɛ] to [i], e.g. יש, שהוא (šɪu, ɪš); and (8) word stress may shift for rhythm, e.g. אמר לנו is [amárlanú] instead of slow [amár lánu].

4.1.5 Phonotactics

Hebrew has a 4 x 4 obstruent system:

pf ts čš kx
bv dz ǧž gʁ

and in addition: c m n l y h ʔ.

4.2 Spelling

This book uses official Israeli spelling, as authorized by the Hebrew Language Academy for unpointed texts. Note that many publishers, schools and members of the public vary in their use of the vowel letters י, ו. ('Pointing', involving 14 signs for the six vowels, plus other signs, is not in general use.)

FURTHER READING
Blanc 1957b, 1964; Bolozky 1977, 1982, forthcoming; Chayen 1973; Devens 1978, 1980, 1981; Enoch & Kaplan 1969; Laufer 1974, 1976; Morag 1973; Ornan 1973; Rabin 1940; Schwarzwald 1972, 1981a; Semiloff-Zelasko 1973; Těné 1962.

5. Definite and indefinite

5.1 Introduction: 'definite article' - ה ha- and 'definite object marker' את et
The definite article is - ה ha-[1] 'the', written as a prefix to the follow-
ing word (as are all one-letter words)[2], e.g. הפיצה ha-pitsa 'the pizza'.
There is no indefinite article, thus:

ha-pitsa	הפיצה
	'the pizza'
pitsa	פיצה
	'a pizza'

But occasionally, with 'countable' nouns, the determiners איזה éze 'some' and
אחד eHad 'a certain' may be used to underscore the indefiniteness, איזה éze
in both singular and plural and אחד eHad just in the singular (see further 9.2,
under paragraphs (d) and (e)):

ani meHapes Haver	אני מחפש חבר
	'I'm looking for a friend'
	(a friend in general or a specific friend)
ani meHapes éze Haver / Haver eHad	אני מחפש איזה חבר / חבר אחד
	'I'm looking for some friend'

- ה ha- is sometimes optional and often impossible with *intrinsically* definite
nouns (e.g. names), thus (ה)שבת (ha-)shabat 'the Sabbath', דוד david 'David',
חברי Haveri 'my friend'.
    In association with - ה ha- one often finds את et, which introduces a 'definite
direct object':

Definite:
tavi li et ha-dag	תביא לי את הדג
bring me OM the fish	

tavi li et david	תביא לי את דוד
bring me OM David	

Indefinite:
tavi li dag	תביא לי דג
bring me fish	

את *et* is usually meaningless. It does not in itself express definiteness and is even omitted occasionally.[3] However, it sometimes serves as a superficial mark of grammatical definiteness where no other mark is evident (see further 5.3.4):

tavi et dov/dov	תביא את דוב/דוב
bring Dov/bear	'Bring Dov (a man's name)/a bear'
pitru nehagey éged	פיטרו נהגי אגד
they-fired drivers-of Eged	'They fired Eged (a bus company) drivers'
pitru **et** nehagey éged	פיטרו **את** נהגי אגד
they-fired OM drivers-of Eged	'They fired **the** Eged drivers'
ani oHel ha-kol	אני אוכל הכל
I eat the all	'I eat anything'
ani oHel et ha-kol	אני אוכל **את** הכל
I eat OM the all	'I eat everything (that's there)'

By making a noun 'definite' (by - ה *ha-*, את *et* or both), one informs the hearers that they know its identity. This usually means that it is a *specific* entity, e.g. 'the (specific) tiger'. But sometimes it means that it is instead 'generic', e.g. 'tigers in general', and in such cases the definite article is just one way of expressing it: הנמר *ha-namer* 'the tiger', נמרים *nemerim* 'tigers'. Section 5.2 discusses 'specific' - ה *ha-* 'the', 5.3 'specifics' with no - ה *ha*, and 5.4 'generic' - ה *ha-*.

5.2 Specific - ה *ha-* 'the'

5.2.1 Referring backwards or forwards

- ה *ha-* 'the' can hark back to a previous mention of (or allusion to) someone/something:

haya kontsert? eH haya **ha-**menatséaH?	היה קונצרט? איך היה **ה**מנצח?
	'There was a concert? How was **the** conductor?'

It can also anticipate the identification of someone/something by an adverbial, relative clause or other modifier that follows; compare 'non-identified idea' with 'identified idea':

heelu raayon she-hitsáti	העלו רעיון שהצעתי
they-raised ⟨an⟩ idea	'They raised an idea
that I-suggested	that I suggested'
heelu et **ha-**raayon she-hitsáti	העלו את **ה**רעיון שהצעתי
they-raised **the** idea that I-suggested	'They raised the idea that I suggested'

5.2.2 Specific to the circumstances

- ה *ha-* 'the' can be referring *out* to something implicit in the broader circumstances, e.g. someone who is visible or something that is well-known. Some such cases tend to have set rules, as in the following examples.

Unique to the world: העולם *ha-olam* 'the world', השמש *ha-shémesh* 'the sun', האדמה *ha-adama* 'the ground', הכוכבים *ha-koHavim* 'the stars' etc. The same holds for times of day, as in:

ba-páam she-avra azávti **ba**-bóker	בפעם שעברה עזבתי **ב**בוקר
	'Last time I left **in the** morning'

and similarly, ביום *ba-yom* 'by day', בצהריים *ba-tsohoráyim* 'at lunchtime', לפני החשיכה *lifney ha-HasheHa* 'before dark'...[4]

Unique to the locality: המשטרה *ha-mishtara* 'the (local) police', החוק *ha-Hok* 'the Law', העירייה *ha-iriya* 'the municipality', הממשלה *ha-memshala* 'the government', הארץ *ha-árets* 'Israel' (literally, 'the land'), הצפון *ha-tsafon* 'the north', בכיתה *ba-kita* 'in class', בגן *ba-gan* 'in kindergarten'[5] etc.

Certain unique personal possessions, for example:

nikit et ha-báyit?	ניקית את הבית?
	'Have you cleaned the [your, our] house?

ha-meHonit be-tikun	המכונית בתיקון
'The [my, our] car's being fixed'	

Parts of the body and clothes being worn: casually, הראש *ha-rosh* 'the head' and suchlike will denote 'my/your/his head' etc., referring back to a possessor in the sentence:

hu melakek et **ha**-sfatáyim	הוא מלקק את **השפתיים**
he's licking OM the lips	'He's licking his lips'

at oméret she-**ha**-rosh ko'ev	את אומרת ש**הראש** כואב
you say that **the** head hurts	'You say your head hurts'

lo orid et **ha**-kóva	לא אוריד את **הכובע**
not I'll-take-off OM **the** hat	'I won't take off my hat'

Casual Hebrew will even insert an anticipatory (pro)noun as part of a special dative ל- *le-* phrase (right after the verb), rather than add 'my/your' etc.:

masháHti **lo** et **ha**-Hultsa	משכתי **לו** את **ה**חולצה
I-pulled **to-him** OM **the** shirt	'I pulled his shirt'

nagáti **la ba**-yad	נגעתי **לה ב**יד
I-touched **to-her on-the** hand	'I touched her hand'

histakálti **le**-david yashar **ba**-eynáyim	הסתכלתי **ל**דוד ישר **ב**עיניים
I-looked **to** David straight **in-the** eyes	'I looked David straight in the eyes'

Formal usage prefers a possessive suffix rather than ה- *ha-* 'the' and dative ל- *le-* phrases:

lo asir et kova'**i**	לא אסיר את כובע**י**
	'I will not remove **my** hat'
nagáti be-yad**a**	נגעתי ביד**ה**
	'I touched **her** hand'

Kinship words: In casual Hebrew, ההורים *ha-horim* 'the parents', הבן *ha-ben* 'the son' etc. can in themselves indicate the parents, the son etc. of someone already mentioned in the sentence:[6]

yóram asa et ze biglal **ha-aH**	יורם עשה את זה בגלל האח
'Yoram did it because of **the** [=his] brother'	
od lo shamáti me-**ha**-horim	עוד לא שמעתי מההורים
'I still haven't heard from **the** [=my] parents'	
at shomáat me-**ha**-yeladim?	את שומעת מהילדים?
'Do you hear from **the** [=your] children?'	
ma shlom **ha**-isha?	מה שלום האשה?
'How's **the** wife?'	

5.3 Absence of -ה *ha-* 'the'

In many cases a noun is 'definite' without -ה *ha*, given the fact that it still requires the object marker את *et* (where appropriate); any accompanying adjectives will themselves take -ה *ha* (see 5.6). For example, note the name משה 'Moshe' (see further 5.3.2):

xibáknu et moshe **ha**-Hamud	חיבקנו **את** משה **ה**חמוד
we-hugged OM Moshe **the** little	'We hugged little Moshe'

In a handful of other cases, a noun refers to something 'definite' and yet is grammatically altogether 'non-definite' – there is no את *et* and no -ה *ha*-; for example (and see 5.3.1):

daHínu siba zo	דחינו סיבה זו
we-rejected reason this	'We rejected this reason'

The main cases are set out in 5.3.1 and 5.3.2.

5.3.1 With 'common nouns'

In 'definite' construct phrases (see ch. 6), though both components are usually felt to be 'definite', -ה *ha-* usually goes just with component B:

tsadim et nimrey **ha**-amakim	צדים את נמרי **ה**עמקים
they-hunt OM tigers-of the valleys	'They hunt the tigers of the valleys'
A B	

Furthermore, when a noun takes a pronoun ('possessive') suffix, creating a type of definite construct phrase in which component B is a *pronoun*, no -ה *ha-* at all is used:

tsadim et nimreyhem	צדים את נמריהם
they-hunt OM tigers-of-them	'They hunt their tigers'
A B	

In two types of apposition

In naming by number (see 36.4), using noun+numeral phrases such as דוגמה שש *dugma shesh* 'example six', עמודים ארבע-שבע *amudim arba-*

shéva 'pages 4-7' with the noun in 'absolute' (apposed) rather than construct form, there is no -ה *ha-* 'the' whatsoever - and yet these are 'definite', for they take the definite object marker את *et:*

hevánti et dugma shesh	הבנתי את דוגמה שש
I-understood OM example six	'I understood example six'

Secondly, in apposition of titles (36.5), several titles are definite without requiring -ה *ha-*: מר *mar* 'Mr', אדון *adon* 'Mr', גברת *gvéret* 'Ms', פרופסור *profesor* 'professor', ד"ר *dóktor* 'Dr', סמל *samal* 'Sergeant' and all military ranks, thus:

takir et adon levi	תכיר את אדון לוי
meet OM Mr Levi	'Meet Mr Levi'

All but מר *mar* 'Mr' (which is never used as an ordinary noun) can take -ה *ha-* 'the' very formally: הגברת מאיר *ha-gvéret me'ir* 'Mme Meir', האלוף הוד *ha-aluf hod* 'Brig. Hod'.

However, most titles *always* have -ה *ha-* (when 'definite'), e.g. המלך דוד *ha-méleH david* 'King David', השר לוי *ha-sar levi* 'Minister Levi', הרב יוסף *ha-rav yosef* 'Rabbi Yosef', ראש הממשלה בגין *rosh ha-memshala bégin* 'Prime Minister Begin'.

Semantically definite but grammatically indefinite

In many expressions and idioms one can choose to make a noun grammatically indefinite, giving it an abstract flavour, e.g. פתח רדיו *pataH rádyo* 'turn on ⟨the⟩ radio', שמע חדשות *shama Hadashot* 'hear ⟨the⟩ news', הרים ידיים *herim yadáyim* 'raise ⟨one's⟩ hands', שם חגורה *sam Hagora* 'put on ⟨one's⟩ belt', מכף רגל עד ראש *mi-kaf régel ad rosh* 'from head to foot', and, sometimes, פעם ראשונה *páam rishona* '⟨for the⟩ first time'.

With אותו *oto* 'that, the same' and (formally in the main) with זה *ze* 'this', a self-evidently 'definite' noun can optionally be treated as grammatically indefinite (see also 9.3):

hu lavash	et oto ha-svéder	את אותו הסוודר
	oto svéder	אותו סוודר
he wore	OM same the sweater	'He wore the same sweater'
	same sweater	

hu lavash	et ha-svéder ha-ze	את הסוודר הזה
	sveder ze	סוודר זה
he wore	OM the sweater the this	'He wore this sweater'
	sweater this	

5.3.2 With 'proper nouns'

Strictly 'proper' nouns rarely have -ה *ha-* 'the',[7] even when qualified by some other word:

shaláHti et moshe sheli		שלחתי את משה שלי
I-sent OM Moshe my		'I sent my Moshe'

tsarfat shel víshi		צרפת של וישי
France of Vichy		'Vichy France'

sára ha-shniya		שרה השנייה
Sara the other		'the other Sara'

yúni ha-ba		יוני הבא
June the next		'next June'

The names for days of the week are proper nouns and do not take -ה *ha-* 'the', despite having the outward appearance of noun+adjective:

be-yom shlishi ha-aHaron		ביום שלישי האחרון
on day third the last		'last Tuesday'

Indeed, their internal structure is that of a construct phrase:

tikaH et **yemey shlishi** ha-notarim		תקח את **ימי שלישי** הנותרים
take OM **days-of third** the remaining		'Take the remaining **Tuesdays**'

Other such items are (...כפור יום ,שבת) ערב *érev (shabat, yom kipur...)* 'the day before (the Sabbath, Yom Kipur...)', ...ליל *leyl...* 'the night of...' and מוצאי *motsa'ey* 'the night after...'.

Names of artistic works, and writers' names transferred to these works, are generally proper nouns:[8]

ra'íti et makbet		ראיתי את מקבת
		'I've seen Macbeth'

lamádeti et agnon		למדתי את עגנון
		'I was studying Agnon'

ani menagen et béthoven		אני מנגן את בייטהובן
		'I'm playing Beethoven'

A notable case of a word made into a name is the numeral, as in:

patárti et árba		פתרתי את ארבע
I've-solved OM four		'I've solved (number) four'

Certain 'uniques' (see 5.2) can be used as proper nouns, notably אלו-הים *elo-him* 'God':

Subject:		
elo-him soléaH	'God forgives'	אלו-הים סולח

Object:		
shibHu et **ha**-elo-him	'They praised God'	שיבחו את ה**אלו-הים**

On אבא *ába* 'father', אמא *íma* 'mother', סבא *sába* 'grandfather', סבתא *sávta* 'grandmother', see note 6.

Conversely, names can often be used as common nouns, in which case the definite form takes -ה *ha-* 'the' and the indefinite does not. For example, when referring to a whole family we might have:

ha-grínbergim ba'im	הגרינברגים באים
	'The Greenbergs are coming'

or, as a 'proper noun':

grínberg ba'im	גרינברג באים
s.	
Greenberg are-coming	'The Greenbergs are coming'

Referring to individuals called by a certain name:

shlosha grínberg(im)	שלושה גרינברג(ים)
pl. SUFF	'three Greenbergs'
sára aHéret	שרה אחרת
	'another Sara'
ha-sára ha-zot	השרה הזאת
the Sara the that	'that Sara'

However, for definite names with adjectives the proper noun is preferred to the common noun:

sára ha-shniya	שרה השנייה
Sara the other	'the other Sara'
*ha-sára ha-shniya	*השרה השנייה
the Sara the other	('the other Sara')

Referring to a type of person, we have:

hayu fróydim ve-yiyu fróydim	היו פרוידים ויהיו פרוידים
	'There have been Freuds and there will be Freuds'

Similarly, names of days of the week or festivals can be both proper and common nouns:[9]

Common noun	
Non-definite:	
bilíta **pésaH** be-yisrael?	בילית **פסח** ישראל?
	'Have you spent ⟨a⟩ **Passover** in Israel?'
Definite:	
bilíti et **ha-pésaH** ha-aHaron sham	ביליתי את **הפסח** האחרון שם
	'I spent **the** last **Passover** there'
Proper noun	
Definite:	
bilíta **et pésaH** be-yisrael?	בילית **את פסח** בישראל?
	'Did you spend **Passover** in Israel?'

The complication here is that these dates as proper nouns have two meanings: 'Passover' etc. in general or 'a particular Passover' etc. This stems from the nature of dates. Notice that את *et* is the crucial sign of a 'proper' or 'definite' noun; ה- *ha-* can be misleading: for example, the set expression ראש השנה *rosh ha-shana* 'the New Year' can be indefinite as well as definite (and similarly, days of the week, which have no ה- *ha-*):

bilíti **rosh ha-shana** eHad sham	ביליתי **ראש השנה** אחד שם
	'I spent a **New Year** there'

5.3.3 With pronouns: זה *ze* 'it', מי *mi* 'who?' etc.

'Definite' pronouns, like 'proper nouns', do not have ה- *ha-* 'the'.[10] But being definite, they take the definite object marker את *et*, and accompanying adjectives have ה- *ha-* (see 5.6):

ani maadif et **ze** ha-aHaron	אני מעדיף את **זה** האחרון
I prefer OM **it** the latter	'I prefer the latter one'

את *et* combined with the 'personal pronouns' for 'I, you, etc.' becomes אותי, אותך... *oti, otHa* etc. 'me, you etc.' (see 42.2.2).

Special note should be taken of the (apparently) semantically *indefinite* pronouns מי *mi* 'who?', מישהו *mishehu* 'someone', אחד *eHad* 'one', כל אחד *kol eHad* 'each one' and אף אחד *af eHad* 'no one'. The first is always *definite* grammatically:

et mi ata maashim?	**את** מי אתה מאשים?
OM who you blame?	'Whom do you blame?'

while the rest can optionally be definite *by association*, i.e. when referring implicitly to part of a 'definite' group:[11]

tsilámti (et) eHad mehem	צילמתי (את) אחד מהם
I-photographed (OM) one of-them	'I photographed one of them'

lo sha'álti (et) af eHad	לא שאלתי (את) אף אחד
not I-asked (OM) single one	'I didn't ask anyone [i.e. of them]'

5.3.4 Names that are common nouns

Names of products are common nouns, and can thus be used definitely or indefinitely:

matsáta nóga/et ha-nóga ?	מצאת נוגה/את הנוגה ?
	'Did you find a Noga/the Noga ?'
	[name of candy bar]

as against the proper noun:

matsáta et nóga?	מצאת את נוגה?
	'Did you find Noga?'
	[girl's name]

Names of prayers are usually indefinite:

gamru minHa ve-matHilim shma   גמרו מנחה ומתחילים שמע
                                          'They've finished Mincha and they're
                                          starting the Shema'

5.4 Generic: 'tigers'

The notion 'all tigers' leaves no doubt as to 'which tigers', so it is often treated as 'definite' and marked by -ה *ha-* 'the'. Thus ambiguity may arise:

ha-namer tsad ba-láyla   הנמר צד בלילה

$$\text{'The tiger} \begin{bmatrix} = \text{all tigers} \\ = \text{that tiger} \end{bmatrix} \text{hunts by night'}$$

In fact, there may be various ways of expressing 'generic', depending on the sort of noun.

The major distinction is between 'countable' and 'non-countable' nouns, as set out in the table:

COUNTABLE NOUNS		
Meaning of noun	'Generic' expressed by:	Examples
Species	s. DEF	ha-namer tsad · הנמר צד · 'The tiger hunts'
	pl. INDEF	ahávti nemerim · אהבתי נמרים · 'I liked tigers'
Social groups	s./pl. DEF	ha-hódi(m) HaHam(im) · ההודי(ם) חכמ(ים) · 'The Indian(s) is/are clever'
	pl. INDEF	ahávti hódim · אהבתי הודים · 'I liked Indians'
Institutions	s. INDEF[1] (sometimes)	hu sone bet-séfer · הוא שונא בית־ספר · 'He hates school'
Types of person	s./pl. DEF	taHshov al ha-ani(im) · תחשוב על העני(ים) · 'Think of the poor'
Times of day	s./pl. DEF	ba'im ba-bóker/bkarim · באים בבוקר/בבקרים · 'They come in the morning'
Sundry	pl. INDEF	térmosim asuyim zeHuHit · תרמוסים עשויים זכוכית · 'Thermoses are made of glass'
		anashim mitlonenim · אנשים מתלוננים · 'People complain'

		NON-COUNTABLE NOUNS	
Meaning of noun	'Generic' expressed by:	Examples	
Substances	S. INDEF	basar hu mazon bari	בשר הוא מזון בריא 'Meat is a healthy food'
		ani sone sukar	אני שונא סוכר 'I hate sugar'
	S. DEF (sometimes)[2]	hu gila et ha-Hankan	הוא גילה את החנקן 'He discovered nitrogen'
Qualities	S. DEF	ha-gaava mesukénet	הגאווה מסוכנת 'Pride is dangerous'
	S. INDEF	gaava doma le-kfira	גאווה דומה לכפירה 'Pride is like heresy'
Diseases	S. DEF[3]	ha-adémet nefotsa	האדמת נפוצה 'Rubella is common'
		mefaHadim me-ha-sartan	מפחדים מהסרטן 'They fear cancer'

Notes:

[1] Similarly, בית־חולים *bet-Holim* 'hospital', בית־סוהר *bet-sóhar* 'prison', בית־שימוש *bet-shimush* 'toilet'.

[2] Non-generically: הוא גילה חנקן *hu gila Hankan* 'he discovered *some* nitrogen'.

[3] Non-generically: קיבלתי אדמת *kibálti adémet* 'I got rubella'.

5.5 -ה *ha-* as 'this' and 'the chief'

With 'time nouns', *ha-* denotes 'this...', i.e. 'the current...' or the one belonging to 'today'. Examples (used mostly as adverbs): היום *ha-yom* 'today', הבוקר *ha-bóker* 'this morning', הערב *ha-érev* 'this evening', and similarly for לילה *láyla* 'night', שבוע *shavúa* 'week', חודש *Hódesh* 'month'. שנה *shana* 'year', רגע *réga* 'moment', פעם *páam* 'instance', עונה *ona* 'season', סמסטר *seméster* 'term', קייץ *káyits* 'summer' and so on.[12]

Stressed -ה *ha-* means 'the chief, the top...':

nirshámti le-**ha**-bet-séfer sham   נרשמתי לה**ה**בית־ספר שם
'I registered for **the top** school there'

For extra emphasis we may have:

ha-bet-séfer be-hey ha-yedia
the school with the definite article   הבית־ספר בה"א הידיעה
'*The* school'

These cases of -ה *ha-* are noteworthy for their syntax - see 5.6.

5.6   - ה *ha-*: where and how often?

The positioning of - ה *ha*

Where the nucleus of a phrase is 'definite', any adjectives,[13] nouns or determiners following as modifiers[14] must themselves be preceded by - ה *ha-*, but not preposition phrases and relative clauses[15] (see further, ch. 12). We therefore have הילד הפרוע *ha-yéled ha-parúa* 'the wild child', דוד הפרוע *david ha-parúa* 'wild David'; החבר העורך־דין *he-Haver ha-oreH-din* 'the lawyer friend'; חיים העורך־דין *Háyim ha-oreH-din* 'Chaim the lawyer'; הילד הזה *ha-yéled ha-ze* 'this child'; but we can *not* have: *הילד הברחוב *ha-yéled ha-ba-reHov* 'the child in the street; *הילד הראיתי *ha-yéled ha-ra'íti* 'the child I saw'.

Deletion of - ה *ha-*

So tightly does - ה *ha-* cohere with its noun etc. that it cannot be omitted to save repetition; therefore we have:

lishtof et **ha**-tsalaHot ve-**ha**-kearot?	לשטוף את הצלחות והקערות?
	'Shall I rinse **the** plates and bowls?'

knafav **ha**-dakot ve-**ha**-Halakot	כנפיו הדקות והחלקות
his wings the thin and the smooth	'his thin, smooth wings'

not:

*lishtof et ha-tsalaHot ve-kearot?	*לשטוף את הצלחות וקערות?
	(except as '...the plates and (any) bowls')

*knafav ha-dakot ve-Halakot	*כנפיו הדקות וחלקות

But note such set phrases as המשא ומתן *ha-masa u-matan* 'the negotiations', הדין וחשבון *ha-din ve-Heshbon* 'the report'.

Conflation of - ה *ha-*

Where the prepositions - ל, - כ, - ב *be-, ke-, le-* precede the definite article they conflate to give - ל, - כ, - ב *ba-, ka-, la-*:

ba-bots (*be-ha-bots)	בבוץ (*בהבוץ)
in-the mud	

Exceptions are as set out in (a) - (d):

(a) Common nouns acting as names, e.g. הארץ *ha-árets* (a newspaper), המשביר *ha-mashbir* (a store), הפועל *ha-po'el* (an organization):

ze haya be-ha-árets	'It was in Haaretz'	זה היה בהארץ

(b) - ה *ha-* as 'the chief', hence:

hu lamad be-ha-bet séfer	הוא למד בהבית־ספר
	'He studied in the top school'

(c) -ה *ha-* as 'this'; here conflation is just occasionally possible:

     gamárti le-ha-réga/le-ha-yom   גמרתי להרגע/להיום

           'I've finished for the moment/for today'

     gamárti   le-ha-shavúa   גמרתי להשבוע

                la-shavúa   לשבוע

           'I've finished for the week'

(d) -ה *ha-* in הכי *haHi* 'the most'. This is treated as a definite article in , e.g. הלחם הכי טוב *ha-léHem ha-Hi tov* (lit. the bread the most good) 'the best bread',[16] in the same way as it is in הללו *halálu* 'these', הלה *hala* 'the latter'; but there is no separate form כי *Hi* (or ללו *lálu,* לה *la*), nor is the -ה *ha-* in הכי *haHi* conflatable:

     ani mitkaven le-haHi tovim   אני מתכוון להכי טובים

      (*laHi tovim)   (*ללכי טובים)

           'I mean the best ones'

Similarly, very casual usage employs הכי *haHi* with an *indefinite* noun (where no specific entity is being referred to):

     at yeHola lehagid mishpatim haHi   את יכולה להגיד משפטים הכי

     ktsarim she-yesh   קצרים שיש

           'You can say ⟨the⟩ shortest sentences that

                                 there are'

FURTHER READING
Agmon-Fruchtman 1981, 1982; Glinert 1978:40ff; Ornan 1978, 1979a: 14ff; Rosén 1977:155ff; Sadka 1981: 198ff.

6. Constructs and possessives

6.1 Introduction
Hebrew has a range of 'genitive' constructions, i.e constructions that are often called 'possessives' in a very loose sense (though only some of them are strictly possessive). There are three main types, as described below.

'Construct phrases' are a particular juxtaposition of nouns, and sometimes of other words:

bigdey shabat	בגדי שבת
clothes Sabbath	'Sabbath clothes'
bigdey ha-tinok	בגדי התינוק
clothes the baby	'the baby's clothes'

'של *shel* phrases' use the preposition של *shel* 'of' to link two nouns as in:

bgadim shel shabat	בגדים של שבת
clothes of Sabbath	'Sabbath clothes'
ha-bgadim shel ha-tinok	הבגדים של התינוק
the clothes of the baby	'the baby's clothes'

In both constructions, where the second item is a personal pronoun, it is suffixed:

bgadav	בגדיו
clothes-him	הבגדים שלו
ha-bgadim shelo	
the clothes of-him	'his clothes'

The third type of genitive, 'construct + של *shel* phrases' ('double genitives'), is a particular blend of the two constructions:

bgadav shel ha-tinok	בגדיו של התינוק
clothes-him of the baby	'the baby's clothes'

Construct phrases are two units grammatically, though semantically often a single idiomatic unit, eg. בית-ספר *bet-séfer* 'school' (בית *bet* = 'house', ספר *séfer* = 'book'). של *shel* phrases are three units in every respect, and belong to a whole range of noun-preposition-noun phrases such as הזבוב על הקיר *ha-zvuv al ha-kir* 'the fly on the wall'. At the other extreme there are 'compounds', which are single units grammatically and only semi-productively coined, eg. כדורגל *kadurégel* 'football'; see 38.4.

In all these phrases the attribute *follows* the nucleus.

6.2 Constructs in general

Constructs can often be distinguished from appositions (see ch. 36, eg. החברים הרופאים האלה *ha-Haverim ha-rof'im ha-éle* 'these doctor friends') and noun+adjective phrases (see ch. 10, eg. החברים הישנים *ha-Haverim ha-yeshanim* 'the old friends') by one or two features. (1) The first word may display a distinct 'construct form':

Havrey ha-rof'im	חברי הרופאים
CONSTRUCT	
friends the doctors	'the doctors' friends'

Our word-for-word gloss is 'friends' rather than 'friends-of' to emphasize that the distinct construct form is often not available

(2) To express 'the', just one ה- *ha-* is used, usually with the second component of the phrase as in the foregoing example (but see 6.8), thus ruling out:

*ha-Havrey (ha-)rof'im	*החברי (ה)רופאים
the friends (the) doctors	

The five types of construct

There are five types of construct phrase as illustrated in (a)-(e) below. For details of type (a), the most widespread and varied, see 6.7-6.17; for the others, see 6.18-6.20.

(a) Noun+noun (the second noun can be a full noun phrase):
Havrey ha-naara ha-zot   חברי הנערה הזאת
friends the girl the that   'that girl's friends'

(b) Quantifier+noun (both components can be a whole phrase):
shivim ve-eHad ha-zkenim   שבעים ואחד הזקנים
seventy and one the elders   'the seventy-one elders'

(c) Adjective+noun ('transferred adjectives'):
ha-ish **ktsar ha-sear**   האיש **קצר השיער**
the man **short the hair**   'the short-haired man' (cf. 'hard of hearing') i.e the man whose hair is short

(d) Adjective+noun (or noun phrase) ('adjective and application'):
sfalim **mele'ey máyim karim**   ספלים **מלאי מים קרים**
cups **full water cold**   'cups full of cold water'

(e) Verbal participle+noun (the noun can be a full noun phrase):
itonim **rodfey sensátsyot**   עיתונים **רודפי סנסציות**
newspapers **seeking sensations**   'sensation-seeking newspapers'

Construct phrase structure in general

Construct phrases have two components, which we call components A and B.[1] Component B is always a noun or noun phrase

kéter zahav	כתר זהב
crown gold	B A
A B	'crown of gold'

Component A is generally a single word.[2] It can, however, be a coordination of words, as in (1) below (condemned by purists), or a complex numeral, as in (2). These, together with the positioning of ה- *ha-* 'the', are the fundamental features of constructs.[3]

(1)	morey ve-talmidey ha-miHlala	מורי ותלמידי המכללה
	teachers and students the college	'the teachers and students of the college'
(2)	arbaim ve-tisha ha-shearim	ארבעים ותשעה השערים
	forty and nine the gates	'the forty-nine gates'

No such restrictions apply to component B; thus it can itself be a construct phrase:

shurat amudey shenhav	שורת עמודי שנהב
A B[A B]	[B A]B A
row columns ivory	'a row of columns of ivory'

Anything qualifying component A, eg. adjectives, must be delayed till after the construct phrase (see further 6.5):

shurat konim **aruka**	שורת קונים ארוכה
line customers **long**	'a **long** line of customers'

6.3   Form of construct component A

6.3.1   Regularities and irregularities

There are certain regularities about the form of construct component A but many semi-regular and irregular features. These involve the construct *endings* and the *internal* shape of the words.

The construct endings stand in a regular relationship to the non-construct ('free') endings,[4] as shown in the table:

	Construct form		Free form	
m.s.	No ending, eg. dod	דוד	No ending, eg. dod	דוד
f.s.	-at ת-	dodat דודת	-a ה-	doda דודה
m.pl.	-ey י-	dodey דודי	-im ים-	dodim דודים
f.pl.	-ot ות-	dodot דודות	-ot ות-	dodot דודות

Examples are: שיר ילדים *shir* yeladim 'children's **song**', לטאה **ארוכת**-זנב *leta'a* **arukat**-zanav '**long**-tailed lizard', שירי ילדים *shirey* yeladim 'children's **songs**', לטאות **ארוכות**-זנב *leta'ot* **arukot** zanav '**long**-tailed lizards'.

When the construct word takes a *suffixed pronoun* there is a slight difference, in that the masculine plural ending disappears phonetically, as in דודיו *dodav* 'his uncles' (i.e uncles-him) - though it shows up in the written shape of the word as the letter *yud*. For all these suffixed forms, see 6.4.

A wide variety of *internal* changes affect certain word patterns or individual words, varying according to particular endings.[5] In many patterns (less so in some casual usage) -*a*- or -*e*- in an open penultimate syllable[6] are dropped, as in:

safa ~ sfat, sfato	'bank'	שפה ~ שפת, שפתו	
safot ~ sfot, sfotav		שפות ~ שפות, שפותיו	
but: shalom ~ shlom, shlomo	'peace'	שלום ~ שלום, שלומו	
zagag ~ zagag, zagago	'glazier'	זגג ~ זגג, זגגו	

These and the distinctive construct forms of certain other noun and adjective patterns are mentioned in chapter 38, where some are shown to be productive and some less so, eg.:

mishtara ~ mishtéret, mishtarto	'police'	משטרה ~ משטרת, משטרתו
braHa ~ birkat, birHato	'blessing'	ברכה ~ ברכת, ברכתו

Examples of individual peculiarities are:

shisha ~ shéshet	'six'	ששה ~ ששת
mlaHa ~ mléHet, mlaHto	'craft'	מלאכה ~ מלאכת, מלאכתו

In some patterns only the plural construct or suffixed construct changes form:

seret ~ sirto, sirtey, sratav	'film'	סרט ~ סרטו, סרטי, סרטיו

Full details are provided in a traditional grammar or a dictionary.

6.3.2   Form of construct numerals

Unlike other quantifiers (see 6.18), numerals require a construct form in some instances and not in others. The numerals 'three' to 'ten' have the construct form if and only if followed by a 'definite' noun, whereas the numeral 'two' has it even with an indefinite noun:[7]

shney dubim CONSTRUCT	'two bears'	שני דובים
shney ha-dubim CONSTRUCT two the bears	'the two bears'	שני הדובים
shisha dubim FREE	'six bears'	ששה דובים
shéshet ha-dubim CONSTRUCT six the bears	'the six bears'	ששת הדובים

All the free and construct forms of numerals are given in 8.9, as are general syntactic details.

Where not qualifying a noun, numerals are by definition not engaged in a construct construction:

kama dubim, **shnáyim?** FREE	'How many bears, **two?**'	כמה דובים, **שניים?**

Compound numerals over 'ten' have no construct form, even where they end in a unit numeral that has one[8] Thus:

esrim ^u-shnáyim ha-saHkanim *u-shney	עשרים ושניים השחקנים *ושני
twenty and two the players	'the 22 players'

The position of ה- *ha-* 'the' shows this to be a construct phrase, though this is not reflected in the form of the numeral.

Exceptionally, ה- *ha-* 'the' in measurement phrases precedes the whole phrase in casual usage, eg.:

éfo ha-árba lírot?	איפה הארבע לירות!
where the four Liras?	'Where are the four Liras?'

A quite distinct construction, using the preposition מ- *me-* 'of, from' instead of the construct, is employed for 'two of the bears' and so on:

shnáyim me-ha-dubim	שניים מהדובים
two of the bears	'two of the bears'

אחד *eHad* 'one' is the exception here, allowing either the construct *or* מ- *me-*. (In the sense of 'one bear' or 'the one bear', however, אחד *eHad* follows its noun.)

eHad me-ha-dubim	'one of the bears'	אחד מהדובים
aHad ha-dubim		אחד הדובים

6.3.3 Words not used as construct component A

Certain types of words are not found as construct component A. Pronouns and names, even when acting as common nouns, cannot be used:[9]

*éle david nignevu	*אלה דוד נגנבו
those David were-stolen	('those of David were stolen')
*máshehu ets	*משהו עץ
something wood	('something of wood')
*tsarfat yemey ha-mluHa	*צרפת ימי המלוכה
France days the monarchy	('France of the days of the monarchy')

Instead, של *shel* 'of' or (in the second example) מ- *mi-* must be interposed:

éle shel david nignevu	אלה של דוד נגנבו
those of David were-stolen	'David's were stolen'

Foreignisms entailing the plural construct suffix י- *-ey* are generally avoided to prevent unstressed י- *-ey*, thus:

student Huts	סטודנט חוץ 'overseas student (m.s.)'
studéntit Huts	סטודנטית חוץ 'overseas student (f.s.)'

studéntiot Huts   סטודנטיות חוץ
                                                    'overseas students (f.pl.)'

but not:

*studéntey Huts   *סטודנטי חוץ
                                                    'overseas students (m.pl.)'

By contrast, the unstressed free construct suffix ת- *-at* (f.s.) is normal:
אוניברסיטת תל-אביב *univérsitat tel aviv* 'Tel Aviv University', as are
unstressed plural suffixes; and where י- *-ey* in a foreignism does take stress, it
is acceptable, as in קורסי יסוד *kurséy yesod* 'foundation courses'.

An idiomatic construct phrase, being felt to be two words, cannot itself ordinarily serve as component A; hence של *shel* 'of' is interposed:

Heyl ha-avir shel shvédya	חיל האוויר של שבדיה
force the air of Sweden	'the airforce of Sweden'
Heyl ha-avir shelánu	חיל האוויר שלנו
force the air our	'our airforce'

There are exceptions, eg. בית-ספר-ערב *bet-séfer-érev* 'evening school',
רב-סמל-משמעת *rav-samal-mishmáat* 'disciplinary sergeant-major'.

6.4   Suffixes as construct component B ('possessive suffixes'): דודי *dodi* 'my uncle'

Where construct component B is to be filled by a personal pronoun,[11]
a *suffix* is generally used. Thus, corresponding to:

sfat ha-nahar	שפת הנהר
bank the river	'the river bank'
A B	

kovshey ha-iyim	כובשי האיים
conquerors the islands	'the islands' conquerors'
A B	

we find:

sfato	שפתו
bank-**it**	'its bank'
A B	

kovshey**hem**	כובשיהם
conquerors-**they**	'their conquerors'
A B	

rather than שפת הוא *sfat hu or כובשי הם *kovshey hem with a separate
pronoun.

Here the suffix amounts to 'my, your, his', etc. and is instrinsically definite,
i.e דירתי *dirati* is 'my apartment' ('the apartment of mine').[12] For '*an* apartment of mine', של *shel* 'of' must be used rather than the construct: דירה שלי
dira sheli. (For של *shel* 'of' in general, see 6.8.)

Suffixes are found with construct quantifiers too (with the exception of numerals over 'four'):

rov ha-skarim most the polls	רוב הסקרים 'most of the polls'

rubam most-**they**	**רובם** 'most of them'

and similarly, שנינו *shnéynu* 'we two, the two of us' (cf. שני המדענים *shney ha-madanim* 'the two scientists'), שלושתכם *shloshteHem* 'you three, the three of you'. But where the construction would ordinarily involve partitive -מ *me-* 'of' rather than the construct (see 8.6), there will be no construct suffix either:[13]

shlosha me-ha-skarim	שלושה מהסקרים 'three of the polls'
shlosha **mehem**	שלושה **מהם** 'three **of them**'

Form of the suffixed pronoun

There are two sets of suffixes, one for singular and one for plural nouns, as illustrated in the table below. The latter set is written with a (sometimes silent) letter *yud*, which originally represented the construct plural suffix י- *-ey* and whose presence is arguably still felt - for nouns with construct plural י- *-ey* drop this before adding the suffixed pronoun.

For the suffixation of possessive של *shel* 'of', see 6.8.

Suffixes for singular nouns		Examples for דוד, דודה *dod, doda* 'uncle, aunt'	
-i 'my'	י-	dodi, dodati 'my uncle, aunt' etc.	דודי, דודתי
-Ha 'your' (m.s.)	ך-	dodHa, dodatHa	דודך, דודתך
-eH 'your' (f.s.)	ך-	dodeH, dodateH	דודך, דודתך
-o 'his, its'	ו-	dodo, dodato	דודו, דודתו
-a 'her, its'	ה-	doda, dodata	דודה, דודתה
-énu 'our'	נו-	dodénu, dodaténu	דודנו, דודתנו
-Hem 'your' (m.pl.)	כם-	dodHem, dodatHem	דודכם, דודתכם
-Hen[1] 'your' (f.pl.)	כן-	dodHen, dodatHen	דודכן, דודתכן
-am 'their' (m.pl.)	ם-	dodam, dodatam	דודם, דודתם
-an[1] 'their' (f.pl.)	ן-	dodan, dodatan	דודן, דודתן
Suffixes for plural nouns		Example for דודים, דודות *dodim, dodot* 'uncles, aunts'	
-ay 'my'	י-	doday, dodotay 'my uncles, aunts' etc.	דודי, דודותי
-éHa 'your' (m.s.)	יך-	dodéHa, dodotéHa	דודיך, דודותיך
-áyiH 'your' (f.s.)	יך-	dodáyiH, dodotáyiH	דודיך, דודותיך
-av 'his'	יו-	dodav, dodotav	דודיו, דודותיו
-éha 'her'	יה-	dodéha, dodotéha	דודיה, דודותיה
-éynu 'our'	ינו-	dodéynu, dodotéynu	דודינו, דודותינו

-eyHem 'your' (m.pl.)	-יכם	dodeyHem, dodoteyHem	דודיכם, דודותיכם
-eyHen[1] 'your' (f.pl.)	-יכן	dodeyHen, dodoteyHen	דודיכן, דודותיכן
-eyhem 'their' (m.pl.)	-יהם	dodeyhem, dodoteyhem	דודיהם, דודותיהם
-eyhen[1] 'their' (f.pl.)	-יהן	dodeyhen, dodoteyhen	דודיהן, דודותיהן

Note: [1]Casually, the masculine plural does service for both.

6.5 Qualifying a construct

yadit ha-délet ha-Huma   ידית הדלת החומה
                                                                              'the brown door handle'

Construct component A and B can both be qualified, but not always simultaneously. Examples (1) and (2) below are acceptable, but (3), with the two 'definite'
adjectives relating to components A and B respectively, is felt to be confusing
and can preferably be rephrased using של *shel* 'of', as in (4), instead of a construct phrase:

(1) megilot ha-kat ha-atika she-avdu   מגילות הכת העתיקה שאבדו
     scrolls the sect the ancient that perished   'The scrolls of the ancient sect that
     pl.   f.s.   f.s.   pl.   perished'

A   B   QUALIFYING B   QUALIFYING A

(2) be-masa hasata adatit akshani   במסע הסתה עדתית עקשני
     meshaHneim aHshav et kulam she..   משכנעים עכשיו את כולם ש...
     in crusade incitement communal determined convince now OM everyone that...
     m.s.   f.s.   f.s.   m.s.

A   B   QUALIFYING B QUALIFYING A
     'In a determined crusade of communal incitement they are now convincing
                                                          everyone that...'

(3) ?megilot ha-kat ha-atika ha-mafliot   ?מגילות הכת העתיקה המפליאות
     scrolls the sect the ancient the amazing 'The amazing scrolls of the ancient
     pl.   f.s.   f.s.   pl.   sect'

(4) ha-megilot ha-mafliot shel ha-kat ha-atika המגילות המפליאות של הכת העתיקה
     the scrolls the amazing of the   'The amazing scrolls of the
       sect the ancient   ancient sect'

One also tends to avoid such ambiguity as the following, by using של *shel* 'of':

mo'étset ha-medina ha-ara'it   מועצת המדינה הארעית
council the state the temporary   'The temporary state council'
f.s.   f.s.   f.s.

A   B   QUALIFYING A OR B?

Further restrictions

There are two cases where an adjective is constrained from 'referring
across' a construct phrase to the first noun. (a) When the first noun is an 'action
noun', its adjective will be as close to it as possible, thus:

ha-hitpatHut ha-mehira shel ha-tsafon	ההתפתחות המהירה של הצפון
the development the rapid of the north	'the rapid development of the north'

haHshara psiHológit shel morim	הכשרה פסיכולוגית של מורים
training psychological of teachers	'psychological training of teachers'

and similarly התפתחותו המהירה *hitpatHuto ha-mehira* 'its rapid development'; but not התפתחות הצפון המהירה* **hitpatHut ha-tsafon ha-mehira* (development the north the rapid), הכשרת מורים פסיכולוגית* **haHsharat morim psiHológit* (training teachers psychological). (b) When the second noun is a name[14], the phrase is generally felt to be too 'open' for an adjective to 'refer across' to the first noun, and so the construct phrase must be broken up:

ha-hatsa'ot (*or* hatsaotéha)	ההצעות/הצעותיה
ha-Hadashot shel sfarad	החדשות של ספרד
the proposals (*or* her-proposals) the new of Spain	'Spain's new proposals'

ákaba, ha-motsa ha-yaHid shel yarden layam	עקבה, המוצא היחיד של ירדן לים
Akaba, the outlet the only of Jordan to-the sea	'Akaba, Jordan's only outlet to the sea'

but not הצעות ספרד החדשות* **hatsaot sfarad ha-Hadashot* (lit. proposals Spain the new), מוצא ירדן היחיד* **motsa yarden ha-yaHid* (lit. outlet Jordan the only).[15]

Similarly, a determiner following a construct phrase can only qualify the last component,[16] except where idiomatic phrases are concerned. Thus instead of השמדת (ה)כפרים (ה)זאת* **hashmadat (ha-)kfarim (ha-)zot* (lit. destruction (the) villages (the) this), הצעתך הזאת* *hatsaatHa ha-zot (lit. proposal-your the this), Hebrew requires:

(ha-)hashmada (ha-)zot shel kfarim	(ה)השמדה (ה)זאת של כפרים
(the) destruction (the) this of villages	'this destruction of villages'

(ha-)hatsa'a (ha-)zot shelHa	(ה)הצעה (ה)זאת שלך
(the) proposal (the) this of-you	'this proposal of yours'[17]

6.6 Agreement with construct phrases

Where a construct phrase is a subject, the predicate generally agrees with component A, this being the nucleus of the phrase:

meamen ha-arayot raad	מאמן האריות רעד
A B PRED	
trainer the lions was-shivering	'The lion trainer was shivering'

But in quantifier+noun phrases it is component B that is the nucleus and determines agreement (including agreement of person):

rov ha-arayot raadu	רוב האריות רעדו
A B	
majority the lions were-shivering	'The majority of the lions were shivering'

rubénu ra'ádnu   רובנו רעדנו
A B   1st pl.
most-us were-shivering   'Most of us were shivering'

For details, see 8.8 and 18.4.

6.7 Noun+noun constructs and other genitives

Noun+noun genitives denote several types of semantic relation between nouns, with concomitant variations in syntax. The chief types, divided according to fairly rough criteria, are described in 6.8-17. They denote possession, action or state of affairs, performer of an action, measures or containers, purpose, identification, attribution and the superlative In addition, there are hosts of semantically idiomatic construct phrases.

These genitives may be in the form of a construct phrase or, in some instances, involve של *shel* 'of'.

Grammatical limitations

One *tends* to avoid a chain of possessive construct nouns by judicious insertion of של *shel* 'of', even in formal usage, or of a 'double genitive'. Thus, instead of למרות תלונות חברי בעלה *lamrot tlunot Havrey baala* 'despite her husband's friends' complaints', one tends to prefer:

lamrot ha-tlunot shel Havrey baala   למרות התלונות של חברי בעלה
despite the complaints of friends   'despite the complaints of her
    husband-her   husband's friends'

lamrot tlunoteyhem shel Havrey baala[18]   למרות תלונותיהם של חברי בעלה
despite complaints-their of   'despite the complaints of her
    friends husband-her   husband's friends'

Even a chain of diverse constructs, involving, for example, action nouns or mere fixed expressions, entitles one to insert של *shel* 'of', though there is nothing gauche about such a chain provided it is not too 'heavy':

en hityaHasut le-fidyon (shel)   אין התייחסות לפדיון (של)
            ACTION GENITIVE
kupot gemel   קופות גמל
FIXED PHRASE
there-is-no reference to redemption   'There is no reference to pension
    (of) funds pension   fund redemption'

parashat nishul arviyey he-harim   פרשת נישול ערביי ההרים
IDENTIFICATION ACTION POSSESSION
episode dislodgement Arabs the mountains   'The episode of the mountain
                                                Arabs' dislodgement'

Conversely, a chain of של *shel* 'of' phrases is avoided in formal style
In possessives, one tends to insert של *shel* 'of' before a name:

ha-motsa ha-yaHid **shel** yarden la-yam   המוצא היחיד **של** ירדן לים
the outlet the sole **of** Jordan to-the sea 'Jordan's sole outlet to the sea'

ba-midbar mats'a matslemato **shel** avraham   במדבר מצאה מצלמתו **של** אברהם
gvul mufshat shel yesodot   גבול מופשט של יסודות
'In the desert Avraham's camera (*lit.* camera-his **of** Avraham)
found an abstract frontier of elements'

In genitives as a whole של *shel* 'of' is inserted to show where an adjective belongs; rather than יעד ההסטוריון העיקרי *yáad ha-historyon ha-ikari* 'the main historian's aim', formal style will prefer:

yaado ha-ikari shel ha-historyon   יעדו העיקרי של ההסטוריון
aim-his the main of the historian   'the main aim of the historian'

Pronoun suffixes are often avoided with uncommon words, as an added ו- *-o* or ה- *-a* etc. would make them even harder to identify, hence:

ha-saman ha-smali shela   הסמן השמאלי שלה
the marker the lefthand of-it   'its lefthand marker'

The same happens *regularly* with words having a foreign stress pattern. Evidently, pronoun suffixes are felt to be even more typically 'native' than the construct suffixes ת- *-at* etc. Thus, rather than סטודנטיותינו **studentiyotéynu*, נובלתו **novelato*, one prefers:

ha-studéntiyot shelánu   'our students'   הסטודנטיות שלנו

ha-novéla shelo   'his novella'   הנובלה שלו

6.8   Possessive constructs and genitives

6.8.1   Four basic structures

Four basic structures are available for the possessive genitive: (1) construct phrases, (2) suffixed construct + של *shel* 'of' phrase ('double genitives'), (3) של *shel* 'of' phrases, (4) משל *mishel* 'of' phrases:

(1)   dirat moshe / dirato   דירת משה/דירתו
apartment Moshe / apartment-his   'Moshe's apartment / his apartment'

(2)   dirato shel moshe   דירתו של משה
apartment-his of Moshe   'Moshe's apartment'

(3)   ha-dira shel moshe / ha-dira shelo   הדירה של משה/הדירה שלו
the apartment of Moshe / the apartment of-him   'Moshe's apartment / his apartment'

(4)   maamar mishel yung / maamar mishelo   מאמר משל יונג/מאמר משלו
article of Jung / article of-him   'an article of Jung's / an article of his own'

These differ both in syntactic and in stylistic distribution. But first their form is described.

For (1) the form of the construct has been described in 6.3. For (2) the 'double genitive' involves a construct suffix referring to and agreeing with the following noun, thus:

dirata shel Havera   דירתה של חברה
apartment-her of girl-friend   'a girl-friend's apartment'

diratam shel Haverim   דירתם של חברים
apartment-their of friends   'some friends' apartment'

However, the use of a double *pronoun*, eg. דירתה שלה *dirata shela* (apartment-her of-her), is emphatic and more formal: 'her apartment'.[19] As for structure (3), של *shel* inflects as follows:

shelánu	'our'	שלנו	sheli	'my'	שלי
shelaHem	'your' (m.pl.)	שלכם	shelHa	'your' (m.s.)	שלך
shelaHen[20]	'your' (f.pl.)	שלכן	shelah	'your' (f.s.)	שלך
shelahem	'their' (m.)	שלהם	shelo	'his'	שלו
shelahen[20]	'their' (f.)	שלהן	shela	'her'	שלה

Structure (4) משל *mishel* inflects like של *shel*, i.e משלך, משלי *misheli, mishelHa* etc.

6.8.2 Syntax and style

Generally speaking, the *construct* possessive is freely coined only in formal usage (with some exceptions)[21]:

With a name:
hatsa'at hódu / hatsaata   הצעת הודו /הצעתה
proposal India / proposal-her   'India's proposal / her proposal'

With a definite noun:
meytrey ha-nével / meytarav   מיתרי הנבל /מיתריו
strings the harp / strings-its   'The harp's strings / its strings'

With an indefinite noun:
anaf ets   ענף עץ
branch tree   'a branch of a tree'

The *double genitive* is freely coined in rather formal usage:

With a name:
hatsaata shel hódu   הצעתה של הודו
proposal-her of India   'India's proposal'

With a definite noun:
meytarav shel ha-nével   מיתריו של הנבל
strings-its of the harp   'the harp's strings'

With an indefinite noun:
anafo shel ets   ענפו של עץ
branch-its of tree   'a branch of a tree'

This last example is indefinite, even though ענפו *anafo* 'its branch' would by itself be definite

The של *shel* possessive is freely coined in all usage, but formal Hebrew is inclined to avoid it except in particular circumstances (outlined in 6.7):

With a name:

hatsa'a shel hódu / shela
proposal of India / of-her

הצעה של הודו / שלה
'a proposal of India's / of hers'

ha-hatsa'a shel hódu / shela
the proposal of India / of-her

ההצעה של הודו / שלה
'India's proposal / her proposal'

With a definite noun:

meytarim shel ha-nével / shelo
strings of the harp / of-it

מיתרים של הנבל / שלו
'some of the harp's strings / of its strings'

ha-meytarim shel ha-nével / shelo
the strings of the harp / of-it

המיתרים של הנבל / שלו
'the harp's strings / its strings'

With an indefinite noun:

anaf shel ets
branch of tree

ענף של עץ
'a branch of a tree'

ha-anaf shel ets
the branch of tree

הענף של עץ
'the branch of a tree'

A general property of של *shel* phrases is that they can appear without a nucleus noun, where this has already been mentioned (and is definite) (see 11.3). Thus:

tmunot? tare li et **shelHa**
ve-**shel dáni**
Pictures? Show me **your** and
of Danny

תמונות? תראה לי את **שלך**
ושל דני
'Pictures? Show me yours
and Danny's'

משל *mishel* is freely used in any register, with a reflexive pronoun suffix rather than a noun; it often qualifies a non-specific indefinite noun, corresponding roughly to English 'of my own'. Contrast:

hu meHapes Haver **shelo**
he searches-for friend **of-his**

הוא מחפש חבר שלו
'He's searching for a friend of his'

hu meHapes Haver **mishelo**
he searches-for friend **of-his**

הוא מחפש חבר משלו
'He's searching for a friend of his own'

A more common use is as emphatic possessive - but generally only with indefinite nouns:[22]

hevéti sidur $\begin{matrix} \text{misheli} \\ \text{sheli} \end{matrix}$!

הבאתי סידור משלי !
שלי
'I've brought my own prayer book!'

Besides these stylistically limited possessives, there is a general use of the *construct* in a host of *generic* expressions, eg. צמר כבשים *tsémer kvasim* 'sheep wool', ענפי תעשיה *anfey taasiya* 'branches of industry', אשת רופא *éshet rofe* 'doctor's wife', תלמיד בית-ספר *talmid bet-séfer* 'school pupil', סוף שבוע *sof shavúa* 'weekend', קרנות נאמנות *karnot neemanut* 'trust funds'. These are sometimes hyphenated, but are generally not felt to be so idiomatic as to preclude expansion, eg. בגדי גברים, נשים וילדים בהנחה *bigdey gvarim, nashim ve-yeladim be-hanaHa* 'men's, women's and children's clothes on discount'. However, being generic, they do not exist as construct+pronoun suffix: צמרם *tsimram* 'their wool' is specific, not generic, and found just in formal usage

-ל *le-* occasionally introduces a possessive: (1) In expressions of the type בשנה השניה לקיום המדינה *ba-shana ha-shniya* **le-***kiyum ha-medina* 'in the second year **of** the State's existence'; (2) with אב/אם (לארבעה ילדים) *av/em (le-arbaa yeladim)* 'a father/mother (of four children)'; (3) as an alternative to של *shel* 'of' in denoting authorship (of classics): "שירה" לעגנון *shíra le-agnon* 'Agnon's "Shira"'.[23]

6.8.3   -ה *ha-* 'the' and definiteness in constructs

Construct phrases have already been shown to inflect for gender and number as *two words:*[24]

meytar nével	מיתר נבל	meytrey nevalim	מיתרי נבלים
string harp	'harp string'	strings harps	'harp strings'

However, the word -ה *ha-* 'the' is limited to just one appearance for the phrase (though the fact that it is generally positioned in front of component B does serve to distinguish the construct phrase from single-word compounds such as הרמזור *ha-ramzor* 'the traffic light'):

meytar **ha-**nével	מיתר הנבל
string **the** harp	'the harp string'

Casually, generic constructs and especially idiomatic expressions often put -ה *ha-* 'the' first:[25]

bet ha-séfer / ha-bet séfer	בית הספר/הבית-ספר	
house the book / the house book		'the school'
meHabey ha-esh / ha-meHabey esh	מכבי האש/המכבי-אש	
extinguishers the fire / the extinguishers fire		'the firemen'

Some idioms actually *require* this, casually, in the singular; in the plural it is just optional (the plural suffix has the effect of 'splitting' the phrase):

ha-ben adam	הבן-אדם
the son man	'the person'

and similarly בן-דוד *ben-dod* 'cousin', בגד-ים *béged-yam* 'swimsuit', עורך-דין *oreH-din* 'lawyer', etc.

The effect of -ה *ha-* 'the' depends on whether the construct phrase is specific or generic: when specific, *both* of its components are felt to become definite; when generic, only component A becomes definite, and component B retains its generic force:

Indefinite construct:		*Specific meaning*	*Generic meaning*
tsémer kvasim	צמר כבשים	'some wool of	'sheep wool'
		some sheep'	(wool of sheep)

Definite construct:
tsémer ha-kvasim צמר הכבשים 'the wool of the sheep' 'the sheep wool'
(the wool of sheep)

Addition of adjectives makes this even clearer:

Specific meaning	*Generic meaning*
Indefinite construct:	
oreH iton yomi עורך עיתון יומי	oreH iton kashish עורך עיתון קשיש
'an editor of a daily newspaper'	'an elderly newspaper editor'

Definite construct:
oreH ha-iton ha-yomi עורך העיתון היומי   oreH ha-iton ha-kashish עורך העיתון הקשיש
'the editor of the daily newspaper'   'the elderly newspaper editor'
                                         (i.e. the elderly editor of newspapers)

An example with just a specific meaning:

atsat shaHen	'a neighbour's advice'	עצת שכן
	(advice of a neighbour)	
atsat ha-shaHen	'the neighbour's advice'	עצת השכן
	(the advice of the neighbour)	

Similarly, where component B is intrinsically definite, i.e. a name, both components are deemed definite: ארצות אפריקה *artsot áfrika* 'the countries of Africa'.

With 'double genitives' too, just one -ה *ha-* 'the' is added and it affects both components: עצתו של שכן *atsato shel shaHen* 'a neighbour's advice', עצתו של השכן *atsato shel ha-shaHen* 'the neighbour's advice'.

By contrast, with של *shel* 'of' phrases one or *two* -ה *ha-* 'the' can be used, yielding four possible senses, of which the second and third are not available in many constructs - hence their use even in formal Hebrew:

etsa shel shaHen	'advice of a neighbour'	עצה של שכן
ha-etsa shel shaHen	'the advice of a neighbour'	העצה של שכן
etsa shel ha-shaHen	'advice of the neighbour's'	עצה של השכן
ha-etsa shel ha-shaHen	'the advice of the neighbour'	העצה של השכן

Naturally, *idiomatic* construct phrases amounting to a single word, e.g. בית-ספר/ *bet-séfer* 'school', become definite as a single unit: בית הספר/ הבית-ספר *bet-ha-séfer* or *ha-bet-séfer* 'the school'. Nevertheless, -ה *ha-* 'the' can usually be interposed *between* the two components.

These rules for the function of -ה *ha-* 'the' require two qualifications:
(a) When the construct denotes 'membership', a 'definite' phrase such as חברי אל-על *Havrey el-al* can mean 'members of El Al' as well as 'the members of El Al', i.e. component A can be *indefinite* even though component B is definite - in which case the 'definite object marker' את *et* is not used: [26]

shitáfnu shisha Havrey el al	שיתפנו ששה חברי אל-על
we-co-opted six members El Al	'We co-opted six El Al members'

Similarly, יליד העיר רחל לוי, תלמידת *yelis ha-ir* '**a** native of the city', התיכון המקומי *raHel levi, talmidat ha-tiHon ha-mekomi* 'Rachel Levi, a pupil of the local highschool', נהג אגד *nehag éged* '**An** Eged driver'.

(b) However, where the definite component B is a name with -ה *ha-* 'the', component A can often be made indefinite by simply omitting this -ה *ha-*, even when not expressing 'possession' or 'membership':

yom **ha**-atsma'ut	יום העצמאות
day **the** independence	'Independence Day'

yom atsma'ut gashum	יום עצמאות גשום
day independence rainy	'**a** rainy Independence Day'

Similarly, הכנסת *ha-knéset* '**the** Knesset' but חבר כנסת *Haver knéset* '**a** Knesset member'.

6.9 Action and state genitives

For most verbs and adjectives there exists a corresponding 'action noun' or 'state noun' ('nominalization'), usually of predictable form, as detailed in 38.2 (patterns 2 and 23):

v: pina 'evacuate'	פינה	action N: pinuy 'evacuation'	פינוי
ADJ: ayef 'tired'	עייף	state N: ayefut 'tiredness'	עייפות

These often serve the same ends as a *subordinate* verb (these and other types of subordination are described in ch. 30):

ad she-**pinu** et ha-ir SUBORDINATE V OBJ	עד שפינו את העיר 'until they **evacuated** the town'
ad **pinuy** ha-ir until **evacuation** the town COMPONENT A COMPONENT B	עד פינוי העיר 'until the evacuation of the town'

Where a verb or adjective would have a subject or direct object, the corresponding noun will usually have a *genitive* construction, as indicated in this last example.

However, whereas a subject generally *precedes* its verb or adjective, the corresponding noun will always *follow* the verbal or adjectival noun: [27]

biglal she-**ha-koHot** nas'u ba-yam	בגלל שהכוחות נסעו בים
'because **the troops** travelled by sea'	3 2 1
1 2 3	

biglal nesiat **ha-koHot** ba-yam	בגלל נסיעת הכוחות בים
'because of the travel of **the troops** by sea'	3 1 2
2 1 3	

The three main types of genitive (6.1) are all available, but not in quite the same way as for possessives (cf. 6.8). As in example (1), construct phrases are freely used in both formal and fairly casual usage, except that with a pronoun suffix they are formal. The 'double genitive' is rather formal, as in (2). The של *shel* 'of' possessive is casual, [28]as in (3). In addition, hosts of *generic* expressions are couched in the construct phrase, as in (4).

(1) hu da'ag la-**aliyat** ha-bat shelo   הוא דאג **לעליית** הבת שלו
     ve-la-klita shela   ולקליטה שלה
     he was-seeing to **immigration** the daughter of-his and to-the absorption of-her

(2) hu da'ag la-**aliyata**   הוא דאג **לעלייתה**
     shel bito ve-li-klitata   **של** בתו ולקליטתה
     he was-seeing to **immigration-her of** daughter-his and to absorption-her

(3) hu da'ag la-**aliya shel** ha-bat shelo   הוא דאג **לעלייה של** הבת שלו
     ve-la-klita shela   ולקליטה שלה
     he was-seeing to-**the immigration of** the daughter of-his and to-the absorption of-her
     Translation for (1-3): 'He was seeing to his daughter's immigration and to her absorption'

(4) mitsmuts eynáyim   'wink of the eyes'   מיצמוץ עיניים
     hatkafat lev   'heart attack'   התקפת לב

'Result nouns' are akin to action nouns, eg. ציור *tsiyur* 'a drawing' (resulting from ציור *tsiyur* 'act of drawing'), תמונה *tmuna* 'picture', התנהגות *hitnahagut* 'behaviour'. They too can take an object or subject noun, eg. הצילום של **התינוק** *ha-tsilum shel* **ha-tinok** 'the photo of **the baby**', but unlike other types of genitive they allow a double של *shel* 'of':

     éfo ha-tsilum shelaH shel sába?   איפה הצילום שלך של סבא!
     where the photo of-you of grandpa?   'Where's your photo of grandpa?'

6.10 Agent genitives: לובשי מדים *lovshey madim* 'wearers of uniform'

To express 'doer' ('agent') plus object, formal Hebrew can make use of the present tense form of a verb as a construct noun plus whatever noun phrase would be the object:[29]

     notney ha-sherutim ha-éle u-**mekableyhem**   **נותני** השירותים האלה **ומקבליהם**
     givers the services the these
     and **receivers**-their   'the givers of these services
                                                        and their recipients'

This is generally limited to verbs taking a direct object.[30] Furthermore, some, perhaps many, such verbs are averse to this construction, thus:

     noaley sandalim tseirim   נועלי סנדלים צעירים
     muzharim bimyuHad   מוזהרים במיוחד
     wearers sandals young   'Young sandal-wearers
     are-warned particularly   are particularly warned'

     ha-séfer meyu'ad li-meviney ha-ivrit הספר מיועד למביני העברית
     the book is-intended for   'The book is intended for
     understanders the Hebrew   those understanding Hebrew'

but not:

*ha-madriH meyu'ad le-sharey shirey am	‏*המדריך מיועד לשרי שירי עם‏
the guide is-intended for	'The guide is intended for
singers songs folk	singers of folksongs'

*gam shom'ey leshon ha-ra ashemim	‏*גם שומעי לשון הרע אשמים‏
also hearers speech the evil	'Hearers of evil speech are
are-guilty	guilty too'

On the other hand, many set phrases of this type appear even in casual Hebrew. eg. (...) ‏מוכר‏ *moHer (...)* '(...) seller', ‏רואה חשבונות‏ *ro'e Heshbonot* 'book-keeper'.

‏של‏ *shel* 'of' cannot be used, but only the construct; indeed these nouns[31] *require* a construct, thus excluding:

*riyánu **mekablim**	('We interviewed **recipients**')	‏*ראיינו מקבלים‏

Other types of 'agent noun' do exist, eg. ‏גנב‏ *ganav* 'thief' (*-a-a-* pattern), ‏סדרן‏ *sadran* 'usher' (*a-an* pattern), but they do not regularly participate in this construction,[32] hence:

gonvey		'the	stealers	of the taxi'	‏גונבי‏
*ganavey	ha-monit		thieves		‏*גנבי‏ המונית

A kindred use of the present tense as a construct, *qualifying* a noun (but not in itself a noun), is described in 6.20:

Hayalim **lovshey jins** lo yurshu	‏חיילים לובשי ג'ינס לא יורשו להיכנם‏
lehikanes	
soldiers **wearers jeans** not	'Soldiers **wearing jeans** will not be
will-be-let enter	admitted'

Two further phenomena can be distinguished. (1) Many present tense forms serve as ordinary nouns, and require no construct, eg. ‏שופט‏ *shofet* 'judge', ‏מפקיד‏ *mafkid* 'depositor', ‏מחנך‏ *meHaneH* 'educator'; thus:

eye meHanéHet	'I will be an educator'	‏אהיה מחנכת‏
meHaneH **shel** yeladim	'educator **of** children'	‏מחנך של ילדים‏

(2) Real present-tense verbs can appear in a headless relative clause with ‏ה-‏ *ha-* meaning 'who/which'; the plural suffix or the position of ‏ה-‏ *ha-* reveal that this is not a construct:

ha-mekablim tipul yeshalmu merosh	‏המקבלים טיפול ישלמו מראש‏
who receive treatment will-pay	'Those receiving treatment will
in-advance	pay in advance'

6.11 'Made of' genitives: ‏שיני זהב‏ *shiney zahav* 'gold teeth'

'Made of' and 'composed of' are freely expressed by the construct in all registers:

shiney zahav	'gold teeth'	שיני זהב
tipat máyim	'drop of water'	טיפת מים
tsévet rofim	'team of doctors'	צוות רופאים
zer praHim	'bouquet of flowers'	זר פרחים

But casual usage avoids unfamiliar or impossible construct forms by interposing
-מ *mi-* 'from' for 'made of', while של *shel* 'of' is common for 'composed of':

praHim mi-plástik	'plastic flowers'	פרחים מפלסטיק
naaley-báyit mi-bad	'cloth slippers'	נעלי-בית מבד
zer shel praHim	'bouquet of flowers'	זר של פרחים

6.12 'Measure and container' genitives: שני בקבוקי יין *shney bakbukey yáyin* 'two bottles of wine'

Measure and container are often expressed by some form of the genitive (but see 8.5 for measurement constructions as a whole and 36.10 for measurement apposition in particular):

Measure:

hiHnásti shney bakbukey yáyin la-marak   הכנסתי שני בקבוקי יין למרק
            CONSTRUCT

I-put-in two bottles wine to-the soup   'I put two bottles of wine in the
                                                                                    soup'

Container:

tavi shney bakbukey yáyin   תביא שני בקבוקי יין
            CONSTRUCT

bring two bottles wine   'Bring two bottles of wine'

For containers, the construct is generally preferred to של *shel* 'of'.[33]

Physical measures, whether using artificial or natural units, sometimes use the construct or של *shel* 'of':

| shney kilo (shel) agasim | שני קילו (של) אגסים |
| two kilo (of) pears | 'two kilos of pears' |

| kapit (shel) sukar | כפית (של) סוכר |
| spoon (of) sugar | 'a spoonful of sugar' |

They commonly also use apposition (36.10), but in most instances this is indistinguishable from the construct.

Abstract measures use either the construct (formal) or apposition (casual):

shisha yemey / yamim tiyul   ששה ימי / ימים טיול

six days (CONSTRUCT) / days (APPOSITION) touring   'six days' touring'

Alternatively, one commonly puts the measure word second and interposes של
shel 'of':

tiyul shel shisha yamim   טיול של ששה ימים
            'a tour of six days'

sherut kéva shel shnatáyim   שירות קבע של שנתיים
'permanent service of two years'

This is particularly frequent when one uses a certain *dimension* of measurement:

kir be-óvi shel méter   קיר בעובי של מטר
wall with thickness of metre   'a wall one metre thick'

héroin be-shóvi shel milyard dólar   הרואין בשווי של מליארד דולר
heroin with value of billion dollar   'heroin with a value of a
                                                             billion dollars'

shilmu be-iHur shel shishim yom   שילמו באיחור של שישים יום
they-paid with arrear of sixty day   'They paid sixty days in arrears'

6.13 Purpose genitives

Purpose is preferably expressed by the construct in a large number
of expressions, and otherwise generally by ל- *le* 'for':

simlat Hatuna   'wedding dress'   שמלת חתונה
kartisey ashray   'credit cards'   כרטיסי אשראי
misrad ha-datot   'the Ministry of Religions'   משרד הדתות
bakbukey yáyin   'wine bottles   בקבוקי יין

as against:

kolar le-kélev   'dog collar'   קולר לכלב
vavim le-kova'im   'hat pegs'   ווים לכובעים

6.14 Identification genitives: מדינת קנסס *medinat kánsas* 'the State of Kansas'

Genitives are involved in two kinds of 'naming': as in (1), attaching
a 'proper name', i.e an identification; or, as in (2), attaching a brand name or
any other 'class name', i.c. an attribute:

(1) har fúji   הר פוג'י   (2) sirtey fúji   סרטי פוג'י
     mountain Fuji   'Mt. Fuji'   films Fuji   'Fuji films'

Section 6.14 deals with the former; the latter, and the other attributive genitives,
are examined in 6.15.

The construct is used generally for specifying names of places and times,
including regions, mountains, rivers, lakes, deserts, airports,[34] hotels, restaurants, universities, days, months, years,[35] etc.:

náHal ha-yarkon   'The River Yarkon'[36]   נחל הירקון
midbar sahára   'The Sahara Desert'   מדבר סהרה
yeshivat mir   'The Mir Yeshiva'   ישיבת מיר
kibuts náHal-oz   'Kibbutz Nahal-Oz'   קיבוץ נחל-עוז
yemey sheni ve-Hamishi 'Monday and Thursday'   ימי שני וחמישי
shnat tashma   'The year 5745'   שנת תשמ"ה

However, עיר *ir* 'town', כפר *kfar* 'village' and the like require *apposition:* העיר חברון *ha-ir Hevron* 'the town of Hebron'; אי *i* 'island' prefers it. Conversely, names of organizations use the construct: מפלגת הלייבור *mifléget ha-léybor* 'the Labour Party'.[37]

The whole phrase is definite by virtue of the proper name, and there is generally no ה- *ha-*'the';[38] if there is, it is affixed to the name, eg. הר האברסט *har ha-éverest* 'Mt Everest' and most mountains.

Apposition is required for naming books, pictures, words and non-places in general (36.4):

ha-mila likud	'the word "Likud"'	המלה "ליכוד"
ha-tarkiv ákamol	'the preparation Akamol'	התרכיב אקמול
dugma shesh	'example six'	דוגמה שש

6.15 Attributive genitives: טילי הוק *tiley hok* 'Hawk missiles'

The construct genitive is used for brand names and other 'class names':

metosey ha-mig	'the Mig planes'	מטוסי המיג
shisha tsmigey alians	'six Alliance tires'	ששה צמיגי אליאנס
shisha atsey brosh	'six cypress trees'[39]	ששה עצי ברוש

The name can itself be a 'proper' or a 'common' noun in origin. In either event, it can take ה- *ha* 'the' when the phrase is definite (see the first example).[40]

The construct is also employed with any noun to append (by hyphen) a small range of nouns, adverbs and miscellaneous words to it. These serve the same purpose as adjectives (and a synonymous adjective often exists),[41] but do not constitute an obvious semantic family:

hearot (ha-)**shuláyim**	הערות-(ה)**שוליים**
remarks (the) **margin**	'(the) **marginal** remarks'
mahalumat (ha-)**néged**	מהלומת-(ה)**נגד**
blow (the) **against**	'(the) **counter** blow'
tsurat (ha-)**yesod**	צורת-(ה)**יסוד**
form (the) **basis**	'(the) **basic** form'

Further 'attributes' are: ביניים *beynáyim* 'intermediate', בכורה *bHora* 'maiden', גומלין *gomlin* 'reciprocal', חול *Hol* 'secular', חינם *Hinam* 'free', יתר *yéter* 'greater', משנה *mishne* 'secondary', נצח *nétsaH* 'eternal', עולם *olam* 'eternal', ענק *anak* 'giant', ערב *arav* 'Arab'. In addition, *idiomatic* constructs exist in which the second component is attributive, eg. חברת אם *Hevrat em* '**parent** company', כלבי זאב *kalbey ze'ev* 'german shepherds', אירגון גג *irgun gag* '**umbrella** organization'.

6.16 Superlative genitives: גדולי האומנים *gdoley ha-omanim* 'the greatest artists'

To express superlatives of the type 'the greatest artist(s)', one generally employs the 'degree words' ביותר *beyoter* or הכי *haHi* 'most' (20.2.2), but formal usage can instead nominalize the adjective and join it to the noun by -שב *she-be-* or by the construct.[42] The construct is generally limited, as in 6.19, to simplex adjectives (rather than verb-based or noun-based adjectives such as מוצלח *mutslaH* 'successful'):

ha-oman(im) ha-tov(im) beyoter the artist(s) the good most	האומנ(ים) הטוב(ים) ביותר
ha-oman(im) ha-Hi tov(im) the artist(s) the most good	האומנ(ים) הכי טוב(ים)
ha-tov(im) she-ba-omanim the good that in-the artists	הטוב(ים) שבאומנים
tov ha-omanim CONSTRUCT(s.) good the artists	טוב האומנים
tovey ha-omanim CONSTRUCT(pl.) good the artists	טובי האומנים
	'the best artist(s)'

This also includes the 'intrinsically superlative' adjectives such as ראשון *rishon* 'first', אחרון *aHaron* 'last'.

6.17 Miscellaneous noun+noun genitives

The noun+noun construct phrase serves to convey many other recurrent semantic relations, in set expressions such as יתוש הקדחת *yetush ha-kadáHat* 'the malaria mosquito' (cause of), מכת חשמל *makat Hashmal* 'electric shock' (caused by), תולעת משי *toláat méshi* 'silkworm' (maker of), סיר לחץ *sir láHats* 'pressure cooker' (works by).

There are also hosts of more idiomatic phrases; the component words themselves may be idiomatic, as well as their semantic relations: אילן יוחסין *ilan yoHasin* 'family tree', חלק הארי *Hélek ha-ari* 'the lion's share'.[43] *Names* involving a genitive are generally construct, eg. ראש העין 'Rosh Haayin' (a village), תוכנית אלון *toHnit alon* 'the Alon plan', מלחמת איראן-עיראק *milHémet iran-irak* 'the Iran-Iraq War'. Some idioms can have a construct *pronoun*, eg. לדעתי *ledaati* 'in my opinion', מיוחד במינו *meyuHad be-mino* 'unique'. A few require של *shel* 'of', eg. לאמיתו של דבר *laamito shel davar* 'in actual fact'.

Two types of construct components, illustrated below, are not otherwise available as nouns.

(1)   Hyphenated prefixes as in:

i-ha-havanot ha-éle		**אי-ההבנות האלה**
non	the understandings the these	'these misunderstandings'
COMPONENT	COMPONENT	
A	B	

| **du-**(ha)-leshoniut | **דו-(ה)לשוניות** |
| **bi-**(the)-lingualism | '(the) bilingualism' |

and similarly -חד *Had-* 'uni-', -רב *rav-* 'multi-', -תת *tat-* 'sub-', -קדם *kdam-* 'pre-', -בתר *batar-* 'post-'. The predicate or modifier of such phrases agrees with component B (the prefix, i.e component A, is unchanging and has no independent existence).[44] Casually, -ה *ha-* 'the' *precedes* the prefix; formally, it usually follows it.

(2)   A few adjectives act as a component B noun, as in כסאות-נוח *kisot nóaH* 'easy-chairs' (כסאות נוחים *kisot noHim* '**comfortable** chairs'), ימי שלישי *yemey shlishi* 'Tuesdays' (ימים שלישיים *yamim shlishiim* 'third days').

6.18   'Quantifier+noun' genitives

Quantifiers are discussed in full in Chapter 8, including several construct and של *shel* 'of' constructions (see 8.5). Briefly, while most quantity is expressed by simple apposition or by partitive -מ *mi-*, there are a few genitive usages.

(1)   Numerals are often in construct relation to their nouns, particularly 'definite' numerals, eg. אלף השנים *élef ha-shanim* 'the thousand years'; and they sometimes have their own construct form, eg. ששת הזוכים *shéshet ha-zoHim* 'the **six** winners'. This is described in general in 6.3 and in detail in 8.9.

(2)   Partitive quantifiers that are intrinsically definite must be construct, eg. מרבית השדרים *marbit ha-shdarim* 'most of the broadcasts'.

(3)   So, too, must fractions of a unit, eg. חצי שעה *Hatsi sha'a* 'half an hour', שני שליש מייל *shney shlish mayl* '⅔ mile'.

(4)   'Loose numerals' too must be construct, eg. מאות נמלים *me'ot nemalim* 'hundreds of ants'.

(5)   Certain regular nouns express quantity; these mostly take של *shel* 'of', eg. שפע של רבנים *shéfa shel rabanim* 'an abundance of rabbis'.

6.19   'Adjective+noun' genitives

There are three main types of adjective+noun genitive, all construct and all acting as adjective phrases (the adjective being the nucleus); they imply some kind of possession.

(1) 'Transferred adjective' (*bahuvrîhi*) constructs:

aHot adumat-eynáyim	אחות אדומת־עיניים
CONSTRUCT (f.s.)	'a red-eyed nurse'
nurse red eyes	(i.e a nurse with red eyes)

(2) 'Adjective and application' constructs:[46]

Hadarim mle'ey ashan	חדרים מלאי עשן
CONSTRUCT (m.pl.)	'smoke-filled rooms'
rooms full smoke	(i.e rooms filled with smoke)

(3) 'Quasi-adjectival' constructs:

musagim baaley Hashivut	מושגים בעלי חשיבות
CONSTRUCT (m.pl.)	'ideas of importance'
ideas having importance	

Types (1) and (2) are freely produced in formal Hebrew whereas casual registers use them just in certain expressions; type (3) is found in all usage but few adjectives are so employed. The adjective must be of the non-suffixed type, eg. גדול *gadol* 'large' or מוקף *mukaf* 'surrounded' and not ענקי *anaki* 'giant'. In all three types, definiteness of the adjective phrase is created by adding ה - *ha* 'the' to the component B noun:[47]

ha-aHot adumat-ha-eynáyim	האחות אדומת־העיניים
the nurse red the eyes	'the red-eyed nurse'

ha-musagim baaley ha-Hashivut	המושגים בעלי החשיבות
the ideas having the importance	'the ideas of importance'

In more detail: type (1) involves nouns denoting a kind of 'inalienable' possession (using this term loosely) - one's body, clothes, mental or spiritual state, traits and various intrinsic aspects of things (but not one's house, car, relatives, etc.). Examples are: רחב־כתפיים *reHav-ktefáyim* 'broad-shouldered', חום־חולצה *Hum-Hultsa* 'brown-shirted', גס־רוח *gas-rúaH* 'vulgar', ארוך־שנים *aroH-shanim* 'long-standing'. A hyphen is used. Among common idioms are קצר־ראיה *ktsar-reiya* 'short-sighted', רב־עוצמה *rav-otsma* 'powerful', קצר־טווח *ktsar-tvaH* 'short-range', יפה־נפש *yefe-néfesh* 'refined'. The ה - *ha-* 'the' in casual usage is sometimes placed in front. This construction is found both attributively and predicatively:[48]

od hayta adumat-eynáyim	עוד היתה אדומת־עיניים
CONSTRUCT	'She was still red-eyed'
still she-was red eyes	

Type (2) freely combines stative verbs or adjectives (which otherwise often take 'applicative' ב - *be-*) with a noun or noun *phrase* This is thus a more flexible construction than (1), and runs parallel to the adjective+object construction (described in 15.8):

isha levushat me'il aroH CONSTRUCT woman dressed coat long	אשה לבושת מעיל ארוך 'a woman dressed in a long coat'

ha-shtiHim meHusey ha-avak CONSTRUCT the carpets covered the dust	השטיחים מכוסי האבק 'the dust-covered carpets'

shney bakbukim mle'ey máyim CONSTRUCT two bottles full water	שני בקבוקים מלאי מים 'two bottles full of water'

These further differ from (1) in being only attributive, i.e they qualify a noun. Predicatively, instead of השטיחים **מכוסי**־אבק* *ha-shtiHim* **meHusey** *avak* 'the carpets are **covered** (CONSTRUCT) with dust', one uses the non-construct form:

ha-shtiHim meHusim avak FREE the carpets covered dust	השטיחים מכוסים אבק 'The carpets are covered with dust'

Besides this freely coined use, there are many kindred *idioms*; being tantamount to simple adjectives, they are available predicatively as well as attributively. For some the genitive is just an option,[49] eg. עשיר ... *ashir...* 'rich (in ...)':

medina	ashirat-neft ashira be-neft	עשירת־נפט עשירה בנפט	מדינה
country	rich (CONSTRUCT) oil rich in oil		'an oil-rich country'

and similarly (שומן,...) דלי *daley (shuman,....)* 'low-(fat,....)', (בהלה,...) אחוזי *aHuzey (behala,....)* '(panic,...)-gripped', זרועי־כוכבים *zeru'ey-koHavim* 'star-spangled', (תורה,...) צמאי *tsme'ey (tora,...)* '(Torah,...)-thirsty' etc. Others *require* the genitive:

yeladim **ivrey-tsva'im** children **blind** colours	ילדים **עיוורי-צבעים** 'colour-**blind** children'

and similarly (רעב,...) מוכי *mukey (ra'av,...)* '(hunger,...)-stricken', אסירי־תודה *asirey-toda* 'grateful'.

Type (3) involves a tiny group of construct adjectives or quasi-adjectives[50] combining freely with a noun. They denote inalienable possession (i.e body, clothes, traits) or lack. All function as attribute or predicate[51]

hem baaley teavon atsum CONSTRUCT they **having** appetite huge	הם **בעלי** תאבון עצום 'They have a huge appetite'

hi Hasrat éreH musari	היא **חסרת** ערך מוסרי
CONSTRUCT	'She lacks moral value'
she **lacking** value moral	

ha-dira bat Hamisha Hadarim	הדירה **בת** חמישה חדרים
CONSTRUCT	
the apartment **consisting** five rooms 'The apartment consists of five rooms'	

A fourth 'adjectival' genitive is casual. It involves של *shel* 'of', but is restricted to a handful of indefinite 'adjectives' - see 9.2, under (n).

hayu sham **yófi shel rakdaniot**	היו שם **יופי של רקדניות**
were there **beauty of dancers**	'There were **beautiful dancers** there'

This actually employs two *nouns*, the first adjective-based (שגעון *shiga'on* 'lunacy', i.e 'amazing', מותק *mótek* 'sweet(ness)') and the second any noun. The second is the nucleus for predicates to agree with.

6.20 'Verbal participle+noun' genitives

itonim rodfey sensátsyot   'sensation-seeking papers'   עיתונים רודפי־סנסציות

Formally, many verbs taking a direct object allow their present tense to be construct in cases where the whole phrase is qualifying a noun:

ההורים של ילדים **מקבלי** טיפול מתבקשים להישאר

ha-horim shel yeladim **mekabley**   tipul mitbakshim lehisha'er
                   CONSTRUCT COMPONENT B
   the parents of children **receiving** treatment are-asked to-remain

More often one uses a relative clause: ילדים המקבלים טיפול *yeladim ha-mekablim tipul* 'children who are receiving treatment'.

This parallels the 'agent construct' described in 6.10.[52]

FURTHER READING
Azar 1977: 2.3-2.4, 1985; Berman 1978: chs. 7, 8, 10, 11; Givón 1979; Glinert 1977a, 1978; Levi 1976; Ornan 1979a: 4.6-4.7; Reif 1968; Rosén 1966a, 1977: 6.5; Seikevicz 1979.

7. Pronouns and other pro-words

7.1 Definitions

A 'pro-word' enables one to refer loosely to a noun, adverb or some other word without the need for detailed repetition. Hebrew has various kinds of pro-words: pronouns, pro-adverbs, pro-verbs, pro-adjectives and pro-quantifiers, for example:

ha-tinok hitorer, ve-**hu** boHe   התינוק התעורר, **והוא** בוכה
'The baby's woken up, and **he's** crying'

nasánu le-tsfat, ki aHoti gára **sháma**   נסענו לצפת כי אחותי גרה **שמה**
'We went to Tsfat because my sister lives **there**'

'Ellipsis' goes one step further than a pro-word: it omits all mention of the word being referred to:

Hashávti lilbosh svéder, ve-lo laváshti   חשבתי ללבוש סוודר, ולא לבשתי
'I thought of wearing a sweater, and I didn't wear ⟨one⟩.'

Ellipsis is dealt with in chapter 17.

7.2-7 DEFINITE PRO-WORDS

7.2 Introduction : definite pro-words

Definition: A 'definite' pro-word refers one to a person or thing whose identity one is thought to know.

Definite pro-words are of five types, described in 7.3-7: (1) personal pronouns, eg. אני *ani* 'I', זה *ze* 'it'; (2) demonstrative pronouns, as in רצו את **זה או את ההוא?** *ratsu et* **ze** *o et* **hahu?** 'Did they want **this one** or **that one**?'; (3) pro-clauses (i.e representing clauses), as in יהיו שינויים אך מכחישים **זאת** *yiyu shinuyim aH makHishim* **zot** 'There will be changes but they deny **it**'; (4) other types of pro-words, eg. שם *sham* 'there, כך *kaH* 'in this way'; (5) anticipatory pro-words ('antecedents'), as in מי שיאחר ייענש *mi she-yeaHer yeanesh* '**Those** who are late will be punished'.

7.3 Personal pronouns : the forms

7.3.1 As subject or predicate

ani	'I'	אני
ata	'you' (m.s.)	אתה
at	'you' (f.s.)	את
hu	'he, it'	הוא
hi	'she, it'	היא
ze	'it'	זה
anáHnu / ánu (F)	'we'	אנחנו / אנו
atem	'you' (m.pl.)	אתם
aten (F)	'you' (f.pl.)	אתן
hem	'they' (m.)	הם
hen (F)	'they' (f.)	הן

Examples of such use are:

ani ha-av	'I am the father'	אני האב
ha-av ze ani	'The father is me'	האב זה אני

The 3rd person pronouns הוא, היא, זה, הם, הן *hu, hi, ze, hem, hen* also act as present tense particles of 'being', eg. הסיפור **הוא** משל *ha-sipur* **hu** *mashal* 'The tale **is** a parable'; see 16.2.

When referring back to someone or something just mentioned, Hebrew generally uses הוא, היא, הם, הן *hu, hi, hem, hen* according to gender and number:

matsu et ha-tabáat, aval **hi** sruta	מצאו את הטבעת, אבל היא שרוטה
f.s. f.s. 'They found the ring, but it ⟨is⟩ scratched'	

But with reference to a thing ('it') in a *preceding sentence*, casual usage can employ masculine זה *ze*, whatever the thing's gender:

yesh kufsa? réga, eH	ze nira (m.s.)	יש קופסה? רגע, איך זה נראה ?
f.s.	hi niret (f.s.)	היא נראית
	'Is there a box? One moment, what does it look like?'	

זה *ze* has a feminine form זאת / זו *zot/zo/zu* and a genderless plural אלה / אלו *éle/élu* when used as a demonstrative pronoun 'this' (7.4), as a reciprocal pronoun 'one another' (7.13) or as a determiner 'this (man, mouse)' (9.2).[1]

Though usually referring *backwards*, these pronouns can refer forwards to something in a containing clause:

be-hityaHaso le-harHakat bérkovits	בהתייחסו להרחקת ברקוביץ
amar ha-meamen ki...	אמר המאמן כי...
'In ⟨his⟩ referring to the sending off of Berkovitz, the trainer said that...'	
(Where there is co-reference between 'his' and 'the trainer')	

While the gender distinction between singular אתה *ata* and את *at* and between הוא *hu* and היא *hi* is rigorously maintained, that between plural אתם *atem* and אתן *aten* and between הם *hem* and הן *hen* is relaxed colloquially - the masculine is preferred. The same holds for the plural *suffixes* in ן- ,ם- - *-m*, *-n*, illustrated in 7.3.2.

7.3.2   In other syntactic roles

Elsewhere, i.e as direct object, modifier or following a preposition, all personal pronouns (except זה *ze* 'it') become suffixes. Examples are given below. For more details, see sections 15.5, 6.2 and 42.2, respectively; full tables are given in traditional grammars.

The direct object suffix is appended directly to the verb, but it is formal and rather uncommon and in all usage the 'direct object marker' *et* generally intervenes and itself takes the pronoun suffix, eg. להזהיר אתכם *lehazhir etHem* 'to warn you':

lehazhiréni	'to warn me'	להזהירני
lehazhirHa	...you (m.s.)	להזהירך
lehazhireH	...you (f.s.)	להזהירך
lehazhiro	...him, it	להזהירו
lehazhira	...her, it	להזהירה
lehazhirénu	...us	להזהירנו
lehazhirHem	...you (m.pl.)	להזהירכם
lehazhirHen	...you (f.pl.)	להזהירכן
lehazhiram	...them (m.)	להזהירם
lehazhiran	...them (f.)	להזהירן

The modifier ('construct, possessive') suffix is appended directly to nouns, in much the same way as noun is juxtaposed to noun in construct phrases. But often, instead, the 'possessive' preposition של *shel* 'of' intervenes, especially in colloquial usage, eg. האיום שלי *ha-iyum sheli* 'my threat' (lit. the threat of-me).

iyumi	'my threat'	איומי
iyumHa	your (m.s.)...	איומך
iyumeH	your (f.s.)...	איומך
iyumo	his, its...	איומו
iyuma	her, its...	איומה
iyuménu	our...	איומנו
iyumHem	your (m.pl.)...	איומכם
iyumHen	your (f.pl.)...	איומכן
iyumam	their (m.)...	איומם
iyuman	their (f.)...	איומן

The only method by which prepositions can take pronouns is by suffixation:

biglali	'because of me'	בגללי
biglalHa	...you (m.s.)	בגללך
biglaleH	...you (f.s.)	בגללך
biglalo	...him, it	בגללו
biglala	...her, it	בגללה
biglalénu	...us	בגללנו
biglalHem	...you (m.pl.)	בגללכם
biglalHen	...you (f.pl.)	בגללכן
biglalam	...them (m.)	בגללם
biglalan	...them (f.)	בגללן

The personal pronouns cannot themselves be qualified; instead, זה, זאת, אלה *ze, zot, éle*, etc. are used, and in a limited way, eg. מה עם **אלה** בצלוחית? *ma im éle ba-tsloHit* 'What about **the ones** in the bowl?'; see 7.7.

7.3.3   Omitting the subject pronoun

Aside from such general processes of omission described under coordination (ch.35) and ellipsis (ch. 17), subject pronouns can be omitted under various circumstances.

With verbs already bearing a 1st or 2nd person affix,[2] i.e past and future tense verbs, the subject pronoun is omitted *generally* in formal usage (example 1), and *often* (depending partly on rhythm and balance) in casual usage (2), except with the 1st person singular future (3).

With verbs inflected for 3rd person[3] and referring to *people*, the subject pronoun is omitted sometimes in formal usage (4) but not in casual usage

Present tense verbs, though they have no person inflection, do sometimes omit the 3rd person pronoun (5).

(1)   asbir zot ba-hemsheH
      1st pers.
      will-explain this later

אסביר זאת בהמשך

'I will explain this later'

(2)   ma (ata) asíta sháma?
         2nd pers.
      what (you) did there?

מה (אתה) עשית שמה?

'What did you do there?'

(3)   ani asbir et ze aHár-kaH
      1st pers.
      I will-explain OM this later

אני אסביר את זה אחר-כך

'I'll explain this later'

(4)   yóav yatsa mukdam. le'et érev (hu)
      Hazar, u-ve-yado tik
         'Yoav left early. Towards evening he returned, with a bag in his hand'

יואב יצא מוקדם. לעת ערב (הוא)
חזר, ובידו תיק

(5)   tsa'ákti lo ve-nofáfti lo be-dgalim lirot.
      (hu) lo yore
         'I shouted to him and waved to him with flags to shoot. He doesn't shoot'

צעקתי לו ונופפתי לו בדגלים לירות.
(הוא) לא יורה

A quite separate phenomenon, and not a real case of pronoun omission, is the 'impersonal 3rd person plural', eg. ירו שם *yaru sham* '⟨they⟩ were shooting there' (see ch. 17).

The subject pronoun cannot be omitted when it undergoes emphasis, focus or coordination, hence:

ata tasbir la	'You will explain to her'	אתה תסביר לה
rak ani yadáti	'Only I knew'	רק אני ידעתי
ani ve-yóni nivHárnu	'Yoni and I were chosen'	אני ויוני נבחרנו

7.4   Demonstrative pronouns

The demonstrative points to items in the physical context or constrasts items in the verbal context.

Physical context

Pointing to things, without contrast, Hebrew uses neuter זה *ze* 'that' and אלה *éle* 'those'. Even though the gender of an object may be evident, one does not use the masculine or feminine pronouns (הוא, היא, הם, הן *hu, hi, hem, hen* and זאת *zot* etc. are considered specifically masculine or feminine):

kaH et ze miyad	'Take that immediately'	קח את זה מיד

(pointing to a lamp, מנורה *menora* (f.)):

eH ze oved	'How does it work?'	איך זה עובד?

Pointing to people, one uses the gender-marked הוא, היא, הם, הן *hu, hi, hem, hen*, but also אלה *éle*; to use זה *ze* and זאת *zot* can be disparaging (similarly, the very casual זאתי *zóti*):

leH tishal	oto	אותו
	et ha-adam ha-ze	לך תשאל את האדם הזה
	'Go and ask	him
		that person

ma	hem	rotsim?	מה הם אלה רוצים?
	éle		

'What do those people want?'

Pointing to things *contrastively:* זה *ze* is both 'this' and 'that', אלה *éle* is 'these, those'. Where a noun was mentioned, gender is expressed: זה, זאת, אלה *ze, zot, éle* 'this one (m.), this one (f.), those ones'. (Formal usage requires a noun with ההוא *hahu* etc., eg. הרכב ההוא *ha-réHev hahu* 'that vehicle'.)

toHal o et **ze** o et **ze**	תאכל או את **זה** או את **זה**
	'Eat either **this** or **that**'
hine smiHot, kaH et *zot*	הנה שמיכות, קח את זאת
	'Here are blankets, take *this one*'
hahem nora yafim	**ההם** נורא יפים
	'**Those ones** are awfully pretty'

Contrastive pointing to people is similar to the non-contrastive usage mentioned above, with the alternative of ההוא *hahu* 'that guy' and its inflections casually, and הלה *hala* 'that man' formally:

al tishal oto éla *oto*,   אל תשאל אותו אלא אותו,
   sháma al-yad ha-kiosk   שמה על-יד הקיוסק!

'Don't ask him, ask *him*, there by the kiosk!'

éle   אלה
      bikshu kódem   ביקשו קודם
hahem   ההם

'Those people asked first'

Verbal context

Referring *back* by a 'demonstrative', as against an ordinary 'definite prounoun' (see 7.3), is by definition a matter of contrast, but this may amount to no more than distinguishing 'the former' or 'the latter'. זה/זאת *ze/zot* and אלה *éle* are used (examples 2-4), or sometimes האחרון *ha-aHaron* 'the latter' and suchlike:

(1) yóav ve-ishto tsiltselu   יואב ואשתו צילצלו
    aval **hem** (*éle) lo hishíru hoda'a   אבל **הם** (*אלה) לא השאירו הודעה
    'Yoav and his wife rang but **they** didn't leave a message'

(2) ha-italkim hiskímu gam panínu el   האיטלקים הסכימו. גם פנינו אל
    ha-shvitsárim aH **éle** hitnagdu   השוויצרים אך **אלה** התנגדו
         DEMONSTRATIVE
    'The Italians agreed. We also asked the Swiss but **the latter** objected'

(3) ba-hafsaka huzaku el ha-yatsía   בהפסקה הוזעקו אל היציע
    rof'a shel ha-po'el ve-ha-mease   רופאה של הפועל והמעסה
    letapel be-ohed she-kibel hetkef lev.   לטפל באוהד שקיבל התקף-לב.
    éle natnu la-ish tipul rishoni ve..   **אלה** נתנו לאיש טיפול ראשוני ו...

'In the interval the Hapoel doctor and the masseur were called
to the stand to treat a fan who had a heart attack.
The former gave the man preliminary treatment and...'

(4) ha-sar bikesh et zHut ha-dibur.   השר ביקש את זכות הדיבור.
    aH **zo** lo nitna lo   אך **זו** לא ניתנה לו
    'The minister requested the right to speak. But **that** was not
                 granted to him'

Correlatives involve two or more of זה/זאת/אלה *ze/zot/éle*:

shneyhem amru she-yavóu,   שניהם אמרו שיבואו,
    aval **ze** be-yavan ve-**ze** be-kafrisin   אבל **זה** ביוון ו**זה** בקפריסין
    'Both said they'd come, but **one**'s in Greece and the **other**'s in Cyprus'

Correlatives are also used in what is not strictly a 'definite' sense, akin to the use of הזה *ha-ze* as 'some' in הבחור הזה *ha-baHur ha-ze* 'this (= some) guy':

éle ohavim oto, éle son'im oto,   אלה אוהבים אותו, אלה שונאים אותו,
ve-éle adishim   ואלה אדישים
'**Some** like him, **some** hate him, and **some** don't care'

ani lo rotsa laasot haHlalot: אני לא רוצה לעשות הכללות:
ha-tseirim kulam ganavim ve-ze ve-ze..   הצעירים כולם גנבים וזה וזה...
'I don't want to make generalizations:
young people are all thieves and **this** and **that**...'

For reciprocal pronouns, related to correlatives, see 7.13. For 'the former... the latter' one uses זה הראשון... זה האחרון *ze ha-rishon... ze ha-aHaron*:

irak ve-luv needru, **zo ha-rishona**   עירק ולוב נעדרו, **זו הראשונה**
be-mikre ve-**zo ha-aHarona** be-Havana   במקרה ו**זו האחרונה** בכוונה
'Iraq and Lybia were absent, **the former** by chance
and **the latter** deliberately'

7.5 Pro-clauses

To refer back to a whole clause, rather than a noun or a phrase, one uses not personal pronouns but 'pro-clauses':

Formal:
zot/ha-davar   זאת/הדבר

yiyu shinuyim, aH makHishim **zot** / **et ha-davar**   יהיו שינויים, אך מכחישים **זאת** / **את הדבר**
'There will be changes, but they deny **it**'

Neutral:
kaH/ken   כך/כן

shovtim? matay hodíu al **kaH**?   שובתים? מתי הודיעו על **כך**?
'They're on strike? When did they announce **it**?'

nifgáshnu kshe-tiyálnu o lifnéy-**Hen**?   נפגשנו כשטיילנו או לפני-**כן**?
'Did we meet while we were touring or before**hand**?'

Casual:
ze   זה

nidme li she-yamshíHu, aval ani néged **ze**   נדמה לי שימשיכו, אבל אני נגד **זה**
'I think they'll go on, but I'm against **it**'

Thus, Hebrew disallows:

*yiyu shinuyim, aH makHishim **oto**   *יהיו שינויים, אך מכחישים **אותו**
'There will be changes, but they deny **it**'

*yiyu shinuyim, im ki **hu** hukHash   *יהיו שינויים, אם כי **הוא** הוכחש
'There will be changes, although **it** has been denied'

There are syntactic limitations on 'pro-clauses'; they function as set out in the following table

AS SUBJECT		AS DIRECT OBJECT[1]	

זאת *zot*

In the idiom:

| zot oméret... | זאת אומרת... | ishru zot | אישרו זאת |
| | 'This means...' | | 'They confirmed it' |

and followed by abstract prepositions, e.g.:

| zot biglal... | זאת - בגלל... | | |
| | 'This is due to...' | | |

| zot lamrot... | זאת - למרות... | | |
| | 'This is in spite of...' | | |

הדבר *ha-davar*

iHárnu. ha-davar	איחרנו. הדבר	ishru et ha-davar	אישרו את הדבר
hivhilam	הבהילם		'They confirmed it'
'We were late. It confounded them'			

כך *kaH*[2]

Before verbs of conjecture:

| kaH nidme li | כך נדמה לי |
| 'It seems so' | |

| kaH omrim | כך אומרים |
| 'So they say' | |

כן *ken*[3]

After - ש *she*[4] - with verbs of conjecture:

| nidme li she-ken | נדמה לי שכן |
| 'It seems so' | |

| omrim she-ken | אומרים שכן |
| 'So they say' | |

זה *ze*

neHtáHti, ve-ze hifHid	נחתכתי, וזה הפחיד	neHtáHti, aval	נחתכתי, אבל
'I got cut, and it was scary'		shaHáHti et ze	שכחתי את זה
			'I got cut, but I forgot it'

AS INDIRECT OBJECT		ADVERBIALLY	

זאת *zot*

With certain prepositions (see 19.3.5), e.g.

| be-zot ani meshuHna | בזאת אני משוכנע | lamrot zot | למרות זאת |
| 'Of this I am convinced' | | | 'despite it' |

הדבר *ha-davar*

| hizhárti me-ha-davar | הזהרתי מהדבר |
| 'I warned against it' | |

AS INDIRECT OBJECT		ADVERBIALLY	

כך *kaH*

kaH mekavim	כך מקווים	With certain prepositions, eg.	
	'So they hope'		
ganvu ve-hodu be-HaH	גנבו והודו בכך	aHár-kaH	אחר-כך
	'They stole and confessed to it'		'afterwards'

כן *ken*

After - ש *she* - with verbs of conjecture: With certain prepositions, eg.

| metsapim she-ken | מצפים שכן | lifney-Hen | לפני-כן |
| | 'They expect so' | | 'beforehand' |

זה *ze*

ganvu ve-hodu be-ze	גנבו והודו בזה	neHtáHti ve-biglal	נחתכתי ובגלל
	'They stole and confessed to it'	ze iHárti	זה איחרתי
		'I got cut, and because of it I was late'	

Notes:
1 זאת *zot* as a 'pro-clause' does not normally accept את *et*; זה *ze* requires it. As personal pronouns, both זה *ze* and זאת *zot* require את *et*.
2 כך *kaH* and כן *ken* as subjects or objects behave almost identically. Instead of שכן *she-ken*, one can use pre-verbal כך *kaH*, with the expected preposition omitted in both instances (but inserted when כך *kaH* follows the verb): קיווה לכך קיווה *kiva le-HaH* 'he hoped so' as against כך קיווה *kaH kiva* or קיווה שכן *kiva she-ken*.
3 An entirely separate use of כן *ken* is as an 'emphatic particle', preceding the predicate: אני כן רופא *ani ken rofe* 'I *am* a doctor'.
4 With verbs implying fact ('factives') rather than conjecture, שכן *she-ken* just functions emphatically: אני זוכר שכן *ani zoHer she-ken* 'I remember that he *did*' (and similar). Adjectives too take כך *kaH*, כן *ken*: כך ברור לי, ברור לי שכן *kaH barur li, barur li she-ken* 'It's clearly so'.

7.6 Other pro-words: שם *sham* 'there', כך *kaH* 'like that' etc.

Besides pro-nouns and pro-clauses, there are other kinds of 'definite pro-word' (for pro-adverb vs. pronoun, see 15.3.7):

Pro-adverb

Of time: az	'then'	אז		aHshav 'now'	עכשיו	
Of place: sham	'there'	שם		kan	'here'	כאן
sháma (C)		שמה		po		פה
Of manner or means: kaH	'in that (or 'this') way'	כך				
káHa		ככה				

For example:

ani medaber be-láHash,   אני מדבר בלחש,
   ki kulam medabrim **kaH**   כי כולם מדברים **כך**
                        'I talk in a whisper, because everyone talks **like that**'

Correlatively, one uses פה... שם *po... sham* 'here.. there':

po haya kise, sham haya shrafraf   פה היה כיסא, שם היה שרפרף
                        'Here there was a chair, there there was a stool'

Pro-verb: עשה *asa* 'do' is used for representing dynamic (but not stative) verbs:

ha-madriH Havash pitom kasda,   המדריך חבש פתאום קסדה,
   az gam ani **asíti** káHa   אז גם אני **עשיתי** ככה
                        'The guide suddenly donned a helmet, so I also **did** so'

Pro-adjective

   kaze (m.s.)   כזה
   kazot/kazo/kazu (f.s.)   כזאת/כזו
   ka'éle/ka'élu (pl.)   כאלה/כאלו

For example.

   sára HesHonit meod,   שרה חסכונית מאד,
      ve-gam bita hi **kazot**   וגם בתה היא **כזאת**
                        'Sara is very frugal, and her daughter is also **like that**'

Pro-quantifier: כך *kaH* 'that number of':

   kiblu méa mígim.   קיבלו מאה מיגים.
      ve-od yoter mi-**kaH** tánkim   ועוד יותר מ**כך** טנקים
                        'They received one hundred Migs, and even more than **that number of**
                                                                        tanks'

7.7   Anticipatory pro-words ('antecedents'): מי שיאחר *mi she-yeaHer* 'those who are late'

7.7.1   Types of anticipatory pro-word

Examples (1) and (2) illustrate the two kinds of anticipatory pro-word, i.e antecedents of relative clauses and antecedents of apposed clauses, respectively:

(1)   ze she-eyno lomed shoHéah   זה שאינו לומד שוכח
                        'He who doesn't study forgets'

(2)   ze she-eynHa lomed madhim oti   זה שאינך לומד מדהים אותי
                        'The fact you don't study astounds me'

In these examples the pronoun does not refer back but forwards - to an unsaid 'someone', subject of לומד *lomed* 'study' in (1), and to the whole apposed clause in (2). In (2) it serves to avoid creating a sentence that itself begins directly with a subordinate clause; introducing this clause with זה *ze* gives it the compactness of a noun phrase

7.7.2 Pro-words as relative antecedents

We illustrate these pro-words in tables, first as *pronouns*, then as *pro-adverbs* 'incorporating' a pronoun. (see pages 61 and 62)

For pronouns, instead of a whole relative clause, a simple adverbial phrase may appear; but then only ...אלה ,זאת ,זה *ze, zot, éle..* (referring back to a certain noun) are used:

kehilot shlemot, kegon	קהילות שלמות, כגון
éle mi-teyman, alu ártsa	**אלה מתימן,** עלו ארצה

'Whole communities such as **those from Yemen** came to Israel'

Whereas זה *ze* as a personal pronoun normally denotes a thing ('it', see 7.3), as an antecedent it can denote a person.

For the pro-adverbs, we distinguish non-specific ש- איפה *éfo she-* 'wherever...' from specific ש- איפה *éfo she-* 'where', the latter casual. All these pro-adverbs can be seen as incorporating a noun, which takes a relative clause For example, איפה *éfo*, which interrogatively means 'where?' (i.e 'in which *place*?') here means 'in a place (in which...)' or (non-specific sense) 'in whichever place (in which...)'. Similarly, ש- מתי *matay she..* 'when/whenever' is 'at a time/at whatever time (at which...)', and so on. The list of such 'interrogatives' acting as 'relatives' also includes כמה *káma* 'how many/however many', איזה *éze* 'which/whichever' (see 33.4.2 for further details).

7.7.3 Pro-words as antecedents of apposed clauses

Many verbs, adjectives, derived nouns and prepositions take a clause directly, without the need for זה *ze* or כך *kaH*, which are then often deemed superfluous:

hitsiu sh-tanúHi	הציעו שתנוחי

'They suggested that you rest'

hatsaatam she-tanúHi niret li	הצעתם שתנוחי נראית לי

'Their suggestion that you rest makes sense'

biglal she-HósheH, nitstareH ligmor	בגלל שחושך, נצטרך לגמור

'Because it's dark, we'll have to stop'

Where the ...ש זה *ze she..* construction is the subject of the whole sentence, as in the first example in the table, זה *ze* can be omitted either if the predicate of the whole sentence comes first (example (1) below) or if a second זה *ze* separates the subject from the predicate (ex. 2); this second זה *ze*, an instance of the verb 'to be' (16.3.8), is casual:

(1)	tov she-bat	טוב שבאת
	PRED SUBJ CLAUSE	'It's good that you came'
	good that you-came	

Pronouns as relative antecedents

PRONOUN		EXAMPLE
Persons[1] mi ze, zot, éle…	מי זה, זאת, אלה…	מי שדפק לא הזדהה זה mi she-dafak lo hizdaha ze 'The person who knocked didn't identify himself'
Referring to a certain noun: ze, zot, éle…	זה, זאת, אלה…	באו הרבה מורים, וגם זה שפגשת אז הם báu harbe morim, ve-gam ze she-pagasht 'Many teachers came, even the one you met'
Things ma	מה	מה שקרה זה טוב ma she-kara ze tov 'What happened is fine'
Referring to a certain noun: ze, zot, éle…	זה, זאת, אלה…	קח נורה, אפילו זו שבתיק kaH nura, afilu zu she-ba-tik 'Take a bulb, even the one that's in the bag'

Note:[1] The personal pronouns (הוא *hu* 'he' etc.) can themselves be antecedents to a relative clause, but only when they are referring backwards, i.e. 'he, who…' rather than 'he who…' (see 33.4.1).

Pro-adverbs as relative antecedents

PRO-ADVERB		EXAMPLE (non-specific)	EXAMPLE (specific) casual
Place:			
éfo	'where' אֵיפֹה	shev éfo she-tirtse שב איפה שתרצה 'Sit where you wish'	shev éfo she-ha-amud שב איפה שהעמוד 'Sit where the pole is'
heHan	'where' (F) הֵיכָן		
le'an	'to where' לְאָן	sa le'an she-nóaH סע לאן שנוח 'Go wherever's easy'	sa le'an she-nasánu kódem סע לאן שנסענו קודם 'Go where we went before'
Time:			
matay	'when' מָתַי	sa matay she-nóaH סע מתי שנוח 'Go whenever's convenient'	eH she-niHnásti, ze nafal איך שנכנסתי, זה נפל 'As I came in, it fell'
eH	'as' (C) אֵיךְ		
Manner:			
kmo	'like' כְּמוֹ	red eH she-tirtse רד איך שתרצה 'Get down the way you want'	tinhag kmo she-ani noheg תנהג כמו שאני נוהג 'Act like I act' (neutral usage)
eH	'like' אֵיךְ		

(2) she-bat ze tov   שבאת זה טוב
     SUBJ CLAUSE PRED   'That you came is good'
     that you-came is good

Where, as in (2), the subject clause comes first, one has the choice between
inserting זה *ze* to show where the subject clause has ended or turning the subject clause into a (more 'manageable') noun phrase by beginning with זה ש- *ze
she-* (as in (3) below). Indeed, both can be found together:

(3) ze she-bat (ze) tov   זה שבאת (זה) טוב
     SUBJ CLAUSE   PRED
                                                            'That you came is good'
     that you-came is good

7.7.4 זה *ze* as 'dummy' subject[4]

A further use of antecedent pronoun זה *ze* is as a 'dummy' subject
for sentences like (1) above, where the subject clause is delayed till after the
predicate. There is, in fact, a whole range of such subject clauses (see 31.4). This
זה *ze* is optional, and most common in casual Hebrew:[5]

     (ze)   tov she-bat   (זה) טוב שבאת
     DUMMY SUBJ SUBJ CLAUSE   'It's good you came'
     (it) good that you-came
     (ze) tov lavo ktsat be-iHur   (זה) טוב לבוא קצת באיחור
                 INFINITVAL CLAUSE   'It's good to come a bit late'
     (it) good to-come a-bit late
     (ze) barur mi hem?   (זה) ברור מי הם?
                 INTERROG. CLAUSE   'Is it clear who they are?'
     (it) clear who they?

This 'dummy זה *ze*' is generally impossible where (a) the predicate is not of
the sort that ever takes a subject: די *day* 'is sufficient', התחשק ל- *hitHashek
le-* 'fancy', אפשר *efshar* 'is possible', מוטב *mutav* 'is better'; as they and many
others do not take a subject noun (thus ruling out *הדבר אפשר* *ha-davar
efshar* 'the thing is possible'), זה *ze* is not needed as a 'dummy' subject:

     (*ze) efshar / mutav lakum   (*זה) אפשר / מוטב לקום
                                                            'It's possible / better to stand up'

Similarly, (b) with certain other predicates, e.g.

     (*ze) mutar / asur latset   (*זה) מותר / אסור לצאת
                                                            'It's all right / forbidden to leave'

Nor is it used (c) where a ל- *le-* 'for, to' phrase accompanies the predicate -
most commonly where this is an experiential adjective such as קשה (לי) *kashe
(li)* 'hard (for me)', נוח (לי) *nóaH (li)* 'convenient (for me)', which tend to have
no subject in any event (see 15.6, 17.3):

Forms and examples of pro-words as antecedents of apposed clauses

		AS SUBJECT	DIRECT OBJECT	INDIRECT OBJECT	ADVERBIAL
ze	זה	זה שֶׁבָּאתָ (זֶה) טוֹב ze she-bat (ze) tov 'The fact that you came is great'	הִזְכִּירוּ אֶת זֶה שֶׁאֵין hizkiru et ze she-en 'They mentioned the fact that there's none'	מִתְנַגְּדִים לְזֶה שֶׁאָבוֹא mitnagdim le-ze she-avo 'They object to my coming'	אֲנִי בְּעַד זֶה שֶׁתֵּלֵךְ ani be'ad ze she-teleH 'I'm all for your going'
ha-davar (F)	הדבר	כְּבָר נִשְׁכְּחָה הַדָּבָר, שֶׁגַּם הֵם זָרִים kvar nishkaH ha-davar, she-gam hem zarim 'It has already been forgotten that they too are aliens'	not in use	not in use	not in use
kaH	כך	not in use	not in use	מִתְנַגְּדִים לְכָךְ שֶׁאָבוֹא mitnagdim le-HaH she-avo 'They object to my coming'	not in use

Note:

[1] כך *kaH* can sometimes be extraposed from the clause it introduces:

be-HaH shona mila zo min ha-aHerot
she-hi rak baalat tafkid
shel kishur
'This word differs from the others **in this respect**: that it only has a connective function'

בְּכָךְ שׁוֹנָה מִלָּה זוֹ מִן הָאֲחֵרוֹת
שֶׁהִיא רַק בַּעֲלַת תַּפְקִיד
שֶׁל קִישּׁוּר

(*זה) נראה לי שצדקו
(*ze) nira li she-tsadku
(it) seems to-me that they-were-right   'It seems to me that they were right'

(*זה) טוב לך שהסכימו
(*ze) tov laH she-hiskimu
(it) good for-you that they-agreed   'It's good for you that they agreed'

7.8 Indefinite pro-words

'Indefinite' pro-words refer to someone/thing not yet identifiable by the addressee, e.g. מישהו *míshehu* 'someone' as against הוא *hu* 'he'.

The positive indefinites are as follows, with the inseparable particle שהו- -*shehu* being added in many cases to the interrogative pro-word.[6]

Persons: מישהו *míshehu* 'someone (m.)', מישהי *míshehi* 'someone (f.)'. The masculine is used whenever 'someone' is not specifically feminine. The plural is כמה אנשים *káma anashim* 'some people' or similar. The correlative מי... ומי *mi...umi* 'some... and some' can be used formally in apposed phrases (cf. מי ש- *mi she-* 'he who...', 7.7):

את זה רואים, מי במידה רבה ומי
et ze ro'im, mi be-mida raba u-mi
במידה פחותה, כערך בפני עצמו
be-mida pHuta, ke-éreH bifney atsmo
'They regard this, some to a greater and some to a lesser extent, as a value in itself'

אחד *eHad*, אחת *aHat* 'someone' (m. and f. respectively), followed by a relative clause, or meaning 'one' with a specific noun in mind:

בלשן זה אחד שמסבך משהו קל
balshan ze eHad she-mesabeH máshehu kal
'A linguist is someone who complicates something easy'

באו שוטרים, ואחד דפק
báu shotrim, ve-eHad dafak
'Some policemen came, and one knocked'

כאלה *ka'éle* 'some (pl.)', with a specific noun in mind; it is not partitive:

דרוזים? יש כאלה בצפון
drúzim? yesh ka'éle ba-tsafon
'Druze? There are some up North'

Things: משהו *máshehu*, דבר-מה *dvar-ma* (F) denote 'something'; אחד *eHad*, אחת *aHat*[7] are 'one' (m. and f. respectively) for a specific noun:

יש עוגות, קח אחת
yesh ugot, kaH aHat
'There are cakes, take one'

כזה/כזאת *kaze/kazot* 'one (m./f.)', כאלה *ka'éle* 'some (pl.)' are for a specific noun; they are not partitive:

שטרודל זה טוב, תאפי פעם כזה
shtrúdel ze tov, tofi paam kaze
'Strudel's nice, bake one sometime'

Place: איפהשהו *éfoshehu* (c), אי-שם *ey-sham* (F) 'somewhere' (commonly also באיזהשהו מקום *be-ézeshehu makom*); לאנשהו *le'ánshehu* (c) 'to somewhere'.

Time: פעם *páam* (c), מתישהו *matáyshehu* (c), אי-פעם *ey-páam* (F) 'some time'.

Manner: איכשהו *éHshehu* 'somehow'.

For *negative* indefinites, eg. אף אחד *af eHad* 'no one', כלום *klum* 'nothing', see 29.10.

7.9   Interrogative pro-words

For מי *mi* 'who?', כיצד *keytsad* 'how?', למה *láma* 'why?' etc., see 26.3.

7.10   Relative pro-words

For such words as הספר שדיברתי עליו *ha-séfer she-dibárti alav* 'the book that I spoke about ⟨it⟩', see 33.3.

7.11   Generic pro-words

A generic pro-word denotes persons or things in general, without explicitly saying כל *kol* 'all'; for example:

le'itim **ata** to'e	'Sometimes **one** is wrong'	לעיתים **אתה** טועה
ze tov po	'It's good here'	**זה** טוב פה

For persons: אתה/את/אתם/אתן *ata/at/atem/aten* 'you (m.s./f.s./m.pl./ f.pl.)'. When addressing a woman or a group, אתה *ata* may used regardless:

leitim ata yodéa she-taíta, śara	לעיתים אתה יודע שטעית, שרה
'Sometimes you (m.s.) know (m.s.) that you were wrong (m.s.), Sara'	

Also, אחד *eHad,* האדם *ha-adam,* (c) הבן-אדם *ha-ben-adam* 'a person':

leitim eHad ro'e she-hu ta'a	לעיתים אחד רואה שהוא טעה
'Sometimes a person sees he was wrong'	

ha-mishmáat meadénet et ha-adam	המשמעת מעדנת את האדם
'Discipline refines a person'	

For the use of the generic 3rd person plural, eg. טועים *to'im* 'people are wrong', see 17.2.

For things (i.e the general environment or ambience): Many predicates are used generically, to describe the general ambience, eg. טוב פה *tov po* '(It's) fine here' (see 17.2). Casual usage can optionally add the generic subject זה *ze* 'it', as in:

(ze) kar	'It's cold'	(זה) קר
(ze) tov po	'It's fine here'	(זה) טוב פה
(ze) nóaH li	'I'm comfortable'	(זה) נוח לי
(ze) magía leHa	'It serves you right'	(זה) מגיע לך

But with predicates that do not take a subject anyway, זה *ze* is not usually added:

(*ze) efshar be-déreH-klal	(*זה) אפשר בדרך-כלל
'⟨It's⟩ possible in general'	

7.12 Reflexive pronouns

By reflexive pronouns one refers back to a noun mentioned in the same finite clause (examples 1, 2 below); by contrast, in referring back to a noun in an 'outer' clause, i.e one containing the clause in question (3), or in a separate clause, one uses a personal rather than a reflexive pronoun (see 7.3):

(1) hu metaken et **atsmo**   הוא מתקן את **עצמו**
     'He corrects **himself**'

(2) shaálti ota al **atsma**   שאלתי אותה על **עצמה**
     'I asked her about **herself**'

(3) ani maadif ┌she-metaknim **oti**┐ (*atsmi)   אני מעדיף שמתקנים **אותי** (*עצמי)
                └ INNER CLAUSE ┘   'I prefer that people correct me'

     OUTER CLAUSE
     I prefer that [people] correct **me** (*myself)

The reflexive pronouns are:

atsmi	'myself'	עצמי
atsmeHa	'yourself' (m.)	עצמך
atsmeH	'yourself' (f.)	עצמך
atsmo	'himself, itself'	עצמו
atsma	'herself, itself'	עצמה
atsménu	'ourselves'	עצמנו
atsmeHem	'yourselves' (m.)	עצמכם
atsmeHen	'yourselves' (f.) (F)	עצמכן
atsmam	'themselves' (m.)	עצמם
atsman	'themselves' (f.) (F)	עצמן

There are two limitations. (a) The verbal pattern התפעל *hitpa'el* is often used instead of the verb + reflexive pronoun construction, thus: התנער *hitna'er*, rather than ניער את עצמו *ni'er et atsmo* 'shake oneself off'. But there is no hard and fast rule; as a simple reflexive pattern based on the simple stem, התפעל *hitpa'el* is generally limited to bodily actions (by contrast, התעורר *hitorer* 'awake' is not equivalent to העיר עצמו *he'ir atsmo* 'wake oneself up', nor can התגלה *hitgala* 'be discovered' mean גילה עצמו *gila atsmo* 'discover oneself'), and even then התפעל *hitpa'el* does not cover all bodily activities, eg. חתך עצמו *HataH atsmo* 'cut oneself' rather than *התחתך *hitHateH.

   (b) In adverbials of time and space, personal pronouns are preferred to reflexives:

raíti svivi (*sviv atsmi) dkalim   ראיתי סביבי (*סביב עצמי) דקלים
                                                       'I saw palms around me'

hináHti oto lefanay (*lifney atsmi)   הנחתי אותו לפני (*לפני עצמי)
                                                       'I placed it in front of me'

Hazárnu etslénu (*étsel atsménu)   חזרנו אצלנו (*אצל עצמנו)
                                                       'We went back home'

Another use of the reflexive pronoun is to emphasize a noun:

sara $\begin{matrix} \text{atsma} \\ \text{be-atsma} \end{matrix}$ (c) lo nohéget   שרה עצמה לא נוהגת
בעצמה
'Sara herself doesn't drive'

taashímu et ha-sar $\begin{matrix} \text{atsmo} \\ \text{be-atsmo} \end{matrix}$ תאשימו את השר עצמו
בעצמו
'Blame the minister himself'

7.13 Reciprocal pronouns

The reciprocal pronouns, denoting 'one another', occur in pairs. In descending order of formality, they are:

ish... $\begin{matrix} \text{Havero} \\ \text{re'éhu} \end{matrix}$ (m.), isha.. $\begin{matrix} \text{Haverta} \\ \text{reuta} \end{matrix}$ (f.)   איש... חברו אשה... חברתה
רעהו רעותה

eHad... mishnéhu (m.), aHat... mishnéha (f.)   אחד... משנהו, אחת... משנה

ze.. ze (m.), zo... zo (f.)   זה... זה, זו... זו

eHad... ha-sheni (m.), aHat... ha-shniya (f.)   אחד... השני, אחת... השניה

Positioning

The *second pronoun* fills the normal slot for objects or adverbials, thus:

ra'ínu ze et **ze**   ראינו זה את זה
      OBJ   'We saw one **another**'

hem lomdim ze mi-**ze**   הם לומדים זה מזה
          ADV   'They learn from each **other**'

Directly preceding the second pronoun is the *preposition*, as required by the particular verb, adjective or derived noun; and directly preceding the preposition is the *first* reciprocal pronoun, which is strictly an 'extra' to the normal structure of a Hebrew clause:

ra'ínu **ze** et ze   ראינו זה את זה
      FIRST   'We saw **one** another'
      PRONOUN
we-saw this OM this

neemanutam **eHad** la-sheni   נאמנותם אחד לשני
      FIRST   'their loyalty to **each** other'
      PRONOUN
their-loyalty one to-the other

Gender and number

When referring to feminine nouns, the pronouns are feminine:

ha-aHayot medabrot aHat al-odot ha-shniya האחיות מדברות אחת על-אודות השניה
'The nurses speak about one another'

But when referring to a combination of masculine and feminine, one commonly uses either two masculine pronouns (the 'unmarked' gender) or one masculine plus one feminine pronoun:

miryam ve-yaakov poHadim ze mi-ze / ze mi-zo מרים ויעקב פוחדים זה מזה / זה מזו
'Miriam and Yaakov are afraid of one another'

For group activity, one uses two plural pronouns, אלה ...אלה *éle.. éle*:

ha-toshavim san'u éle et éle התושבים שנאו אלה את אלה
the inhabitants hated these OM these   'The inhabitants hated one another'
                                         (i.e one group hated the other)

as against זה את זה ... ...*ze et ze* '...one another' (i.e each person hated the other).

FURTHER READING
Berman 1979a, 1980, b; Bin-Nun 1979; Dahan 1980; Givón 1973; Glinert 1978; Levenston 1976; Rubinstein 1968, 1971:83ff., 2.4, 1973; Sadka 1978: 298ff., 1981:192 ff., 222 ff; Schwarzwald 1979b.

8. Quantifiers

8.1 Introduction

Quantifiers are a part of speech denoting *quantity* (and including numerals). Rather like nouns, they act as subject, object etc. or, most commonly, they qualify a noun:

hayu	shesh	'There were six'	שש היו
	káma	'a few'	כמה
	SUBJ		
	harbe	'a lot'	הרבה
asíti	maspik	'I did enough'	עשיתי מספיק
	Hétsi	'half'	חצי
	et ha-rov	'most'	את הרוב
	OBJ		
od		'more	עוד
ktsat	balátot	'a few tiles'	קצת בלטות
hamon		'loads of	המון
she'ar		'the rest of	שאר
kol	ha-dibrot	'all commandments'	כל הדיברות
aséret		'the ten	עשרת

For 'measure phrases', as in the following example, see 36.10.

knu **esrim méter** dikt		קנו **עשרים מטר** דיקט
MEASURE PHRASE		
buy **twenty metres** plywood		'Buy **twenty metres** of plywood'

8.2 Quantifiers: general form

Quantifiers have no special shape or inflection, except that (1) numerals inflect in a way somewhat reminiscent of nouns[1] for gender, number and construct (see 8.9); and (2) fractions for 5th to 10th and for 100th are derived from the feminine form of the ordinals - חמישית *Hamishit* '1/5th', מאית *me'it* '1/100th', etc.

The difference between quantifiers and degree words is essentially that the latter generally relate to a verb or adjective: גאה {קצת/מאד} {*ktsat/me'od*} ge'e '{slightly/very} proud'. With abstract nouns, however, quantifiers will themselves denote 'degree': גאווה {קצת/הרבה} {*ktsat/harbe*} gaava '{slight/much} pride'.

Quantity can also be expressed by certain (irregular) adjectives, e.g. מרובה *merube*, 'many, much', מעט *me'at* 'a little, few', אחדים *aHadim* 'a few'. See 8.15.

8.3 Quantifying what?

Quantifiers generally state *amount* or *portion*, i.e. they are 'amount quantifiers'[2] or 'partitive quantifiers' respectively (a distinction that helps explain their behaviour), either for an explicit noun or for one directly implied. Many quantifiers can act as both amount and partitive quantifiers; others are intrinsically partitive, e.g. רוב האנשים *rov ha-anashim* 'most of the people', or intrinsically express amount, e.g. יותר מדי אנשים *yoter miday anashim* 'too many people'.

Amount quantifiers:
ratsíti Hamisha dapim, ve-hevet shisha רציתי חמשה דפים והבאת ששה
           EXPLICIT N   N IMPLIED
I-wanted five sheets and you-brought six

Partitive quantifiers:
Hamisha me-ha-sfarim nimkeru ve-Hélek חמשה מהספרים נמכרו וחלק
hushalu הושאלו
       EXPLICIT N   N IMPLIED
five of the books were-sold and a-portion were-lent

Amount quantifiers can also be 'open-ended', i.e. relate to *non-specific thing(s)* (but not people):[3]

harbe kara li	'A lot happened to me'	הרבה קרה לי
hevet yoter miday	'You brought too much'	הבאת יותר מדי

This is not possible for 'precise' numerals[4] (unless, of course, referring back to a noun just mentioned): מליון יתנגדו* *milyon yitnagdu* 'A million will object'. Here a word like אנשים *anashim* 'people' is needed.

8.4 Definite and non-definite, singular and plural quantifiers
Quantifiers are more restricted than nouns.

Amount quantifiers
Aside from numerals, which can be either definite or non-definite,
e.g.

kaH	shesh	'Take	six'	שש קח
	et ha-shesh ha-éle		these six'	את השש האלה

most amount quantifiers are indefinite,[5] as in example (1) and ruling out example (2):

(1)
ktsat	'A bit		קצת
harbe	nizrak	'A lot is thrown out'	הרבה נזרק
káma	'How much		כמה

(2)
*ha- ktsat/harbe	she-nish'ar...	'The little/lot that remains...'	...ה קצת/הרבה שנשאר*

Partitive quantifiers

Fractions are generally indefinite, eg. (...מ) ריססתי עשירית *risásti asirit (mi...)* 'I sprayed a tenth (of...)', (...מ) תן לי חצי *ten li Hétsi (mi...)* 'Give me half (of...)'.[6] חלק *Hélek* 'part, some' is similar.

The following partitives are generally definite: הרוב *ha-rov* 'most', מרבית -ה *marbit ha-* 'most of the' (only construct); הכל *ha-kol* 'all, everything, everyone'; השאר/היתר *ha-she'ar/ha-yéter* 'the rest'. With a noun -ה *ha-* 'the' will appear only on the noun, as is usual with construct constructions (8.5):

rov **ha**-etim dolfim	רוב העטים דולפים
most **the** pens leak	'Most pens leak'
	'Most of the pens leak'

kol **ha**-Hatulim tsadim	כל החתולים צדים
all **the** cats hunt	'All cats hunt'
	'All the cats hunt'

yéter **ha**-Heshbonot nisgeru	יתר החשבונות נסגרו
rest **the** accounts were-closed	'The rest of the accounts were closed'

The noun can be intrinsically definite:

kol	aHyotay	'all	my sisters'	אחיותי
	éle		these'	כל אלה

As for the noun, it must be definite in its own right when introduced by a partitive quantifier:

heHzárti	éser		me-**ha**-kosot	מהכוסות	עשר
	Hélek			חלק	החזרתי

'I returned	ten	of **the** cups'
	some	

except where the fractions, especially with units of measurement, express *amount* rather than 'part of something' (forming construct phrases), eg. רבע שעה *réva shaa* '1/4 hour' (a quarter-hour), חצי משרה *Hatsi misra* 'a half (i.e half-time) job', as against חצי מהמשרה *hétsi me-ha-misra* 'half of the job', etc.[7]

Only fractions go into the plural, eg. שתי עשיריות *shtey asiriyot* '2/10', כמה אחוזים *káma aHuzim* 'how many percent'.[8]

8.5   The join between quantifier and noun

8.5.1   Types of link

Quantifiers are linked to their nouns in three main ways:
By the preposition -מ *mi-*:

shisha me-ha-nerot	ששה מהנרות
six of the candles	'six of the candles'

By the construct construction:

    shéshet ha-nerot   שֵׁשֶׁת הנרות
    CONSTRUCT
    six the candles   'the six candles'

By mere juxtaposition:

    shisha nerot   שִׁשָׁה נרות
    six candles   'six candles'

In the 'construct' (6.2), הـ *ha-* 'the' leapfrogs to the last word, and the quantifier has a special construct form where this is available (see below and 8.9). Occasionally the preposition של *shel* 'of' is used instead.

The choice between these three types of join depends on the type of quantifier, as illustrated in the following sections.

8.5.2   Partitive quantifiers

Partitive quantifiers that are always definite (8.4) require the construct:[9]

maHatsit		'half of'		מחצית
marbit		'most of'		מרבית
rov		'most of'		רוב
kol	ha-shdarim	'all of'	the messages'	כל השדרים
she'ar		'the rest of'		שאר
yéter		'the rest of'		יתר

Pronouns are suffixed (שאר *she'ar* disallows them), with phonetic adjustments in the following quantifiers:

ruba, rubénu, rubHem...	'most of it, etc.'	רובה, רובנו, רובכם...
kula, kuleH, kulánu..	'all of it, etc.'	כולה, כולך, כולנו...
yitra, yitrénu, yitram...	'the rest of it, etc.'	יתרה, יתרנו, יתרם...

Most other partitives require מـ *mi-* when preceding a definite noun:
Fractions:

réva	me-ha-kartisim	'a quarter	of the cards'	מהכרטיסים
	mehem		of them'	מהם
				רבע

and similarly, חלק *Hélek* 'part, some', חצי *Hétsi* 'half', etc.[10]
Other quantifiers:

Hamisha	me-ha-kartisim	'five	of the cards'	מהכרטיסים
	mehem		of them'	מהם
				חמשה

and similarly, מאות *me'ot* 'hundreds', כמה *káma* 'a few', הרבה *harbe* 'lots' etc.

However, אחד, אחת *eHad, ahat* 'one'[11] can take either מـ *mi-* or the construct.[12] Its construct form is אחד *aHad* (masculine) and אחת *aHat* (feminine):

eHad me-ha-vradim	'one of the roses'	אחד מהוורדים
aHad ha-vradim		אחד הוורדים

8.5.3 Amount quantifiers

Within a 'definite' noun phrase (eg. 'the six boys'), numerals from 'two' upwards require the construct. Some even have a special construct form (8.9).

Definite		*Indefinite*	
élef ha-shanim	אלף השנים	élef shanim	אלף שנים
1000 the years	'the 1000 years'	1000 years	'1000 years'
shéshet ha-bragim	ששת הברגים	shisha bragim	ששה ברגים
CONSTRUCT		FREE FORM	
six the screws	'the six screws'	six screws	'six screws'
shloshténu	שלושתנו	shlosha meitánu	שלושה מאתנו
three-us	'the three of us'	three of-us	'three of us'

Similarly, מעט *me'at* 'little' (no suffixes or construct form):

me'at ha-yedi'ot ha-magi'ot	מעט הידיעות המגיעות
little the news that arrives	'the little news that arrives'

as against ...מעט מה *me'at me-ha...* 'a little of the..'.

Fraction + unit of measurement is treated as 'amount', not 'partitive'; it requires the construct:

Hatsi sha'a	'1/2 hour'	חצי שעה
shney shlish mayl	'2/3 mile'	שני שליש מייל

The 'imprecise' numerals (which are in several respects not strictly numerals) can use the construct, eg. עשרות *asrot* 'tens (of...)', מליוני *milyoney* 'millions (of...)', as does מספר *mispar* 'a number of'.[13]

Other quantifiers, and numerals within *indefinite* noun phrases (eg. 'six boys'), are simply juxtaposed to their noun. They usually precede it:

harbe Hanuyot	'**many** shops'	הרבה חנויות
kaful Hanuyot	'**twice as many** shops'	כפול חנויות
be-**mínimum** hotsa'ot	'with **a minimum of** expenses'	במינימום הוצאות

However, שניים, שתיים *shnáyim, shtáyim* 'two (m.,f.)' becomes construct to its noun: שתי גרביים *shtey garbáyim* 'two socks'; in formal usage, די *day* 'sufficient' becomes די *dey*: די מאמצים *dey maamatsim* 'sufficient efforts'.[14]

A few juxtaposed quantifiers *follow* their noun, notably אין-ספור *en-sfor* 'countless', למכביר *lemaHbir* 'abundant', also:

shéled eHad	שלד אחד	hafta'ot la-rov	הפתעות לרוב
skeleton one	'one skeleton'	surprises abundant	'abundant surprises'

A few can either precede or follow, notably מספר *mispar* 'a number of' (casually it precedes), בלי-סוף *bli-sof* 'countless' and אין-סוף *en-sof* 'countless'.[15]

Certain nouns whose pattern of agreement shows them to be quantifiers too can take the construct or של *shel*, eg.

mabul
shéfa (shel) omanim **omdim** larédet alénu   מבול (של) אומנים **עומדים** לרדת עלינו
שפע

a-torrent
a-host (of) artists **are-due** to-descend on-us

8.5.4 Measure expressions

Measure expressions are usually juxtaposed to their noun (see also 36.10). Example of physical measurements are:[16]

shloshim méter bad	שלושים מטר בד
thirty metre cloth	'thirty metres of cloth'

ha-kílo batsal	הקילו בצל
the kilo onion	'the kilo of onions'

Time and other abstract measurements are often juxtaposed, or use של *shel* 'of' with inverse word order, expecially in casual usage:

tiyul shel shisha yamim = shisha yamim tiyul	טיול של ששה ימים = ששה ימים טיול
trip of six days = six days trip	'a six-day trip'

maasar shel esrim shana = esrim shana maasar	מאסר של עשרים שנה = עשרים שנה מאסר
jail of twenty year = twenty year jail	'twenty years' jail'

hishtatfut shel méa aHuz = méa aHuz hishtatfut	השתתפות של מאה אחוז = מאה אחוז השתתפות
participation of 100% = 100% participation	'100% participation'

Formal usage prefers the construct: ששה ימי טיול *shisha yemey tiyul* (six days-of trip).

8.6 Partitive מ- *mi-* in general

8.6.1 Types of partitive construction

Partitives usually involve a quantifier + *plural* noun, eg. שניים מהחיילים *shnáyim me-ha-Hayalim* 'two of the **soldiers**'. They can however involve *collective* nouns, eg. שניים מהיחידה *shnáyim me-ha-yeHida* 'two of the **platoon**'; here שניים *shnáyim* 'two' represents 'two persons', not 'two platoons'.[17]

Not only quantifiers but also certain pronouns take a partitive מ- *mi-*:

míshehu mehem hilshin	**someone** of-them informed	מישהו מהם הלשין

af eHad ish mehem lo notar	**no one** of-them remained	אף אחד מהם לא נותר איש

mi		who
éze mi-banav huHtar?		which of his-sons was-crowned? ?

מי
איזה

éle miken she-yad'u..   **those** of-you that knew...   ...אלה מכן שידעו

A distinctive trait of these pronouns is that they often become definite in anticipation of a following definite noun, witness the direct object marker את *et*. So
too does אחד *eHad* 'one (of...)'. מי *mi* 'who?' is intrinsically definite

hitstarHu laatsor et míshehu mehem   הצטרכו לעצור את מישהו מהם
they-had to-arrest OM someone of-them   'They had to arrest one of them'

Neither nouns nor adjectives are followed by partitives with -מ *mi-*:

af katsin mehem...   ...אף קצין מהם
no officer of-them...

ha-ktsinim meitánu (✓ she-benénu)   (הקצינים מאתנו (✓ שבינינו
the officers of-us (that are among-us)

ha-svuHa me-ha-baayot (✓ ba-baayot)   (הסבוכה מהבעיות (✓ בבעיות
the thorniest of-the problems (in-the problems)

8.6.2 Four (formal) partitive constructions

Partitive phrases can introduce an exceptional relative clause of
'being', lacking a relative conjunction and explicit word for 'be':

ha-ulam yipataH bifney élef tsofim,   ,האולם ייפתח בפני אלף צופים
rubam yisreelim bimkoram, she..   ...רובם ישראלים במקורם, ש
PARTITIVE
PHR
the hall will-open to 1000 spectators, **most-of-them** Israelis by-origin, who...

They also introduce regular relative clauses (or even main clauses); the -מ *mi-*
+ noun can be separated from the quantifier:

ha-shana tipálnu be-He-élef olim,   ,השנה טיפלנו בכאלף עולים
she-**mehem** nikletu ba-avoda   שמהם נקלטו בעבודה
me'al shésh-me'ot   מעל שש-מאות
this year we-handled about 1000 immigrants, that **of-them** [=of whom] were-
absorbed in work **over 600**   PARTITIVE
PARTITIVE

Equivalent to 'appositional' כולל *kolel* 'including' (after a comma) is מהם
mehem 'of them', which introduces a quantifier (alternatively: בהם *bahem* +
noun or ביניהם *benehem* + noun or quantifier):

ha-shana nirshemu matáyim Hiburim,   ,השנה נרשמו מאתיים חיבורים
mehem shloshim be-anglit   מהם שלושים באנגלית
this year were-registered 200 theses, **of-which 30** [are] in English

Unlike the three foregoing constructions, the fourth does not necessarily refer
back. The quantifier 'one' or 'some' (...of them, of the chairs - and particularly

'superlatives': ...of the best, of the shortest) can be left unsaid in certain contexts - at the head of a major phrase, but for perceptual reasons not ahead of the verb. Examples are set out below.

Superlatives following a verb (*mostly as direct object*):

shaláHnu **mi-meytav** saHkanéynu   שלחנו **ממיטב** שחקנינו
we-sent [some] **of the-best-of** our-players

Predicate (casual usage too):

im ata rotse she-ha-báyit yiye naki,   אם אתה רוצה שהבית יהיה נקי,
   lo **me-ha-nekiyim beyoter** aval...   לא **מהנקיים ביותר** אבל...
               'If you want the house to be clean,
                 not ⟨one⟩ **of the cleanest** but...'

mitkan ze hu **min ha-dugma'ot**   מתקן זה הוא **מן הדוגמאות**
le-pituHim she-bahem tomeH ha-váad   לפיתוחים שבהם תומך הוועד
               'This installation is ⟨one⟩ **of the examples**
               of developments that the committee
               is supporting'

Subject:

haya bo **mi-tmimut** ha-yeladim   היה בו **מתמימות הילדים**
was in-him **of naivety** the children   'There was something of a
               child's naivety in him'

Apposition:

alfey bney nóar she-shahu etslénu   אלפי בני-נוער ששהו אצלנו
zman rav, **mehem** afîlu shanim,...   זמן רב, **מהם** אפילו שנים,...
               'Thousands of young people that stayed
               with us a long while, ⟨some⟩ **of them**
               even years,...'

nimtsa be-yaday miHtav mi ***,   נמצא בידי מכתב מ ***,
   mi-baaley ha-moadon   **מבעלי** המועדון
               'I have in my hands a letter from ***,
               ⟨one⟩ **of the owners of** the club'

Parenthesis:

nimtse'u sham tseirim nilhavim   נמצאו שם צעירים נלהבים
   (**mehem** hispíku le-hipared me-rik'am)   (**מהם** הספיקו להיפרד מרקעם)
               'There were present excited youngsters
               (⟨some⟩ **of whom** had managed to break
               away from their background)'

Attribute:

yesh kan rúaH leHima kmo   יש כאן רוח לחימה כמו
be-yeHida kravit **me-ha-meulot**   ביחידה קרבית **מהמעולות**
               'There is here a fighting spirit like in the best
               combat units (*lit.* unit combat **of the best**)'

8.7 Types of quantified noun

Most quantifiers take both singular 'mass' and plural 'countable', and both human and non-human, nouns:

káma mesibot, harbe?	how-many parties, a-lot?	כמה מסיבות, הרבה?
PL.		
COUNTABLE		
káma óHel, harbe?	how-much food, a-lot?	כמה אוכל, הרבה?
S.		
MASS		

However, only the plural is used with non-interrogative כמה *káma* 'a few', eg. כמה מסיבות *káma mesibot* 'a few parties', not *כמה אוכל *káma óHel* 'a few food' (except כמה זמן *káma zman* 'a little while'). Similarly, מספר *mispar* 'a few', and the quantity adjectives (8.15) אחדים *aHadim*, ספורים *sfurim* 'a few' use the plural.

A plural or an *abstract* mass singular noun is generally used with רב *rav*, מרובה *merube* 'much/many', מעט *me'at*, מועט *mu'at* 'a little/ a few', eg. מסיבות רבות/מעטות *mesibot rabot/meatot* 'many/ a few parties', סבלנות מרובה/מעטה *savlanut meruba/meata* 'much/a little patience', but not **ריבה מעטה *riba meata* 'a little jam'.[18]

קצת *ktsat* is not commonly used with *plural human* nouns, hence **קצת בגדים** *ktsat bgadim* **'a few** clothes' but **כמה אנשים** *káma* anashim **'a few** people'.

עוד *od* 'more, another' takes both countable and mass nouns in the singular:

od sug	'another sort'	עוד סוג	od tal	'more dew'	עוד טל
od sugim	'more sorts'	עוד סוגים	MASS		
COUNTABLE					

8.8 Quantifiers and their predicate: agreement

8.8.1 Quantifier without noun

Quantifiers without a noun are masculine when referring to a *thing* even where one has a specific feminine noun in mind:

káma bíra nishpeHa ve-káma **nish'ar** (*nishara)?   כמה בירה נשפכה וכמה **נשאר** (*נשארה)?
f.   f.   m.   f.
how-much beer spilled and how-much **is-left** (*is-left)?

For *plural things*, quantifiers adopt the gender of what they refer to:

	Hélek	חלק
káma pitriyot aHilot, ve-	ha-she'ar marilot	כמה פטריות אכילות ו השאר מרעילות
	ha-rov	הרוב
f.pl. f.pl.	f.pl.	

                                                some
some mushrooms [are] edible and the rest   [are] poisonous
                                    the majority

For *people*, natural sex and number prevails:[19]

éfo ha-yeHida?	ha-rov	yeshenim (*yeshena)	איפה היחידה? הרוב ישנים (*ישנה)
f.s.	m. pl.	f.s.	

Where's the unit? The majority are-asleep (*is-asleep)

8.8.2 Quantifier + noun

With a construct or a juxtaposed quantifier (8.5), agreement of the predicate is generally determined by the noun (i.e in כל המלון *kol ha-melon* 'all the melon', the quantifier is modifier and the noun is nucleus).[20] When the noun is a personal pronoun, i.e a suffix, agreement of person ensues:

she'ar	ha-dira	meluHléhet	שאר הדירה מלוכלכת
CONSTRUCT	f.s.	f.s.	'The rest of the flat is dirty'
rest	the flat	dirty	

me'at	gvina	nafla	מעט גבינה נפלה
CONSTRUCT	f.s.	f.s.	
a-little	cheese	dropped	

yoter miday	Hem'a	nitsreHa	יותר מדי חמאה נצרכה
JUXTAPOSED	f.s.	f.s.	
too much	butter	was-consumed	

kulánu / rubénu	shárnu		כולנו/רובנו שרנו
1st pl. 1st pl.	1st pl.		
all-of-us/most-of-us	sang		

With a partitive מ- *mi-*, either the noun or its quantifier determines agreement (the latter according to its inherent masculine or feminine shape) when referring to *singular things:*

Hétsi me-ha-Humtsa	neegar (m.s.)		נאגר חצי מהחומצה
	neegéret (f.s.)		נאגרת
m.s.	f.s.		
half of the acid	is-stored		
	is-stored		

For *people* or *plural things*, the quantifier tends to adopt their natural sex and number, not their person:[21]

Hétsi me-ha-Hatsaiyot	pgumot	חצי מהחצאיות פגומות
f.pl.	f.pl.	
half of the skirts [are] faulty		

	mikem			מכם
Hélek	2nd pl.	yad'u		חלק מהיחידה ידעו
	me-ha-yeHida	3rd pl.		
	f.s.			
some	of-you	knew		
	of the unit			

8.8.3 Measure expression + noun

Physical measurements (8.5.4) tend to determine agreement:

נשפכו לי עשרים ליטר דלק

nishpeHu li esrim li̱ter délek
  AGREEMENT   AGREEMENT
were-spilled to-me twenty litre fuel   'I had a spill of twenty litres of fuel'

With abstract measurements the noun tends to determine agreement, as in:

היתה לפחות עשרים אחוז השתתפות

ha̱yta lefaHot esrim aḢuz hishtatfut
f.s.   AGREEMEENT   f.s.   AGREEMENT
there-was at-least 20% participation   'There was at least a 20% participation'

8.9-11 NUMERALS

8.9 Cardinals (1, 2 etc.)

8.9.1 'Free' and 'construct' structures

The 'free' form of the numeral expresses *amount* with an indefinite noun, as in example (1) below, or with no noun, as in examples (2,3). It is also used with partitive -מ *mi-* 'of', as in example (4):

(1)	shisha rofim	'six doctors'	<div dir="rtl">ששה רופאים</div>
(2)	shaalu shisha	'They asked six'	<div dir="rtl">שאלו ששה</div>
(3)	shaalu et ha-shisha	'They asked the six'	<div dir="rtl">שאלו את הששה</div>
(4)	shisha me-ha-rofim	'six of the doctors'	<div dir="rtl">ששה מהרופאים</div>

The construct construction, in which some numerals have a special construct form, expresses amount for a *definite* noun. Where -ה *ha-* 'the' is involved, it leapfrogs to the last noun, as is usual with constructs:

shéshet ha-rofim ve-shéshet aHeyhem   ששת הרופאים וששת אחיהם
CONSTRUCT   CONSTRUCT   'the six doctors and their
six the doctors and six brothers-their   six brothers'

shéshet   aHey ha-méleH   ששת אחי המלך
CONSTRUCT CONSTRUCT
six brothers the king   'the six brothers of the king'

8.9.2 Masculine and feminine numerals

Masculine and feminine cardinal numerals usually go with masculine and feminine nouns, respectively. These nouns may be explicit or just implied:

bikshu Hamisha tikim ve-hevénu shisha   ביקשו חמשה תיקים והבאנו ששה
     m.   m.   m.
they-wanted five bags and we-brought six

However, some numerals have just one form for both genders. Moreover, casual (and above all, substandard) usage sometimes simply employs the feminine form for 'two' to 'ten', particularly for 'two'; for '11' to '19' this practice is especially widespread:

ratsíti shésh-esre banim ve-shésh-esre banot		רציתי שש־עשרה בנים ושש־עשרה
f. form m. f. form f.		בנות
I-wanted 16 boys and 16 girls		

Feminines also serve as 'neutrals', to denote a number in the abstract:[22]

aHat-shtáyim-shalosh!	'One-two-three!'	אחת־שתיים־שלוש!
	(eg. in races)	
lispor ad éser!	'Count to ten!'	לספור עד עשר!

Numeral forms under 100

	MASCULINE			FEMININE		
	Free		Construct	Free		Construct
1	eHad	אחד	aHad· אחד	aHat	אחת	aHat אחת
2	shnáyim	שניים	shney שני	shtáyim	שתיים	shtey שתי
3	shlosha	שלושה	shlóshet שלושת	shalosh	שלוש	shlosh[1] שלוש
4	arba'a	ארבעה	arbáat ארבעת	árba[2]	ארבע	
5	Hamisha	חמשה	Haméshet חמשת	Hamesh	חמש	as
6	shisha	ששה	shéshet ששת	shesh	שש	in
7	shiv'a	שבעה	shivat שבעת	shéva	שבע	free
8	shmona	שמונה	shmonat שמונת	shmóne[2]	שמונה	form
9	tish'a	תשעה	tishat תשעת	tésha/téysha	תשע	
10	asara	עשרה	aséret עשרת	éser	עשר	

	MASCULINE		FEMININE[3]	
11	aHád-asar	אחד־עשר	aHát-esre	אחת־עשרה
12	shném-asar	שנים־עשר	shtém-esre	שתים־עשרה
13	shloshá-asar	שלושה־עשר	shlósh-esre	שלוש־עשרה
14	arba'á-asar	ארבעה־עשר	arbá-esre	ארבע־עשרה
15	Hamishá-asar	חמשה־עשר	Hamésh-esre	חמש־עשרה
16	shishá-asar	ששה־עשר	shésh-esre	שש־עשרה
17	shivá-asar	שבעה־עשר	shvá-esre	שבע־עשרה
18	shmoná-asar	שמונה־עשר	shmóne-esre[4]	שמונה־עשרה
19	tish'á-asar	תשעה־עשר	tshá-esre	תשע־עשרה
20		esrim	עשרים	
21	esrim ve-eHad	עשרים ואחד	esrim ve-aHat	עשרים ואחת
22	esrim ve-shnáyim[5]	עשרים ושניים	esrim ve-shtáyim	עשרים ושתיים
30		shloshim[6]	שלושים	
40		arba'im	ארבעים	
50		Hamishim	חמשים	
60		shishim	ששים	
70		shiv'im	שבעים	
80		shmonim	שמונים	
90		tish'im	תשעים	

Notes:

[1] Casually, the masculine construct is preferred: שלושת *shlóshet* and similarly חמשת *Haméshet*, ששת *shéshet* (creating pre-final stress throughout the feminine construct).

[2] In puristic usage *arbá*, *shmoné*; also in the numerals 24, 28, 34, etc.

[3] Feminines are shaped differently than those for 1-9, but like 3-9 of 300-900.
Casual speech may drop the first *e* in *esre*, giving *aHát-sre*, etc.
All of these are indivisible compounds - not phrases, thus not *חמש או שש־עשרה *Hamesh o shésh-esre* '15 or 16'.

[4] Casually also *shmoná-esre*, in line with *shvá-esre tshá-esre*

[5] Also, particularly in formal usage, ושניים... ...*u-shnáyim*, ושמונה... ...*u-shmone* in '22, 28' etc.

[6] 30-90 are based on the 3-9 masculine stem.

8.9.3 Syntax

'1', alone among numerals, follows its noun, eg. גל אחד *gal eHad* 'one wave', except in the partitive sense of 'one of...': אחד מהגלים, אחד הגלים *eHad me-ha-galim, aHad ha-galim* 'one of the waves'. As part of a larger number, too, it precedes its noun: שבעים ואחד זקנים *shivim ve-eHad zkenim* '71 elders'. Similarly, אחד עד שלושה שופטים *eHad ad shlosha shoftim* 'one to three judges'. Thus אחד *eHad* is only a *quasi*-adjective[23]

'2', alone among numerals, uses its construct form with indefinite as well as definite nouns, when *directly* preceding them: שני דגים *shney dagim* 'two fish', but שניים או שלושה דגים *shnáyim o shlosha dagim* 'two or three fish' and גם לי יש שניים *gam li yesh shnáyim* 'I've also got two'. Nor is its construct form (or indeed any construct numeral form) used in *compounds*, i.e where it is part of a larger numeral:

> esrim ve-**shtáyim** otiyot   עשרים ושתיים אותיות
> 'twenty-**two** letters'

'21, 22' etc. and all additive combinations, eg. 670, 1245, are made by stringing numerals together, with higher before lower.[24] In casual usage ו- *ve-* 'and' is usually inserted before the final numeral, if this is a numeral from 1 to 9,[25] eg. מאה ששים ושלוש *méa shishim ve-shalosh* '163' as against מאה ששים *méa shishim* '160'. Purist usage, however, makes no distinction: מאה ושישים *méa ve-shishim* '160'.

8.9.4 Numerals over 100

Numeral forms from 100 onwards

100	méa[1]	מאה	600	shésh-me'ot	שש-מאות
200	matáyim[2]	מאתיים	700	shvá-me'ot	שבע-מאות
300	shlósh-me'ot[3]	שלוש-מאות	800	shmóne-me'ot	שמונה-מאות
400	arbá-me'ot	ארבע-מאות	900	tshá-me'ot	תשע-מאות
500	Hamésh-me'ot	חמש-מאות			

1000 élef	אלף	6000 shéshet-alafim	ששת-אלפים
2000 alpáyim[2]	אלפיים	7000 shivát-alafim	שבעת-אלפים
3000 shlóshet-alafim[4]	שלושת-אלפים	8000 shmonát-alafim	שמונת-אלפים
4000 arbáat-alafim	ארבעת-אלפים	9000 tishát-alafim	תשעת-אלפים
5000 Haméshet-alafim	חמשת-אלפים	10000 aséret-alafim	עשרת-אלפים

11,000	aHád-asar élef[5]	אחד-עשר אלף
~	~	~
~		~
~		
23,000	esrim-ve-shlosha élef	עשרים-ושלושה אלף
~		~
~		~
~		~
1,000,000	milyon[6]	מליון
~		~
~		~
~		~
3,000,000	shlosha milyon[7]	שלושה מליון
~		~
~		~
~		~
100 million	milyard[8]	מליארד

Notes:

[1] Purists require *me'á*. There is an optional construct מאת *me'at*.

[2] This involves the true dual suffix ‎ים- *áyim* (8.11). Jerusalem dialect pronounces it *ma'atáyim*.

[3] These are semi-compounds (see note 24); the definite form is not שש המאות **shesh ha-me'ot* (six the hundreds) as in open phrases. Whereas the second element is the regular word for 'hundreds', the first is an exceptional form of the numerals 3 to 9 akin to those in 13 to 19.

[4] These are akin to open phrases, hence ששת האלפים *shéshet ha-alafim* (six the thousand) 'the six thousand'. The second element is the regular word for 'thousands' but the first is the *construct* form of 3 to 10 (a unique use of these constructs). However, as the ‎ת- *-et* suffix becomes ‎ת- *-t* in casual speech (*shlóshtalafim* '3000'), all these forms may be reanalysed as ‎תלפים... ...*talafim*, giving rise to substandard כמה 'תלפים *káma talafim* 'a few thousand', מלאן 'תלפים *malan talafim* 'umpteen thousand'.

[5] All these phrases involve the masculine numeral + singular אלף *élef*. (Its singularity is due to a 'depluralizing' rule, see 39.12)

[6] As a whole, the numbering of millions etc. involves no construct forms or peculiarities. Thus one can add אחד *eHad* as with a noun: מליון (אחד) *milyon (eHad)* 'one/a million' but not אלף אחד **élef eHad* 'one thousand', מאה אחת **méa aHat* 'one hundred'; similarly חצי מליון *Hatsi milyon* 'half a million' but not חצי אלף **Hatsi élef* 'half a thousand' etc.

[7] מליון *milyon*, מליארד *milyard* remain singular with any numeral.

[8] This is the American 'billion'.

8.9.5 Other features of cardinals

או *o* 'or' can be dropped when one means 'or maybe':[26]

shtáyim shalosh (dakot etc.)	'two or three (minutes etc.)'	שתים שלוש (דקות...)
Hamisha shisha (yamim etc.)	'five or six (days etc.)'	חמשה ששה (ימים...)

ה- *ha* 'the' in casual usage tends not to leapfrog to the last noun when this is a unit of measurement ('30 Shekels' being not 30 individual Shekels but a measurement), thus:

ha-shloshim shékel	'the 30 Shekels'	השלושים שקל
ha-méa kílo	'the 100 kilos'	המאה קילו

'1½, 2¼' etc. are usually of the form:

aHat va-Hétsi	'one and ⟨a⟩ half'	אחת וחצי
shtáyim va-réva	'two and ⟨a⟩ quarter'	שתיים ורבע

Similarly, when the fraction comes with a noun, the usual order is:[27]

shnáyim va-Hétsi Hadarim	'two and ⟨a⟩ half rooms'	שניים וחצי חדרים

But when definite, the 'whole number' in the fraction tends to adopt neutral, i.e feminine form (rather than construct or even 'free' masculine form):

shalosh va-Hétsi ha-amudim	שלוש וחצי העמודים
f. m.	
three and half the pages	'the three and a half pages'

Cardinals are used in neutral form as *serial numbers:* קו עשר *kav éser* 'route 10' (contrast with הקו העשירי *ha-kav ha-asiri* 'the tenth route'), דוגמה שבע *dugma shéva* 'example 7', etc. The noun is juxtaposed, not in construct form. They also denote the day of the month (masculine, like the word יום *yom* 'day'), the year (feminine, like שנה *shana* 'year'), and hours and minutes (the latter masculine, although דקה *daka* 'minute' is feminine). Ordinals too can denote the day of the month:

ad shiv'a be-merts/ha-shvi'i be-merts	עד שבעה במרץ/השביעי במרץ
m	
till seven in March/the seventh in March	'till March 7'

me'az shloshim ve-shéva	מאז שלושים ושבע
	'since 37 (= 1937)'

aHshav Hamisha le-Hamesh	עכשיו חמשה לחמש
m. f.	'It's now five (m.) to five (f.)'

Pronoun numerals are of three kinds. כך *kaH* refers back to a stated number:

méa narkisim ve-od yoter mi-**kaH** kalaniyot   מאה נרקיסים ועוד יותר מ**כך** כלניות
'a hundred daffodils and even more than **that number of** anemones'

For an indefinite number כך וכך *kaH ve-kaH* is used:

tlushim be-shóvi shel **kaH ve-kaH** shkalim   תלושים בשווי של **כך וכך** שקלים
'coupons with a value of so many (lit. **such and such**) shekels'

As part of a larger number כמה *káma* is employed:

leHidat shishim **ve-Háma** naHatim   לכידת ששים **וכמה** נחתים
'the capture of sixty plus (lit. sixty **and a few**) marines'

'Hundreds (of...)' etc., i.e the *imprecise numbers*, are expressed by the regular plurals of the numerals:[28] עשרות *asrot* 'tens', מאות *me'ot* 'hundreds', אלפים *alafim* 'thousands', רבבות *revavot* 'tens of thousands', מליונים *milyónim* 'millions'. When followed by a noun they are construct.

bulim? yesh li káma asrot   בולים? יש לי כמה עשרות
stamps? are to-me a-few tens   'Stamps? I have a few score'

me'ot rabanim ba'im[29]   מאות רבנים באים
'Hundreds of rabbis are coming'

8.10   Ordinals (1st, 2nd, etc.)
Ordinals from *1st to 10th* are regular adjectives derived from the feminine cardinal numerals (except 1), with an ...*i*...+ *suffixed -i* pattern from *3rd to 10th*:

gamárti rishon	'I finished 1st'	גמרתי ראשון
sheni	2nd	שני
shlishi	3rd	שלישי
revi'i	4th	רביעי
Hamishi	5th	חמישי
shishi	6th	שישי
shvi'i	7th	שביעי
shmini	8th	שמיני
tshi'i	9th	תשיעי
asiri	10th	עשירי

The feminine form is ראשונה *rishona* '1st', שנייה *shniya* '2nd'; otherwise add ת- *-t*.

For '11th' onwards, one employs the *cardinal* numerals (8.9) directly as ordinals, agreeing with their noun, eg.:

ha-ish ha-esrim u-shlosha[30]   האיש העשרים ושלושה
  m.   m.
the man the twenty and three   'the 23rd man'

Note also בפעם המי-יודע-כמה *ba-páam ha-mi yodéa káma* 'for the umpteenth (lit. who knows how many) times'. These occur only with definite nouns, which rules out:

*kol ish esrim   *כל איש עשרים
every man twenty   ('every 20th man')

gamárti esrim[31]   גמרתי עשרים*
('I finished 20th (lit. twenty)')

Digital vs. non-digital

There is thus a major divide between the numerals 1-10 ('digitals') and 11+. Digitals are simpler in basic shape, yet have special construct forms, ordinal adjectives and obligatory gender distinction.

Note, however, that construct *syntax* is possible with numerals over 10 too:

shlósh-me'ot **ha**-shanim   שלוש מאות השנים
three hundreds **the** years   '**the** three-hundred years'

The numerals from 11 upwards also allow 'plural-loss' (39.12) in certain nouns, eg. שלושים שנה *shloshim shana* 'thirty year [i.e years]'.

8.11 Dual

With time units, Hebrew expresses 'two' by the dual suffix ים-- *-áyim*, not by שתיים *shtáyim*:[32]

shaatáyim	'two hours'	שעתיים
yomáyim	'two days'	יומיים
shvu'áyim	'two weeks'	שבועיים
Hodsháyim	'two months'	חודשיים
shnatáyim	'two years'	שנתיים

Strictly speaking, ים-- *-áyim* generally denotes 'two consecutive (days etc.)'; thus:

hitsáti **shney** yamim aHerim   הצעתי שני ימים אחרים
                                             'I suggested **two** other days'

A consequence of ים-- *-áyim* being a numeral is the construction יומיים שלושה *yomáyim shlosha* (days-two three) 'two or three days', שעה שעתיים *sha'a shaatáyim* (hour hours-two) 'an hour or two', which is parallel to שתיים שלוש דקות *shtáyim shalosh dakot* 'two or three minutes' (8.9). Nor is a further numeral allowed: שני יומיים* **shney yomáyim* (two days-two)

However, ים-- *-áyim* is often just a plural suffix, notably with nouns for things typically in pairs: שתי/שש} רגליים} {*shtey/shesh*} *ragláyim* '{two/six} legs'. See 39.11.

8.12 Individual quantifiers: further details

אחד *eHad* 'one': As a partitive (using construct or -מ *mi-*), it is optionally definite by association with its definite noun, bence את *et* (5.1) may be used (optionally):

sha'álti (et) eHad me-ha-morim   שאלתי (את) אחד מהמורים
I-asked (OM) one of the teachers

The same holds for -כל אחד מ *kol eHad mi-* 'each of', -אף אחד מ *af eHad mi-* 'none of', and possibly even מ- שניים *shnáyim mi-* 'two of'. It is also a pronoun denoting 'someone' (see 7.8).

כל *kol* with the meaning 'every/any' is used with indefinite nouns, and belongs with 'determiners' (9.2):

eyn kol sakana	'There isn't any danger'	אין כל סכנה
yesh kol sug	'There's every type'	יש כל סוג

עוד *od*, unlike other quantifiers, qualifies pronouns, eg. מי עוד *mi od* 'who else', עוד מישהו *od míshehu* 'someone else', and even already quantified nouns: עוד נמלה אחת *od nemala aHat* 'one **more** ant'.

'The least' is expressed by הכי מעט *ha-Hi me'at* (the most little) or especially often הכי פחות *ha-Hi paHot* (the most less). However, Hebrew does not allow **ha-Hi yoter* (the most more) הכי יותר* for 'the most'; instead one uses הכי הרבה *ha-Hi harbe* (the most much) - a combination of the superlative particle (see ch. 20 on 'degree words') and the quantifier הרבה *harbe* 'much', eg.:

mi aHal ha-Hi harbe dag?   'Who ate the most fish?'   ?מי אכל הכי הרבה דג

פי *pi* + numeral expresses '... times as (many, much) ...', followed by the comparative conjunction מ- *mi-* or מאשר *measher*. The numeral is usually in neutral, i.e feminine, form; purists require the masculine:

yesh pi shalosh anashim measher...	...יש פי שלוש אנשים מאשר
there-are times three people than...	'There are three times as many people as...'

In this example it is inherently comparative; but it can itself take יותר *yoter* 'more' (never פחות *paHot* 'less'):

yesh pi méa yoter neft measher...	...יש פי מאה יותר נפט מאשר
there-is times a-hundred more oil than...	'There is a hundred times more oil than...'

כפליים *kifláyim* 'twice as (many)...' (formal) and its casual synonym כפול *kaful* are inherently comparative with nouns:

kataft **kaful** tmarim miména	קטפת **כפול** תמרים ממנה
you've-picked **double** dates than-her	'You've picked twice as many dates as her'

8.13 Qualifying the quantifier: כ- *ke-* 'about', לפחות *lefaHot* 'at least', etc.

Certain quantifers accept qualification by degree words or other quantifiers.

מעט *me'at* 'little, few', הרבה *harbe* 'a lot, many' accept the same degree words (מאד *me'od* 'very', כל-כך *kol-kaH* 'so' etc.) as the related adjectives מעט *me'at* 'few', רב *rav* 'much, many', unlike their near-synonyms קצת *ktsat* and המון *hamon*, which are not adjective-related in this way:

nora harbe bizbuz	נורא הרבה בזבוז
awful much waste	'an awful lot of waste'

harbe me'od késef　　　　　　　　　　　　　　הרבה מאד כסף
a-lot very money　　　　　　　　　　　　　　'very much money'

kol-kaH me'at mazal　　　　　　　　　　　　כל-כך מעט מזל
so little luck　　　　　　　　　　　　　　　'so little luck'

These and most other quantifiers and numerals accept עוד *od* 'more', as in עוד
קצת *od ktsat* 'a little more', עוד הרבה *od harbe* 'much more'.

The comparative quantifiers יותר *yoter* 'more', פחות *paHot* 'less', יותר מדי
yoter miday 'too much' themselves take quantifiers (as do the comparative
degree words (20.6)), which precede them:

{od/harbe} yoter késef　　　　　　　　　　{עוד/הרבה} יותר כסף
{still/much} more money

ktsat yoter miday of　　　　　　　　　　　　קצת יותר מדי עוף
a-little too much chicken

By contrast, the 'precision quantifers' (i.e numerals and fractions, as against
הרבה *harbe* 'much', יותר *yoter* 'more', etc.) can be qualified by a range of prepositions, focus adverbs (see ch. 22) and other adverbs, with varying syntactic
results, as set out below.

Directly preceding the precision quantifier:[33]

od		another		עוד
éze/ke-		some		איזה/כ-
karov le-		nearly		קרוב ל-
yoter mi	esrim	more than	twenty	יותר מ-	עשרים
me'al le-		over		מעל ל-
paHot mi-		less than		פחות מ-

Directly preceding the quantifier or following the whole noun phrase (cf.
22.4):[34]

nifgeshu im	kim'at lefaHot	élef ish		כמעט לפחות	אלף איש	נפגשו עם

they-met with　almost　a-thousand people
　　　　　　　at-least

Preceding the quantifier *and* any prepositions, or following the noun phrase:

nifgeshu	beéreH/bekeruv bidiyuk rak mínimum	im élef ish	בערך/בקירוב בדיוק רק מינימום	עם אלף איש	נפגשו

they-met　roughly　with 1000 people
　　　　　exactly
　　　　　only
　　　　　minimum

...im élef ish bekeruv　　　　　　　　　　...עם אלף איש בקירוב
...with 1000 people roughly

8.14   Quantifiers as predicates

Though operative at most points where nouns are used (recall 8.1), quantifiers do not normally occur as predicate - except for numerals and the group of 'quantity adjectives' (8.15):

tsraHéynu hem Hamisha			צרכינו הם חמשה
our-needs are five			

baayotéynu hen	rabot/merubot[35]		רבות/מרובות בעיותינו הן
	meatot		מעטות

our-problems are	many	
	few	

8.15   Adjectives of quantity

The adjectives of quantity are as set out below. They are irregular adjectives rather than quantifiers.

rav, raba, rabim, rabot		'much, many'	רב, רבה, רבים, רבות
-	meruba, merubim, merubot	'much, many'	מרובה, מרובים, מרובות -
mu'at, muata, muatim, muatot		'a {little/few}	מועט, מועטה, מועטים, מעטות
-	meata, meatim, meatot[36]	'a {little/few}	מעטה, מעטים, מעטות -
-	-	aHadim, aHadot	'a few'	אחדים, אחדות - -
-	-	sfurim, sfurot	'a few'	ספורים, ספורות - -

Qualifying a noun, they (a) follow it, and (b) agree with it, in definiteness too:

yesh ahada meata	יש אהדה מעטה
there's sympathy little	'There's little sympathy'

ha-hashpa'a ha-raba asher raHash	ההשפעה הרבה אשר רכש
the influence the much which he-acquired	'the great infuence which he acquired'

Moreover, they are used as predicate too (unlike some quantifiers; see again note 35):

baayotay hen {rabot/merubot}	בעיותי הן {רבות/מרובות}
my-problems are many	

They take degree words and comparatives, just like adjectives:

la-atsotav hashpa'a	raba yoter[37]		רבה יותר לעצותיו השפעה
	ko meruba		כה מרובה

to his-advice effect	great more	'His advice has	a greater effect'
	so great		so great an effect'

...baal ha-hashpa'a ha-raba beyoter	...בעל ההשפעה הרבה ביותר
...with the effect the great most	'...with the greatest effect'

metoséynu hayu meatim mehem   מטוסינו היו מעטים מהם
our-planes were few than-them   'Our planes were fewer than theirs'

They need no noun, if one is plain from the context:

hayu nisyonot? ken, hayu **aHadim**   היו נסיונות? כן, היו **אחדים**
there-were attempts? Yes, there-were **a-few**

ratsínu lehakir anashim, aH lo hispáknu   רצינו להכיר אנשים, אך לא הספקנו
  lehakir **rabim**   להכיר **רבים**
we-wanted to-know people, but we-didn't manage to-get-to-know **many**

But this construction is not possible with mass nouns:[38]

*ratsu **hitkadmut**, aH husga **meata** me'od   *רצו **התקדמות**, אך הושגה **מעטה** מאד
they-wanted **progress**, but was-achieved **little** very [= very little was achieved]

or where no specific noun is understood:

*asínu {rav/mu'at}   *עשינו {רב/מועט}
we-did {much/a little}

Instead, one uses the quantifiers רבה *harbe*, מעט *meat* (the latter being an uninflected quantifier as well an adjective).[39]

Unlike adjectives, (1) they are not used with *concrete* mass nouns, except רב *rav* in the sense of 'considerable': כסף, נשק רב *késef, néshek rav* 'considerable money, weaponry' but not *חלב רב* *Halav rav* 'considerable milk', *גבינה מעטה* *gvina meata* 'a little cheese'; and (2) they lack certain forms, as set out above

FURTHER READING
Glinert 1976a, 1977a, 1978; Grosu 1969: 45ff; Ornan 1979a: 81ff.

9. Determiners

9.1 Introduction

Determiners are a small class of words, accompanying the noun and determining its precise *identity* or its *very degree of identity*. Examples are:

ze	'this, that'	זה
éze	'which?'	איזה
kólshehu	'any'	כלשהו
kaze	'such'	כזה
af	'no'	אף
kol miney	'all kinds of'	כל מיני
me'en	'a sort of'	מעין

Determiners are distinct syntactically from nouns. The verb agrees with their accompanying noun, even though they themselves may often look like construct nouns and would as such have been expected to determine agreement:

min klala rovétset aléha   מין קללה רובצת עליה
DET N(f.) v(f.)   'A kind of curse rests on her'
a-kind-of curse rests on-her

ikar ha-baaya niftera   עיקר הבעיה נפתרה
DET   N (f.)   v (f.)   'The basic problem was solved'
basis the problem was-solved

Many determiners are themselves required to agree with their noun:

oto ish	**אותו** איש	ota isha	**אותה** אשה
m. m.	'that man'	f. f.	'that woman'

Determiners are distinct from quantifiers, eg. הרוב *ha-rov* 'most', and adjectives in that they rarely occur without their noun (see 9.5).

A few other items have the syntax of determiners, although in meaning they amount to adjectives, eg. (casual):

hayu sham **yófi shel** naarot!   !היו שם **יופי של** נערות
v (pl.)   DET   N (pl.)
there-were there **beauty of** girls   'There were beautiful girls there!'

91

9.2 Form and meaning

Determiners have no special shape or inflection. Some inflect (each in their own way) for gender and number, and some do not. This section gives the main morphological details, according to the semantic classes of determiner. Syntax is discussed in subsequent sections.

(a) *Demonstratives, i.e 'this, that'*:
זה *ze* 'this' (here, just mentioned)' or 'that (there)';[1] The feminine singular forms are זאת *zot*, זו *zo* (F)/*zu*[2]; plural forms are אלה *éle* or אלו *élu*

הללו *halálu* 'these (here, just mentioned)' or 'those (there)':[3] occurs in the plural only.

ההוא *ha-hu* 'that (there, then)': the feminine form is ההיא *ha-hi*; masculine plural ההם *ha-hem*; feminine plural ההן *ha-hen* (F).

אותו *oto* 'that (there, then, aforesaid) as in 'that other idea', 'that (familiar)' as in 'just one of those things': the feminine singular form is אותה *ota*; masculine plural אותם *otam*; feminine plural אותן *otan* (F). The plural is also used in the context 'those.. who...'.

(b) *'the same'*
אותו *oto* (inflected like אותו *oto* above), as in:

kanínu otam kelim we-bought (the) same dishes	קנינו אותם כלים

(c) *'such'*
כזה *kaze*, שכזה *she-kaze* (inflected like זה *ze* above, eg. כזאת *kazot* etc).[4]
כיוצא באלה *kayotse ba-éle* 'other such' occurs only in plural form:

méshek Hay katan ve-kayotse ba-éle shaashu'im	משק חי קטן וכיוצא באלה שעשעים
	'a small animal farm and other such amusements'

(d) *Indeterminate: 'some..(or other)'*
איזה *éze*:[5] feminine singular forms are איזה *éze* (C), איזו *ézo* (F);[6] plural forms are איזה *éze*, אי-אלו *ey-élu* (F) as in:

bishvil éze mesiba	'for some party'	בשביל איזה מסיבה
yesh laH éze hatsa'a?	'Do you have some suggestion?'	יש לך איזה הצעה?

איזה שהוא *éze shehu*:[7] feminine singular forms are איזה שהיא *éze shehi* (C), איזו שהיא *ézo shehi* (F); masculine plural איזה שהם *éze shehem*; feminine plural איזה שהן *éze shehen* (F). These are sometimes written as one word, without the final *alef*, eg. איזהשהו, in the same way as מישהו *míshehu* 'someone', כלשהו *kólshehu* 'any'. Alternatively, שהוא *shehu* etc. can follow the noun, which it regularly does as part of the expressions כל... שהוא *kol...shehu* 'any... whatsoever', אף... שהוא *af... shehu* 'none..whatsoever' (see type (i) below):

ézeshehen shitot		איזהשהן שיטות
éze shitot shehen	'some methods or other'	איזה שיטות שהן

כלשהו *kólshehu* (slightly formal):[8] feminine singular form כלשהי *kólshehi*; masculine plural כלשהם *kólshehem*; feminine plural כלשהן *kólshehen* (F).

> tsariH latet tshuva kólshehi   צריך לתת תשובה כלשהי
> 'You have to give *some* answer'

(e) *'a certain'*

אחד *eHad* (this is unstressed; when stressed, it means 'one'): feminine singular form אחת *aHat*; there is no plural.

> (eze) shnórer eHad   (איזה) שנורר אחד
> 'a certain scrounger'

> yesh laH roman eHad beshem...?   ?...יש לך רומן אחד בשם
> 'Do you have a certain novel called...'

זה *ze* (inflected like זה *ze* in type (a)):

> nigéshet elay ha-isha **ha-zot**   **הזאת** ניגשת אלי האשה
> '**This** woman comes up to me..'

(f) *Ill-defined: 'a sort of...'*

מין *min* is only used with singular nouns:[9]

> (éze) min klala rovétset aléha   (איזה) מין קללה רובצת עליה
> DET DET N(f.) v(f.)
> (some) sort-of curse rests on-her

כזה *kaze* (C): inflection and agreement are as with כזה *kaze* 'such' (type (c.)). It is unstressed:

> hu lavash kfafot **kaéle**   **כאלה** הוא לבש כפפות
> 'He wore gloves **of some sort**'

> éze angli meshune **kaze**[10]   **כזה** איזה אנגלי משונה
> 'some **sort of** weird English guy'

Three determiners are drawn from the ranks of prepositions (with related meaning): כמו *kmo*,[11] מעין *me'en* (F) and כעין *ke'en* (F) 'like'. A further kindred determiner is כמין *ke-min*. Examples of these forms used as determiners are:

> hirgáshti **kmo** zérem me-ha-Hayalim ba-ulam הרגשתי **כמו** זרם מהחיילים באולם
> I-felt **like** [= a sort of] a-current from the soldiers in-the hall

> huHlat al **me'en** pagrat káyits ba-siHot הוחלט על **מעין** פגרת קייץ בשיחות
> they-decided on **like** [= a sort of] summer recess in-the talks

> hayta **ke'en** brit histórit   היתה **כעין** ברית היסטורית
> there-was **like** [= a sort of] historical alliance

As prepositions they occur in, eg.:

> kmo   כמו
> be-Héder me'en ze mutkan manóa   בחדר מעין זה מותקן מנוע
> ke'en   כעין
> in a–room like this is–fitted a motor 'in a room like this a motor is fitted'

משום *mishum* 'something of...' (F)[12] is limited to the construction ...ב יש
...משום 'there is [or any other verb of being] in... something of a...', i.e '...
constitutes something of a...'. This and the next three items are the only cases
of DET+N being restricted as to their function in the sentence:

hayta ba-Hidush mishum sakana	היתה בחידוש משום סכנה
v (f,) N (f.)	'The idea was something of danger'
AGREEMENT	
there-was in-the idea something-of danger	

Similarly, בגדר *be-géder*, בחינת *bHinat*, בבחינת *bi-vHinat* (F) 'in the nature
of...'[13] are found only with a noun predicating a verb of being:

dvarav hem **bHinat** shvu'at shav	דבריו הם **בחינת** שבועת שווא
his-words are in-the-nature-of	'His words are **in the nature of** a false
oath false	oath'

(g) *'the very...' (only with abstract nouns)*
עצם *étsem*[14] is used, as in:

étsem ha-maHshava margiza oti	עצם המחשבה מרגיזה אותי
N(f.) v(f.)	'The very thought angers me'
very the thought angers me	

(h) *'the main, the basic'*
עיקר *ikar*[15] is used, as in:

ikar he-arim	**עיקר** הערים
	'the **main** cities'

ikar ha-sheela sovévet sviv...	עיקר השאלה סובבת סביב...
N(f.) v(f.)	
basis the question revolves around...	'The basic question revolves around...'

(i) *Generalizing (see also 29.9 on 'negative words')*
כל *kol* with indefinite nouns denotes (1) 'every, each', and (2), in negatives,
questions and conditionals (i.e non-assertive clauses), 'any' (F):

ra'íti **kol** shinuy	'I saw **every** change'	ראיתי **כל** שינוי
im ra'íti **kol** shinuy...	'If I saw **any** change..'	אם ראיתי **כל** שינוי...

With definite nouns, by contrast, כל *kol*, or הכל *ha-kol*, is best considered a
quantifier (see 8.5) meaning 'all, the whole of', and in such cases it needs no
noun, unlike most determiners:

ra'íti hakol	'I saw everything'	ראיתי הכל

כלשהו *kólshehu* 'any' means 'absolutely any' in 'assertive' clauses and 'any'
(= כל *kol*) in negatives, questions and conditionals. It inflects like כלשהו
kólshehu of type (d):

ani muHan la-gur be-dira **kólshehi**	אני מוכן לגור בדירה **כלשהי**
	'I am willing to live in **any** apartment'

yesh shinuy **kólshehu?** יש שינוי **כלשהו?**
'Is there **any** change?'

שהו - -*shehu* 'whatsoever' and the next item below are optional 'tags' to nouns already qualified by איזה *éze* 'some',[16] כל *kol* 'any' and (in the case of שהוא- -*shehu*) אף *af* or שום *shum* 'no'. The feminine singular form is שהיא *shehi;* masculine plural שהם *shehem*; feminine plural שהן *shehen* (F).

éze hatsa'a **shehi**	'some proposal **or other**'	איזה הצעה **שהיא**
{af/shum} hatsa'a **shehi**	'no proposal **whatsoever**'	{אף/שום} הצעה **שהיא**
kol hatsa'a **shehi**	'any proposal **whatsoever**'	כל הצעה **שהיא**

שלא יהיה *she-lo yiye* 'whatsoever' (literally 'that there will not be') inflects יהיה *yiye* as in its normal role as future tense verb. The feminine singular form is תהיה *tiye*; the plural is יהיו *yiyu*:

kaH éze kaftor she-lo yiye	קח איזה כפתור שלא יהיה
take some switch that not will-be	'Take any switch whatsoever'

(i) *'all sorts of'*

כל מיני *kol miney*[17] is related to מין *min* 'a sort of' (type (f.)) and the noun מין *min* 'sort':

kol miney kushiyot olot tamid	כל מיני קושיות עולות תמיד
N(f.pl.) v(f.pl.)	'All sorts of problems always arise'
AGREEMENT	
all sorts problems arise always	

(k) *'X sorts of'*

Quantifiers + מיני / סוגי *miney/sugey* 'sorts of' combine to make a determiner, when the noun is *plural*.[18] Note the agreement of the verb with the *noun*:

shney sugey **ha-parot** adáyin **nimtsa'ot** kan   שני סוגי **הפרות** עדיין **נמצאות** כאן
N(f.pl.)   v(f.pl.)   'The two sorts of **cows** still **exist** here'

(l) *Negatives (details are given in 29.9, 29.11)*

שום *shum* 'no', אף *af* 'not a single..':

lo matsáti ᵉʰᵘᵐ iparon

lo matsáti ^{shum}_{af} iparon   לא מצאתי שום עיפרון
אף

'I didn't find ^{any}_{a single} pencil'

(m) *Interrogative and exclamatory*

איזה *éze* 'which? (i.e out of a number of known alternatives)', 'what?',[19] 'what (a)...!' in casual usage is uninflected, but formal usage employs the feminine singular form איזו *ézo*, and plural אילו *éylu* (very formal):

éze teruts yesh lo?	איזה תירוץ יש לו?
	'What excuse does he have?'

איזה מין *éze min* 'what sort of...' optionally has a feminine singular form איזו מין *ézo min* (F):

איזו מין שנה תצמח פה?

ézo min shena titsmaH po?
N(f.)   v(f.)
'What sort of sleep will sprout here?'

(n) *Descriptive (non-indentificatory)*

Casually, the abstract adjectival nouns יופי *yófi* 'beauty', מותק *mótek* 'sweetness', חומד *Hómed* 'cuteness' and שגעון *shiga'on* 'lunacy' themselves act like adjectives meaning 'beautiful, sweet, cute, incredible'; but syntactically they are like determiners (particularly in exclamations): they precede a noun and this noun controls agreement.[20] For example:

יופי
איזה מותק של בחורה היתה שמה!
חומד

	yófi			
éze	mótek	shel	baHura hayta	sháma!
	Hómed		baHurot hayu	

	beauty			
what	sweetness of	girl was	there!
	cuteness	girls were	

איזה מותק של בחורה היתה שמה!
בחורות היו

	beautiful		
'What (a)	sweet	girl was	there!'
	cute	girls were	

(o) *Superlative*

מיטב, מבחר *meytav*,[21] *mivHar*[22] 'the best of...' and מירב *meyrav* 'the maximum...' are used as in:

mivHar ha-megilot shmurot ba-martef   מבחר המגילות שמורות במרתף
       N(f.pl.)   v(f.pl.)   'The best scrolls are kept in the basement'
best-of the scrolls are-kept in-the basement

kdey le-hafik et **meyrav** ha-to'élet   כדי להפיק את מירב התועלת
so-as to derive OM **maximum** the use   'so as to derive the maximum use'

9.3   The accompanying noun

9.3.1   Definite or indefinite

Most determiners (unlike adjectives) are limited to either a definite or an indefinite noun,[23] generally depending on their semantic type Following the examples, certain aspects are discussed in detail:

Examples of determiners with *definite* nouns only:

type a	ha-adam hahu	'that guy'	האדם ההוא
{in part):	ha-anashim halálu[24]	'these people'	האנשים הללו
	ha-talmid denan	'the foregoing student'	התלמיד דנן
type g, h:	{étsem/ikar} ha-baaya	'the {very/main} problem'	(עצם/עיקר) הבעיה
type o:	meytav ha-sfarim	'the best books'	מיטב הספרים

Examples of determiners with *indefinite* nouns only:

type c:	ish kaze	'such a man'	איש כזה
type d:	éze témbel	'some idiot'	איזה טמבל
type e:	shaHen eHad	'a certain neighbour'	שכן אחד
type f:[25]	min shastom	'a sort of valve'	מין שסתום
type i:	kol sheela shehi	'any question'	כל שאלה שהיא
type j:	kol miney barvazim	'all sorts of ducks'	כל מיני ברוזים
type l:	shum safam	'no moustache'	שום שפם
type m:[26]	éze katse	'which end'	איזה קצה
type n:	yófi shel meil	'a beautiful coat'	יופי של מעיל

Examples of determiners used with either definite or indefinite nouns (only in type k does this affect the meaning):

type a	ha-talmid ha-ze[27]	'this student'	התלמיד הזה
(in part):	talmid ze		תלמיד זה
	otam (ha-)mikrim	'those cases'	אותם (ה)מקרים
type b:	otam (ha-)shemot	'the same names'	אותם (ה)שמות
type k:	shney miney (ha-)kapot	'(the) two sorts of spoons'	שני מיני (ה)כפות

When the determiner agrees in definiteness

When a determiner with a definite noun *precedes* this noun (see 9.4 for details), the definite article precedes the noun as usual (as when a quantifier precedes the noun):

otam **ha**-shemot	אותם **ה**שמות
same **the** names	'the same names'

éle **ha**-dapim	אלה **ה**דפים
these **the** pages	'these pages

But when following a definite noun, determiners must have a -ה *ha-* of their own:[28]

ha-daf **ha**-ze	הדף **ה**זה
the page **the** this	'this page'

ha-dapim **ha**-hem	הדפים **ה**הם
the pages **the**-they	'those pages

Semantic definiteness with no את *et*

The definite object marker את *et* does not occur before phrases of the type שיא זה *si ze* 'this record', שיאים אלה *si'im éle* 'these records', even though they are semantically definite:

leaHar she-kaváta (*et) si'im éle..	לאחר שקבעת (*את) שיאים אלה
after you-set (*OM) records these..	'After you set these records...'

Conversely, את *et* tends to be used (except by purists) before אותו *oto* 'that, same' even with no -ה *ha-*:[29]

kalátnu et otam	taHanot		תחנות	קלטנו את אותם התחנות
	ha-taHanot		התחנות	
we-picked-up OM {same/those}	stations	'We picked up	the same	stations'
	the stations		those	

Restrictions on demonstratives

With demonstratives, the definite noun can be a proper name (אותו איינשטיין *oto áynshtayn* 'that Einstein') but not, as in example (1) below, *noun + possessive*, nor, as in example (2), any other '*open construct phrase'* (see 6.5). An open construct phrase is one equivalent to 'the..of the..' as against a mere idiomatic compound:

(1) *rishumi ha-ze / ha-hu   רישומי הזה / ההוא
    drawing-my the-that   'that drawing of mine'

    *oto rishumi   *אותו רישומי
    that drawing-my   'that drawing of mine'

(2) *haftsatsat ha-kfarim ha-zot   *הפצצת הכפרים הזאת
    bombing the villages the this   'this bombing of the villages'

    *bney ha-kibuts ha-éle[31]   *בני הקיבוץ האלה
    members the kibbutz the these   'these members of the kibbutz'

Instead, של *shel* 'of' must be interposed between the nouns, and the determiner follows the first noun, eg.:

    ha-rishum ha-ze sheli   הרישום הזה שלי
    the drawing the this of-me   'this drawing of mine'

9.3.2 Singular or plural noun

Most determiners allow either a singular or a plural noun, but a few are idiosyncratically restricted.

The following require a singular noun: משום *mishum* 'something of', כמין *kemin* 'a sort of', מין *min* 'a sort of' (with plural nouns one uses מיני *miney* 'sorts of'), עצם *étsem* 'the very', כל *kol* 'each, every' (...כל ה *kol ha-...* 'all the..' is used with plurals), כל *kol* 'no' (usually), אף *af* 'no' (it requires *countable* singulars).
The following require a plural: הללו *halálu* 'these', כיוצא באלה *kayotse ba-éle* 'other such', כל מיני *kol miney* 'all sorts of'.

9.4 Positioning the determiner

Vis-à-vis the noun. Most determiners precede their noun (as do most quantifiers). The exceptions are somewhat arbitrary: Those which follow the noun are: זה *ze* 'this',[32] הללו *halálu* 'these', ההוא *hahu* 'that' (but אותו *oto* 'that' precedes), אחד *eHad* 'a certain', כלשהו *kólshehu* 'any', שהוא *shehu* 'some ...or other', שלא יהיה *she-lo yiye* 'whatsoever' (איזהשהו *ézeshehu* 'some..or other' can follow or precede), שכזה *shekaze* 'such' (כזה *kaze* 'such' can follow or, in casual usage, even precede).

Vis-à-vis other words. Determiners and other modifiers of the noun generally observe the 'degree of closeness'[33] to the noun indicated in the diagram, whether preceding or following it:

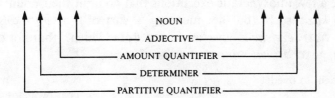

Examples are:

rov otan menorot	רוב אותן מנורות
PART. DET.	'most of those lamps'
most those lamps	

kol otam milyon ha-boHarim she..	כל אותם מליון הבוחרים ש...
PART. DET. AMOUNT	'all those million voters who...'
all those million the voters that...	

efsharut noséfet aHat kazot	אפשרות נוספת אחת כזאת
ADJ. AMOUNT DET.	'one such added possibility'
possibility added one such	

9.5   Determiners with no noun: ההוא *hahu* 'that one', כל מיני *kol miney* 'all sorts'

A characteristic of most determiners is that they *cannot* omit their noun, unlike quantifiers or adjectives, for example:

éle ha-rishumim shelaH? *gam li yesh **éze**	אלה הרישומים שלך? *גם לי יש **איזה**
DET.	
(✓...éze rishumim)	(✓....איזה רישומים)
'Are these your sketches? I also have **some** sketches'	

as against:

...gam li yesh **káma**	...גם לי יש **כמה**
QUANT.	'...I also have a few'
also to-me is **a-few**	

...li yesh **katan** ve-**gadol**	...לי יש קטן וגדול
ADJ. ADJ.	'...I have a small one and a big one'
...to-me is **small** and **big**	

Further examples of the need for a noun with the determiner are:

*lahem yesh kol-kaH harbe neft ve-lánu	*להם יש כל-כך הרבה נפט ולנו
en **shum** (✓...shum neft)	אין **שום** (✓....שום נפט)
'They have so much oil and we do not have **any** oil'	

laH yesh teyp? *li yesh **oto** (✓...oto teyp)	לך יש טייפ? *לי יש **אותו** (✓....אותו טייפ)
'You have a tape-recorder? I have the **same** tape-recorder'	

Nor does Hebrew have the equivalent of the pronoun 'one' (as in 'the same one, this one'); the noun must be repeated.[34]

There are a few idiosyncratic exceptions that do omit their noun: ההוא *hahu* 'that', כזה *kaze* 'such' (but not meaning 'a sort of'), כלשהו *kólshehu* 'any', איזה שלא יהיה *éze she-lo yiye* 'any', איזה *éze* 'which?' (but not exclamatory 'what a...!'), כל מיני *kol miney* 'all sorts of', eg.:

hahi lo ovédet
ההיא לא עובדת
'That ⟨woman⟩ doesn't work'

ha-taba'ot tovot? az ten li ka'éle
the washers good? then give me such
הטבעות טובות? אז תן לי כאלה
'Are the washers good? Then give me some like that'

mikserim? yesh kol miney
מיקסרים? יש כל מיני
'Mixers? There are all sorts'

True pronouns

Certain determiners have a second function as true pronouns. For example, זה *ze* 'this' and its inflections can be pronouns:

ten li kasda aHéret, ani sone et **zot**
תן לי קסדה אחרת, אני שונא את **זאת**
'Give me another helmet, I hate **this** ⟨one⟩'

ha-baaya hi **zot**
הבעיה היא **זאת**
'The problem is **this**'

There are several indications that this is a pronoun. (1) Unlike the determiner זה *ze* and unlike noun-less adjectives, it cannot take -ה *ha-*: הקסדה הזאת *ha-kasda ha-zot* (the helmet the this, with the determiner *zot*) 'this helmet' as against אני שונא את (ה*)זאת *ani sone et (*ha-)zot* (I hate (*the) this). (2) In the first example above, the pronoun זאת *zot* is introduced by the 'definite object' marker את *et*; were it a determiner, as in קסדה זאת *kasda zot* 'this helmet', it would be considered *indefinite* and would not allow את *et* (see 9.3.1).[35] Additionally, הזה *ha-ze* and its inflections are used very casually as a regular *noun* meaning 'that/those thing(s)':

ten li et **ha-ze**
'Give me **that thing**' .
תן לי את **הזה**

Plural כאלה *ka'éle* is like a pronoun in being able to act as an antecedent to a relative clause, i.e 'some who..., some which...' (in the same way as זה ש- *ze she-* 'the one who', אלה ש- *éle she-* 'those who'):

balátot? yesh **ka'éle** she-nidbakot maher
tiles? there-are **such** [= some] that stick quickly
בלטות? יש **כאלה** שנדבקות מהר

By contrast, as a determiner it would mean 'such': בלטות כאלה *balátot ka'éle* 'such tiles'.

Plural אותם *otam* 'those' (ϝ) is used without a noun, as an antecedent to a relative clause: 'those who...'; this is a pronoun, not a determiner implying a particular noun previously mentioned:

hatsaga zo mumlétset le-**otam she**-eynam   הצגה זו מומלצת ל**אותם שאינם**
ohavim sratim   אוהבים סרטים

> 'This show is recommended for **those who**
> do not like films'

9.6   Clauses complementing a determiner: ...**כמו**...**אותו** *oto...kmo*...'the same..as...'

Many determiner+noun expressions are followed by a relative clause, eg. ...ש האדם הזה *ha-adam ha-ze she*.. 'that man who...'. Of course, the relative clause depends on there being a noun, not on the determiner. However, as illustrated below, אותו *oto* 'the same' and כזה *kaze* 'such' are two determiners that can be followed by a clause specifically complementing them.

אותו *oto* 'the same' is complemented by a clause beginning with כמו *kmo* 'like' + the conjunction ש- *she-* 'that', rather as in a comparative clause (see 20.4):[36]

yesh li ota meHonit	kmo she-yesh laH she-yesh le-nisim	כמו שיש לך שיש לנסים	יש לי אותה מכונית
is to-me same car	like that is to-you that is to Nissim	'I have the same car	as you have' as Nissim has'

כזה *kaze* 'such' is complemented by a clause beginning with ש- *she-*, the conjunction that introduces most subordinate clauses. This is not a relative clause but a result clause, just as in ש... טוב כל-כך *kol kaH tov she*... 'so good **that**....' (see 20.5). Note that כזה *kaze* 'such' has two meanings, one amounting to 'so' (the counterpart of exclamatory איזה *éze* 'what a...!') and the other amounting to 'of such a type' (counterpart of איזה *éze* 'which?'):

hu idyot **kaze she**-enéni medaber elav	הוא אידיוט **כזה שאינני** מדבר אליו
he idiot **such that** I-not speak to-him	'He is **such an** idiot **that** I don't speak to him'

yesh sidur **kaze she**-ani ken yaHol linsóa	יש סידור **כזה שאני** כן יכול לנסוע
there's arrangement **such that** I indeed can go	'There's an arrangement **such that** I can indeed go'

FURTHER READING
Glinert 1977a, b, 1982a; Kaddari 1982; Ornan 1968, 1979a: 53, 82; Rosén 1966a: 51f, 283, 1977: 117ff, 160ff; Sadka 1981: 103ff.

10. Adjectives as modifiers

10.1 Introduction

Adjectives are used both *attributively*, i.e qualifying a noun (the noun + adjective together just form a phrase), and *predicatively* (the adjective is predicate and completes the sentence):[1]

Attributive:
ha-yaréaH **ha-atsuv**　　　　　　　　　　　　　　　　　**הירח העצוב**
the moon **the sad**　　　　　　　　　　　　　　　　　'the sad moon'

Predicative:
ha-yaréaH **atsuv**　　　　　　　　　　　　　　　　　　**הירח עצוב**
the moon **sad**　　　　　　　　　　　　　　　　　　'The moon is sad'

This chapter describes adjective phrases in general and the syntax of attributive adjectives in particular. For predicative adjectives, see chapters 16 and 17. For the *form* of all adjectives and their inflection, see chapter 41.

The distinction between adjective, noun and verb is described in 41.2. Adjectives are fairly distinct from verbs in not having past and future tense inflection, for example:

eye gadol　　　　　　　　'I will be big'　　　　　　　אהיה גדול
　　ADJ
egdal　　　　　　　　　　'I will grow'　　　　　　　　אגדל
V

Admittedly, they can easily have the same form as nouns; but (example (1) below) they do not take possessive suffixes; as predicates they can be used impersonally with no subject as in (2); and they do not need (but can have) a copula הוא, היא, הם *hu, hi, hem* to express 'is, are', as in example (3):

(1) aniyéynu 'our poor'　עניינו　　　　　　zkenéynu 'our old'　זקנינו
　　　N!　SUFF　　　　　　　　　　　　　　N!　SUFF

　　*aHeréynu　√ha-aHerim shelánu　　　　　*אחרינו　√האחרים שלנו
　　ADJ　　　　　　　　　　　　　　　　　　　　　　'our other ones'
　　others-our

(2) ani ro'e she-kvar ayefim　　　　　　　　אני רואה שכבר עייפים
　　I see that already tired　　　　　　　'I see that they are already tired'
　　and not:
　　*ani ro'e she-kvar horim　　　　　　　　*אני רואה שכבר הורים

| I see that already parents | 'I see that they are already parents' |

(3)   avazim ksherim   'Geese ⟨are⟩ kosher'   אווזים כשרים

All adjectives can be used attributively but few nouns.[2]

10.2   Positioning of adjectives

In general, adjectives directly follow the noun they are qualifying - except when the noun is part of a construct noun phrase, in which case the adjective must follow the whole noun phrase:

| maase mevadéaH | מעשה מבדח |
| incident amusing | 'amusing incident' |

sipur yeladim mevadéaH	סיפור ילדים מבדח
CONSTRUCT PHR m.s.	
story children amusing	'amusing children's story'
	(i.e the *story* is amusing)

As an adjective can qualify either the final noun in such construct phrases or a preceding noun, ambiguity sometimes arises when adjective agreement offers no clue:

memshélet ha-medina ha-ara'it	ממשלת המדינה הארעית
f.s. f.s. f.s.	'the provisional [government of the state]'
government the state the provisional	'the government of the provisional
	state'

However, where a של *shel* 'of' phrase is used instead of a construct phrase (ch. 6), the adjective must follow the noun it qualifies:

ha-memshala ha-ara'it shel ha-medina	המדינה של הארעית הממשלה
the government the provisional of the state	'the provisional government of
	the state'

If there is a determiner or quantifier after the noun, it generally follows the adjective (if any):

Determiner:

toHnit Hadasha **zo**/	/**זו** חדשה תוכנית
/ha-toHnit ha-Hadasha **ha-zot**	**הזאת** החדשה התוכנית
program new **this**/the program the new **the this**	'this new program'

| alim metim **ka'éle** | **כאלה** מתים עלים |
| leaves dead **such** | '**such** dead leaves' |

Quantifier:

| aHbar iver **eHad** | **אחד** עיוור עכבר |
| mouse blind one | 'one blind mouse' |

However, any words for 'this, that' involving -ה *ha*- 'the', and the word אחד *eHad* 'one', can instead *precede* the adjective:

ha-toHnit ha-zot ha-Hadasha	התוכנית הזאת החדשה
the program the this the new	'this new program'

aHbar eHad iver	עכבר אחד עיוור
mouse one blind	'one blind mouse'

Casual Hebrew uses מותק של *mótek shel* 'sweetness of', חומד של *Hómed shel* 'niceness of', יופי של *yófi shel* 'beauty of', שיגעון של *shiga'on shel* 'madness of' (and a few other nouns) as uninflected adjectives *preceding* the noun:

hayu li yófi shel naaláyim	היו לי יופי של נעליים
pl. m.s. f.pl	
there-were to-me beauty of shoes	'I had some beautiful shoes'

10.3 Adjective agreement[3]

Attributive adjectives agree in gender, number and definiteness with their noun:[4]

sir Hum	סיר חום	sira Huma	סירה חומה
m.s. m.s.	'a brown pot'	f.s. f.s.	'a brown boat'
pot brown		boat brown	

ha-sir ha-Hum	הסיר החום	ha-sirot ha-Humot	הסירות החומות
m.s. m.s.	'the brown pot'	f.pl f.pl	'the brown boats'
the pot the brown		the boats the brown	

By contrast, predicative adjectives agree in gender and number but *not* in definiteness - this indeed is the commonest way of distinguishing a phrase from a full sentence:

ha-sir ha-Hum	הסיר החום	'the brown pot' vs.	ha-sir Hum	הסיר חום
the pot the brown			the pot brown	'the pot is brown'

10.4 Multiple adjectives: stacking

Two (occasionally more) attributive adjectives can be combined by 'stacking' or by coordination. Adjectives of disparate semantic type are combined by stacking, i.e one simply follows the other without pause, comma or link-word, like 'layers' of adjectives:[5]

betoH mita ktana smuHa le-mitati	בתוך מיטה קטנה סמוכה למיטתי
in bed small close to my-bed	'in a small bed close to my bed'

ha-tnu'a ha-avirit ha-pnimit	התנועה האווירית הפנימית
the traffic the aerial the internal	'the internal air traffic'

This can be analysed as:

[[[NOUN] ADJ] ADJ]

Most such combinations simply cannot use coordination as an alternative, owing to the very disparateness of the adjectives.[6] Stacking is required:

ha-balash ha-prati ha-yaHid	הבלש הפרטי היחיד
	'the only private detective'
mumiya mitsrit atika	מומיה מצרית עתיקה
	'an ancient Egyptian mummy'

The first stacked adjective is often a noun-based adjective such as that in בחירה פרלמנטרית *bHira parlamentárit* 'parliamentary election', הפעלה ידנית *hafala yadanit* 'manual operation', הצעה מצרית *hatsa'a mitsrit* 'Egyptian proposal'. This is easily paraphrased using a noun:

bHirat parlament	בחירת פרלמנט
election [of] parliament	
hafalat yad	הפעלת יד
operation [of] hand	
hatsa'at mitsráyim	הצעת מצריים
proposal [of] Egypt	

and so almost always occurs attributively rather than predicatively (see 10.6):

*ha-hatsa'a mitsrit	*ההצעה מצרית
	'The proposal ⟨is⟩ Egyptian'

It will thus be stacked closest to the noun; indeed, adjectives corresponding to a subject or object noun will precede adjectives corresponding to an adverb:

ha-bHira ha-parlamentárit ha-yardénit	הבחירה הפרלמנטרית הירדנית
the election the parliamentary the Jordanian	'the election of Parliament in Jordan'

Adjectives particularly associated with the noun will also take precedence; superlatives (including האחרון *ha-aHaron* 'the last', היחיד *ha-yaHid* 'the sole') and ordinals (eg. השישי *ha-shishi* 'the 6th') are last of all.

For contrast's sake, however, the order of adjectives can change (example (1) below) and even adjectives of similar semantic type will be stacked rather than coordinated, as seen in examples (2,3):

(1)	ha-hatsa'a ha-Hadasha ha-*mitsrit*	ההצעה החדשה המצרית
	the proposal the new the *Egyptian*	'the new *Egyptian* proposal'
(2)	ha-kélev ha-gadol ha-*lavan*	הכלב הגדול הלבן
	the dog the large the *white*	'the large *white* dog'
(3)	ha-kélev ha-lavan ha-*gadol*	הכלב הלבן הגדול
	the dog the white the *large*	'the *large* white dog'

10.5 Multiple adjectives: coordination

Adjectives of like semantic type are generally combined by coordination. ‑ו *ve-* 'and' can be omitted as in general coordination (35.2); to cut the
final ‑ו *ve-* is typically literary (final example):

kélev gadol ve-lavan dog big and white	כלב גדול ולבן 'a big white dog'
anashim rogzim va-alutim people angry and dark	אנשים רוגזים ועלוטים 'dark angry people'

panav ha-gasim, he-avim
  ve-ha-metumtamim kim'a
face-his the crude, the thick and the
  stupid slightly
	פניו הגסים, העבים
	והמטומטמים קמעה
	'his crude, thick, slightly
	  stupid face'

aviv raH, aroH me'od, nifla bimyuHad spring soft, long very, wonderful particularly	אביב רך, ארוך מאד, נפלא במיוחד a soft, very long, particularly wonderful Spring'

However, the definition of what counts here as 'like semantic type' is complex:
for example, that a dress is 'lovely' is not as newsworthy a quality as its being
'green', hence שמלה יפה ירוקה *simla yafa yeruka* 'a lovely green dress' without ‑ו *ve-*, as against תוכנית יפה ואנושית *toHnit yafa ve-enoshit* 'a lovely **and**
humane programme'. Similarly, colours tend to follow other adjectives but
'newsworthiness' can affect this.

10.6 'Attributive only' adjectives

Certain types of adjective are generally only attributive - however,
they otherwise behave no differently from others. Five types can be distinguished.

Types 1 and 2 below can be explained as 'transferred epithets': the adjective
is semantically equivalent to an adverbial or noun, thus *it does not characterize
its noun* and cannot act predicatively.

(1) *Adverbial adjectives*

ha-yoshev-rosh ha-noHeHi (*hu noHehi)	'the current chairman' 'He is current'	היושב-ראש הנוכחי (*הוא נוכחי)
be-hizdamnut kodémet	'on a previous occasion'	בהזדמנות קודמת
yoresh efshari	'a possible successor'	יורש אפשרי
ha-nasi ha-manóaH	'the late president'	הנשיא המנוח

as against:

hi rakdanit tova	'She's a good dancer'	היא רקדנית טובה
ha-rakdanit ha-zot tova	'That dancer's good'	הרקדנית הזאת טובה

(2) *Noun-like adjectives*

Most noun-based adjectives have a suffix ‑י *-i*. Qualifying a noun, they are often equivalent to a construct genitive (recall 10.4):

kénes miflaga ~ kénes **miflagti**	כנס מפלגה ~ כנס **מפלגתי**
N N N ADJ	'a party congress'

siHat télefon ~ siHa **telefónit**	שיחת טלפון ~ שיחה **טלפונית**
N N N ADJ	'a phone call'

Only occasionally are they predicative, mostly in technical usage:

ha-kénes hu miflagti	הכנס הוא מפלגתי
	'The congress is a party congress'

ha-imunim hayu tsvaiim	האימונים היו צבאיים
	'The training was military'

Alternatively, the adjective may have another commonly predicative sense:

sheela Hukit	שאלה חוקית
	'a legal question' (= 'pertaining to or allowed by law')

ha-sheela Hukit	השאלה חוקית
	'The question is legal' (again ambiguous)

One type of noun-based adjective (condemned by purists) is often equivalent to the subject of a sentence:

ha-hatkafa ha-romit	ההתקפה הרומית
	'the Roman attack'

i.e	
ha-hatkafa bidey ha-romaim	ההתקפה בידי הרומאים
	'the attack by the Romans'

ha-siHot ha-luviyot-marokáiot	השיחות הלוביות-מרוקאיות
	'the Lybian-Moroccan talks'

i.e	
ha-siHot beyn...	השיחות בין...
	'the talks between...'

No predicative use is possible:

*ha-hatkafa hayta romit	'the attack was Roman'	*ההתקפה היתה רומית

עצמי *atsmi* 'self' is equivalent to a sentence subject or object:

limud atsmi	'self-learning'	לימוד עצמי
sherut atsmi	'self-service'	שירות עצמי

(3) *'Degree word'-like adjectives (cf. ch. 20):*

ta'ut **gmura**	'a **complete** mistake'	טעות **גמורה**
Haver **tov**	'a **good** friend'	חבר **טוב**
	(= very much a friend)	

(4) *Determiner-like adjectives (cf. ch. 9)*

yéled **mesuyam**	'a **certain** boy'	ילד מסויים
ha-siba ha-**ikarit**	'the **main** cause'	הסיבה העיקרית
séret **aHer**	'**another** film'	סרט אחר

(5) *Miscellaneous*

ha-délet ha-**(lo) neHona**	'the **(in)correct** door'	הדלת ה(לא) נכונה
be-shlav **rishon**	'at the **first** stage'	בשלב ראשון

10.7 Restrictive and non-restrictive

Like relative clauses (ch. 33), most attributive adjectives can be restrictive or non-restrictive (meaning and context permitting), as in English: 'colourful Brazilians' may be referring to *some* Brazilians, i.e restrictive, or to *all* Brazilians, i.e non-restrictive The ambiguity of the following Hebrew examples is often avoided by stressing the restrictive adjective, but this is not essential; and written Hebrew does not generally take any evasive action:

Restrictive	*Non-restrictive*
ishto ha-angliya אשתו האנגליה	ishto ha-angliya אשתו האנגליה
his-wife the English	his-wife the English
'his English (not his other) wife'	'his wife, who is English'
me'ot zkenim adukim מאות זקנים אדוקים	me'ot zkenim adukim מאות זקנים אדוקים
'hundreds of pious (as against other) elders'	'hundreds of pious (naturally!) elders'

10.8 Semi-compounds: השנות-טובות *ha-shanót-tovot* 'the New Year cards'

Casual Hebrew treats some 'noun + adjective' combinations as semi-compounds, as if they were felt to express a single indivisible concept.

Graphically, they are hyphenated; grammatically, they take just one -ה *ha-* 'the', before the first word while, however, still inflecting each compound element with gender-number suffixes:

ha-shaná-tova ~ ha-shanót-tovot	השנה-טובה ~ השנות-טובות
f.s. f.s. f.pl. f.pl.	
the year good the years good	'The New Year ⟨card ~ cards⟩'

This particular example and a few other semi-compounds are even distinct phonetically from noun+adjective phrases, by stressing just the first word (the noun)[7] and thus creating a contrast with, eg.:

shaná tová	'a good year'	שנה טובה

Further examples (those marked on the first word are commonly stressed there) may very often be a semi-compound:

mazál-tov	'congratulations'	מזל-טוב
kipá-sruga	'knitted skullcap'[8]	כיפה-סרוגה
magen-david-adom	'ambulance service'	מגן-דוד-אדום
yéled-tov	'goody-goody'	ילד-טוב

or sometimes a semi-compound:

et-novéa	'fountain pen'	עט-נובע
or-yarok	'green light' (go-ahead)	אור-ירוק

Literary/technical usage sometimes hyphenates a noun+adjective (as an alternative to quotation marks) to give the impression of a distinct concept, as in example (1) below. But where there is -ה *ha-* 'the', it must be on both parts, and we no longer have a semi-compound, as in (2):

(1) teurim shel Hayatiut-enoshit   תיאורים של חייתיות-אנושית
     descriptions of bestiality-human   'descriptions of human bestiality'

(2) ha-Hayatiut ha-enoshit   החייתיות האנושית
     the bestiality the human   'the human bestiality'

10.9   The overall adjective phrase

Which types of words accompany adjectives, to form adjective phrases, depends on whether the adjective is predicate of the clause or just attribute of a noun. When predicate, it can take a genitive, a degree word, an object, and a large range of adverbials:

hu me'od ge'e ba-méshek aHshav   הוא מאד גאה במשק עכשיו
    DEGREE   OBJ   ADV
    WORD
he very proud of-the farm now   'He's very proud of the farm now'

When attribute, the adjective phrase is kept fairly simple: it can involve genitives and degree words (these being tightest to the adjective structurally, see ch.6), but few types of objects and few adverbials, except where the adjective is a past participle Thus:

with construct genitives:
dardakim shzufey-shémesh u-kHuley-eynáyim   דרדקים שזופי-שמש וכחולי-עיניים
    CONSTRUCT   N   CONSTRUCT   N
    ADJ   ADJ   'sun-tanned, blue-eyed children'

with degree words:[9]
hu-tinok **me'od** atsbani   הוא תינוק **מאד** עצבני
                                                  'He's a **very** irritable baby'

ramat miskal gvoha **min ha-memutsa**   רמת משכל גבוהה **מן הממוצע**
'a higher **than average** level of intelligence'

Most objects are ruled out:[10]

*mats'u me'il shayaH **laH**   *מצאו מעיל שייך **לך**
'They found a coat belonging **to you**'

*tish'al míshehu nasuy **le-yisraelit**   *תשאל מישהו נשוי **לישראלית**
'Ask someone married **to an Israeli**'

Most adverbials are ruled out:[11]

*yesh la tinok **tamid** atsbani   *יש לה תינוק **תמיד** עצבני
'She has an **always** irritable baby'

*dirot éle noadu le-anashim   *דירות אלה נועדו לאנשים
nesu'im **kvar**   נשואים **כבר**
'These apartments are meant for **already** married people'

However, adjectives acting as true past participles of verbs may take objects and adverbials:[12]

ha-tsibur maadif neyarot **tsmudim la-dólar**   הציבור מעדיף ניירות **צמודים לדולר**
PART   OBJ
'The public prefers bonds **linked to the dollar**'

horénu lahem linHot be-téHnika   הורינו להם לנחות בטכניקה
mekubélet ba-avir   **מקובלת באוויר**
PART   ADVERBIAL
'We instructed them to land by a technique **accepted in the air**'

10.10   Noun-less ('headless') adjectives

Adjectives can optionally forgo a nucleus noun when this has just been mentioned - and they agree with whatever their nucleus noun would have been, as in (1) below. They can be definite or indefinite (2):[13]

(1) ra'íti shtey **toHniyot** be-emtsa ha-láyla.   ראיתי שתי **תוכניות** באמצע הלילה.
f.pl.
ha-**rishona** aska be..   **הראשונה** עסקה ב...
f.s.
'I saw two **programmes** in the middle of the night.
The **first** dealt with...'

(2) ha-**tmarim** nora yekarim. im eyn yoter **zolim**...   ה**תמרים** נורא יקרים. אם אין יותר **זולים**...
m.pl.   m.pl.
'The **dates** are very expensive
If there aren't **cheaper** ⟨ones⟩...'

A case of anticipation of the noun is the (formal) superlative construction:

ha-svuHa ba-baayot hi ha-aliya	הסבוכה בבעיות היא העליה
f.s. f.pl.	(= הבעיה הסבוכה ביותר...)
(= ha-baaya ha-svuHa beyoter...)	
the thorny among-the problems	'The most thorny problem
is immigration	is immigration'

ha-yedu'a she-bahen hayta neHáma láybovits	הידועה שבהן היתה
f.s. f.pl.	נחמה לייבוביץ
the well-known that among-them was	'The best known of them
Nechama Leibowitz	was Nechama Leibowitz'

A kindred construction, restricted to a few adjectives, is the following:

prévin, me-Hashuvey ha-menatsHim	פרווין, מחשובי המנצחים
ba-olam,.../...mi-gdoley.../...me-aHaroney...	בעולם,.../...מגדולי.../...מאחרוני...
previn, of important-of the	'Previn, one of the most important
conductors in-the world/...	conductors in the World.../...
of great-of.../of last-of...	of the greatest/...of the last...'

Non-contextualized omission

As subject or predicate in certain constructions, a masculine singular adjective can denote an abstract 'something -, the - thing', with *no* foregoing noun implied:

ha-muzar ve-ha-meanyen (ba-davar)	המוזר והמעניין (בדבר)
hu she-hiskímu	הוא שהסכימו
the odd and the interesting (in-the thing)	'The odd and interesting thing
is that they-agreed	is that they agreed'

ha-dome/ha-shone bi-shney ha-mikrim	הדומה/השונה בשני המקרים
- ha-ratson leharshim	- הרצון להרשים
'The similar/different ⟨thing⟩ in the two cases ⟨is⟩ the desire to impress'	

lo haya be-oto shavúa **patéti yoter**	לא היה באותו שבוע **פתטי יותר**
mi-tguva meumétset be-miktsat	מתגובה מאומצת במקצת
la-dádaizm	לדאדאיזם
'There was not that week ⟨anything⟩ **more pathetic**	
than a slightly strained reaction to Dadaism'	

Adjective-based nouns

Unlike the foregoing, certain human-related adjectives such as זקן *zaken* 'old', צעיר *tsa'ir* 'young', ותיק *vatik* 'old', עשיר *ashir* 'rich', עני *ani* 'poor', משוגע *meshuga* 'crazy' can act as nouns. As such, they cannot take degree words - see (1) below[14] - indeed, they take possessive suffixes like any noun (2):

(1) *pagáshti **zaken me'od** ve-sipárti lo   *פגשתי **זקן מאד** וסיפרתי לו*
      I-met **old-man very** and I-told him   ('I met a very old man and I told him')

(2)   ani ge'e be-vatikéynu   אני גאה בוותיקינו
                                                     'I am proud of **our** oldtimers'

FURTHER READING
Barri 1978; Sadka 1981.

11. Preposition phrases and adverbs as modifiers

11.1 Introduction

Like adjectives (ch.10) and nouns (ch.36), one may use preposition phrases or simple adverbs in two closely related roles: as predicates and as modifiers ('attributively');[1] for example:

Predicative:

ha-shi'ur hu **al iyov** PREP. PHR	השיעור הוא **על איוב** 'The lesson is **on Job**'
ha-shi'ur hu **lemáta** ADV.	השיעור הוא **למטה** 'The lesson is **downstairs**'

Attributive:

ha-shi'ur al iyov lemáta butal	השיעור על איוב בוטל למטה

'The lesson on Job downstairs was cancelled'

For preposition phrases in general, see chapter 19; for predicates, see chapter 16.

Predicates and attributes are closely related in that an attribute is usually equivalent to 'is+PREDICATE':

ha-shi'ur **al iyov** butal   השיעור **על איוב** בוטל
= ha-shi'ur she-**hu al iyov** butal   = השיעור שה**וא על איוב** בוטל
'The lesson **on Job** was cancelled
= The lesson that **is on Job** was cancelled'

11.2 'Objects' of verbal nouns

tikva **la-mashíaH**	'hope **for the Messiah**'	תקווה **למשיח**
bogdim **ba-medina**	'traitors **to the state**'	בוגדים **במדינה**

'Action or product nouns' correspond closely to verbs, and 'state nouns' to adjectives (see 30.6):

tikva ~ kiva	'hope ~ to hope'	תקווה ~ קיווה
truma ~ taram	'contribution ~ to contribute'	תרומה ~ תרם

113

ayefut ~ ayef   'tiredness ~ tired'   עייפות ~ עייף

So too do their 'objects' ('complements'). With the exception of objects with the object marker את *et*, all objects are the same for the verbal or adjectival noun as for the corresponding verb or adjective (את *et* is replaced by של *shel* 'of' or by the construct genitive):[2]

{taram ~ truma} le-tsáhal   {תרם ~ תרומה} לצה"ל
                                   '{donate ~ donation} to the Army'

{ayef ~ ayefut} mi-ktiva   {עייף ~ עייפות} מכתיבה
                                  '{tired ~ tiredness} from writing'

'Agent nouns' correspond less closely;[3] in particular, it is often cumbersome to add an object ('complement') introduced by the usual verbal 'case preposition':

?nifgáshti sham be-Háma **tomHim ba**-nasi   ?נפגשתי שם בכמה **תומכים בנשיא**
                        CASE PREP
                                   'There I met some **supporters [of] the** president'

?ha-mishtara menasa laatsor   ?המשטרה מנסה לעצור
   moHrey samim li-tseirim   **מוכרי סמים לצעירים**
                                   'The police try to detain **sellers of drugs to** young people'

yesh[4] lehilaHem néged **maaminim**   יש להילחם נגד **מאמינים**
   be-datot shuliot   **ב**דתות שוליות
                                   'One must fight against **believers in** fringe religions'

Adding ה- *ha*- helps. ה- *ha*- is felt to mean 'who...', creating a ('headless') relative clause: '(Those) who support the president':

ha-tomHim ba-nasi   'the supporters of the president'   התומכים בנשיא

Many such nouns can be used with a construct genitive complement (but not without a complement), even where the corresponding verb takes a preposition, eg.:

                                   תמך ב... ~ תומכי הנשיא
tamaH be..   'to support....' ~ tomHey ha-nasi   'the supporters of the
   PREP   CONSTRUCT   president'

                                   בא אל... ~ באי הכנס
ba el...   'to come to...' ~ ba'ey ha-kénes   'the participants at the congress'
   PREP   CONSTRUCT

                                   ישב ב... ~ יושבי מערות
yashav be..   'dwell in...' ~ yoshvey mearot   'cave dwellers'
   PREP   CONSTRUCT

11.3 Modifiers using של *shel* **'of'**

As detailed in chapter 6, של *shel* 'of' covers many things, including:

(1) *Possession*:
ha-mitriya ha-aHéret shelánu

המטריה האחרת שלנו
'our other umbrella'

(2) *Composition*:
dira shel shney Hadarim

דירה של שני חדרים
'a flat of two rooms'

(3) *Implied object of a thing*:
tmuna shelánu

תמונה שלנו
'a picture of us'

(4) *Subject/object of action*:
ha-kavana shelánu le-terorístim

הכוונה שלנו לטרוריסטים
'our reference to terrorists'

The של *shel* 'of' phrase will directly follow any adjectives, as in (1) above, and precede any complements (4).[5]

A nucleus noun, when definite, can be omitted rather than repeated:

ha-meHkar shel pnína Harif,
   aval **shel náama** shitHi lemaday
the research of Pnina shrewd,
   but of Naama superficial quite

המחקר של פנינה חריף,
אבל **של נעמה** שטחי למדי
'Pnina's research is shrewd,
but **Naama's** is fairly superficial'

tmunot? ten li lir'ot et **shelHa**
pictures? Let me see OM **of-you**

תמונות? תן לי לראות את **שלך**
'Pictures? Let me see the ones **of you**'
(or '**yours**')

haftsatsa shel eyzorey taasiya mutsdéket,
   aval **shel arim** u-kfarim asura
beheHlet

הפצצה של איזורי תעשיה מוצדקת,
אבל **של ערים** וכפרים אסורה
בהחלט
'Bombing of industrial areas is justified,
but ⟨**that**⟩ **of towns** and villages is absolutely unwarranted'

11.4 Adverbials as modifiers

martse im jins   'a lecturer in jeans'   מרצה עם ג'ינס

Adverbials as modifiers ('attributive') *follow* any adjective or של *shel* phrase:

ha-miHtav ha-aroH shelHa **la-menahel**
the letter the long of-you **to-the manager**   'your long letter **to the manager**'

המכתב הארוך שלך **למנהל**

There can be a sequence of several disparate kinds of adverbial, as in (1), while similar kinds of adverbial can be coordinated or, as in (2), stacked:

(1) ha-miHtav **miméni la-mol**   המכתב **ממני למו"ל**
        ADV   ADV

'the letter **from me to the publisher**'

(2)   me-ha-taHana be-talbíye, bi-reHov márkus...   ...מרכוס ברחוב בטלבייה, מהתחנה
            ADV   ADV

                           'from the stop in Talbiye, on Marcus St...'

Most types of adverbials - adverb, preposition+noun, preposition+clause - can be used with nouns. They are the equivalent of 'which/who is...':[6]

     ha-lulav **sham** pasul   פסול **שם** הלולב
                      'The palm-branch **there** is not kosher'

     af élu **ba-tsloHit** ksherim   כשרים **בצלוחית** אלו אף
                      'Even those **in the bowl** are kosher'

     ha-martse **im jins** HatiH   חתיך **ג'ינס עם** המרצה
                      'The lecturer **in jeans** is cute'

     ha-shir **lifney she-motsi'im**   **שמוציאים לפני** השיר
     et ha-tora yafe me'od   מאד יפה **התורה את**
                  'The song **before they take out the Tora** is very beautiful'

Where the adverbial denotes נמצא *nimtsa* 'is located', the particle -ש *she-* 'which/who' tends to be inserted to introduce it in formal usage; even for past events, just -ש *she-* and no היה *haya* 'was' is needed:[7]

     me'al-gabey ha-miznon **she-meaHorav**,   **שמאחוריו,** המזנון מעל-גבי
     hita elav et oznav ha-kvedot   הכבדות אוזניו את אליו היטה
               'From the sideboard **which ⟨was⟩ behind him,**
                 he inclined his heavy ears towards him'

     hityatsávti be-taHanat ha-mishtara   המשטרה בתחנת התייצבתי
     bi-reHov jabotínski **she-be-rámat-gan**   **שברמת-גן** ז'בוטינסקי ברחוב
              'I reported to the police station in Jabotinski St.
                   which ⟨is⟩ in Ramat Gan'

'Location' does not include cases like הבעיות בהולנד *ha-baayot be-hóland* 'the problems in Holland', hence no -ש *she-*. For adverbs of 'location in time', של *shel* 'of' is possible:

     bar-ha-samHa **shel** az, yadin   ידין אז, **של** בר-הסמכא
                  'the authority **of** then, Yadin'

     ha-tsarot **shel** ha-yom   היום **של** הצרות
                  'the troubles **of** today'

Some adverbials cannot act attributively, notably בסדר *beséder* 'all right', לבד *levad* 'alone', ביחד *beyáHad* 'together', and 'affective' -ל *le-* (cf.21.10):

     *lamrot ha-driHa **la-shHena** al ha-déshe..   ...הדשא על **לשכנה** הדריכה למרות*
     despite the treading **to-the neighbour**   ('Despite treading on the
     on the grass...   neighbour's grass...')

FURTHER READING
Berman 1978: 11.3; Ornan 1968, 1979: 4.8; Sadka 1981: 13.6.

12. Agreement in the noun phrase

12.1 Definition of 'agreement'

A word borrowing some intrinsic grammatical property of another word, with which it is in context, is said to 'agree' with it. Thus, the words determining agreement in the following examples are הקופסה *ha-kufsa* and הארגז *ha-argaz*, and the other words agree with them in gender, number and (except the word ריק(ה) *rek(a)*) definiteness:

ha-kufsa	ha-Huma	ha-zot	reka		הקופסה החומה הזאת ריקה
f.s.	f.s.	f.s.	f.s.		'This brown box is empty'
the box	the brown	the this	empty		

ha-argaz	ha-Hum	ha-ze	rek		הארגז החום הזה ריק
m.s.	m.s.	m.s.	m.s.		'This brown trunk is empty'
the trunk	the brown	the this	empty		

Although agreement does not affect 'lexical' meaning, it sometimes indicates syntactic structure Thus the ה- *ha-* of החומ(ה) *ha-Hum(a)* above tells one that חומ(ה) *Hum(a)* is part of the same noun phrase and not a predicate ('the box is brown'). See further 18.7.

This chapter discusses the modes of agreement within the noun phrase and their syntactic expression. Agreement between subject and predicate is set out in chapter 18 ('agreement in the clause'). For the *forms* of agreement prefixes and suffixes in general, see chapter 8 (quantifiers), chapter 9 (determiners), chapter 40 (verbs) and chapter 41 (adjectives). Chapter 39 describes gender and number *inherent* in nouns; chapter 5 describes inherent definiteness.

12.2 Nucleus and modifiers

Noun phrases usually consist of a 'nucleus noun', sometimes accompanied by one or more 'modifiers'. The full range of possible modifiers (in their likely order) is:

Partitive quantifier + determiner + amount quantifier + *nucleus* + adjective + determiner + adverb or preposition phrase + relative clause

For instance:

shisha	me-otam	tish'a	parparim	levanim	ששה מאותם תשעה פרפרים לבנים
QUANT	DET	QUANT	N	ADJ	מהודו שהזמנת
me-hódu	she-hizmant				
PREP PHR	REL				'Six of those nine white butterflies from India that you ordered'

This order has a bearing on agreement. The 'outer' modifiers - adverb or preposition phrase and relative clause - do not undergo agreement; the others usually do.

The modes of agreement are gender (masculine or feminine), number (singular or plural) and definiteness (indefinite or definite).

12.3 Quantifier agreement

Of the quantifiers, whether partitive or amount quantifiers (see ch. 8), only numerals undergo agreement - and in gender alone[1] The numerals for 'one' to 'ten' and those ending in these (eg. 1099, 110 but not 111, 120) agree with their noun in all registers except (sometimes) in substandard or very casual usage,[2] thus:

shisha rabanim		ששה רבנים	shesh rabaniyot		שש רבניות
m.	m.pl.	'six rabbis'	f.	f.pl.	'six rabbis' wives'

méa ve-shisha iyim		מאה וששה איים	méa ve-shesh Havot		מאה ושש חוות
	m. m.pl.	'106 islands'		f. f.pl.	'106 farms'

The numerals for 11-19 tend to agree only in somewhat formal Hebrew. Otherwise the 'feminine' form is preferred, eg.:

shvá-esre yeladim (casual)	'17 boys'	שבע־עשרה ילדים
f.		
shivá-asar yeladim (somewhat formal)	'17 boys'	שבעה־עשר ילדים
m.		

The numerals for the tens, hundreds, thousands etc. do not agree
   See 8.9 for the form of these inflections.

12.4 Determiner agreement

A majority of determiners precede the noun and a substantial minority can follow it (a few precede or follow), as elaborated in 9.4. This has some effect on agreement.

Determiners preceding the noun

Among the determiners that can precede the noun are אותו *oto* 'that', כזה *kaze* 'such' (c), איזהשהו *ézeshehu* 'some.. or other', איזה *éze* 'some.. or other', איזה *éze* 'which?', מין *min* 'a sort of', עצם *étsem* 'the very...', כל *kol* 'any, every', שום *shum* 'any', אף *af* 'not a single', כל מיני *kol miney* 'all sorts of', מיני ... ...*miney* '...sorts of'.

The first three of these determiners must agree for gender, in both the singular and the plural; while איזה *éze*, in both its senses, does so in the singular in formal Hebrew (see 9.2 for the formal inflections). The remainder do not agree.

The same three determiners must agree for number; so too must איזה *éze* 'which?' in formal usage, but not usually איזה *éze* 'some'. The remainder do not agree.

There is no agreement for definiteness. Nor is there for other *modifiers* preceding the noun.

Determiners following the noun

The notable determiners that can follow the noun are זה *ze* 'this', הללו *halálu* 'these', ההוא *hahu* 'that', כזה *kaze* 'such', כלשהו *kólshehu* 'any', אחד *eHad* 'a certain', שהוא *shehu* 'whatsoever', שלא יהיה *she-lo yiye* 'whatsoever', איזהשהו *ézeshehu* 'some.. or other', כזה *kaze* 'a sort of'.

All agree for gender, except the plural forms of זה *ze*, הללו *halálu* and כזה *kaze* All agree for number (except that הללו *halálu* is only used with plural nouns and אחד *eHad* with singular).

For definiteness, הללו *halálu and* ההוא *hahu* are inherently definite, and כזה *kaze*, כלשהו *kólshehu* and most others inherently indefinite Only זה *ze* 'this' has the option of accompanying a definite *or* an indefinite noun, and agrees by taking -ה *ha-* 'the' when its noun does - though the only difference thereby is stylistic, namely that the indefinite variety is more formal:

ha-Hag ha-ze	החג הזה	Hag ze	חג זה
the festival the this	'this festival'	festival this	'this festival'

ha-Hagim ha-éle	החגים האלה	Hagim éle	חגים אלה
the festivals the these	'these festivals'	festivals these	'these festivals'

12.5 Adjective agreement

Nearly all adjectives agree with the noun they qualify, in gender, number and definiteness, eg.:

kala yafa	כלה יפה	kalot yafot	כלות יפות
f.s. f.s.	'a lovely bride'	f.pl. f.pl.	'lovely brides'
bride lovely		brides lovely	

ha-kala ha-yafa	הכלה היפה	ha-kalot ha-yafot	הכלות היפות
the bride the lovely	'the lovely bride'	the brides the lovely	'the lovely brides'

or yafe	אור יפה	orot yafim	אורות יפים
m.s. m.s.	'a lovely light'	m.pl. m.pl.	'lovely lights'
light lovely		lights lovely	

Agreement is not a matter of adjectives agreeing in *suffix shape* with their noun. In the foregoing example, אורות *orot* is masculine despite its ות- *ot* suffix, hence the adjective displays the masculine plural suffix of all adjectives, ים- -*im*. (For adjectival inflectional forms, see 41.6-9.) Similarly, names are definite in function but not usually in shape:

sara **ha**-yafa	שרה **ה**יפה
Sara **the** lovely	'lovely Sara'

The only significant group of adjectives that do not agree in *gender* is ordinal adjectives (see 8.10) for '11th, 12th' onwards. Those for numbers ending in a zero have just one form for both genders; the others have separate masculine and feminine forms in formal usage, but in casual usage the feminine tends to do service for both:[3]

ha-shana ha-shtém-esre		השנה השתים־עשרה
f.s. f.s.		'the 12th year'

ha-shévet	ha-shném-asar (m.s., F)	השנים־עשר
	ha-shtém-esre (f.s., C)	השבט השתים־עשרה
		'The 12th tribe'

Compounds of adjectives usually mark *definiteness* on the first component only, although both components inflect for gender and number.[4] There are three major types, exemplified by

ha-siHot ha-yisreeliyot-mitsriyot[5]	השיחות הישראליות-מצריות
f.pl. f.pl. f.pl.	'the Israeli-Egyptian talks'
the talks the Israeli-Egyptian	

ha-sfina ha-shHora-levana	הספינה השחורה־לבנה
f.s. f.s. f.s.	'the black and white ship'
the ship the black-white	

ha-meHonit ha-yeruka behira	המכונית הירוקה בהירה
f.s. f.s. f.s.	'the bright green car'
the car the green bright	

12.6 Agreement with coordinate phrases

A coordination of masculine and feminine nouns requires *masculine* plural agreement in its modifiers. This amounts to 'neuter' gender:

otam ish ve-/o isha	אותם איש ו-/או אשה
m.pl. m.s. f.s.	'that man and/or woman'
those man and/or woman	

ha-yéled ve-ha-yalda hahem	הילד והילדה ההם
m.s. f.s. m.pl.	'that boy and girl'
the boy and the girl those	

ha-yéled ve-ha-yalda ha-tovim beyoter	הילד והילדה הטובים ביותר
m.s. f.s. m.pl.	'the best boy and girl'
the boy and the girl the good most	

FURTHER READING
Berman 1974; Ornan 1968; Schwarzwald 1979c.

13. Tense, modality and aspect

13.1 Introduction

This chapter deals primarily with the choice of grammatical tense, using the forms known as 'past, present, future' and 'compound past' tense. The *shape* of these forms is given in chapter 40.

Tenses denote in fact a whole range of semantic time relationships, as well as certain semantic modalities and aspects. For example, in (1) the present tense denotes future time; in (2), the past tense denotes a hypothetical present time - 'hypothetical' being a different *modality*, i.e. a different 'kind of reality', than a 'declaration' or a 'request'; in (3) compound past tense denotes habitual past time - 'habitual' being a particular *aspect*, i.e. a particular structuring or conception of the event:

(1) maHar ani ba   מחר אני בא
       PRES   'I'm coming tomorrow'

(2) lu zaHárti aHshav,...   לו זכרתי עכשיו,...
       PAST   'If I remembered now,...

(3) ba-Hufshot hayíti mishtolel   בחופשות הייתי משתולל
       COMPOUND PAST   'In the holidays I used to run wild'

The terms 'present, past, future tense' (or 'form') will be retained for simplicity's sake.

This chapter also indicates some other, more widespread, ways of expressing modality and aspect - by lexical rather than grammatical means.

13.2-7 TENSE IN MAIN CLAUSES

13.2 Tense in main clauses: introduction

Main and subordinate clauses are similar for tense: there are no 'sequence of tense' rules to complicate subordinate clauses as in English. The basic 'tense and time rule' is 'The time of a situation is expressed from the vantage point of the person most directly contemplating it.'

Examples

(1) dov yada she-**nisha'er**   דוב ידע שנישאר
       FUT   'Dov knew that **we'd stay**'

The 'staying' is in future time as seen by the person doing the 'knowing', Dov, hence the future tense נישאר *nisha'er*. Despite there being a further vantage point here - the speaker's (as in every sentence) - from which the 'staying' could be seen as being in the past, one cannot say נשארנו *nishárnu* (past tense), for it is Dov who is most directly contemplating the 'staying'.

(2) nishma   'We'll hear'   נשמע
      FUT

Here the 'hearing' is in future time as seen by the speaker. No other vantage point is involved, hence the future tense

(3) eH neda im nitsáHnu?   איך נדע אם ניצחנו?
            PAST   'How will we know if we've won?'

Even if the 'winning' here is in the future of the speaker, the 'tense and time rule' relates to the most direct vantage point, i.e the knower's. The 'winning' is in the past of the 'knower'.

13.3 Present form

The Hebrew present form denotes a time *coinciding with* or *including* the vantage point of the contemplator.

There are six notable uses, some involving particular 'aspects' and 'modalities':

(1) *Here-and-now present*

         ani maklit otaH   'I am recording you'   אני מקליט אותך

(2) *Up-to-now present* for an event embracing the past that extends to include the present. This is found particularly with מאז *me'az* 'since' and מזה/זה/כבר *mize/ze/kvar* 'for':[1]

         paamáyim Hazárti me'az she-ani **gar** po   פעמיים חזרתי מאז שאני גר פה
             PAST   PRES
                           'I've been back twice since I've **been living** here'

         ani menase kvar shana   אני מנסה כבר שנה
            PRES   'I've been trying for a year'

         káma zman at melamédet?   כמה זמן את מלמדת?
              PRES   'How long have you been teaching?'[2]

(3) *Habitual present* for an event that recurs:

         ani shote ba-tsohoráyim   אני שותה בצוהריים
            PRES   'I drink at lunchtime'

(4) *Present of intent* for an event that is *presently intended* (by whomsoever) to happen in the future, i.e a special modality of viewing future reality, distinct from the central uses of the present tense:

         shovtim maHar   '⟨They⟩ are striking tomorrow'   שובתים מחר
            PRES

By contrast, ישבתו מחר *yishbetu maHar* 'They will strike tomorrow' is a prediction. Often the distinction between prediction and plan is not so apparent, especially in the 1st person.

(5) *Present of ultimatum* is a modality akin to 'intent':

ata mitnatsel ad maHar!   אתה מתנצל עד מחר!
PRES   'You're apologizing by tomorrow!'

ata mitnatsel ad maHar! PRES	אתה מתנצל עד מחר! 'You're apologizing by tomorrow!'
o she-kulam yoshvim o she-ani ozev either that everyone sits or that I leave	או שכולם יושבים או שאני עוזב 'Either everyone sits down or I leave'

(6) *Narrative present* is a modality of past time for vivid personally involved description:

az hi tsoHéket ve-oméret day PRES PRES	אז היא צוחקת ואומרת "די!" 'Then she laughs and says, "Stop it!"'

13.4 Future form

The future form mostly denotes a time in the future of the person contemplating the event. There are two main uses (see 13.10 and 13.13 for other uses of this tense):

Future of prediction:

tafsik kenir'e be-shesh FUT	תפסיק כנראה בשש 'You will stop at six apparently'

Future of request denotes future time with a modality of request (as against declaration):

tafsik be-shesh FUT	תפסיק בשש 'Stop at six'

There are two restrictions on the 'future of request', discussed more fully in chapter 28. Firstly, 2nd person requests in formal usage tend to employ the 'imperative form' rather than the 'future form', eg. הפסק *hafsek* 'Stop!', and certain verbs prefer it even in casual usage, eg. סע *sa* 'Go!'. However, *negative* requests in all usage use future and not imperative form, as in:

al tafsik NEG FUT	אל תפסיק 'Don't stop'	lo tafsik NEG FUT	לא תפסיק 'You won't stop'

The distinction here between request and prediction is conveyed by the choice of negator. In the positive, however, one must resort to intonation and context:

tafsik	'Stop ~ You will stop'	תפסיק

Secondly, 1st and 3rd person requests (singular or plural) occasionally use the bare future form, but more usually add a prefix - formal usage adds non-inflected הבה *háva* for the 1st person, casual usage adds the inflecting verb בוא *bo* for 1st and the conjunction -ש *she-* for 3rd (and sometimes 1st) person:

naHazor le-nos'im polítiyim 1st FUT	נחזור לנושאים פוליטיים 'Let us return to political topics'

aH yiten bevakasha et daato al ze she..   אך יתן בבקשה את דעתו על זה ש...
   3rd FUT   'But let him please consider the fact that...'

háva nish'al   הבה נשאל
   1st FUT   'Let us ask'

{ bo } nish'al   בוא נשאל
{ bóu }   בואו

{ come m.s. } 1st FUT { to one addressee   }
{   pl. }   { to several addressees }   'Let's ask'

she-hem yenasu   שהם ינסו
   3rd FUT
that they try   'Let them try'

13.5 Another 'aspect' of future time: עמד ל- *amad le-*, הלך ל- *halaH le-*

The verbs עמד *amad* and הלך *halaH*[3] in their various tenses, with an infinitive, denote a particular 'modality' or 'aspect' of futurity - as viewed either by the person contemplating the event or from some other vantage point in the past or future

עמד *amad* denotes futurity with more certainty than the simple future form:

ha-rakévet omédet / amda linsóa be'od sha'a   הרכבת עומדת / עומדה לנסוע בעוד שעה

'The train is going / was going to leave in an hour'

ha-négev omed liyot gan éden yom eHad   הנגב עומד להיות גן עדן יום אחד
                                          'The Negev is going to be a Paradise one day'

הלך *halaH*, by contrast, is casual; it denotes imminence or intent:

ha-rakévet mamash **holéHet** linsóa   הרכבת ממש הולכת לנסוע
                                         'The train really **is about** to go'

ata **holeH** lehagid lo ba-sof?   אתה הולך להגיד לו בסוף?
                                     'Are you **going** to tell him in the end?'

13.6 Simple past form

The simple past form mostly denotes the contemplator's *past*. (For another use, in hypothetical conditionals, see 13.12.) This time relationship can be 'basic' or 'complex':

(1) Basic:[4]

```
        O ◄─────────── X
     EVENT        CONTEMPLATOR
```

(2) Complex (a series):

```
        O ◄─────────────────── X
     EVENT IN QUESTION  FURTHER EVENT   CONTEMPLATOR
```

(3) Complex (event within event):

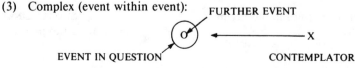

```
                    FURTHER EVENT
                    ⊙ ◄────── X
     EVENT IN QUESTION      CONTEMPLATOR
```

Examples

(1) gamárti be-shesh   'I finished at six'   גמרתי בשש

(2) Usually with an added adverbial, eg. כבר *kvar* 'already, יום קודם *yom kódem* 'a day earlier' (English might here use the pluperfect):

   kshe-amart ligmor, hu kvar **gamar** ve-**araz**   הוא כבר **גמר וארז**, כשאמרת לגמור
   PAST   PAST   PAST   'When you said he should
                                           finish, he **had finished**
                                           and **packed** already'

(3) Usually with an added adverbial, notably בדיוק *bidiyuk* 'just' (English uses the past continuous):[5]

   kshe-tsiltsalt, ani bidiyuk **difdáfti** bo   כשצילצלת, אני בדיוק **דיפדפתי** בו
   PAST   PAST   'When you rang, I **was** just **leafing**
                                    through it'

13.7 Compound past form

'Compound past' involves the past form of the verb 'to be', i.e היה *haya*,[6] plus the present form of the appropriate verb, both inflected in regular fashion: From הלך *halaH* 'go' → היה הולך *haya holeH*, היינו הולכים *hayínu holHím* etc.

For the verb היה *haya* 'be' itself, which has a 'zero' present tense form, the compound past form is simply היה *haya* etc., identical to the simple past. Thus היו *hayu* can mean 'were' and 'would be'.

The 'compound past' has three general uses and a further substandard (dialectal) use: (1) ordinary past time, for a few verbs; (2) habitual past time and (3) durative past time (substandard), these both being aspectual; (4) hypothetical past, present and future time, this being a modality (described in 13.12).

Ordinary past time

A few verbs can or must express past time by using the compound past, each in its own way. These verbs would otherwise have been mostly ambiguous between present and past tense; however, many other verbs of the selfsame verbal patterns tolerate such ambiguity and do not use the compound past.

גר *gar* 'lived (=resided)': the 3rd person singular גר *gar* (m.), גרה *gára* (f.) acts as both present and past form,[7] but compound past היה גר *haya gar*, היתה גרה *hayta gára* are often used when ambiguity might arise 1st and 2nd person and 3rd plural have no such ambiguity, hence the final example:

   napólyon gar po   'Napoleon lived here'   נפוליון גר פה
   PAST

   yóske haya gar be-Hevron   'Yoske lived in Hebron'   יוסקה היה גר בחברון
   COMPOUND PAST

yóske ve-dína gáru	'Yoske and Dina lived	יוסקה ודינה גרו
PAST	in Yamit'	בימית
be-yamit		

חי *Hay* 'lived': the 3rd person singular חי *Hay* (m.), חיה *Háya* (f.) acts as present and past form even when ambiguous; however, the compound past היה חי *haya Hay*, היתה חיה *hayta Háya*, and even 3rd plural היו חיים *hayu Hayim*, are used in addition.

נחשב *neHshav* 'was considered': the 3rd masculine singular נחשב *neHshav* can act as present and past form even when ambiguous, though some would then prefer היה נחשב *haya neHshav* as past.

נקרא *nikra* 'was called' behaves like נחשב *neHshav*, except that היה נקרא *haya nikra*, היתה נקראת *hayta nikret* (f.s.) היו נקראים *hayu nikra'im* (pl.) are also common.

יכול *yaHol* 'can': the 3rd masculine singular past is היה יכול *haya yaHol* or יכול היה *yaHol haya*.[8] (יכל *yaHal* is substandard and יכול *yaHol* as past form is puristic.) Even היתה יכולה *hayta yeHola* (f.s.) and היו יכולים *hayu yeHolim* (pl.) are possible, despite the availability of יכלה, יכלו *yaHla*, *yaHlu*

Habitual past time

Habitual past time can be conveyed by (1) the simple past form, using תמיד *tamid* 'always' or some other suitable context; (2) the verb נהג *nahag* 'be wont to' plus infinitive (rather formal); or (3) היה *haya* plus present form, i.e the compound past. Semantically, the main difference is in emphasis:[9]

tamid bikárti sham	תמיד ביקרתי שם
tamid nahágti levaker sham	תמיד נהגתי לבקר שם
tamid hayíti mevaker sham	תמיד הייתי מבקר שם
	'I always used to visit there'

Syntactically, היה *haya* plus present form is limited to past time, unlike נהג *nahag*, thus ruling out:

*yavo ha-yom ve-**niye mevakrim** ba-yaréaH   *יבוא היום **ונהיה מבקרים** בירח
('The day will come when **we'll be visiting** the Moon')

Durative past time

In some Oriental casual Hebrew, the compound past also denotes a durative past action, against the background of a momentary action:

hayiti yashen kshe-partsu   **הייתי ישן** כשפרצו
'**I was sleeping** when they broke in'

13.8-10 TENSE IN ADVERBIAL CLAUSES

13.8 Tense in time adverbials

Time adverbials mostly observe the basic 'tense and time rule' stated in 13.2. The exceptions are clauses introduced by -כש *kshe-* 'while' and its synonyms.

13.8.1 'Before, after'
The basic 'tense and time rule' yields the following:

Past time

yarad shéleg lifney she-**yarad** géshem **fell** snow before that **fell** rain	ירד שלג לפני שירד גשם 'It snowed before it rained'
yarad géshem aHarey she-**yarad** shéleg **fell** rain after that **fell** snow	ירד גשם אחרי שירד שלג 'It rained after it snowed'

The fact that the 'rain' is in the future of the 'snow' is immaterial; only the contemplator (here the speaker) is relevant.[10]

Present time In habitual present time, both events are taken as embracing the vantage point of the contemplator rather than being in his future or past, i.e this is an 'extended present':

bedéreH-klal mishtaHrerim   lifney   לפני   בדרך־כלל משתחררים
PRES   aHarey   אחרי   שמתחתנים
      she-mitHatnim
       PRES

'One usually gets discharged before/after one marries'

Using present of intent (see 13.3), both the main and the subordinate verb are present tense:

ani gomer   lifney   she-ani mitkaléaH   לפני   שאני מתקלח   אני גומר
PRES   aHarey   PRES   אחרי

'I'm finishing before/after I have a shower'

Future time

ze yered lifney she-ze yaale FUT FUT	זה ירד לפני שזה יעלה 'It will drop before it rises'
ze yaale aHarey she-ze yered FUT FUT	זה יעלה אחרי שזה ירד 'It will rise after it has dropped'

As with past time, only the contemplator is relevant. However, some 'before' clauses infringe the 'tense and time rule' when the event they describe is a 'non-event' - see 13.10.

13.8.2 'Until, since'
The basic 'tense and time rule' yields cases such as the following.
עד *ad* 'until':

avádeti ad she-**gamárti**		עבדתי עד שגמרתי
PAST	PAST	'I worked until **I finished**'

tamid ovdim ad she-**gomrim**		תמיד עובדים עד שגומרים
PRES	PRES	'One always works till **one has finished**'

amshiH ad she-**egmor**		אמשיך עד שאגמור
FUT	FUT	'I'll continue till **I've finished**'

In the last two examples, the second verb is in the 'extended present' and future (respectively) of the speaker.[11]

מאז *me'az* 'since':

rómi hitnavna me'az **hitatsma**		רומי התנוונה מאז **התעצמה**
PAST	PAST	'Rome declined since **becoming mighty**'

ani ohev et tsfat me'az **gárti** sham		אני אוהב את צפת מאז **גרתי** שם
PRES	PAST	'I've liked Tsefat since **I lived** there'

ani ohev et tsfat me'az ani **gar** sham		אני אוהב את צפת מאז אני **גר** שם
PRES	PRES	'I've liked Tsefat since **I've been living** there'

In the second case the 'living' is in one's past but the 'liking' is continuing, hence its present tense; in the third, the 'living' too is continuing, hence the two present tenses. However, מאז *me'az* 'since' plus future form is impossible, as מאז *me'az* intrinsically means 'something beginning in one's *past*'. Instead, one uses מהרגע ש- *me-ha-réga she-*.

tafsiki me-ha-réga she-**eshrok**		תפסיקי מהרגע שאשרוק
	FUT	'Stop as soon as **I whistle**'

13.8.3 'When, while'

בזמן ש- , *kshe-*, כאשר *kaasher*, - (ב)שעה ש *(be-)sha'a she-*, *bizman she-* all have two senses:

(1) 'when',[12] as in:

adaber ito kshe-yaHzor	אדבר אתו כשיחזור
	'I'll speak to him when he returns'

(2) 'at the same time as it is a *fact* that', as in:

láma ata shovet aHshav, kshe-kibálta		למה אתה שובת עכשיו, כשקיבלת
PRES	PAST	העלאה?
haala'a?		'Why are you striking now, when you've had a raise?'

With sense (1) the 'when' clause either observes the 'tense and time rule' or in formal usage (see the third example below) it can use the vantage point of *the action in the main clause*, in which case the simultaneity of the events is emphasized:[13]

	TIME				TIME	
06.00	──────────→	09.00		06.00	──────────→	09.00

GETTING ON   X   X   GETTING ON
GETTING OFF   CONTEMPLATOR   CONTEMPLATOR   GETTING OFF

Fig. 1   Fig. 2

yarádeti kshe-hu **ala**   ירדתי כשהוא **עלה**
       PAST (Fig. 1)   'I got off when he **got on**'

ered kshe-hu **yaale**   ארד כשהוא **יעלה**
       FUT (Fig. 2)   'I'll get off when he **gets on**'

yarádeti kshe-hu **ole**   ירדתי כשהוא **עולה**
       PRES (Fig. 1)   'I got off as he **got on**'

With sense (2) the 'when' clause uses the vantage point of *the action in the main clause*:

ma yiye im míshehu yaale kshe-ani   מה יהיה אם מישהו יעלה כשאני
lo yarádeti?   **לא ירדתי?**
       PAST   'What will happen if someone gets on when I ⟨still⟩
                            haven't got off?'

hu yashen kshe-horav **yagiu** be'od sha'a!   הוא ישן כשהוריו **יגיעו** בעוד בשעה!
       FUT   'He's asleep when his parents **will be here**
                            in an hour!'

'Time expressions' are involved in two other adverbial constructions that do not strictly denote time: ‏ש -‏(ב)שעה‎ *(be-)sha'a she-*, ‏ש - בזמן‎ *bizman she-* and formal ‏(ש-) בעוד‎ *be'od (she-)* can mean 'whereas'. The tense observes the 'tense and time rule', as in:

aleksánder bikesh kavod, bizman she-yorshav   אלכסנדר ביקש כבוד, בזמן שיורשיו
bikshu ósher   **ביקשו** עושר
       PAST   'Alexander sought glory, whereas his heirs
                            sought wealth'

Second, ‏כש-‎ *kshe-*, ‏כאשר‎ *kaasher*, ‏תוך ש-‎ *toH she-* and ‏ו -‎ *ve-* introduce 'circumstantial clauses' (see 21.6, 32.4), denoting 'while at the same time', though not for the purpose of locating an event in time. Present tense is required:

makabi Heyfa balma et hapoel Hadéra,   מכבי חיפה בלמה את הפועל חדרה,
       PAST   תוך שהיא **מעניקה** למאמן
toH she-hi **maanika** la-meamen   הפסד ראשון
       PRES
hefsed rishon   'Maccabi Haifa repulsed Hapoel Hadera, **giving**
                          the coach ⟨his⟩ first defeat'

13.9   Tense in other adverbial clauses

Conditional: 'if, unless'

The real-world conditional (as against the 'hypothetical' conditional - see 13.12) follows the 'tense and time rule' (13.2): the contemplator's vantage point is crucial.

im **gamárta**, Hake!
PAST

אם **גמרת**, חכה!
'If you **have finished**, wait!'

im ata **gomer** kvar, Hake!
PRES

אם אתה **גומר** כבר, חכה!
'If you **are** already **finishing**, wait!'

im ata **ba**, ten tsiltsul
PRES

אם אתה **בא**, תן צילצול
'If you **are coming** [=mean to come], give a ring'

im **tavo**, tir'e
FUT

אם **תבוא**, תראה
'If **you come**, you will see'

lo navo éla-im-ken **yeshalmu**
                FUT

לא נבוא אלא־אם־כן **ישלמו**
'We won't come unless **they pay**'

Purpose: 'in order that, so that; in case'

Future tense is obligatory in adverbial clauses of purpose (unless they are infinitival), whatever the vantage point of the contemplator. This is a 'subjunctive' use, 'in order that' seeming to imply an intent on someone's part:[14]

avádeti kemo meturaf, kdey she-ze
yetse kvar etmol
FUT

עבדתי כמו מטורף, כדי שזה
יצא כבר אתמול
'I worked like crazy, so that it **would go** yesterday'

lo bodkim et kulam, she-ze **yeleH**
                        FUT
aHat shtáyim

לא בודקים את כולם, שזה **ילך**
אחת שתיים
'They don't check them all, for it **to go**
nice and quick'

The same is true when כדי, בשביל *kdey, bishvil* '(in order) that' appear following מספיק *maspik* 'enough', מדי *miday* 'too', יותר מדי *yoter miday* 'too much' (see 20.5) with no suggestion of 'purpose':

yóna lo haya maspik mevugar bishvil
she-**negale** lo
FUT

יונה לא היה מספיק מבוגר בשביל
שנגלה לו
'Yona was not old enough for us **to tell** him'

Cause, concession and result

Clauses introduced by כי *ki* 'because, על אף *al af* 'although', כך ש- *kaH she-* 'with the result that' and their synonyms observe the 'tense and time rule':

báti ki haya riv
PAST   PAST

באתי כי היה ריב
'I came because there was [*or*: had been] an argument'

13.10   Tense in 'quasi-negative' adverbials

Clauses introduced by בלי, מבלי *bli, mibli* 'without', במקום *bimkom* 'instead of', sometimes בטרם *betérem* 'before', and those of the type מה שלא יהיה *ma she-lo yiye* 'whatever happens' are felt to be quasi-negative

They allow or require the future tense, as a kind of subjunctive 'modality', whatever the vantage point of the contemplator.

In 'without' clauses there is usually a choice between the 'tense and time rule' and a fixed future tense (sometimes more formal):[15]

ha-gvéret natna sukariyot bli she-horim	הגברת נתנה סוכריות בלי שהורים
{hivHinu/yavHinu} ba-ze	{הבחינו/יבחינו} בזה
PRES FUT	'The lady gave sweets without parents **noticing**'

láma hu medaber bli	למה הוא מדבר בלי
she-{shom'im/yishme'u} oto?	ש{שומעים/ישמעו} אותו?
PRES FUT	'Why does he talk without anyone **being able to hear** him?'

במקום *bimkom* 'instead' requires future tense (however, the simple infinitive is altogether more common):

ha-rofe hevi otánu le-Hadro, bimkom	הרופא הביא אותנו לחדרו, במקום
{she-neshev/lashévet} ba-Huts	{שנשב/לשבת} בחוץ
FUT INFIN	'The doctor brought us to his room, instead of **us sitting** outside'

The words for 'before', בטרם *betérem* (F) and לפני *lifney*, require especial care The former can convey a clear negative implication that something has not transpired at all, by using a fixed future tense (Past or present tense leave this unsaid.)

hem soHrim yáHad dira betérem yaamidu	הם שוכרים יחד דירה בטרם **יעמידו**
FUT	חופה וקידושין
Hupa ve-kidushin	'They are renting an apartment together before **getting married**'

hu nilkaH meitánu betérem	הוא נלקח מאתנו בטרם
{hishlim/yashlim} et mesimato	{השלים/ישלים} את משימתו
PAST FUT	'He was taken from us before **completing** his mission'

Conversely, in casual usage לפני *lifney* clauses depicting a *future* event that is not due to transpire at all generally use *past* (or present) tense:[16]

tistakel, hu lokéaH li et ha-tsaláHat lifney	תסתכל, הוא לוקח לי את הצלחת לפני
PRES	**שגמרתי**
she-**gamárti**	'Look, he's taking my plate away
PAST	before **I've finished**'

The negative ש-, איך ש-, מה ש- *ma she-, eH she-* 'whatever, however' construction (cf. 32.11.4) mostly involves the 'tense and time rule' (vantage point of the contemplator):

ma she-lo **hitsáti**, tamid hiskímu	מה שלא **הצעתי**, תמיד הסכימו
what that not **I-suggested**, always they-agreed	'Whatever **I suggested**, they always agreed'

eH she-lo **avashel** lehába,...　　　　איך שלא **אבשל** להבא,...
　　　　FUT　　　　　　　　　　　　'However **I cook** henceforth,...'

ma she-ani lo **osa**,...　　　　　　מה שאני לא **עושה**,...
　　　　PRES　　　　　　　　　　　　'Whatever **I do**,...'

But with 'present habitual' time (i.e the previous example), the future form is also used:

ma she-lo **eese**,...　　　　　　　　מה שלא **אעשה**,...
　　　　FUT　　　　　　　　　　　　'Whatever **I do**,...'

A type of 'result clause' following a negative or interrogative (i.e 'non-assertive') main clause requires future tense:

kan lo
ha'im kan　　bet-séfer yesodi, she-**teleH**　　בית־ספר יסודי, שתלך　　כאן לא
　　　　　　　　　　　　　　FUT　　　　　להתאונן לפני המורה　　האם כאן
　　lehitonen lifney hamora
　　　　　　　　　　'This is not
　　　　　　　　　　'Is this　　an elementary school that **you should go**
　　　　　　　　　　　　　　　　to complain to the teacher'

13.11　Tense in other subordinate clauses

As in adverbial clauses (13.8-9), so in other subordinate clauses it is mostly the vantage point of the most direct contemplator that determines tense (the 'tense and time rule').[17]

Object clauses (see 31.2) follow the 'tense and time rule',[18] thus:

06.00 ——TIME→ 09.00

　　　X　　　X
FALLING THINKING SPEAKER

Hashávti she-hi nafla　　חשבתי שהיא נפלה
　　　　　　　PAST
　　　'I thought she had fallen'

FALLING
　X　　　　　　　X
THINKING　　　　SPEAKER

Hashávti she-hi nofélet　　חשבתי שהיא נופלת
　　　　　　　PRES
　'I thought she was falling'

　X　　　　　X
THINKING FALLING SPEAKER

Hashávti she-hi tipol　　חשבתי שהיא תפול
　　　　　　FUT
　　'I thought she would fall'

Indirect questions (see 26.) count as object clauses, thus (as in the preceding example):

dina shaala matay yosef **yagía**　　דינה שאלה מתי יוסף **יגיע**
　　　　　　　FUT　　　'Dina asked when Yosef **would arrive**'

Subject clauses (see 31.4) may observe the 'tense and time rule', depending on the predicate of the main clause. With words such as ברור *barur* 'clear' or בטוח *batúaH* 'certain' as predicates they do so (the implication being 'it is clear to so-and-so' etc.), thus:

haya barur be-arba'im ve-shalosh she-ánu	היה ברור בארבעים ושלוש שאנו
{mitgabrim/nitgaber} al ha-oyev	{מתגברים/נתגבר} על האויב
PRES FUT	

'It was clear in 1943 that we {were defeating/would defeat} the enemy'

But adjectives of 'attitude', e.g. מוזר *muzar* 'odd', טבעי *tiv'i* 'natural', מפתיע *maftía* 'surprising', tend not to be treated as words of 'contemplation', so the 'contemplator' in examples like the following is likely to be the speaker (i.e. the 'invasion' is seen from the present):

ze haya muzar she-napolyon **palash** le-rúsya ba-stav	זה היה מוזר שנפוליון **פלש**
PAST	לרוסיה בסתיו

'It was odd that Napoleon **was invading** Russia in the autumn'

Apposition clauses (see ch. 34) follow the 'tense and time rule', except that the 'contemplator' is often just *understood* from context, as with subject clauses (as if ידיעה *yedi'a*, אפשרות *efsharut* etc. below were verbs):

ha-yedi'a she-ha-oniya **továat** lo hivhíla otánu	הידיעה שהאוניה **טובעת** לא הבהילה
(CONTEMPLATOR) PRES	אותנו

'The news that the ship **was sinking** did not alarm us'

ha-efsharut she-hem **yeaHru** garma la linhog maher	האפשרות שהם **יאחרו** גרמה
(CONTEMPLATOR) FUT	לה לנהוג מהר

'The possibility that they **would be late** made her drive fast'

Relative clauses (see ch. 33) usually observe the 'tense and time rule'. Thus in the next example the 'contemplator' is the speakers themselves: הודעה *hoda'a* 'message' plus relative clause, unlike ידיעה *yedi'a* 'news' plus apposition clause in the foregoing examples, does not act like a *verb* of contemplation.

kaavor yomáyim kibálnu hoda'a she-ba **hodu** ba-ashma	כעבור יומיים קיבלנו
ANTEC PAST	הודעה שבה **הודו** באשמה
REL CLAUSE	

'Two days later we received a message, in which they **admitted** guilt'

But formal usage permits one, unusually, to treat the antecedent noun itself as the vantage point for tense in the relative clause:[19]

bismark kibel hoda'a, she-ba **modim** ba-ashma	ביסמארק קיבל הודעה, שבה
ANTECEDENT PRES	**מודים** באשמה

'Bismarck received a message, in which they **admitted** guilt'

hu Hafan bi-smolo et ha-betsa she-klipata	הוא חפן בשמאלו את הביצה שקליפתה
meruséket ve-hitHil leHayeH	**מרוסקת** והתחיל לחייך
PRES	

'Into his left hand he scooped the egg whose shell **was crushed** and began to smile'

After a 'non-specific' antecedent, present tense can be used instead of future tense:

ershom **kol mila** she-ani {eshma/shoméa}   ארשום **כל מלה שאני** {אשמע/שומע}
      NON-SPECIFIC   FUT   PRES

'I'll jot down **every word** that I **hear**'

batúaH she-hu yivke   בטוח שהוא יבכה
ba-páam ha-rishona she-hu {yipol/nofel}   **בפעם הראשונה** שהוא {יפול/נופל}
       NON-SPECIFIC   FUT   PRES

'Of course he's going to cry **the first time** he falls over'

13.12   Hypothetical tense

'Hypothetical' is a modality denoting the unreal - as against the 'declarative' modality. It is often expressed by choice of tense

13.12.1   Hypothetical conditionals

Hypothetical conditionals imply that the supposition being made is unreal:

lu hayíta shotek,   hayíti nish'ar   לו היית שותק, הייתי נשאר
CONDITIONAL CLAUSE CONSEQUENT CLAUSE
     (HYPOTHETICAL)

'If you kept quiet, I would stay'

Both the 'conditional' clause and the 'consequent' clause require a past tense of some kind. What such 'hypotheticality' and past **time** have in common is in conveying something that is neither actual nor potential.[20]

The conditional clause

'Hypothetical' and 'real' conditionals are usually distinguishable by tense: the former generally require conpound past tense, whereas the latter rarely have it (and then only as specified by 13.7):[21]

Hypothetical:
im **hayíta ba**,   hayíti kam   אם **היית בא**, הייתי קם
  COMPOUND PAST

'If you **came**, I'd get up'

Real:
im **báta**, láma shatákta?   אם **באת**, למה שתקת?
    PAST

'If you **came**, why did you keep quiet?'

However, conditional clauses introduced by the rather formal לו, אילו *lu, ílu* 'if' and formal לולא, אלולי, אלמלא *lule, ilule, ilmale* 'if...not' can opt for simple past tense; these words are intrinsically hypothetical, so no confusion with 'real conditionals' occurs:

lu {yadáta/hayíta yodéa}, hayíti shav   לו {ידעת/היית יודע}, היית שב
    PAST   COMPOUND PAST

'If you knew, you would return'

lule {báta/hayíta ba}, hayíti mevatélet   לולא {באת/היית בא}, הייתי מבטלת
     PAST COMPOUND PAST

'If you had not come, I would have cancelled'

The consequent clause

The consequent clause of a hypothetical conditional requires compound past tense, even where the conditional makes do with simple past tense:[22]

lu Halit, hayíti tsam	לו חלית, **הייתי צם**
COMPOUND PAST	'If you fell sick, **I would fast**'

Time in hypotheticals

The simple or compound past tense is all that is available to convey past, present and future time in this hypothetical modality. Thus context is critical. The following sentence theoretically has three (or even more) meanings:

im hayit tása, hayíti nivhal	אם היית טסה, הייתי נבהל
COMPOUND COMPOUND PAST	'If you had flown, I would have panicked'
PAST	'If you were flying, I would be panicking'
	'If you were to fly, I would panic'

13.12.2 'Wishing' clauses

'Wishing' clauses with an assumption of 'unreality', introduced by ו- / -ש הלוואי *halvay she-/ve-* 'if only' (C) or its synonyms אילו רק, אם רק *ílu rak, im rak*, require simple or compound past tense - whatever 'time' is intended (as in 13.12.1):

halvay she-	limádnu	tanaH	תנ"ך	לימדנו הלוואי ש
	hayínu melamdim		מלמדים	היינו
	PAST/COMPOUND PAST		'If only we (had) taught the Bible'	

But a wish need not involve the unreal, thus:

halvay she-nelamed	הלוואי שנלמד
FUT	'I hope we teach'

13.12.3 'As if' clauses

כאילו *ke'ílu* 'as if' is hypothetical in meaning but not in syntax, particularly not in the tense it takes - neither hypothetical past nor compound past tense, but a tense in keeping with the 'tense and time rule' (13.2), i.e from the contemplator's vantage-point, or alternatively (final example, present tense) a tense as seen from the event closest to the 'as if' clause, as though an on-the-spot viewer were enunciating the 'as if':[23]

ata mitnaheg ke'ilu (she-)ata **lo yodéa** aHshav	אתה מתנהג כאילו (ש)אתה **לא יודע** עכשיו
PRES	'You're behaving as if you **didn't know** now'

at nir'et ke'ilu od lo **ikalt**	את נראית כאילו עוד לא **עיכלת**
PAST	'You look as if you **have** not yet **digested**'

izével nahaga ke'ílu hi adáyin   איזבל נהגה כאילו היא עדיין
paHada/mefaHédet   **פחדה / מפחדת**
PAST   PRES   'Jezebel acted as if she **were** still **afraid**'

13.13 Modality and aspect in general

As already indicated, tense can express particular modalities: the desired, the occasional, the hypothetical in conditionals and wishes, the negative in quasi-negatives and in certain other constructions. But many other notions of modality are expressed not by such grammatical means but *lexically*.

Drawing a basic line between 'epistemic' and 'deontic' modality, i.e degree of certainty about things vs. an objective ability or need to do or be, one might point to such expressions as (*inter alia*):

Epistemic

Possibility: יכול להיות ש- *yaHol liyot she-* 'maybe', יתכן ש- *yitaHen she-* 'it may be that...'

Probability: עשוי ל- ....*asuy le-* '...is likely to', עלול ל-.......*alul le-* '...is likely to', כנראה (ש-) *kenir'e (she-)* 'apparently', בטח (ש-) *bétaH (she-)* 'probably'.

Certainty: בטוח ש- *batúaH she-* 'certain that', צריך ל-........*tsariH le-* '...must be'.

Deontic

Ability: יכול ל-......*yaHol le-* '...can', אפשר ל- *efshar le-* 'one can'.

Permissibility: יכול ל-......*yaHol le-* '...may', אפשר ל- *efshar le-* 'one may', אסור ל- *asur le-* 'one may not'.

Necessity: צריך ל-.....*tsariH le-* '...must', צריך ל- *tsariH le-* 'one must'.

There is no clear grammatical difference between epistemic and deontic; thus 'impersonal' (i.e subject-less) and 'personal' expressions are found among both. Lexically, although words for 'possibility' vs. 'ability' are generaly kept distinct, 'certainty' and 'necessity' share many words, eg. צריך *tsariH* (both with a subject and without), חייב *Hayav*, מוכרח *muHraH*. Whether the past/future marker היה *haya* precedes or follows these words[24] has nothing to do with their meaning, thus היה צריך *haya tsariH* and צריך היה *tsariH haya* both mean 'he was bound to' and 'he had to' - as well as 'he should have';[25] postposed היה *haya* is usually simply more formal (except in the negative). As for 3rd person יכול היה *yaHol haya* 'was able, (conditional) could', it too is formal; but in the negative לא יכול היה *lo yaHol haya* is generally preferred[26] to לא היה יכול *lo haya yaHol*.

hu   haya tsariH   leshaker   הוא היה צריך לשקר
      tsariH haya   צריך היה
            'He was bound to lie/was forced to lie/should have lied'

13.14   Other grammatical modalities

Modality of 'modest assertion'

To tone down a wish or statement, the verb of 'wishing or stating' may be put into the compound past tense (in whatever person is required):

hayíti maadif le..   ...הייתי מעדיף ל

'I'd prefer to...'

hi hayta rotsa od eHad   היא היתה רוצה עוד אחד

'She would like another one'
(The verb רוצה *rotsa* ordinarily signifies 'want'.)

hayíti omer she-shneyhem to'im   הייתי אומר ששניהם טועים

'I'd say both are wrong'

The verb ביקש *bikesh* 'ask' in the 1st person *future* tense can express a more lofty request:

avakesh lehitkadem!   !אבקש להתקדם

'Could I ask you to move along'

Other verbs, such as הזהיר *hizhir* 'warn', הזכיר *hizkir* 'mention', do not have this facility.

Modality of the occasional

Future tense is sometimes used in casual Hebrew to express the 'occasional':

anáHnu lo Haverim *tovim* - lifamim   אנחנו לא חברים טובים - לפעמים
    ani **agid** lo shalom aval ze ha-kol   אני **אגיד** לו שלום אבל זה הכל
    FUT

'We aren't *good* friends - sometimes **I'll say** 'hello' to him but that's all'

kore lifamim she-noséa **yekalel** nehag   קורה לפעמים שנוסע **יקלל** נהג
    FUT

'It happens sometimes that a passenger **will curse** a driver'

shamáta páam she-shoter **yaatsor** katsin?   שמעת פעם ששוטר **יעצור** קצין?
    FUT

'Have you ever heard of a policeman **stopping** an officer?'

This future modality is not possible in a past tense framework (eg. 'It *happened* sometimes that...'), unlike other uses of the future tense in 13.4.

Aspect in general, eg. perfective, inchoative, repetitive, is largely expressed by the *binyanim* (verb patterns) and aspectual verbs. See 40.3.2. and 31.3.

FURTHER READING
Berman 1978: ch. 5, 1980a; Kopelovich 1982; Landau 1975; Rosén 1977: 179 ff.

14. Active and passive

14.1 Introduction

The passive is an alternative grammatical means of expressing the subject-verb-object relationship (the active construction). Occasionally, however, it is not available The passive has up to three possible features, set out below.

Verb conversion

The verb always converts to a different *binyan* (pattern), often a special passive pattern:

surtat	'was drawn'	סורטט	⇐	*sirtet*	'drew'	סירטט

Subject-object switching

Usually, the *object* of the active becomes the *subject* of the passive (thus controlling agreement of the verb):

dolárim husteru   **דולרים** הוסתרו   ⇐   histir **dolárim**   הסתיר דולרים
'**Dollars** were hidden'   'He hid **dollars**'

Concomitantly, the *subject* of the active may become the *complement* of the passive, i.e introduced by על־ידי *al-yedey* or בידי *ḇidey* 'by' and occupying object position. Alternatively, it is simply omitted:

ráfi histir et ha-dolárim   הדולרים הוסתרו על־ידי רפי ⇐ רפי הסתיר את הדולרים
⇒ ha-dolárim husteru al-yedey ráfi   'Rafi hid the dollars' ⇒
                                                       'The dollars were hidden by Rafi'

× aHal et ha-ugiyot ⇒ ha-ugiyot neeHlu   העוגיות נאכלו ⇐ אכל את העוגיות ×
× has-eaten the cookies ⇒ the cookies have-been-eaten

The passive is a *secondary* construction: there will always be an active sentence but not always a passive equivalent.[1]

14.2 Functions of the passive

14.2.1 To 'play down' an object

In active sentences, the subject is commonly first noun phrase and thus commonly 'known' information, whereas the object is commonly 'new' information, i.e it is *salient:*

138

sára tsav'a kise	'Sara painted ⟨a⟩ chair'	שרה צבעה כיסא
KNOWN NEW		

But where the object is to be 'known' information, eg. הכיסא הזה *ha-kise ha-ze* 'this chair', Hebrew can either simply put the object first, by (a) topicalization or (b) dislocation ('copying'); or else it can (c) change the object to subject (subject still coming first) while 'passivizing' the verb to indicate that this has been done:

(a) Topicalization:

et ha-kise ha-ze tsav'a sára	את הכסא הזה צבעה שרה
OM the chair the this painted Sara	'This chair Sara painted'

(b) Dislocation:

ha-kise ha-ze sára tsav'a oto	הכסא הזה שרה צבעה אותו
the chair the this Sara painted it	'This chair, Sara painted it'

(c) Passive:

ha-kise ha-ze nitsba bidey sára	הכסא הזה נצבע בידי שרה
the chair the this was-painted by Sara	'This chair was painted by Sara'

14.2.2   To gloss over a subject

To be vague about a subject, Hebrew again has various ploys. (1) When 'human', the subject can simply be left blank, and the verb (or adjective), still 'active', is put into 3rd person plural. (2) Alternatively, the subject is 'generic' אתה *ata* 'you'. (3) Using the passive: for *any* type of subject, one may promote object to subject, passivize the verb, and simply drop the 'underlying' subject:[2]

(1)	hizíku et ha-mishtara	הזעיקו את המשטרה
		'⟨One/you⟩ called the police'

(2)	ata hizákta et ha-mishtara	אתה הזעקת את המשטרה
		'One/you called the police'

(3)	ha-mishtara huzaka	המשטרה הוזעקה
		'The police were called'

14.2.3   Other constructions functioning as passives

Other, minor constructions functioning like passives are the following:

Locative subject

By a kind of 'metaphorical transfer', verbs like המה *hama* 'hum', זלג *zalag* 'flow' (i.e tears) can switch locative noun to subject, while subject becomes an apparent object (see further 15.8); the verb does *not* change pattern. The meaning now becomes 'The city swarmed all over' in our example:

nemalim shartsu ba-ir   נמלים שרצו בעיר
ants swarmed in-the city

ha-ir   shartsa nemalim   העיר שרצה נמלים
LOCATIVE
SUBJ
the city swarmed [with] ants

Using another *binyan*

Certain words allow one to switch to another, *non*-passive *binyan* ('pattern'). Object becomes subject, and subject becomes indirect object:

x meabed y	⇒	y ovdim le-x	x-אובדים ל ⇐	x מאבד y
x Haser y	⇒	y Haserim le-x	x-חסרים ל ⇐	x חסר y

                   'x loses y' ⇒   'y are lost to x'
                   'x lacks y' ⇒ 'y are lacking to x'

Using 'helper verbs' + action noun

ניתח *nitaH* 'operate', בדק *badak* 'test' and many other verbs can be turned into an 'action noun', introduced by עבר *avar* 'undergo', קיבל *kibel* 'get' or other 'helper verbs':

avárti {nitúaH/bdika}   עברתי {ניתוח/בדיקה}
                   'I underwent an {operation/test}'
                   (= 'I was operated on', etc.)

kibálti {ezra/maka}   קבלתי {עזרה/מכה}
                   'I received {help/a blow}'

14.3 How much are passives used?

Passives are fairly common formally (particularly in technical usage), but litttle used casually, despite the near-automatic availability of *pu'al* and *huf'al* verbs and the common use of the *nif'al* pattern for other functions at least. Topicalization and 3rd person impersonal verbs (14.2) are much preferred.[3]

14.4 Passive *binyanim* (verb patterns)

14.4.1 Passivization

The passive verb is formed near-automatically, using fairly distinctive patterns (see ch. 40 for *binyanim* in general):

pa'al	פעל	yields	*nif'al*	נפעל
hif'il	הפעיל	→	*huf'al*	הופעל
pi'el	פיעל	→	*pu'al* or *hitpa'el*	פועל/התפעל

Examples are:

> *pa'al* → *nif'al*:
> zarak   'threw'   זרק → nizrak   'was thrown'   נזרק
> *hif'il* → *huf'al*:
> hizrik   'injected'   הזריק → huzrak 'was injected'   הוזרק
> *pi'el* → *pu'al*:
> miHshev 'computerized' מיחשב → muHshav 'was computerized' מחושב
> *pi'el* → *hitpa'el*:
> pina   'evacuated' פינה → hitpana 'was evacuated'   התפנה

Active verbs in the *nif'al* and *hitpa'el* patterns have no passive, e.g. נהנה *nehena* 'enjoy', התנגד *hitnaged* 'oppose'.

14.4.2   General exceptions to passivization

Nearly all verbs taking a direct object can be passivized, but very many taking an indirect object cannot, e.g. -ל חיכה *Hika le-* 'wait for'. For details see 14.6.

Pre-emption. Several passives are inadmissible, having been pre-empted for a non-passive or simply another sense of the word, e.g. נפגש *nifgash* 'met' (*'was met'), נאחז *neeHaz* 'seized' (*'was seized'), נחצה *neHtsa* 'was divided' (*'was traversed'), אוחר *uHar* 'was delayed' (*'was missed'), חופש *Hupas* 'was dressed up' (*'was sought'). But Hebrew frequently tolerates such ambiguity, e.g. נענה *naana* 'responded, was answered', נעצר *neetsar* 'halted, was stopped', הושלם *hushlam* 'was completed, was perfected'.

Several *state verbs* ('non-ergatives') have no passive, e.g. (physical) ארך *araH* 'last', שקל *shakal* 'weigh', עלה *ala* 'cost', מנה *mana* 'number (= amount to)', הכיל *heHil* 'contain', היווה *hiva* 'constitute', גבל *gaval* 'border'; (psychological) עניין *inyen* 'interest', הרגיז *hirgiz* 'anger', העריך *heeriH* 'admire', שנא *sana* 'hate', אהד *ahad* 'sympathize with'.

Some state verbs express the passive by the statal passive adjective (passive participle) instead:

> shéleg kisa et ha-ir
>
> שלג כיסה את העיר
> 'Snow covered the town'
>
> ha-ir hayta meHusa (*kusta) shéleg
>
> העיר היתה מכוסה (*כוסתה) שלג
> 'The town was covered ⟨in⟩ snow'

14.4.3   Exceptional use of individual *binyanim*

pa'al → *nif'al*

Pa'al → *nif'al* passivization is lacking in certain instances: (a) where there is no passive, e.g. עבר *avar* 'pass', נהג *nahag* 'drive', ירק *yarak* 'spit', טעם *ta'am* 'taste', רעה *ra'a* 'graze', הרה *hara* 'conceive' and (b) where a different *binyan* is used, as in הציל *hitsil* 'save' ~ ניצל *nitsal*, שר *shar* 'sing' ~ הושר *hushar*.

Passive *nif'al* must be distinguished from the following uses of *nif'al* (see further ch.40):

(a) Occasional statal passives, i.e past participles (adjective or noun) akin to the *pa'ul* pattern (14.5): נרצח *nirtsaH* 'murdered' (no רצוח* *ratsúaH*), נבחר *nivHar* 'chosen' (no בחור* *baHur*), נפגע *nifga* 'injured'.

(b) Widespread middle voice, i.e autonomous action corresponding to a transitive action in *pa'al/pi'el/hif'il*: נאלץ *neelats* 'had to' (אולץ *ulats* = 'was forced by someone'), נפתח *niftaH* 'opened', נמנע *nimna* 'refrained' (also 'was prevented'), נשמע *nishma* 'sounded' (also 'was heard'), נרטב *nirtav* 'got wet' (הורטב *hurtav* 'was wetted').

(c) Frequent aspectual variations on *pa'al*, eg. שכב *shaHav* 'lay down/was lying' ~ נשכב *nishkav* 'lay down', פגש *pagash* 'met' (unplanned) ~ נפגש *nifgash* 'met' (planned).[4]

hif'il → huf'al, pi'el → pu'al

Among verbs with a direct object but with no passive are הרויח *hirvíaH* 'earn', הפסיד *hifsid* 'lose', הושיע *hoshía* 'save', כילה, סיים *siyem, kila* 'finish', חיבב *Hibev* 'like', סייר *siyer* 'patrol'. Among verbs using *hitpa'el* (see also below) as their passive are הוסיף *hosif* 'add', העיר *he'ir* 'wake', קיבל *kibel* 'receive', ביקש *bikesh* 'request', מילא *mile* 'fill'.

Neither *hif'il* nor *pi'el* have any other general functions.

pi'el → hitpa'el

Occasionally, *hitpa'el* acts as the passive *instead* of *pu'al*, and sometimes in addition:

ביצע *bitsa*	~	בוצע/התבצע *butsa/hitbatséa*	'perform'
גילה *gila*	~	גולה/התגלה *gula/hitgala*	'discover, uncover'
קיבל *kibel*	~	התקבל *hitkabel*	'receive'
ביקש *bikesh*	~	התבקש *hitbakesh*	'request'

This passive use of *hitpa'el* may be spreading - not surprisingly, as the commonest function of *hitpa'el* is as 'middle voice', denoting autonomous action (see 40.9), eg. פיתח *pitaH* 'develop (something)' ~ התפתח *hitpatéaH* 'develop by itself'.[5]

14.5   Pa'ul and other past participles: statal passives

To indicate 'in a state of having been done' (statal passive) as against 'being done', certain verb-based adjectives exist.

The *pa'al* supplies a special semi-automatic adjective, *pa'ul*, for verbs denoting physical action but not, for example, for שמע *shama* 'listen to':[6]

hem niftaHim	'They are opened'	הם נפתחים
hem nifteHu	'They were opened'	הם נפתחו
but: hem ptuHim	'They are open'	הם פתוחים

nishbarim	'are being broken'	נשברים
nishberu	'were broken'	נשברו
but: shvurim	'are broken' (state)	שבורים

The *huf'al* and *pu'al* present tense doubles automatically as statal passive adjectives:

hem Hulku	'They were distributed'	הם חולקו
hem meHulakim	'They are being distributed'	הם מחולקים
	most commonly:	
	'They are distributed (already)'	

For their non-passive meaning (eg. ממושקף *memushkaf* 'bespectacled'), see 41.3.1.

These forms, though derivable from passives, are not fully passive: no על-ידי / בידי *al-yedey/bidey* 'by' phrase is ordinarily possible (except as in note 6, example (2)); the following is therefore ruled out:

*ha-vitrína shvura al-yedey ganavim   *הוויטרינה שבורה על-ידי גנבים

('The showcase is broken by thieves')

Indeed, strictly speaking, the participle does not imply a past action: פתוח *patúaH* 'open' does not imply 'was opened (and was beforehand closed)'.

14.6 Structural obstacles to the passive

Just as nearly all direct objects of the active can become subjects of the passive, losing their את *et* case-preposition completely, so too do many indirect objects with על, -ב *be-*, *al* and occasionally -ל *le-*, eg. -ב טיפל *tipel be-* → טופל *tupal:*[7]

ha-telefónim tuplu (*be-) midey yom   הטלפונים טופלו (*ב) מדי יום

the telephones were-dealt (*with) every day 'The telephones were dealt with every day'

Further examples of passive '-ב *be-*' verbs are: נבגד *nivgad* 'betrayed', נבעט *niv'at* 'kicked', נדון *nadon* 'discussed', נורה *nura* 'shot', נחשד *neHshad* 'suspected', נפגע *nifga* 'hit', נתמך *nitmaH* 'supported'.

Examples of 'על *al*' verbs are: דווח *duvaH* 'reported', הוחלט *huHlat* 'decided', הוכרז *huHraz* 'proclaimed', הומלץ *humlats* 'commended', הושפע *hushpa* 'influenced', נחתם *neHtam* 'signed', נאסר *neesar* 'forbidden'.

Examples of '-ל *le-*' verbs are: הורשה *hursha* 'permitted', נעזר *neezar* 'helped', נענה *naana* 'answered', נקרא *nikra* 'called'.

Constraints

Case prepositions have a hierarchy. את *et* is 'weakest', in that (1) it occurs only with definite nouns; (2) even as such it is sometimes omitted in literature; (3) it can drop in relativized nouns (see 33.3.2) eg. האיש שראיתי (אותו) *ha-ish she-ra'íti (oto)* 'the man that I saw (him)', and must drop for action nouns, eg. הארכת השביתה *haaraHat ha-shvita* '⟨the⟩ prolongation ⟨of⟩ the strike'.

The prepositions ל-, על, ב- *be-, al, le-* are intermediate in rank; and עם, אל, מ- *im, el, mi-* are 'strongest' - they usually stand farther from the verb than all the others (especially as clitics with pronoun suffixes - see 15.7).

This hierarchy has five notable consequences. First, when a verb can take a *double object* - which almost invariably involves a 'direct' object with את *et* plus an 'indirect object' - the direct object can be made subject of passive but the indirect object cannot (example (1) below), not even where the direct object is unspecified, as in example (2):[8]

> (1) katvu lo shney miHtavim ⇒   כתבו לו שני מכתבים ⇐
>   shney miHtavim niHtevu lo   שני מכתבים נכתבו לו
>
>   they-wrote to-him two letters ⇒
>   two letters were-written to-him
>
>   *but*
>   *hu niHtav shney miHtavim   *הוא נכתב שני מכתבים
>   he was-written two letters
>
> (2) katvu lo kol shavúa ⇏   כתבו לו כל שבוע⇐
>   *hu niHtav kol shavúa   *הוא נכתב כל שבוע
>
>   they-wrote to-him every week ⇏
>   he was-written every week

Secondly, many if not most indirect objects do not undergo passivization in any event, thus ruling out such forms as: זולזל* *zulzal* ('was looked down on'), נעסק* *neesak* ('was dealt with'), אויים* *uyam* ('was threatened'), הוגב* *hugav* ('was reacted to'), הוקשב* *hukshav* ('was listened to'), צופה* *tsupa* ('was expected').

Thirdly, no indirect object with מ-, עם, אל *mi-, im, el* can undergo passivization.

Fourthly, even in the rare event of a double object with את *et*, a hierarchy is at work: only the first object can become subject of passive:

> shoalim harbe anashim sheelot ⇓   שואלים הרבה אנשים שאלות ⇓
>   OBJECT A   OBJ B
> they-ask many people questions
> harbe anashim nishalim sheelot   הרבה אנשים נשאלים שאלות
>   SUBJECT
> many people are-asked questions

and:

> harbe sheelot nishalot   הרבה שאלות נשאלות
> many questions are-asked

but:

*sheelot nishalot harbe anashim   *שאלות נשאלות הרבה אנשים
questions are-asked many people

Fifthly, and rather similarly, verbs whose meanings change according to whether they have a direct or an indirect object generally passivize only in the former case, as in example (1) below:

(1) *Direct object*

radaf oto   ⇒   hu nirdaf   הוא נרדף ⇐   רדף אותו
                                     'persecuted him   ⇒   he was persecuted'

(2) *Indirect object*

radaf aHarav   ⇒   no passive   רדף אחריו
                                       'chased after him'

Further examples: הואץ *hu'ats* 'was hurried', הוכר 'was known' (the active verbs with an indirect object mean 'urge' and 'give recognition to', respectively).

14.7 Complements of the passive, eg. בידי *bidey* 'by'

The active subject is usually represented in the passive by using בידי *bidey* or על-ידי *al-yedey* 'by'. בידי *bidey* is formal and appears mostly with verbs implying physical action:

ha-tsiyurim tsuyeru **bidey** yéled iver   הציורים צויירו **בידי** ילד עיוור
                'The drawings were drawn **by** a blind boy'

ha-dvarim she-hushme'u **al-yedey** ha-sar...   הדברים שהושמעו **על-ידי** השר...
                'the words uttered **by** the minister...'

על-ידי *al-yedey* is used otherwise, but there are many exceptions for psychological 'non-ergatives', i.e. verbs denoting non-deliberate actions as set out under (a) and (b) below:

(a) *Psychological effect on someone*:

yaakov	zuaza mi- hushpa... neelav... hufta...	'Yaakov was	shocked at...' influenced by... offended by... surprised at...	יעקב זועזע מ-... הושפע מ-... נעלב מ-... הופתע מ-...
hu	sanu al yaakov ahuv al... meHubad al...	'He is	hated by Yaakov' loved by... respected by...	הוא שנוא על יעקב אהוב על מכובד על

(b) *Awareness of someone/something*:[11]

ze yuvan laH im...	'It will be understood by you if...'	זה יובן לך אם...
ze zaHur li	'It is remembered by me'	זה זכור לי
ze yadúa li	'It is known to me'	זה ידוע לי
hu mukar li	'He is known to me'	הוא מוכר לי

Verbal 'action nouns' (see 30.6) correspond to the *active* verb patterns and are strictly active, thus allowing example (1) below but not (2):

(1) ha-aHot tipla ba-inyan   האחות טיפלה בעניין
         ACTIVE
         the nurse dealt with-the matter
         ⇒
         tipul ha-aHot ba-inyan   טיפול האחות בעניין
         [the] dealing [of] the nurse with-the matter

(2) ha-inyan tupal   העניין טופל
         PASSIVE
         the matter was-dealt [with]
         ⇏
         *tipul ha-inyan   *טיפול העניין
         [the] dealing [of] the matter

But though active, action nouns can express their 'subject' by a על-ידי *al-yedey* phrase or the equivalent:[12]

         ha-hitnagdut le-yidish **al-yedey**...   ...ההתנגדות ליידיש **על-ידי**
                                'the opposition to Yiddish **by**...'

In contrast, adjectival state nouns never allow such semi-passive 'by' phrases:

         *ha-shayaHut le-mitsráyim **al-yedey**... (√shel...)   (...שׁל√) *השייכות למצרים **על-ידי**...
         the relevance to Egypt **by**... (of...)

14.8 Non-inverted ('impersonal') passives

         In some cases where a passive (as so far described) is impossible, a non-inverted, i.e 'impersonal', passive is available: for verbs of saying or knowing being used with an object clause or with an indirect object noun:

         yarshu lo leashen   ירשו לו לעשן
         [they] will-permit to-him to-smoke   'They will permit him to smoke'

         sikmu she-neHalek   סיכמו שנחלק
         [they] decided that we'll-share   'They decided we'd share'

         dibru al hafuga   דיברו על הפוגה
         [they] talked of [a] truce   'They talked of a truce'

When the subject is understood as an impersonal 'we', 'you' or 'they', the verb can be passivized in form (always 3rd masculine singular, the unmarked form), without subject and object being inverted; instead, the object remains as it is and the subject, being impersonal, is omitted (rather than being able to show up as a ...על-ידי *al-yedey*... 'by...' phrase). Thus the functional effect is roughly the same as for the 3rd person plural impersonal (see 14.2.2.), viz. subject removal without 'object promotion'.

         yurshe lo leashen   יורשה לו לעשן
         [it] will-be-permitted to-him to-smoke   'He'll be permitted to smoke'

         sukam she-neHalek[13]   סוכם שנחלק
         [it] was-decided that we'll-share   'It was decided we'd share'

dubar al hafuga   דובר על הפוגה
was-talked of [a] truce   'A truce was talked about'

Another verb allowing this construction is החל ב- *heHel be-* 'begin on':

huHal be-hakamat kur   הוחל בהקמת כור
was-begun on building [a] reactor   'The building of a reactor was begun'

The very fact that nouns do not invert here means that indirect object verbs like דיבר על *diber al* 'talk of', ordinarily not passivizable, are free to become passive

FURTHER READING
Azar 1977:41f; Ben-Asher 1972:ch.2; Berman 1979b, 1980b, 1982a; Rosén 1977:190ff; Rubinstein 1971:2.5; Sadka 1978:5.1; Stern 1979, 1981.

15. Object phrases

15.1 Introduction
Verbs and adjectives may 'govern' one or two objects - or none:

ten **smartut le-ába**	'Give **a rag to Daddy**'	תן **סמרטוט לאבא**
OBJ OBJ		

ani ashema **ba-avera**	'I'm guilty **of the offence**'	אני אשמה **בעבירה**
OBJ		

The object can be (1) a noun phrase,[1] (2) an infinitive verb phrase, or (3) a finite clause - depending on the verb or adjective governing it.[2] This chapter describes (1); for (2,3), see chapters 30 and 31. Examples of the three forms are:

(1)   ratsíti havana
       I-wanted understanding   רציתי הבנה

(2)   ratsíti lehavin
       I-wanted to-understand   רציתי להבין

(3)   ratsíti she-taviní
       I-wanted that you'd-understand [you to understand]   רציתי שתביני

15.2 Object or subject?
Object and subject are ordinarily quite distinct:
(1) The object follows the verb/adjective (save for emphasis); the subject precedes.
(2) The object can be introduced by case prepositions, eg. ב- , את *et, be-*; the subject cannot.
(3) The subject, not the object, determines verb agreement.

       ha-nemerim son'im et ha-aklim   הנמרים שונאים את האקלים
       SUBJ (m.pl.) v(m.pl.) OM OBJ
       the tigers hate OM the climate

Exceptions
The subject-object distinction is blurred in the cases of יש / היה *yesh/haya* + noun 'there is...' and יש / היה *yesh/haya* + ל- *le* + noun + noun '...has...' (see ch.16). For example:

| yesh baayot | 'There are problems' | יש בעיות |
| yesh le-yigal baayot | 'Yigal has problems' | יש ליגאל בעיות |

In formal Hebrew, the noun that 'exists' or 'is possessed' (here: בעיות *baayot*) generally follows this verb (like an object); but it has no case preposition (like a subject) and it determines the agreement of the verb (like a subject):

| gam kan hayu ha-baayot ha-éle | | גם כאן היו הבעיות האלה |
| also here were the problems the these | 'Here too there were these problems' | |

| hayu le-yigal baayot | | היו ליגאל בעיות |
| were to Yigal problems | 'Yigal had problems' | |

In casual Hebrew, this noun is more decidedly an object:[3] it generally follows the verb and it has the direct object preposition את *et* (when definite, as is the rule for את *et*); but it has one subject-like characteristic: it does *tend* to determine verb agreement - less so when there is את *et* present:

| gam kan haya et ha-baayot ha-éle | | גם כאן היה את הבעיות האלה |
| also here was OM the problems the these | 'Here too there were these problems' | |

hayta (f.s.)	lahem mamash baaya		היתה
?(haya) (m.s.)	f.s.		(והיה)
was to-them really problem		'They really had a problem'	להם ממש בעיה

The same blurring of the subject-object distinction is found in casual usage with certain verbs of possession or acquisition where the 'possessor' is marked by -ל *le-*, eg. מגיע *magía* 'be entitled to', חסר *Haser* 'lack' and, very casually, even נשאר *nishar* 'be left' and נולד *nolad* 'be born':

magía li botnim?		מגיע לי בוטנים?
m.s. m.pl.		
comes to-me peanuts?	'Am I entitled to peanuts?'	

nolad lo bat		נולד לו בת
m.s. f.s.		
was-born to-him girl	'He's had a girl'	

15.3   Object or adverbial?

15.3.1   General semantics

Objects express *participants* in an event. The noun is the main feature of an object; prepositions, if any, contribute much less to its meaning.

Adverbials, and specifically adjunct adverbials, *describe* an event or convey its *circumstances*. They fall into semantic groups, and the choice of preposition determines the exact meaning, eg.:

Means:	be..	'with...'	...ב
Time:	be..	'at...'	...ב
	ad...	'until...'	...עד
Place where:	me'al...	'above..'	...מעל
	sviv...	'around...'	...סביב

This is a rough distinction. There are several intermediate types, which for less evident reasons have been grouped in this chapter or with adjuncts in ch.21:

OBJECTS

Recipient: le- -ל (15.6)
    ten oto le-dáni

תן אותו לדני
'Give it to Danny'

Specification: be- -ב (15.8)
    ze male be-aley tey

זה מלא בעלי-תה
'It's full of tea-leaves'

ADVERBIALS (ADJUNCTS)

Affectee: le- -ל (21.10)
    tidroH lo al ha-déshe

תדרוך לו על הדשא
'Step on his grass'

Benefactee: le- -ל (21.10)
    bishálti lo

בישלתי לו
'I was cooking for him'

Possessor: le- -ל (21.10)
    tiga lo ba-af

תגע לו באף
'Touch him on the nose'

*Autonomous
agent*:   le- -ל (21.10)
    yashavt laH sham

ישבת לך שם
'You were sitting there'

*Destination or
origin*:   le- -ל (21.8)
    ruts la-mora

רוץ למורה
'Run to the teacher'

15.3.2   Object and adverbial propositions

Objects and adverbials may look alike as both are commonly introduced by the following prepositions:

-ב	-ל	על	עם	-מ	אל	-כ	מפני	אחרי
be-	le-	al	im	mi-	el	ke-	mipney	aHarey

There is a further preposition, used exclusively with direct objects: את *et*.
Objects and adverbials are often apparently easy to distinguish:

Object:
histakálti **ba-shamáyim**   'I was looking **at the sky**'   הסתכלתי בשמיים

Adverbial:
áfti **ba-shamáyim**   'I was flying **in the sky**'   עפתי בשמיים

However, the criteria are not always clear-cut; the remainder of this section describes various phenomena for which objects and adverbials differ to various extents.

15.3.3 Meaningful and meaningless prepositions

Quite generally, object prepositions are intrinsicaly meaningless whereas adverbial prepositions are intrinsically meaningful:

	OBJECT	
re'u **et** ha-anak	'See the giant'	ראו **את** הענק
taHlit **al** máshehu	'Decide **on** something'	תחליט **על** משהו
	ADVERBIAL	
leH **im** dáni	'Go **with** Danny'	לך **עם** דני
shev **al** ze	'Sit **on** this'	שב **על** זה

But these are just the two extremes of a whole spectrum of meaningfulness in prepositions, which we discuss below.

Grammatical 'case' - the least 'meaningful'

Many verbs and adjectives 'govern' a preposition which has *no* obvious relevance to their meaning, eg. **-ל** הקשיב *hikshiv le-* 'listen **to**', **על** החליט *heHlit al* 'decide **on**'. There may even be a meaningless *choice* of prepositions: **-ל** / **-כ** מינה *mina ke/le* 'appoint as', אחרי / את חיפש *Hipes et/aHarey* 'search for', **-ב** / **את** החזיק *heHzik et/be* 'hold', **עם** / **-ב** התחשב *hitHashev be/im* 'take into consideration'.

Many verbs etc. can vary their meanings by choice of preposition while the preposition itself still has no *intrinsic* meaning: **-ל** הצביע *hitsbía le-* 'vote for' ~ **על** הצביע *hitsbía al* 'point to'; **-ל** אחראי *aHra'i le-* 'responsible for' ~ **על** אחראי *aHra'i al-* 'in charge of'; **את** הכיר *hikir et* 'know' ~ **-ב** הכיר *hikir be-* 'recognize'; **-ל** קינא *kine le-* 'jealous for' ~ **-ב** קינא *kine be-* 'jealous of'.

Semi-grammatical 'case'

Various prepositions are indeed likely with certain semantic classes of verb etc., though the preposition will not have this particular meaning elsewhere Thus, adjectives denoting 'emotionally affected by' (eg. מרוצה, מבסוט, מופתע **-מ** *merutse, mabsut, mufta mi-* 'glad, pleased, surprised at/with') tend to govern **-מ** *mi-*, and verbs denoting 'transfer of objects or information' (eg. נתן, אמר *natan, amar* 'give, say') tend to govern **-ל** *le-* for the recipient, whereas זה מדני, המלח לדני *ze mi-dáni, ha-mélaH le-dáni* could only mean 'it's *from* Danny' and (unlikely) 'the salt's *to* Danny'. See further 15.6.

For both types, particular verbs may be 'weakly' or 'strongly' transitive, i.e they *allow* or *require* an object. Examples of weakly transitive verbs are (...ל) הקשיב *hikshiv (le..)* 'listen' (to...)', (...ל) איחר *iHer (le..)* 'be late (for...)'; and of strongly transitive verbs **את** / **-ב** החזיק *heHzik be-/et* 'hold', **-ב** השתמש *hishtamesh be-* 'use'.

If strongly transitive, the verb may be regarded as having a 'built-in' preposition, though in fact it can easily be separated from it:

hishtamesh aHshav be-peHam	השתמש עכשיו בפחם
use now coal	'Use coal now'

Semantic 'case'

Some verbs etc. govern a preposition with its normal adverbial meaning - but only *one particular preposition*, even when there are others, similar in meaning, that might have served a similar purpose:

amad bifney (*lifney)	עמד בפני (*לפני)
	'stand up to, i.e facing (*in front of)'

hoda al (*legabey)	הודה על (*לגבי)
	'thank for (*concerning)'

nifgash, rav im (*beyáHad im)	נפגש, רב עם (*ביחד עם)
	'meet, fight with (*together with)'

Sometimes this follows from the intrinsic meaning of the verb:

hitgaagéa el (*letoH, *meaHorey)	התגעגע אל (*לתוך, *מאחורי)
	'yearn for (to)' (*into, *behind)

Conversely, some verbs allow additional prepositions not available in adverbials:

akav aHarey/**aHar**	'follow (= comprehend)'	עקב אחרי/**אחר**...
baraH mi-/**mipney**	'flee from'	ברח מ/**מפני**...

Free semantic selection - the most 'meaningful'

Some verbs etc. can take *any preposition* with an appropriate meaning - which would make this a clear case of an adverbial except that it *coheres tightly* to the verb (see 15.3.5):

gar be-/meaHorey/al	'live in/behind/on...'	גר ב-/מאחורי/על...
diber al/odot/legabey	'speak about...'	דיבר על/אודות/לגבי...

Sometimes, indeed, one may choose either a clearly 'grammatical' or a semantic preposition, thus (respectively):

neHshávti **le-ga'on**	'I was regarded **as a genius**'	נחשבתי **לגאון**
neHshávti **ke-ga'on**		נחשבתי **כגאון**

15.3.4   How many objects?

A double object is possible but not a triple, in all obvious cases of objects. In the case of the types listed at the start of 15.3, verbs taking 'recipient' -ל *le-* or 'specification' -ב *be-* take just one other object, thus:

masar et...le..	'hand...to...'	...מסר את...ל
hoda le..al...	'thank...for...'	...הודה ל...על
kisa et...be..	'cover...with...'	...כיסה את...ב-
hikif et...be..	'surround...with...'	...הקיף את...ב-

However, 'affective', 'benefactee', 'possessor' -ל *le-* and 'destination/origin' adverbials can clearly be added *in addition to* a verb's single or double object:

láma irbavt li et ha-sukar im ha-kémaH?   ?למה עירבבת לי את הסוכר עם הקמח
    AFFECTEE   OBJ 1   OBJ 2
why did-you-mix to-me OM the sugar with the flour?
    'Why did you go and mix the sugar with the flour?'

tafárti laH et ha-kfafot la-me'il   תפרתי לך את הכפפות למעיל
    POSSESSOR OBJ 1   OBJ2
I've-sewed to-you OM the gloves to-the coat
    'I've sewed your gloves to your coat'

tishlaH li et ze mi-óksford   תשלח לי את זה מאוקספורד
    OBJ1 OBJ2   ORIGIN
send me OM it from Oxford   'Send it to me from Oxford'

15.3.5   Cohesion to the verb: tight objects and loose adverbials
Many types of adverbial can be 'set off' by pause from the rest of the sentence, or preposed without any special emphasis:

be-shéva, ha-yeladim od lo yeshenim   בשבע, הילדים עוד לא ישנים
    'At seven, the kids still aren't asleep'

biglal ha-ráam, ha-yeladim od lo yeshenim   בגלל הרעם, הילדים עוד לא ישנים
    'Because of the thunder, the kids still aren't asleep'

However, objects ('participants in the action') cannot be set off, nor preposed except for emphasis or de-emphasis:

et ha-yeladim od lo hilbáshti   **את הילדים** עוד לא הלבשתי
EMPH OBJ   'I still haven't dressed **the kids**'

Thus Hebrew can (though it often does not) distinguish between object prepositions and adverbial prepositions:

ba-minhara lo histakálti   **במנהרה** לא הסתכלתי
EMPH OBJ   'I didn't look **at the tunnel**'

ba-minhara, lo histakálti   במנהרה, לא הסתכלתי
ADVERBIAL   'In the tunnel, I didn't look'

Neither, however, can so-called 'adverbials' of (1) means, (2) manner and (3) extent be set off or routinely preposed (see ch. 21); nor can (4) 'adverbials' of destination or origin (these, after all, do not express 'circumstance'); nor can (5) 'adverbials' of place, time, topic serving verbs like גר *gar* 'live', התקיים *hitkayem* 'take place', דיבר *diber* 'talk', whose very sense involves place, time and topic, respectively; nor can (6) affectee or possessor adverbials with - ל *le-*:[4]

(1) pitsHu et ha-egozim **be-patish**   פיצחו את האגוזים **בפטיש**
'They cracked the nuts **with a hammer**'

(2) nigáshti **le'at** el ha-monit   ניגשתי **לאט** אל המונית
'I **slowly** approached the cab'

(3) ani kore tanaH **hamon**   אני קורא תנ"ך **המון**
'I read the Bible **an awful lot**'

(4) rátsnu **min he-Hatser el ha-masa'it**   רצנו **מן החצר אל המשאית**
'We ran **from the yard to the truck**'

(5) gárnu **be-efrat**   גרנו **באפרת**
'We lived **in Efrat**'

(6) Hafáfnu **la-tinok** et ha-rosh   חפפנו **לתינוק** את הראש
'We washed **the baby's** hair'

15.3.6 Word order

The order of objects and adverbials partly reflects the 'degrees of cohesion' in 15.3.5, in the following ways.

Objects and means/manner/extent adverbials are all likely to follow the verb closely:

dibárti **tov** sínit   דיברתי **טוב** סינית
sínit **tov**   סינית **טוב**

I spoke **well** Chinese
Chinese **well**   'I spoke Chinese well'

Place, time, cause and other adverbials are frequently less close to the verb. However, affectee and possessor - ל *le-* must precede even the direct object (conceivably because they almost always involve people, not things):

kilkálti **la-shaHen** et ha-déshe   קילקלתי **לשכן** את הדשא
I-ruined **to-the-neighbour** OM the lawn   'I went and ruined the neighbour's
lawn'

Adverbials of destination or origin, save where *required* by a verb (eg. גר *gar* 'live'), behave like other adverbials of place or time:

higánu el ha-gésher be-sha'a aHat   הגענו אל הגשר בשעה אחת
be-sha'a aHat el ha-gésher   בשעה אחת אל הגשר

we-got to the bridge at one o'clock
at one o'clock to the bridge

lo gárti sham az   לא גרתי שם אז
'I didn't live there then'

Among the various objects themselves there are further ordering restrictions;
see 15.7.

15.3.7   Object and adverb pronouns

Special one-word pronouns are a feature of *some* adverbials, whereas
objects always need to display their preposition (?במי *be-mi*? 'whom?', etc).

Place and time: איפה, לאן *éfo, le'an* 'where, to where', מתי *matay* 'when',
and שם *sham* 'there', אז *az* 'then'. Purpose/cause: למה *láma* 'why'. Means/
manner: איך *eH* 'how'. Extent: כמה *káma* 'how much' and others. All these
refer to things, places etc., not to people; thus לאן *le'an* 'where to' would not
expect the answer לדני *le-dáni* 'to Danny'.[5] For fuller lists, see chapters 25 and
26.

15.3.8   Object preposition deletion

Object prepositions usually drop before an object *clause*, a further
example of their weakness (see 19.5):

Hashash **mi-**	חשש מ-
be-afraid **of**	

Hasháshti she-tipol	חששתי שתפול
OBJ CLAUSE	
I-was-afraid that you'd-fall	

15.3.9   Other phenomena

Gerunds. Gerunds occur in adverbials but not in objects (for details,
see 30.5):

be-kablo et ha-igéret...	...בקבלו את האיגרת
	'on his receiving the letter...'

'Internal objects'. These are in fact adverbials of manner (see 21.4.2):

amádnu amida eytana	עמדנו עמידה איתנה
we-stood a-stand firm	'We stood firm'

'Middle objects'. קרן *karan* 'shine with', נטף *nataf* 'drip with', and several other
verbs take a 'middle object', an *apparent object* which is strictly non-definite
and always has a freer, near-synonymous equivalent involving a *subject* + the
same verb (see further, 15.8):

ha-kvish zorem máyim	הכביש זורם מים
MIDDLE OBJ	'The road is flowing ⟨with⟩ water'

máyim zormim ba-kvish	מים זורמים בכביש
SUBJ	'Water is flowing on the road'

15.4   Transitive and intransitive

15.4.1   Introduction

There are three degrees of *transitivity*, each involving numerous verbs and adjectives, though not on any recognized semantic basis:

Intransitives:
no object, eg.   gasas   גסס   shamen   שמן
                                   'be dying'   'fat'

Weakly transitive:
optional object, eg.   aHal   אכל   merutse   מרוצה
                                    'eat'   'satisfied (with...)'

Strongly transitive:
obligatory object, eg.   hekim   הקים   asuy   עשוי
                                     'construct'   'likely (to...)'

A subject-less verb or adjective too may have no object: אמרתי שנוח *amárti she-nóaH* 'I said that ⟨it's⟩ **comfortable**'. Action/state nouns corresponding to strongly transitive verbs, eg. הגנה *hagana* 'defence' (corresponding to הגן *hegen* 'defend'), often need no 'object'; however, הקמה *hakama* 'construction', לבישה *levisha* 'wearing' and many others generally require a further noun (eg. הקמת בתים *hakamat batim* 'construction of houses').

Similarly for agent nouns: מגינים *meginim* 'defenders' and זוכים *zoHim* 'winners' need no further noun, but לובשים *lovshim* 'wearers' does.

More examples of transitive verbs

Weakly transitive: קנה *kana* 'buy', כתב *katav* 'write', שאל *sha'al* 'ask', הציץ *hetsits* 'peep', הודה *hoda* 'confess', דילג *dileg* 'skip', חזר *Hazar* 'return', הועיל *ho'il* 'be of use', המתין *himtin* 'wait', נפגש *nifgash* 'meet together', התקשר *hitkasher* 'phone up', רב *rav* 'quarrel'.

Strongly transitive: לבש *lavash* 'wear, put on', קיים *kiyem* 'keep', עשה *asa* 'make, do', דן *dan* 'discuss', הבחין *hivHin* 'notice', חשד *Hashad* 'suspect', הגן *hegen* 'defend', הסתמך *histameH* 'rely', ער *er* 'aware', האזין *heezin* 'listen in', התמסר *hitmaser* 'be addicted', נחלץ *neHlats* 'escape', סלד *salad* 'dislike', נפטר *niftar* 'get rid of'.

15.4.2   Transitives and object deletion

Absence of an object can arise in two ways: example (1) below features a weakly transitive verb; examples (2-4) feature indefinite object deletion, where a particular indefinite object, even of a strongly transitive verb, is left to be deduced from context. Ambiguity sometimes arises:[6]

(1)   aHálti   אכלתי
      'I've eaten' (i.e 'I've eaten something')

(2) aHalt anavim? ken, aHálti   אכלת ענבים? כן, אכלתי
'Have you eaten any grapes? Yes, I've eaten ⟨some grapes⟩'

(3) ratsiti laasot skandal, ve-**asíti**   רציתי לעשות סקנדל, **ועשיתי**
'I wanted to make a scandal, and **I made** ⟨one⟩'

(4) im dalya lovéshet Hagora, gam ani **elbash**   אם דליה לובשת חגורה, גם אני **אלבש**
'If Dalya is wearing a belt, I'll also **wear** ⟨one⟩'

15.4.3 Obligatory adverbials and transitive verbs: גר *gar* 'live'
Certain verbs require an adverbial; they too can be termed 'strongly transitive':[7]

gur/hitgorer ba-négev   גור / התגורר בנגב
'Live in the Negev'

yom kipur Hal be-yom he   יום כיפור חל ביום ה'
'Yom Kipur falls on Thursday'

nahagu bi be-Humra   נהגו בי בחומרה
'They treated me severely'

15.5 Direct objects and their preposition את *et*
Direct objects differ somewhat in form and syntax from indirect objects.

15.5.1 Form
Direct objects are introduced (a) by the preposition את *et* when they are definite, and (b) by no preposition otherwise Thus they often *directly* follow their verb:

baláti zvuv   בלעתי זבוב
I-swallowed fly   'I swallowed a fly'

baláti **et** ha-zvuv   בלעתי **את** הזבוב
I-swallowed OM the fly   'I swallowed the fly'

Indirect objects, by contrast, nearly always must (and always can) be introduced by a preposition:[8]

hitsbáti **al** zvuv   'I pointed **to** a fly'   הצבעתי **על** זבוב

hitsbáti **al** ha-zvuv   'I pointed **to** the fly'   הצבעתי **על** הזבוב

Dropping את *et*: further details
את *et* is more restricted than other object prepositions: it has no 'free' meaning of its own; it requires a definite noun; and it is the most easily omissible preposition, in five respects as set out in (a)-(e) below:
(a) Verbs taking את *et* are much more likely to have a passive equivalent (by

which את *et* drops); see further, 15.6: הזבוב נבלע *ha-zvuv nivla* 'The fly was swallowed'.

(b) In 'telegraphic' usage, eg. headlines, את *et* is often omitted with definite nouns, especially when not *directly* followed by ‑ ה *ha-* 'the':[9]

ha-tsinor Hadal lemale **yiudo**   הצינור חדל למלא **ייעודו**

'The pipe ceased to fulfil **its purpose**'

ha-shovtim alulim lehashbit **ha-tnu'a**   השובתים עלולים להשבית **התנועה**

'The strikers are liable to stop **the traffic**'

ha-matara hi lehavtíaH **merav ha-sherut**   המטרה היא להבטיח **מירב השירות**
la-tsibur   לציבור

'The aim is to ensure **the maximum service** to the public'

(c) Instead of אותי, אותך *oti, otHa* 'me, you' etc., very formal Hebrew occasionally opts for *verbal suffixes*:

bikshu leyatser **otam** ~ bikshu leyatsram   ביקשו לייצר **אותם** ~ ביקשו לייצרם

'They sought to manufacture **them**'

Full lists are found in traditional grammars (many forms are learnéd or non-existent).[10] These suffixes are also found, idiomatically in the main, with a few *indirect* object verbs, eg.:

avakesh lehodiaHa...   'I wish to make known ⟨to⟩ **you**..'   אבקש להודיעך...

harshúni lomar...   'Allow **me** to say...'   הרשוני לומר...

(d) In relative clauses (ch.33), relative pronouns involving את *et*, i.e אותו, אותה *oto, ota* etc, are usually omitted. Contrast אותו *oto* with, eg., the pronoun בו *bo*:

éfo ha-et she-katávti **bo**?   איפה העט שכתבתי **בו?**

'Where's the pen that I wrote **with [it]**?'

éfo ha-et she-kaníti **(?oto)**?   איפה העט שקניתי **(?אותו)?**

'Where's the pen that I bought **[it]**?'

(e) 'Action nouns' (30.6) corresponding to a verb that takes את *et*, as in example (1), introduce their 'object' with של *shel* 'of' (2) or with the construct (3), not with את *et*:

(1)   sagru et ha-namel   סגרו את הנמל
      they-closed ᴏᴍ the port

(2)   ha-sgira shel ha-namel   הסגירה של הנמל
      the closure of the port

(3)   sgirat ha-namel   סגירת הנמל
      closure-of the port

15.5.2   Syntax and semantics of the direct object

The direct object commonly precedes the indirect object (see 15.7).
Many more verbs take direct than take indirect objects, and the sizeable
minority of verbs with a double object nearly always have a direct object as one
of these But very few adjectives take a direct object; the most common are חייב
hayav 'owe', מלא *male* 'full', שווה *shave* 'worth', טעון *ta'un* 'in need of':

ze lo shave et ha-maamats	זה לא שווה את המאמץ
it's not worth OM the effort	

Which verbs take direct objects?

There are no recognized semantic criteria as to which verbs take
direct objects - except negative ones, eg. 'recipients' normally have -ל *le-* rather
than את *et*; 'topics of discussion' normally have על *al* etc; and especially, one
object in a double object is usually direct.[11] See 15.6.

Several verbs allow את *et* and -ב *be-* with the same meaning, eg. בחר *baHar*
'choose', חקר *Hakar* 'research', בעט *ba'at* 'kick', החזיק *heHzik* 'hold'. However, -ב *be-* with some verbs of damage denotes 'part of': ב / השמיד את -
hishmid et/be- 'destroy', כירסם *kirsem* 'gnaw', קיצץ *kitsets* 'cut'. On the other
hand, the sense may differ totally: פתח את *pataH et* 'open' vs. -ב פתח *pataH*
be- 'begin'.

15.6   Indirect objects and their prepositions

Indirect objects commonly have the prepositions:[12]

be-, le-, al, el, im, mi-	ב-, ל-, על, אל, עם, מ-

and less often:

ke-, beyn, mipney, aHarey, bifney	כ-, בין, מפני, אחרי, בפני

These also double as adverbial prepositions - see 15.3.3. For the form of these
prepositions and their suffixes (בו, עליך *bo, aléHa* etc.), see chapter 42.
There are certain *syntactic* differences among these prepositions. (a) Objects
with -ל *le-*, notably when denoting 'recipient' (suffixed form לי, לך *li, leHa*,
etc.), are more likely to precede the direct object than are objects with עם, -ב
be-, im etc. (15.5.2). (b) Objects with על, -ל, -ב *be-, le-, al* are the only ones to
have a corresponding passive (and even then not for all verbs), eg. ~ ב - בגד
נבגד *bagad be-* ~ *nivgad* 'betrayed' ~ was betrayed' (see ch. 14).[13]

Examples and individual semantic/syntactic properties
With -ב *be-*

Miscellaneous: גאה *ge'e* 'proud', התגאה *hitga'a* 'take a pride in', האשים
heeshim 'accuse of', בחר *baHar* 'choose', דן *dan* 'discuss', תמך *tamaH* 'support', זיכה *zika* 'award' etc.

Many verbs of visual/physical contact: הבחין *hivHin* 'notice', עיין *iyen* 'study', הביט *hibit* 'look at', הסתכל *histakel* 'look at', הציץ *hetsits* 'peep at', צפה *tsafa* 'view', נגע *naga* 'touch', אחז *aHaz* 'seize', משך *mashaH* 'pull', בעט *ba'at* 'kick' etc.

For *be-* of 'specification', eg. מילא ב- *mile be-* 'fill with', see 15.8.

With -ל le-; suffixed form לי, לך... *li, leHa etc.*

Miscellaneous: אחראי *aHara'i* 'responsible for', מודע *muda* 'aware of', שייך *shayaH* 'belong to', הרביץ *hirbits* 'hit', נגע *naga* 'pertain to', חיכה *Hika* 'wait for', דמה *dama* 'resemble' etc.

For certain adjectives, the 'experiencer' is an *object* with -ל *le-*, not a subject, eg. קשה לי *kashe li* 'it's hard for me', קר לי *kar li* 'I'm cold', נוח לי *nóaH li* 'I'm comfortable', משעמם לי *meshaamem li* 'I'm bored', טוב לי *tov li* 'I'm OK', עצוב לי *atsuv li* 'I'm sad'. Unlike other -ל *le-* objects, these can *precede* the adjective, as in (1), with no special emphasis - except when suffixed ('clitic'), as in (2) - and even clitics tend to precede the adjective where there is an 'auxiliary' היה/יהיה *haya/yihye* for them to follow (3):[14]

(1)	la-tinok kar	to-the baby cold	לתינוק קר
	kar la-tinok	cold to-the baby	קר לתינוק
			'The baby's cold'
(2)	kar lo	cold to-him	קר לו
			'He's cold'
(3)	haya lo kar	was to-him cold	היה לו קר
			'He was cold'

Subject-less adjectives/verbs in general express the 'human agent' (in such cases usually a 'thinker' or 'feeler' rather than a 'doer' - or at least suggestive of a lesser degree of 'human agency') by an object with -ל *le-*. But this generally *follows* the adjective/verb:

| im lo haya mistader le-dáni... | אם לא היה מסתדר לדני... |
| if not were sort-itself-out to Danny... | 'If Danny weren't managing...' |

Similarly, נראה ל- *nir'a le-* 'seem right to', התחשק ל- *hitHashek le-* 'fancy', מובן ל- *muvan le-* 'make sense to', and others.

'Recipients' (of things, information) usually have -ל *le-* (alternating ל/אל *le-/ el* in one-object verbs of communication - see below): מסר *masar* 'hand to', החזיר *heHzir* 'restore to', הביא *hevi* 'bring to', אמר *amar* 'tell'. They are usually human, but note ייחס *yiHes* 'attribute to', הוסיף *hosif* 'add to' etc. Similarly, 'something being attached to': הצמיד *hitsmid* 'attach to', צירף *tseref* 'join to', קשר *kashar* 'tie to' etc.

With על al

Miscellaneous: שנוא *sanu* 'hateful to', החליט *heHlit* 'decide on', הקפיד *hikpid* 'insist on', הצביע *hitsbía* 'point to', דילג *dileg* 'skip', הגן *hegen* 'defend', חזר *Hazar* 'repeat', חתם *Hatam* 'sign up for' etc.

Many verbs of 'domination': ציווה צ tsiva 'order', אסר asar 'forbid', צעק
tsa'ak 'shout at', צחק tsaHak 'laugh at', התלבש hitlabesh 'take advantage of',
השפיע hishpía 'influence' etc.

Verbs of 'referring' favour על al or other words for 'concerning': דיבר diber
'speak of', קרא kara 'read about', שר shar 'sing of', העיר he'ir 'comment on',
לימד limed 'teach about' etc.

With -ל *le- (formally also* אל *el); suffixed form only* ...אליך, אלי elay, eléHa *etc.*
Verbs of 'address', taking single objects: דיבר diber 'talk to', כתב katav 'write
to', פנה pana 'apply, turn to', התקשר hitkasher 'phone' etc. These amount to
verbs of 'motion', as in:

hitkasher mi-ashdod habáyta

התקשר מאשדוד הביתה
'Phone home from Ashdod'

Verbs of 'joining', taking single objects: הצטרף hitstaref 'join', התלווה
hitlava 'accompany' etc.

Verbs of 'referring': התכוון hitkaven 'mean', התייחס hityaHes 'relate to,
treat' etc.

With עם *im*
Most verbs of 'reciprocal action', as in:

יורם נאבק עם גד ~ יורם וגד נאבקים
yoram neevak im gad ~ yoram ve-gad neevakim
Yoram is-wrestling with Gad ~ Yoram and Gad are-wrestling

and other such verbs: נפגש nifgash 'meet', התקוטט hitkotet 'quarrel', השלים
hishlim 'make peace with', השתווה hishtava 'equal', התייעץ hitya'ets 'consult',
דיבר diber 'speak with' etc.

Many verbs of 'association': הזדהה hizdaha 'identify with', התקשר
hitkasher 'contact', השווה hishva 'compare with', הפגיש hifgish 'have someone
meet...' etc.[15]

With -מ *mi-*
Denoting most 'sources of an experience': פחד paHad 'fear', סלד salad 'dislike', נהנה nehena 'enjoy', התפעל hitpa'el 'be impressed with', מבסוט mabsut
'glad at', התייאש hitya'esh 'despair with' etc.

With most verbs of 'distancing': נזהר nizhar 'beware of', נחלץ neHelats
'escape', נפטר niftar 'be rid of', הסתייג histayeg 'have reservations about',
הסתיר histir 'conceal from', רחוק raHok 'distant' etc.

Denoting most 'sources of things or information' (mirroring 'recipient' -ל le-
(above)): קיבל kibel 'receive', למד lamad 'learn', שמע shama 'hear' etc.[16]

With -כ *ke-*[17]
Only with verbs of 'status': These may denote 'having status', as in נחשב
neHshav 'be regarded as', שימש shimesh 'serve as', תיפקד tifked 'function as',
התחזה hitHaza 'masquerade as'; or 'giving status', as in תפס tafas 'regard as',
בחר baHar 'choose as', מינה mina 'appoint as', ראה ra'a 'see as', הכריז

hiHriz 'proclaim as'. The preposition can be ל- *le-* with מינה *mina* 'appoint as', בחר *baHar* 'choose as', התחזה *hitHaza* 'masquerade as', and נחשב *neHeshav* 'be regarded as'; and may even be omitted for indefinite nouns with מינה *mina* 'appoint as' and שימש *shimesh* 'serve as'. The exceptional omission of the preposition reflects the fact that כ- *ke-* = '...is something', 'serve as' = '...as being', 'choose as' = '...as being'. Indeed, a noun following כ- *ke-* generally *agrees* with the foregoing noun, unlike other object nouns:

tafásti otam ke-bogdim	תפסתי אותם כבוגדים
pl. pl.	'I regarded them as traitors'

Moreover, some 'status verbs' also take an adjectival or even a verbal phrase, and are best classed among the *complements of verbs of 'being'*, which behave in most respects like objects.

Complements of verbs of 'being'

The verb היה *haya* 'be', discussed in chapter 16, and several verbs denoting 'being, becoming, remaining' and the like take a complement noun phrase, adjective phrase or occasionally even a verb phrase that is in most respects a kind of 'object'.[18] At the same time, these complements agree with the subject (or, if there is a direct object, with this) in the same way as any predicate of a verb of 'being' (see 18.2.1):[19]

avital neesta baalat-tshuva	אביטל נעשתה בעלת-תשובה
f.s. N(f.s.)	'Avital became ⟨a⟩ newly-observant Jew'

In detail, חשב *Hashav* 'consider' and its passive נחשב *neHshav* 'be considered' usually take ל- *le-*, as in (1) below, or (more formal) כ- *ke-*, and occasionally no preposition; whereas תפס *tafas* 'consider' requires כ- *ke-* and ראה *ra'a* 'view' usually requires it. Of the verbs of 'becoming', נעשה *naasa* and נהיה *niya* have no preposition (2), while הפך *hafaH* usually takes ל- *le-* and literary היה ל- *haya le-* is distinguished from היה *haya* 'be' by the very presence of its ל- *le-* (3). Of the verbs of 'making', i.e 'causing to become', עשה *asa* always takes ל- *le-*, as in (4), and הפך *hafaH* usually does so. נשאר *nish'ar* and נותר *notar* 'remain' and נמצא *nimtsa* 'turn out to be' have no prepositon:

(1) hem neHshavim le-ánglo-sáksim   הם נחשבים לאנגלו-סקסים
'They are considred Anglo-Saxons'

(2) hi niyeta sávta   היא נהיתה סבתא
'She's become a grandmother'

(3) ha-shamáyim hayu le-kodrim   השמיים היו לקודרים
'The heavens became dark'

(4) ze asa oto le-(adam) meyu'ash   זה עשה אותו ל(אדם) מיואש
'It made him ⟨a⟩ desperate (man)'

With בין *beyn*

Only for verbs of 'separation'/'joining'. Either one plural object or a sequence of:

uveyn...	...ובין
beyn... leveyn...	בין... לבין...
ve..	...ו

eg. הבדיל *hivdil* 'discriminate', תיווך *tiveH* 'mediate'.

With מפני *mipney*

Alternative (formally) to -מ *mi-* with verbs of 'fear, dislike, protection', eg. ירא *yare* 'fear', הבטיח *hivtíaH* 'protect'.

With אחרי *aHarey*

Only for a few verbs etc. of 'pursuit' or 'interest', eg. רדף *radaf* 'pursue', עקב *akav* 'follow' (= understand), מצוד *matsod* 'pursuit', משוגע *meshuga* 'crazy (about)'. A more formal alternative is אחר *aHar*.

With בפני *bifney*

With עמד *amad* 'withstand' and עמיד *amid* 'resistant'. Most terms of 'protection' take -מ *mi-* or מפני *mipney* (see above).

15.7 Double objects

15.7.1 Types of double object

Many verbs allow two objects - one of them usually with את *et* (thus no adjectives take two objects) and the other not.[20] The only common ...את...את *et...et...* verbs are לימד *limed* 'teach', שאל *sha'al* 'ask (a question)' and העביר *heevir* 'take..across (the road etc.)'.

Examples are:

hitna	et...be..	'make..conditional on...'	התנה את...ב...
kibed		'honour...with...'	כיבד
hisgir	le..et...	'hand over...to...'	הסגיר ל...את...
her'a		'show...to...'	הראה
hit'im	et...le..	'adapt...to...'	התאים את...ל...
hirgil		'get...used to...'	הרגיל
hifkid		'put...in charge of...'	הפקיד
kafa	et...al...	'foist...on...'	כפה את...על...
asar		'forbid...to...'	אסר
mana	et...im...	'count...among...'	מנה את...עם...
hishva		'compare..with...'	השווה
ga'al	et...mi...	'redeem...from...'	גאל את...מ...
mana		'deny...to...'	מנע
siveg et...ke..		'classify...as...'	סיווג את...כ...
hoda le..al...		'thank...for...'	הודה ל..על...

15.7.2   Word order

The order of direct vs. indirect object and even vs. adverbial is largely a matter of information and emphasis - notably, 'known information' (in particular, a definite noun) generally precedes 'new information' (an indefinite noun), as in (1,2); plus a secondary factor: the short tends to precede the long. Where both objects are definite, there is no clear-cut preference (3):

(1) lamádeti me-ha-aH sheli káma dvarim   למדתי מהאח שלי כמה דברים
     I-learned from the brother my a-few things 'I learned a few things from my
                                                                  brother'

(2) HataHt ba-sakin ha-ze máshehu bsari?   חתכת בסכין הזה משהו בשרי?
     you-cut with-the knife the this something meaty?   'Did you cut something
                                                                meaty with this knife?'

(3) tuHal latet   la-yéled haze et ha-talit ha-zot   לילד הזה את הטלית הזאת?   תוכל לתת
                   et ha-talit ha-zot la-yéled haze   את הטלית הזאת לילד הזה?
                   'Can you give   [to] this boy this prayer-shawl   ?
                                   this prayer-shawl to this boy

But where both objects are indefinite ('new information'), direct objects precede most types of indirect objects, as listed in 15.7.1 above[21]

Object *pronouns* have their own word order, being 'clitics', i.e unstressed words. This even extends to adverbial use of pronouns, eg. בו *bo* meaning 'with it'; thus this is a 'lexical rule'.

Vis-à-vis a noun we have:

li	bi	oti		אותי	בי	לי
leHa	beHa	otHa		אותך	בך	לך
.	.	.		.	.	.
.	.	.		.	.	.
etc.	etc.	etc.				

which must precede an object noun

alay	miméni	iti	elay		אלי	אתי	ממני	עלי
aléHa	mimHa	itHa	eléHa		אליך	אתך	ממך	עליך
.	.	.	.		.	.	.	.
.	.	.	.		.	.	.	.
etc.	etc.	etc.	etc.					

which generally either precede or follow an object noun

Examples are:

emor **lo** káma milim   אמור **לו** כמה מלים
                                               'Say some words **to him**'

ten **otam** le-ári   תן **אותם** לארי
                                               'Give **them** to Ari'

hu yazik **bo** le-míshehu   הוא יזיק **בו** למישהו
                                               'He'll injure someone **with it**'

nisiti lehafgish **itHa** et ha-menahel   ניסיתי להפגיש **אתך** את המנהל
et ha-menahel **itHa**   את המנהל **אתך**

'I tried to have **you** meet with the manager'

Vis-à-vis a second pronoun, the order hierarchy is more complex and variable
It is approximately:

(1) lo לו

⇓ ⇓

(2) bo בו

⇓ ⇓

(3) oto אותו

⇓ ⇓

(4) alav, miménu עליו, ממנו

⇓ ⇓

(5) ito אתו

⇓ ⇓

(6) elav אליו

Sometimes (2, 3) may rank equal in terms of order, and similarly (3, 4). Examples are:

takir **lánu** oto   תכיר **לנו** אותו

'Introduce him **to us**'

ha-miktsóa ha-ze, mi inyen   המקצוע הזה, מי עניין **בו**
{**bo** otam/otam bo}   אותם/אותם בו

'This subject, who interested them **in it**?'

timtsa niyar atifa ve-taatof   תמצא נייר עטיפה ותעטוף
{**bo** otam/otam bo}   **בו** אותם/אותם בו

'Find wrapping paper and wrap them **in it**'

ha-ishun ze she-him'is **oto** alay   העישון זה שהמאיס **אותו** עלי

'Smoking is what put me **off him**'

nisiti lehafgish **oto** ita   ניסיתי להפגיש **אותו** אתה

'I tried to have **him** meet her'

ze asuy lehargil **otaH** elav   זה עשוי להרגיל **אותך** אליו

'It's likely to get **you** used to him'

ב- *be-* and ל- *le-* are phonologically weaker than את *et*, in that most of the pronouns that they form (...לך, לי, *li, leHa* etc.) are shorter than those formed by את *et* (...אותך, אותי *oti, otHa* etc.).[22] The overall 'weakness' of ל-, ב-, את *le-, be-, et* objects also shows up in the fact that they are sometimes (and את *et* usually) able to become subjects by means of passivization, the preposition dropping in the process (see 14.6); so too do על *al* objects.

If the object is a clause or infinitive, it must *follow* any other object:

osrim al nashim lehatsbia   אוסרים על נשים להצביע

'They forbid women to vote'

15.8   Specification objects: נוטף מים *notef máyim* 'dripping with water'

There are two types of 'quasi-object', denoting not the object of a physical or mental activity but rather *specifying the activity*: 'direct objects of specification', as in example (1), and '־ב *be-* objects of specification', as in (2, 3):

(1)   ha-nahar shorets neHashim
      the river is-swarming snakes

הנהר שורץ נחשים
'The river is swarming with snakes'

(2)   ha-kfar mukaf (be-)ginot
      the village is-ringed (with) gardens

הכפר מוקף (ב)גינות
'The village is ringed with gardens'

(3)   kisit otánu (be-)avak!
      you've-covered us (with) dust!

כיסית אותנו (ב)אבק!
'You've covered us with dust!'

These objects are unlike other objects: (1) The quasi-'direct object' cannot be made definite nor passivized. This is a 'middle object'. (2) The quasi-'־ב *be-* object' is unlike all other indirect objects: it has the option of dropping ־ב *be-*, provided the noun is indefinite and the word order is verb-object. It involves a stative verb or adjective, commonly a passive participle as in (2), or one implying a state, as in (3).

These quasi-object constructions can be explained in terms of their semantics: they are semantically akin to two constructions which have a *subject* instead of a quasi-object, and a locative adverbial (example 1 below) or an object (2, 3) instead of the subject seen in the examples above[23]

(1)   neHashim shortsim ba-nahar
      snakes are-swarming in-the river

נחשים שורצים בנהר
'Snakes are swarming in the river'

(2)   ginot makifot et ha-kfar
      gardens ring OM the village

גינות מקיפות את הכפר
'Gardens ring the village'

(3)   avak meHase otánu
      dust is-covering us

אבק מכסה אותנו
'Dust is covering us'

Note, however, that the quasi-object construction suggests a 'superlative' state of affairs; the verbs in the first set of examples above can take 'superlative stress', denoting 'absolutely swarming with' and so on. It furthermore suggests an unmethodical or non-deliberate situation. Where a deliberate action is intended, ־ב *be-* tends to be retained:

ha-kos mele'a be-máyim

הכוס מלאה במים
'The glass is full of [= *lit.* filled with] water'

ha-mita mele'a máyim

המיטה מלאה מים
'The bed's full of water'

kisiti oto be-smiHot

כיסיתי אותו בשמיכות
'I covered him with blankets'

kisit otánu (be-)avak!   !כיסית אותנו (ב)אבק

'You've covered us in dust!'

Further examples of quasi-object constructions of type (1) are (מים...) נטף *nataf (máyim....)* 'drip with (water,...),' (שאט־נפש...) שפע *shafa (sheat-néfesh....)* 'brim with (revulsion,...),' (אושר) קרן *karan (ósher)* 'beam with (happiness)'; of type (2): גדוש ב- *gadush be-* 'brimming with', אחוז ב- *aHuz be-* 'gripped with'.

Quite distinct from such 'open' verb/adjective + object constructions are 'construct' phrases (described in 6.19), as in :

    hem ashirey-neft   הם עשירי־נפט

    CONSTRUCT (m.pl.)   'They are oil-rich'

    they rich oil

These are of three general types. (a) Sometimes they have no 'open' equivalent, eg. עיוורי־צבעים *ivrey-tsva'im* 'colour blind', מלאי־תקווה *mele'ey-tikva* 'hope-filled', הרי־אסון *harey-ason* 'pregnant with danger'. (b) Often they are *idiomatic* derivatives of 'quasi-object' ב- *be-*, eg. עשירי־נפט *ashirey-neft* 'oil-rich', מוכי־פחד *mukey-páHad* 'fear-struck', ספוגת־דמעות *sfugat-dma'ot* 'tear-soaked', אפופי־עשן *afufey-ashan* 'smoke-wreathed'. (c) Rarely, they derive from another open equivalent חסרים בית ~ חסרי־בית *Hasrey báyit ~ Haserim báyit* 'lacking a home', צמאים לתורה ~ צמאי־תורה *tsme'ey-tora ~ tsme'im le-tora* 'Torah-thirsty'.

FURTHER READING
Azar 1972, 1977: 2.6; Ben-Asher 1972: ch. 4; Berman 1982a,b; Cole 1976a; Gil 1982; Rabin 1974b; Rosén 1966b; Rubinstein 1971: 2.1, 5.5, 6; Sadka 1981: ch.15; Stern 1977, 1979, 1981; Ziv 1976.

16. 'Be' and 'have' constructions

16.1 Introduction

Clauses expressing 'be', 'exist' and 'have' have much in common. In *past, future, infinitive and imperative* clauses, they generally involve a form of the verb היה *haya*:

'be':	ha-méleH **haya** sémel	המלך **היה** סמל
	the king **was** symbol	'The king **was** a symbol'
'exist':	**haya** méleH	**היה** מלך
	was king	'There **was** a king'
'have':	**haya** le-yarden méleH	**היה** לירדן מלך
	was to-Jordan king	'Jordan **had** a king'

In *present tense* clauses they occasionally employ no verb or particle whatsoever, but more commonly 'be' employs 'present tense copulas' (henceforth termed 'copulas') such as הוא *hu* 'is' and the negative אין *en* 'is not'; and 'exist' and 'have' employ the verb יש *yesh* 'there is' and the negative אין *en* 'there is not' (though in slightly different fashion):

'be':	ha-méleH hu sémel	המלך הוא סמל
	the king is symbol	'The king is a symbol'
'exist':	yesh méleH	יש מלך
	there-is king	'There is a king'
'have':	le-yarden yesh méleH	לירדן יש מלך
	to Jordan there-is king	'Jordan has a king'

Alternatively, 'be', 'exist' and 'have' may be expressed by words such as היווה *hiva* 'constitute', קיים *kayam* 'exist', בעל *báal* 'possessor' respectively, but these are not major constructions in themselves.

This chapter deals with the major 'be/have' constructions, focusing first on the 'copula' (16.2-8) and then on 'existential' (16.9) and 'have' (16.10) constructions.

16.2 The copula in general

The copulas הוא *hu*, זה *ze* and formal הנ- *hin-* appear (if at all) between subject and predicate, where English would use the present tense of the verb 'to be'. אין *en* denotes the negative of 'be' in formal usage

הוא *hu* and זה *ze* inflect as follows:

m.s.	hu	הוא	ze	זה
f.s.	hi	היא	zot, zo, zu (C)	זאת, זו
m.pl.	hem	הם	éle, élu	אלה, אלו
f.pl.	hen (F)	הן		

The inflections of -הנ *hin-* and אין *en* are listed in 18.2.4, together with an overall account of the way in which copulas *agree* with their subject or predicate

הוא *hu*, זה *ze* and their inflections are weak particles quite unlike verbs or other parts of speech, including the verb היה *haya*.[1] They can only occur between the subject and predicate,[2] unlike היה *haya* or other verbs:

láma $^{haya}_{*hu}$ ha-shatíaH baaya ?למה היה* השטיח בעיה

'Why $^{was}_{*is}$ the carpet ⟨a⟩ problem?'

ata tsimHoni? gam avi $^{haya}_{*hu}$ אתה צמחוני? גם אבי היה*

'Are you a vegetarian? My father also$_{*is}^{was,}$'

By contrast, formal -הנ *hin-* and negative אין *en* have a somewhat broader function: they can appear between subject and *verb*, as in example (1), unlike הוא *hu*, זה *ze* and English 'be' - and in fact are a 'halfway house' between a copula and a true verb, being able to do without a subject pronoun (2,3) just like a verb (4):[3]

(1) ha-méleH eno zoHer
    the king NEG + SUFF remembers
    המלך אינו זוכר
    'The king does not remember'

(2) (ani) enéni zoHer
    (I) NEG + SUFF remember
    (אני) אינני זוכר
    'I do not remember'

(3) (ata) hinHa mitHayev leshalem
    (you) COP + SUFF undertake to-pay
    (אתה) הנך מתחייב לשלם
    'You undertake to pay'

(4) (ani) zaHárti
    (I) V + 1st s. SUFF
    (אני) זכרתי
    'I remembered'

אין *en* is discussed in detail with other negators in chapter 29. Thus this chapter focuses on הוא *hu* and זה *ze* (-הנ *hin-* is ordinarily possible wherever *hu* is possible)[4] For their agreement, see 18.2.4 and 18.3.1.

Copula vs. pronoun

הוא *hu*, זה *ze* and their inflections act both as copulas and as pronouns meaning 'he, it' etc. (see ch. 7). A distinction must therefore be drawn between example (1), with its *copula*, and examples (2,3), with the noun set off earlier in the sentence and taken up again by what is a *subject pronoun*:[5]

(1) ha-méleH hu general   המלך הוא גנרל
         COP   'The King is a general'

(2) ha-méleH - **hu** general   המלך - **הוא** גנרל
              PRONOUN   'The King - **he** is a general'

(3) gam ha-méleH safek im **hu** yofia   גם המלך ספק אם **הוא** יופיע
                     PRONOUN   'It is doubtful if the King will appear
                                                        either'

16.3 'Be' in noun+noun clauses

16.3.1 Introduction

Noun+noun clauses are those where both subject and predicate are a noun (or a noun with modifiers), eg.:

ha-malka hi sémel amami   המלכה היא סמל עממי
   N   N
NOUN PHR NOUN PHR   'The queen is a popular symbol'

Noun+noun clauses are of seven types, as shown in the following table:

subject	+	predicate	example	
Pronoun	+	Noun	at ktsina	את קצינה 'You are an officer'
Possessive definite noun	+	Noun	aHoti ktsina	אחותי קצינה 'My sister is an officer'
Proper noun	+	Noun	orit ktsina	אורית קצינה 'Orit is an officer'
Definite noun with ה - *ha-* 'the'	+	Noun	ha-pamot hu matana	הפמוט הוא מתנה 'The candlestick is a gift'
Indefinite noun	+	Noun	betsim hen mazon nóaH	ביצים הן מזון נוח 'Eggs are a convenient food'
Non-specific phrase	+	Noun	ma she-maftía ze kolo	מה שמפתיע זה קולו 'What's surprising is his voice'
Subordinate clause	+	Noun	lehizdaken ze busha?	להזדקן זה בושה? 'Is getting old a disgrace'?

These seven types of subject all differ in the behaviour of their copula. Following details of this, an explanation will be offered in the form of a 'scale of definiteness' in 16.3.9.

16.3.2 'Be' with a pronoun as subject

Neither definite pronouns, eg. אני *ani* 'I' and זה *ze* 'it', nor indefinite pronouns, eg. מישהו *míshehu* 'someone', generally use a copula:

aHshav ani ha-sho'er	עכשיו אני השוער
now I the goalkeeper	'Now I'm the goalkeeper'

zot ha-siba	זאת הסיבה
that the reason	'That is the reason'

míshehu shakran	מישהו שקרן
someone liar	'Someone's a liar'

There are three important exceptions, all involving copular הוא *hu* rather than זה *ze*:

Demonstrative subject pronouns, i.e זה *ze* 'this' and its inflections, optionally allow the copula הוא *hu* (and its inflections) in most instances:[6]

hayínu ba-tanur - zé**hu** mapal	היינו בתנור - **זהו** מפל
máyim adir ba-galil	מים אדיר בגליל
	'We were at the Tanur. This **is** a huge waterfall in the Galilee'

éle **hen** ha-breHot ha-rashiyot	אלה **הן** הבריכות הראשיות
	'These **are** the main pools'

In the other two exceptions a copula is *obligatory* because the predicate is more definite than the subject: the subject may be an indefinite pronoun whereas the predicate is a definite noun (1), or the predicate may simply be not only definite but the 'given' (as against the 'new') information in the clause (2,3):

(1)	míshehu **hu** ha-ganav	מישהו **הוא** הגנב
	DEF N	'Someone **is** the thief'

(2)	az at **hi** ha-gvéret	אז את **היא** הגברת
	she-meHapéset bébisiter?	שמחפשת בייביסיטר?
		'So you **are** the lady who's looking for a baby-sitter?'

(3)	ani **hu** ze she-piHákti	אני **הוא** זה שפיהקתי
		'I **am** the one who yawned'

16.3.3 'Be' with a possessive definite noun as subject

Possessive definite nouns involve a suffixed pronoun, and are thus akin to pronouns themselves (see 16.3.2). The use of the copula depends largely on the predicate: with an *indefinite* predicate, the copula is uncommon, otherwise it is usual.

ishti (**hi**) ktsina be-tsáhal	אשתי (**היא**) קצינה בצה"ל
	'My wife **is** an officer in the Forces'

ishti **hi** ha-mearáHat maHar   אשתי **היא** המארחת מחר
'My wife **is** the hostess tomorrow'

This copula can be זה *ze* and its feminine forms (for agreement see 18.2.4) in casual usage when the predicate noun denotes someone/something already identifiable in advance, i.e 'given':[7]

mi ze baali? baali **ze** ha-baHur   מי זה בעלי? בעלי **זה** הבחור
she-nivHar la-tafkid she-ratsíta   שנבחר לתפקיד שרצית
'Who's my husband? My husband **is** the guy
who was picked for the post you wanted'

as against a case where the predicate is not a person already known (here הוא *hu* is required):

*baali **ze** aHshav ha-menahel shel ha-snif   *בעלי **זה** עכשיו המנהל של הסניף
'My husband **is** now the manager of the branch'

16.3.4 'Be' with a proper noun as subject

Whether a proper noun uses a copula depends on the predicate With an *indefinite* predicate, the copula is uncommon except where the predicate is 'heavier' (in length or complexity) than its subject, as in (3) below:[8]

(1) orit zaméret   אורית זמרת
'Orit ⟨is⟩ a singer'

(2) gam raHel íma tova   גם רחל אמא טובה
'Even Rachel ⟨is⟩ a good mother'

(3) orit **(hi)** shminístit tipusit   אורית **(היא)** שמיניסטית טיפוסית
     COP   'Orit **is** a typical eighth-grader'

But with a *definite* predicate, the copula is obligatory:[9]

orit **hi** ha-rishona   אורית **היא** הראשונה
DEF   'Orit **is** the first'

The use of זה *ze* as copula is as in 16.3.3.

16.3.5 'Be' with a definite noun as subject (with -ה *ha-* 'the')

Here the copula is common, particularly when the subject is 'heavy', i.e long or, as in example (3), complex by virtue of containing a relative clause or the like; the copula helps keep in mind that a subject noun has been mentioned (see 16.3.9, 16.5). The copula is obligatory when the predicate too is definite, as in (4):

(1) ha-mezuza (hi) matana   המזוזה (היא) מתנה
     DEF   INDEF   'The mezuza is gift'

(2) ha-míkser (hu) lo matana   המיקסר (הוא) לא מתנה
     DEF   INDEF   'The mixer isn't a gift'

(3) ha-tsaatsu'im she-arázti hem matana
    DEF   REL CLAUSE   INDEF
    הצעצועים שארזתי הם מתנה
    'The toys that I packed are a gift'

(4) ha-mezuza hi ha-matana sheli
    DEF   DEF
    המזוזה היא המתנה שלי
    'The mezuza is my gift'

Casual זה *ze* and its feminine forms are more common as copulas than in 16.3.3-4: they are found even with *indefinite* predicates, provided these are inanimate:

    ha-méHes ze sipur aHer
              INANIMATE PRED
    המכס זה סיפור אחר
    'The customs is another story'

16.3.6 'Be' with an indefinite noun as subject

Here the copula is obligatory in most usage הוא *hu* is the most flexible:

    shisha biskvítim **hem** lo aruHa
             m.pl.   m.pl.
    ששה ביסקוויטים **הם** לא ארוחה
    'Six biscuits **are** not a meal'

    betsim **hen** mazon nóaH
    f.pl.   f.pl.
    ביצים **הן** מזון נוח
    'Eggs **are** a convenient food'

    sukar **hu** klala
    m.s. m.s.
    סוכר **הוא** קללה
    'Sugar **is** a curse'

זה *ze* and its feminine forms are also common, casually, either with a 'given' predicate (see 16.3.3) or with an inanimate predicate (particularly where the subject too is inanimate):

    iton eHad **ze** me'at me'od dapim
    m.s.   m.s.
    עיתון אחד **זה** מעט מאד דפים
    'One newspaper **is** very few pages'

    sufot reamim {**ze/zu**} **tofa'a muzara**
    f.pl.   m.s./f.s.
    סופות רעמים {**זה/זו**} תופעה מוזרה
    'Thunderstorms **are** a strange phenomenon'

    rof'im **ze** mikre meyuHad
    m.pl. m.s. INANIMATE PRED
    רופאים **זה** מקרה מיוחד
    'Doctors **are** a special case'

as against:

    rof'im **hem** anashim metuHim
            ANIMATE PRED
    רופאים **הם** אנשים מתוחים
    'Doctors **are** tense people'

16.3.7 'Be' in clauses of specification, i.e. a non-specific subject

Clauses of specification involve a non-specific subject such as מה ...ש *ma-she-...* 'what...', הראשון *ha-rishon* 'the first one', הטוב ביותר *ha-tov beyoter* 'the best'. A copula is necessary – הוא *hu* in formal usage, זה *ze* otherwise (For agreement, see 18.2.4 and 18.3.1):[10]

    ma she-matrid oti **ze** ha-dam
    what that bothers me **is** the blood
    מה שמטריד אותי **זה** הדם
    'What bothers me **is** the blood'

ha-taHshir ha-ya'il beyoter   התכשיר היעיל ביותר
{**hu/hi**} tamtsit te   {**הוא/היא**} תמצית תה
'The most efficacious preparation is tea essence'

16.3.8 'Be' with a subordinate clause as subject

By 'subordinate clause' we mean infinitive clauses (eg. להגיד לו
lehagid lo 'to tell him') as well as finite clauses (eg. שיגידו לו *she-yagídu lo*
'that they will tell him'). The copula זה *ze* is required here, even in formal
usage:[11]

<u>(ze) she-en la raHamim</u> ze busha   (זה) שאין לה רחמים **זה** בושה
FINITE CLAUSE   'That she has no pity **is** a disgrace'

<u>lehizdaken káHa</u> ze davar meHubad   להזדקן ככה **זה** דבר מכובד
INF CLAUSE   'To age that way **is** an honourable thing'

16.3.9 The copula in noun+noun clauses: summary

The role of the copula is akin to that of 'agreement suffixes': rather
than having inherent meaning (in most cases), it makes it clearer where subject
ends and predicate begins. But this is at best an approximation - consider examples (1,2):

(1) ha-Hom (hu) baaya   'The heat is a problem'   החום (הוא) בעיה

(2) azbest mesukan   'Asbestos is dangerous'   אזבסט מסוכן
or 'dangerous asbestos'

(1) is clearly a whole sentence even without a copula, while (2) is allowed to be
ambiguous (either subject+predicate or a simple 'noun+modifier' phrase) with
no insistence on use of the copula.

The definiteness hierarchy

The role of the copula is rather to 'reinforce' a subject that is relatively 'indefinite' (and apparently in need of special marking, inasmuch as subjects are typically *definite*).

(1) When the subject is a pronoun - the peak of definiteness - the copula is generally not used.

Otherwise:

(2) Where the predicate is itself definite, it detracts from the 'weight' of the subject and necessitates a copula in most instances.

But where the predicate is *indefinite*:

(3) The copula is fairly uncommon with a suffixed possessive noun or proper
noun as subject.

(4) The copula is likely with a somewhat less definite subject, i.e a noun with
ה- *ha-* 'the'.

(5) The copula is obligatory with an indefinite subject. The least definite are the non-specific subject (definite only by virtue of the predicate specifying them) and especially the subject clause;[12] and it is no coincidence that the copula זה *ze* is so common with the former and obligatory with the latter (rather than הוא *hu*), for it is related to the pronoun זה *ze* which is more neuter and impersonal than the pronoun הוא *hu* (see ch. 7).

16.4 'Be' in noun+clause clauses

Subordinate clauses are akin to nouns, both as subjects (see 16.3.8) and as predicates. As predicates, where the subject is a non-specific noun (see 16.3.7), they make the copula very likely:

ha-kavana **hi** she-ha-ti'ul meyushan
CLAUSE

הכוונה **היא** שהתיעול מיושן

'The meaning **is** that the sewerage is antiquated'

ha-matara **hi** liklóa kol páam
CLAUSE

המטרה **היא** לקלוע כל פעם

'The aim **is** to score a hit every time'

Where the subject is a suffixed noun - more 'definite' - the copula is common (save where the predicate clause is 'subjunctive' rather than 'factive', see 30.2.2):

kavanaténu **hi** she-ha-shalom shone mi-du-kiyum
FACTUAL CLAUSE

כוונתנו **היא** שהשלום שונה מדו-קיום

'Our meaning **is** that peace differs from co-existence'

kavanaténu she-yeHonan shalom be-ezorénu
MODAL CLAUSE

כוונתנו שיכונן שלום באיזורנו

'Our intention ⟨is⟩ that peace be established in our region'

16.5 'Be' in noun+adjective clauses

Here the copula depends on the nature of the noun phrase and adjective phrase In any event, it is usually הוא *hu* (and its inflections).[13]

Ambiguity is a factor. Since *indefinite noun+adjective* can in principle be either a mere phrase or a whole clause, it tends to have a copula when it is a clause - in casual usage:

Hatsilim **hem** teimim   'Eggplants **are** tasty'   חצילים **הם** טעימים

Conversely, *definite noun + adjective* can only be a whole clause anyway, so a copula is unnecessary:[14]

ha-Hatsilim teimim   'The eggplants ⟨are⟩ tasty'   החצילים טעימים

However, even more crucial is the relative 'weight' of the subject and predicate, in all usage With a heavier predicate, the copula is rendered less likely, as in examples (1,2); with heavier subjects the copula is favoured, as a 'boundary marker' recalling that a subject noun has been mentioned (3):[15]

(1) Hatsilim teimim yoter   חצילים טעימים יותר
      eggplants tasty more   'Eggplants are tastier'

(2) biskvítim mele'im be-sukar   ביסקוויטים מלאים בסוכר
     biscuits full of sugar   'Biscuits are full of sugar'

(3) ha-biskvítim she-natat li etmol **hem** ayumim   הביסקוויטים שנתת לי אתמול
           SUBJ   **הם** איומים
                                         'The biscuits you gave me yesterday **are** awful'

16.6 'Be' in noun+adverbial clauses

The copula here depends on definiteness and the type of adverbial.
It cannot be זה *ze*

With a highly definite subject (pronoun, proper noun, suffixed noun) copulas
are unlikely:

moshe be-paris	'Moshe ⟨is⟩ in Paris'	משה בפריס
ani lo ba-inyanim	'I⟨'m⟩ not in the swing of things'	אני לא בעניינים
míshehu ba-Huts	'Someone⟨'s⟩ outside'	מישהו בחוץ

With a definite noun with -ה *ha-* 'the', the copula is commonly used to 'reinforce' the subject (as in 16.3.9 for noun+noun clauses) - but less often with lit-
eral adverbials of *place*:

ha-sha'on **hu** le-kishut   השעון **הוא** לקישוט
                                    'The watch **is** for decoration'

ha-magafáyim **hem** shel yáakov   המגפיים **הם** של יעקב
                                    'The boots **are** Yaakov's'

ha-matlim ba-aron   המתלים בארון
                                    'The hangers ⟨are⟩ in the closet'

The question does not arise with indefinite subjects: with or without a copula,
they are impossible:[16]

*kélev (hu) ba-salon   *כלב (הוא) בסלון
dog is in-the lounge   ('A dog is in the lounge')

*atifa na'a (hi) la-séfer   *עטיפה נאה (היא) לספר
cover nice is to-the book   ('The book has a nice cover')

16.7 'Be' with 'question words'

'Question words', eg. מי *mi* 'who', can be subject or predicate of 'be'.
The distinction is a delicate one, as they come first in the clause in either event.
This distinction is best seen as 'given' vs. 'new' information, rather than 'subject' vs. 'predicate'. In example (1) below מי *mi* 'who' may be 'given' and thus
mean 'who of certain people already under discussion?'; in example (2) מי *mi*
is definitely 'new', i.e an open 'who?':

(1)   mi   ha-bos   מי הבוס?
{ GIVEN NEW }   'Who (is) the boss?'
{ NEW   GIVEN }

(2)   mi hu ha-bos?   מי הוא הבוס?
       NEW   GIVEN   'Who is the boss?'

Only in type (2) is the copula used.

With a proper noun[17] as 'given'
Here a copula is usually required, formally הוא *hu* and casually זה
ze (for agreement see 18.2.4):[18]

   mi {hu/ze} éli?   'Who is Eli?'   מי {הוא/זה} עלי?

   ma {hi/ze/zot} Herut?   'What is liberty?'   מה {היא/זה/זאת} חרות?

   ma {hem/ze} Hukim?   'What are laws?'   מה {הם/זה} חוקים?

   efo {hi/ze} arad?   'Where is Arad?'   איפה {היא/זה} ערד?

   matay {hu/ze} purim?   'When is Purim?'   מתי {הוא/זה} פורים?

With a common noun as 'given'
Here the copula is mostly optional, though with מי *mi* 'who' it can
affect the meaning. It is usually הוא *hu*, rarely זה *ze*:

   mi ha-gavóa sham?   מי הגבוה שם?
                  'Who is the tall fellow over there?'
(expecting a proper noun in reply, eg. הדיקן *ha-dikan* 'the dean')

   mi hu ha-gavóa sham?   מי הוא הגבוה שם
                  'Who is the tall fellow over there?'
(expecting a proper noun in reply, eg. מר לוי *mar levi* 'Mr Levi')[19]

   ma (hi) ha-siba?   מה (היא) הסיבה?
                  'What is the reason?'

   éze hu ha-mivne ha-tov beyoter?   איזה הוא המבנה הטוב ביותר?
                  'What is the best structure?'
(copula obligatory)

   efo (hu) ha-sakin?   איפה (הוא) הסכין?
                  'Where is the knife?'

For places (as against people, things) the copula is uncommon:

   éfo beyto shel ha-rav?   'Where's the Rabbi's house?'   איפה ביתו של הרב?

   matay ha-kontsert?   'When is the concert?'   מתי הקונצרט?

   bat káma (hi) aHotHa?   'How old's your sister?'   בת כמה (היא) אחותך?

16.8 The copula in relative clauses, and 'hanging copulas'

Relative clauses frequently omit the relative pronoun referring back to the antecedent noun (see ch.33), thus:

ata ha-ish	she-ani rotse	אתה האיש שאני רוצה
ANTECEDENT	REL CLAUSE	
you the man	that I want	'You're the man that I want'

This includes (in casual usage) relative pronouns that would be understood as predicate of 'be':

shakranim ze ma she-ha-politikáim ha-éle	שקרנים זה מה שהפוליטיקאים האלה
	'Liars is what these politicians ⟨are⟩'

taamod éfo she-ha-paH zével	תעמוד איפה שהפח-זבל
stand where that the garbage can	'Stand where the garbage can ⟨is⟩'

However, the process of indefinite object deletion (see 15.4), which even deletes the predicate of the verb היה *haya* 'be' (1), is incapable of deleting the predicate of the present tense copula (2):

(1) enéni kohen, aval ani Hoshev   אינני כהן, אבל אני חושב
she-savi **haya**   שסבי **היה**
'I am not a priest, but I think that my grandfather **was**'

(2) *...aval ani Hoshev she-savi   ...אבל אני חושב שסבי*
'...but I think that my grandfather ⟨is⟩'

In either event, the copula itself cannot be left 'hanging' at the end of the clause (see 16.2):

tafran ze ma she-ha-shaHen hu   תפרן זה מה שהשכן הוא
hard-up is what that the neighbour is

16.9 Existential clauses: יש נמלים *yesh nemalim* 'There are ants'

Existential clauses denote 'there is...' or 'there exists...' or 'the.. is found in...':[20]

(1) yesh nemalim!   'There are ants!'   !יש נמלים

(2) yesh (et) ha-nemalim ha-éle ba-árets   יש (את) הנמלים האלה בארץ
exist (OM) the ants the these in Israel   'These ants are found in Israel'

They are a verb+noun phrase construction.[21] The verb is usually יש *yesh* (not a copula) for the present tense and a form of היה *haya* 'be' for other tenses. The verb precedes the noun, except for contrast. This in itself does not make the noun the *object* of the verb, but in fact casual Hebrew treats it as such (see further 15.2) by inserting the 'object marker' את *et* when the noun is definite, as in example (2) above Formal Hebrew tends not to,[22] which reflects the fact that formally the existential verb must agree openly with the noun in all tenses but the present, as in examples (1,3), and even there it can agree sometimes (see 18.2.2 for details) - and all verbs agree with their *subject*:

(1)   **hayu** nemalim   'There were ants'   **היו** נמלים
    pl.   pl.

(2)   תברר באיזה אבקת ניקוי "יש" (ה)תמונות של השחקנים ישנם

tevarer be-éze avkat nikuy $\genfrac{}{}{0pt}{}{\text{yesh}}{\text{yeshnam (pl.)}}$ (ha-)tmunot shel ha-saHkanim

    'Check up in which washing powder there are (the) pictures of the players'

In casual usage, however, the verb היה *haya* sometimes fails to agree, i.e it is frozen as 3rd masculine singular, especially when there is a definite noun introduced by את *et* (18.2.2, examples 3,4).

The negative of יש *yesh* is never לא יש* *lo yesh (as against לא היה... *lo haya...* 'was not...', ...הוא לא *hu lo...* 'is not...'), but rather אין *en*:

    en nemalim   'There aren't ⟨any⟩ ants'   אין נמלים

Where there is a noun accompanied by an adverbial of place, no verb is needed in formal Hebrew, provided the adverbial comes first and the noun is 'quantified':[23]

    be-shida zot shesh megerot   בשידה זאת שש מגירות
    in chest-of-drawers this six drawers   'In this chest-of-drawers are six drawers'

A quite distinct construction is 'noun+agreeing יש *yesh*, אין *en* or היה *haya*' denoting 'is in, is present'. This is a subject+verb construction in every sense, with standard word order, though clearly related to existentials (for agreement, see 18.2.2):

    hi hayta aval hi **enéna** aHshav   היא היתה אבל היא **איננה** עכשיו
    she was but she **is-not** now   'She was in but she **isn't in** now'

Another distinct construction is the 'situational generic' (described in 17.3). This can use certain nouns or adjectives as clauses in their own right, a kind of predicate without a subject. Existential יש *yesh* is not used here, nor אין *en* in the negative, but rather לא *lo* 'not'; in other tenses היה *haya* is used, as a tense marker:

    kenire she-HósheH kvar   כנראה שחושך כבר
    apparent that darkness already   'Apparently it's dark already'

16.10   'Have' clauses

'Have' clauses are structurally akin to existential clauses: they are generally as illustrated below. The verb is יש *yesh* (or negative אין *en*) in the present tense and a form of היה *haya* in other tenses:

le-míri   yesh   priHa   למירי יש פריחה
POSSESSOR 'HAVE' POSSESSED   'Miri has a rash'
PREP PHR   V   N PHR
to Miri exists rash

or:

yesh   le-míri   priHa   יש למירי פריחה
'HAVE' POSSESSOR   POSSESSED   'Miri has a rash'
V   PREP PHR   N PHR
exists to Miri rash

Thus, as in existentials, the verb generally precedes the noun phrase; the added element in 'have' clauses is the -ל *le-* preposition phrase, which may either precede or follow the verb but *must* precede the noun phrase[24] (i.e 'possessor' precedes 'possessed', as in English 'have'). However, where the 'possessor' is a suffixed pronoun (a 'clitic', see 15.7), the usual non-contrastive order is verb+'possessor'+'possessed':

yesh la priHa   יש לה פריחה
exists to-her rash   'She has a rash'

As in existentials, the 'possessed' noun is treated as the object in casual Hebrew by insertion of the 'definite object marker' את *et* (examples (1,2)); and even formal usage tacitly concedes this: it avoids using את *et* but it also tends to avoid *not* using it, especially with a pronoun (examples (3,4)), by having recourse to some different construction (such as example (5)):[25]

(1)   yiye lánu et ha-néshek bekarov   יהיה לנו את הנשק בקרוב
       will-exist to-us OM the weaponry shortly 'We will have the weaponry shortly'

(2)   yiye lánu oto bekarov   יהיה לנו אותו בקרוב
       will-exist to-us it (OBJ) shortly   'We will have it shortly'

(3)   yiye lánu ha-néshek bekarov   יהיה לנו הנשק בקרוב
       will-exist to-us the weaponry shortly   'We will have the weaponry shortly'

(4)   *yiye lánu hu bekarov   *יהיה לנו הוא בקרוב
       will-exist to-us it (SUBJ) shortly   ('We will have it shortly')

(5)   yiye lánu bekarov   יהיה לנו בקרוב
       will-exist to-us shortly   'We will have it shortly'

As for agreement, in formal and some casual usage the 'have' verb agrees with its 'possessed' noun (which ordinarily follows it, see above), as in (1) below, but casually the verb may be frozen into 3rd masculine singular, especially where there is את *et*, as in (2).[26] This is as in existentials; the difference is that 'have' clauses do not allow יש *yesh* to take suffixes (3), these being reserved for 'existentials' in the narrow sense of the word:

(1)   hayta li brera?   !היתה לי ברירה
       f.s.   f.s.   'Did I have a choice?'

(2) haya li gam et ha-kosot ha-éle   היה לי גם את הכוסות האלה
     m.s.   f.pl.   'I also had these glasses'

(3) *yeshnam lánu harbe sugim   *ישנם לנו הרבה סוגים
     m.pl   m.pl.   ('We have many types')

The same 'adverbial' inversion is available as in existentials, and without a verb:

le-yisra'el milyon nesi'im   לישראל מליון נשיאים
to Israel million presidents   'Israel has a million presidents'

FURTHER READING

Azar 1976, 1977: ch.4, 1978; Berman 1978: ch.6, 1980b; Hayon 1971, 1972, 1973; Rubinstein 1968; Sadka 1981; Schwarzwald 1982a; Turkel 1976; Ziv 1976.

17. Ellipsis and subject-less clauses

17.1 Introduction

The lack of a subject, verb or object is sometimes due to general processes avoiding repetition: 'conjunction reduction' and 'gapping', as in examples (1,2) below, are described in chapter 35.[1]

(1) ata lokéaH oto o **mash'ir oto**?　　　**!אתה לוקח אותו או משאיר אותו**

'Are you taking it or **leaving it**?'

(2) ha-gvarim Hovshim kova'im　　　הגברים חובשים כובעים
ve-ha-nashim mitpaHot　　　**והנשים - מטפחות**

'The men wear hats **and the women kerchiefs**'

But sometimes more restricted processes of ellipsis are at work; and sometimes the lack of a subject is not a matter of ellipsis but of a fundamentally subject-less verb or predicate

17.2 Ellipsis of the definite and the indefinite

The omission of subject pronouns is described in 7.3. They are already explicitly marked in the past and future tense affixes, and here the separate subject pronouns are often omitted - the 1st and 2nd person pronouns meticulously so in formal usage, the 3rd person pronoun less often and only when referring to *people*:

ha-aHot hevía me'il.　hayta nekia ve-na'a　היתה נקיה ונאה .האחות הביאה מעיל
　　　　　　　　*haya naki ve-na'e　*היה נקי ונאה

the nurse brought coat.　was (f.) clean and nice
　　　　　　　　*was (m.) clean and nice
　　　　　　　　'The nurse brought a coat. She (*it) was clean and nice'

The *object* may be omitted if just mentioned, provided it is *non-specific* and the previous mention was indefinite:[2]

im at hizmant tayar(im) habáyta,　　　אם את הזמנת תייר(ים) הביתה,
　　　INDEF　　　　　　　　גם לי מותר להזמין
gam li mutar lehazmin　　　'If you've invited (a) tourist(s) home,
　　　　　　　　I can also invite ⟨one/some⟩'

aHarey she-éytan matsa késef,　　　אחרי שאיתן מצא כסף,
kulam matsu　　　　　　　כולם מצאו
　　　　　'After Eytan found money, they all found ⟨some⟩'

17.3 Subject-less generics

In place of a *generic subject* denoting 'things in general' or 'people in general', Hebrew often can, and sometimes must, do without a subject. This is not ellipsis: no repeated material is being omitted and indeed the subject-less construction is often the basic construction.

Generic things: situational and experiential

Verbs, adjectives and nouns describing the situation or its effect on feelings ('experience') need no subject if a generic 'it' (i.e no reference to any particular noun) is intended (cf. 7.11):

yadáti she-tov po	'I knew that ⟨it's⟩ fine here'	ידעתי שטוב פה

Subject זה *ze* 'it' is sometimes added colloquially:

yadáti she-ze tov po	'I knew that it's fine here'	ידעתי שזה טוב פה

Further examples of predicates needing no subject:[3] חם *Ham* 'it's hot', נקי *naki* 'it's clean', צפוף *tsafuf* 'it's crowded', נחמד *neHmad* 'it's nice', קשה *kashe* 'it's hard', מזל *mazal* 'it's lucky', חבל *Haval* 'it's a pity', אכפת *iHpat* 'it matters', ...ש חזקה *Hazaka she..* 'it can be assumed that...', כיף *kef* 'it's fun', מפריע לי *mafría li* 'it bothers me'.

By contrast, certain verbs and other predicates *never* have a subject. Most express a feeling or experience, using -ל *le-* (the dative marker) rather than the 'direct object marker' את *et* for the person involved - thus suggesting a less deliberate action by an impersonal 'agent', namely a non-specific 'situation', while at the same time the person involved is a passive experiencer:[4]

tov **lo** aHshav fine **to-him** now	טוב לו עכשיו 'He's fine now'

meshaamem **le**-miryam bores **to** Miriam	משעמם למרים 'Miriam's bored'

but:

ze meshaamem et miryam it bores ᴏᴍ Miriam	זה משעמם את מרים 'It (i.e something specific) bores Miriam'

Further examples (when used without -ל *le-*, some of these do take a subject): רע לי *ra li* 'I feel bad', קר לי *kar li* 'I'm cold', קשה עלי *kashe alay* 'it's hard for me', בא לי *ba li* 'I fancy', מסתדר לי *mistader li* 'I'm managing', מתבלבל לי *mitbalbel li* 'I'm getting confused', ...ש מוטב *mutav she..* 'it is better that...', ...אם די *day im...* 'it is sufficient if...', אפשר *efshar* 'it's possible'. One verb that takes את *et* is צריך *tsariH*: צריך את אלה *tsariH et éle* 'There is a need for these'.

Other predicates never introduced by a subject זה *ze* 'it' but usually 'anchored' by an adverbial of time or place are terms for telling the time or date and certain other 'environmentals':

oy - aHshav éser!	אוי - עכשיו עשר!
oh - now ten!	'Oh no, it's ten o'clock!'

ata yodéa she-(ha-sha'a) éser va-réva?	אתה יודע ש(השעה) עשר ורבע?
you know that (the hour) ten and quarter?	'Do you know that it's 10.15?'

kenir'e she-HosheH ba-Huts	כנראה שחושך בחוץ
apparent that darkness outside	'It's apparently dark outside'

A further class of 'non-activity' verb, expressing 'having' and 'being', is generally treated as subject-less in casual usage, for the item 'possessed' or 'existing' acts as object in certain respects - see 15.2 and 16.9-10:

yesh **baayot**	יש **בעיות**
OBJ	'There are **problems**'

en li et ha-baaya ha-zot	אין לי את הבעיה הזאת
there-isn't to-me OM the problem the this	'I haven't got this problem'

Similarly, חסר *Haser* 'is lacking', מגיע לי *magía li* 'I'm entitled to'.

Generic people

A *3rd person masculine plural* verb or adjective with no subject is a sign of a *generic* subject. What 'generic' means varies with context; it can be much less general than English 'one' or 'you':[5]

ba-yamim ha-hem, kshe-**hitatslu**, neenshu	בימים ההם, כשה**תעצלו**, נענשו
	'In those days, when **one was idle**, one was punished'

kshe-**atsbaniyim**, kashe lilmod	כשע**צבניים**, קשה ללמוד
	'When **you're upset**, it's hard studying'

yod'im?	'Does anyone (here) know?'	יודעים?

But a predicate *noun* requires a subject, thus ruling out the following:

*im **atslanim**, kashe lilmod	*אם **עצלנים**, קשה ללמוד
	('If you're **a lazybones**, it's hard studying')

An *infinitive* not preceded by a noun that could be its subject is generally credited with a generic subject.[6] As with the 3rd person plural, 'generic' varies with context:

kal lishon	קל לישון
INFIN	'It's easy to sleep' (i.e. for one/you/me.. to sleep)

ze keday laséget	זה כדאי לסגת
	'It's worth withdrawing'

efshar liftóaH Halon?	אפשר לפתוח חלון?
	'Is it possible to open a window?' (i.e. for one/you/me to open a window)

FURTHER READING
Berman 1979b, 1980b, 1982a; Bin-Nun 1979; Schwarzwald 1979b.

18. Agreement in the clause

18.1 Introduction

Agreement operates (1) betwen the nucleus noun of a noun phrase and its adjectives, quantifiers etc., and (2) between the subject (occasionally the predicate) of a clause and its verb, adjective etc. The former are described in chapter 12; this chapter deals with the latter.

18.2 Agreement with the subject

The subject is the controlling element in most agreement. The predicate very occasionally determines agreement for copulas and 'neuter' subject pronouns (see 18.3).

18.2.1 Verb and adjective agreement

Verbs and adjectives always agree with their subject, if any.[1] Past and future tense verbs agree for gender, number and person; present tense verbs, and adjectives, agree for gender and number. There is no agreement for definiteness. For example:

at	teasi	mefunéket	את תיעשי מפונקת
f.s.	FUT(2nd f.s.)	ADJ(f.s.)	'You will become spoilt'
you	will-become spoilt		

hem	yeasu	mefunakim	הם ייעשו מפונקים
m.pl.	FUT(3rd m.pl.)	ADJ(m.pl.)	'They'll become spoilt'
they	will-become spoilt		

Details of the inflectional forms of verbs and adjectives are set out in chapters 40 and 41, respectively.

A subject-less (impersonal) verb or adjective uses the 'unmarked,' i.e 3rd person masculine singular, form - or the 3rd masculine plural form where there is an *animate* impersonal subject:

lo hitHashek li	לא התחשק לי
3rd m.s.	'I didn't fancy'
not fancied to-me	

yitragzu	יתרגזו
3rd m.pl.	'⟨They⟩ will be angry'

Subject or object?

To state that verbs or adjectives agree with their subject is to beg the question of what is the subject. For instance, the verb חסר *Haser* 'lack' agrees with the noun ordinarily following it, in formal but not in casual usage:

Formal:

Haser lo séHel		חסר לו שכל
m.s. m.s.		'He lacks sense'
lacks to-him sense		

Hasera lo em		חסרה לו אם
f.s. f.s.		'He lacks a mother'
lacks to-him mother		

Casual:

Haser lo	séHel	חסר לו שכל
	em	אם
		'He lacks sense'
		a mother'

It might at first appear that this verb does not agree with its subject in casual usage However, the fact that many verbs and adjectives do not need or permit a subject (eg. התחשק *hitHashek* 'fancy', illustrated above) raises the possibility that casual חסר *Haser* 'lack' takes just an object, hence its non-agreement. And indeed it requires the object marker את *et* when the noun is definite:

Casual:

| Haser lo et ha-késef | חסר לו את הכסף |
| lacks to-him oM the money | 'He lacks the money' |

Thus verbs and adjectives may be said to agree with their subject in all usage

Further examples are discussed more fully in 15.2, including the tricky case of יש/היה *yesh/haya* 'there is/was' (whose agreement is discussed in the next subsection).

18.2.2 Agreement of the existential verbs יש *yesh*, אין *en* 'there are/aren't'

יש *yesh* and אין *en* serve as present tense existential verbs, meaning 'there is/are' (or '...is/are present') and their negative, respectively; in the other tenses one uses the regular forms of היה *haya* 'be' and its negative לא היה *lo haya*.[2] For existentials in general, see 16.9.

There are two existential uses, involving different types of agreement. In the sense 'is present, is not present', in the present tense, יש *yesh* and אין *en* are used freely with a 3rd person (human) subject. They follow it and agree with it in gender and number, inflecting as follows:

m.s.	yeshno	ישנו	enénu[3]	איננו
f.s.	yeshna	ישנה	enéna	איננה
m.pl.	yeshnam	ישנם	enam	אינם
f.pl.	yeshnan (F)	ישנן	enan (F)	אינן

sávta yeshna	סבתא ישנה	hem enam	הם אינם
Grandma is-present (f.s.)		they not-present (m.pl.)	
	'Grandma's in'		'They aren't in'

But after a 1st or 2nd person pronoun only casual usage employs יש *yesh* and אין *en*, often still with their 3rd person suffix rather than ישני *yeshni*, איננּי *enéni* etc.:

im ani **enénu**, az ani metalfen	אם אני **איננו**, אז אני מטלפן
If I **am-not-present**, then I ring	'If **I'm not there**, I ring'

For the other tenses, similarly following the subject, היה *haya* is used in its regular gender, number and person inflections:

ata **hayita** lifney réga?	אתה **היית** לפני רגע?
2nd m.s.	'**Were** you **in** a moment ago?'

In the looser sense 'there is, there exists' and its negative, one again uses יש *yesh*, אין *en* and היה *haya*, but preceding the noun (except for contrast):

haya minyan? - minyan lo haya	היה מניין? - מניין לא היה
was prayer-quorum? - prayer-quorum not was	'Was there a quorum? - There wasn't'

אין *en* 'there is not' does not inflect. Nor does יש *yesh* in the sense 'there is/are', but in the stronger sense 'there exist(s)' it can optionally inflect as in the paradigm above: ישנו *yeshno*, ישנה *yeshna* etc.:

yesh	mazkirot	מזכירות	יש
en			אין
	'There are		
	'There aren't ⟨any⟩	secretaries'	

yesh(nam) kshayim o en?	ישׁ(נם) קשיים או אין?
	'Are there difficulties or aren't there?'

היה *haya* agrees and inflects fully, except that in casual usage - with the strong tendency to treat existential nouns as object, by inserting the object marker את *et* for 'definite' nouns, as in examples (1, 2) below - היה *haya* sometimes does not agree, especially where את *et* is present (3, 4). See also 15.2.

(1) yesh sham gam et sávta   יש שם גם את סבתא
     there-is there also OM Grandma   'There's also Grandma there'

(2) ba-árets en et ha-baaya ha-zot   בארץ אין את הבעיה הזאת
     in Israel there-isn't OM the problem the this   'Israel doesn't have this problem'

(3) haya (m.s.)   היה
     hayta (f.s.) sham simHa gdola   היתה שם שמחה גדולה
              f.s.   'There was great revelry there'
     was there revelry great

(4) gam kan haya et ha-baaya ha-zot   גם כאן היה את הבעיה הזאת
          m.s. OM   f.s.   'Here too there was such a problem'
     also here was the problem the this

18.2.3   Predicate noun agreement

Gender

When a noun is predicate in a noun+noun clause (see 16.4), it some-times agrees with its subject *in gender*, if the noun concerned is ordinarily capable of an intrinsic change in natural gender:

Hevrat bóing hi ha-**yatsranit** ha-biladit   חברת בואינג היא **היצרנית** הבלעדית
f.s.   f.s.   The Boeing Company is the sole **manufacturer**'

mif'al nésher hu ha-**yatsran** ha-biladi   מפעל נשר הוא **היצרן** הבלעדי
m.s.   m.s.   'The Nesher Works is the sole **manufacturer**'

as against

Hevrat bóing hi **taagid** anaki   חברת בואינג היא **תאגיד** ענקי
f.s.   m.s.   'The Boeing Company is a giant **corporation**'

While תאגיד *taagid* 'corporation' is solely masculine, יצרן *yatsran* 'manufac-turer' has a feminine counterpart יצרנית *yatsranit*. So predicate noun agree-ment is favoured, where possible, even for the sake of purely 'grammatical' rather than 'natural' gender.

Another noun capable of a change in natural gender is חבר *Haver* 'member'; hence it agrees with its subject even when strictly inanimate and non-natural:

ha-i ha-katan hu **Haver** ba-um   האי הקטן הוא **חבר** באו"ם
m.s.   m.s.   'The tiny island is a **member** of the UN'

maurítsius hi **Havera** ba-um   מאוריציוס היא **חברה** באו"ם
f.s.   f.s.   'Mauritius is a **member** of the UN'

But no agreement takes place when the predicate noun itself has a natural gen-der that has to be expressed:

ha-tsipor ha-zot hi **avaz**   הציפור הזאת היא **אווז**
f.s.   m.s.   'That bird is a **goose**'

Which nouns allow intrinsic change in gender is a complex matter (see ch. 39). Thus, for example, Israeli military rank has feminine forms in casual usage, but not officially:

aHoti hi {rabat/rabátit}   אחותי היא {רב"ט/רב"טית}
f.s.   m.s. f.s.   'My sister is a corporal'

Number

Predicate nouns do not 'agree' in number. Thus in:

ha-tsiporim ha-éle hen **avazim**   הציפורים האלה הן **אווזים**
f.pl.   m.pl.   'Those birds are **geese**'

plurality is an intrinsic semantic choice for the predicate, unaffected by the grammar of the subject noun.

18.2.4 Copula agreement

By 'copula' are meant the particles -הוא, זה, אין, הנ *hu, ze, en, hin-* (and their inflections), meaning 'is/are (not)' and introducing a noun or adjective (see 16.3), as in:

ha-sha'on **hu** matana	'The clock **is** a present'	השעון **הוא** מתנה
éyfo **ze** báyit-vegan?	'Where **is** Bayit Vegan?'	איפה **זה** בית-וגן?

הוא *hu*

The copula הוא *hu* and its inflections היא *hi* (f.s.), הם *hem* (m.pl.), הן *hen* (f.pl. F)) generally take their gender and number from the subject:

ha-sha'on **hu** matana		השעון **הוא** מתנה
m.s. m.s.		'The clock **is** a present'
ma **hi** Herut?		מה **היא** חירות?
f.s. f.s.		'What **is** freedom?'
ma **hem** nimusim?		מה **הם** נימוסים?
m.pl. m.pl.		'What **are** manners?'
éyfo **hen** ha-bahurot?		איפה **הן** הבחורות
f.pl. f.pl.		'Where **are** the girls?'

Sometimes agreement is controlled by the predicate noun instead (see 18.3.1.).

זה *ze*

By contrast, copula זה *ze* allows its feminine and plural forms (זו / זאת *zo/zu/zot* and אלה / אלו *éle/élu* respectively) to be used for agreement on a limited scale only, as described below:

In *declarative* clauses (except specificationals, see below), copula זה *ze* is strictly casual. It agrees for gender, not number[4] - but usually with its predicate, not its subject (examples (1,2)); and where the subject is generic, זה *ze* tends to be uninflected (examples (3,4)):[5]

(1) ha-báyit shelHa zot dugma tova		הבית שלך זאת דוגמה טובה
m.s. SUBJ f.s. f.s. PRED		'Your house is a good example'
(2) ha-kapiyot zu matana		הכפיות זו מתנה
f.pl SUBJ f.s. f.s. PRED		'The spoons are a present'
(3) herayon ze lo maHala		היריון זה לא מחלה
zu		זו
m.s. SUBJ m.s./f.s. NEG f.s. PRED		'Pregnancy is not a disease'
(4) diburim ze lo maasim		דיבורים זה לא מעשים
m.pl. SUBJ m.s. NEG m.pl. PRED		'Words aren't deeds'

In *specificational* clauses, i.e sentences of the kind 'x is y' where it is the very identity of 'x' that is being established, זה *ze* is not necessarily casual. It agrees for number as well as gender with its predicate, or more casually is uninflected:[6]

אלה קטעים שכולם אוהבים המוסיקה שבחרתי
זה

ha-músika she-baHárti	éle ze	ktaim she-kulam ohavim
f.s.	{pl./m.s.}	m.pl.

'The music I picked is pieces everyone loves'

אלה המסיבות של ליל שבת מה שאני שונא
זה

ma she-ani sone	éle ze	ha-mesibot shel lel shabat
m.s.	{pl./m.s.}	f.pl.

'What I hate is Friday night parties'

In clauses beginning with an *interrogative* word, the copula in casual Hebrew is commonly uninflected זה *ze* - in cases where the noun is the *subject*, i.e where the clause is defining or identifying a given thing or person or locating a place:[7]

ma ze yófi? m.s.	'What is beauty?'	מה זה יופי?
ma ze Herut? f.s.	'What is freedom?'	מה זה חירות?
ma ze halaHot? f.pl.	'What are laws?'	מה זה הלכות?
mi ze ha-banim sham? m.pl.	'Who are the boys over there?'	מי זה הבנים שם?
éfo ze zámbia? f.s.	'Where is Zambia?'	איפה זה זמביה?

In formal as well as casual מה/מי... *mi/ma...* 'who/what...' questions, copula זה *ze* can be used in gender agreement with a singular subject, as in examples (1,2). Formal Hebrew also uses מי אלה... *mi éle..* 'who are..', as in (3). In all usage, the copula הוא *hu* and its inflections can be used instead:

(1)	ma zot Herut fs. f.s.	'What is freedom?'	מה זאת חירות?
(2)	mi zo ha-tabaHit ha-Hadasha? f.s. f.s.		מי זו הטבחית החדשה? 'Who's the new cook?'
(3)	mi éle ha-baHurim ha-shezufim? pl. m.pl.		מי אלה הבחורים השזופים? 'Who are the sun-tanned fellows?'

אין *en*, **-הנ-** *hin-*

Formal Hebrew can use אין *en* as a negative copula meaning 'not',[8] and suffixed -הנ *hin-* occasionally as a positive copula.[9] Following their subject, they agree with it in gender, number and person. (As with inflected verbs, the agreement inflections enable one to omit the subject pronoun.) After the inflection table, we give examples:

1st s.	eni/enéni	איני/אינני	hineni	הנני
2nd m.s.	enHa	אינך	hinHa	הנך
2nd f.s.	eneH	אינך	hinaH	הנך
3rd m.s.	eno/enénu	אינו/איננו	hino	הנו
3rd f.s.	ena/enéna	אינה/איננה	hina	הנה
1st pl.	enénu	איננו	hinenu	הננו
2nd m.pl.	enHem	אינכם	hinHem	הנכם
2nd f.pl.	enHen	אינכן	hinHen	הנכן
3rd m.pl.	enam	אינם	hinam	הנם
3rd f.pl.	enan	אינן	hinan	הנן

ha-malka **hina** merutsa f.s. 3rd f.s.	'The queen **is** satisfied'	המלכה **הנה** מרוצה
ani **enéni** merutse 1st s.	'I **am not** satisfied'	אני **אינני** מרוצה

Unlike the other copulas, which simply signify 'be', the negative אין *en* can (immediately) precede the subject. In this case there is no agreement:

en ha-malka merutsa	'The queen **is not** satisfied'	**אין** המלכה מרוצה
en ani merutse	'I **am not** satisfied'	**אין** אני מרוצה

18.2.5 Reflexive and reciprocal pronoun agreement
See 7.12 and 7.13.

18.3 Agreement with the predicate
הוא *hu* and זה *ze* and their respective inflections are both pronouns (see 7.3) and copulas. In 18.2.4 copular זה *ze* was seen to agree sometimes with its predicate; the same holds for copular הוא *hu* and for זה *ze* and הוא *hu* as subject pronouns. This section deals with predicate agreement as a whole

18.3.1 Agreement by the copula
זה *ze* often agrees with the predicate (1) Casual זה *ze* in most declaratives agrees for gender with a singular predicate (examples (1,2) in 18.2.4), except that after a generic subject it tends to be uninflected (examples (3,4) there). (2) Specificational זה *ze* in formal or casual usage either agrees for gen-

der and number with its predicate or (more casually) remains uninflected; see the examples in 18.2.4.

הוא *hu* in most declaratives can optionally agree for gender with its predicate, in casual usage,[10] if both subject and predicate are singular. (Otherwise it agrees with its subject.)

ha-shóHad	hu hi	baaya		בעיה	הוא היא	השוחד
m.s.	{m.s./f.s.}	f.s.				'Bribery is a problem'

הוא *hu* in specificationals tends to agree with the predicate:

ma she-mad'ig **hi**	sheelat ha-máyim	מה שמדאיג **היא** שאלת המים
m.s. f.s.	f.s.	'What is worrying **is** the question of water'

18.3.2 Agreement by the subject

The pronoun זה *ze*, when *subject* of a noun+noun clause, usually agrees with the predicate noun, in gender and number. This holds both for the 'empty' זה *ze* that means no more than the verb 'to be', as in (1), and for זה *ze* that refers to a foregoing noun, as in (2):

(1) taamin li,   תאמין לי, זאת

zot   sheela meanyénet, matay hu yevater   שאלה מעניינת, מתי הוא יוותר
f.s. SUBJ f.s. PRED
    AGREEMENT
'Believe me, it ⟨is⟩ an interesting question when he's going to give up'

(2)   היינו בגבעת המורה. זהו הר בודד בגליל
hayínu be-givat ha-more zehu   har boded ba-galil
f.s.   m.s.SUBJ m.s. PRED.
                            AGREEMENT
'We were at Givat Hamore **It** is an isolated mountain in the Galilee'

However, with appropriately adjusted intonation, pronoun זה *ze*, be it subject, object or whatever, can agree with whatever it is referring back to:

ze *ken* sheela kasha	זה כן שאלה קשה
m.s. f.s. PRED	'That *is* a difficult question'

Agreement

הוא *hu* too, as subject of a noun+noun clause, will on occasion agree with the predicate:[11]

uvda hi, she-ha-hanaka adifa   עובדה היא, שההנקה עדיפה
f.s.   f.s.
PRED SUBJ
fact it that the breast-feeding preferable   'It is a fact [=the fact is] that breast-feeding is preferable'

18.4   The nucleus in control of agreement

The noun phrase controlling agreement may contain more than one noun. If the nouns are coordinated, e.g. by ‏-ו‎ *ve-* 'and', they are often counted together for purposes of agreement - see 18.6.3. If, conversely, they qualify one another (as in the following example), it is usually the first noun that is the 'nucleus' and thus controls agreement; here it is 'the attorney', not 'the accused', that is angry:

ha-praklit shel ha-neeshamim ka'as   ‏הפרקליט של הנאשמים כעס‎
  N(m.s.)   N(m.pl.)   v(m.s.)   'The attorney of the accused was
NUCLEUS └_____↑   angry'
          AGREEMENT

Occasionally in genitive constructions, i.e. construct and ‏של‎ *shel* 'of' phrases (see ch.6), the first word is not functioning as a noun but as a quantifier, determiner or even adjective:

me'ot   horim ba'im   ‏מאות הורים באים‎
QUANT m.pl.   m.pl.   'Hundreds of parents come'
hundreds parents come

ikar ha-sakana hurHeka   ‏עיקר הסכנה הורחקה‎
DET f.s.   f.s.   'The basic danger has been removed'
basis the danger has-been-removed

yófi shel tsmidim hayu la   ‏יופי של צמידים היו לה‎
ADJ   m.pl.   pl.   'She had beautiful bracelets'
beauty of bracelets were to-her

In such cases, the first word is not the nucleus; the first true noun controls agreement. Details are given in 8.8. (quantifiers), 9.2 (determiners) and 12.2 (adjectives).

18.5   Agreement of peripherals

Having described agreement of the central elements in the clause - subject, predicate, copula, object pronouns (reflexive and reciprocal) - we discuss the agreement of structurally peripheral elements with the subject or the object.

18.5.1   Complements of 'impression verbs'

Certain verbs denoting 'impression' may take an adjective. When the adjective describes the impression itself, it employs a non-agreeing masculine singular form, i.e. it is a kind of 'manner adverb' (see 21.4):

at   nir'et   nehedar   ‏את נראית נהדר‎
f.s. v(f.s.)   ADJ(m.s.)   'You look gorgeous'

hi   nishmáat muzar   ‏היא נשמעת מוזר‎
f.s. v(f.s.)   ADJ(m.s.)   'She sounds odd'

hem margishim tov   הם מרגישים טוב
m.pl. v(m.pl.)   ADJ(m.s.)   'They feel good'

Compare מראה נהדר *mar'e nehedar* 'a gorgeous look', קול מוזר *kol muzar* 'an odd voice', הרגשה טובה *hargasha tova* 'a good feeling'.

When describing the subject, however, the adjective agrees with it, as if it were simply predicate to the subject:

at nir'et nehedéret   את נראית נהדרת
f.s. v(f.s.) ADJ(f.s.)   'You look a gorgeous sort'

hi nishmáat muzara   היא נשמעת מוזרה
f.s. v(f.s.)   ADJ(f.s.)   'She sounds an odd person'

18.5.2 Complements of 'state verbs'

Certain verbs incorporating a notion of 'being' may take an adjective or noun agreeing with the subject (or, for some verbs, the object). Such verbs include היה *haya* 'be', הפך *hafaH* 'become', נעשה *na'asa* 'become', עשה *asa* 'make', נשאר *nish'ar* 'remain', נחשב *neHshav* 'be considered'. Thus:

hem   hayu / naasu   kenim   הם היו / נעשו כנים
m.pl.   ADJ(m.pl.)
                       'they were / became honest'

asíti otam   kenim   עשיתי אותם כנים
v   OBJ(m.pl.) ADJ(m.pl.)   'I made them honest'

A kindred construction is the 'circumstance' predicate (see 21.6), notably in formal Hebrew, linked by comma or pause to a preceding clause:

karánu itonim,   קראנו עיתונים,
kosesim et tsipornéynu me-rov metiHut   **כוססים** את ציפורנינו מרוב מתיחות
v(m.pl.)
       'We read newspapers, **chewing** our nails in our tension'

hiHnásnu ota mi-ba-Huts, **kofet** ve-**ro'édet**   הכנסנו אותה מבחוץ, **קופאת ורועדת**
f.s.   v(f.s.)   v(f.s.)
     'We brought her in from the outside, **frozen** and **shivering**'

The predicate relates to and agrees with the main subject, or even, where context assists, with the main object (as in the second example).

18.5.3 Complements of 'perceptional verbs'

ראה *ra'a* 'see', שמע *shama* 'hear', תפס *tafas* 'catch', מצא *matsa* 'find' are among verbs expressing perception. Their object can be followed by a participle phrase, a phrase relating to and agreeing with it (see 21.6, 30.3):

tafásti otam   mitpartsim la-dira   תפסתי אותם מתפרצים לדירה
v   OBJ(m.pl.) v(m.pl.)   'I caught them breaking into the apartment'
        AGREEMENT

When such verbs are in the passive, this predicate will naturally agree with the subject:

hem nir'u mitpartsim la-dira	הם נראו מתפרצים לדירה
m.pl. v v(m.pl.)	'They were seen breaking into the apartment'

AGREEMENT

18.6   Some complications in agreement

18.6.1   Agreement with 'neutral' pronouns

אני *ani* 'I', אנחנו *anáHnu* 'we' are masculine *or* feminine, with the suffix of the predicate often deciding the issue, e.g. אני קם *ani kam* (m.s.) vs. אני קמה *ani káma* (f.s.) 'I get up'. In casual Hebrew this is often true of the other *plural* personal pronouns, i.e. אתם *atem* 'you', הם *hem* 'they', and any other words incorporating these pronouns (e.g. אותם *otam,* להם *lahem*); thus:[12]

atem holHot?	!אתם הולכות
f.pl.	'Are you going?'

hem maskimot	הם מסכימות
f.pl.	'They agree'

18.6.2   Agreement with 'de-pluralized' nouns

Number agreement is geared to the form of a noun, not to its meaning. Thus שמיים *shamáyim* 'sky', צוהריים *tsohoráyim* 'lunchtime' are plural and קבוצה *kvutsa* 'team', ועד *váad* 'committee' singular. But several plural nouns, when preceded by certain numerals, actually tend to be singular in form, although *plural* for purposes of agreement (see 39.12). For example:

	avru	עברו
esrim yom	v(m.pl)	עשרים יום
	*avar	*עבר
N(m.s.)	v(m.s.)	
twenty day passed		'Twenty days passed'

	soarot	סוערות
shmonim shana	ADJ (f.pl)	שמונים שנה
	*soéret	*סוערת
N (f.s.)	ADJ (f.s.)	
eighty year stormy		'Eighty stormy years'

18.6.3   Agreement with coordinated phrases

Conjunction

A conjunction of masculine and feminine nouns requires masculine agreement. This amounts to 'neuter' gender. Thus:

ha-kir ve-ha-tikra meluHlaHim	הקיר והתקרה מלוכלכים
N (m.s.) N (f.s) ADJ (m.pl.)	'The wall and the ceiling are dirty'

dorit, sára ve-shimon meHayeHim			דורית, שרה ושמעון מחייכים
f.	f.	m.	v (m.pl.)	'Dorit, Sara and Shimon are smiling'

Regarding the conjunction of two different 'persons': agreement requires the lowest person present; thus with 2nd and 1st person, agreement requires 1st person (plural), while 2nd and 3rd person require 2nd person, and so on:

ani ve-ata
ata ve-ani neshane et ha-kol   אני ואתה
1st pl.   אתה ואני   נשנה את הכל

'I and you
'You and I   will change it all'

at ve-ha-baHur ha-keréaH asitem et ze			את והבחור הקרח עשיתם את זה
f.s.	m.s.	2nd m.pl.	'You and the bald guy did it'

ani ve-hem yarádnu   אני והם ירדנו
1st pl.   'I and they got out'

Disjunction

A disjunction of nouns ('A or B', 'not A but B') complicates agreement.

A or B. In questions, two uses of או *o* 'or' are found. Thus in:

ha'im yisrael o mitsráyim be-makom sheni?   האם ישראל או מצרים במקום שני?
'Are Israel or Egypt in second place?'

או *o* 'or' may be strictly 'either / or' (the reply being ישראל *yisrael* 'Israel' or מצרים *mitsráyim* 'Egypt') or not (the reply: כן / לא *ken / lo* 'yes / no'). In both events there is apparently no clear-cut rule for agreement: when או *o* is 'either / or', the last noun tends to control agreement:

o nóami o sára titstareH lavo   או נעמי או שרה תצטרך לבוא
v (f.s)   'Either Naomi or Sara will have to come'

ha'im yisrael o mitsráyim nitsHa?   האם ישראל או מצרים ניצחה?
v (f.s.)   'Did Israel or Egypt win?'

When או *o* takes the second sense, the tendency is to do as with conjunction:

kos te o uga yeraanenu oti   כוס תה או עוגה ירעננו אותי
v (pl.)   'A cup of tea or a cake will perk me up'

ha'im yisrael o mitsráyim nitsHu?   האם ישראל או מצרים ניצחו?
v (pl.)   'Did Israel or Egypt win?'

Not A but B. Here again there is no clear-cut rule The second element tends to determine agreement. Where there is a clash in person, 3rd person is likely:

lo amos éla yeHezkel amar zot   לא עמוס אלא יחזקאל אמר זאת
v (m.s.)   'Not Amos but Ezekiel said this'

	haya		היה
lo ani éla ata	3rd m.s.	ashem אשם	לא אני אלא אתה
1st s. 2nd m.s.	hayíta		היית
	2nd m.s.		'Not I but you were to blame'

A favoured alternative is to hold back the '*éla* phrase' to the end:

lo ani hayíti ashem éla ata	לא אני הייתי אשם אלא אתה
1st s.	'Not I was to blame but you'

18.6.4   1st and 2nd person nouns

Following *subject pronoun* + *'non-specific' predicate*, such as אני
ש- היחידי *ani ha-yeHidi she-* 'I am the only one that ...', אתה האדם השני ש-
ata ha-adam ha-sheni she-...' you are the second person who ...', the verb in
the relative clause has the option of agreeing with the *subject* of the main clause
(instead of with the antecedent):

ani ha-yeHidi {she-nehenéti/she-nehena}   {אני היחידי {שנהניתי/שנהנה

SUBJ ANTECEDENT   1st s.   3rd.m.s.

REL CLAUSE   'I am the only one who enjoyed it'

AGREEMENT

ani ze {she-nehenéti/she-nehena}   {אני זה {שנהניתי/שנהנה

    1st s.   3rd m.s.   'I am the one that enjoyed it'

SUBJ   REL CLAUSE

AGREEMENT

ata ha-adam ha-sheni she-{badákta / badak} oto   אתה האדם השני ש

      2nd m.s. 3rd m.s.   {בדקת/בדק} אותו

SUBJ   REL CLAUSE

AGREEMENT

      'You are the second person who has checked him'

It is as if the subject pronoun had transferred its 'person' to the non-specific
predicate, creating 1st and 2nd person *nouns*. (Ordinarily, 1st and 2nd person
is only in personal pronouns.)

A kindred construction is the 'cleft construction': זה *ze* + *pronoun* + *clause*
(see 37.9), as in:

ze ata (she-)mesaken otánu	זה אתה (ש)מסכן אותנו
it you (that) endanger us	'It's you that endanger us'

The personal pronoun can be considered as antecedent to a relative clause,
which thereby agrees with it:[13]

ze ata   (she-)sikánta otánu   זה אתה (ש)סיכנת אותנו

PRONOUN   2nd m.s.   'It's you that endangered us'

AGREEMENT

      REL CLAUSE

18.7 The function of agreement

While agreement usually adds nothing to meaning, it sometimes serves to mark out the structure of a sentence and occasionally even intrinsically affects gender and definiteness.

(1) Agreement is sometimes crucial to the major distinction between a complete clause and a mere phrase:

ha-léHem raH	הלחם רך
the bread soft	'The bread is soft'

ha-léHem **ha-ṛaH**...	...הלחם הרך
‾‾‾‾‾‾ AGREEMENT	'The soft bread...'
the bread **the** soft...	

(2) Gender and number agreement sometimes shows which modifier belongs to which noun:

baalat ha-kélev ha-tokpanit	בעלת הכלב התוקפנית
f.s. m.s. f.s.	'The aggressive owner of the dog'
owner the dog the aggressive	

baalat ha-kélev ha-tokpani	בעלת הכלב התוקפני
f.s. ⎿ m.s. m.s. ⏌	'The owner of the aggressive dog'
N PHR	

(3) Definiteness agreement allows one to distinguish 'definite' and 'indefinite' use of proper nouns (see 5.3.2):

lemáan yisrael yafa	למען ישראל יפה
INDEF	'For a beautiful Israel'
for Israel beautiful	

lemáan yisrael **ha**-yafa	למען ישראל היפה
DEF	
for Israel **the** beautiful	'For beautiful Israel'

(4) A similar distinction can be made between masculine and feminine nouns that look the same:[14]

yóna lo nimtsa	יונה לא נמצא
m.s.	'Yona [boy's name] isn't here'

yóna lo nimtset	יונה לא נמצאת
f.s.	'Yona [girl's name] isn't here'

ma {amar / amra} rosh ha-memshala?	מה {אמר/אמרה} ראש הממשלה?
m.s. f.s.	'What did the Prime Minister say?'

FURTHER READING
Azar 1977: ch.4; Berman 1974; Ornan 1979a: 7.6; Rosén 1965; Schwarzwald 1979a,c, 1982b; Ziv 1976.

19. Preposition phrases

19.1 Introduction

Nouns or subordinate clauses are sometimes introduced by a preposition. This expresses their relationship to the verb, adjective or other sentence part which they complement (or qualify). What a preposition introduces is termed its 'complement' (which can be regarded as its 'object'). For example:

nikfots be-shabat
     PREP COMP
נקפוץ בשבת
'We'll come by **on** Shabat'

ha-gézer me-ha-marak bishvileH
     PREP COMP
הגזר מהמרק בשבילך
'The carrot from the soup is for you'

titsak kdey she-yinbaH
     PREP   COMP
תצעק כדי שינבח
'Shout so that he barks'

Prepositions have no distinctive form, and often resemble construct nouns (as explained in 42.1).[1] Much of the detail that follows, and much more, is examined from a different angle in the chapters on object phrases (ch. 15), adjunct adverbials (ch. 21) and adverbial clauses (ch. 32).

19.2 Semantic relationships expressed by prepositions

The semantic relationships expressed by prepositions are diverse: time and space relationships of various kinds, cause, purpose, and so on. There are also 'non-semantic' relationships, helping to indicate the meaning of some other word, as in examples (1, 2), or just indicating the structure of the clause, as in (3):

(1) tishmor et   ha-késef
      V   PREP   N
תשמור את הכסף
'Keep the money'

(2) tishmor al   ha-késef
      V   PREP   N
תשמור על הכסף
'Guard the money'

(3) ha-shir mazkir le- yitsHak et   ha-shir
      SUBJ   V   PREP IND OBJ   PREP DIR OBJ
      ha-aHer
השיר מזכיר ליצחק את השיר
האחר
'The song reminds Yitshak of the other song'

Many such relationships can or must be expressed by prepositions. Among semantic and non-semantic relationships *almost always* expressed by prepositions are:[2]

Location:
Hake **be**-malon   'Wait **in** ⟨a⟩ hotel'   חכה **במלון**
Destination:
sa **le**-malon   'Go **to** ⟨a⟩ hotel'   סע **למלון**
Cause:
eleH **mishum** she-tsariH 'I'll go **because** I must'   אלך **משום** שצריך
Indirect object:
tistakel **be**-ze   'Look **at** this'   תסתכל **בזה**

Among relationships *sometimes* expressed by prepositions are:

Duration:
Hake (**lemésheH**) shavúa 'Wait (**for**) a week'   חכה (**למשך**) שבוע
Purpose:
Hake (**kdey**) she-teda   'Wait **so** you'll know'   חכה (**כדי**) שתדע
Possession:
ale (**shel**) péraH   'a petal **of** a flower'   עלה (**של**) פרח

The chief relationships not involving prepositions are:

Subject:
HósheH ba   'Darkness came'   חושך בא
Indefinite direct object:
kaH kosit   'Take ⟨a⟩ glass'   קח כוסית
Complement of 'be':
hayiti sayar   'I was ⟨a⟩ scout'   הייתי סייר

See 15.3 for detailed discussion of the various degrees to which prepositions are meaningful or meaningless. The present chapter begins with the internal structure of preposition phrases, followed by their role as objects and adverbials.

19.3   Internal structure of the preposition phrase

19.3.1   Preposition phrases vs. verb and noun phrases

The preposition is verb-like in one respect and noun-like in certain others. Like verbs, it requires the clauses it introduces to begin with a conjunction (see 19.3.3 for exceptions), usually -ש *she-*:

Preposition:
aHarey she- yafsiku   אחרי שיפסיקו
    CONJ   CLAUSE   'after they stop'

Verb:
hitsáti she- yafsiku   הצעתי שיפסיקו
    CONJ   CLAUSE   'I suggested that they stop'

Like nouns, a preposition directly taking a personal pronoun will suffix it (see 42.2). Verbs do so occasionally (see 15.5), and nouns very often (see 6.4), but verbs usually prefer instead to insert את *et* before the pronoun or noun that they introduce, while nouns often insert של *shel*:

Preposition:
  bishvil**Hem**   'for **you**'   בשבילכם
Verb:
  minu**Hem**   'appointed **you**'   מינוכם
  minu et**Hem**   מינו אתכם
Noun:
  beyt**Hem**   '**your** house'   ביתכם
  ha-báyit shela**Hem**   הבית שלכם

and not בית אתם* *מינו אתם *בשביל אתם **bishvil atem,* **minu atem,* אתם בית*
*beyt atem with the 'free' pronoun אתם *atem* 'you'. The actual suffixes too are
usually the same as for nouns (see 42.2).

19.3.2   Noun or clause as complement

Many prepositions require a noun as their complement, many a
clause, and many take either[4] - somewhat arbitrarily. The only major restriction
is that where a preposition introduces an *object*, rather than an adverbial, this
will generally be an object *noun*; with an object clause, the expected preposition
is usually omitted (see 19.5). For the conjunction - ש *she-* introducing the clause,
see 19.3.3.

In the following table are listed some prepositions used with particular complements.

Only with nouns			Only with clauses		
étsel	'"chez"'	אצל	af-al-pi	'although'	אף-על-פי
bemésheH	'during'	במשך	baasher	'insofar as'	באשר
be-	'in, with'	ב-	biHdey	'in order'	בכדי
be'ad	'for'	בעד	ho'il	'since'	הואיל
Huts mi-	'except'	חוץ מ-	heyot	'seeing as'	היות
le-	'to, for'	ל-	ke-[1]	'when'	כ-
le'or	'in view of'	לאור	kdey[2]	'in order'	כדי
legabey	'concerning'	לגבי	keshem	'just as'	כשם
lelo	'without'	ללא	(mi)kevan	'since'	(מ)כיוון
leumat	'as against'	לעומת	mishum	'because'	משום
milvad	'besides'	מלבד	mipney[3]	'because'	מפני
avur	'for'	עבור	al-menat	'in order'	על-מנת
al-pi	'according to'	על-פי	af[4]	'although'	אף
im	'with'	עם	uvilvad	'provided'	ובלבד
	etc.			etc.	

With nouns and clauses					
lifney	'before'	לפני	aHarey	'after'	אחרי
mi-	'than'	מ-	biglal[5]	'because'	בגלל
me'az	'since' (time)	מאז	(mi)bli	'without'	(מ)בלי
ad	'until'	עד	bimkom	'instead of'	במקום
al	'on, about'	על	bishvil	'for'	בשביל
al-af	'despite'	על-אף	kmo	'like'	כמו
toH-kdey	'while'	תוך-כדי	lamrot	'despite'	למרות
ilmaley[6]	'were it not for'	אלמלא			
	etc.				

Notes:

[1] -כ *ke-* takes a noun in the separate (though kindred) senses כשלג *ke-shéleg* 'like snow', כרב *ke-rav* 'as a rabbi'. Similarly כמו *kmo* 'while' and 'like'.

[2] כדי *kdey* takes a noun in the sense כדי עשר מעלות *kdey éser maalot* 'as much as ten degrees'.

[3] מפני *mipney* takes a noun formally.

[4] אף *af*, בלבד *bilvad* and three other 'focus adverbs' introduce clauses in this way, and are perhaps not prepositions at all.

[5] בגלל *biglal* takes a clause in casual usage

[6] אלמלא *ilmaley* takes the full rather than suffixed pronoun: אלמלא אתה *ilmaley ata* 'were it not for you', as if a quasi-conjunction. Other 'if' words are conjunctions.

Thus the following are ungrammatical:

bemésheH she-aHlu CONJ	*במשך שאכלו ('during [=while] they ate')
mishum shvita	*משום שביתה ('because of a strike')

Alternatives to a complement clause

Prepositions taking nouns but no clauses can frequently take a verbal noun or a gerund (see 30.5-6) instead, particularly in formal Hebrew:

le'or **hitpatruto**	'in view of **his resignation**'	לאור **התפטרותו**
le'or **heyoto** po	'in view of **his being** here'	לאור **היותו** פה

Another common way of avoiding לאור ש- * *le'or she-* 'in view of + clause' and other such ungrammaticalities is to use זה ש- *ze she-* and (with 'governed prepositions', see 19.4) כך ש- *kaH she-* or (implying a fact) העובדה ש- *ha-uvda she-* 'the fact that':

le'or ha-uvda she-avart   לאור העובדה שעברת
in-view-of the fact that you-passed

Huts mi-ze she-hu po   חוץ מזה שהוא פה
except for it that he here   'except for the fact that he's here'

ani mitnaged le-HaH she-teshalem maHar   אני מתנגד לכך שתשלם מחר
I object to it that you'll-pay tomorrow   'I object to you paying tomorrow'

19.3.3 Complement clauses in detail

Finite and infinitival clauses

A few prepositions can take an infinitival clause, as do many verbs (see 30.4 on infinitivals as against 30.2 on finite clauses): (1) purpose prepositions, i.e כדי *kdey*, בכדי *biHdey*, על־מנת *al-menat*, בשביל *bishvil* 'in order (to)'; and (2) 'quasi-negative' prepositions, i.e במקום *bimkom* 'instead of' and (מ)בלי *(mi)bli* 'without' (see 32.8 and 13.10 respectively). Examples are:

kámti kdey likro	'I got up in order to read'	קמתי כדי לקרוא
barHu bimkom lehilaHem	'They fled instead of fighting'	ברחו במקום להילחם
mezog bli livHosh	'Pour without stirring'	מזוג בלי לבחוש

The conjunction in complement clauses

In finite clauses. -ש *she-* (joined to the next word) normally introduces the complement clause:

kfi she-tsipíti	'as I expected'	כפי שציפיתי
bli she-yadat	'without you(r) knowing'	בלי שידעת

-ש *she-* or -ו *ve-* (distinct from -ו *ve-* 'and') are found with the following:

me'aHar	she- ve-	'since'	מאחר	-ש -ו	heyot	she- ve-	'since'	היות -ש -ו
ho'il	she- ve-	'since'	הואיל	-ש -ו	be-mida	she- ve-	'if'	במידה -ש -ו

כי *ki* and אשר *asher* are occasionally used in formal אף כי *af ki* or -אף ש *af she-* 'although' and formal עד כי *ad ki* or עד אשר *ad asher*, as well as neutral עד ש *ad she-* 'until'. Formal כאשר *kaasher* 'when' is idiomatically related to -כש *kshe-*. באשר *baasher* 'insofar as' has no corresponding -בש *be-she*[5]

No conjunction need be used with a few prepositions: מאז (-ש) *me'az (she-)* 'since' (in time), בעוד (-ש) *be'od (she-)* 'while', בטרם (-ש) *betérem (she-)* 'before', כאילו (-ש) *ke'ílu (she-)* 'as if'.

The following never use a conjunction, and are probably best considered conjunctions in their own right, for they take clauses but never nouns: אם, אילו, לו *im, ilu, lu* 'if', אלמלא *ilmale* and its synonyms 'if...not', אלא־אם־כן *éla-im-ken* 'unless', אם כי *im ki* 'even though',[6] כי *ki* 'because', שכן, שהרי *she-ken, she-harey* 'for [= because]', שמא *shéma* 'lest'. However, למען *lemáan* 'so that, for the sake of' takes clauses and nouns.

For a general discussion of conjunctions in subordinate clauses, see 30.2.1.

In infinitival clauses. No conjunction is used with infinitivals, save in certain object clauses (which do not belong here).

19.3.4 Where there is no complement

Like verbs (15.4), prepositions are absolutely/weakly transitive (require or do not require a complement). The few prepositions not requiring a complement are acting casually. The missing complement is understood as a *specific* noun (contrast אכלתי *aHálti* 'I've eaten (something)'):

hizmant kafe im Halav o **bli**?	הזמנת קפה עם חלב או **בלי**?
you-ordered coffee with milk or **without**?	'Did you order coffee with milk or **without**?'

ata no'em **lifney** o aHarey?	אתה נואם **לפני** או **אחרי**?
you speak **before** or **after**?	'Are you speaking **before** or **after**?'
(more common: לפני-כן, לפניו *lifnéy-Hen, lefanav* etc. 'beforehand')	

but not, for example:

> *yesh leHa máshehu liHtov al?   ‏*יש לך משהו לכתוב על?‏
> exists to-you something to-write on?   ('You have something to write on?')

> *ze ha-tik she-báti im   ‏*זה התיק שבאתי עם‏
> this the bag that I-came with   ('This is the bag I came with')

19.3.5 Pro-clauses as complements: ‏כן‏ *ken,* ‏כך‏ *kaH,* ‏זה‏ *ze*

Pro-words representing clauses, as described in 7.5, can never take
the form of a suffix. Thus:

> heviu et gad u-viglal **ze** hiskámnu   ‏הביאו את גד ובגלל זה הסכמנו‏
> ‾‾‾‾‾‾‾‾‾‾‾‾‾
>   CLAUSE   PRO-CLAUSE   'They brought Gad and because of **it**
>   we consented'

not: ...‏ובגללו‏...* *u-viglalo...* '...and because-of-**it**...'

Certain prepositions require ‏כך‏ *kaH* as their pro-clause, others ‏כן‏ *ken,* others
even ‏זה,זאת‏ *ze, zot* - with no apparent reason, except an historical one; the
table on page 000 gives the pattern. In ‏בכך‏ *be-HaH* 'thus', ‏לכן‏ *laHen* 'therefore', ‏על-כן‏ *al-ken* 'therefore', ‏עם-זאת‏ *im zot* 'notwithstanding', the preposition has an idiomatic sense.

19.4 'Governed' vs. 'free' prepositions

The complex distinction between 'preposition in object' and 'preposition in adverbial' ('governed' vs. 'free' prepositions) is made in detail in 15.3.
(Many verbs can take a double object - see 15.7.) The syntactic and semantic
choice among governed prepositions is discussed in 15.5-6, while 32.3-13 set
out the variety of free prepositions.

Briefly, verbs and adjectives (and the action/state nouns derived from them)
generally require a particular preposition in front of their object or complement:

> ra'u **et** david   ‏ראו **את** דוד‏
>   OBJ   'They saw David'

> amádnu **al** ha-kshayim   ‏עמדנו **על** הקשיים‏
>   OBJ   'We comprehended the difficulties'

Only a few prepositions function in this way; sometimes they are meaningful,
sometimes not:

> et, be-, le-, al, im, mi-, el, ke-,   ‏את, ב-, ל-, על, עם, מ-, אל, כ-,‏
>   mipney, aHarey   ‏מפני, אחרי‏

But these (except ‏את‏ *et*) and the numerous other prepositions are used with a
well-defined meaning in adverbials; for example, the particular ones just listed
can mean 'in, to, on, with, from, to, as, because, after'.

19.5 Omitting the governed prepositions

Governed prepositions drop in certain environments, for they are often meaningless and are in any event determined by the verb or adjective This section describes two constructions where they must drop, and mentions two prepositions particularly prone to omission.

Before an object clause

Governed prepositions are always omitted before a finite clause, and usually before an infinitive[8] (except in very casual speech). The same applies with the pro-clause ככה/כך *kaH/káHa* if it precedes its verb, as in (6) below:

(1) ani ge'e be- hatslaHata　　　　　　　　אני גאה בהצלחתה
　　　　　　PREP N　　　　　　　　　　　'I am proud **of** her success'

(2) ani ge'e {she- / *be- she-} hitsliHa　　אני גאה {ש/*בש}הצליחה
　　　　　CONJ PREP CONJ CLAUSE　　　'I am proud that she succeeded'

(3) paHádti **mi-** nehiga　　　　　　　　פחדתי מנהיגה
　　　　　　PREP N　　　　　　　　　　'I was afraid **of** driving'

(4) paHádti linhog　　　　　　　　　　　　פחדתי לנהוג
　　　　　CLAUSE　　　　　　　　　　　'I was afraid to drive'
　　(*very casually*: **mi-**linhog)　　　　　(מלנהוג
　　　　　　PREP+CLAUSE

(5) ani asuk **be-** tsvia　　　　　　　　　אני עסוק בצביעה
　　　　　PREP　　　　　　　　　　　　'I'm busy painting'
　　(*very casually*: ani asuk **be-**litsbóa)　(אני עסוק בלצבוע

(6) téHef neda, o kaH ani metsapa　　　　תכף נדע, או כך אני מצפה
　　　　　　　　　　　　　　　　　　'Soon we'll know, or so I expect'

A few verbs governing מ- *mi-* retain it before an infinitive, notably נזהר *nizhar* 'beware of', מנע *mana* 'prevent', נמנע *nimna* 'be prevented', and (מ- *mi-* optional) נמנע *nimna* 'refrain'.

Governed prepositions do not take gerunds even though gerund phrases are functionally like noun phrases rather than clauses (see 30.5).

Active and passive

Many 'active' verbs have a 'passive' counterpart in another *binyan* (verb pattern). Thus:

x shamar y ~ y nishmar al-yedey x　　　x שמר y ~ y נשמר על-ידי x
　　　　　　　　　　　　　　　　　'x keep y ~ y be kept by x'

x kibel y ~ y hitkabel al-yedey x　　　x קיבל y ~ y התקבל על-ידי x
　　　　　　　　　　　　　　　　　'x receive y ~ y be received by x'

Choice of prepositions for pro-clause

Only כך *kaH*	Only כן *ken*	Only זה *ze*	זאת *zot* / זה *ze*	כך *kaH* / זה *ze*
אחר־כך aHar-kaH[1] 'afterwards'	אף־על־פי־כן af-al-pi-Hen 'nevertheless'	בגלל זה biglal ze 'because of it'	לעומת זאת/זה leumat zot/ze 'as against this'	בכך, בזה be-HaH/ze 'thus'
לשם כך leshem kaH 'for that purpose'	אחרי־כן aHarey-Hen[2] 'afterwards'	. . . *and other prepositions*	למרות זאת/זה lamrot zot/ze 'despite this'	בתוך כך/זה betoH kaH/ze 'within this'
משום כך mishum kaH 'because of this'	כמו־כן kmo-Hen 'likewise'			על כך/זה al kaH/ze 'about this'
תוך־כדי־כך toH-kdey-kaH 'in the course of this'	לאחר מכן leaHar mi-ken 'afterwards'			על־ידי כך/זה al-yedey kaH/ze 'by this'
	לפני־כן lifney-Hen 'beforehand'			
	מפני־כן mipney-Hen 'because of it'			
	קודם לכן kódem la-Hen 'beforehand'			

Notes:

1 אחר־כך aHar-kaH and אחרי־כן aHarey-Hen mean both 'after what happened' and 'in a short while' (i.e. 'after *now*').

2 זה אחרי aHarey ze 'afterwards' and זה לפני lifney ze 'beforehand' are found casually.

The 'active' object usually becomes subject in the passive, and the governed preposition must drop from any such object that becomes subject. For details, see 14.6 and 14.8.

Two commonly omitted prepositions: את *et*, ‑ב *be‑*

את *et* is more restricted than other governed prepositions: it requires a 'definite' object, and has no 'free' meaning of its own.[9] Also, not only is את *et* the most easily omissible preposition when switching active to passive but it alone can ‑ or must ‑ be omitted in telegraphic usage (eg. headlines), with object suffixes, in relative clauses and after action nouns. For details, see 15.5.

‑ב *be‑* 'with, in' can specify the nature of an action: כיסה בשלג *kisa be‑shéleg* 'cover with snow', חבוש בכובע *Havush be‑kova* 'dressed in a hat', עטף בניילון *ataf be‑náylon* 'wrap in plastic' etc. ‑ as against the means: כיסה באת *kisa be‑et* 'cover with a spade', עטף בחבל *ataf be‑Hével* 'wrap with string'. This '*be‑* of specification' is sometimes omitted formally; see 15.8.

19.6   Order within the preposition phrase

Prepositions must precede their complement. Nothing can normally intervene between preposition and complement (as aginst verb and object), thus not:

*amlits	al	**afilu** dégem ze	*אמליץ על **אפילו** דגם זה
	PREP	N	

rather:

amlits **afilu**	al	dégem ze	אמליץ **אפילו** על דגם זה	
	PREP	N	'I'll **even** recommend this model'	

Only occasionally can the complement be dropped, leaving a 'hanging' preposition (see 19.3.4), and never can the complement actually be moved away from the preposition (unlike English). Therefore, not:

*mi rávta im?	*מי רבת עם?
who you‑argued with?	'Who were you arguing with?'

but rather:

im mi rávta?	עם מי רבת?
with who you‑argued?	

FURTHER READING
Azar 1972; Ben-Asher 1974; Cole 1976b; Glinert 1982b; Ornan 1979a: 116f; Rosén 1955: 115ff., 1966a: 184ff; Sadka 1981: 78.

20. Degree words and comparatives

20.1 Introduction

This chapter describes the behaviour and effect of a small, semi-productive class of words expressing 'degree', eg. מאד *me'od* 'very', קצת *ktsat* 'a little', יותר *yoter* 'more'. Though traditionally classed with adverbs of time, manner etc., they are distinct semantically and syntactically.

Semantically, degree words supply the information 'to what extent', with respect to properties, emotions and the like:

hu kol-kaH dabran	'He's so talkative'	הוא כל-כך דברן
hem kol-kaH heelívu oto	'They so offended him'	הם כל-כך העליבו אותו

By contrast, with a verb such as דיבר *diber* 'talk' a degree word would be inappropriate - there is no 'property' to measure; instead one might measure 'how long' or 'how often':

*hem kol-kaH dibru ito	('They so spoke to him')	*הם כל-כך דיברו אתו
hem dibru **harbe**	'They spoke **a lot**'	הם דיברו **הרבה**

Syntactically, it must be emphasized that 'degree' is not restricted to adjectives. Some Hebrew verbs and some, but not all, adjectives denote or imply a property and thus take a degree word; the same is true for some adverbials and quantifiers, but nouns generally do not take a degree word:[1]

Verb:
me'od **ahávti** otam

מאד **אהבתי** אותם
'I very much **liked** them'

Adverb:
ze mudbak yoter miday **lemáala**

זה מודבק יותר מדי **למעלה**
'It's stuck too **high**'

Quantifier:
en **harbe** me'od

אין **הרבה** מאד
'There isn't very **much**'

As against:

Nouns:
*zu me'od **Hutspa**

*זו מאד **חוצפה**
('It's very **a cheek**')

*zu hayta dey **hatslaHa**   *זו היתה די **הצלחה***
('It was quite **a success**')

*gmishut **kol-kaH**   *גמישות **כל-כך***
('so **flexibility**')

tsaar me'od   ***צער* מאד**
('**very** regret')

Nouns can instead be graded by, say, an adjective, as in חוצפה **גדולה** *Hutspa* ***gdola*** 'a **great** cheek', by an adverbial phrase such as במידה רבה *be-mida raba* 'to a great extent', במידה מסויימת *be-mida mesuyémet* 'to a certain extent', or by determiner as in גמישות **כזאת** *gmishut **kazot*** '**such** flexibility'.[2]

Degree words are further restricted *positionally*. Generally they directly precede their adjective or verb,[3] or follow it at any distance (not all do both - see 20.2), whereas a comparable *adverbial* has no such restrictions (see 21.2.1); thus:

ani me'od maariH nashim ka'éle   אני **מאד** מעריך נשים כאלה
SUBJ DEGREE V   OBJ PHR   '**I very much** admire women like that'

ani maariH **me'od** nashim ka'éle   אני מעריך **מאד** נשים כאלה
          DEGREE   'I **very much** admire women like that'

ani maariH nashim ka'éle **me'od**   אני מעריך נשים כאלה **מאד**
                 DEGREE   'I **very much** admire women like that'

be-mida raba ani maariH nashim ka'éle   **במידה רבה** אני מעריך נשים כאלה
ADVERBIAL   SUBJ V   OBJ PHR
                   '**To a great extent** I admire women like that'

ani **be-mida raba** maariH nashim ka'éle   אני **במידה רבה** מעריך נשים כאלה
      ADVERBIAL   '**To a great extent** I admire women like that'

ani maariH **be-mida raba** nashim ka'éle   אני מעריך **במידה רבה** נשים כאלה
          ADVERBIAL   '**To a great extent** I admire women like that'

ani maariH nashim ka'éle **be-mida raba**   אני מעריך נשים כאלה **במידה רבה**
             ADVERBIAL   '**To a great extent** I admire women
                                 like that'

Degree words are easily confused with quantifiers (see ch.8). Indeed, the same word is often employed for both, eg. יותר *yoter* 'more', קצת *ktsat* 'a little', טיפ-טיפה *tip-tipa* 'a tiny bit'. Quantifiers denote quantity for nouns or extent in time for verbs (see ch.21 'Adjunct adverbials'); quantifiers that are *not* degree words include הרבה *harbe* 'a lot', עוד *od* 'more':

*hu gavóa harbe   ('He's tall a lot')   *הוא גבוה הרבה*

Quantifiers must normally *follow* their verb, whereas most degree words can directly precede it:

Degree:

| hu | yoter Hole / Hole yoter | miméni | 'He's more ill than me' | הוא יותר חולה ממני / חולה יותר |
| hu | me'od Hole / Hole me'od | | 'He's very ill' | הוא מאד חולה / חולה מאד |

Quantity (of time):

| hu Hole **yoter** miméni | 'He's ill **more** than me' | הוא חולה **יותר** ממני |
| hu Hole **harbe** | 'He's ill **a lot**' | הוא חולה **הרבה** |

20.2 Degree words with verbs and adjectives

20.2.1 Positioning

The following is a list of notable degree words, by meaning type and position *vis-à-vis* their adjective or verb.

Most degree words treat adjectives and verbs alike:

i-efshar lehanot miménu **beyoter**
V
impossible to-enjoy it **extremely**   'It is impossible to enjoy it very much'   אי-אפשר ליהנות ממנו **ביותר**

kashe **beyoter**
ADJ
hard **extremely**   'It is extremely hard'   קשה **ביותר**

ze **dey** matsHik oti
V
it **quite** amuses me   'It quite amuses me'   זה **די** מצחיק אותי

ze yiye **dey** matsHik
ADJ
it will-be **quite** amusing   'It will be quite amusing'   זה יהיה **די** מצחיק

But מדי *miday* 'too' is one degree word that tends to follow verbs but not necessarily adjectives. When such words as יותר *yoter* 'more' and מספיק *maspik* 'enough' act as 'time quantifiers', they usually *follow*; see the end of 20.1. Where the degree word can either precede or follow its verb or adjective, to follow is often somewhat more formal. Otherwise the table on page 00 shows that neither the register of usage nor the meaning type has a marked effect on the positioning of degree words.

Directly preceding		Following	Both	
Interrogative and exclamatory				
káma	כמה 'how!'		keHol sheyiye	ככל שיהיה 'however'
ma	מה 'how!' (F)			

Directly preceding		Following		Both	
(ad) káma	(עד) כמה 'how?'				
Comparative					
káma ... she-efshar	... כמה שאפשר 'as ... as possible' (c)	ha-Hétsi	החצי 'half' (c)	yoter	יותר 'more'
		leen aroH	לאין ערוך 'incomparably' (F)	paHot[1]	פחות 'less'
Superlative					
haHi	הכי 'most' (c)	beyoter	ביותר 'most' (F)		
Boosters					
ko	כה 'so' (F)	bimyuHad	במיוחד 'particularly'	kol-kaH	כל-כך 'so'
kaze	כזה 'so' (c)[2]	beyoter	ביותר 'extremely'	ad-kdey-kaH	עד-כדי-כך 'so'
méa aHuz	מאה אחוז 'totally' (c)	laHalutin	לחלוטין 'totally'	legámrey	לגמרי 'totally'
yotse min ha-klal	יוצא מן הכלל 'exceptionally' (c)	máshehu lo normáli	משהו לא נורמלי 'incredibly' (c)	me'od	מאד 'very'
				nora	נורא 'very' (c)
Downtoners					
tip-tipa	טיפ-טיפה 'a tiny bit' (c)	kólshehu	כלשהו 'slightly' (F)[2]	ktsat	קצת 'slightly'
		kim'a	קמעה 'slightly' (F)	me'at	מעט 'slightly' (F)
		kaze	כזה 'sort of' (c)[2]		
Others					
dey/day	די 'quite'	lemaday	למדי 'quite' (F)	yaHasit	יחסית 'relatively'
maspik	מספיק 'enough'	dayo	דיו 'sufficiently'(F)[2]	paHot o yoter	פחות או יותר 'more or less'

Directly preceding	Following	Both
יותר פחות (עד) כמה ש (ad) kámá she- yoter paHot 'as ... as possible' little..	miday	מדי 'too'
yoter miday 'too' (c) יותר מדי		
miday 'too' (c) מדי		

Notes:
1 פחות *paHot* is particularly formal when following its verb or adjective
2 This agrees with the same noun as its adjective, eg. היא מוזרה כזאת *hi muzara kazot* 'She's sort of strange' and הסמים חזקים דיים *ha-samim* (N pl.) *Hazakim dayam* (DEG pl.) 'The drugs are **sufficiently** powerful'.

20.2.2   Details of individual types of degree word

Interrogative and exclamatory

מה *ma* 'how' (F) is chiefly exclamatory, eg. מה יפה! *ma yafe!* 'How beautiful!'[4] But כמה *káma* has three roles: exclamatory as in example (1); the construction כמה שיותר/שפחות *káma she-yoter* (or *paHot*), as in example (2); and denoting 'as' in the construction כמה ... שאפשר *káma...she-efshar*, as in example (3):[5]

(1)   kámá tov lashir!   כמה טוב לשיר!
                                                          'How good to sing!'

(2)   hem medabrim kámá she-yoter amami   הם מדברים כמה שיותר עממי
      they talk how-much that more colloquial   'They talk as colloquial as possible'

(3)   hem medabrim kámá amami she-efshar   הם מדברים כמה עממי שאפשר
      they talk how-much colloquial that possible   'They talk as colloquial as
                                                     possible'

ככל שיהיה *keHol she-yiye*, in which יהיה *yiye* agrees with the same noun as its adjective, amounts to an idiomatic relative clause Its very meaning (as seen from this example) is appropriate only to adjectives:

ha-mutsarim, meshuHlalim keHol she-yiyu,   המוצרים, משוכללים ככל שיהיו,
   hem naHalat ha-avar   הם נחלת העבר
the products, sophisticated as-all that they-will-be, are legacy the past
'The products, as sophisticated as they may be, are a legacy of the past'

Comparatives

See 20.4.

Superlatives

The commonest superlatives are ביותר *beyoter* (F) and הכי *haHi* (C):

ha-pe'a ha-kveda beyoter	'the heaviest wig'	הפאה הכבדה ביותר
ha-pe'a haHi kveda	'the heaviest wig'	הפאה הכי כבדה

ביותר *beyoter* means 'the most, -est' with definite nouns but 'extremely' with indefinite: פאה כבדה ביותר *pe'a kveda beyoter* 'an extremely heavy wig'.

הכי *haHi* merits particular attention. It is not composed of -ה *ha-* 'the' plus כי *Hi*: כי *Hi* is not a distinct word, and furthermore very casual usage can employ הכי *haHi* with an indefinite noun too:

rak nehagim haHi tovim osim káHa	רק נהגים הכי טובים עושים ככה
only drivers most good do that	'Only the best drivers do that'

However, the -ה *ha-* of agreement cannot be prefixed to הכי *haHi*, as if it were itself ה+כי *ha+Hi*:[6]

ha-ets ha-gavóa	העץ הגבוה
the tree the tall	'the tall tree'

ha-ets (*ha-)haHi gavóa	העץ (*ה)הכי גבוה
the tree (*the) most tall	'the tallest tree'

הכי *haHi* qualifies adverbs too (unlike its synonym ה...ביותר *ha-...beyoter*):[7]

mi rats haHi maher?	מי רץ הכי מהר?
who runs most quickly?	'Who runs the fastest?'

*mi rats ha-mahir beyoter?	*מי רץ המהיר ביותר?
who runs the quick most?	

To express 'the most' as a *quantifier*, Hebrew employs not the construction:

*mi matsa haHi shgi'ot?	*מי מצא הכי שגיאות?
who found most mistakes?	

but rather:

mi matsa **haHi harbe** shgi'ot?	מי מצא **הכי הרבה** שגיאות?
who found **most many** mistakes?	'Who found **the most** mistakes?'

But to express 'the least', casual Hebrew uses הכי פחות *haHi paHot* (most less),[8] as a degree word and as a quantifier (formal usage: המעט ביותר *ha-me'at beyoter* 'the most little', or similar):

shvédya savla **haHi paHot**	שבדיה סבלה **הכי פחות**
	'Sweden suffered **the least**'

ze lakaH **haHi paHot** zman	זה לקח **הכי פחות** זמן
	'This took **the least** time'

Formal usage also occasionally employs יותר *yoter* and פחות *paHot* which ordinarily mean 'more' and 'less':

ha-pe'a ha-	yoter paHot	kveda	הפאה ה יותר כבדה פחות

the wig the	more less	heavy	'The most least heavy wig'

Other formal superlative constructions are exemplified by the following (in (1) and (2) the adjective can be singular or plural, and in (3) the noun):

(1) tovey ha-manHim   טובי המנחים
CONSTRUCT   'the best presenters'
good the presenters

ha-aruka ba-sfinot   הארוכה בספינות
f.s.   f.pl.   'the longest ship'
the long in-the ships
(see 6.16.)

(2) ze ha-kaved mi-kulam   זה הכבד מכולם
this the heavy of all-of-them   'This is the heaviest of all'

(ha-)sridim (ha-)zaaruriyim she-ba-zaaruriyim   (ה)שרידים (ה)זעירוריים שבזעירוריים
m.pl.   m.pl.   m.pl.
(the) remnants (the) minuscule which in-the minuscule
'The most minuscule of remnants'

ha-sridim ha-zaaruriyim she-hitgalu   השרידים הזעירוריים שהתגלו
ba-maaréHet   במערכת
the remnants the minuscule that were-discovered
in-the system
'The most minuscule remnants discovered'
in the system'

(3) *Partitive*:
mitvaH Hadish min ha-meshuHlalim   מטווח חדיש מן המשוכללים
(ba-olam)   (בעולם)
range modern of the sophisticated (in-the world)
'One of the most sophisticated ranges (in the world)'

When the precise scope of the superlative is thus delimited (by ב- *be-*, מ- *mi-*, ש- *she-*), there is no need for the degree word ביותר *beyoter*.[9]

Boosters

משהו *máshehu*, literally 'something', combines with certain 'superlative' adjectives to form 'degree phrases' of the type:

ha-tmunot yafot máshehu yotse-min-ha-klal   התמונות יפות משהו יוצא-מן-הכלל
DEGREE PHR   'The pictures are exceptionally lovely'
the pictures lovely something exceptional

עד-כדי-כך *ad-kdey-kaH* 'so' requires a 'complement clause' (see 20.5) except when negated:

hu tov ad-kdey-kaH she...	'He's so good that...'	...הוא טוב עד-כדי-כך ש
hu lo ad-kdey-kaH tov	'He's not so good'	הוא לא עד-כדי-כך טוב

כזה *kaze*, casually 'so' or 'sort of', is homophonous with the *determiner* כזה *kaze* 'such a' or 'a sort of' which precedes or follows nouns:

kaze muzar	כזה מוזר	kaze tof	כזה תוף
DEGREE ADJ	'so odd	DET N	'such a drum'

As a degree word, כזה *kaze* means 'so, such' when preceding, and 'sort of' when following, its adjective (it is not found with verbs):

tof **kaze** muzar	'**such** an odd drum'	תוף **כזה** מוזר
ze muzar **kaze**	'It's **sort of** odd'	זה מוזר **כזה**

But grammatically כזה *kaze* seems more like a determiner than a degree word: (1) It is not found with verbs, (2) it agrees with its adjective, (3) its adjective must be relating to a noun:

(1)	*hu kaze itsben oti	('He so annoyed me')	*הוא כזה עיצבן אותי
(2)	kursa kazu muzara	'such an odd armchair'	כורסה כזו מוזרה
(3)	*haya kaze kar	('⟨It⟩ was so cold')	*היה כזה קר

To express 'very' without a degree word, casual or fictional style may repeat an adjective:

ze katan katan	זה קטן קטן
it little little	'It's very little'

aHyotáyiH tevashálna **hetev hetev**	אחיותיך תבשלנה **היטב היטב**
	'Your sisters will cook **very well**'

20.3 Degree words with adverbials

Degree words occur with one-word adverbs (e.g. תמיד *tamid* 'always') and with adverbials of the form ב- *be*+abstract noun (e.g. בסבלנות *be-savlanut* 'with patience, patiently'), but with several limitations.

First, whereas *manner* adverbs of one word, e.g. לאט *le'at* slowly', take any degree word just like adjectives:

sa le'at me'od	'Go very slowly'	סע לאט מאד

adverbs of *place*, e.g. למעלה *lemáala* 'up', בפנים *bifnim* 'inside', אחורה *aHóra* 'behind', מערבה *maaráva* 'westwards', take just certain degree words and only in casual usage, as in:

ze **nora** lemáta	זה **נורא** למטה
	'It ⟨is⟩ **very low down**'

ha-kfar nimtsa tsafóna **yoter**   הכפר נמצא צפונה **יותר**
the village is-situated northwards **more**   'The village is **more** to the North'

The same is true for פחות *paHot* 'less', כל-כך *kol-kaH* 'so', קצת *ktsat* 'a bit', יותר מדי *yoter miday* 'too'. By contrast, מדי *miday* 'too', which otherwise tends to follow its adjective, generally *precedes* its adverb; as for מאד *me'od* 'very', it is scarcely used with adverbs.

Second, adverbial phrases of the type בסבלנות *be-savlanut* 'with patience' accept all degree words, in casual usage, but some of these generally must *precede* the adverbial, e.g.:

nahagu bi-zhirut	yoter kol-kaH	יותר כל-כך	נהגו בזהירות
they-drove with care	more so	'They drove more carefully' so	

sa	me'od nora	bi-zhirut	מאד נורא	בזהירות	סע
go	very	with care	'Go very carefully'		

But where adverbials have an explicit adjective, the norm is:

sa be-ófen me'od zahir   סע באופן מאד זהיר
go in way very careful   'Go very carefully'

rather than *...מאד באופן זהיר* * *...me'od be-ófen zahir* (...very in way careful).

20.4 Comparatives

The comparative structures which follow are employed with comparative *quantifiers* as well as with degree words; in addition there are intrinsically comparative verbs and adjectives such as העדיף *heedif* 'prefer', עדיף *'preferable'* and שונה *shone* 'different'.

'More, less'

יותר *yoter* 'more' and פחות *paHot* 'less' are the basic comparative terms. (Other terms such as כפליים *kiflásim* 'double' are discussed in 20.6.) They can introduce parts of clauses or simple phrases.

Comparative *clauses* are introduced by the conjunctions מאשר *measher* 'than' or its synonyms מש- *mi-she* (F), מכפי ש- *mi-kfi she-* (E) or ממה ש *mi-ma she-* (sometimes C):[10]

ani tsame yoter **measher** hayíti kódem   אני צמא יותר **מאשר** הייתי קודם
I thirsty more **than** I-was before   'I'm more thirsty **than** I was before'

ani mevashélet yoter ugiyot **mi-ma she**-ani   אני מבשלת יותר עוגיות **ממה שאני**
yeHola leeHol   יכולה לאכול
'I cook more cookies **than** I can eat'

Comparative *phrases* are of various degrees of 'heaviness', affecting the choice of introductory word. The 'lightest', consisting just of a personal subject pronoun, are preferably introduced by the preposition -מ *mi-* 'from, than'; the subject pronoun becomes a suffix to it:

<table>
<tr><td>hu atsma'i yoter **miméni**</td><td>הוא עצמאי יותר **ממני**</td></tr>
<tr><td>PREP+PRONOUN</td><td>'He's more independent **than me**'</td></tr>
<tr><td>he independent more **than-I**</td><td></td></tr>
</table>

Those consisting of a subject or object noun (without modifiers) can be introduced by -מ *mi-* or by the 'heavier' conjunction מאשר *measher* (also used with clauses - see above):

<table>
<tr><td>ani yoter ohev tey Ham **mi-shóko Ham**</td><td>אני יותר אוהב תה חם **משוקו חם**</td></tr>
<tr><td>I more like tea hot **than cocoa hot**</td><td>'I like hot tea more **than hot cocoa**'</td></tr>
</table>

Slightly 'heavier' are those with an object ('case') marker + object pronoun or noun, eg. אותי *oti* 'DIRECT OBJ me',[11] לו *lo* 'DATIVE him', את התה *et ha-tey* 'DIRECT OBJ the tea'. They are mainly introduced by מאשר *measher*:

<table>
<tr><td>ze yoter meanyen et eyran measher oti</td><td>זה יותר מעניין את עירן מאשר אותי</td></tr>
<tr><td>it more interests OM Eyran than OM-me'</td><td>'It interests Eyran more than me'</td></tr>
</table>

Other words or phrases (notably adverbials) are generally introduced by מאשר *measher* or also by formal -מש *mi-she-* as in (1) below. Single-word adverbs, however, are 'light' enough to allow simple -מ *mi-* too, as in (2):

<table>
<tr><td>(1)</td><td>kan yoter kar</td><td>measher
mi-she-</td><td>be-odésa</td><td>כאן יותר קר מאשר
מש- באודסה</td></tr>
<tr><td></td><td>here more cold than in Odessa</td><td></td><td></td><td>'Here it is colder than in Odessa'</td></tr>
</table>

<table>
<tr><td>(2)</td><td>yoter kar</td><td>measher
mi-</td><td>kódem</td><td>יותר קר מאשר
מ- קודם</td></tr>
<tr><td></td><td></td><td></td><td></td><td>'(It's) colder than before'</td></tr>
</table>

Omission of the degree word יותר *yoter* 'more' is possible, in formal usage with non-derived adjectives,[12] if the conjunction is -מ *mi-* followed by a noun phrase, i.e in the 'lighter' type of comparative:

<table>
<tr><td>hu yiye **gavóa mi-**kol eHav</td><td>הוא יהיה **גבוה מכל** אחיו</td></tr>
<tr><td>he will-be **tall from** all brothers-his</td><td>'He will be **taller than** all his brothers'</td></tr>
</table>

whereas the following are impossible: **gavóa measher...* גבוה מאשר * ('tall than...') or **margiz mi...* מרגיז מ- * ('annoying than...').

Truncation of comparative clauses is usual when they contain a verb of 'thinking' or 'saying'.[13] The conjunction is -מש *mi-she-* or ש ממה *mi-ma she-* rather than מאשר *measher*:

<table>
<tr><td>ze kehe yoter mi-ma she-tsipíti</td><td>זה כהה יותר ממה שציפיתי</td></tr>
<tr><td>it dark more from what that I-expected</td><td>'It is darker than I expected'</td></tr>
</table>

The fuller form would be

<table>
<tr><td>...mi-ma she-tsipíti she-yiye</td><td>ממה שציפיתי שיהיה</td></tr>
<tr><td></td><td>'...than I expected that it would be'</td></tr>
</table>

'As...as...'

To denote 'as...as...', Hebrew does not use a degree word except (optionally) in negative:

hu gavóa kamoH he tall like-you	הוא גבוה כמוך 'He's as tall as you'

hu lo (kol-kaH) gavóa kmo tal he not (so) tall like Tal	הוא לא (כל־כך) גבוה כמו טל 'He's not as tall as Tal'

These examples could also mean, with an intonational break, 'He is (not) tall, like you', etc.

However, 'as many as, as much as' is not הרבה כמו *harbe kmo...* 'many/much like..'; not only the degree word for 'as' but even the quantifier for 'many, much' is omitted in casual usage:

yesh po anashim kmo etmol there-are here people like yesterday	יש פה אנשים כמו אתמול 'There are as many people as yesterday here'

In the negative, כל־כך הרבה *kol-kaH harbe* is possible:

en po (kol-kaH harbe) anashim kmo kódem there-aren't here (so many) people like before	אין פה (כל־כך הרבה) אנשים כמו קודם 'There aren't as many people here as before'

Equally commonly, ...אותו מספר של...כמו *oto mispar shel...kmo...* 'the same number of...as...' or ...אותה כמות של...כמו *ota kamut shel...kmo...* 'the same amount of...as...' are used.

'Detached' comparatives

Besides expressing 'degree' with respect to a trait or property, comparative clauses can express the degree to which *something is true* They are then treated as separate ('disjunctive' - see ch. 23) from the main body of the clause:[14]

ani Hayat, kmo she-avi haya I tailor, like that father-my was	אני חייט, כמו שאבי היה 'I am a tailor, like my father was'

יותר *yoter* 'more (i.e rather)', פחות *paHot* 'less' and לא כל־כך *lo kol-kaH* 'not so much' are similarly employed, though not necessarily 'disjunctively':

ze **yoter** tamlilan measher maHshev it **more** word-processor than computer	זה **יותר** תמלילן מאשר מחשב 'It is **more** a word-processor than a computer'

20.5 כל־כך קל ש... *kol-kaH kal she..* 'so easy that...', קל מדי ל... *kal miday le..* 'too easy to...'

The ensuing 'complement clauses', like those for comparatives in

20.4, are used whether these words are degree words or quantifiers.

With ‏כל־כך‏ kol-kaH 'so' and its synonyms the complement clause, if any, is introduced by the conjunction ‏ש‏ -she- or ‏עד ש‏ -ad she- (F):

kol-kaH kar she-kashe lishon so cold that hard to-sleep	‏כל־כך קר שקשה לישון‏ 'It's so cold that it's hard to sleep'

With ‏(יותר) מדי‏ (yoter) miday 'too' and ‏פחות מדי‏ paHot miday 'too un-' the complement clause is introduced indiscriminately by ‏מכדי‏ miHdey,[15] ‏בשביל‏ bishvil[16] (c) or zero, and is either a finite or an infinitival[17] clause ‏כדי‏ kdey too is occasionally used:

haya zaken miday (miHdey) lishmóa he-was old too (than-for) to-hear	‏היה זקן מדי (מכדי) לשמוע‏ 'He was too old to hear'
yesh li yoter miday avoda (bishvil) laazor there's to-me too much work (for) to-help	‏יש לי יותר מדי עבודה (בשביל) לעזור‏ 'I have too much work to help'
ha-shéleg amok miday (miHdey) she-nisa the snow deep too (than-for) that we'll-go	‏השלג עמוק מדי (מכדי) שנסע‏ 'The snow is too deep for us to go'

With ‏מכדי‏ miHdey especially, the degree word for 'too' is often omitted in formal usage, leaving just an adjective:[18]

ha-davar murkav harbe miHdey she-nenatHo the matter complex much than-for that we-shall-analyse-it	‏הדבר מורכב הרבה מכדי שננתחו‏ 'The matter is much too complex to analyse'
ze ktsat raHok bishvil lir'ot it a-bit far for to-see	‏זה קצת רחוק בשביל לראות‏ 'It's a bit too far to see'

A common alternative to these 'too'+clause constructions is ‏כל־כך‏ kol-kaH 'so' +negative:

haya zaken kol-kaH she-lo shama he-was old so that not he-heard	‏היה זקן כל־כך שלא שמע‏ 'He was so old that he did not hear'

With ‏מספיק‏ maspik 'enough' and its synonyms, the complement clause begins indiscriminately with ‏כדי‏ kdey 'so (that)' or ‏בשביל‏ bishvil (c) or zero, and is either finite or infinitival:[19]

hu maspik Hazak (kdey) laruts he enough strong (so-as) to-run	‏הוא מספיק חזק (כדי) לרוץ‏ 'He is strong enough to run'
ani lo maspik batúaH be-atsmi (bishvil) she-uHal lehotsi et ze haHútsa	‏אני לא מספיק בטוח בעצמי‏ ‏(בשביל) שאוכל להוציא‏ ‏את זה החוצה‏ 'I am not sure enough of myself for me to be able to get it out in the open'

20.6   Specifiers of comparison

Comparison phrases can themselves be qualified, particularly by quantifiers such as הרבה *harbe* 'much', קצת *ktsat* 'a bit', עוד *od* 'more (i.e still)', directly preceding the comparative words יותר *yoter* 'more' and פחות *paHot* 'less'.[20] The whole phrase thus formed can precede or follow the adjective or verb:

hu Hamud **harbe paHot** he cute **much less**	הוא חמוד **הרבה פחות** 'He is **much less** cute'
ze **od yoter** madhim oti it **still more** appalls me	זה **עוד יותר** מדהים אותי 'It appalls me **still more**'

Precise specifiers

"(Two, three,...) times more..' is expressed by the particle פי *pi* + numeral (usually feminine but masculine in puristic usage). 'Double as...' or 'double as many' can alternatively be expressed by כפליים *kifláyim* (F) or כפול *kaful* (C). These are in fact degree words and quantifiers:

ha-oféret Hazaka pi shalosh the lead tough *pi* three	העופרת חזקה פי שלוש 'Lead is three times more tough'
kaH me-ha-bulim sheli, li yesh pi éser take from the stamps my, to-me are *pi* ten	קח מהבולים שלי, לי יש פי עשר 'Take from my stamps, I've got ten times as many'
yesh po kifláyim anashim measher... there-are here double people than...	יש פה כפליים אנשים מאשר... 'There are double as many people here as...'

יותר *yoter* 'more' can be optionally added[21] for פי *pi* + numeral. When quantifying a noun these specifiers precede the noun; as 'degree words' they can precede *or* follow, and can even follow the whole comparative phrase as a kind of adverbial:

ha-oféret kveda me-ha-avats **pi shalosh** the lead heavy than the zinc **pi three**	העופרת כבדה מהאבץ **פי שלוש** 'Lead is **three times** heavier than zinc'

'Measure phrases' specifying a comparative are introduced by the preposition ב- *be-* 'in, with'. Like פי *pi* above, they can be positioned like degree words, or at some distance like adverbials; they need no יותר *yoter* 'more', provided a מ- *mi-* 'than' phrase is explicitly mentioned:

ze **be-shiva méter** (yoter) aroH mi... it **by seven metres** (more) long than...	זה **בשבעה מטר** (יותר) ארוך מ... 'It's **seven metres** longer than...'
ze (paHot) yakar mi... be-esrim aHuz it (less) expensive than... by 20%	זה (פחות) יקר מ... בעשרים אחוז 'It's 20% less expensive than...'

but:

hu lo **ha-Hétsi** HaHam mimHa   הוא לא **החצי** חכם ממך
he not **the half** clever from-you   'He's not **half** as clever as you'

Such measure phrases go mainly with *comparatives*. Hebrew lacks the construction:

*ze (be-)shiva méter aroH   *זה (ב)שבעה מטר ארוך
it (by) seven metres long   ('It is seven metres long')

and instead employs an abstract noun, as in:[22]

orko shiva méter   אורכו שבעה מטר
length-its seven metres   'It is seven metres long'

FURTHER READING
Azar 1977: 5.6.5; Ben-Asher 1972: 91-101, 1977; Glinert 1988a; Rubinstein 1975; Sadka 1981:262-8.

21. Adjunct adverbials

21.1 Introduction

A fundamental syntactic and semantic distinction must be drawn between five kinds of adverbial: degree adverbs (ch. 20), adjunct adverbials (this chapter), focus adverbs (ch. 22), disjunct adverbials (ch. 23) and link adverbials (ch. 24). By 'adverb' we mean a one-word 'adverbial'.

(1) *Degree adverbs* denote 'degree' for verbs or adjectives expressing a property, eg. מאד *me'od* 'very', כל־כך *kol-kaH* 'so'.

(2) *Adjunct adverbials*[1] elaborate on the event/situation and its circumstances - how, where, when etc., eg. יפה *yafe* 'nicely', בעיר *ba-ir* 'in town', בגלל זה *biglal ze* 'because of this'.

(3) *Focus adverbs* are logical particles that focus on one word or phrase, eg. גם *gam* 'also', רק *rak* 'only'.

(4) *Disjunct adverbials* comment on the statement itself, eg. בוודאי *bevaday* 'certainly', אישית *ishit* 'personally speaking'.

(5) *Link adverbials* express a logical connection between sentences, eg. הרי *harey* 'after all', אמנם *omnam* 'indeed'.

In terms of sentence structure, the first three are 'inner adverbials', being an integrated part of the clause,[2] and the last two are 'outer adverbials', often being set off by pause, commas or the like Of the first three, degree and focus adverbs are tightly associated with their verb, noun etc. and are syntactically distinctive in several other ways (see the relevant chapter) from adjuncts, the topic of this chapter.

A further distinction must be made between adverbials and *objects*, as illustrated (see 15.3 for details):

áfu **ba-shamáyim**	'They flew **in the sky**'	עפו **בשמיים**
ADVERBIAL		

hibítu **ba-shamáyim**	'They looked **at the sky**'	הביטו **בשמיים**
OBJ		

Adjuncts have a wealth of diverse semantic, syntactic and morphological properties. Indeed, they are not amenable to watertight subdivision. We can ony survey their form and syntax according to the main rough semantic types: extent, manner, means, circumstance, time, place, status; and various semi-adverbial datives using -ל *le-*, namely affectee, benefactee, possessor and autonomous agent.

This chapter deals with adjunct phrases. (Adjunct *clauses*, including further semantic types such as 'cause' and 'result', are described in ch. 32). Adjunct phrases generally involve a single word (an 'adverb'), a preposition+noun phrase, or occasionally a noun phrase with no preposition:

maHar	'tomorrow'	מחר
be-oto yom	'on that day'	באותו יום
oto yom	'that day'	אותו יום

21.2 The general syntax of adjuncts

21.2.1 Syntactic function

Adjuncts qualify the predicate or verb, as in (1) below, or a noun, as in (2),[3] or else themselves function as predicate, as in (3):

(1) ze ba **mi-yapan**   זה בא **מיפן**
'It comes **from Japan**'

(2) ha-séret **mi-yapan** lo ra   הסרט **מיפן** לא רע
'The film **from Japan** ⟨is⟩ not bad'

(3) ha-séret **mi-yapan**   הסרט **מיפן**
'The film ⟨is⟩ **from Japan**'

Adjuncts vary in their cohesion to a verb. Extent, manner and quantifier adjuncts and those complementing verbs of time, place and status are 'tight': there is no pause, and they usually follow the verb. Other adjuncts, eg. most time and place adjuncts, are 'loose': they can precede the verb and be set off by a pause or comma. Thus:

gárnu be-arad	'We lived in Arad'	גרנו בערד
TIGHT		

be-arad, kibálti maanak	'In Arad, I got a grant'	בערד, קיבלתי מענק
LOOSE		

Adverbials do not usually go with a verb, adjective or adverbial that is itself qualifying something.[4] Contrast:

ha-tinok **tamid** {atsbani/boHe}   התינוק **תמיד** {עצבני/בוכה}
'The baby ⟨is⟩ **always** {tetchy/crying}'

ha-juk **aHshav** táHat ha-tanur   הג'וק **עכשיו** תחת התנור
'The roach ⟨is⟩ **now** under the oven'

with the unacceptable:

*yesh la tinok **tamid** {atsbani/boHe}   *יש לה תינוק **תמיד** {עצבני/בוכה}
is to-her baby **always** {tetchy/crying}   ('She has an **always** {tetchy/crying} baby')

*ha-juk **aHshav** táHat ha-tanur megared   *הג'וק **עכשיו** תחת התנור מגרד
the roach **now** under the oven is-scratching

21.2.2 Qualifying an adverbial

A 'measure phrase' or 'degree word' (see ch. 20) can be placed in front of[5] a 'measurable' adverbial of time, place or comparison, thus qualifying the adverbial:

káma dakot	leaHar ha-pitsuts...	...כמה **דקות** לאחר הפיצוץ
MEASURE PHR	TIME ADV	'Some minutes after the bombing...'

hi nimtset	**méa méter** raHok mi-kan	היא נמצאת **מאה מטר** רחוק מכאן
	MEASURE PHR PLACE ADV	'It is situated **100 metres** distant from here'

ze **nora**	lemáala	זה **נורא** למעלה
DEGREE WORD	PLACE ADV	'It's **awfully** high up'

ze **ktsat**	kmo jez	זה **קצת** כמו ג'ז
DEGREE WORD	COMPARISON ADV	'It's **a bit** like jazz'

21.2.3 Adverbial 'reference'

The adjunct usually 'refers' to the *event*. (Manner adverbials may refer to the *subject* of the clause - see 21.4.1.)

nafálti	hayom pit'om	=		היום פתאום =	נפלתי היום פתאום
nefilati hayta	ha-yom pitomit		נפילתי היתה פתאומית		
I-fell	today suddenly	= my-fall was	today sudden		

Occasionally too, adjuncts of time or place (also circumstance and status, see 21.6, 21.9) can refer to the *object* - with verbs of perception, expecting, arranging, having and suchlike (context etc. permitting):

metaHnenim tfilot **maHar ba-meara**	מתכננים תפילות **מחר במערה**
	'⟨They⟩ are planning prayers **tomorrow in the cave**'
	(The *prayers* are in the cave tomorrow or the *planners* are)

hu ahav aruHat-érev **be-shesh ba-salon**	הוא אהב ארוחת־ערב **בשש בסלון**
	'He liked supper **at 6 in the lounge**'

ra'íti naHash **ba-nahar**	ראיתי נחש **בנהר**
	'I saw a snake **in the river**'

Shifting and pausing is possible with both subject and object 'reference':

be-toH ha-máyim, ra'íti zug tamnunim	**בתוך המים**, ראיתי זוג תמנונים
	'**In the water**, I saw a pair of octopuses'

21.2.4 'Adverbial' verbs: מיהר לקום *miher lakum* 'was quick to get up'

Several verbs related by root to adverbs can do some - but by no means all - of these adverbs' work[6] in formal usage They mostly take an infinitive Some notable examples are listed here

Time verbs:[7]

miher	ledaber ve-diber	לדבר מיהר ודיבר	= diber mehera	דיבר מהרה
was-quick	to-speak and spoke	'quickly spoke'	spoke quickly	'quickly spoke' (i.e 'soon spoke')
	hikdim lehagía was-early to-arrive	הקדים להגיע 'arrived early'	= higia mukdam arrived early	הגיע מוקדם 'arrived early' (i.e earlier than expected)
	shav ve-hidgish returned and stressed	שב והדגיש 'stressed again'	= hidgish shuv stressed again	הדגיש שוב 'stressed again'

Manner verbs:

	hetiv lenagen did-well to-play	היטיב לנגן 'played well'	= nigen hetev played well	ניגן היטב 'played well'
	halaH ve-nivna went and was-built	הלך ונבנה 'was being built gradually'	= nivna be-hadraga was-built gradually	נבנה בהדרגה 'was being built gradually'

By contrast, the verbs in the following example are not synonymous with the corresponding manner adverbials בשמחה *be-simHa* 'happily', בקפדנות *be-kafdanut* 'carefully' and בעקשנות *be-akshanut* 'determinedly', and so are not strictly adverbial verbs:

samáHti			שמחתי
hikpádeti	liyot sham		הקפדתי להיות שם
hitakáshti			התעקשתי
	I was happy		
	' I was careful	to be there'	
	I was determined		

Extent verbs:[8]

hirba ledaber	הרבה לדבר	= diber harbe	דיבר הרבה
did-a-lot to-speak	'spoke a lot'	spoke a-lot	'spoke a lot'

Most 'adverbial verbs' can instead take an object phrase, involving the preposition -ב *be-*+an abstract noun,[9] as in:

hirba be-dibur	הרבה בדיבור
did-a-lot in speaking	'spoke a lot'

21.3   Extent adverbials

To express the extent to which an action accumulates, certain quantifiers (see ch.8) can be employed as 'extent adverbs' with the verb - for example, הרבה *harbe* 'a lot', קצת *ktsat* 'a bit', עוד *od* 'more', and also the feminine plural רבות *rabot* 'much':[10]

et ha-olam ra'íti ad az **dey harbe**	את העולם ראיתי עד אז **די הרבה**
	'I'd seen the world by then **quite a lot**'

ha-ivrit hushpe'a mimena **rabot**	העברית הושפעה ממנה **רבות**
Hebrew was-influenced by-it **much**	'Hebrew was **much** influenced by it'

nase **od**	נסה **עוד**
	'Try ⟨some⟩ **more**'

They occasionally express degree of a *quality* or *state*, but this is usually done by 'degree words' (ch.20):

ze	hishtana ka'av	me'od		זה	השתנה כאב	מאד
		DEGREE WORD				
it	changed hurt	very		'It	changed hurt	a lot'

The position of extent adverbials is after the verb or its object (like manner and means adverbials), i.e they are 'tight' adjuncts.

21.4   Manner adverbials

Manner adverbials express the manner in which something is done, eg. 'behave *nicely*', 'behave *like me*'.

21.4.1-4   FORMS OF MANNER ADVERBIALS

21.4.1   Preposition phrases

Manner adverbials are regularly formed as phrases, built around either an adjective or an abstract noun (usually adjective-based or verb-based):

(1)	be-	ófen tsura + ADJ óraH (F)		אופן ב צורה + ADJ אורח

in way + ADJ
(i.e "in a ADJ way")

(2)   -ב *be* + adjective-based noun

(3)   -ב *be* + verb-based noun

Examples are:

(1) hu po'el **be-ófen Hofshi**   הוא פועל **באופן חופשי**
     he acts **in way free**   'He acts **freely**'

(2) hu po'el **be-Hofshiyut**   הוא פועל **בחופשיות**
     he acts **with freedom**   'He acts **freely**'

(3) hitkarvu **be-hisus**   התקרבו **בהיסוס**
     they-approached **with hesitation**   'They approached **hesitantly**'

A negative adverbial can regularly take various forms (see ch.29):

be-ófen **lo** Hofshi   'in an **unfree** way'   באופן **לא** חופשי
be-**Hóser** Hofshiyut   'with **lack** of freedom'   **בחוסר** חופשיות
lelo hisus   '**without** hesitation'   **ללא** היסוס

and a less common, formal practice is to insert שלא *she-lo* (in which -ש *she-* has no clear function) in front of the whole adverbial phrase:

she-lo beHofshiyut   '**not** freely'   **שלא** בחופשיות

באופן *be-ófen*, בצורה *be-tsura* and באורח *be-óraH* 'in a...way' generally go with adjectives applicable to things:

ze hishtana		maftia	מפתיע		זה השתנה
	be-ófen	maH'is	מכעיס	באופן	
hitnahagt		meaHzev	מאכזב		התנהגת

it changed		surprising	'It changed	surprisingly'
	in way	annoying		annoyingly'
you-acted		disappointing	'You acted	disappointingly'

and not:[11]

	mufta	מופתע	
*hegávnu be-ófen	ko'és	כועס	*הגבנו באופן
	meuHzav	מאוכזב	

	surprised		surprisedly'
we-reacted in way	angry	('We reacted angrily'	)
	disappointed		disappointedly'

By contrast, -ב *be*+abstract noun tends to be used of persons[12] (though such qualities or actions as 'freedom, speed, hesitation' will obviously relate simultaneously to the act too: 'quick at..., free with...'):

| hitHabku be- | hisus | | היסוס | התחבקו ב |
| | shtika | | שתיקה | |

                                        'They embraced hesitantly'
                                                        silently'

saper be-	Hofshiyut	חופשיות
	mehirut	מהירות	ספר ב
	kafdanut	קפדנות
	tamtsitiyut	תמציתיות

'Tell ⟨it⟩ freely'
quickly'
scrupulously'
concisely'

and not:

*ha-**máyim** zarmu be-Hofshiyut   *המים זרמו בחופשיות
('The **water** flowed freely')

*ha-**zérem** mitnatek be-otomátiyut   *הזרם מתנתק באוטומטיות
('The **current** shuts off automatically')

*ha-**shana** heHéla be-idud   *השנה החלה בעידוד
('The **year** began encouragingly')

(rather: באופן חופשי/אוטומטי/מעודד *be-ófen* Hofshi / otomáti / meoded)
Casual usage sometimes employs a further construction with adjectives
expressing an extreme:

hitnahagt **máshehu**	meyuHad	מיוחד	התנהגת משהו
	lo normáli	לא נורמלי	

you-behaved **something**   special
extraordinary   'You behaved extraordinarily'

21.4.2 'Echo' manner phrases (traditionally: 'internal objects')
As an alternative to the foregoing, formal Hebrew sometimes inserts
an 'echo noun' - a noun, mostly abstract, corresponding regularly to the verb or
adjective in hand - and adds to it an *adjective* (or even a relative clause or other
phrase), usually to specify manner. The adjective agrees with the echo noun:[13]

(1) nitsHu otam **nitsaHon muHlat**   ניצחו אותם נצחון מוחלט
     ECHO N   MANNER ADJ
     they-defeated them **defeat decisive**   'They defeated them **decisively**'

(2) neenáHti **shalosh anaHot arukot**   נאנחתי שלוש אנחות ארוכות
     I-sighed **three sighs long**   'I sighed **three long sighs**'

(3) ha-gufot nikberu sham **kvura zmanit**   הגופות נקברו שם קבורה זמנית
     the bodies were-buried there **burial temporary**
          'The bodies were buried there **temporarily**'

(4) gam im nenatséaH et ha-nitsaHon   גם אם ננצח את הנצחון
     ha-muHlat beyoter...   המוחלט ביותר...
     even if we-defeat OM the defeat the decisive most...
          'Even if we inflict the most decisive defeat...'

(5)   giborat ha-séret yafa **yófi she-kashe**   גיבורת הסרט יפה **יופי שקשה**
      letaaro   **לתארו**
      heroine-of the film beautiful **beauty that hard to-describe-it**
                                          'The film's heroine is **indescribably** beautiful'

21.4.3   Adjectives as adverbs

There are much less productive adjective-based patterns for manner adverbials. First, several 'passive participle' adjectives, and certain others, can be introduced by the preposition -ב *be-* to form a manner adverb, eg. בגלוי *be-galuy* 'openly', במודגש *be-mudgash* 'emphatically'. These 'words' are not usually coined freely; and though the -ב *be* is equivalent to באופן... *be-ófen...* (see 21.4.1), the adjective involved cannot in most cases be qualified: not *במדוייק מאד *be-meduyak **me'od** ('**very** accurately') but באופן מדוייק מאד *be-ófen meduyak me'od* 'in a very accurate way', etc.

Second, some adjectives are in themselves also manner adverbs. They do not agree with the subject. They are of the types listed in (a)-(d).

(a)   Several, and in casual usage very many, *masculine singular* adjectives (but none ending in a derivative suffix such as י- *-i*), eg.[14] טוב *tov* 'well', יפה *yafe* 'nicely', ברור *barur* 'clearly', and more casually דחוף *daHuf* 'urgently', מצויין *metsuyan* 'excellently'.

(b)   Several, and in formal usage many, *feminine singular inanimate* adjectives (i.e pertaining to actions, not persons) ending in ית- *-it*, i.e based on a masculine singular in י- *-i*, eg. אוטומטית *otomátit* 'automatically', אלכסונית *alaHsonit* 'diagonally'.

(c)   Feminine plural adjectives (inanimate again) partly complement the foregoing, by providing many manner adverbs in ות- *-ot* (and not יות- *-iyot*, the plural of adjectives in י- *-i*), mostly in formal usage, eg. ארוכות *arukot* 'at length', בטוחות *btuHot* 'confidently'.

(d)   A few infinitive verbs denoting 'extreme' qualities are best considered degree adverbs (ch.20): להפליא *lehafli* 'wonderfully', להפתיע *lehaftía* 'surprisingly', להדהים *lehadhim* 'frighteningly', as in:

      hu armumi lehadhim   הוא ערמומי להדהים
      he cunning to-frighten   'He's frighteningly cunning'

21.4.4   Specialized manner adverbs and miscellaneous

A few manner adverbs are special words or phrases of no general pattern, eg. מהר *maher* 'quickly', היטב *hetev* 'well', הישר *haysher* 'directly', פה אחד *pe eHad* 'unanimously'.

Unrelated to any adjectives or abstract nouns are three fairly productive 'double noun' patterns, listed in (a)-(c) below.

(a)   A repeated plural noun denoting 'in lots of...', as in:

      bad meshubats **ribu'im ribu'im**   בד משובץ **ריבועים ריבועים**
      cloth chequered **squares squares**   'cloth chequered **in squares**'

hitgodedu **Havurot-Havurot**   התגודדו **חבורות-חבורות**
they-banded-together groups groups (i.e 'in groups')

(b) A repeated singular noun denoting '...by...', as in:

bedakuha se'if-se'if   בדקוה סעיף-סעיף
they-checked-it section section (i.e 'section by section')

(c) אחרי *aharey* 'after' can be inserted between the singular nouns:

tsáad aHarey tsáad   'step by step'   צעד אחרי צעד

Finally, 'manner' can be expressed by a 'comparative construction' using כמו
kmo 'like' (see ch.20), as in:

titnaheg kmo limor   'Behave like Limor'   תתנהג כמו לימור

21.4.5-8 SYNTAX OF MANNER ADVERBIALS

21.4.5 Function

Manner adverbials generally qualify a verb (or adjective *directly*
related to it, i.e a present or past participle):[15]

titlabesh **yafe**   'Dress **nicely**'   תתלבש **יפה**

hayínu levushim yafe   'We were dressed nicely'   היינו לבושים יפה
    PAST PART ADV

The whole adjective+adverbial can itself be used to qualify a noun:

mosifim klipat tapuz megurédet dak   מוסיפים קליפת תפוז מגורדת דק
   N   N   ADJ   ADV
add peel orange grated finely   'Add finely grated orange peel'

Manner adverbials are not used as predicates themselves, nor where the predicate is merely a noun:[16]

hi   tov   טוב היא
    be-savlanut   בסבלנות

she   good (m.s.)
    with patience

hu rofe   be-savlanut   בסבלנות הוא רופא
    be-ófen simpáti   באופן סימפטי

he doctor   with patience
    in way friendly

A few verbs (נראה *nir'e* 'seem', נשמע *nishma* 'sound', הרגיש *hirgish* 'feel'
etc.) that otherwise take a noun or adjective as their predicate, can take a
non-agreeing adjective - describing the appearance, feel etc. (rather than the person) but not strictly a manner adverb:

hem nir'im {muzar/tov}
they look {odd/good}

הם נראים {מוזר/טוב}
'They look {odd/good}'

hem nir'im (anashim) {muzarim/tovim}
they look (people) {odd/good}

הם נראים (אנשים) {מוזרים/טובים}
'They look like {odd/good} people'

21.4.6 Word order and adverbial combination

Manner (and extent and means) adverbials are 'tightest' to the verb, in the sense that they generally follow the verb or its object (see (1) below). The general order of object *vis-à-vis* adverbial tends to involve putting the shortest element first, (compare (2)). Time, place and other adverbials denote more 'extrinsic' circumstances, and are thus 'looser' and unlikely to come between verb and manner adverbial (3):

(1) hadaft **metsuyan** et ha-kadur
        et ha-kadur **metsuyan**

מצויין את הכדור   הדפת
את הכדור **מצויין**

you-stopped **excellent** OM the ball
                OM the ball **excellent**

'You stopped the ball **excellently**'

(2) hu hadaf **metsuyan** et kadur ha-késhet
     he stopped **excellent** OM ball the curve

הוא הדף **מצויין** את כדור הקשת
'He stopped the curved ball
excellently'

(3) be-Hatsot he'árti oto ba-adinut
     at midnight I-woke him gently
     or:
     he'árti oto ba-adinut be-Hatsot
     I-woke him gently at midnight

בחצות הערתי אותו בעדינות

הערתי אותו בעדינות בחצות

Manner adverbials jar with two other 'tight' adverbials, 'degree words' and quantifiers of extent or time (though *logically* compatible), as if competing for the same 'slot':[17]

*me'od hishtanet maher
very you've-changed quickly

*מאד השתנית מהר
('You've very much changed quickly')

?enéni oved kashe kol-kaH harbe
NEG-I work hard so much

?איננו עובד קשה כל-כך הרבה
('I don't work hard such a lot')

Nor do two manner adverbials generally co-occur, except joined by -ו *ve-* 'and':[18]

*sámti oto **maher bi-zhirut** ba-makom

*שמתי אותו **מהר בזהירות** במקום
('I put it **quickly carefully** away')

21.4.7 Qualifying manner adverbials

Manner adverbials comprising *adjectives* and *nouns* can mostly be qualified in ways usual for adjectives and nouns:[19]

adjective + degree word
avad be-tsura **yoter** ye'ila
worked in way **more** efficient

עבד בצורה **יותר** יעילה
'worked **more** efficiently'

noun + adjective

badak be-yeilut {maflia/raba}	בדק ביעילות {מפליאה/רבה}
checked with efficiency {amazing/great}	'checked {amazingly/very} efficiently'

Note also the formal particle יתר *yéter* 'more' (related to the degree word יותר *yoter* 'more'), used in adverbial constructions of the type ביתר *be-yéter* + abstract noun:

be-yéter yeilut	ביתר יעילות
with more efficiency [=more efficiently]	

Furthermore, casual Hebrew can use most degree words in front of adverbials of the ביעילות *be-yeilut* 'with efficiency' type, and a few (but not, eg., מאד *me'od* 'very' and יותר *yoter* 'more') after them (see 20.3):

me'od be-yeilut	מאד ביעילות
very with efficiency	'very efficiently'

A general constraint is that adjectives and nouns in manner adverbials do not usually take their customary objects (but see 21.4.8). Contrast:

at Hofshit **mi-leHatsim**	'you're free **from pressure**'	את חופשית **מלחצים**
Hofshiyut **mi-leHatsim**...	'freedom **from pressures**...'	חופשיות **מלחצים**...

with the unacceptable:

*at mesaHéket	be-ófen Hofshi	באופן חופשי
	be-Hofshiyut mi-leHatsim	מלחצים בחופשיות

you play	in way free in freedom	from pressures	

21.4.8   Manner vs. circumstance

Circumstance adverbials (21.6, 32.4) can overlap with manner adverbials:

míshehi tilfena elay **nirgéshet me'od**	מישהי טילפנה אלי **נרגשת מאד**
f. CIRCUMSTANCE	
someone phoned me **excited (f.) very**	'Someone phoned me **very excited**'

...be-hitragshut raba	...בהתרגשות רבה
MANNER	
...with excitement great	'...very excitedly'

Briefly, they involve any adjective or participle, expressly describing the *subject* (or object) and *agreeing* with it. These adjectives or participles readily take their customary objects:

at mesaHéket Hofshit mi-leHatsim	את משחקת חופשית מלחצים
f.s.f.s. f.s.	
you play free from pressures	

21.5 Means ('instrumental') adverbials

The means by which something is done is usually expressed by the preposition -ב *be-*, or in casual usage by עם *im* (condemned by purists). Sometimes בעזרת/באמצעות *be-ezrat/be-emtsa'ut* are used, but not for bodily actions:

tohal	be-/im	kaf	'Eat with a spoon'	תאכל ב כף עם
hivkáti	ba-/im ha-	rosh	'I scored with my head'	הבקעתי ב ראש עם ה

But note -ב *be-* (not עם *im*) for travel by vehicle:

eH nasat, be-meHonit?   'How did you go, by car?   איך נסעת, במכונית?

Among the few one-word 'means adverbials' is טלפונית *telefónit* 'by phone'.

Word order

Means adverbials generally follow the verb or object closely:

patáHti oto bi-mhirut be-yaday / be-yaday bi-mhirut / toH-kedey dibur   במהירות בידי / בידי במהירות תוך-כדי דיבור פתחתי אותו

I-opened it quickly with my-hands / with my-hands quickly while speaking

But they can come first for contrast:

{be-/im} maftéaH kaze, efshar liftóaH ha-kol   {ב/עם} מפתח כזה, אפשר לפתוח הכל
with a-key like-this, you-can open anything

Means adverbial vs. specification object

Contrast the 'means phrase' in example (1) below with the 'specification object phrase' in (2). -ב *be-* regularly introduces such object phrases for verbs of the 'fill/cover/surround/swarm with' type (see 15.8). This -ב *be-* can be omitted in formal usage; the appropriate interrogative word is במה *be-ma* 'with what', as with all objects, rather than איך *eH* 'how' as with means adverbials:

(1) ataf be-Hével   'wrap with [=by means of] string'   עטף בחבל
(2) ataf (be-)niyar   'wrap with [=in] paper'   עטף (ב)נייר

21.6 Circumstance adverbials

Circumstance adverbials convey all kinds of accompanying circumstances - pertaining to the 'actors' themselves (their place, mode of action, etc.) or their possessions or even someone/something extraneous.

21.6.1 Preposition phrases

-ב *be-* can signal information about bodily circumstances - when followed by a noun phrase (indefinite) involving an adjective:[20]

dibárnu be-yadáyim meshulavot	דיברנו בידיים משולבות
N (f.pl.) ADJ (f.pl.)	'We spoke with folded arms'
we-spoke with arms folded	

An alternative and more flexible construction employs the preposition עם *im*. This signals information about one's person or even one's possessions, particularly in casual usage Instead of just an indefinite noun phrase, as in (1) below, it can involve a quasi-clause (2), i.e subject+present tense predicate (which may be adjective, noun, verb or adverbial):[21]

(1)	dibárnu im yadáyim meshulavot	דיברנו עם ידיים משולבות
	we-spoke with arms folded	

		lo mesurak yafe	לא מסורק יפה
(2)	yats'u im ha-se'ar	zva'a	זוועה
		meHase et ha-panim	מכסה את הפנים
		ba-eynáyim	בעיניים

	not combed nicely
	a-disgrace
they-went-out with the hair	covers OM the face
	in-the eyes

A non-circumstantial use of עם *im* 'with' + noun phrase, expressing 'I have.. with me' rather than 'my... is...', is as follows. Here -ב *be-* is uncommon and the opposite of עם *im* is בלי *bli* 'without':

yatsáti im mitriya yeshana	יצאתי עם מיטריה ישנה
I-went-out with umbrella old	'I went out with an old umbrella'

For circumstantial *clauses*, introduced by -ו *ve-* and כאשר *kaasher*, see 32.4.

21.6.2 Circumstance predicates

To a sentence one may append a clause *minus its subject*, i.e a predicate, relating to the subject or object (direct or indirect) of that sentence The 'clause without subject' usually features a verb or adjective, occasionally a noun (or adverbial) - with any attendant object etc. - which naturally agree with the subject or object they relate to.[22]

Relating to the subject:

zéhu, hi amra,	yodáat she-ze yargia oti	יודעת שזה ירגיע אותי
	menasa liyot adiva	מנסה להיות אדיבה
	CIRCUMSTANCE PRED	

זהו, היא אמרה,

'that's-it', she said,
   knows [=knowing] that this will-calm [=would calm] me
   tries [=trying] to-be courteous

Hazárnu ayefim legámrey   חזרנו עייפים לגמרי
m.pl.   m.pl.
we-returned tired completely   'We returned completely tired out'

hu shav habáyta **loHem menuse**   הוא שב הביתה **לוחם מנוסה**
he returned home **fighter experienced**   'He returned home **an experienced fighter**'

Relating to the object:

החזקנו בה חזק ,רועדת מקור, והזזנו אותה
heHzáknu ba Hazak, ro'édet mi-kor, ve-hezáznu ota
    f.s.   f.s.
we-held her tight, shivers [=shivering] with cold, and moved her

They occasionally precede the sentence (unlike - ו *ve* or -כש *kshe-* clauses); but whatever their position, agreement plus context enable one to relate them to subject or object (where doubtful, they usually relate to what is nearest):

ro'édet mi-kor, heHzáknu ba Hazak ve..   ...רועדת מקור, החזקנו בה חזק ו
OBJ-RELATED
shivers [=shivering] with cold, we-held her tight and....

One- or two-word circumstance predicates have no preceding comma or gap.[23] They are common in any usage (whereas more complex predicates are more formal):

hu met **milyoner**   'He died ⟨a⟩ **millionaire**'   הוא מת **מליונר**

hem tamid yod'im **(ha-)rishonim**   הם תמיד יודעים **(ה)ראשונים**
they always know **(the) first**

...pítot? oHlim otan **Hamot!**   ...פיתות! אוכלים אותן **חמות!**
       f.pl.   f.pl.
...pittas? ⟨One⟩ eats them **warm**

21.7 Time adverbials

21.7.1 Form

Time adverbials can have the forms as set out in the following table (For 6,7 see chs. 30, 32.)

1 *Special 1-word adverb*	yashánti kódem	I-slept first	ישנתי קודם
2 *Quantifier*	harbe	... a lot	הרבה ...
3 *Noun phrase*	shtey dakot	... two minutes	שתי דקות ...
4 *Preposition + noun phrase*	ad ha-érev	... till the evening	עד הערב ...
5 *Preposition + adverbial*	ad aHarey ha-ne'um	... till after the speech	עד אחרי הנאום ...
6 *Preposition + clause*	ad she-bat	... till that you-came [= till you came]	עד שבאת ...
7 *Preposition + gerund*	ad bo'eH	... till coming-of-you	עד בואך ...

Special one-word adverbs have no distinctive form, here as elsewhere, eg. תמיד *tamid* 'always', אמש *émesh* 'last night', עתה *ata* 'now'.[24]

Quantifiers (see ch. 8), such as קצת *ktsat* 'a bit' and יותר מדי *yoter miday* 'too much', may express frequency. As they can also express 'extent' with many verbs, ambiguity may arise:

ra'iti et mitsráyim **dey harbe**	ראיתי את מצרים **די הרבה**
I've-seen OM Egypt **quite a-lot**	
[= 'often' or 'a fair amount']	

Noun phrases

A few types of time phrase can consist just of a noun phrase - though the preposition -ב *be-* 'at' is often prefixed (and *must* be with most other time phrases - see below).

Of point of time Phrases with the determiners אחד *eHad* 'one' and (formal) אותו *oto* 'that' (more neutrally באותו *be-oto*);[25] also formal -ש (ב)שעה *(be-)sha'a she-* 'when' and literary עת *et* 'when':

bóker eHad yatsánu..	בוקר אחד יצאנו...
	'One morning we went out...'

rádyo peking shider (be-)**ota sha'a**	רדיו פקינג שידר **(ב)אותה שעה**
shirey am siniim	שירי עם סיניים
	'Peking Radio was transmitting ⟨at⟩ **that moment** Chinese folksongs'

et palash ha-oyev...	**עת** פלש האויב...
time invaded the enemy...	'**When** the enemy invaded...'

Of frequency. In phrases with כל *kol* 'every' or רוב *rov* 'most', the preposition -ב *be-* can drop, as in (1, 2) below; it must drop for כל *kol* + a number (3), but כל *kol* meaning 'any' requires -ב *be-* (4):

(1) **(be-)kol yom sheni** yesh maHaze   **(ב)כל יום שני** יש מחזה
  'On every Monday there's ⟨a⟩ play'

(2) **(be-)rov ha-yamim** hayta menamnémet   **(ב)רוב הימים** היתה מנמנמת
  'On most ⟨of⟩ the days she'd doze'

(3) **kol Hamesh dakot** yesh monit   **כל חמש דקות** יש מונית
  'Every five minutes there's ⟨a⟩ cab'

(4) hu tsariH lavo **be-Hol réga**   הוא צריך לבוא **בכל רגע**
  'He's due to come **at any moment**'

With פעם *páam* 'time', -ב *be-* is impossible (save for point-of-time, eg. בפעם השניה *ba-páam ha-shniya* 'for the second time'):[26]

she'al káma peamim	שאל כמה פעמים
	'Ask several times'

af páam en uga	אף פעם אין עוגה
no time there-isn't cake	'There's never any cake'

Of duration. For duration, extending either forwards or backwards, the prepositions במשך *bemésheH* and זה *ze* or מזה *mize* are just optional, provided a time, such as יומיים *yomáyim* 'two days', is specified:

yashánti (bemésheH) shavuot	ישנתי (במשך) שבועות
I-slept (for) weeks	'I slept for weeks'

kama zman at po? - (mize) Hódesh	כמה זמן את פה? - (מזה) חודש
how-much time you here? -	'How long have you been here? -
(since) month	A month'

dibárta bemésheH kol ha-kontsert	דיברת במשך כל הקונצרט
you-spoke during all the concert	

Of time relationship. Phrases of the type פעם ראשונה *páam rishona* '(for the) first time' take no preposition. An alternative is בפעם הראשונה *ba-páam ha-rishona* (on-the time the first), with a preposition and definite but identical in meaning. A separate (casual) construction is דבר ראשון *davar rishon* 'first thing' etc:

ani mitbayesh lomar zot ve-lo páam	אני מתבייש לומר זאת ולא פעם
rishona	ראשונה
I'm ashamed to-say this and not time first	'...and not for the first time'

davar rishon badku oti ve-az...	דבר ראשון בדקו אותי ואז...
thing first they-checked me and then...	'First they checked me and then...'

Preposition + noun phrase

Point of time 'Co-temporal' is usually expressed by -ב *be-*, e.g. ביום שני הזה/שעבר *be-yom sheni haze/she-avar* 'this/last Monday' (on Monday the this/that passed), בימי שני *bi-ymey sheni* 'on Mondays', ב(שעה) שש *be-(sha'a) shesh* 'at six (o'clock)'.

21.7.2 Syntax

Function

Time adjuncts generally qualify a predicate:

hem tamid {ravim/kenim}	הם תמיד {רבים/כנים}
	'They're always {arguing/honest}'

Adjuncts of specific time (not e.g. תמיד *tamid* 'always') can also be predicate themselves, as in (1) below, and can by the same token qualify nouns (2):

(1) matay ha-Hazarot, {ha-yom/kol sha'a}? מתי החזרות, {היום/כל שעה}?
   when [are] the rehearsals, {today/every hour}?

(2) saper al ha-mesiba etmol ספר על המסיבה אתמול
   tell about the party yesterday [= the party which was yesterday]

Frequency quantifiers

הרבה *harbe* 'a lot', כמה *káma* 'how much' and suchlike can generally be used like הרבה פעמים *harbe peamim* 'often' etc., though rarely with adjectives (see example (3)) or their derivatives (4):[27]

(1)   aHshav ze kore yoter   עכשיו זה קורה יותר
'Now it happens more'

(2)   hu yoter miday étsel horav   הוא יותר מדי אצל הוריו
'He's too much at his parents'

(3)   hi ayefa { *harbe / harbe peamim }   *הרבה / היא עייפה
הרבה פעמים
'She's tired {*a lot/often}'

(4)   *ze mishtane harbe   *זה משתנה הרבה
'It changes a lot'

Adverbial + -ש *she-*

'Duration since' adjuncts can take a 'dummy' conjunction -ש *she-*, when preceding the clause:

{mi-ze/kvar} káma Hodashim (she-)hem shovtim   {מזה/כבר} כמה חודשים (ש)הם שובתים
{for/already} several months (that) they're striking   'It's several months that they've been striking'

Positioning

Most time adjuncts can appear virtually anywhere except between subject and verb/adjective, and there too for emphasis - but the exceptions are important. (Naturally, the subtle forces of balance, context and emphasis also intervene) בשבת *be-shabat* 'on Saturday' is typical; '∧' in the example marks where it will appear (with no special emphasis):

láma ata ko'es?   למה אתה כועס?
ki ∧ bni kibel ∧ doH-Hanaya∧   כי ∧ בני קיבל ∧ דו"ח חנייה ∧
'Why are you angry? Because ∧ my son got ∧ a parking ticket ∧'

This holds for place adjuncts too (21.8). As usual, longish adjuncts generally gravitate to either end of the clause Exceptions, listed under (a)-(e) below, mostly involve one-word adverbs.

(a)   Between subject and verb (or anywhere else): פעם *páam* 'once (upon a time)', אז *az* 'then [= at that time]', עכשיו *aHshav* 'now', תמיד *tamid* 'always' and many others.

(b)   Somewhere before the verb: תכף *téHef* 'soon' (with present or future tense).[28]

(c)   Somewhere after the verb: מוקדם *mukdam* 'early', מאוחר *meuHar* 'late', מחדש *meHadash* 'anew', עוד, שוב, יותר *od, shuv, yoter* 'ever again', and the quantifiers such as הרבה *harbe* 'a lot' (so too quantifiers of extent; see 21.3).

(d) Initial: אז *az* 'then [= after that]'.

(e) Directly before the verb: רק ,אך *aH, rak* 'only just', טרם *térem* 'not yet', עוד *od* 'still' (c).

All of these are unamenable to focusing, eg. negation.

If the adverbial comes first, the verb can optionally come next (balance etc. permitting):

kvar ata	ha-Hevra mekabélet... mekabélet ha-Hevra...	...החברה מקבלת	כבר עתה
		...מקבלת החברה	
already now	the company receives... receives the company...	'Now already the company receives...'	

Positioning *vis-à-vis* one another

There is no general priority between various time adjuncts, eg. (all else being equal):

yesh kénes Hashuv	be-Hol Hódesh ha-shana ha-shana be-Hol Hódesh	בכל חודש השנה	יש כנס חשוב
		השנה בכל חודש	

'There's an important conference {every month this year/this year every month}'

Similarly when they are initial; but when one is initial and the other(s) elsewhere, the initial must be the most general (except for emphasis):

kol yom yesh tsofar be-shesh   כל יום יש צופר בשש

GENERAL   SPECIFIC   'Every day there's a siren at six'

every day there's siren at six

'Tight' time adjuncts

Some verbs of *occurence* or *duration* take time adjuncts 'tightly', without pause, often because they require such an adjunct:

be'od shavúa yaHul pésaH   **בעוד שבוע** יחול פסח

in week will-fall Pesach   'Pesach is **in a week**'

ha-tisa arHa **sha'a**   הטיסה ארכה **שעה**

         'The flight lasted ⟨an⟩ **hour**'

21.8 Place adverbials

21.8.1 Form

Place adverbials can have the following forms:[29]

Special one-word adverb :	tásnu lemáala we-flew upwards	טסנו למעלה
Adjective :	... gavóa ba-shamáyim ... high in the sky	...גבוה בשמיים

Noun phrase of distance :	... élef kilométer ... 1000 km	...אלף קילומטר
Preposition + noun phrase :	... le-sin ... to China	...לסין
Preposition + place adverbial :	... le-sham ... to there	...לשם

Special one-word adverbs. These have no distinctive form, eg. איפה *éfo* 'where', פה *po* 'here', סביב *saviv* 'around'. Several idiomatically attach the prepositions -מ *mi-*, -ל *le-* or the unstressed suffix ה- *-a* to nouns, other prepositions or non-independent bases, eg. מצפון *mi-tsafon* 'in/from the North', ממול *mi-mul* 'opposite', מאחור *meaHor* 'behind'.

Adjectives. Among the few adjectives used as place adverbs (and not agreeing with the subject) are רחוק *raHok* 'far away' and נמוך *namoH* 'low down':

tásnu **namoH** min ha-ragil pl. m.s. we-flew **low** than the usual	טסנו **נמוך** מן הרגיל 'We flew **lower** than usual'

Noun phrases of distance Like duration adverbials (חכה שעה *Hake sha'a* 'wait an hour', 21.7.1), there are distance adverbials, usually a noun phrase of measure Here there is *no* optional preposition like במשך *bemésheH* 'during', just את *et* where definite (just as in 'echo adverbials', 21.4.2):

sa Hamishim kilométer	סע חמשים קילומטר 'Go 50 kilometers'

nasáti et	ha-méa mayl kol ha-déreH	le-elat	נסעתי את	המאה מייל לאילת כל הדרך
I-went OM	the 100 miles all the way	to Elat		

ha-kli'im hayu neutsim **Hatsi méter** betoH ha-Homa the bullets were lodged **half ⟨a⟩ metre** in the wall	הקליעים היו נעוצים **חצי מטר** בתוך החומה

Preposition + noun phrase All place adjuncts denoting location, 'to' or 'from' require a preposition (rarely, the suffix ה- *-a*) with any noun phrase The most general are -ב *be-* 'at, in', -ל *le-* 'to'[30] and -מ *mi-* 'from'.[31]

Preposition + place adverbial. Permitted combinations are a rather arbitrary matter, eg. מכאן *mi-kan* 'from here' but not בתוך כאן *betoH kan* ('inside here'), אל מאחורי... *el meaHorey...* 'to behind...' but not ...למאחורי *le-meaHorey...* ('to behind...').

21.8.2   Syntax

Function

Place adverbials can qualify a predicate, be predicates themselves, or modify nouns:[32]

hu mesaHek **ba-Huts**	'He plays **outside**'	הוא משחק **בחוץ**
hu **ba-Huts**	'He's **outside**'	הוא **בחוץ**
ha-kise **ba-Huts** nirtav	'The chair **outside** got wet'	הכיסא **בחוץ** נרטב

Motion adverbials require a motion verb.[33]

Positioning

Place adjuncts (like time, 21.7.2) can appear - with or without pause - before the subject or after the verb etc., except for tight adjuncts (below); and there are no exceptions among the one-word adverbs.

Relative positioning (of specific *vis-à-vis* general, place vs. time, verb when preceded by adjunct etc.) is as in 21.7.2.

Tight place adjuncts

Many verbs of motion or location take place adjuncts 'tightly', without pause, often because they require such an adjunct, eg. גר *gar* 'live', שהה *shaha* 'stay', מצוי *matsuy* 'situtated', התגעגע *hitgaagéa* 'yearn':

bi-tHuma **metsuyim** rov ha-mekarke'in   בתחומה **מצויים** רוב המקרקעין
'In its area ⟨are⟩ **situated** most ⟨of⟩ the lands'

Apparently indistinguishable in sentence structure from 'objects' (ch.15), these are adverbials semantically; thus the appropriate interrogative word is איפה *éfo* 'where' or לאן *le'an* 'to where'.[34]

21.9   Status ('as') adverbials

The prepositions בתור ,-כ *ke-*, *betor* 'as' introduce at least three related adjunct constructions:

(1)   **ke-morim**, ánu mitnagdim   **כמורים**, אנו מתנגדים
        as teachers we object   ('as' = *qua*)

        liglegu alay, **ke-more**   ליגלגו עלי, **כמורה**
        they-mocked at-me **as [a] teacher**

(2)   liglegu alay, **ke-yéled**   ליגלגו עלי, **כילד**
        they-mocked at-me, **as [a] child**   ('as' = 'when')

(3)   avádnu bishvilo ke-morim   עבדנו בשבילו כמורים
        we-worked for-him as teachers

        liglegu alay {ke-/ke-al} baHyan   ליגלגו עלי {כ/כעל} בכיין
        they-mocked at-me {as/as at} [a] crybaby

This - כ *ke-* is distinct from כמו *kmo* 'like' (whose formal alternative is also - כ *ke-*) - and the appropriate 'question word' is not איך *eH* 'how'. As in circumstance adverbials (21.6) the noun identified in bold type here relates to and (where feasible) agrees with the object or the subject.

Whereas constructions (1) and (2) are 'loose adverbials', capable of shifting around with pauses, construction (3) generally follows the verb 'tightly', without pause, like 'tight' time and place adverbials - it is tied to verbs of status. These may be (a) verbs of 'having status', eg. עבד *avad* 'work', תיפקד *tifked* 'function', התחזה *hitHaza* 'masquerade' - here it is subject-related; or (b) verbs of 'creating status', eg. התייחס *hityaHes* 'treat', השתמש *hishtamesh* 'use', הגדיר *higdir* 'define', הכריז *hiHriz* 'proclaim', ראה *ra'a* 'view', בחר *baHar* 'choose'; and of 'attitude', eg. התלונן *hitlonen* 'criticize', שיבח *shibaH* 'praise' - here it is object-related (and when passivized it becomes subject-related) and can be expanded to a whole verb phrase:[35]

ra'u trufa zo **ke-potéret** kama	ראו תרופה זו **כפותרת** כמה
ve-Hama baayot	וכמה בעיות
'They saw this medicine **as solving** several problems'	

Some verbs let - כ *ke-* interchange with - ל *le-* (notably התחזה *hitHaza* 'masquerade as', מינה *mina* 'appoint as', בחר *baHar* 'choose as', חשב *Hashav* 'regard as') or even drop (שימש *shimesh* 'serve as').[36]

An alternative to construction (3) with some verbs, if the object has prepositions other than את *et*, is an object+object clause, as in:

liglegu **alav** she-hu yéled péle	ליגלגו **עליו** שהוא ילד פלא
they-mocked **at-him** that he's child wonder	'They mocked **him as** a wonder child'

Many verbs (including some taking את *et*) take object clauses without there being a preceding object noun such as עליו *alav*: examples are התלונן *hitlonen* 'complain', זכר *zaHar* 'remember', ראה *ra'a* 'see'. But this will not always do the same job as 'as' phrases - contrast:

ra'u **she-ani** ga'on	'They saw **that** I'm a genius'	ראו **שאני** גאון
ra'u **oti ke**-ga'on	'They saw **me as** a genius'	ראו **אותי כ**גאון

And some 'as' verbs require an object before a clause, eg. ליגלג *ligleg* 'mock', ריחם *riHem* 'pity'.

21.10 Semi-adverbial datives

Four types of dative, i.e - ל *le-* phrases, are to be regarded as on the border between object and adverbial: they denote affectee, benefactee, possessor and 'autonomous agent'.

Affectee To denote the person (occasionally, the thing) tangentially affected by an action,[37] the dative can be added between verb and object (if any). This commonly serves to achieve a mention of an animate participant before the inanimate participant. It is a casual construction:

liHláHta **le-ishti** et ha-mitbaH!   ‏ליכלכת **לאשתי** את המטבח!‏
you've-dirtied **to my-wife** OM the kitchen!   'You've dirtied the kitchen **for my wife!**'

hu pataH **li** tik   ‏הוא פתח **לי** תיק‏
'He opened a file **against me**'

hi nirdema **lo**   ‏היא נרדמה **לו**‏
'She fell asleep **on him**'
(i.e in his presence)

Benefactee To denote the person benefitting from an action, the dative can be added after the verb (sometimes after the object), particularly typically benefactive verbs such as רקד *rakad* 'dance', ניגן *nigen* 'play', בנה *bana* 'build', בישל *bishel* 'cook':[38]

hishkéti   **la-shaHen** et ha-praHim   ‏**לשכן** את הפרחים‏
         et ha-praHim **la-shaHen**   ‏את הפרחים **לשכן**‏

I-watered   **for-the neighbour** OM the flowers
         OM the flowers **for-the neighbour**

hu pataH **li** tik   ‏הוא פתח **לי** תיק‏
     'He opened a file **for me**'

There may be different degrees of benefaction:

hi mevashélet **li**   ‏היא מבשלת **לי**‏
     'She cooks **for me** (i.e to eat)'

hi mevashélet **bishvili**   ‏היא מבשלת **בשבילי**‏
     'She cooks **for me** (i.e as a job)'

A pair of datives tends to be avoided:

ulay tar'e **li** et ze **le-édna**   ‏אולי תראה **לי** את זה **לעדנה**‏
perhaps you'll-show **to-me** OM this **to Edna**
     'Could you show it **to Edna for me**'

Possessor. When reference is made to part of someone's body (whether as subject, object or adverbial), casual usage tends to specify *whose body* by the dative, occasionally by the possessive (שלי *sheli* 'my', שלו *shelo* 'his' etc.). Formal usage requires possessive suffixes, as in בטנו *bitno* 'his stomach'. The dative comes between verb and object (if any), thus again mentioning the animate participant ahead of the inanimate:[39]

yaakov sirek **le-aHoto** et ha-se'ar   ‏יעקב סירק **לאחותו** את השיער‏
Yaakov combed **to his-sister** OM the hair   'Yaakov combed his sister's hair'

histakálti **le-Hána** ba-enáyim   ‏הסתכלתי **לחנה** בעיניים‏
I-looked **to Hana** in-the eyes   'I looked Hanna in the eyes'

Autonomous agent. Particularly, but not exclusively, in formal Hebrew, the *reflexive dative* serves to emphasize the autonomy of an action, especially with verbs[40] of movement and stationary or engrossed activity. The reflexive uses the ordinary, non-reflexive pronoun, unlike objects; but unlike adverbials, including the other datives in this section, the 'autonomy dative' cannot be focused or emphasized. It is thus like a suffix, indeed a 'subject suffix' highlighting that the subject is his 'own free agent':

ha-tsofe nimnem lo	הצופה נימנם לו
the scout was-dozing to-him	'The scout was dozing away'

she-teleH la!	שתלך לה!
that she-go to-her	'Away with her!'

FURTHER READING
Agmon-Fruchtman 1980, 1984; Amit 1976; Avineri 1962; Azar 1977: ch.5; Ben-Asher 1972: ch.2; Berman 1978: 10.4, 1980b, 1982a, b; Blau 1957, 1973; Chayen & Dror 1976: ch.7; Friedman 1971; Glinert 1974; Kaddari 1985; Lerner 1976; Mackenzie 1978; Ornan 1979a: 5.12, ch.6; Ravid 1977; Ring 1971; Rosén 1962, 1966a: ch.3, 1977: 134; Rubinstein 1970, 1971; Sadka 1977, 1978, 1981; Schwarzwald 1976b, 1977a.

22. Focus adverbs

22.1 Introduction

Focus adverbs are a small class of words expressing such 'logical' relationships as 'also, even, especially, either, only, at least', and focusing on (i.e stressing) individual words, phrases or clauses - or occasionally even on the whole sentence[1] Examples are:

ra'ínu sham **gam** atsmot pilim	ראינו שם **גם** עצמות פילים
we-saw there **also** bones elephants	'We also saw elephant bones there'

laHen, **aH** tiv'i ha-davar she..	לכן, **אך** טבעי הדבר ש...
therefore, **only** natural the fact that...	'Therefore it is only natural that...'

bikshu **rak** she-naHrish	ביקשו **רק** שנחריש
CLAUSE	
they-asked **only** that we-keep-quiet	'They only asked that we keep quiet'

nirshámti, **rak** she-lo shilámti	נרשמתי, **רק** שלא שילמתי
I-registered, **only** that not I-paid	'I registered, only I didn't pay'

They tend to stand close to the word etc. on which they focus - even in speech, where intonation already shows what is being stressed. Indeed, Hebrew quite generally indicates stress by special word order on top of special intonation (see ch. 37):

atsmot *pilim* ra'íta?	עצמות פילים ראית?
bones elephants you-saw?	'Did you see *elephant* bones?'

22.2 Form and meaning

Focus adverbs have no distinctive shape, and are not productively coined. Notable examples, grouped by semantic type, are given below (F = formal, C = casual).

Additive:

גם *gam,* גם כן *gam ken* (C), אף *af* (F), ...אף הוא/היא., גם הוא/היא *gam hu/hi* etc., *af hu/hi* etc. (F) 'also, even'.
וכן *ve-Hen* 'and also'.
אפילו *afílu,* ולו *ve-lu* (F) 'even' (see 22.5)

245

Restrictive ('only'):

רק rak,[2] אך aH (F), אך ורק aH ve-rak (F), בלבד bilvad (F), לבד levad (F),[3] לבדי/לבדך... levadi/levadHa (F) etc. (agrees with the noun it focuses on), or a combination of any negator with אלא éla 'but' (F):

lo matsáti éla shnáyim	לא מצאתי אלא שניים
not I-found but two	'I only found two'

Specific:

במיוחד bimyuHad, בייחוד beyiHud [4] 'especially'.

דווקא dávka[5] 'of all things/people, precisely', e.g. דווקא שמיר dávka shamir 'Shamir of all people'.

(ב)עצמי (be-)atsmi[6] 'myself' (emphatic), 'as for myself', כשלעצמי ke-she-le-atsmi 'as for myself' (F), (both agree with focused noun, thus עצמה atsma 'herself' etc.).

אני-, אתה-... -ani/-ata etc.[7] (F) 'own', as in:

artsénu-ánu	ארצנו-אנו
land-our we	'our own land'

Essential:

גופא gufa (F), גופו gufo etc. (F) (agrees with focused noun) 'proper':

ha-maamar gufo	'the article proper'	המאמר גופו

לפחות lefaHot 'at least'.

לא lo 'not'.[8]

A fortiori ('all the more so'):

לא כל שכן, על אחת כמה וכמה lo kol she-ken, al aHat kama ve-Hama (F), as in:

be-ásya... u-ve-áfrika lo kol she-ken	באסיה... ובאפריקה לא כל שכן
	'In Asia... and how much more so in Africa'

Correlatives:

גם ...(ו)גם..., הן ...והן... gam... (ve-)gam..., hen... ve-hen 'both... and...' (F); בין ...(ו)בין..., אם ...ואם... ben... (u-)ven..., im... ve-im... 'whether... or...' (F); או ...או... o... o... 'either... or...'; לא... ולא... lo... ve-lo... 'neither... nor...'.

22.3-6   FOCUS ON PART OF A SENTENCE

22.3   Focus on what?

Most focus adverbs can focus on any part of speech occupying any position, e.g.:

rak mimHatot **levanot** mutarot	רק ממחטות לבנות מותרות
└─FOCUS─→ ADJ	FOCUS
only hankies **white** are-allowed	'Only white hankies are allowed'

kaH **gam** et ha-késef ha-katan ba-**kufsa**   קח **גם** את הכסף הקטן **בקופסה**

      N PHRASE   FOCUS

   FOCUS

'**Also** take the small change in the **box**'

and even on a pronoun suffixed to a preposition:[9]

yaru **alav** {bilvad/levado/af hu}   ירו **עליו** {בלבד/לבדו/אף הוא}

   PRONOUN

they-shot at-**him** {alone /also}

Clauses too can undergo focus:

afilu **im nisog**...   ...אפילו **אם נסוג**

   CLAUSE

even **if we-withdraw**...

hitsíu gam **she-ashaker**   הציעו גם **שאשקר**

      CLAUSE

they-proposed also **that I-lie**

More than one per clause is conceivable:

yéter ha-atarim she-ba-galil **af hem**   יתר האתרים שבגליל **אף הם**

heHélu lif'ol **gam** ba-Hóref   החלו לפעול **גם** בחורף

      'The other sites in the Galilee **too** began operating in winter **too**'

hu eyno aHra'i **éla** le-aHzaka **bilvad**   הוא אינו אחראי **אלא** לאחזקה **בלבד**

      'He is **only** responsible for maintenance **alone**'

Restrictions

There are a few restrictions on focus (and many on *positioning* the focus adverb - see 22.4).

The only focus adverbs to focus on possessive suffixes are the hyphenated personal pronouns, and this is their only use as focus adverbs:[10]

mishpaHti-ani   family-me I   'my own family'   משפחתי-אני

     PRONOUN

baayotav-hu   problems-him he   'his own problems'   בעיותיו-הוא

     PRONOUN

The following focus only on definite nouns: focus adverbs incorporating a pronoun agreeing with a preceding noun, e.g. אף הוא *af hu* 'also', לבדו *levado* 'alone', עצמו *atsmo* 'oneself', גופו *gufo* 'proper', and הוא- *-hu* 'one's own'; thus:

yisrael **levada** nishala   Israel **alone** was-asked   ישראל **לבדה** נשאלה

but not:

*horim levadam (✓bilvad) nishalu   *הורים לבדם (✓בלבד) נשאלו

   INDEF

parents alone were-asked

Items focusing only on noun/preposition/adverb phrases are לא כל שכן,
על אחת כמה וכמה *lo kol she-ken, al aHat káma ve-Háma* 'all the more so'.
An item focusing only on verbs or adjectives is אך *aH* 'only', thus:

isuk ze aH mevazbez et zmana
עיסוק זה אך מבזבז את זמנה
'This activity only wastes her time'

and not:

*isuk ze hino aH masve
*עיסוק זה הינו אך מסווה
('This activity is only ⟨a⟩ cover')

רק *rak* and בלבד *bilvad* (not אך *aH* etc.) can go with numerals to denote 'no
more than', eg. מאה מטר בלבד *méa méter bilvad* '100m. only'. See 22.4.3 for
positioning, and 8.13 for other words (non-focusing) that qualify numerals,
denoting 'roughly, more than, barely' etc.

22.4   Positioning

22.4.1   Outline: focusing from close up

Focus adverbs can, and most tend to, appear *alongside* the word(s)
in focus:

gam *mifalénu* orez teenim
also *our-factory* packs figs
גם מפעלנו אורז תאנים
'Our factory too packs figs'

mifalénu gam *orez* teenim
Our-factory also *packs* figs
מפעלנו גם אורז תאנים
'Our factory also *packs* figs'

mifalénu orez gam *teenim*
our-factory packs also *figs*
מפעלנו אורז גם תאנים
'Our factory packs *figs* too'

However, in negative sentences focus adverbs readily go with the 'negative' word
rather than just with the word being focused:

hu {gam/afilu} lo ohev et makártni
he even not likes OM makártni
הוא {גם/אפילו} לא אוהב את מקרטני
'He doesn't even like Macartney'

hu lo ohev {gam/afilu} et makártni
he not likes even OM makártni
הוא לא אוהב {גם/אפילו} את מקרטני
'He doesn't even like Macartney'

ze eyno rak osek be-yahalomim
     eyno osek rak
זה אינו רק עוסק ביהלומים
    אינו עוסק רק

it not only deals with diamonds
    not deals only
'It doesn't only deal with diamonds'

Furthermore, focus adverbs incorporating a pronoun occur *anywhere* after the
focused word (by virtue of the referring pronoun) - except לבד/לבדו
levad/levado 'alone', which thus (example (3)) avoids confusion with לבדו
levado 'unaided' (example (4)):

(1) ha-méleH **(be-)atsmo** tsaHak   המלך **(ב)עצמו** צחק

(2) ha-méleH tsaHak **be-atsmo**   המלך צחק **בעצמו**
'The king **himself** laughed'

(3) hu **levado** noheg   הוא **לבדו** נוהג
'He **alone** drives'

(4) hu noheg **levado**   הוא נוהג **לבדו**
'He drives **by himself**'

Moreover, in casual usage (especially) other focus adverbs too can operate 'at a distance':[11]

ha-mifal {rak/gam} orez *tapuHim*   המפעל {רק/גם} אורז תפוחים
'The factory {only/also} packs *apples*'

yibáshti et ha-kosiyot gam ken   ייבשתי את הכוסיות גם כן
'I *dried* the glasses also'

In general, where ambiguity of focus is a danger, the adverb is presumed to focus on the nearest appropriate word.

22.4.2   Before or after the focused item?

Here as so often, there is no semantic basis for the positioning of individual words: the table below illustrates the pattern.

Examples
Only preceding the focused word :
af   'also'   אף
רק, אך, אך ורק
rak, aH, aH ve-rak   'only' ha-méshek mevusas aH ve-rak al... המשק מבוסס אך ורק על...
'The economy is based only on...'
lo   'no'   לא
All correlatives
Only following the focused word :
gam ken   'also'   גם כן
bilvad, levad 'only' בלבד, לבד   avur naHim bilvad   'For invalids only'   עבור נכים בלבד
All pronoun-incorporating adverbs: levado לבדו, af hu אף הוא
Preceding or following the focused word :
gam   'also'   גם[1]   ata **gam** ba/**gam** ata ba?   אתה **גם** באי/**גם** אתה באי
'Are *you* coming **too**?'

			Examples
			zéhu, ze **gam**!/zéhu, **gam** ze! !זהו, זה **גם**!/זהו, **גם** זה 'This is it, that **too**!'
afilu	'even'	אפילו[1]	lo ratsíti litsHok **afilu** לא רציתי לצחוק **אפילו** not I-wanted to-laugh **even** lo ratsíti **afilu** litsHok לא רציתי **אפילו** לצחוק *Transl. for both*: 'I didn't even want to laugh'
dávka	'precisely'	דווקא	láma baHar **dávka** be-varod? ?למה בחר **דווקא** בוורוד why he-chose precisely pink? láma baHar be-varod **dávka**? ?למה בחר בוורוד **דווקא** *Transl. for both*: 'Why did he choose *pink*?'
beyiHud bimyuHad	'especially'	בייחוד[2] במיוחד	
lefaHot	'at least'	לפחות	**lefaHot** be-inyan ze efshar le.. ...**לפחות** בעניין זה אפשר ל **at-least** in matter this one may... be-inyan ze, **lefaHot**, efshar le.. ...בעניין זה, **לפחות**, אפשר ל *Transl. for both*: 'In this matter at least one may...'
lo kol she-ken לא כל שכן על אחת כמה וכמה al aHat kama ve-Hama 'all the more so'			

Notes:
[1] This follows only in casual usage
[2] In initial position, במיוחד *bimyuHad* means 'just': באתי במיוחד בשבילך *báti bimyuHad bishvileH* 'I came just for you'.

22.4.3 Restrictions on positioning

לא *lo* 'not' must precede the verb, if any, as in (1) below - unless the focus explicitly involves *contrast*, i.e 'not mice but rats', in which case, as in (2,3), it may instead precede the focused words:

(1) hu **lo** ko'es aláyiH   הוא **לא** כועס עליך
     he **not** is-angry at-you   'He's not angry at you'

(2) hu **lo** ko'es aláyiH éla alay   הוא **לא** כועס עליך אלא עלי
     he **not** is-angry at-you but at-me   'He's not angry at you but at me'

(3) hu ko'es **lo** aláyiH éla alay   הוא כועס **לא** עליך אלא עלי
     he is-angry **not** at-you but at-me   'He's not angry at you but at me'

Similarly, לא *lo* must precede the verb when part of the לא...אלא *lo...éla* 'only' construction - here אלא *éla* (ordinarily = 'but rather') is not contrastive:

hem lo hisigu éla heskem Helki   הם לא השיגו אלא הסכם חלקי
they not reached but agreement partial   'They only reached a partial agreement'

This construction, strictly speaking, involves any negator (ch.29), even בלי *bli* 'without'; and there must be some item intervening between its two components (as if to give the negator something to negate), even just a suffix:

hu ey**no** éla mashle atsmo   הוא אינו אלא משלה עצמו
he is-not-SUFFIX but deluding himself   'He is only deluding himself'

*hu lo éla hishla atsmo   *הוא לא אלא השלה עצמו
he not but deluded himself   ('He was only deluding himself')

Crossing into noun phrases etc.
Focus adverbs can be conceived of as issuing from some central point to the various parts of the sentence, and they encounter obstacles - they cannot usually 'cross' into noun phrases or preposition phrases:

baHanu **gam** yeladim *du-leshoniyim*   בחנו **גם** ילדים דו־לשוניים
        N   PHR   'They also tested *bilingual* children'
they-tested **also** children *bilingual*

and not:

*baHanu yeladim **gam** du-leshoniyim   *בחנו ילדים **גם** דו־לשוניים
they-tested children **also** bilingual

Similarly:

daber **afilu** al ze   דבר **אפילו** על זה
speak **even** about that
*daber al **afilu** ze   *דבר על **אפילו** זה
speak about **even** that

A result of this is the distinction between אף *af* as a focus adverb (= 'even') and as a negative determiner (= 'no'; see ch. 9):

af be-iton   'even in ⟨a⟩ newspaper'   אף בעתון
be-af iton   'in no newspaper'   באף עתון

22.5   Syntactic restrictions
Three (formal) focus adverbs introduce *apposed* words or clauses, the first two always and the third usually:

ve-lu   'even'   ולו
im... $\genfrac{}{}{0pt}{}{\text{ve-im}}{o}$ ...   'whether...or...' $\genfrac{}{}{0pt}{}{\text{ואם}}{\text{או}}$ ...אם...
ben... (u)ven...   'whether...or...'   בין...(ו)בין...

ולו *velu* (related to -ו *ve-* 'and' plus hypothetical לו *lu* 'if'; cf. 32.11.2) is strictly hypothetical and may be rendered 'even if it be..', unlike the other word for 'even' אפילו *afilu*:

ha'im yesh sikuy, velu ha-kal beyoter,...?   ‏האם יש סיכוי, ולו הקל ביותר,...?‏
'Is there a chance, even the slightest,...?'

keHol she-ha-mitsva heHraHit yoter,   ‏ככל שהמצווה הכרחית יותר,‏
{ben/im} mitsad ha-adam,   ‏בין/אם} מצד האדם,}‏
{ben/im/o} mitsad ha-makom   ‏בין/אם/או} מצד המקום}‏
{u-ven/ve-im/o} mitsad ha-zman,...   ‏ובין/ואם/או} מצד הזמן,...}‏

'The more the precept is essential, whether in terms of man or in terms of
place or in terms of time,...'

By contrast, ...אי...או *o...o...* 'either...or...' and other correlatives (see 22.6) are
not limited to apposition:

hishtamesh o (*im) be-neft o be-peHam   ‏השתמש או (*אם) בנפט או בפחם‏
'Use either oil or coal'

A more general restriction is that when the focused noun is *unsaid*, focus is
impossible - thus ruling out the following relative clause:[13]

dov, she-gam (√she-gam hu) ahav dikduk...   ‏דב, שגם (√שגם הוא) אהב דיקדוק...‏
Dov, that also (√that also he) liked grammar   ('Dov, who also liked grammar')

Conversely, there is nothing to stop one focusing on a focus adverb itself, eg.
negating, questioning or otherwise emphasizing בלבד , רק *rak, bilvad* 'only',
דווקא *dávka* 'precisely', and (ב)עצמו *(be-)atsmo* 'oneself'. לא *lo* 'not' too is
questioned and emphasized. Thus:

lo rak yisra'el éla...   ‏לא רק ישראל אלא...‏
'not only Israel but...'

22.6   Correlatives: גם...ו... *gam...ve..* 'both...and...',   או...או... *o...o...*
'either...or...' etc.

'Correlative focus adverbs' focus in *series*, usually in pairs, on (conjoined) words or phrases; some examples are listed below.

...ולא...לא *lo...ve-lo...* 'neither...nor...' (*lit.* 'not...and not...'), when following
the verb, comes *in addition* to the usual לא *lo* 'not' which precedes the verb
(see also ch. 29):

ani lo
eynéni   rotse lo ezra ve-lo raHamim   ‏אני לא‏   ‏רוצה לא עזרה ולא רחמים‏   ‏איננו‏
I not want not help and not pity   'I want neither help nor pity'

lo rómi lo yavan ve-lo kartágo hitslíHu..   ‏לא רומי לא יוון ולא קרתגו הצליחו‏
not Rome not Greece and not Carthage succeeded...

...גם(ו)...גם *gam...(ve-)gam...* 'both...and...' is literally 'also...and also' - but
here the two גם *gam* relate to one another and not to the foregoing; -ו *ve* 'and'
can drop formally:

...להילחם **גם** ככוח מוצנח, **גם** בנחיתה מהים, **(ו)גם** כחיל רגלים
...lehilaHem **gam** ke-kóaH mutsnaH, **gam** bi-neHita me-ha-yam,
   (ve-)gam ke-Heyl raglim
   '...to fight **both** as a paratroop force, **and** by seaborne landing,
   and as infantry'

הן...והן... *hen...ve-hen...* 'both...and...' is used only correlatively. As for
או...או... *o...o...* 'either...or...', although single או *o* is the conjunction 'or' and
not a focus adverb (thus: הוא **גם** מצייר *hu* **gam** *metsayer* 'he **also** paints', and
not *הוא **או** מצייר* *hu* **o** *metsayer* 'he **or** paints'), correlative ...או...או... *o...o...*
is strictly a focus adverb:[14]

שבי **או** עם דליה **או** עם ליאורה

shvi **o** im dálya **o** im lióra
sit **either** with Dalya **or** with Liora

In all the above, the second of the pair can be tagged to the *end* of the sentence
(as is common with conjoined phrases, see ch. 35):

לא המשטרה הוזעקה ולא הצבא

lo ha-mishtara huzaka ve-lo ha-tsava
not the police was-called and not   'Neither the police were called nor
the army   the army'

בין...(ו)בין... *ben...(u)ven...* and ...אם...{או/ואם} *im...{o/ve-im}* 'whether...
or...' are used only correlatively, the latter only in apposition (see 22.5).

22.7 Focus on whole sentences: רק *rak* 'only', לא ש- *lo she-* 'not that...'

Certain types of focus adverb, *initial* in a sentence, can focus on the
whole sentence rather than on individual words - setting it against the adjoining
discourse They are thus equivalent to 'link adverbs' (ch. 24), whose *only* role is
to signal the logical ties between sentences, eg. כמו-כן *kmo-Hen* 'likewise'.
'*Also*':

		גם
	gam	
baali be-Hul ve-	*gam ken* aHoti Hola	בעלי בחו"ל ו גם כן אחותי חולה
	af	אף

'My husband (is) abroad and **also**
[= moreover] my sister (is) ill'

'*Only*': רק ש- *rak she-* 'only',[15] לא רק ש- , לא זו בלבד ש-[17] *lo rak she*,[16] *lo zo
bilvad she-* (F) 'not only':

אתן לו ללכת ברצון, **רק שהוא**
עכשיו חולה...

éten lo laléHet be-ratson, **rak she-hu**
aHshav Hole..
   'I will allow him to go willingly, **only** [= however]
   he is now ill...'

{לא רק/לא זו בלבד} שקיום יש הרבה
זוגות צעירים אלא...

{lo rak/lo zo bilvad} she-kayom yesh harbe
zugot tseirim éla...
not only that nowadays there-are many   'Not only are there nowadays many
   couples young but...   young couples but...'

'*Not*': לא ש- *lo she-* 'not that' (c):

לא שאני רוצה לאיים אבל...

lo she-ani rotse leayem aval...
Not that I want to-threaten but...

The two foregoing types are the only focus adverbs to allow (and require) -ש *she-*; there is no -ש גם* *gam she-* ('also that') or -ש לפחות* *lefaHot she-* ('at least'):[18]

'At least' (not only initial) :

בוא נלך. הגשם נפסק **לפחות**

bo neleH. ha-géshem nifsak **lefaHot**
'Let's go. The rain's stopped **at least**'

'Either...or...' :

או שהוא רב **או** שהוא צורח

o she-hu rav **o** she-hu tsoréaH
or that he quarrels **or that** he yells
'Either he quarrels or he yells'

The double -ש *she-* is obligatory (see note 15).[19] The second clause can be reduced to a mere tagged phrase:

או שהוא ידע או **שאת**

o she-hu yada o **she-at**
either that he knew or **that you**
'Either he knew or you did'

22.8   Focus on a camouflaged subordinate clause: אפילו *afilu* 'even if' etc.

Four focus adverbs are also used like prepositions introducing a clause; they are אפילו *afilu* 'even', אף *af* 'even', במיוחד *bimyuHad* 'especially' and בייחוד *beyiHud* 'particularly'. Examples and forms are listed here אפילו *afilu* 'even if':

אפילו כל העולם יצעק, ...

afilu kol ha-olam yits'ak,...
'Even if all the world screams,...'

-ש אפילו *afilu she-* 'even though' (i.e. 'even with the fact that'):

אני מחייך אליו אפילו שאינני
סובל אותו

ani meHayeH elav afilu she-enéni
sovel oto
'I smile at him even though I can't stand him!'

-ש אף *af she-* 'even though'.
כי אף *af ki* 'even though'.
-ש במיוחד *bimyuHad she-* 'particularly as':

מה אם יהיו סופות רעמים, במיוחד
שבא החורף?

ma im yiyu sufot reamim, bimyuHad
she-ba ha-Hóref?
'What if there are thunderstorms, particularly as
winter's coming?'

-ש בייחוד *beyiHud she-* 'particularly as'.

These four focus adverbs are focusing on a camouflaged *adverbial clause* ('if, despite, as'). אפילו *afilu* here is to be contrasted with אפילו *afilu* 'even' which focuses on a noun, as in example (2); the former tends to be followed directly by the verb, as in (1):[20]

(1)   afilu yitsaku Haveray,...   אפילו יצעקו חברי, ...
'Even if my friends scream, ...'

(2)   afilu Haveray yitsaku   אפילו חברי יצעקו
'Even my friends will scream'

FURTHER READING
Azar 1981: 138f; Blau 1966: 45,66; Chayen & Dror 1976: 142; Glinert 1978: 61.

23. Disjunct adverbials

23.1 Introduction

Disjuncts are 'fringe adverbials'. In terms of sentence structure, they are typically 'parenthetical'. Semantically, their main role is to evaluate a sentence or one's intentions in producing it - from three angles:

Truth disjunct :	**אולי** זה מדבק
ulay ze medabek	**'Maybe** it's catching'

Comment disjunct :	**לצערי,** זה קרוע
le-tsaari, ze karúa	**'Unfortunately** it's torn'

Manner of speaking disjunct :	**אישית,** אני בעד
ishit, ani be'ad	**'Personally,** I'm in favour'

However, a few disjuncts have a somewhat different role semantically, eg. ...למרות *lamrot*... 'despite..'; see 23.5.

As with all adverbial types, 'disjunct' denotes a specific *role* in sentence meaning and structure - filled by (1) a single word, (2) a phrase, or (3) a clause:

(1)	**ishit**, ani be'ad	**אישית,** אני בעד
		'Personally, I'm in favour'

(2)	**be-ófen ishi**, ani be'ad	**באופן אישי,** אני בעד
		'Personally, I'm in favour'

(3)	**lomar laH be-Henut**, ani be'ad	**לומר לך בכנות,** אני בעד
		'To put it candidly, I'm in favour'

This chapter deals with words ('adverbs') and phrases. For disjuncts as clauses, see chapter 32 (especially 32.1 and 32.12). For an overview of adverbials other than disjuncts, see 21.1. Contrast particularly with 'link adverbials' (ch. 24).

23.2-5 TYPES OF DISJUNCT
Most disjuncts are found in any position *vis-à-vis* subject, verb and object (balance and emphasis permitting); exceptions will be noted. Many disjuncts can potentially be marked off by pause or comma, i.e they are phonetically as well as semantically 'on the sidelines'.

23.2 Truth disjuncts

Truth disjuncts evaluate the likelihood of a sentence being true, in terms of (1) how definite? (ranging from 'undoubtedly' to 'in no way') and (2) in whose opinion? Since an exhaustive list and a precise translation of the various truth, comment and 'manner of speaking' disjuncts is beyond the scope of this book, examples will be given in context.

Examples of truth disjuncts

hem avaryanim pliliyim **beheHlet**　　　　הם עבריינים פליליים **בהחלט**
'They're **certainly** criminal offenders'

hu *bétaH* putar　　　　הוא **בטח** פוטר
'**Sure** he's been sacked'

hu **bétaH** putar　　　　הוא **בטח** פוטר
'He's **probably** been sacked'

he **beemet** yotser araHim　　　　הוא **באמת** יוצר ערכים
'He **really** creates values'

beHayay she-ani mefaHed　　　　**בחיי** שאני מפחד
'**Am I scared!**'

uvda, ze po'el　　　　**עובדה**, זה פועל
'**The fact is** - it works'

hagdarat tnu'a **omnam** titaHen, aH...　　　　הגדרת תנועה **אמנם** תיתכן, אך...
'Defining a vowel is **admittedly** possible, but...'

ve-**aHen**, tsadákti　　　　ו**אכן**, צדקתי
'And **indeed**, I was right'

halo ani makir otHa　　　　**הלא** אני מכיר אותך
'I know you **after all**'

hu met **ke'ilu**　　　　הוא מת **כאילו**
'He is dead, **so as to speak**'

gam ba-maHatsit ha-shniya **kmo**　　　　גם במחצית השניה **כמו**
nirata ba-migrash rak kvutsa aHat　　　　נראתה במגרש רק קבוצה אחת
'Even in the second half only one team **as it were** could be seen on the pitch'

ha'im barHu o **shéma** neHtefu　　　　האם ברחו או **שמא** נחטפו?
'Did they flee or **else** were they seized?'

ledaatam shel ha-shnáyim, tsriHot　　　　**לדעתם של השניים**, צריכות
ha-rashuyot lehitarev　　　　הרשויות להתערב
'**According to both**, the authorities must intervene'

Form of truth disjuncts

Truth disjuncts have no distinctive form. Many are also used for other purposes, eg. כמו *kmo* also means 'like' and בחיי *beHayay* 'good heavens!', but Hebrew has no regular means of creating new disjuncts.[1] בטוח *batúaH* 'certain(ly)' is one of the few adjectives also used as disjunct (see also פשוט *pashut* 'simply' in 23.4) and can be qualified:[2]

hi kim'at **batúaH** be-Hufsha	היא כמעט **בטוח** בחופשה
f.s. m.s.	
she almost **certain** on holiday	'She's almost **certainly** on holiday'

Syntax of truth disjuncts

Position . A few truth disjuncts are restricted in position, for reasons apparently unconnected with their meaning. These particular disjuncts are mostly 'integrated' into the sentence, with no pause or comma.

Clause-initial truth disjuncts include: בחיי *beHayay* 'really', הלא *halo* 'after all', שמא *shéma* 'perhaps',[3] אפשר *efshar* 'perhaps'; initial or within the clause: בטח, בטוח *bétaH, batúaH* 'certainly/probably'; directly preceding the verb: כן *ken* 'certainly',[4] ממש *mamash* 'really', כמו *kmo* 'as it were'; and within the clause or final: כאילו *ke'ilu* 'as it were'. עובדה *uvda* 'the fact is' and אמת (נכון) *emet* (*naHon*) 'admittedly', both clause-initial, are followed by either a colon or a comma.

The בוודאי ש- *bevaday she-* construction

For emphatic (ב)וודאי *(be)vaday* 'certainly' and כמובן *kamuvan* 'of course' to occur in initial position, one generally appends what is apparently the conjunction ש- *she-*, although this has little in common with that conjunction (see below):

bevaday she-Hankan hu yesod	בוודאי שחנקן הוא יסוד
	'Of course nitrogen is an element'

The same holds for בטח, בטוח *bétaH, batúaH* 'certainly/probably', בהכרח *beheHraH* 'inevitably', באמת, בחיי *beemet, beHayay* 'really', מכל שכן *mikol sheken* 'all the more so'. Two non-emphatic disjuncts, which allow an optional ש- *she-*, are כנראה *ke-nir'e* 'apparently' and כידוע *ka-yadúa* 'as is well-known':

ke-nir'e she-ha-nura nisrefa	כנראה שהנורה נשרפה
	'Apparently the bulb has gone'

Though superficially resembling the widespread 'predicate + subordinate clause' construction, as in (1), the truth disjunct+-ש *she-* is a law unto itself - it can be inserted (casually) in mid-sentence, directly preceding the predicate:[5]

(1)	barur she-ha-nura nisrefa	ברור שהנורה נשרפה
		'⟨It is ⟩ clear that the bulb has gone'
(2)	*ába shelo bevaday (she-)rotse laazov*	אבא שלו בוודאי (ש)רוצה לעזוב
	father his certainly (that) wants to-quit	'His father certainly wants to quit'
(3)	ani beemet (she-)lo mevin ota	אני באמת (ש)לא מבין אותה
	I really (that) not understand her	'I really don't understand her'

Free-standing truth disjuncts

Truth disjuncts denoting certainty, probability, 'apparently' as well as
אולי *ulay* 'perhaps' and ברצינות *birtsinut* 'seriously' (virtually a truth disjunct)
can stand alone, often as answers or questions:

smeHim? - bétaH	'Happy? - Sure!'	שמחים? - בטח
smeHim? - kenir'e	'Happy? - Apparently.'	שמחים? - כנראה
Ham! - be-emet?	'It's hot! - Really?'	חם! - באמת?
Ham! - birtsinut?	'It's hot! - Seriously?'	חם! - ברצינות?

Double verb constructions

Literary Hebrew can convey future certainty by 'double verb' constructions: (a) indeclinable gerund + future tense verb, eg. בוא יבוא *bo yavo*
'come it will'; (b) future + *gam* + future; eg. יבוא גם יבוא *yavo gam yavo* 'come
it will'.

23.3   Comment disjuncts

Comment disjuncts embroider a statement with a comment on its
impact, desirability, or the way in which it is known - often taking its 'truth' for
granted, unlike 'truth disjuncts' in 23.2.

Examples of comment disjuncts

be-oto yom pagash **le-tadhemato** et kraus	באותו יום פגש **לתדהמתו** את קראוס
	'That day he met Kraus **to his horror**'
ha-metsi'ut, **le-tsaari**, hayta shona	המציאות, **לצערי**, היתה שונה
	'Reality, **regrettably**, was otherwise'
le-marbe ha-pli'a he'ira bat-tsHok et panav	**למרבה הפליאה** האירה בת-צחוק את פניו
	'**Amazingly**, a smile lit up his face'
eni tovéa **Halila** she-yiye adiv	איני תובע **חלילה** שיהיה אדיב
	'I'm not demanding, **perish the thought**, that he be polite'
hu mistapek be-manganon metsumtsam, **ka-amur**	הוא מסתפק במנגנון מצומצם, **כאמור**
	'He makes do with a reduced apparatus, **as stated**'

Semantically, most comment disjuncts are equivalent to nouns or adjectives
(predicating the clause):

le-haftaati, hi HiyHa = ze she-hi HiyHa garam li hafta'a	להפתעתי, היא חייכה = זה שהיא חייכה גרם לי הפתעה
	'To my surprise, she smiled' = 'That she smiled caused me surprise'
ha-menayot yatsivot, be-ófen lo tsafuy = ze she-ha-menayot yatsivot lo tsafuy	המניות יציבות, באופן לא צפוי = זה שהמניות יציבות לא צפוי
	'Shares are unexpectedly steady' = 'That shares are steady is unexpected'

Two other, more productive alternatives to comment disjuncts are:

ha-maftia (ba-davar) hu she..   ...המפתיע (בדבר) הוא ש
the surprising (in-the thing) is that...

ma she-maftia hu she..   ...מה שמפתיע הוא ש
what that surprising is that...

Both :

'What's surprising (about it) is that...' (= surprisingly,...')

Another, common equivalent to most comment disjuncts of the type כאמור
ka-amur 'as stated' is a whole clause (see 32.6):

kfi
    she-tsafuy, hu..   ...כפי שצפוי, הוא
kmo   כמו

'As is expected, he..'

Form of comment disjuncts

To express 'impact', Hebrew has three constructions, limited to a
small set of nouns or adjectives[6] (except in 'creative' styles):

-ל *le* + abstract construct noun:

le-aHzavata   'to her disappointment'   לאכזבתה
le-simHat aviv   'to his father's pleasure'   לשמחת אביו

למרבה *le-marbe* or למרבית *le-marbit* + abstract (definite) noun:[7]

le-marbe ha-tsáar   'regrettably'   למרבה הצער
le-marbit ha-mazal   'luckily'   למרבית המזל

באופן *be-ófen* or באורח *be-óraH* (F) + adjective:[8]

be-ófen paradoksáli   'paradoxically'   באופן פרדוקסלי
be-óraH lo tsafuy   'unexpectedly'   באורח לא צפוי

However, to express 'the way in which something is known', Hebrew employs
the construction *ka* 'as' + passive participle on a fairly productive scale:[9]

ka-mudgam   'as illustrated'   כמודגם
ka-nizkar   'as mentioned'   כנזכר
ka-mutsa   'as proposed'   כמוצע

In addition, a motley of other expressions act as comment disjuncts, eg.
ברוך ה' *baruH hashem* 'thank Heaven', במפתיע *be-maftia* 'surprisingly'.

Syntax of comment disjuncts

Most comment disjuncts can occur in any position, above all initially,
and can be marked off by pause or comma. However, חלילה *Halila* 'Heaven
forbid' and its synonyms do not occur initially.

Comment disjuncts can generally be expanded where appropriate:

le-tsaari **ha-rav**   'to my **great** regret'   לצערי **הרב**
be-óraH paradoksáli **me'od**   '**very** paradoxically'   באורח פרדוקסלי **מאד**
ka-yadúa **be-artsot arav**   'as known **in Arab countries**'   כידוע **בארצות ערב**

But most ‑כ *ke‑* type disjuncts will prefer to be expanded into a *full* clause:

kfi she‑nizkar (not: ka‑nizkar)   כפי שנזכר (׳כנזכר)
kvar ba‑pérek ha‑kodem,...   כבר בפרק הקודם,...
   'as was mentioned already in the previous chapter'

Negation is by שלא *she‑lo*, notably:

she‑lo le‑hafta'at...   'not surprisingly (for...)'   ...שלא להפתעת
she‑lo be‑tsédek   'unjustly'   שלא בצדק
she‑lo ka‑tsafuy   'unexpectedly'   שלא כצפוי

23.4 'Manner of speaking' disjuncts

'Manner of speaking' disjuncts convey the way a sentence is intended, usually by describing the 'manner of speaking' (typically one's own).

Examples of 'manner of speaking' disjuncts

ishit, ani sone hódu   אישית, אני שונא הודו
   'Personally, I hate turkey'

ktsat savlanut, **be‑emet!**   קצת סבלנות, באמת!
   'A little patience, **really!**'

ani, **pashut**, lo yadáti al ze   אני, פשוט, לא ידעתי על זה
   '**I simply** didn't know about it'

kan, **birshutHa**, ani mafsik   כאן, ברשותך, אני מפסיק
   'Here, **with your indulgence,** I shall stop'

be‑ófen klali turkav ha‑maskóret   באופן כללי תורכב המשכורת
me‑ha‑tosafot ha‑ba'ot   מהתוספות הבאות
   '**Generally speaking** the salary will be composed of the following incre‑
                ments'

Semantically, these often have an equivalent in a disjunct *conditional clause*:

im ledaber be‑ófen ekroni...   ...אם לדבר באופן עקרוני
   'If one may speak in a principled way...'

Distinguish also between the following. Example (2) is not a disjunct:

(1) **be‑ófen teoréti** hu mad'an tov   באופן תיאורטי הוא מדען טוב
  in way theoretical he scientist good   'Theoretically, he's a good scientist'

(2) **mi‑bHina teorétit** hu mad'an tov   מבחינה תיאורטית הוא מדען טוב
  from aspect theoretical he scientist   'In theoretical matters, he's a good
  good   scientist'

Form of 'manner of speaking' disjuncts

Three distinctive constructions are used as 'manner of speaking' disjuncts:[10]

(1) באופן *be-ófen* + adjective:

be-ófen rishmi	'officially speaking'	באופן רשמי

(2) Adjectives with a feminine ending in ית- *it-*:

rishmit	'officially speaking'	רשמית

(3) ב *be+* abstract noun, eg.

be-Henut	'honestly speaking'	בכנות

Construction (1) is productive: any appropriate adjective may appear. But construction (2), and especially (3), are used in just a few cases (except in creative styles), thus example (1) below is possible but not example (2):

(1) im ledaber ba-adivut,...   ...אם לדבר באדיבות
                                          'If one may put it politely,...'

(2) *ba-adivut,...   ...*באדיבות
                                          'Politely speaking,...'

Various other expressions are used, eg. דרך אגב *déreH agav* 'incidentally', פשוט *pashut* 'simply', בינינו *benénu* 'confidentially', בבקשה *bevakasha* 'please', להלכה *laHalaHa* 'theoretically'.

Syntax of 'manner of speaking' disjuncts

Most such disjuncts occur in any position, above all initially, and can be marked off by pause or comma. However, אנא *ána* 'please' (F) is only initial, and נא *na* 'please' (F) only follows the verb, without pause, often hyphenated to it.[11] Both, unlike בבקשה *bevakasha* (the commonest word for 'please'), generally require a verb in a command form, i.e imperative or future:

mesor na et shmam	מסור נא את שמם
give please OM their-name	'Please give their name'

ani rotse shlosha kartisim, bevakasha	אני רוצה שלושה כרטיסים, בבקשה
I want three tickets, please	

נא *na* and בבקשה *bevakasha*, but not אנא *ána*, also take an infinitive (giving a remote, lofty tone):

bevakasha lehamtin	בבקשה להמתין
please to-wait	'Wait please'

Most 'manner of speaking' disjuncts do not allow 'expansion' (or negation):

*be-ófen ishi **me'od**	'**very** personally'	*באופן אישי **מאד**
*birtsinut **raba**	'**very** seriously'	*ברצינות **רבה**

23.5 Other disjuncts

Several other types of word, phrase and clause are disjuncts in terms of *sentence structure*, though not serving semantically to 'evaluate a sentence or one's intentions in producing it.' (For clauses, see ch.32.) Notable examples are set out here.

Concessive ('although..., despite...'):

lamrot ha-kor, natan lo viter		למרות הקור, נתן לא ויתר
	'Despite the cold, Natan did not give in'	

Additives and subtractives ('besides, including, except...'):

(be-)nosaf le/al...		...(ב)נוסף ל/על
milvad...(F)	'besides, in addition to'	...מלבד
Huts mi-...[12]		...חוץ מ
Huts mi-...		...חוץ מ
milvad (F)...	'except for'[13]	...מלבד
lehotsi...		...להוציא
prat le-...		...פרט ל
kolel	'including'	כולל
lerabot (F)		לרבות

Syntax

מלבד *milvad* 'except' and כולל *kolel* 'including' can act like coordinators or like prepositions; as coordinators:

badákti be-Hol ha-Hadarim, milvad **ba**-salon	בדקתי בכל החדרים, מלבד **בסלון**
I-checked in all the rooms, except **in-the** lounge	

hizmánti et kulam, kolel **et** dan		הזמנתי את כולם, כולל **את** דן
I-invited OM all-of-them, including OM Dan	'I invited them all, including Dan'	

Compare the same repetition of prepositions after the coordinator -ו *ve-* 'and':

...ve-lo **ba**-salon	'...and not **in** the lounge'	...ולא **בסלון**
...ve-gam et dan	'...and also Dan'	...וגם **את** דן

As prepositions, and with exactly the same meaning, they are directly followed by the noun (and can even occur in initial position); no preposition can intervene:

badákti be-Hol ha-Hadarim, milvad ha-salon	בדקתי בכל החדרים, מלבד הסלון
I-checked in all the rooms, except the lounge	

חוץ מ- *Huts mi-* 'except' can act either as a simple preposition or as a kind of comparative particle (meaning 'other than'), in which case -מ *mi-* can be replaced by the 'than' conjunction מאשר *measher* (see 20.4):

...Huts me-ha-salon	חוץ מהסלון
	'...except the lounge'
...Huts measher ba-salon	חוץ מאשר בסלון
	'...except (than) in the lounge'

23.6　Shared syntactic traits of disjuncts

Sentence processes

Whether phonetically detached or not, disjuncts are structurally detached in being outside the focus of the 'sentence processes' - negation, questioning, contrastive emphasis. This rules out:[14]

ata ozev? - *lo bétaH	אתה עוזב? - *לא בטח
you leaving? - *not certainly	('Are you leaving? It isn't certain')
*ha'im le-aHzavateH hi putra?	*האם לאכזבתך היא פוטרה?
Q-word to your-disappointment she was-fired?	('Are you disappointed she was-fired?)'

Rather:

ze lo batúaH	זה לא בטוח
	'It isn't certain'

at meuHzévet she..?	את מאוכזבת ש...?
	'Are you disappointed that...?'

Disjuncts do allow negation etc. - they are simply outside it:

ani bétaH lo ozev!	אני בטח לא עוזב!
	'Of *course* I am not leaving!'

Comment disjuncts, implying a fact, do not mix with questions or commands in general:

*le-tsaari, al titnadev	*לצערי, אל תתנדב
	'Unfortunately, don't volunteer'

Word order after disjuncts

Disjuncts can but need not affect word order. In initial position, with or without pause, they will allow, but not compel, subject-predicate inversion (compare ch.21 - they are just like other adverbials):[15]

la'amito shel davar yaHol ha-adam.../	לאמיתו של דבר יכול האדם.../
ha-adam yaHol...	האדם יכול...
in actual fact can Man.../Man can... [same meaning: 'Man can...']	

As initial disjuncts can stand 'detached', further adverbials can directly follow without making the sentence top-heavy:

kenir'e, **bi-yshivat ha-memshala** hualta sheela zo	כנראה, **בישיבת הממשלה** הועלתה שאלה זו
	'Apparently, **at the Cabinet meeting** this question was raised'

Disjuncts readily occur in subordinate clauses:

omrim she-kenir'e lo yiyu hozalot	אומרים שכנראה לא יהיו הוזלות
	'They say that apparently there will not be reductions'

FURTHER READING
Azar 1977: 5.4; Blau 1977b; Chayen & Dror 1976: ch. 7; Kaddari 1977; Levenston 1970; Rubinstein 1970; Sadka 1981: 186ff.

24. Link adverbials

24.1 Introduction

Link adverbials express a logical connection between sentences:[1]

az hi lo báa?	'So she isn't coming?'	אז היא לא באה?
hu **omnam** bari, aH...	'He is **indeed** healthy, but...'	הוא **אמנם** בריא, אך...
any **harey** ben-adam	'I am a person, **after all**'	אני **הרי** בן-אדם

Thus link adverbials differ in function from other types of adverbial, set out in general in 21.1. But in common with disjunct adverbials (ch. 23), they are 'fringe adverbials', parenthetical in a semantic and syntactic sense: they can usually be set off by pause or comma, and most can be positioned anywhere *vis-à-vis* subject, verb and object - though most commonly at the front of their clause:

im ken, láma leakev et ze	'If so, why hold it up?'	**אם כן**, למה לעכב את זה?
láma, **im ken**, leakev et ze	'Why, if so, hold it up?'	למה, **אם כן**, לעכב את זה?
láma leakev et ze, **im ken**	'Why hold it up, if so?'	למה לעכב את זה, **אם כן**?

A handful are less obviously 'fringe elements' - they resist any pause or punctuation; and most require front position:

yesh laH? **az** tamshiHi	'Got it? **Then** go on'	יש לך? **אז** תמשיכי

Link adverbials are mostly one-word adverbs. They have no distinctive form, and often have other diverse functions. Though not productively coined, they are too numerous to list here exhaustively, so we give examples of the main types.

24.2 Main types of link adverbial

Enumeration[2]

kódem-kol	'first of all'	קודם-כל
lesiyum	'to conclude'	לסיום

Addition[3]

yéter-al-ken/gam zot	'moreover'	גם זאת/יתר-על-כן
gám ken/ken[4]/od	'likewise'	עוד/כן/גם-כן
beétsem	'in actual fact'	בעצם
omnam	'admittedly'	אמנם

Transition[5]

aHshav éfo hayit etmol?	עכשיו איפה היית אתמול?

'**Now** where were you yesterday?'

káma yesh? - **uvHen** yesh shney sugim		כמה יש? - **ובכן** יש שני סוגים
	'How many there are? - **Well** there are two sorts'	

legabey.../(ba)asher le..	'as regards...'	(ב)אשר ל.../לגבי..

Summing up [7]

lesikum	'to sum up'	לסיכום
bekitsur	'in a nutshell'	בקיצור

Reformulation [8]

bifrat	'specifically'	בפרט
(de)háynu	'namely'	(ד)היינו
mutav	'or rather'	מוטב

For example [9]

ledugma/déreH mashal	'for example'	דרך משל/לדוגמה

Result [10]

az	'so' (clause-initial)	אז
efo	'therefore' (not clause-initial)	אפוא
im ken/im kaH	'thus' (any position)	אם כן/אם כך

Inference [11]

im ken/im kaH	'if so' (any position)	אם כן/אם כך
az	'so' (clause-initial)	אז

Alternatives [7]

miHad...meidaH...	'on the one hand...on the other...'	מחד...מאידך...

Antithesis [7]

lehéfeH	'quite the opposite' (clause-initial)	להפך
leumat ze	'by contrast'	לעומת זה

Reservation [7]

beHol zot	'nevertheless'	בכל זאת
kaH o kaH	'anyway'	כך או כך

Explanation

hen (clause-initial)/harey (any position)	'after all'	הרי/הן

24.3 Link adverbials and their clause

Sentence focusing

Link adverbials are 'signposts' showing the logical links between sentences - and they are felt to be on the sidelines, transcending *sentence focusing*; eg. one does not negate them, ask about them, or otherwise single them out for contrastive attention. Thus Hebrew does not say:

*lo **laHen** (√biglal ze) sha'álti	*לא **לכן** (√בגלל זה) שאלתי
not **therefore** (√because-of that) I-asked	'That's not why I asked.'

However, some such items accept emphasis but not negation or questioning, thus (1) below is good but not (2):[12]

(1)	*laHen* sha'álti	לכן שאלתי
	therefore I-asked	'That's why I asked'

(2)	*ani *efo* sha'álti	*אני אפוא שאלתי
	I *therefore* asked	('That's why I asked')

Similarly, בכל זאת *beHol zot* and למרות זאת *lamrot zot* 'nevertheless' and all terms denoting 'anyway' allow emphasis, but not ואולם *ve-ulam* or עם זאת *im zot* 'however'.

Several link adverbials also act as adjunct adverbials (see ch.21), as in:

bekitsur, daber bekitsur	בקיצור, דבר בקיצור
LINK ADV ADJUNCT	'In brief, speak in brief'

lehéfeH, hu mitnaheg lehéfeH	להפך, הוא מתנהג להפך
LINK ADV ADJUNCT	'Quite the opposite, he acts the opposite'

Indeed, link adverbials are sometimes best seen as part of an unexpressed 'I'm telling you (briefly, first of all,...) that...'

Free-standing link adverbials
Certain such items, by virtue of their meaning, can be free-standing, notably:

hem enam Hofshiyim? - **lehéfeH**	הם אינם חופשיים? - להפך
	'They aren't free? - **Quite the opposite**'

asur lehisha'en? - **ádraba**	אסור להישען? - אדרבה
	'Can't one lean? - **Far from it**'

Word order
Most link adverbials are 'parenthetical', i.e potentially set off by pause or comma, while a few are compulsorily integrated into the sentence, notably כן *ken* 'likewise', עכשיו *aHshav* 'now', אז *az* 'so', הן *hen* 'after all'. The latter are almost invariably clause-initial, no doubt affording easier comprehension, while the former often trigger inversion of subject and verb (just like adjunct adverbials); contrast examples (1) and (2):[13]

(1)	i-leHaH, tehe af ha-hityaHasut eléha	אי-לכך, תהא אף ההתייחסות אליה
	hityaHasut ambivaléntit	התייחסות אמביוולנטית
	as-a-result, will-be too the relation to-her relation ambivalent	
		'As a result, the relation to her too will be ambivalent'

(2)	az kulam tsriHim lishkav	אז כולם צריכים לשכב
	so everyone has to-lie-down	

The 'closely integrated' type of link adverbial has an extra-close relationship to the foregoing clause: not even -ו *ve-* 'and' can come between them. It is thus somewhat akin to a coordinator (-ו *ve-* 'and', אך *aH* 'but' etc.)[14] or conjunction (כי *ki* 'for', שמא *shéma* 'lest' etc.). Compare the two types of link adverbial:

Parenthetical

.... ve-yéter-al-ken...	'and moreover ....'	... ויתר-על-כן ...
.... aH af-al-pi-Hen...	'but nevertheless...'	... אך אף-על-פי-כן ...
.... ve-tsariH, efo,...	'and one must thus...'	...וצריך, אפוא,...

Integrated[15]

| kar hayom, (*ve-)az tsariH kóva | קר היום, (*ו)אז צריך כובע |
| cold today, (*and) so need hat | 'It's cold today, so you need a hat' |

| hayta teuna, (*ve-)ma od she-ha-nehagim shavtu | היתה תאונה, (*ו)מה עוד שהנהגים שבתו |
| '⟨There⟩ was ⟨an⟩ accident, ⟨and⟩ what's more, the drivers were striking' | |

However, the two clauses can be separated by a semi-colon or full stop (see 24.4):

| kar hayom. az tsariH kóva | קר היום. אז צריך כובע |
| | 'It's cold today. So you need a hat' |

| hayta teuna. ma od she.. | היתה תאונה. מה עוד ש... |
| | 'There was an accident. What's more,...' |

Several link adverbials, mostly of *enumeration*, *summing up* and *reformulation* (a distinct group in itself), are always detached from their clause, and tend to precede it. No subject-verb inversion occurs. Thus:

| **davar rishon**, ha-mimshal asuy levater | **דבר ראשון,** הממשל עשוי לוותר |
| | '**Firstly**, the regime ⟨is⟩ likely to yield' |

be-mikre ze yukdam ha-póal. **kelomar:**	במקרה זה יוקדם הפועל. **כלומר:**
ha-póal yikdam le-nos'o	הפועל יקדם לנושאו
'In this case the verb will be brought forward, **i.e**,	
the verb will precede its subject'	

24.4 Link adverbials and the preceding clause

Most such items are linked to the preceding clause by comma, semi-colon, full stop (or their spoken equivalent), with or without -ו *ve-* 'and' or אבל *aval* 'but' etc., as meaning may require:[16]

| ...; ve-yoter mi-ze, ani... | ...; ויותר מזה, אני... |
| | '...; and furthermore, I...' |

The tie between link adverbial and preceding clause results in the fact that, by and large, the clause with the link adverbial *directly* follows that clause Thus[17] (where the link to the previous clause is indicated by arrows):

... **u-Hemo-Hen** en ha-tsilumim moHiHim   וכמו-כן אין הצילומים מוכיחים...
davar kshe-en bakara maspéket   דבר כשאין בקרה מספקת
'... **and similarly** the photos prove nothing when there is no adequate control'

but not:

*...u-kshe-en bakara maspéket, **kmo-Hen**   וכשאין בקרה מספקת, כמו-כן*
en ha-tsilumim moHiHim davar   אין הצילומים מוכיחים דבר
('... and when there is no adequate control, **similarly** the photos prove nothing')

Beyond this, there are few special restrictions. The preceding clause can be subordinate as in (1) below, as can the link adverbial clause (2) or both (3):

(1)   af im yeshanu et ha-Hok, yitstarHu   אף אם ישנו את החוק, יצטרכו
       belav-haHi leshalem   בלאו-הכי לשלם
       'Even if they change the law, they'll have to pay **anyway**'

(2)   ani oved kashe, ki **laHen** báti le-Han   אני עובד קשה, כי לכן באתי לכאן
       'I'm working hard, because **that's why** I came here'

(3)   mitbarer she-hayta takala, **az** hu hitakev   מתברר שהיתה תקלה, אז הוא התעכב
       'It turns out that there was a mishap **so** he was held up'

Link adverbials as 'echoes'

Semantically, many link adverbials do the same job as a preposition:

x, laHen y=kevan she-x, y   'x, thus y=because x,y'   לכן y=כיוון ש- x, y, x

x, im zot y=im ki x, y   'x, however y=though x, y'   עם זאת y=אם כי y, x, x

And Hebrew occasionally uses both link adverbial and preposition together, one echoing the other:[18]

lamrot she-te'ur ze mekubal mize   למרות שתיאור זה מקובל מזה
shanim rabot, **be-Hol zot** en hu   שנים רבות, בכל זאת אין הוא
te'ur tov   תיאור טוב
'**Although** this description has been accepted for many years, **nevertheless** it is not a good description'

keshem she-en lehitragesh mehem,   כשם שאין להתרגש מהם,
kaH suma alénu lehizaher...   כך שומה עלינו להיזהר
'**Just as** one must not become excited about them, **so** it is necessary to beware...'

FURTHER READING
Chayen & Dror 1976: ch.7; Glinert 1987; Landau 1985: 309ff; Ornan 1979a: 92; Sadka 1981: 186f.

25. Pro-adverbs

Pro-adverbs, words representing adjuncts of extent, manner, means, place, time, purpose and cause, are described together with pronouns in chapter 7: section 7.6 deals with 'definite pro-adverbs' such as אז *az* 'then', שם *sham* 'there', כך *kaH* 'in that way'; section 7.7 describes 'anticipatory pro-adverbs' as in (1) below; and 7.8 discusses 'indefinite pro-adverbs' such as איפהשהו *éfoshehu* 'somewhere'. On interrogative pro-adverbs, eg. those for 'where, why', see 26.3; on negative pro-adverbs, eg. for 'nowhere, never', see 29.11; and on relative pro-adverbs as in (2) below, see chapter 33.

(1) sa **le'an** she-nóaH   'Go **wherever** easy'   סע **לאן** שנוח

(2) ha-ir **sham** noládeti...   'the city **where** I was born...'   ...העיר **שם** נולדתי

Not all semantic classes of adjunct have special pro-adverbs: for example, 'purpose' and 'cause' have a special interrogative למה *láma* 'why?' whereas 'for that purpose' must be expressed by phrases such as לשם כך *leshem kaH* or בשביל זה *bishvil ze*, and 'for that reason' is usually rendered by a phrase such as משום כך *mishum kaH*.

Furthermore, pro-adverbs such as לאן *le'an* 'where to' and שם *sham* 'there' refer to places, whereas 'people' require למי *le-mi* 'to whom':

le-mi nasáta?   'Who were you going to?'   !למי נסעת

As for the general distinction between pro-adverbs and pronouns, see 15.2.5:

éfo nilHámta   'Where were you fighting?'   !איפה נלחמת
ba-me nilHámta   'What were you fighting?'   !במה נלחמת

269

26. Questions

26.1 Definition of 'question'

One must distinguish between 'question' as a syntactic construction and as an act. The *act* of questioning (as against stating, warning, etc.), in Hebrew as in English, uses various *constructions*, e.g. declarative 'I want to know the time', imperative 'Tell me the time', and interrogative 'What is the time?'. The interrogative is the 'question construction' *par excellence*, and the subject of this chapter.

Note, however, that the interrogative may fail to 'act' as a question:

ani yodéa ma ha-sha'a	אני יודע **מה השעה**
I know **what the time**	'I know **what the time is**'

Such interrogatives too are described here (26.7).

26.2 Yes /no questions in main clauses

There are two types of interrogatives: those expecting a 'yes /no' reply, i.e. 'yes /no' questions, as in example (1) below, and those asking 'who, what, where, how' etc., i.e. '*wh-*' questions, as illustrated here in examples (2,3):

(1)	at ofa máshehu?		?את אופה משהו
	you bake something?		'Are you baking something?'

(2)	ma at ofa?		?מה את אופה
	what you bake?		'What are you baking?'

(3)	matay at ofa?		?מתי את אופה
	when you bake?		'When do you bake?'

First we describe yes /no questions; for '*wh-*' questions see 26.3-6. For their subordinate and infinitival varieties, see 26.7 etc.

In casual usage

Casual speech usually distinguishes yes /no questions from statements by intonation:

yesh makóm	יש מקוֹם
there-is room	'Is there room?'

yesh makòm	יש מקוֹם
there-is room	'There's room'

Casual writing uses a question mark, ordinarily with no extra 'question particle' or word order change (though the question particle האם *ha'im* is occasionally used):

yesh makom?	יש מקוֹם?
there-is room?	'Is there room?'

In formal usage

In formal speech and writing, yes/no questions usually begin with the question particle האם *ha'im* :[1]

ha'im yesh makom?	האם יש מקוֹם?
PARTICLE there-is room?	'Is there room?'

Instead of האם *ha'im*, literature also uses the particles כלום *klum*, וכי *ve-Hi*, and -ה *ha-* (in main clauses):

ve-Hi hiskámnu?	'Did we agree?'	וכי הסכמנו?

-ה *ha-* also figures in a few less literary idioms, e.g. היתכן? *ha-yitaHen* ? 'can that be?' ...ל התוכל *ha-tuHal le*... 'can you...?'

Negative yes/no questions: 'Isn't he?'

Negative yes/no questions allow two meanings: either simply asking for confirmation (with stressed לא *lo* 'not'):[2]

(ha'im) *lo* yashnu?	'They *weren't* asleep?'	האם לא ישנו?

or, more commonly, expressing a fond hope for the answer 'yes':

(ha'im) lo yashnu?	'Weren't they asleep?'	האם לא ישנו?

26.3-6 'WH-' QUESTIONS IN MAIN CLAUSES

26.3 The various 'wh-' words

'*Wh-*' words are the interrogative pronouns (and pro-adverbs, pro-adjectives, etc.) for the various parts of speech, listed below.

Nouns: מי *mi* 'who', מה *ma* 'what'.

Adjectives: איך *eH*:

eH hu, neHmad?	'What's he like, nice?'	איך הוא, נחמד?

Adverbs of manner and means: איך *eH*, כיצד keytsad (F) 'how':

eH shárti, beséder?	איך שרתי, בסדר?
	'How did I sing, OK?'

eH shárti, be-mikrofon?	איך שרתי, במקרופון?
	'How did I sing, with a microphone?'

Adverbs of extent: כמה *káma* 'how much (eg. did you sleep?)'.
Adverbs of place: איפה *éfo*, היכן *heHan* (F) 'where'; לאן *le'an*, לאיפה/איפה *le-éfo/éfo* (very casual), להיכן *le-heHan* (F) 'where...to'[3]; מאיפה *me-éfo* (C), מאין *me'áyin* (F), מהיכן *me-heHan* (F) 'where...from'.
Adverbs of time: מתי *matay* 'when'.
Adverbs of purpose and cause: למה *láma*, מה *ma* (C), מדוע *madúa* (F) 'why'.
Quantifiers: כמה *káma* 'how many, how much'.
Determiners: איזה *éze* 'which, what':[4]

éze brerot?	'What alternatives?'	איזה ברירות?

Degree words: עד כמה *ad káma*, מה *ma* (literary) 'how':

ad káma hu meshuHna?	'How convinced is he?'	עד כמה הוא משוכנע?

Special properties

מי *mi* 'who' can be feminine but not plural (even when a group of people is implied):

banot, mi gamra? f.s.	'Who's finished, girls?'	בנות, מי גמרה?

*banot, mi gamru? pl.	('Who have finished, girls?')	*בנות, מי גמרו?

Acting as direct object, מי *mi* 'who' requires the 'direct object particle' את *et*, ordinarily only found with '*definite*' pronouns (eg. את זה *et ze* 'this', see 15.5). By contrast, מה *ma* 'what' takes את *et* only in 'echo questions', as in (2):

(1) *et mi naashim?*   את מי נאשים?
     OM who we-will-blame?   'Whom shall we blame?'

(2) *ratsiti et ze - et ma?*   רציתי את זה - את מה?
     I-wanted OM this - OM what?   'I wanted this - You wanted what?'

איך *eH* representing an adjective can be predicate as in (1) below, but not modifier (2); instead, something like (3) is employed:

(1) *eH hu, hu simpáti?*   איך הוא, הוא סימפטי?
     PRED   PRED
     how he, he nice?   'What's he like, is he nice?'

(2) **eH baHura Hipásta, baHura shketa?*   *איך בחורה חיפשת, בחורה שקטה?
     how girl you-looked-for, girl quiet?
                       ('What sort of girl did you look for, a quiet girl?')

(3) *éze sug shel baHura*   'What sort of girl?'   איזה סוג של בחורה?

מה *ma* is used for 'why' rhetorically, conveying 'you mustn't' or 'I'm not!':

ma at boHa!	'What are you crying for!'	מה את בוכה!
ma ani ashem!	'Why am I to blame!'	מה אני אשם!

עד כמה *ad káma* 'how' is not strictly a degree word, in respect of its positioning. Unlike degree words (example (1)), it cannot directly adjoin its adjective (2):[5]

(1) **dey** Hazak   די חזק
     'Quite strong'

(2) ad káma hu Hazak?   עד כמה הוא חזק?
    how he strong?   'How strong is he?'

26.4 Positioning of 'wh-' words

'*Wh-*' words are usually put as close as possible (with restrictions as listed below) to the front of the question clause, thus:

ma Hashavt?   'What did you think?'   מה חשבת?
OBJ

ma ha-liHluH ha-ze?   'What is this filth?'   מה הליכלוך הזה?
PRED

Restrictions

Where a '*wh-*' word forms part of a larger noun phrase (eg. בעיית מי *baayat mi* problem who = 'whose problem') or preposition phrase (eg. עם מי *im mi* 'with whom') it cannot by itself be lifted out to the front of the clause Instead, the whole phrase is shifted *en bloc* to the front of the question clause:[6]

baayat mi zot?   בעיית מי זאת?
N PHR
problem who this?   'Whose problem is this?'

im mi   at nosáat?   עם מי את נוסעת?
PREP PHR
with whom you are-going?   'Who are you going with?'

baala shel mi   ashem?   בעלה של מי אשם?
             PREP PHR
N PHR
her-husband of whom at-fault?   'Whose husband is at fault?'

But Hebrew can begin questions with '*wh-*' words that *logically* belong not to the main clause but to a subordinate clause embedded within it.[7] (Roughly speaking, what works for English works for Hebrew). Thus:

éfo Hashavt **she-eshev**, al ha-gag?   איפה חשבת **שאשב**, על הגג?
where you-thought **that I'd-sit**, on the roof?
         SUBORD CLAUSE
                     'Where did you think that I'd sit, on the roof?'
                         (='You thought that I'd sit where?')

26.5   More on word order: subject-verb inversion

Following the 'wh-' word, the verb often leapfrogs over the subject (unlike in statements):

ha-bos halaH	'The boss went'	הבוס הלך

but:

le'an halaH ha-bos?		?לאן הלך הבוס
where went the boss?	'Where did the boss go?'	

There are three restrictions. First, subject *pronouns* do not usually permit inversion, hence:

le'an **hu** halaH?		לאן **הוא** הלך
where **he** went?	'Where did he go?'	

Second, phonetic and semantic balance in the sentence play a subtle part in whether one inverts. Third, prescriptive grammarians bar inversion for present tense verbs, preferring:

ma ha-ayalot osot?		?מה האיילות עושות
what the deer are-doing?	'What are the deer doing?'	

Such subject-verb inversion is part of a wider tendency for verbs to cross in front of subjects, once some other word has taken over clause-initial position (see 37.4, 37.13):

gam etmol ba ha-ganan		גם אתמול בא הגנן
also yesterday came the gardener	'The gardener came yesterday also'	

26.6   'Wh-' words in non-questions

Most 'wh-' words have five further functions that have little to do with questions. Rather than being basically 'interrogative', 'wh-' words are more like multi-purpose pronouns:

(1) As 'whatever, wherever' (the first example is a concessive conditional clause):

et mi she-lo tishal, lo tekabel tshuva	את מי שלא תשאל, לא תקבל תשובה
OM who that not you'll ask,	'Whomever you ask,
not you'll-get reply	you'll get no reply'

kaH ma she-tirtse	קח מה שתרצה
take what that you'll-want	'Take whatever you want'

(2) As 'the thing (that), the place (where)' etc. (Both (1) and (2) involve ש - *she-* + clause):

ze ayom, ma she-amart	זה איום, מה שאמרת
it frightful, what that you-said	'It's frightful, what you said'

be-mi she-ani ge'a ze be-yóni	במי שאני גאה זה ביוני
of who that I proud is of Yoni	'The person I'm proud of is Yoni'

(3) As 'something, somewhere' etc, with the suffix שהו -*shehu*:

máshehu nafal   'Something fell'   משהו נפל

(4) As relative pronouns 'which, where' etc. (notice the infinitive that follows them):

yesh harbe ma lehosif   יש הרבה מה להוסיף
there-is a-lot what to-add   'There is a lot to add'

(5) In exclamations:

eH rakádnu!   'How we danced!'   איך רקדנו!

For details, see (1) 32.11, 33.4.2, (2) 33.4.2, 37.9, (3) 7.8, (4) 37.9, and (5) 27.2.

Three '*wh-*' words have yet other functions that even create possible ambiguity; these are איזה *éze* (see 9.2), כמה *káma* and מה *ma*:

éze núdnik tilfen   'Some pest phoned'   איזה נודניק טילפן
éze núdnik tilfen?   'Which pest phoned?'   איזה נודניק טילפן?

káma izim niHnesu   'A few goats got in'[8]   כמה עזים נכנסו
káma izim niHnesu?   'How many goats got in?'   כמה עזים נכנסו?

מה *ma* ('what') also means 'some' in some idioms (F), when it is hyphenated to an abstract noun in 'construct state':

zman-ma   זמן-מה   be-midat-ma   במידת-מה
time some   'a while'   in extent some   'to some extent'

26.7 Subordinate questions

26.7.1 Function

Subordinate questions are subordinate clauses having question *form* (they begin with '*wh-*' words or 'question particles'), though they do not necessarily have the *effect* of reported questions. Thus the subordinate question in example (1) reports on a question; in example (2) it expresses a mere non-certainty, and in example (3) a failure to specify:

(1) sha'alt **éfo hayiti**   שאלת **איפה הייתי**
     you-asked **where I-was**   'You asked where I was'

(2) lo barur **mi brógez**   לא ברור **מי ברוגז**
     not clear **who angry**   'It isn't clear who's angry'

(3) ani yodéa **mi hitatesh**   אני יודע **מי התעטש**
     I know **who sneezed**   'I know who sneezed'

26.7.2 Form

Subordinate yes/no questions. These usually begin with the question particle אם *im* 'whether',[9] rarely with formal האם *ha'im*. No special question intonation is used. (By contrast, *main* yes/no questions (26.2) use האם *ha'im* or simply special intonation, not אם *im*.)

Subordinate question:

tishal im ze met	תשאל אם זה מת
ask whether it dead	'Ask whether it is dead'

Main question:

(ha'im) ze met?	(האם) זה מת?
(Q PARTICLE) it dead?	'Is it dead?'

Subordinate 'wh-' questions. These are usually as in main clauses. Word order too is the same:

Subordinate question:

sha'álti matay ze met	שאלתי מתי זה מת
I-asked when it died	'I asked when it died'

sha'álti matay méta ha-para	שאלתי מתי מתה הפרה
I-asked when died the cow	'I asked when the cow died'

Main question:

matay ze met?	מתי זה מת?
when it died?	'When did it die?'

matay méta ha-para?	מתי מתה הפרה?
when died the cow?	'When did the cow die?'

But in casual usage the conjunction ‑ש *she-* can be inserted (an optional extra with no meaning) after the '*wh-*' word:

lo sha'alt éfo she-ani gar	לא שאלת איפה שאני גר
not you-asked where that I live	'You haven't asked where I live'

sha'alt im mi she-ani meshatéfet	שאלת עם מי שאני משתפת
you-asked with who that I share	'You asked who I'm sharing with'

Tense

Tense in all subordinate questions is as in subordinate clauses as a whole: by the 'tense and time rule' the vantage point of the person directly contemplating the action - not necessarily the speaker - determines its tense (see ch.13):

gad sha'al matay yósef yagía	גד שאל מתי יוסף יגיע
VANTAGE　　　　　　　　FUT	
POINT (PAST)　　　　　TENSE	'Gad asked when Yosef would arrive'

26.7.3　Role of subordinate questions within main clauses

Like subordinate 'statements' and 'requests', questions can be subordinated in a number of ways (for details see ch.31 and 34).
As subject of the main clause:

mi hifsid od lo barur	**מי הפסיד** עוד לא ברור
SUBJ	
who lost still not clear	'Who lost is still not clear'

lo barur **mi hifsid**   לא ברור **מי הפסיד**
    SUBJ
not clear **who lost**   'It is not clear who lost'

As *dislocated* subject of the main clause:

aHshav ze barur **mi yashar**   עכשיו זה ברור **מי ישר**
           DISLOCATED SUBJ
now it clear **who honest**   'Now it's clear who's honest'

As object of the main clause:

ata batúaH **ma beséder**   אתה בטוח **מה בסדר**
you certain **what OK**   'You're certain what's OK'

In apposition to a noun:[10]

ha-sheela **eH ze kara**   lo huvhara   השאלה **איך זה קרה** לא הובהרה
 N   APPOSED CLAUSE
the question **how it happened** not has-been-clarified
                  'The question of how it happened has not been clarified'

Note that the noun cannot be in the construct relationship (שאלת *sheelat*) to the apposition clause

26.8 Infinitival questions

Besides the 'finite' questions (questions with an inflected verb) described so far, Hebrew has a range of 'infinitival' questions (with an infinitive). They convey 'should (I, one)?' generally:

eH lehagiv?   איך להגיב?
how to-react?   'How should I (*or*: one) react?'

(ha'im) leHabot?   (האם) לכבות?
(Q PARTICLE) to-switch-off?   'Shall I (*or*: ought one) switch off?'

As the infinitive in 'statements' basically conveys a *request* (לכבות! *leHabot*! 'switch off!'; see 28.4), the infinitive in 'questions' is a question about a request, i.e 'should (I, one)?'

Subordinate infinitival questions

Infinitival questions turn up as subordinate clauses in the same way as do finite questions:

lo barur **ma lemalot**   לא ברור **מה למלאות**
not clear **what to-fill-in**   'It is not clear what to fill in'

taHlit kvar **im laHtom**   תחליט כבר **אם לחתום**
decide already **whether to-sign**   'Decide, will you, whether to sign'

How the subject of the infinitive verb is understood depends on the verb in the main clause (infinitives lack a subject). Following אמר *amar* 'tell', לימד *limed* 'teach' and other verbs of 'instruction', the infinitive will relate to the *object* of these verbs, i.e to the person *being* instructed (as in English):

amárti lo ma laasot

אמרתי לו מה לעשות
'I told him what to do'
(= what *he* should do)

hisbárti laH ma laasot

הסברתי לך מה לעשות
'I explained to you what to do!'
(= what *you* should do)

With any other verbs, adjectives, etc., the infinitive will relate to the *subject* of the verb, adjective, etc.:[11]

shaalu oti matay lavo

שאלו אותי מתי לבוא
'They asked me when to come'
(= when *they* should come)

enéni batúaH matay lavo

אינני בטוח מתי לבוא
'I'm not sure when to come'
(= when *I* should come)

An alternative to the infinitive: future tense

'Questions about requests' can be conveyed instead by future tense questions:

ma ani **eese**?

מה אני **אעשה**
'What should I do?'

ani **alamed** gam et ze?

אני **אלמד** גם את זה?
'Shall I teach this as well?'

In principle, future tense here can be taken, as usual, as 'will I' (a question about a statement) besides 'shall I' (a question about a request).

26.9   Truncated 'wh-' questions

Questions can be spared needless repetition by 'truncation':[12]

az kanu tanur... aval éze kanu?   אז קנו תנור... אבל איזה קנו?
so they-bought a-stove.. But which   'So they bought a stove.. But which did
   they-bought   they buy?'

MAIN CLAUSE
TRUNCATION
yields:

az kanu tanur... aval éze?   אז קנו תנור... אבל איזה?
so they-bought a-stove.. But which?

yiye tov, aH mi yodéa matay yiye tov?   יהיה טוב, אך מי יודע מתי יהיה טוב?
it-will-be good, but who knows when it-will-be good?

SUBORDINATE
TRUNCATION
yields:

yiye tov, aH mi yodéa matay?   יהיה טוב, אך מי יודע מתי?
it-will-be good, but who knows when?

26.10 ‮יש משהו?‬ yesh máshehu? 'Is there anything?'

In questions, wherever English uses special 'non-specific' pronouns and pro-words, i.e 'anyone, anything, any, at all, ever', Hebrew tends simply to use ‮משהו‬ máshehu 'something', ‮מישהו‬ míshehu 'someone', ‮כלשהו‬ kólshehu 'some or other', ‮בכלל‬ biHlal 'at all', ‮פעם‬ páam 'once' (and formal ‮אי-פעם‬ ey-paam 'once' and ‮אי-שם‬ ey-sham 'somewhere') - words not limited to questions:

ha'im tafsu míshehu? Q PARTICLE they-caught someone?	‮האם תפסו מישהו?‬ 'Did they catch anyone?'
todía li im máshehu Haser tell me if something is-missing	‮תודיע לי אם משהו חסר‬ 'Tell me if anything is missing'

lo yadúa heHan hitgala givun kólshehu
not known where was-detected
  variation some
	‮לא ידוע היכן התגלה גיוון כלשהו‬
	'It is not known where any variation
	  was detected'

Halamt paam? you-dreamed once?	‮חלמת פעם?‬ 'Did you ever dream?'

However, formal Hebrew has an optional alternative: 'non-specific' pronouns etc. which are indeed special to questions (and to conditionals, negative statements and anything else that is not a positive assertion):[13]

'Non-specific' word			Example (in questions)	
ish	'anyone'	‮איש‬	ha'im sipru le-ish?	‮האם סיפרו לאיש?‬ 'Did they tell anyone?'
davar	'anything'	‮דבר‬	ha'im nish'ar davar?	‮האם נשאר דבר?‬ 'Did anything remain?'
kol	'any'	‮כל‬	ha'im gila kol havana?	‮האם גילה כל הבנה?‬ 'Did he show any understanding?'
klal	'at all'	‮כלל‬	safek im vitru klal	‮ספק אם ויתרו כלל‬ 'It is doubtful whether they yielded at all'

FURTHER READING
Ben-Horin 1976; Chayen & Dror 1976: ch.5; Cole et al. 1977; Glinert 1982a; Laufer 1974; Malisdorf 1979; Rosén 1977: 8.5.3; Sadka 1981.

27. Exclamations

27.1 Introduction

This chapter describes three exclamatory constructions: question-like exclamations, 'relative clause' exclamations (negative and positive), and infinitival exclamations.

First, however, mention should be made of the host of idiomatic expressions of exclamation like those in (1) below, of such exclamatory degree words as כל־כך *kol-kaH* 'so' and מאד *me'od* 'very', and of the regular conversion of statements into exclamations by exclamation marks or by exclamatory intonation, as in examples (2,3) - although no intonation pattern is exclamatory *per se*:

(1) shtūYOT   שטויות!
                                      'nonsense!'

     nēeDAR   נהדר!
                                      'gorgeous!'

(2) ze ‚lo yitaHÈN   זה ‚לא יתכן
     it not is-possible   'It can't be!'

(3) ata ma'mash neHMAD   אתה ממש נחמד
     you really nice   'You're really nice!'

27.2 Question-like exclamations

Question-like exclamations convey extremes of degree or quantity. They are introduced by:

éze	'what'	איזה
káma	'what a lot of; how'	כמה
eH	'how'	איך

Qualifying a noun

> *Degree:*[1]
> éze krav mishtolel sham!   איזה קרב משתולל שם!
> what battle rages there!   'What a battle is raging there!'

> *Quantity:*
> káma shgiot hu asa!   כמה שגיאות הוא עשה!
> how-many mistakes he made!

280

Qualifying an adjective[2]

> káma tov lanúaH!   כמה טוב לנוח!
> how good to-rest!

Adverb to the verb phrase

> *Degree*:
> káma hu nire muzar!   כמה הוא נראה מוזר!
> how he looks odd!   'How odd he looks!'

> *Quantity*:
> káma hu mefatpet!   כמה הוא מפטפט!
> how-much he chatters!

> *Degree* (*of unsaid adverb*):
> eH hi rakda!   איך היא רקדה!
> how she danced!

An optional -ש *she-*, identical to the subordinating conjunction -ש *she-* but here devoid of meaning, is often inserted after the opening phrase (as in questions; see 26.7):[3]

> éze terutsim she-hu mamtsi!   איזה תירוצים שהוא ממציא!
> what excuses that he invents!   'What excuses he invents!'

> éze ga'on she-hu!   איזה גאון שהוא!
> what genius that he!   'What a genius he is!'

> káma she-hu nire muzar!   כמה שהוא נראה מוזר!
> how that he looks odd!   'How odd he looks!'

> eH she-hi rakda!   איך שהיא רקדה!
> how that she danced!   'How she danced!'

Casual usage, rather than using כמה *káma* 'how many, how' with nouns and adjectives, tends to prefer quite different constructions. Instead of:

> káma origináli!   'How original!'   כמה אוריגינלי!
> káma shgiot...!   'How many mistakes...!'   כמה שגיאות....!

it prefers:

> éze origináliut!   איזה אוריגינליות!
>   'What originality!'

> hu kol-kaH origináli!   הוא כל-כך אוריגינלי!
>   'He ⟨is⟩ so original!'

> hu asa hamon shgiot!   הוא עשה המון שגיאות!
>   'He made loads of mistakes!'

The 'question-like' exclamation is impossible with other '*wh-*' words or with yes/no questions:[4]

> *éfo hi hayta!   *איפה היא היתה!
> where she has-been!

*ha'im ani ra'ev!		‏*האם אני רעב!‏
Q PARTICLE I hungry!		('Am I hungry!')

Exclamation clauses can be cut back to simple phrases:[5]

éze kravot!	'what battles!'	‏איזה קרבות!‏
káma shgi'ot!	'what a lot of mistakes!'	‏כמה שגיאות!‏
káma matsHik!	'how funny!'	‏כמה מצחיק!‏
ve-od eH!	'and how!'	‏ועוד איך!‏

27.3 'Relative clause' exclamations - negative

One particular type of relative clause has no overt antecedent noun, and an 'interrogative-like' relative pronoun (described in 33.8); the '∧' symbol indicates here that the antecedent noun 'anyone' is understood:

lo haya li el mi lifnot	‏לא היה לי אל מי לפנות‏
not was to-me ∧ to who to-turn	'I did not have anyone to whom to turn'

This construction is also used in exclamations - but with the conjunction ‏ש‏- *she-* plus finite verb rather than with an infinitive, and strictly in the negative:[6]

el mi she-lo paníti!	‏אל מי שלא פניתי!‏
to who that not I-turned!	'Who I only turned to!'
mi she-lo haya sham!	‏מי שלא היה שם!‏
who that not was there!	'Who was only there!'
ma she-hi lo yodáat!	‏מה שהיא לא יודעת!‏
what that she not knows!	'What she only knows!'
éfo she-lo hayínu hayom!	‏איפה שלא היינו היום!‏
where that not we-were today!	'Where we've only been today!'

These exclamations convey not extremes of degree/quantity (as in 'question-shaped' exclamations earlier) but rather that 'everyone/everything' etc. is involved - thus contrast the following:

eH she-hu lo nisa!	‏איך שהוא לא ניסה!‏
how that he not tried!	'How he only tried!'
	(= he tried everything)
eH she-hu nisa!	‏איך שהוא ניסה!‏
how that he tried!	'How ⟨hard⟩ he tried!'

Less colloquially, the conjunction ‏ש‏- *she-* can drop, but still with the negative - a 'blend' between a relative clause and the 'question-shaped' exclamations of 27.2:

ma hi lo yodáat!	‏מה היא לא יודעת!‏
what she not knows!	'What she only knows!'

27.4 'Relative clause' exclamations - positive

Noun + relative clause - with a stated antecedent and strictly using the positive - can convey an exclamation equivalent to ...איזה *éze..* 'what a ...!':

ha-balagan she-hu ose po!	הבלגן שהוא עושה פה!
the mess that he makes here!	

ha-dvarim she-hi oméret!	הדברים שהיא אומרת!
the things that she says!	

27.5 Infinitival exclamations

Verbs of perception are used in the infinitive (with no subject noun, as usual) to express 'to see..!, to hear...!' and the like:

lishmóa eH hu maaliv ota!	לשמוע איך הוא מעליב אותה!
to-hear how he insults her!	'To hear how he insults her!'

kshe-hitHálnu, kol méshek gidel levad,   כשהתחלנו, כל משק גידל לבד,
ve-lir'ot eH ze mitpatéaH,   **ולראות איך זה מתפתח,**
ba'im zugot Hadashim, mishpaHot...   באים זוגות חדשים, משפחות...
'When we started, each farm farmed by itself, and **to see how it's developing**, new couples, new families are coming...'

FURTHER READING
Laufer 1974.

28. Requests

28.1 Definition of 'request'

This chapter deals with constructions that typically convey a request (or 'command' - the term is meant loosely). Of chief concern are particular uses of the future tense, the imperative form and the infinitive:[1]

Future tense:	taatsor!	'Stop!'	תעצור!
Imperative form:	atsor!	'Stop!'	עצור!
Infinitive:	laatsor!	'Stop!'	לעצור!

Such future tense and infinitive requests occur in subordinate clauses too ('reported requests'):

amárti **she-yaatsor**	אמרתי שיעצור
FUT	
I-said **that he-stop**	'I said that he should stop'
amárti **laatsor**	אמרתי לעצור
INF	
I-said **to-stop**	'I said to stop'

The chapter is organized in the main according to function and level of diction; 28.10 sets out the facts again, tense by tense.

28.2-8 MAIN CLAUSE REQUESTS

Requests may be made in the 1st, 2nd or 3rd person, though of course requests to the addressee (2nd person) are most common. Direct 2nd person requests chiefly involve the imperative form (mainly in formal usage), the future tense (mainly casual), and the infinitive (neutral), as described below.[2]

28.2 Formal 2nd person requests

Formal usage, e.g. literature, officialese, the press, printed instructions, and much careful educated usage, generally employs the imperative form in 2nd person requests (except in the negative):

habet	'Look'	הבט
knu kóka-kóla	'Buy Coca-Cola'	קנו קוקה-קולה

In the negative, not the imperative but the future tense is used, and the negator is אל *al*, not לא *lo*:[3]

al tabit	'Do not look'	אל תביט
al tiknu	'Do not buy'	אל תקנו

284

In these and all other requests in this chapter, other words can be brought to the front of the sentence, as in:

et ze ten le-ába	את זה תן לאבא
OM this give to Daddy	'Give this to Daddy'

אתה *ata* 'you' and other terms for 'you' cannot be added as subject to an *imperative*, except as a vocative, meaning 'hey you...'. For אתה *ata* 'you' in other 2nd person requests, see 28.5.

28.3 Casual 2nd person requests

The general rule for positive requests: future tense

For positive 2nd person requests, casual Hebrew mostly uses the future[4] form, e.g. תזכור *tizkor* 'remember', with no subject אתה *ata* 'you' except for emphasis (see 28.5).

What distinguishes future tense requests (in the positive) from future tense predictions is (1) an exclamation mark, or (2) suitable intonation and context, or (3) just context:

(1)	tizkor!	'Remember!'	!תזכור
(2)	ˈtizKÒR	'Remember'	ˈתזכור
(3)	tizkor bevakasha	'Please remember'	תזכור בבקשה

vs.

téHef tizkor	'Soon you'll remember'	תכף תזכור

The exception: use of the imperative form

For a request expecting an immediate result, e.g. 'Tidy up' as against 'Tidy up tomorrow morning', casual Hebrew offers the option of using either the future or the imperative form, if one is using a verb that can form the imperative by the simple method of lopping off its future tense prefix ת- *ti-* / *ta-* / *te-*. Only two verb patterns meet this criterion, the *kal* (also called *pa'al*) and the *pi'el* patterns:[5]

Imperative form			Future form	
meshoH	'Pull'	משוך	timshoH	תמשוך
sa	'Proceed'	סע	tisa	תסע
kum	'Stand up'	קום	takum	תקום
sader	'Tidy'	סדר	tesader	תסדר

By contrast, verbs of the *nif'al*, *hif'il* and *hitpa'el* patterns do not employ an imperative of the normative type (as listed in traditional grammars) in casual usage, for it cannot be formed by simply omitting the future tense prefix:

Normative Imperative			Future	
hikanes	'Enter'	היכנס	tikanes	תיכנס
hakshev	'Listen'	הקשב	takshiv	תקשיב
hitlabesh	'Dress'	התלבש	titlabesh	תתלבש

The distinction is seen in the following example:

tafsik livkot ve-**ptaH** et ha-délet	**תפסיק** לבכות ו**פתח** את הדלת
HIF'IL KAL	
FUT IMP	'**Stop** crying and **open** the door'

While most *kal* and *pi'el* imperatives in casual usage are fairly elegant in style (though not formal or pedantic) and immediate, even slightly brusque in meaning, a minority are often more or less *identical* in style and meaning with the future tense request - particularly *kal* imperatives of the form consonant + vowel (± consonant), such as: בוא *bo* 'come', גע *ga* 'touch', גש *gash* 'approach', דון *dun* 'discuss', לך *leH* 'go', סע *sa* 'go', צא *tse* 'leave', קח *kaH* 'take', רד *red* 'get down', רוץ *ruts* 'run', שב *shev* 'sit', שים *sim* 'put', תן *ten* 'give'; and among *pi'el* forms: חכה *Hake* 'wait', כבה *kabe* 'turn off'.

leH maHar, mótek	'Go tomorrow, sweetheart'	לך מחר, מותק

A new imperative form

Casual usage has created a new imperative כנס *kanes* 'Come in' (and its inflections) alongside the future form תיכנס *tikanes*.

Very casually, *hitpa'el* verbs too have a new imperative by dropping the prefix תֿ- *ti-*:

titlabesh→tlabesh	'Get dressed'	תתלבש←תֿלבש
tistakli→stakli	'Look'	תסתכלי←סתכלי

Negative requests

In the negative, casual usage has the negator אל *al* + future tense throughout (even with *kal* and *pi'el* verbs, for the imperative form is not negatable):

al tisa	'Don't go'	אל תסע
al takum	'Don't stand up'	אל תקום

There is no confusion with future tense *predictions*, as their negator is לא *lo*, not אל *al*:

lo tisa	'You won't go'	לא תסע

-ש *she-* + future tense: a forceful request

Casually, -ש *she* + 2nd person future (and indeed with 1st person, see 28.7) conveys a more forceful tone:

she-terdi be-atsmeH that you-get-down by yourself	שתרדי בעצמך 'Get down by yourself, will you'

she-lo tishkaH that not you-forget	שלא תשכח 'Don't you forget'

The conjunction ש *she* and the use of negator לא *lo* rather than אל *al* make this construction akin to a subordinate request: 'I insist that you etc.'.

28.4 2nd person requests: the 'remote' infinitive

An infinitive has no person, number or gender; nor has it a subject. Aptly, a main clause infinitive expresses a request more remote in tone than the future tense or imperative - and appropriate to persons of authority or written instructions:

(1) *Museum attendant*:

laavor bevakasha to-move-along please	לעבור בבקשה 'Move along, please'

(2) *Teacher to pupils*:

kulam lakum everyone to-stand-up	כולם לקום 'All stand'

(3) *Mother to child* (*distantly*):

lo lingóa not to-touch	לא לנגוע 'No touching'

Negation uses לא *lo*. By contrast, the use of negative אין *en* ('there is not') + infinitive, as in אין לעשן *en leashen* (there-is-not to-smoke), does not create a specifically *2nd* person request but rather a general request: 'Smoking is forbidden'.

נא *na* or בבקשה *bevakasha* 'please' can be placed in front of the infinitive to render it more polite and less remote (בבקשה *bevakasha* following it has no such effect, see example (1) above):[6]

na laavor please to-move-along	נא לעבור 'Would you please move along'

bevakasha lakum please to-stand-up	בבקשה לקום 'Could you please stand'

For the infinitive of request in *questions*, see 1st person requests (28.7):[7]

lehagid la? to-tell her?	להגיד לה? 'Should I tell her?'

28.5 Use of the subject in 2nd person requests

Though the average request (future tense, imperative, infinitive) tends not to use אתה/את/אתם *ata/at/atem* 'you', they can sometimes appear - with future tense and imperative.[8] Following the verb, they do not affect meaning or tone substantially:[9]

{leH/teleH} ata letalfen   {לך/תלך} אתה לטלפן
  IMP FUT
{go/go} you to-phone   'Go and phone'

teleH letalfen ata   תלך לטלפן אתה
go to-phone you   'Go and phone'

Preceding the future tense verb, the 2nd person pronoun sounds emphatic, even brusque (preceding imperative requests, it is felt to be set off by a comma, i.e. 'Hey you,...'):

ata tatir oto   '*You* undo it'   אתה תתיר אותו
  FUT

ata, zuz tipa   'You, move a bit'   אתה, זוז טיפה

28.6 3rd person requests

Formal

Official or literary usage sometimes employs the bare 3rd person future, as in (1) below, with the verb often initial, as in (2). The negative uses אל *al*, as in all 'bare future' requests, or (particularly in legalese) לא *lo*. נא *na* 'please' or similar is often added, making it look more clearly a request. However, formal Hebrew generally prefers a paraphrase, such as (3):

(1)   yizkor (na) zot   יזכור (נא) זאת
      he-will-remember (please) this   'Let him remember this'

(2)   yishtamesh sabal letsóreH isko be-agala   ישתמש סבל לצורך עסקו בעגלה
      will-use porter for his-trade   'A porter shall use a trolley for
          trolley   his trade'

(3)   alav lizkor zot   עליו לזכור זאת
      on-him to-remember this   'He must remember this'

Casual

Casual usage has ש- *she-* + 3rd person future, the conjunction ש- *she-* representing roughly אני מבקש ש *ani mevakesh she* 'I request that':[10]

she-hem yizkeru aval   שהם יזכרו אבל
that they will-remember though   'They'd better remember, though'

she-aviv lo yagid klum   שאביו לא יגיד כלום
that his-father not will-tell   'His father had better not say
     anything   anything'

28.7 1st person requests

1st person requests denote a request/insistence for oneself ('*Let me* warn you') or oneself-plus-addressees ('*Let's* go').

Formal

Formal usage employs the 1st person future, usually followed by נא
na 'please' or preceded by the special particle הבה *háva*:

urshe na lefaret   אורשה נא לפרט
I-will-be-allowed please to-specify   'Might I be allowed to specify'

nizkor na zot   נזכור נא זאת
we-will-remember please this   'Please let us bear this in mind'

háva neleH   הבה נלך
PARTICLE we-will go   'Let us go'

Negation involves אל *al* (with optional נא *na*) + 1st person future:

al (na) nishkaH zot   אל (נא) נשכח זאת
not (please) we-will-forget this   'Let us not forget this'

Casual: בוא נלך *bo neleH* 'Let's go'
The future tense by itself cannot express 'let's' in casual Hebrew;[11]
thus:

nisa ba-rakévet   נסע ברכבת
FUT   'We'll (*not*: 'let's') go by train'

Casual usage can employ -ש *she*- + 1st person future (as with 3rd person
requests):

she-*ani* eten laH   שאני אתן לך
that *I* will-give you   'Let *me* give you'

she-nizkor et ze   שנזכור את זה
that we-will-remember OM it   'Let's bear it in mind'

Additionally, the casual 1st person request has its own specialized - and less
insistent - construction: the inflected imperative בוא *bo* (otherwise meaning
'come!') plus 1st person future - with the specific implication that the addressee
participates somehow in the action (rather than just 'allowing' the action).
Thus:

bo eten leHa   בוא אתן לך
come I-will-give to-you   'Let me give you'

bo naHshov réga   בוא נחשוב רגע
come we-will-think moment   'Let's think for a moment'
                                           ('us' includes the addressee)

and not the following (the addressee is 'on the sidelines'):

*bo eten lo   *בוא אתן לו
come I-will-give to-him   ('Let me give him')

*bo aHshov réga	בוא אחשוב רגע*
come I-will-think moment	('Let me think for a moment')

The word order is as follows. The subject pronoun אני *ani* 'I', but not אנחנו *anáHnu* 'we', can optionally be used - between בוא *bo* and the verb. Nothing else can come between them except לא *lo* 'not' (see below). As for inflection, בוא *bo* inflects in accordance with the *addressee* and the future tense verb in accordance with the *speaker*:

to a male: m.s.	bo	בוא
to a female: f.s.	bói	בואי
to two or more people: pl.	bóu	בואו

bo		leHa		you (m.s.)'	בוא לך
bói	eten	laH	'Let me give	you (f.s.)'	בואי אתן לך
bóu		laHem		you (pl.)'	בואו לכם

bo			to a male	בוא
bói	nafsik		to a female	בואי נפסיק
bóu			to two or more	בואו

'Let's stop'

The negative requires לא *lo*, following בוא *bo*:

bo lo nariv	בוא לא נריב
come not we-will-quarrel	'Let's not quarrel'

Neutral: the infinitive and ‎-ש‎ *she-* + future in questions

For the quite distinct notion of *being* requested, the bare infinitive can be used - in questions:[12]

leHayeg aHshav?	?לחייג עכשיו
to-dial now?	'Should I/we dial now?

laanot?	?לענות
to-answer?	'Should I/we answer?'

Hebrew also uses ‎-ש‎ *she-* + future (not particularly casual in questions), which enables one to put stress on the subject

she-*ani* aHayeg?	?שאני אחייג
that *I* will-dial?	'Should *I* dial?'

28.8 Present tense requests

Sharp requests or instructions can be conveyed, casually, by present tense (as well as by the infinitive) - and in the 3rd person too. The subject is used and negation is with לא *lo* or אין *en*, as in ordinary present tense clauses:

atem mesadrim et kol ha-balagan	אתם מסדרים את כל הבלגן
you are-cleaning-up OM all the mess	'You're cleaning up all the mess'

aHshav kol eHad lokéaH et	עכשיו כל אחד לוקח עט
now every one takes pen	'Now everyone take a pen'

28.9   Subordinate requests
Subordinate requests tend to be of the form:

darshu she-yazuz	'They asked that he move'	דרשו שיזוז

Subordinate requests are just part of a whole spectrum of subordinate wishes and requests ('modal clauses'), introduced by verbs etc., such as:

tsiva (she/le...)	'order (that/to...)'	ציווה (ש/ל...)
darash (she/le...)	'request (that/to...)'	דרש (ש/ל...)
kiva (she/le...)	'hope (that/to...)'	קיווה (ש/ל...)
adif (she/le...)	'preferable (that/to...)'	עדיף (ש/ל...)
hamlatsa (she/le...)	'recommendation (that/to...)'	המלצה (ש/ל...)

In fact, despite the title of this section, there is no clear-cut 'request construction' among subordinate clauses, nor an obvious semantic division between wishing and requesting; nonetheless, notice that two of the three general 'request' forms (future tense and infinitive, but not imperative) are used in subordinate clauses and in much the same way - in formal as well as casual Hebrew.

Subordinate future tense requests
With some verbs, e.g. ציווה *tsiva* 'order', - ש *she-* + future tense automatically conveys a request:

tsivíti she-yisog	צוויתי שייסוג
I-ordered that he-will-retreat	'I ordered him to retreat'

Some others allow either predictions or requests, context deciding. Thus:

amárti laH		אמרתי לך
hodáati laH	she-titsHaki	הודעתי לך שתצחקי
hizhárti otaH	FUT	הזהרתי אותך

'I told you
'I informed you that   you would laugh'
'I warned you   you should laugh'

As with main clause requests introduced by - ש *she-* (28.6-7), negation is by לא *lo*, not אל *al*.

The infinitive, e.g. לבדוק *livdok* 'to check', can generally substitute for ש *she* + future in subordinate clauses like these, as is now shown.

Subordinate infinitive requests
Subordinate (as opposed to main clause) infinitives are in no way 'remote'. Many verbs can govern infinitive as well as future tense requests - with the same meaning:

amárti laH	litsHok	אמרתי לך לצחוק
hizhárti otaH	INF	הזהרתי אותך

'I told you   to laugh'
'I warned you

Some verbs prefer an infinitive to -ש *she-* + future, and some *vice versa*:

napolyon kara le-ángliya **lehikana**   נפוליון קרא לאנגליה **להיכנע**
INF

'Napoleon called on England **to surrender**'
(rather than שתיכנע* *she-tikana ('that it surrender'))

hodáati le-róni she-yitslol   הודעתי לרוני שיצלול
FUT

'I told Roni that he should dive'
(rather than לצלול* *litslol ('to dive'))

There is a limitation on infinitive requests: their subject is not stated, and must be taken to refer back to the object (if any) of the preceding, i.e. 'governing', verb. Thus in example (1) below it must be the 'lady' who should not scream, whereas in example (2) the future tense verb permits mention of some other word as subject:[13]

(1)   avakesh me-ha-gvéret lo **litsróaH**   אבקש מהגברת לא **לצרוח**
INF   'Might I ask the lady not **to scream?**'

(2)   avakesh me-ha-gvéret she-bita lo **tidHof**   אבקש מהגברת שבתה לא **תדחוף**
SUBJ   FUT 'Might I ask the lady that her daughter should not **push**'

28.10   Structure-by-structure summary

Type of structure	In main clause	In subordinate clause
Bare future tense (תלך *teleH*)	2nd person request (casual in the positive); negative uses אל *al*	-
ש *she* + future tense	1st/2nd person firm request (casual); 3rd person request (casual); 1st/3rd person request in questions	With certain verbs of wishing and requesting
בוא *bo* + future tense	1st person request, with addressee's participation (casual)	-
Imperative (לך *leH*)	2nd person request (formal, save certain *kal* and *pi'el* verbs)	-
New imperative	2nd person request for certain *nif'al* and *hitpa'el* verbs (casual)	-
Infinitive	1st person request in questions; 2nd person request of 'remoteness'	With certain verbs of wishing and requesting
Present tense	Any person. Sharp request.	With verbs of stating

FURTHER READING
Bar-Adon 1966; Bolozky 1979, 1980: 13-15; Rabin 1958; Rosén 1955:217ff, 1977:198ff; Sadka 1981:60.

29. Negation

29.1 Definitions

The 'negator' is the word expressing negation ('not, non-' etc.) - very roughly as described in the following table.

Negator		Details in	Function	Example	
lo	לא	29.2-4	All-purpose negator	lo eleH	לא אלך 'I won't go'
		29.4	'No'	lo!	לא! 'No!'
		29.8	Contrastive/emphatic 'not'	lo hu ba	לא הוא בא '*He* isn't coming'
al	אל	29.3	'Don't' in some future tense requests	al teleH	אל תלך 'Don't go'
en	אין	29.2,29.6	'Not'/'is not' in present tense	dan eno ba	דן אינו בא 'Dan does not come'
		29.7	Negative of 'exist', 'be present'	dan enénu	דן איננו 'Dan isn't present'
i- Hóser	אי חוסר	29.8	'Non-' (with nouns)	i-tipul	אי-טיפול 'non-treatment'
bilti-	בלתי	29.8	'Non-' (with adjectives)	bilti-Huki	בלתי-חוקי 'illegal'

Further concepts used in this chapter

'Complex negators' (29.12) express negation as a component of their meaning, e.g. בלי *bli* 'without' (= not with).

'Quasi-negators' (29.12) appear negative in meaning, but do not behave so syntactically, e.g. סירב *serev* 'refuse' (= not accept).

'Negative words' often accompany the negator. They reinforce or just extend the application of the negation (29.9-10):

shum kavana	'**no** intention'	שום כוונה
lo haya **klum**	'There wasn't **anything**'	לא היה **כלום**

Sometimes the negator is left unsaid and these words themselves do the negating, e.g. כלום - מה חסכתי *ma HasáHti - klum* 'What did I save - nothing' (29.11).

Negation is of two basic kinds: 'sentence negation', as in example (1) (see 29.2-7), and 'word or phrase negation' as in example (2) (see 29.8):

(1)	lo hiskamt	'You did not agree'	לא הסכמת
(2)	i-haskama	'non-agreement'	אי-הסכמה

29.2-7 SENTENCE NEGATION

29.2-3 'NOT': לא *LO*, אל *AL*, אין *EN*

29.2 'Not' in statements and questions
With past, future and infinitive, only לא *lo* is used:[1]

lo {zázu/yazúzu}	לא {זזו/יזוזו}
not {they-moved/they-will-move}	'They {did not/will not} move'

notim lo lazuz	נוטים לא לזוז
	'⟨They⟩ tend not to move'

With the present tense, 'not' is אין *en* (F) and לא *lo* (c):[2]

hu eno mevashel	הוא אינו מבשל
he not + SUFF cooks	'He does not cook'

hu lo mevashel	הוא לא מבשל
he not cooks	'He doesn't cook'

אין *en*
Ordinarily אין *en* directly precedes the verb or other predicate, as in example (1). Very formally, it may directly precede the subject, as in (2):

(1)	ha-tsav eno {zaz/ra'ev}		הצב אינו {זז/רעב}
	the tortoise not + SUFF {move/hungry}	'The tortoise is not {moving/hungry}'	
(2)	en ha-tsav {zaz/ra'ev}		אין הצב {זז/רעב}
	not the tortoise {move/hungry}	'The tortoise is not {moving/hungry}'	

אֵין *en* takes suffixes agreeing with its subject (except when it precedes its subject), as follows:

Subject		Form of אֵין *en*		Subject		Form of אֵין *en*	
ani 'I'	אני	eni enéni	אֵינִי אֵינֶנִּי	anáHnu 'we'	אנחנו	enénu	אֵינֶנּוּ
ata 'you (m.)'	אתה	enHa	אֵינְךָ	atem 'you (m.pl.)'	אתם	enHem	אֵינְכֶם
at 'you (f.)'	את	eneH	אֵינֵךְ	aten 'you (f.pl.)'	אתן	enHen	אֵינְכֶן
3rd person m.s.		eno enénu	אֵינוֹ אֵינֶנּוּ	3rd m.pl.		enam	אֵינָם
3rd person f.s.		ena enéna	אֵינָהּ אֵינֶנָּה	3rd f.pl.		enan	אֵינָן

Sections 29.5-7 give fuller details of the general behaviour of אֵין *en* as 'not' and as the negative of 'be, exist, be present'.

לֹא *lo*

לֹא *lo* directly precedes the verb or other predicate[3] - except where contrastive ('not this but that'; see 29.8). It never inflects.

ha-tsav lo {zaz/ra'ev}	הצב לא {זז/רעב}
the tortoise not {moving/hungry}	'The tortoise isn't {moving/hungry}'

29.3 'Not' in requests

Request constructions employ the future tense, imperative, particle + future tense, infinitive and present tense (see ch.28).

For the simple future tense, the negator is אַל *al*, directly preceding the verb. The imperative (the basic form in formal usage) cannot be negated - it converts instead to the simple future tense, taking אַל *al*, as shown in the table below.

		Positive		Negative	
2nd person	Casual	takshiv SIMPLE FUT	תקשיב 'Listen'	al takshiv	אל תקשיב 'Don't listen'
	Formal	hakshev IMP	הקשב 'Listen'		
1st/3rd person	Formal	navo SIMPLE FUT	נבוא 'Let us come'	al navo	אל נבוא 'Let us not come'
		yavóu SIMPLE FUT	יבואו 'Let them come'	al yavóu	אל יבואו 'Let them not come'

Elsewhere, the request negator is לא *lo*; and with present tense requests, formal usage prefers (as always) אין *en*:

> *Particle + future*:
> bo lo naníaH she-ken
> come not we-will-assume that so
>
> בוא לא נניח שכן
> 'Let's not assume so'
>
> she-lo yafríu
> that not they-will-bother
>
> שלא יפריעו
> 'They'd better not bother me'
>
> *Infinitive*:
> lo legared!
> not to-scratch!
>
> לא לגרד!
> 'No scratching!'
>
> *Present*:
> lo doHafim!
> not they-push!
>
> לא דוחפים!
> 'No pushing!'

29.4   'No!' לא *lo*

'No' as a one-word statement or request is לא *lo*.[4] Alternatively, the request 'Don't' can be conveyed by אסור! *asur*! (= forbidden).

אין *en* on its own means 'There isn't any' (29.7). אל *al* is not used on its own.

29.5-7   'IS/HAS NOT, IS NOT PRESENT, THERE IS NOT': אין *EN*

29.5   אין *en*: an overview

אין *en* is a negator with five functions, all related:

(1)   A simple negator, somewhat like לא *lo* (though strictly speaking a 'semi-verb'), as described in 29.2; see further, 29.6.

(2-5) Semantically, a combination of negator and verb

(2)   A semi-verb meaning 'be not' in formal usage[5]

(3)   A verb meaning 'there {is/are} not' (the negative of יש *yesh* 'there is/are')

(4)   A verb meaning 'have not', used with the preposition -ל *le-* (the negative of ל... יש *le... yesh* 'have')

(5)   A verb meaning 'be not present' (the negative of ישנו *yeshno* etc. 'be present')

Examples of these functions are:

(1)   hu eno bo'et
he not + SUFF kicks

הוא אינו בועט
'He does not kick'

(2)   dov eno av
Dov not + SUFF father

דוב אינו אב
'Dov is not a father'

(3)	en brera	אין ברירה
	there-is-not choice	'There is no choice'

(4)	le-úri en musag	לאורי אין מושג
	to Uri there-is-not idea	'Uri has no idea'

(5)	dána enéna	דנה איננה
	Dana is-not-present	'Dana is not present'

29.6   אין *en* as the semi-verb 'not, be not'

As illustrated in 29.2, אין *en* is the present tense negator in formal usage. Further, it serves as the negative of the present tense particle 'be',[6] covering those situations where a positive sentence would need an explicit word for 'be', e.g. (ch.16) where subject and predicate are both indefinite nouns, thus:

matsberim hem baaya   מצברים הם בעיה
'Batteries are ⟨a⟩ problem'

matsberim **enam** baaya   מצברים **אינם** בעיה
'Batteries **are not** ⟨a⟩ problem'

These two אין *en* have much in common, and often act syntactically rather like verbs, as is now described.

Ordinarily אין *en* precedes the verb or other predicate, as is example (1) below; very formally, it can directly precede its subject, as in (2). In the first case it must take suffixes; in the second it must not.[7] (For inflections, see 29.2).

(1)	dov eno tas	דב אינו טס
	Dov not + SUFF flies	'Dov does not fly'

(2)	en dov tas	אין דב טס
	not Dov flies	'Dov does not fly'

When inflected, אין *en*, like an inflected past or future tense verb, needs no pronoun subject:

(ani) enéni toféret   'I do not sew'   (אני) אינני תופרת
(hi) ena tipusit   'She is not typical'   (היא) אינה טיפוסית

Where the subject is unstated and understood as non-specific זה *ze* 'it', one rarely uses אין *en* (see examples (1,2) below); לא *lo* is preferred or where possible זה *ze* is added, giving אין זה *en ze* (examples (3,4)). Casual Hebrew always uses לא *lo* or זה לא *ze lo*. But some predicates, e.g. חם *Ham* 'it is hot', do not usually occur with זה *ze* as a non-specific 'it' (see ch.17), nor consequently with אין זה *en ze* in the negative; they prefer לא *lo*, as in (5):[8]

(1)	en kal linhog	אין קל לנהוג
		'⟨It is⟩ not easy to drive'

(2)	ha'im en Haval?	?האם אין חבל
	Q PARTICLE not pity?	'Is it not a pity?'

(3) lo kal linhog
                                         לא קל לנהוג
                                        '⟨It is⟩ not easy to drive'

(4) en ze kal linhog
     not it easy to-drive
                                           אין זה קל לנהוג
                                          'It is not easy to drive'

(5) lo Ham kan
     not hot here
                                           לא חם כאן
                                          'It is not hot here'

אין *en* as such a semi-verb needs something to follow it,[9] thus ruling out:

*ha-kiyorim nekiyim, aH ha-aronot **enam**   *הכיורים נקיים, אך הארונות **אינם**
                   'The sinks ⟨are⟩ clean, but the cupboards **are not**'

29.7 אין *en* as the verb 'there is not, not have, not be present'

'There is not, not have'

The difference between 'There is not' and 'not have', as in the following examples, is often just the possessor phrase ...ל *le...* (see further, ch.16).

en of
there-is-not chicken
                                   אין עוף
                               'There is no chicken'

la-samal en of
to-the sergeant there-is-not chicken
                               לסמל אין עוף
                       'The sergeant has no chicken'

אין *en* is the negative form of יש *yesh*, so לא יש *lo yesh* and אין יש *en yesh* are impossible. But in other tenses אין *en* gives way to לא היה *lo haya* 'was not' and the like:

la-samal lo yiye of
to-the sergeant not will-be chicken
                             לסמל לא יהיה עוף
                    'The sergeant will have no chicken'

The positioning of אין *en* is as for יש *yesh* (described in 16.9-10): it generally precedes the noun that 'exists/is possessed', as in examples (1,2) below, save for emphasis (3) or de-emphasis (4). By 'precedes' is not meant 'directly precedes' - the 'possessor' noun can intervene, as in (5):

(1) en mits
     there-isn't juice
                                         אין מיץ
                                   'There's no juice'

(2) le-tal en mits
     to-Tal there-isn't juice
                                      לטל אין מיץ
                                   'Tal has no juice'

(3) *mits* en, aval yesh bíra
     juice there-isn't, but there's beer
                               מיץ אין, אבל יש בירה
                        'Juice there isn't, but there's beer'

(4) lo, baayot be'étsem en li
     no, problems actually there-aren't to-me
                                לא, בעיות בעצם אין לי
                 'No, I don't actually have any problems'

(5) en le-tal mits
     there-isn't to Tal juice
                                     אין לטל מיץ
                                   'Tal has no juice'

As with יש *yesh* (16.9-10), this word order suggests that מיץ *mits* is not subject but *object* of אין *en* (there are several verbs with no subject, see ch. 17), and indeed casual Hebrew inserts the 'object particle' את *et* (provided this noun is 'definite'):[10]

en et ze be-hódu	אין את זה בהודו
there-is-not OM this in India	'There isn't such a thing in India'

le-dov en et ha-maftéaH?	לדב אין את המפתח?
to Dov there-is-not OM the key?	'Dov hasn't got the key?'

This אין *en* never inflects, unlike אין *en* in 29.6.[11]

'Not be present'

אין *en* is also the negative of the present tense verb יש *yesh* 'be present, be there' (see 16.9). Both must follow their subject, usually 3rd person (other verbs need not), and must inflect.[12] The endings are:

enénu איננו	enéna איננה	enam אינם	enan אינן
3rd m.s.	3rd f.s.	3rd m.pl.	3rd f.pl.

An example:

nóa enéna karéga	נועה איננה כרגע
Noa is-not-here right-now	

29.8 Word or phrase negation

Word or phrase negation focuses on a particular word or phrase, whether for contrast or emphasis or other reasons. This is sometimes effected by intonation, but we concentrate here on the use made of grammar and syntax.

Contrastive negation: 'not this but that'

Contrastive negation employs three devices:

(1) Stress or underlining or suchlike on the negated word(s):

lo *hirbátsti* leHa	לא **הרבצתי** לך
	'I didn't *hit* you (but rather...)'

(2) Appending a contrastive phrase with אלא *éla* 'but':

lo hirbátsti éla daHáfti	לא הרבצתי אלא דחפתי
	'I didn't hit but shoved'

(3) Shift in word order: לא *lo* 'not' (but not אל *al or* אין *en*) can optionally be repositioned directly ahead of the word(s) to be negated:

nikiti lo be-spónja éla be-smartut	ניקיתי לא בספונזה אלא בסמרטוט
I-cleaned not with mop	'I cleaned not with a mop
but with rag	but with a rag'

lo ani be'ad	לא אני בעד
not I for	'*I'm* not for it'

Conversely, where negative stress is non-contrastive, לא *lo* stays directly in front of its verb:

אינני יודע מה הם רצו
אבל אני לא בעד

enéni yodéa ma *hem* ratsu
aval *ani* lo be'ad
'I don't know what *they* wanted but *I'm* not for it'

Strings of 'nots': 'neither....nor'

For emphasis in a string of two or more negated words or phrases, one may insert גם...גם...וגם *gam...gam...ve-gam* 'also...also...and also' (or an equivalent using הן *hen*), or לא...לא...ולא *lo...lo...ve-lo* 'not...not...and not'. This is like English 'neither...nor', except that the Hebrew particles can be repeated any number of times:

גם אדמת וגם שחפת לא חוסלו

gam adémet ve-gam shaHéfet lo Huslu
also rubella and not TB not were-eradicated
'Neither rubella nor TB were eradicated'

לא אדמת ולא שחפת חוסלו

lo adémet ve-lo shaHéfet Huslu
not rubella and not TB were-eradicated
'Neither rubella nor TB were eradicated'

As the foregoing example shows, the main sentence negator (לא *lo* or אין *en*) drops after לא...ולא *lo...ve-lo*; but it can be kept when preceding לא...ולא *lo... ve-lo* :

אפשר ש(לא) יבחרו לא בזה ולא בזה

efshar she-**(lo)** yivHaru lo be-ze ve-lo be-ze
possible that **(not)** they-will-vote
not for this and not for this
'Maybe they will not vote for either'

Negation (non-emphatic) of particular parts of speech

This mostly involves repositioning לא *lo* (never אין *en*); but note the special particles בלתי *bilti* and אי *i*.
With *adjectives,* לא *lo* is used with all styles, whereas בלתי *bilti* is formal and used particularly with adjectives formed from verbal participles (see ch.41):

bilti-mekubal   'unacceptable'   בלתי-מקובל

Many other verb-based and noun-based adjectives, of two syllables or more, take בלתי *bilti*, e.g. בלתי-כביס/לא כביס *bilti-kavis/lo kavis* 'unwashable', חוקי בלתי-חוקי/לא *bilti-Huki/lo Huki* 'illegal'. But some take only לא *lo*, e.g. פגיע לא *lo pagía* 'invulnerable', דתי לא *lo dati* 'non-religious', לא ישראלי *lo yisreeli* 'non-Israeli'. A few take only בלתי *bilti*, e.g. בלתי-נראה *bilti-nir'e* 'invisible', בלתי-נודע *bilti-noda* 'unknown'. אל *al* is rare, e.g. אל-אנושי *al-enoshi* 'non-human'.

Negated word or phrase	Negator	Example
Adjective	lo לא	haya dey **lo** nóaH היה די **לא** נוח 'It was quite **un**pleasant'
		haya **lo** simpáti היה **לא** סימפטי 'He was **un**likeable'
	bilti בלתי	hu **bilti**-yatsiv הוא **בלתי-**יציב 'He's **un**stable'
Some quantifiers	lo לא	yesh **lo** me'at batlanim יש **לא** מעט בטלנים there-are **not** few layabouts 'There are a good few layabouts'
Some degree words	lo לא	*hu* haya **lo** paHot kene הוא היה **לא** פחות כנה '*He* was **no** less sincere'
Adverbial[1]	(she-)lo (של)לא	**lo** mizman bikru **לא** מזמן ביקרו **not** long-ago they-visited 'They visited not long ago'
		hegávti she-lo הגבתי שלא be'emtsa'ut ha-váad באמצעות הוועד I-responded that not through the committee 'I responded without going through the committee'
		she-lo kmo yerivay, hitHálti... שלא כמו יריבי, התחלתי... that not like my-foes, I-began... 'Unlike my foes, I began...'
Action and state nouns[2] (see 30.6)	Hóser- חוסר- -i אי-	{Hoser-/i-} te'um {חוסר-/אי-} תיאום '{lack of/non-} coordination'
		i-mesirat Havilot אי-מסירת חבילות 'non-delivery of parcels'
		{Hóser-/i-} sviut ratson {חוסר-/אי-} שביעות-רצון 'dissatisfaction'

Notes:

[1] Formal usage tends to add - ש *she-* (no obvious connection with the conjunction - ש *she-* 'that') to the לא *lo*, when negating adverbials of more than one word and when negating infinitives:

     heedáfti (she-)lo lehitarev   העדפתי (ש)לא להתערב
     I-preferred (CONJ) not to-interfere   'I preferred not to interfere'

[2] Nouns denoting a person or 'agent' do not regularly have a negative, but לא *lo* does sometimes do the job: לא-יהודי *lo-yehudi* 'non-Jew', לא-מאמינים *lo-maaminim* 'non-believers', קרון ללא-מעשנים *karon le-lo-meashnim* 'carriage for non-smokers'. אל *al* is limited to a handful of compounds, e.g. אלמוות *almávet* 'immortality'.

Nouns denoting a real action take אי- *i-*, not חוסר- *Hóser*:

i-tipul (be...)	'non-treatment (of...)'	(...ב) אי-טיפול
vs.		
Hóser-tipul	'lack of treatment'	חוסר-טיפול

Otherwise, אי *i* and חוסר *Hóser* are often interchangeable. חוסר *Hóser* often suggests a human quality, though this is a very relative matter:

i-aHarayut   אי-אחריות
'non-responsibility'

Hóser-aHarayut   חוסר-אחריות
'lack of responsibility'

i-havana   אי-הבנה
'a misunderstanding'

Hóser-havana   חוסר-הבנה
'lack of understanding'

i-neimut   אי-נעימות
'unpleasantness' (notably, of a situation)

Hóser-neimut   חוסר-נעימות
'unpleasantness' (notably, of a person)

Hóser-savlanut   חוסר-סבלנות
'impatience'

(There is no *i-savlanut אי-סבלנות*)

29.9-13 'NEGATIVE WORDS': 'NOTHING, NEVER, NONE, NO' ETC.

29.9 Terms for 'no, any': אף *af*, שום *shum* etc.

אף *af*, שום *shum*, כל *kol* and כלשהו *kólshehu* (see also ch.9) can be added to an indefinite noun, thus extending or just reinforcing the negation - corresponding to English 'no, any'; strictly speaking, אף *af* means '(not) a single':

lo ra'iti (af) shoter   לא ראיתי (אף) שוטר
not I-saw (any) policeman   'I did not see a (single) policeman'

(shum) shedim lo nir'u   (שום) שדים לא נראו
(any) ghosts not were-seen   'No ghosts were seen'

en (kol) tsóreH   אין (כל) צורך
there-is-not (any) need   'There is no need'

lo haya sikun (kólshehu)   לא היה סיכון (כלשהו)
not was risk (any)   'There was not any risk'

אף *af*, שום *shum*, כל *kol* only *precede* their noun, with the option of an added particle שהו *-shehu* 'whatsoever'. כלשהו *kólshehu* as a single word only follows its noun:[13]

| lo heeléti | af hatsa'a shehi
hatsa'a kólshehi | | אף הצעה שהיא
הצעה כלשהי | לא העליתי |

| not I-raised | any proposal whatsoever
proposal any | | 'I didn't raise any proposals
whatsoever' |

Both שהו *-shehu* and כלשהו *kólshehu* agree with the noun, like the pronoun הוא *hu*; they have the following endings:

| *m.s.* | -hu | -הו | | *f.s.* | -hi | -הי |
| *m.pl.* | -hem | -הם | | *f.pl.* | -hen | -הן |

How negative are these 'negative words'?

אף *af* and שום *shum*, typically found where there is already a negator (e.g. לא *lo*) in the same clause, are equivalent to 'any' - save in clause fragments (discussed in 29.11):

| hayu neumim aH **shum havtaHot** | היו נאומים אך **שום הבטחות** |
| | 'There were speeches but **no promises**' |

By contrast, כל *kol* and כלשהו *kólshehu* are not limited to negative clauses. כל *kol* is also 'all, every', כלשהו *kólshehu* is also 'some... or other', and both denote 'any' in questions as well as negations (see 26.10 and 9.2):

| ha'im yesh | kol tsóreH?
tsóreH kólshehu? | | כל צורך?
צורך כלשהו? | האם יש |
| | | | 'Is there any need?' |

The negative determiners differ as to which type of noun they introduce:

With single *countable* *nouns:*[14]	lo hayta... ...af hatsa'a ...shum hatsa'a ...hatsa'a kólshehi ...kol hatsa'a	'There was not...' '...a single suggestion'	...לא היתה ...אף הצעה ...שום הצעה ...הצעה כלשהי ...כל הצעה
	lo hayu... ...shum hatsa'ot ...hatsa'ot kólshehen ...kol hatsa'ot	'There weren't...' '...any suggestions'	...לא היו ...שום הצעות ...הצעות כלשהן ...כל הצעות
With mass *nouns:*[15]	en... ...shum siyúa ...siyúa kólshehu	'There is not...'	...אין ...שום סיוע ...סיוע כלשהו
With *abstract* *mass* *nouns, also:*	...kol siyúa	 '...any aid'	...כל סיוע

29.10 Terms for 'no one, nothing, never, nowhere'

These, like the terms for 'no' (29.9), are in fact usually equivalent to 'anyone, anything, ever, anywhere', as they typically occur where there is already a negator in the clause, as in (1,2) below - though as fragments they look negative in themselves (3), as described in 29.11:

(1) lo tafásti klum
     not I-caught anything
     'I did not catch anything'
     לא תפסתי כלום

(2) ish eno kore
     anyone not calls
     'No one calls'
     איש אינו קורא

(3) ve-ma kara? klum
     and what happened? nothing
     'And what happened? Nothing'
     ומה קרה? כלום

'No one' is אף אחד *af eHad*[16] and איש *ish* (F).[17] 'Nothing' is כלום *klum*,[18] מאומה *me'úma* (F), דבר *davar* (fairly formal),[19] שום דבר *shum davar* (c). 'Never' is אף פעם *af páam*,[20] לעולם *leolam*,[21] מעולם *meolam* (F) and the very formal מימי, מימיך *mi-yamay, mi-yaméHa* etc. and מעודי, מעודך *meodi, meodHa* etc.

All 'never' words but אף פעם *af páam* are restricted. לעולם *leolam* is not used for past time in formal usage, and is not used for present time in casual usage. The rest denote only past time:

Future: af páam lo ashuv
           leolam lo ashuv
           'I shall never return'
           אף פעם לא אשוב
           לעולם

Present: af páam lo onim
           leolam en onim (F)
           'They never answer'
           אף פעם לא עונים
           לעולם אין עונים

Past: af páam lo rávnu
           meolam lo rávnu
           'We (have) never argued'
           אף פעם לא רבנו
           מעולם

'Nowhere' is בשום מקום *be-shum makom* (*lit.* 'in no place').

General features

The two-word negatives, i.e. אף אחד *af eHad*, שום דבר *shum davar*, אף פעם *af páam* and בשום מקום *be-shum makom*, are fixed phrases - שום אחד *shum eHad*, אף דבר *af davar* and the like are rare.

One can add adjectives to שום דבר *shum davar*, דבר *davar* and אף אחד *af eHad*, but not to כלום *klum*, מאומה *me'úma* and איש *ish*:

shum davar meanyen   'nothing interesting'   שום דבר מעניין
af eHad aHer   'no one else'   אף אחד אחר

More than one negative word can figure in a sentence:

meolam lo heelávnu ish   מעולם לא העלבנו איש
ever not we-offended anyone
'We never offended anyone'

29.11 'Negative words' as free-standing negatives

Casually, many of the negative words of 29.9-10 occur without a negator לא *lo* or אין *en*, as 'free-standing negatives,[22] as shown in the table:

Negative words		Examples	
af	אף	hayu hamon shvarim aval af para	היו המון שוורים אבל אף פרה
		'There were many bulls but ⟨not⟩ a single cow'	
shum	שום	shum hitkadmut?	שום התקדמות!
		'No progress?'	
af eHad	אף אחד	mi ba? - af eHad	מי באז - אף אחד
		'Who came? - No one'	
klum/	כלום/	ma nafal? - klum	מה נפלז - כלום
shum davar	שום דבר	'What fell? - Nothing'	

The same holds for אף פעם *af páam* 'never' and בשום מקום *be-shum makom* 'nowhere'.

The negator can be added to most such free-standing negative words (before כלום *klum* but after the others) and is favoured by purists:

hizmánta mishehi? - lo, af eHad lo	הזמנת מישהיז - לא, אף אחד לא
you-invited someone? - no, anyone not	'Did you invite anyone? - No one'

ma haya sham? - lo klum	מה היה שם? - לא כלום
what was there? - not anything	'What was there? - Nothing'

'Negative' כל *kol*, כלשהו *kólshehu* 'any', מאומה/דבר *me'úma/davar* 'anything', לעולם/מעולם *leolam/meolam* 'ever', איש *ish* 'anyone', כלל *klal* 'at all', בשום אופן *be-shum ófen* 'under any circumstances' *require* a negator.

29.12 Complex and quasi-negators

Complex negators

Besides לא *lo*, אין *en* and אל *al* 'not', several other words are negators or incorporate a negator ('complex negators'). As a result, one can even use the 'negative words', e.g. שום *shum* 'no' and כלום *klum* 'nothing' (see 29.9-10), in such a context. Thus:

gamru **bli**	klum	גמרו **בלי** כלום
COMPLEX NEG	NEG	'They ended **without** anything'
NEG	WORD	

Other 'complex negators' are:[23]

mibli, lelo, belo	'without'	מבלי, ללא, בלא
leval	'lest'	לבל
asur, en	'it is forbidden (to...)'	אסור, אין
i-efshar	'it is impossible (to...)'	אי-אפשר
en	'there is not'	אין

Quasi-negators

Many more words, e.g. סירב *serav* 'refuse', are quasi-negative - they are akin to, but subtly different from, negators, and so do not allow strictly 'negative words' like כלום *klum* 'anything' and אף *af* 'any'; instead, one uses positive pronouns such as משהו *máshehu* 'someone' or words that are not limited to negation, e.g. כל *kol* 'any' and איש *ish* 'anyone':

máshehu	משהו
servu laasot davar	סירבו לעשות דבר
*klum	*כלום
they-refused to-do anything	
QUASI-NEG	

Other quasi-negators are: אסר *asar* 'to forbid', חסר *Haser* 'to lack', במקום *bimkom* 'instead of', טרם *térem* 'not yet', הכחיש *hiHHish* 'to deny' and בלתי *bilti* 'non-, un-'.

29.13 Direction and reach of negation

Direction of negation

When negative words, e.g. אף אחד *af eHad* 'anyone' and כלום *klum* 'anything', come first in sentences, the negator must still be put in: 'nothing remained' is כלום לא נשאר *klum lo nishar*, not *כלום נשאר *klum nishar*. כלום *klum* in fact amounts to English 'anything', as is clear from turning it around:

lo nishar **klum**	לא נשאר **כלום**
not remained anything	'(There did) not remain **anything**'

The difference between them is that English 'anything, anyone' etc. must *follow* the negator ('not'), whereas their Hebrew counterparts can *precede* (technically, Hebrew negates backwards or forwards). And Hebrew has no exact counterparts for 'no one, nothing', words which carry the negator in them, as in 'nothing remained'.[24] More examples are:

ish lo ra'inu	איש לא ראינו
anyone not we-saw	'We did not see anyone'
kol shinuy lo nirsham	כל שינוי לא נרשם
any change not was-recorded	'No change was recorded'

Quantifiers, and some time adverbs, are also negated backwards:

shinuyim rabim lo Hálu ba-matsav	שינויים רבים לא חלו במצב
changes many not occurred in-the situation	
BACKWARDS	'Not many changes occurred in the situation'
{yoter/shuv} lo nipagesh	{יותר/שוב} לא ניפגש
again not we'll-meet	'We shall never meet again'
BACKWARDS	

Reach of negation

Negators can act on the infinitive clauses they introduce, as in (1) below, and with 'mental verbs' such as חשב *Hashav* 'think' and ציפה *tsipa* 'expect' they act on a 'finite clause' too, as in (2):[26]

enéni rotse lashir **klum**   אינני רוצה לשיר **כלום**

NEG   INF   'I don't want to sing **anything**'

enéni maamin she-**shum davar** mutsdak   אינני מאמין ש**שום דבר** מוצדק

'I do not believe that **anything**
[= a single thing] is justified'

FURTHER READING

Altbauer 1964; Ben-Asher 1972: 72-90; Berman 1978: ch.6; Chayen & Dror 1976: ch. 5; Givón 1978; Glinert 1982a; Horn 1978; Levenston 1970: 7.5; Malisdorf 1979; Mirkin 1962; Rabin 1958; Rosén 1977: 8.3; Zilkha 1970.

30. Types of subordination

30.1 Introduction

To express a sentence within a sentence, a 'subordinate (= embedded) clause', Hebrew has five regular methods at its disposal, depending partly on the function of the subordination and its meaning: these are set out in a table.

Method	Example
Finite clause: Involving a verb with tense, as in an independent sentence	Hake ad she-ha-shearim yaalu חכה עד שהשערים יעלו 'Wait till [that] the rates rise'
Participle phrase: Involving a tenseless verb (identical to present tense) with gender and number but no subject of its own	ha-shearim heHélu olim השערים החלו עולים 'The rates began rising'
Infinitive phrase Involving a special tenseless form of verb, with no subject of its own	ha-shearim heHélu laalot השערים החלו לעלות 'The rates began to rise'
Gerund clause: Involving a special tenseless form of verb, with its own subject	Hake ad alot ha-shearim חכה עד עלות השערים 'Wait until ⟨the⟩ rising ⟨of⟩ the rates'
Action/state noun phrase: Involving a noun, but accompanied by many of the items that accompany verbs	Hake ad aliyat ha-shearim חכה עד עליית השערים 'Wait until ⟨the⟩ rising ⟨of⟩ the rates'

After discussion of these subordination types in this chapter, subsequent chapters describe specific uses made of them: as object clauses, relative clauses and so on.

30.2 Finite clauses

30.2.1 Subordinating conjunctions ('complementizers')

'Finite' signifies 'having a tense'. Most 'main' (i.e. 'non-embedded') clauses have a tense; so do many embedded clauses, but these nearly always begin with a subordinating conjunction ('complementizer'), whose prime role is

Choice of subordinating conjunction

Conjunction	Function of clause	Example	
-שׁ *she-* (the 'unmarked', all-purpose conjunction)	Complement	hodáati she-báta	הודעתי שֶׁבָּאתָ 'I announced that you came'
	Apposition	ha-hoda'a she-báta	הַהודעה שֶׁבָּאתָ 'the announcement that you came'
	Relative	ha-hoda'a she-báa	הַהודעה שֶׁבָּאה 'the announcement that came'
	Adverbial (mostly after prepositions)	ad she-báta	עד שֶׁבָּאתָ 'till [that] you came'
אשׁר *asher* (F)	Relative	ha-hoda'a asher báa	הַהודעה אשׁר בָּאה 'the announcement that came'
	Adverbial (after certain prepositions)	ad asher báta	עד אשׁר בָּאתָ 'till [that] you came'
כי *ki*	Complement (F)	hodáati ki báta	הודעתי כי בָּאתָ 'I announced that you came'
	Apposition (F)	ha-hoda'a ki báta	הַהודעה כי בָּאתָ 'the announcement that you came'
	Adverbial (= 'because', otherwise rare)	nish'árti ki báta	נשׁארתי כי בָּאתָ 'I stayed because you came'
-ה *ha-*	Relative	hoda'a ha-magi'a	הודעה הַמַגִּיעַ 'an announcement that arrives'
-ו *ve-*	A few complements and adverbials	meaHar ve-higáta	מאחר וְהִגַּעְתָּ 'as [that] you came'

to 'signpost' embedded clauses.[1] The table on page 309 gives a rough outline of which conjunction is used for which type of clause.

In addition to those in the table, there are conjunctions with more specific meaning, e.g. to signal questions (אם, האם *ha'im, im* '*est-ce que*, whether'), conditionals (אילו, אם *im, ílu* 'if') and apprehension (שמא *shéma* 'lest'). Some also introduce main clauses: -ש *she-* for casual requests with future tense, and האם *ha'im* or (literary) -ה *ha-* for questions:

she-yeHaku!	'Let them wait!'	שיחכו!
ha'im yeHaku?	'Will they wait?'	האם יחכו?

They are discussed in the relevant chapter.

The only cases where *no* conjunction is needed for subordination are (1) clauses already introduced by question words, (2) some relative clauses (see 33.7), and (3) a few adverbial clauses:

(1)	tevarer **matay** ze haya	'Check **when** it was'	תברר **מתי** זה היה
(2)	ha-báyit **bo** yashánu	'the house **in which** we slept'	הבית **בו** ישנו
(3)	me'az rávnu	'since we quarrelled'	מאז רבנו

30.2.2 Finite clauses: function

Finite clauses can appear in any sentence 'slots', as illustrated in 30.2.1, i.e. complement (subject, object or predicate), apposition, relative and adverbial[2] - but subject to their intrinsic 'truth status' and to the particular class of verb (or even the individual verb) to which they are subordinated. Contrast them with infinitives (set out in 30.4): (a) 'Factive' clauses (i.e. 'presupposing' that something is a fact) and 'assertions' can usually be finite, never infinitival:

muzar she-matsat kétem		מוזר שמצאת כתם
FACTIVE	'It's odd that you found a stain'	

amart she-matsat kétem		אמרת שמצאת כתם
ASSERTIVE	'You said that you found a stain'	

(b) 'Subjunctive' clauses (i.e. expressing an intention or the like) tend to be finite *or* infinitival:

bikáshti	she-teshev		ביקשתי שתשב
	lashévet		לשבת
I-asked	that you'll-sit	'I asked you to sit'	
	to-sit		

me'il	she-yilbash		מעיל שילבש
	lilbosh		ללבוש
coat	that he'll-wear	'a coat to wear'	
	to-wear		

kdey	she-eda ladáat		כדי שאדע לדעת
in-order	that I'll-know to-know		'for me to know/ in order to know'

Examples of the many individual words unexpectedly not taking finite clauses: עקב *ékev* 'as a result of', הקשיב *hikshiv* 'listen', דיבר *diber* 'speak'.

30.3 Participle phrases

Structure

Participle phrases consist of a present tense verb ('participle'), with no overt subject but with attendant objects, adverbials etc. The participle must agree with the noun that is understood as its subject; this noun is the subject or object of the main verb.[3]

shamáti	otan		sharot	shirim	שמעתי אותן שרות שירים
MAIN V	OBJ, understood as SUBJ of →		PARTICIPLE V f.pl.	OBJ	'I heard them singing songs'

I-heard them singing songs

ha-banot	heHélu	loHashot	הבנות החלו לוחשות
SUBJ f.pl.	V	PARTICIPLE V f.pl.	'The girls began whispering'

The girls began whispering

Function

Participle phrases can be object or adverbial. As adverbials they are not specifically *participles* but rather predicates of *various* kinds, described in 21.6 as 'circumstantial predicates'. Here they are described *qua* objects: (a) objects to a small group of verbs of 'noticing' and 'finding', notably שמע *shama* 'hear',[4] מצא *matsa* 'find', ראה *ra'a* 'see'; (b) objects to two verbs of 'beginning' (formally): התחיל, החל *hitHil, heHel*,[5] as in:

heHélu yorim	'They began firing'	החלו יורים

Those in the former group usually have an object noun somewhere to refer back to, even at a distance:

gam **otam** shamáti sharim	גם **אותם** שמעתי שרים
OBJ PARTICIPLE	'Even **them** I heard singing'

Being objects (not adverbials) of the wider sentence, these participle phrases cannot be set off by commas, nor indeed preposed or parted from the object noun being referred back to (save for emphasis) - unlike circumstantial predicates (21.6) such as:[6]

heHzáknu ba Hazak, roédet mi-kor f.s.	החזקנו בה חזק, רועדת מקור

we-held her tight, shivering with cold

30.4   Infinitive phrases

30.4.1   Form of the infinitive
The infinitive (traditional term: 'infinitive construct') is a totally non-finite verb form, i.e. it has no mark of tense, nor number and gender, unlike participles (30.3). Contrast:

Participle:	
hi hitHila melamédet	היא התחילה מלמדת
	'She began teaching'
Infinitive:	
hi hitHila lelamed	היא התחילה ללמד
	'She began to teach'

The infinitive always has a - ל *le-* prefix, inseparable from it (and thus unlike the conjunction - ש *she-*), hence לא ללמד *lo lelamed* 'not to teach' rather than **le lo lamed*.[7] **ללא למד* The only possible suffixes to the infinitive are 'object suffixes' - formal and optional, e.g. ללמדו *lelamdo* 'to teach **him**'. (See further, 15.5.1).

Infinitives are regularly available from almost any verb (see 40.10, 40.16).

30.4.2   Structure of the infinitive phrase
The infinitive (like the participle phrase, 30.3) has no overt subject but has attendant objects, adverbials, etc., like any verb.[8] Thus:

ratsiti	levaker oto levakro	bekarov	בקרוב	לבקר אותו לבקרו	רציתי
	INF OBJ				

means 'I wanted to visit him soon', not 'I wanted him to visit soon'.

The infinitive need not be first word in the infinitive phrase. Thus question words come to the front, as with any verb (1), so too can contrasted words (2), and the negator לא *lo* 'not' precedes its infinitive as it would precede any verb[9] (3):

(1) tish'al eH linhog   'Ask how to act'   תשאל איך לנהוג

(2) az at rotsa kan lashévet?   אז את רוצה כאן לשבת?
     so you want here to-sit?   'So you want to sit *here* ?'

(3) tenase lo legalot   'Try not to tell'   תנסה לא לגלות

The *understood subject* of the infinitive is normally the preceding noun of the main clause (assuming neutral word order):[10]

dov mesarev aHshav lazuz   **'Dov** refuses now to move'   **דב** מסרב עכשיו לזוז

sára biksha mi-**dov** lazuz   'Sara asked of **Dov** to move'   שרה ביקשה מ**דב** לזוז

kashe **li** lehaamin	'(It's) hard for **me** to believe'	קשה לי להאמין
mesarvim aHshav lazuz	'(They're) refusing now to move'	מסרבים עכשיו לזוז

(The last of the group above is an impersonal construction, i.e. there is no subject.)

However, this preceding noun must itself sometimes be inferred from context. Firstly, certain verbs can drop their object, e.g. ציווה *tsiva* 'order', דרש *darash* 'require', אמר *amar* 'tell', הציע *hitsia* 'suggest':

bikáshti lishtok	ביקשתי לשתוק
	'I asked (you, him, them...) to be quiet'

Furthermore, with an infinitive as subject of the main clause, the noun is often vague - but always 'human':

kashe laakov	קשה לעקוב
INF SUBJ	'It's hard (for me, you, one...) to follow'
lamut ze davar tiv'i	למות זה דבר טבעי
INF SUBJ	'To die is natural'

Conversely, the understood subject can be the noun *before* the preceding noun, context permitting:

ani bikáshti me-ha-more latset li-shniya	אני ביקשתי מהמורה לצאת לשניה
I asked of the teacher to-go-out (= if	
{I could/he could} go out) for a second	
sára hivtíHa li **laazor**	שרה הבטיחה לי **לעזור**
Sara promised me **to-help**	'Sara promised me that she'd help'

30.4.3 Function of the infinitive phrase

Infinitive phrases can appear in any 'sentence slot', though less freely than finite clauses (30.2), because of their 'truth status': infinitives express not a fact but rather (a) an intention or ability,[11] (b) the mere notion of some state of affairs, or (c) they accompany verbs/nouns of aspect (starting, continuing, habit...), modality (possibility, certainty)[12] or manner - especially when the subordinate subject has something to refer back to in the main clause.

The various functions of the infinitival phrase are set out below.

Subject of the clause:

   Notion:

meanyen ladáat	מעניין לדעת
	'It's interesting to know'

(Contrast:

meanyen she-yod'im	מעניין שיודעים
	'It's interesting that they know')
lishmóa ze baaya	לשמוע זה בעיה
	'To hear is a problem'

Predicate of the clause:

> *Notion*:
> ha-baaya hi lehagia

הבעיה היא להגיע
'The problem is to get there'

> *Intention*:
> ha-kavana hi lehikana

הכוונה היא להיכנע
'The intention is to surrender'

Object of the clause[13]:

> *Intention*:
> kivíti/tsivíti laatsor

קיוויתי/ציוויתי לעצור
'I hoped/gave an order to stop'

> *Aspect*:
> nahágti laatsor

נהגתי לעצור
'I was wont to stop'

> *Modality*:
> hu asuy laatsor

הוא עשוי לעצור
'He's likely to stop'

> *Manner*:
> hu marbe laatsor

הוא מרבה לעצור
'He stops a lot'

Within adverbials (only non-factive, hence):

> *Intention*:
> yatsátsi {lirot/kdey lirot}

יצאתי {לראות/כדי לראות}
'I went to see'

> '*Without*':
> bli lirot

בלי לראות
'without seeing'

> '*Instead*':
> bimkom lirot

במקום לראות
'instead of seeing'

Apposition (as with objects):

> ha-tikva laatsor   'the hope of stopping'   התקווה לעצור

Relative clause:

> *Intention/possibility*:
> sratim lirot

סרטים לראות
'films to see'

> (Contrast factive or non-factive *finite* relative clauses:
> sratim she-er'e

סרטים שאראה
'films I will/could see')

However, some verbs idiosyncratically do not take an infinitive:

> *yitaHen lehaskim

*יתכן להסכים
('It is possible to agree')

> *hem yitaHnu lahaskim

*הם יתכנו להסכים
('They may agree')

tsafuy ladáat behekdem   צפוי לדעת בהקדם
it-is-anticipated to-know soon

30.5 Gerund clauses

Gerunds (traditionally called 'infinitive construct', like infinitives - see 30.4.1) differ slightly from infinitives in form, and greatly in structure and function. The handful of 'noun-like gerunds' are discussed separately in 30.5.3.[14] Stylistically, gerunds are particularly formal.

30.5.1 Form of the gerund

Gerunds, like infinitives, are a totally non-finite verb form: they have no inherent mark of tense, nor person, number or gender:

im hagía ha-noamim la-duHan...   ...עם הגיע הנואמים לדוכן
with reaching the speakers to-the rostrum   'On the speakers' reaching
                                         the rostrum...'

They may have a suffix, but this is the actual *subject* of the gerund, not an agreement ending:

im hagi'**am**...   עם הגיעם
with reaching-**their**   'on **their** reaching...'

They are mostly identical to infinitives (and akin to the future stem).[15] They are formed regularly, as illustrated in the table below, and with regular meaning. The suffixed gerund is the most common.

Verb pattern	Simple gerunds			Suffixed gerunds	
Pa'al	pkod	'enumeration'	פקוד	pokdo etc.	פוקדו
Nif'al	hipaked	'absence'	היפקד	hipakdo etc.	היפקדו
Hif'il	hafkid	'deposit'	הפקיד	hakfido etc.	הפקידו
Pi'el	paked	'command'	פקד	pakdo etc.	פקדו
Hitpa'el	hitpaked	'enumeration'	התפקד	hitpakdo	התפקדו

Although the gerund's suffix gives it the appearance of a noun, the structure of the whole gerund clause (below) will show it to be a verb.

30.5.2 Structure of the gerund clause

What accompanies the gerund gives it the general appearance of a verb within a clause. Firstly, it requires a subject,[16] thus ruling out:

bi-shmóa et ha-yedia...   ...בשמוע את הידיעה
on hearing OM the news...

but:

bi-shmóa **miryam** et ha-yedia...	...בשמוע **מרים** את הידיעה
SUBJ	
on hearing **Miriam** OM the news...	'On **Miriam** hearing the news...'

Secondly, it can take objects and adverbials in the same manner as the corresponding verb (1), and unlike nouns it cannot take adjectives (2):

(1) be-haariHénu me'od gam itsur ze...   ...בהאריכנו מאד גם עיצור זה

            ADV   ADV OBJ

       on prolonging-our very also   'On very much prolonging this

       consonant this...   consonant too...'

(2) *im aloto ha-pitomi (✓pit'om) la-shilton...   (פתאום) עם עלותו הפתאומי*

                 ADJ   ...לשלטון

      *on rising-his the sudden (✓suddenly) to power...

                                   'On his sudden rise to power...'

Thirdly, the word order is as flexible as in any clause, except that the gerund *must come first* [17] - and so the subject (in ordinary clauses usually, but not inevitably, first) leapfrogs:

(a) If a pronoun, it will have to be suffixed:

leaHar hagi'**o**	לאחר הגיעו
after arrival-**his**	'After **his** arrival'

(b) If a noun, it will simply follow the gerund, though (unlike genitives, e.g. constructs) not always directly:

be-hilakaH mehem **rabam**...	...בהילקח מהם **רבם**
GERUND SUBJ	
on being-taken from-them **their-rabbi**...	'on **their rabbi's** being taken from them'

However, negation is impossible - perhaps because the negator in clauses must always *precede* the verb, and in 'gerund clauses' nothing can:[18]

*be $\begin{matrix} \text{lo} \\ \text{i-} \end{matrix}$ hadgisho et ha-tnaim	לא הדגישו את התנאים... ב* אי-
	('In not stressing the conditions...')

30.5.3 Function of the gerund clause

Gerund clauses are only used *adverbially*, most commonly with time prepositions, especially ב - *be*- 'in, on'. (The only cases of infinitives used adverbially are for 'in order to, without, instead of...'; see 30.4.3). Thus:

be-yoshveHa mul méir nizkar ata she...   ...בישבך מול מאיר נזכר אתה ש

                     'On sitting facing Meir you remember that...'

biglal/lamrot hibaHaro le-tafkid ze...   ...בגלל/למרות היבחרו לתפקיד זה

                    'Because of/despite his being elected to this post...'

and not:

*kiblu et hibaHaro be-simHa	*קיבלו את היבחרו בשמחה
OBJ	('They greeted his being elected joyously')

*hitnagdu le-dabro be-yídish	*התנגדו לדברו ביידיש
DATIVE	
OBJ	('They objected to his speaking in Yiddish')

Further, only noun-governing prepositions (see 19.3.2) take gerunds,[19] ruling out:

*ki/mikevan/af-al-pi hibaHaro la-tafkid,...	...,*כי/מכיוון/אף-על-פי היבחרו לתפקיד
('because/since/although his being elected to the post,...')	

Note that some noun-governing prepositions do not take finite clauses at all: עם היכנסו *im hikanso* 'on his entering' has no finite counterpart, for עם שנכנס *im she-niHnas* means 'although he entered'; similarly for -ב *be-*. Nor are gerunds quite the same as action/state nouns; thus the following two uses of -ב *be-* are special to gerunds:

meHakim, amárti, **be-hitkavni** le-vólvo	מחכים, אמרתי, **בהתכווני** לוולוו
adom she...	...אדום ש
they're waiting, I-said, **in referring-my** to volvo red that...	
'They're waiting, I said, **referring** to a red volvo that...'	

bi-yoto aHad ha-mitstaynim ba-yeHida,	**בהיותו** אחד המצטיינים ביחידה
omdim lishlóaH oto le-Hul	עומדים לשלוח אותו לחו"ל
in being-his one the best in-the unit, they-are-due to-send him abroad	
'**As he is** one of the best in the unit, they are due to send him abroad'	

30.5.4   Noun-like gerunds

shuvo shel natan	שובו של נתן
return-his of Natan	'Natan's return'

A few gerunds are in some ways like nouns, forming a scale of 'noun-ness', notably:

More	(a) bo	'coming'	בוא
	(b) shuv	'returning'	שוב
	(c) tset	'leaving'	צאת
	(d) header	'absence'	היעדר
	(e) healem	'disappearing'	היעלם
	(f) himatse	'presence'	הימצא
Less	(g) heyot	'being'	היות

They all function as subject, object, modifier, as well as adverbial, just like nouns - (g) less readily perhaps:

hudgash she-**headro shel ha-méleH** yigrom beayot	הודגש שהיעדרו של המלך
SUBJ	יגרום בעיות

it-was-stressed that [the] absence of the King will-cause problems

ze yasim kets li-**yotam mi'ut**	זה ישים קץ להיותם מיעוט
OBJ	

it will-put [an] end to their-being [a] minority

uvdat **heyoteH sefaradit**...	עובדת היותך ספרדית...
MODIFIER	

[the] fact-of your-being Sephardi...

The 'double genitive' is used, notably with (a)-(c) but not with (g). (With 'true' gerunds, the 'genitive' is not one at all - cf. the end of 30.5.2.) The 'double genitive' involves an anticipatory possessive suffix plus a further possessive phrase - see 6.8:

headro **shel** ha-méleH	היעדרו **של** המלך
absence-his of the king	'the king's absence'

Gerunds (a) and (b) take adjectives, as in (1) below. The negator -**אי** *i-* is sometimes used, as with action nouns, described in 30.6.2. (2). None of these noun-like gerunds occur without a genitive suffix, nor in the plural (3):

(1)	im bo'o/shuvo ha-pitomi	עם בואו/שובו הפתאומי
	on arrival-his/return-his the sudden	'On his sudden arrival/return'

(2)	i-heyota ba-inyanim	אי-היותה בעניינים
	non-being-her in the matters	'her not being involved'

(3)	*ha-bo/bo'im shelo	*הבוא/בואים שלו
		('his arrival(s)')

In fact, (a), (b) and (e) make up for the lack of a common action noun.

30.6   Action/state noun phrases

bikuro ba-kótel	ביקורו בכותל
visit-his to-the Wall	'his visit to the Wall'

30.6.1   Range of action/state nouns

Action/state nouns have all the hallmarks of nouns, and several of verbs. Like infinitives and gerunds, they express action or state, based on both verbs and adjectives:

yitsur	'production'	ייצור	(yitser	'to produce'	(ייצר
metikut	'sweetness'	מתיקות	(matok	'sweet'	(מתוק

In actual fact there is a complex *range* of adjective-based and verb-based nouns, expressing various lesser degrees of abstraction: an individual act (event) and its result, abstract or concrete. Often one word covers it all:[20]

haka'a	'act of hitting'	הכאה	(maka	'blow' (action or wound)	(מכה
shira	'singing'	שירה	(shir	'song'	(שיר
adifut	'priority'	עדיפות	(adifut	'a priority'	(עדיפות

This chapter deals with *abstract* action/state nouns only.

30.6.2 Form of the action/state noun

Action nouns have five shapes - parallel to five *binyanim* (verb patterns); see 38.2 for details.

Action nouns			Verb		
pkida	'enumeration'	פקידה	pakad	'enumerate'	פקד
hipakdut	'absence'	היפקדות	nifkad	'be absent'	נפקד
hafkada	'deposit'	הפקדה	hifkid	'deposit	הפקיד
pikud	'command'	פיקוד	piked	'command'	פיקד
hitpakdut	'enumeration'	התפקדות	hitpaked	'be enumerated'	התפקד

Like gerunds and infinitives, action nouns do not exist for *huf'al* and *pu'al* - these have only *finite* forms. But where these *binyanim* express a 'state of mind', e.g. -מ מאוכזב ,-מ מופתע *mufta mi-, meuHzav mi-* 'surprised, disappointed at...', *hif'il* or *pi'el* nouns often step in: הפתעה *hafta'a* 'being surprised', אכזבה *aHzava* 'being disappointed'.

State nouns are usually formed from adjectives. Those ending in *-i* י- add *-ut* ות-, as do many of the כבוד ,כביד *CaCiC, CaCuC* pattern (adjusting to *CCiCut* כבידות) and many others. There are many less common derivations; see further, 38.2.

shlili~shliliut	'negative~negativity'	שלילי~שליליות
matun~metinut	'moderate~moderation'	מתון~מתינות
bahir~bhirut	'bright~brightness'	בהיר~בהירות
tipesh~tipshut	'stupid~stupidity'	טיפש~טיפשות

Like any noun, action/state nouns mark gender, number and definiteness, and have no tense:

medubar be-tikun ha-kavéret   מדובר בתיקון הכוורת
'We're talking about the repair (e.g. yesterday, now, soon) of the hive'

30.6.3 Structure of the action/state phrase

Internally, the action/state phrase has all the features of a noun phrase, plus a few of a verb phrase, illustrated by the following sentences:

(1) giluy   ha-ikar ha-yashish etmol   גילוי האיכר הישיש אתמול
     ACTION N 'SUBJ'   'ADV'   'The old peasant's discovery yesterday'
     discovery the peasant the old yesterday

     giluyo hayom   גילויו היום
     discovery-his today   'his discovery today'

(2) ha-giluy he-Hadash shel ha-ikar ha-yashish   גילוי החדש של האיכר הישיש
     ACTION N   'SUBJ'   'the new discovery of the
     the discovery the new of the peasant the old   old peasant'

     ha-giluy he-Hadash shelo   הגילוי החדש שלו
     the discovery the new of-him   'his new discovery'

(3) ha-giluy al-yedey ha-ikar ha-yashish   הגילוי על־ידי האיכר הישיש
                       'SUBJ'   'the discovery by the old peasant'

(4) giluy ha-mamot (al-yedey ha-ikar)   גילוי הממות (על־ידי האיכר)
          'OBJ'   'SUBJ'   'the discovery of the mammoth
     discovery the mammoth (by the peasant)   (by the peasant)'

     giluyo (al-yedey ha-ikar)   גילויו (על־ידי האיכר)
     discovery-its (by the peasant)   'its discovery (by the peasant)'

(5) ha-giluy shel ha-mamot (al-yedey ha-ikar)   הגילוי של הממות (על־ידי האיכר)
                  'OBJ'   'SUBJ'
     the discovery of the mammoth (by the peasant)

     ha-giluy shelo (al-yedey ha-ikar)   הגילוי שלו (על־ידי האיכר)
     the discovery of-it (by the peasant)

(6) giluy   ha-ikar ha-yashish et ha-mamot   גילוי האיכר הישיש את הממות
     ACTION N 'SUBJ'   'OBJ'   הקפוא
     ha-kafu
     discovery the peasant the old   'the old peasant's discovery of
       OM the mammoth the frozen   of the frozen mammoth'

There can be a (notional, underlying) 'subject', 'object' or 'adverbial', as with verbs or adjectives, but with the following stipulations.

The 'subject' always *follows* the action/state noun, and mostly in genitive relation to it, i.e. the order is nucleus + modifier, as is typical of noun phrases (and as with gerunds, see 30.5.2). Anything else too must follow the action/state noun, e.g. the adverbs in example (1) above.[21] This genitive relation can involve the 'construct', as in (1), or the preposition של *shel* 'of', as in (2), or indeed the 'double genitive', as normal for genitives in general (see 6.8):[22]

Double genitive:
giluyo shel ha-ikar   גילויו של האיכר
discovering-his of the peasant   'the peasant's discovery'

With action (but not state[23]) nouns an *agent phrase* using על־ידי *al-yedey* 'by'
is sometimes employed as 'subject', as in (3). Such agent phrases are typically
associated with passive verbs (see 14.7) but with action nouns they are used
even where the action has no passive equivalent:

lamrot ha-hitnagdut ha-aza al-yedey ha-oyev   למרות ההתנגדות העזה על־ידי האויב
'despite the strong resistance by the enemy'

The 'object' too is generally in a genitive relation if the corresponding verb
takes the *direct* object: the 'construct', as in (4), or של *shel*, as in (5), or the
double genitive may be used. Thus ambiguity can arise between 'subject' and
'object' genitives:

ahavat nashim   אהבת נשים
'love for women/love by women'

When the corresponding verb or adjective governs some other preposition, this
preposition must appear, rather than a genitive:

hityaHasut   התייחסות **לתורה**
shayaHut   **la**-tora   שייכות
reference   **to** the Torah
relevance

To express subject and object together, either the subject is genitive (preferably a construct genitive) and the object is introduced by a preposition, even by
את *et*, as in (6),[24] or else the subject is a 'by' phrase and it is the object that
uses a genitive, as in (4).

Subjects are unnecessary; so are objects, even where the corresponding verb/
adjective does require one. Action nouns thus differ markedly from gerunds
(which are verbs, not nouns - see 30.5.1); and the implied subject need not be
'human'. All this is illustrated by:

gidul ze Hashuv   גידול זה חשוב
growth is important (of people, plants etc.)

One-word 'degree' and 'manner' adverbs are generally not used, but rather
the corresponding adjective.[25] (Other adverbials are permitted.)

*ahavato me'od (√ha-raba) le-rótev   *אהבתו מאד (√הרבה) לרוטב
*love-his very (√the great) for gravy   'his great love of gravy'

*ktivato hetev (√ha-tova)   *כתיבתו היטב (√הטובה)
*writing-his well (√the good)   'his good writing'

*leaHar ne'imut kol-kaH (√kazot)   *לאחר נעימות כל־כך (√כזאת)
*after niceness so (√such)   'after such niceness'

Adjectives regularly qualify action/state nouns, as in example (2) above.
Alone among modifiers of action/state nouns, ־אי *i*- 'non-' *precedes* them.
לא *lo* 'not' is impossible:

i-yatsivut	'non-stability'	אי־יציבות
i-mesirat Havilot	'non-delivery of parcels'	אי־מסירת חבילות

30.6.4 Function of the action/state phrase

Action/state nouns occur in the same sentence 'slots' as other nouns (and see also 21.4.2 'echo nouns').

Subject:
ha-shimush be-samim holeH ve-gadel

השימוש בסמים הולך וגדל
'The use of drugs is growing'

Object:
badku et ha-shimush besamim

בדקו את השימוש בסמים
'They checked the use of drugs'

Within adverbial:
im knisato kámu kulam

עם כניסתו קמו כולם
'On his entry they all rose'

Construct:
hashlamat ha-tipul

השלמת הטיפול
'the completion of the treatment'

Finite clauses and infinitives are restricted to particular verbs (see 30.3.4) and have a rather different distribution from action/state nouns and nouns in general:

kidmu et gidul ha-moshav

קידמו את גידול המושב
'They promoted ⟨the⟩ growth ⟨of⟩ the Moshav'

but:

*kidmu she-ha-moshav yigdal
they-promoted that the Moshav grow

*קידמו שהמושב יגדל

amru she-ha-matsav Hamur

אמרו שהמצב חמור
'They said that the situation ⟨is⟩ serious'

but:

*amru et Humrat ha-matsav
they-said the seriousness-of the situation

*אמרו את חומרת המצב

aléHa lishtok
[it is] on-you to-be-quiet

עליך לשתוק
'You should be quiet'

but:

*aleHa ha-shtika
[it is] on-you quietness

*עליך השתיקה

hitkavánti laalot

התכוונתי לעלות
'I meant to immigrate'

but:

hitkavánti la-aliya

התכוונתי לעלייה
'I meant immigration'
(*not*: 'I meant (= intended) to immigrate')

The truth-status of action/state noun phrases

Depending in part on the governing verb and the context, such noun phrases can express (a) 'the fact that...', (b) 'the notion that...' (both senses especially with the construct genitive - examples (1, 2)),[26] though this is not always the right paraphrase - see example (3). They can even express (c) 'the way in which' (4):

(1) azivateH
    retsinuteH   tatrid oto   תטריד אותו   עזיבתך
                                               רצינותך

    'The idea/fact that you're ${}^{\text{leaving}}_{\text{serious}}$ will bother him'

(2) ani mitnaged le- azivateH
                      retsinuteH   אני מתנגד ל עזיבתך
                                                     רצינותך

    'I object to the fact that you're ${}^{\text{leaving}}_{\text{serious}}$'

(3) leaHar knisat napolyon   לאחר כניסת נפוליון
                          'after the entry of Napoleon'

(4) ha-nehiga shelo madhima oti   הנהיגה שלו מדהימה אותי
    the driving of-him appalls me   'The way he drives appalls me'

FURTHER READING
Ben Asher 1972, 1976; Bendavid 1956; Berman 1976, 1978; Blau 1977a; Gordon 1982; Ornan 1979a; Reif 1968; Rubinstein 1971; Sadka 1981.

31. Complement clauses

31.1 Introduction

31.1.1 Types of complement clause

Clauses can be used as 'complements' to a verb or other predicate, i.e. as *subject* or *object*; or as 'specificational' predicates complementing verbs or particles of 'being'. Thus, they parallel nouns.

Subject clause:

she-yikashel barur la-kol	שייכשל ברור לכל
'That he will fail is plain to all'	

Object clause:

heedáfti she-hu yishtok	העדפתי שהוא ישתוק
'I preferred that he keep quiet'	

Predicate clause:

efsharut noséfet hi she-yitpater	אפשרות נוספת היא שיתפטר
'A further possibility is that he'll resign'	

For the general features of subordinate clauses, see chapter 30.

Finite, infinitival and participial clauses

Complement clauses can be finite, infinitival or participial[1]:

Finite:

bikáshti she-teshev	'I asked that you sit down'	ביקשתי שתשב

Infinitival:

bikáshti lashévet	'I asked (i.e. you) to sit down'	ביקשתי לשבת

Participial:

heHélu yorim	'They began shooting'	החלו יורים

A general description, set against the broader context of adverbial, relative and other clauses, is provided in 30.1-4.

Declarative, subjunctive and interrogative clauses

Subject, object and predicate clauses can be declarative, subjunctive or interrogative - depending on the nature of the main verb (or, in the case of predicates, of the main subject). The very difference between declarative and subjunctive in subordinate clauses is not one of form: subjunctives require the same 'future form' as used for the declarative future tense.[2]

Subject clauses:

> *Declarative*:
> **she-tiye kaduraglan** ze lo matrid oti   שתהיה כדורגלן זה לא מטריד אותי
> **'That you'll be a footballer'** doesn't bother me'

> *Subjunctive*:
> adif **she-tiye kaduraglan**   עדיף שתהיה כדורגלן
> 'It's preferable **that you be a footballer'**

> *Interrogative*:
> **ma hu asa** lo barur li   מה הוא עשה לא ברור לי
> **'What he did** ⟨is⟩ not clear to me'

Object clauses:

> *Declarative*:
> amárti **she-ha-géshem yafsik**   אמרתי שהגשם יפסיק
> 'I said **that the rain will stop'**

> *Subjunctive*:
> amárti **she-tafsik**   אמרתי שתפסיק
> 'I said **that you should stop'**

> *Interrogative*:
> amárti laH **ma lehagid**   אמרתי לך מה להגיד
> 'I told you **what to say'**

Predicate clauses:

> *Declarative*:
> ha-kavana hi **she-ze yafsik**   הכוונה היא שזה יפסיק
> 'The meaning is **that it will cease'**

> *Subjunctive*:
> ha-kavana hi **she-ze yafsik**   הכוונה היא שזה יפסיק
> 'The intention is **that it should cease'**

> *Interrogative*:
> ha-baaya hi **káma leshalem**   הבעיה היא כמה לשלם
> 'The problem is **how much to pay'**

31.1.2 Clause vs. noun phrase

Complement clauses (and indeed adverbial and other clauses) differ markedly from noun phrases, both in external function and in internal structure:

External function

Many verbs can take object *clauses* without being able to take object *noun phrases*:

natáti lo **lehikanes**   נתתי לו **להיכנס**
'I allowed him **to enter**'

shiHne'u oto **laalot**   שיכנעו אותו **לעלות**
'They persuaded him **to go up**'

mutav **she-lo yeda**   מוטב **שלא ידע**
'It's better **that he does not know**'

Unlike noun phrases, clauses cannot ordinarily be referred to by the pronoun הוא *hu* 'it' or by suffixed forms of this pronoun as found in עליו *alav* 'about it', אינו *eno* 'is not', עצמו *atsmo* 'itself' and so on. However, זה *ze* 'it' does stand for a clause,[3] and so do on occasion the 'sentence pronouns' כך *kaH* 'it' and זאת *zot* 'it' (see 7.5):[4]

keday she-titlabesh yafe, ki *ze* *hu yaase róshem   כדאי שתתלבש יפה, כי זה *הוא יעשה רושם
'It's good that you should dress well, because **it** will make an impression'

láma amra davar kaze *lo* *eno barur   למה אמרה דבר כזה לא *אינו ברור
'Why she said such a thing **is not** clear'

Complement clauses, including those introduced by זה ש... *ze she...* 'the fact/notion that...', cannot readily coordinate with nouns (except when both are introduced by את *et* or another preposition):

*tsiyánti et Hóser-ha-nisayon shela   *ציינתי את חוסר-הניסיון שלה
ve-**she**-yesh la mishpaHa   ו**שיש** לה משפחה
'I mentioned her lack of experience and **that** she has a family'

However, like any subject or object noun, complement clauses can be responses to question words:[5]

ma at rotsa, she-ekana?   מה את רוצה, שאכנע?
'What do you want, that I surrender?'

Internal differences

ש- *she-* versus זה ש- *ze she-*. Many factive verbs and adjectives, e.g. הצטער *hitsta'er* 'regret', מופתע *mufta* 'surprised', may choose to introduce their object clause and their subject clause with זה ש- *ze she-* as in (1) below; and some must, to contrast with their use as verbs of *assertion*, as in examples (2-5):

(1) ani mufta (mi-ze) she-diyakt   אני מופתע (מזה) שדייקת
     I surprised (at it) that you-were-punctual 'I'm surprised you were punctual'

(2)   ani maariH she...   אני מעריך ש...
                                                    'I imagine that...'

(3)   ani maariH et **ze** she...   אני מעריך את **זה** ש...
                                                    'I admire **the fact** that...'

(4)   ani mevin she...   אני מבין ש...
                                          'I understand that [=I gather that...]'

(5)   ani mevin et **ze** she...   אני מבין את **זה** ש...
                                                    'I understand **the fact** that...'

Extraction

An interrogative or relative pronoun can be brought to the front, even where this involves 'extracting' it out of an object clause,[6] as in (1,2) below. But ש זה *ze she-* (illustrated above) introducing the object clause acts like a noun introducing an apposed clause: the whole structure is a kind of noun phrase, and 'extraction' is rendered impossible - see example (3) below:[7]

(1)   **ma**   metsapim she-eese?   מה מצפים שאעשה?
      PRONOUN   OBJ CLAUSE
      what they-expect that I'll-do?   'What do they expect that I should do?'
          EXTRACTION

(2)   ha-délet she-miména Hashvu she-etse   הדלת שממנה חשבו שאצא
                    PRONOUN   OBJ CLAUSE
      the door that from-it they-thought that I'd-leave
                                    EXTRACTION
                                            'the door they thought I'd leave by'

(3)   *ma metsapim le-ze she-eese?   *מה מצפים לזה שאעשה?
      what they-expect for it that I'll-do?   ('What do they expect I should do?')
          EXTRACTION

31.2   Object clauses

31.2.1   Object of what?

Object clauses generally complement a verb or adjective, or occasionally an idiomatic phrase such as:

mazal yesh la she-lo badku et ha-tik   **מזל יש לה** שלא בדקו את התיק
                    OBJ CLAUSE
luck there-is to-her that they-didn't check OM the bag
                                    '**She's lucky** they didn't check her bag'

ma daateH she-neleH?   **מה דעתך** שנלך?
                OBJ CLAUSE
what's your-view that we-go?   'What do you say that we go?'

Most but not all verbs or adjectives governing a semantic *proposition* use an object clause to express it. Some cannot, and may instead use ...זה ש *ze she...* or ...כך ש *kaH she...* (pronoun + apposed clause), as long as the meaning is 'the fact that...' or 'the notion that...':

> dibárti al **kaH she**-alíti ártsa   דיברתי על **כך שעליתי** ארצה
> I-spoke about **it that** I-went to-Israel   'I spoke about my going to Israel'

> ánu tomHim be-**ze she**-yipaslu   אנו תומכים **בזה שייפסלו**
> we support **it that** they'll-be-disqualified 'We support their disqualification'

Others take neither object clause nor ...זה/כך ש *ze/kaH she-...*, but just an object action noun (30.6); but they do not form a definable semantic group:

> siyámti et ha-shvita (*...lishbot,   סיימתי את השביתה (*...לשבות,
> *...et ze she-shaváteti)   *...את זה ששבתתי)
> I've-ended the strike (*...to strike, *...it that I-was-striking)

Parallel, but somewhat different, is the structure 'action/state noun + apposed clause', described in ch.34:

> ha-tvi'a she-nafsik...   ...התביעה שנפסיק
>   'the demand that we stop...'

paralleling:

> tav'u she-nafsik   תבעו שנפסיק
> V   OBJ CLAUSE   'They demanded that we stop'

No more than *one* object clause is possible. Two object *nouns* are allowed (see 15.3), but there too, only one of them represents an 'abstract proposition'.

Non-subordinate 'object clauses'
   Two types of request use what appears to be an object clause with an unsaid 'I request...' (see further 28.3-4): (1) lofty 2nd person requests using an infinitive: לעבור! *laavor*! 'pass along'!; (2) (casual) use of ש *she* + finite clause: שלא תשכח! *she-lo tishkaH*! 'Don't you forget!'

31.2.2 Object clause vs. adverbial clause: preposition omission
   Contrast:

heHlit al...	'He decided on...'	...החליט על
heHlit she-esha'er	'He decided that I'd stay'	החליט שאשאר
muda le...	'aware of...'	...מודע ל
hu muda she-hem gerim	'He's aware that they're converts'	הוא מודע שהם גרים
ge'e be...	'proud of...'	...גאה ב
ani ge'e lehakir otHa	'I'm proud to know you'	אני גאה להכיר אותך

The differences between object and adverbial are set out in 15.3. Object and adverbial *clauses* are even more dissimilar: most adverbial clauses begin with a preposition, whereas object clauses - such as those highlighted above - do not. They *omit the governed prepositions* so often required by verbs or adjectives (see further 19.5).

A further characteristic of object clauses is that, unlike adverbial clauses, they allow 'extraction' as described at the end of 31.1.2.

31.2.3 Word order

Where there is an object noun and an object clause, the latter comes second (even though the corresponding action noun might otherwise come first), so affording balance and unambiguity:

> asru al yehudim **lilmod ivrit**   אסרו על יהודים **ללמוד עברית**
>
> OBJ CLAUSE   'They have forbidden Jews **to study Hebrew**'

> asru **limud ivrit** al yehudim   אסרו **לימוד עברית** על יהודים
>
> 'They have forbidden **the study of Hebrew** to Jews'

Object clauses can even come after adverbials, less commonly after an adverbial clause:

> maniHim **beHól-zot** ki ha-tmuna mezuyéfet   מניחים **בכל-זאת** כי התמונה מזוייפת
>
> ADV
>
> 'They assume **nonetheless** that the picture ⟨is⟩ forged'

31.2.4 Direct and indirect speech

As object (rarely as subject), Hebrew may use a direct quotation, i.e. something actually said or thought, generally preceded by a colon; this is not a subordinate clause in any formal sense:

> bóaz omer: ani gam nehene lir'ot eH   בועז אומר: אני גם נהנה לראות איך
> mamtinim li-fgisha imi   ממתינים לפגישה עמי
> 'Boaz says: "I also enjoy seeing how they wait for ⟨a⟩ meeting with me"'

When following the quotation (or interposed), the subject + verb inverts (see also 37.11); this is formal usage:

> ani gam nehene lir'ot eH mamtinim   אני גם נהנה לראות איך ממתינים
> li-fgisha imi, **omer bóaz**   לפגישה עמי, **אומר בועז**
> '"I also enjoy seeing how they wait for ⟨a⟩ meeting with me", **says Boaz**'

An indirect quotation too can be made the main clause (*style indirecte libre*) - note the הוא *hu* 'he' rather than אני *ani* 'I' - with the 'main' subject + verb now following it or interposed, as in the following examples:

(1) hu gam nehene lir'ot, omer bóaz, eH   הוא גם נהנה לראות, אומר בועז, איך
     mamtinim li-fgisha imo   ממתינים לפגישה עמו
     he also enjoys seeing, says Boaz, how they-wait for [a] meeting with him
     (Boaz speaking of himself)

(2) rak aHi, kaH yesh lesha'er, yirtse leherashem   רק אחי, כך יש לשער, ירצה להירשם
     only my-brother, so one-must assume, will-want to-register

In (2), the inserted clause begins with כך *kaH*, a pronoun for the 'object clause', and is thus complete in itself: 'One must assume so'.[8] זה *ze* or זאת *zot* can be used instead of כך *kaH*:

> ha-refu'a, **be-zot ani batúaH**, tishtane
> me'od bekarov
> 'Medicine, **of this I'm sure**, will change a lot soon'

> הרפואה, **בזאת אני בטוח**, תשתנה
> מאד בקרוב

31.2.5 'How' object clauses

איך *eH* or כיצד *keytsad* (ordinarily meaning 'how') can act as conjunctions equivalent to -ש *she-* 'that', to introduce object clauses of certain verbs of 'fact', notably of 'seeing' and 'describing' - as if to underline that the description is indeed fact and not an assertion (other conjunctions are given in 30.2):

> hanehagim Hazu peurey pe
> **keytsad** mitmotétet tikrat ha-beton
> 'The drivers watched open-mouthed
> [**how**] the concrete ceiling collapsed'

> הנהגים חזו פעורי פה
> **כיצד** מתמוטטת תקרת הבטון

> sipárti lo eH aHad ha-anashim diber
> aléha be-ahada
> 'I told him how one of the men spoke about her
> sympathetically'

> סיפרתי לו איך אחד האנשים דיבר
> עליה באהדה

31.2.6 Distinguishing object clause from subject clause

Many verbs and adjectives cannot take a subject. Any clause they take is thus an object clause, e.g. ...(אי-)אפשר ל *(i-)efshar le...* 'it is (im) possible to...', ...בא לי ל *ba li le...* 'I fancy...', ...מתחשק לי ל *mitHashek li le...* 'I fancy...', ...טוב לי ל *tov li le...* 'I'm OK (doing that etc...)', ...מוטב ש *mutav she...* 'It's better that...', ...די ל *day le...* 'It's enough to...', ...לא אכפת לי מה *lo iHpat li ma...* 'I don't care what...', ...הוחלט ל *huHlat le...* 'it was decided to...', ...נמסר ש *nimsar she-...* 'it was reported that...'.

By contrast, ...כדאי ל *keday le...* 'it's worthwhile...', ...יתכן ש *yitaHen she...* 'it's possible that...' and many other verbs and adjectives take a *subject* clause. See further 31.4.3.

31.3 'Raising' in object clauses

Three semantic classes of verb or adjective take object clauses of a special kind: the object clause is semantically *not* subordinate to the verb or adjective governing it, and it is the subject that is subordinate.[9] Thus the example

> yosef alul **lenatséaH**
>   ADJ   OBJ CLAUSE
> Yosef is-likely **to-win**

> יוסף עלול **לנצח**

is semantically as follows:

עלול שיוסף ינצח

alul she-yosef yenatséaH
[It is] likely that Yosef will-win

The three semantic types are:

Type 1. Aspectuals, e.g. עמד *amad* 'due to', הלך *halaH* 'going to', התחיל *hitHil* 'begin', המשיך *himshiH* 'continue', הפסיק *hifsik* 'stop', גמר *gamar* 'finish', נהג *nahag* 'be wont to', נטה *nata* 'tend', חזר *Hazar* '...again'.

Type 2. Modals, e.g. צריך *tsariH* 'must',[10] חייב *Hayav* 'must', יכול *yaHol* 'might', עלול *alul* 'liable', עשוי *asuy* 'likely', אמור *amur* 'supposed to...'.

Type 3. Adverbial types, e.g. (see further 21.2.4) מיהר *miher* 'be quick to', הקפיד *hikpid* 'be careful to', שמח *samaH* 'be pleased to', היטיב *hetiv* '...well', ...ו הלך *halaH ve...* '...increasingly', הרבה *hirba* 'do a lot of...', מיעט *mi'et* '...little'.

The object clause is mostly infinitive, its implied subject being *identical* with the actual subject:[11]

mihárti **latset**	'I quickly **left**'	**מיהרתי לצאת**
hitHálti **litsHok**	'I began **to laugh**'	**התחלתי לצחוק**

Aspectuals and modals, and the adverbial-type verbs הרבה *hirba* 'do a lot of...', מיעט *mi'et* '...little' and ...ו הלך *halaH ve...* '...increasingly', are particularly distinct from usual object clause structures; the whole structure is best regarded as having the following abstract syntax:

ABSTRACT   ABSTRACT
[she-ha-shéleg kofe] note⇒ ha-shéleg note likpo   השלג נוטה לקפוא ⇐נטה [שהשלג קופא]
[that the snow freezes] tends ⇒the snow tends to freeze

Here, what seems to be the subject of these verbs or adjectives is not in fact such - their subject is a whole *clause*, i.e. they are the result of 'subject raising'. This explains how these verbs[12] contrive to admit *inanimate* subject nouns:

maHshirey video marbim lehiganev	מכשירי וידיאו מרבים להיגנב
video sets do-a-lot-of being-stolen	
[= get stolen a lot]	
ha-shikun holeH ve-nivne	השיכון הולך ונבנה
the estate goes and is-built	'The estate is gradually being built'

A further peculiarity is that most such clauses cannot be represented by pronouns such as זה *ze* 'it', מה *ma* 'what':[13]

*gamart leeHol? ani lo gamárti et ze   *גמרת לאכול? אני לא גמרתי את זה
('Finished eating? I haven't finished **it**'
[i.e. eating])

Those verbs that take a 'raised' object clause, as in (2) below, do not usually allow 'object deletion' (see 15.3.9). Contrast:

(1)   dror tsariH <u>liyot toran maHar</u>   דרור צריך להיות תורן מחר
        TRUE OBJ CLAUSE   וגם אשתו **צריכה**
ve-gam ishto **tsriHa**
Dror has to-be on-duty tomorrow and his-wife too **has-to**

(2)   ?*dror tsariH <u>liyot adam meanyen</u>   ?*דרור צריך להיות אדם מעניין
        RAISED OBJ CLAUSE   וגם אשתו **צריכה**
ve-gam ishto **tsriHa**
*Dror must be [= is surely] an interesting person and his-wife too must**

Furthermore, none of these verbs etc. can be replaced by an equivalent action noun,[14] thus:

    gamárti lehitgaléaH   'I have finished shaving'   גמרתי להתגלח

but:

    *gmira lehitgaléaH   ('finishing shaving...')   *גמירה להתגלח

also:

    yaHol liyot she-shikru   יכול להיות ששיקרו
                       'It may be that they lied'

but:

    *ha-yeHólet liyot she-shikru   *היכולת להיות ששיקרו...
    the ability to-be that they-lied...   ('The possibility that they lied...')

היה *haya* + participle

By contrast, the verb היה *haya* 'be' - as habitual 'was wont to' or conditional 'would' - is merely an 'auxiliary': it only occurs in past tense, and never takes an infinitive but only a participle, which is best considered its main verb rather than its object clause (see further 13.7):[15]

    az hayíti meashen   אז הייתי מעשן
    then I-used-to smoke

    lu hayíti meashen...   לו הייתי מעשן...
    if I-were-to/I-had smoked...

31.4   Subject clauses

31.4.1   Structure

Subject clauses act as subject for any verb (or predicate) for which 'the act of...', 'the fact that...', 'the notion that...' is an appropriate subject. Thus, unlike object clauses, they are not dependent on the whim of the individual verb. Examples - using (1) finite and (2) infinitive verbs,[16] both (a) declaratively and (b) interrogatively:

(1) a.   tir'e, **she-zo ta'ut** barur li   תראה, **שזו טעות** ברור לי
           'Look, **that this ⟨is a⟩ mistake** ⟨is⟩ plain to me'

she-lo hivHant be-ze kódem	שלא הבחנת בזה קודם
me'od maftia oti	מאד מפתיע אותי

'**That you didn't notice it before** very much surprises me'

b. aval *eH* **higáta la-maskana** lo barur li   אבל *איך הגעת למסקנה* לא ברור לי
'But *how* **you reached the conclusion** isn't clear to me'

(2) a. laazov be-shesh ba-bóker lo yaHbid aléha   לעזוב בשש בבוקר לא יכביד עליה
'To leave at six in the morning won't be hard on her'

lehavin et ze kashe	**להבין את זה** קשה

'**To understand this** ⟨is⟩ difficult'

b. **ma lilbosh** biHlal lo barur li   **מה ללבוש** בכלל לא ברור לי
'**What to wear** ⟨is⟩ not at all clear to me'

These subject clauses, in typical 'subject' position, have a particular 'focus' or emphasis expressed by intonation, pause or the like.

31.4.2 Position
Subject clauses more usually *follow* their predicate:[17]

barur li **she-zo ta'ut**	ברור לי **שזו טעות**

'⟨It's⟩ plain to me **that this ⟨is a⟩ mistake**'

lo yaHbid aléha **laazov be-shesh ba-bóker**	לא יכביד עליה **לעזוב בשש בבוקר**

'⟨It⟩ won't be hard on her **to leave at six in the morning**'

A further constraint is that subject clauses cannot occupy subject position in subordinate clauses (an especial perceptual difficulty):

*ha-shofet amar she-**she-hu Hole** ze	*השופט אמר ש**שהוא חולה** זה
lo relevánti	לא רלוונטי
the judge said that **that he is-ill** is	
not relevant	

*tsariH od Hakirot, ki **madúa ha-sHum**	*צריך עוד חקירות, כי **מדוע הסכום**
hufkad be-Hul térem hitbarer	**הופקד בחו"ל** טרם התברר
it-needs more investigation, as **why the sum**	
was-deposited abroad has-not-yet become-apparent	

31.4.3 The distinction between subject and object clauses
Although subject clauses like those in 31.4.2 look much like object clauses, they are evidently *subject* when complementing the many verbs or adjectives that *require* a subject, e.g. in the (a) example in each of the following pairs:

a. margiz ota **she-haláHta**	מרגיז אותה **שהלכת**
SUBJ CLAUSE	

[it] annoys her **that you-went**

b. ani Hoshev she-**ze** margiz ota אני חושב שזה מרגיז אותה
     REQUIRED 'I think that **it** annoys her'
     SUBJ

a. keday **lemaher** כדאי למהר
    [it's] worthwhile **hurrying**
b. ani Hoshev she-**ze** keday אני חושב שזה כדאי
    I think that **it** [is] worthwhile

a. barur **she-yiyu skandálim** ברור שיהיו סקנדלים
    [it's] obvious **that there'll-be scandals**
b. ani Hoshev she-**ze** barur אני חושב שזה ברור
    I think that **it** [is] obvious

Further examples of words requiring a subject (be it a noun or a clause) are: שיעמם *shiamem* 'bore', מפתיע *maftia* 'surprising', מצחיק *matsHik* 'funny', מעצבן *meatsben* 'annoying', עדיף *adif* 'preferable', חשוב *Hashuv* 'important', מוזר *muzar* 'odd', יפה *yafe* 'lovely', טוב *tov* 'good', מותר *mutar* 'permissible', יתכן *yitaHen* 'is possible'.

By contrast, a ...ש *she*... or ...ל *le*... clause occuring with words such as אפשר *efshar* 'it-is-possible', טוב לי *tov li* 'I'm OK' - not capable of subjects (see 31.2.6) - is evidently an object clause.

31.5 Empty זה *ze* 'it' with subject clauses
Besides the structures in 31.4, Hebrew - particularly casual Hebrew - often uses the 'empty' pronoun זה *ze* 'it' in creating its subject clauses:

ze margiz ota she-**haláHta** זה מרגיז אותה שהלכת
it annoys her that you-went

ze keday laléHet זה כדאי ללכת
it's worthwhile going

ze barur eH latset mi-sham זה ברור איך לצאת משם
it's obvious how to-get-out of there

This זה *ze* fills the normal subject slot, the subject clause preferring to *follow* the predicate.[18]

Curiously, verbs are averse to having both a 'postposed' subject clause and an object noun - although an object pronoun (i.e. a clitic), such as אותי *oti* or לו *lo*, is acceptable. Even adding 'empty' זה *ze* 'it' makes no improvement - see (1) below; instead, Hebrew prefers (2). By contrast, adjectives cause no trouble (3):

(1) ?*(ze) margiz et yedidéha shel yisra'el ?*(זה) מרגיז את ידידיה של ישראל
    she-en tiHnun שאין תיכנון
    ?*(it) annoys OM friends of Israel that
    there-is-no planning

(2) ze she-en tiHnun margiz et yedidéha   זה שאין תיכנון מרגיז את ידידיה
     shel yisra'el   של ישראל
     it that there-is-no planning annoys OM friends
     of Israel

(3) (ze) barur li-ydidéha shel yisra'el   (זה) ברור לידידיה של ישראל
     she-en tiHnun   שאין תיכנון
     (it) clear to friends of Israel that there-is-no planning

Formal Hebrew too can use 'empty' זה *ze* 'it', but only to create an elevated
inversion of order, using the tense particle היה *haya* or negator אין *en*:

     haya ze meanyen ladáat   היה זה מעניין לדעת
     would-be it interesting to-know   'It would be interesting to know'

     en ze barur matay niftar   אין זה ברור מתי נפטר
     not it clear when he-died   'It is not clear when he died'

Three further uses of זה *ze*
This same 'empty ' זה *ze* occasionally serves to anticipate an *object*
clause:

     Hashavt al $\frac{kaH}{ze}$ káma hen yitsHaku?   חשבת על כך כמה הן יצחקו!
                    OBJ CLAUSE   זה
                                                  'Have you thought about [it]
                                                  how much they'll laugh?'

Inseparable ...ש זה *ze she...* can signify 'the fact that...'/'the notion that...',
introducing both subject and object clauses (details in 7.7):

     ze she-zo ta'ut barur li   זה שזו טעות ברור לי
     it that it mistake plain to-me   'That it's a mistake is plain to me'

     mi hitsia et ze she-tilmad be-yeshiva?   מי הציע את זה שתלמד בישיבה!
     who suggested it [= the idea] that you-should-learn in Yeshiva?

It is quite unrelated to 'empty' זה *ze* (though neither can take a resumptive
pronoun) for it does not go with subject infinitives or interrogatives. So examples (1, 3) cannot be rephrased as (2, 4):

(1) ze Hashuv ladáat   זה חשוב לדעת
     it important to-know   'It is important to know'

(2) *ze ladáat Hashuv   *זה לדעת חשוב
     it to-know important

(3) en ze barur keytsad hitsliaH   אין זה ברור כיצד הצליח
     not it clear now he-managed   'It is not clear how he managed'

(4) *ze kaytsad hitsliaH eno barur   *זה כיצד הצליח אינו ברור
     it how he-managed not clear

Following an initial subject clause (even beginning with ...ש זה *ze she...* 'the fact that...'), casual and even formal usage tends to insert זה *ze* to mark the end of the subject clause:[19]

> she-hu meayem aléHa **ze** lo madig oti   שהוא מאיים עליך **זה** לא מדאיג אותי
> 'That he's threatening you **[it]** doesn't worry me'

> étsem **ze** she-HósheH ba-láyla **ze** mar'e laH   עצם **זה** שחושך בלילה **זה** מראה לך
> ad kama ha-olam meshuHlal   עד כמה העולם משוכלל
> 'The very fact that it's dark at night **[it]**
> shows you how sophisticated the world is'

31.6 Predicate clauses

As predicate specifying an (abstract) subject noun (e.g. 'what the problem is is that...'), one may use a clause.[20] The subject is commonly an action/state noun:

> retsoni (hu) <u>leHashev et maslul ha-til</u>   רצוני (הוא) לחשב את מסלול הטיל
>   INF CLAUSE
> 'My intention is to calculate the
> trajectory of the missile'

> sheela noséfet hayta <u>kama ola vila</u>   שאלה נוספת היתה כמה עולה וילה
>   INTERROG CLAUSE
> 'A further question was how much
> a villa costs'

> uvda (hi) <u>she-ha-toHna Hasera máshehu</u>   עובדה (היא) שהתוכנה חסרה משהו
>   FINITE CLAUSE
> 'The fact is that the software
> lacks something'

Sometimes the noun is not directly verb-based, e.g. מגמה *megama* 'trend', תכונה *teHuna* 'characteristic', בעיה *baaya* 'problem'. There is usually a parallel with a noun + apposed clause (34.4):

> tsiyánti retsoni lehinase   ציינתי רצוני להינשא
> 'I mentioned my wish to marry'

A few one-word expressions create what looks like a predicate clause but is in fact not:[21]

> *Apposed clause*:
> hi oHélet? - siman **she-hi beséder**   היא אוכלת? - סימן **שהיא בסדר**
> she's eating? - [sure] sign **that she's OK**

> *Subject clause*:
> mazal **she-ze nidHa**   מזל **שזה נדחה**
> luck [= lucky] **that it's-been-postponed**

> *Object clause*:
> im ata merugaz, **zHutHa laazov**   אם אתה מרוגז, **זכותך לעזוב**
> if you're angry, your-right [= you have
> the right] **to-quit**

FURTHER READING
Berman 1980b; Kopelovich 1982; Landau 1975; Malisdorf 1979; Rubinstein 1971; Schwarzwald 1976b.

32. Adverbial clauses

32.1 External function of adverbial clauses

Adverbials can involve (1) single words, (2) phrases or (3) clauses. This chapter describes clauses (for single words or phrases see chs 20-25).

(1)   leH miyad   'Go immediately'   לך מיד

(2)   leH ad ha-gan   'Go as far as the park'   לך עד הגן

(3)   leH kshe-tirtse   'Go when you want'   לך כשתרצה

Unlike subjects and objects, adverbials are not 'central' to the sentence - see the overall introduction in 21.1. Of the various types of adverbial described there, two can involve a clause, either adjunct or disjunct.

Adjunct clauses[1] elaborate an event or situation: how, where, why, etc. These are 'core adverbials', in terms of not needing a comma or pause and of coming within the scope of 'sentence activities' such as negation, questioning and other forms of focus, by means of רק *rak* 'only', אפילו *afîlu* 'even' and emphasis (cf. ch. 21 'Adjunct adverbials'):[2]

lo himrénu *lifney* **she-hem yaru** éla aHarey ze   לא המראנו **לפני שהם ירו**
                    └──────CLAUSE──────┘   אלא אחרי זה
         └────── ADJUNCT ADVERBIAL ──────┘
                                        'We didn't take off *before* **they fired** but after that'

                    את מדליקה נרות **משום שזאת מסורת** או מסיבה אחרת?

at madlika nerot **mishum she-zot masóret** o mi-siba aHéret
                  └────── CLAUSE ──────┘
         └────── ADJUNCT ADVERBIAL ──────┘
                    'Do you light candles **because it is a tradition** or for another reason?'

Adjuncts can also qualify a noun:

ma daateH al **ha-ráash** kshe-ani martse?   מה דעתך על **הרעש** כשאני מרצה?
              N   ADJUNCT ADVERBIAL
                    'What do you think of **the noise** when I lecture?'

Disjunct clauses generally relate to the very act of uttering or writing the sentence - justifying it, drawing conclusions from it, indicating how it was intended etc.:

הזיהום הולך ופוחת, שכן מבעירים פחות פחם

ha-zihum holeH u-foHet, <u>she-ken mavirim paHot peHam</u>

DISJUNCT CLAUSE

'Pollution is steadily decreasing, for people are burning less coal'

im ledaber be-Henut, ze madhim   אם לדבר בכנות, זה מדהים

DISJUNCT CLAUSE

'To speak candidly, it's appalling'

These are 'fringe adverbials', typically set off by comma or pause, and not subject to negation, questioning etc. (cf. ch. 23 'Disjunct adverbials'). Hence one cannot say:[3]

*hu holeH u-foHet lo she-ken mavirim   *הוא הולך ופוחת לא שכן מבעירים

paHot peHam éla she-ken...   פחות פחם אלא שכן...

it is steadily decreasing not for [people] are-burning less coal but for...

Both adjuncts and disjuncts readily precede or follow the main clause, or even interrupt it (exceptions will be noted) - subject to the 'information lay-out' of the paragraph (see ch. 37):

aHarey she-titHatni, mi yaazor li?   אחרי שתתחתני, מי יעזור לי?

'After you get married, who'll help me?'

mi yaazor li, aHarey she-titHatni?   מי יעזור לי, אחרי שתתחתני?

'Who'll help me after you get married?'

32.2   Internal structure of adverbial clauses

32.2.1   With and without a preposition

Adverbial clauses involve two kinds of internal structure: most commonly, a preposition[4] introduces the adverbial clause:

me'az she- báti   'since I came'   **מאז שבאתי**

PREP   CONJ CLAUSE

bimkom le-barber   'instead of jabbering'   **במקום לברבר**

PREP   INF

        CLAUSE

The adverbial clause itself, like other subordinate clauses, ordinarily begins with a subordinating conjunction ('complementizer'): -ש *she-*, כי *ki*, -ו *ve-*, אשר *asher*. (For conjunctions in general, see 30.2.)

Occasionally there is no preposition and instead the form of the verb is crucial:

ha-yeladim rátsu la-migrash **lesaHek**   הילדים רצו למגרש **לשחק**

INF   'The children ran to the lot to play'

et ha-mapa atáfti, **she-lo yir'u** ota   את המפה עטפתי, **שלא יראו** אותה

FUT

'I wrapped the tablecloth ⟨so⟩ that they shouldn't see it'

Circumstantial clauses (see further 21.6) actually involve any type of present tense predicate, even a mere noun phrase:

Hazárti ha-báyta **loHem menuse**   חזרתי הביתה **לוחם מנוסה**
I-returned home **fighter experienced**   'I returned home an experienced fighter'

Finite and infinitive

Both with and without a preposition, adverbial clauses can involve a finite or an infinitive clause. The infinitive has (a) no subject and (b) an uninflected verb prefixed by *-ל le-*, depending on the type of adverbial and preposition. In a general sense, finite clauses express *either* a fact/assertion *or* an intention/possibility/mere notion etc., whereas infinitives do *not* express the former (for finite vs. infinitive in general, see ch. 30).[5] Examples are:

Finite
yaríti bli she-yadáti   יריתי בלי שידעתי
                                         'I fired without knowing'
                                         (*lit.* without that I-knew)
yaríti ki yadáti   יריתי כי ידעתי
                                         'I fired because I knew'

Infinitive
yaríti bli ladáat   יריתי בלי לדעת
                                         'I fired without knowing'
yatsáti leeHol   יצאתי לאכול
                                         'I went out to eat'

For the *order* of subject-verb-object within adverbial clauses, see 37.13. For *tense* in adverbial clauses, see 13.8-10.

32.2.2 Shortened adverbial clauses

Many adverbial clauses can be represented by a pronoun[6] having several forms, e.g. לאחר מכן *leaHar mi-ken* 'afterwards', משום כך *mishum kaH* 'because of **that**', אם כן *im ken* 'if so', but not, e.g., *בעוד כן* * *be'od ken* ('while **that**'), *היות כן* * *heyot ken* ('as **that**').[7] See 19.3.5 for details of which preposition takes which pronoun.

Conditional clauses introduced by אם *im* 'if' and its synonyms, -במקרה ש *bemikre she-* or -במידה ש *bemida she-* (or -ו *ve-*) can be reduced to לא *lo* 'not' or its opposite, stressed כן *ken*.[8] The conjunction -ש *she-* or -ו *ve-* is retained;

tsaltsel. im lo, az tiHtov   צלצל. אם לא, אז תכתוב
                                         'Phone. If not, write'

bemida ve-lo,...   ...,במידה ולא
                                         'if not,...'

lo nire li she-eda. bemikre   לא נראה לי שאדע. במקרה
she-ken, odia laH   שכן, אודיע לך
'I don't think I'll know. If I do, I'll let you know'

Two kinds of adverbial clause, concessive conditionals and comparative clauses, allow 'flexible' ellipsis, of virtually anything in the clause that happens to be repeated material. Both types serve to juxtapose facts in one way or another, and are thus akin to coordination (see ch. 35), which allows unrestricted ellipsis of repeated material.

Concessive conditionals (see 32.11) expressing 'if not..., then at least...' (quite distinct semantically from ordinary 'if not' and concessive 'although'), and introduced by אם *im* 'if' or אם כי *im ki* 'though', are reduced to a noun or preposition phrase:[9]

im lo ata, az aHotHa tavo, naHon?   ‏**אם לא אתה**, אז אחותך תבוא, נכון?
'**If not you**, then [= at least] your sister will come, no?'

shaálti et rov ha-teHna'im,   שאלתי את רוב הטכנאים
im ki lo et kulam   ‏**אם כי לא את כולם**
'I've asked most of the technicians, **though not all**'

im li lo, az le-mi titen?   ‏**אם לי לא**, אז למי תתן?
'**If not to me**, who will you give to?'

Comparative clauses with כמו ש- *kmo she-*... 'like...', ...יותר מאשר *yoter measher*... 'more than...' contract even more freely, as do comparative-like relative clauses. (See further 32.5.)

32.2.3 Alternatives to an adverbial clause

There are many alternatives to an adverbial clause, using a noun + relative/appositional clause such as:

Time:
me-ha-réga she-hitgala ha-davar, heHélu   מהרגע שהתגלה הדבר, החלו
maariHim oto   מעריכים אותו
     N   REL CLAUSE
'From the moment that the matter got out, they began admiring him'

Purpose:
hitsávnu maHsomim **be-matara** letofso   הצבנו מחסומים **במטרה** לתופסו
'We set up road-blocks **with the aim** of catching him'

Result:
tásti namoH be-**ófen** she-lo hivHínu bi   טסתי נמוך ב**אופן** שלא הבחינו בי
'I flew low in ⟨such⟩ **a way** that they didn't notice me'

In fact there is a spectrum of such expressions, from syntactically regular nouns through semi-exceptional nouns to specialized prepositions. For example, במטרה *be-matara* 'with the aim of' is regular; כדרך *ke-déreH* 'in ⟨the same⟩ way as' involves the noun דרך *déreH* 'way' but an idiomatic preposition -כ *ke-* and a clause which, unlike relative clauses, does not allow a relative pronoun

בה *ba* 'in which'; but על-מנת *al-menat* 'in order that' involves the preposition על *al* plus a word that is not recognizably a noun or anything else, so it is a specialized preposition.

A notable series of 'quasi-relative' adverbial clauses involves regular combinations of 'pro-adverb' + -ש *she-* clause, e.g. מתי ש- *matay she-* 'when(ever)', איפה ש- *éfo she-* 'where(ver)':

matay she-hishta'álti,...	...,מתי שהשתעלתי
when that I-coughed,...	'Whenever/when I coughed,...'

These may be analysed syntactically as 'at the time that, at the place that...' etc. and are discussed with relative clauses in 33.3.3.

32.3-13 ADVERBIAL CLAUSES BY SEMANTIC TYPE
Adverbial clauses are described by semantic type, as this involves many syntactic distinctions.

32.3 Time clauses
Time clauses involve preposition[10]+finite clause, notably: -כש, כאשר, עת (ש-) *kshe-, kaasher, et (she-)* 'when'; כמו ש- *kmo she-*, איך ש- *eH she-* 'just as'; בעוד (ש-), שעה ש- *be'od (she-), sha'a she-* 'while'; כל עוד *kol od* 'as long as'; עד ש-/אשר *ad she-/asher* 'until'; מש-, מאז (ש-) *meaz (she-)*, *mi-she* 'since'; לאחר ש-, אחרי ש- *leaHar she-, aHarey she-* 'after'; לפני ש-, קודם ש-, בטרם *lifney she-, kódem she-, betérem* 'before'.

Several are introduced by an expression on the border between noun and preposition (the clause rarely or never contains a relative pronoun): בזמן ש-, בעת ש-, בשעה ש- *bi-zman she-, be-et she-, be-sha'a she-* 'at a time that (i.e. while)' or מזמן ש- *mi-zman she-* etc. 'from the time that', and כל זמן ש- *kol zman she-* 'as long as'.[11] These are thus quasi-relative clauses.

The conjunction can be omitted where in parentheses in the above list, thus:

meaz (she-)neHtam ha-heskem, doéHet ha-merida	מאז (ש)נחתם ההסכם דועכת המרידה
	'Since the agreement was signed, the revolt has been dying out'

The preposition -כ *ke-* in -כש *kshe-* 'when' can drop in casual usage following another time adverbial:

lifamim, **she**-ani metsayer, ani matHil laHlom	לפעמים, שאני מצייר, אני מתחיל לחלום
sometimes, **that** [= when] I paint, I begin dreaming	

בעוד *be'od* 'while' followed by a subject pronoun can suffix it in formal usage (as if it were -ב *be-* + separate adverb עוד *od* 'still'), compare:

élsint tagia la-shuk **be'odo** be-ibo	אלסינט תגיע לשוק **בעודו** באיבו
	'Elsint will arrive in the market **while it is** in its infancy'

odo be-ibo   עודו באיבו
still-it [= it is still] in its-infancy

A few of these clauses are disjuncts, and so not negated, emphasized etc. (see 32.1), notably those introduced by: איך *eH she* 'just as', (ש) בעוד *be'od* (*she*) 'while', עת (ש) *et* (*she*) 'when', מש *mi-she* 'since', כל עוד / כל זמן ש *kol zman she/kol od* 'as long as'.

Structurally idiomatic, but conveying the same notion as a time adverbial clause, are:

rak báti ve-hitHílu le...   ...רק באתי והתחילו ל
'I'd only arrived and they began to...'

lo yatsáti u-Hvar hitHílu le...   ...לא יצאתי וכבר התחילו ל
'I hadn't left and they'd already begun to...'

32.4 Circumstantial clauses

Circumstantial clauses (formal usage) often convey 'while at the same time...', though not for the purpose of placing an event in time. They involve (1) -כש, כאשר, תוך, ו- *kshe-, kaasher, toH* or *ve-* plus finite clause, 'frozen' into the present tense, or (2) a mere predicate (i.e. a clause minus its subject):

(1) ha-shi'ur yinaten kol yom, kshe-páam   השיעור יינתן כל יום, כשפעם
     ha-martse hu ha-rav ve-páam Hatano   המרצה הוא הרב ופעם חתנו
     'The lesson will be given daily, now the lecturer being (lit. while one time the lecturer is) the Rabbi and now his son-in-law'

(2) zéhu, hi amra, koráat et ha-toHnit   זהו, היא אמרה, קורעת את התוכנית
        V   OM OBJ
     '"That's it", she said, tearing up the programme'

Both types are disjuncts. The latter is described in 21.6 with circumstance phrases; here we describe the former. It always comes at the *end* of the main clause. When introduced by the conjunction -ו *ve-*,[12] it must refer back by the first word in the clause to a person/thing mentioned in the main clause or to something of theirs, as in (1) below; the other conjunctions impose no such restriction (2).

(1) sára raHva al ha-ofanáyim ve-hi   שרה רכבה על האופניים והיא
     maHzika be-yada agasim   מחזיקה בידה אגסים
     Sara rode on the bicycle **and** [= while] she holds [= held] in her-hand pears

(2) ha-roma'im palshu la-heHal,   הרומאים פלשו להיכל,
     kshe-ha-kohanim mamshiHim ba-avoda   **כש**הכוהנים ממשיכים בעבודה
     ke'ilu lo kara klum   כאילו לא קרה כלום
     'The Romans invaded the temple, **while** the priests continued the service as if nothing happened'

32.5 Manner clauses: 'like..., as if...'
Manner clauses are of three types, as described in 32.5.1-3.

32.5.1 'Like, as...'
'Real world' manner equivalence, i.e. 'like, as...', employs the prepositions כמו *kmo* or כשם, כפי *kfi*, *keshem* (rather and very formal, respectively):

ha-malka levusha kmo she-hi hayta	המלכה לבושה כמו שהיא היתה
levusha etmol! CONJ	לבושה אתמול!
the queen is-dressed like [that] she was dressed yesterday	

Such clauses can supply the manner adverbial required by 'manner verbs' such as התנהג *hitnaheg* 'behave':

hu tamid mitnaheg kmo she-ha-aHerim	הוא תמיד מתנהג כמו שהאחרים
mitnahagim	מתנהגים
'He always behaves like the others behave'	

Like manner phrases (see 21.4), they cohere more 'tightly' to the verb than time and cause adverbials etc., and rarely occur ahead of the main verb or with a separating pause or comma.

כמו *kmo* 'like' clauses (not כפי, כשם *kfi*, *keshem*) are commonly reduced to a noun phrase, preposition phrase or adverb[13] - but the conjunction -ש *she-* optionally remains on occasions (casually):

ani lo mityaHes le-Haveray kmo (she-)ishti	אני לא מתייחס לחברי כמו (ש)אשתי
'I don't relate to my friends like my wife does'	
(lit. like that my wife)	

...kmo le-ishti	...כמו לאשתי
...like to my-wife	
'Like I do to my wife'	

...kmo (she-)lifney shana	...כמו (ש)לפני שנה
'... like [that] a year ago'	

כמו *kmo* 'like' requires that immediate personal pronouns be suffixed, as in (1) below, and any prepositions preceding the personal pronoun must remain, as in (2):

(1)	ani lo mityaHes le-Haveray kamoH	אני לא מתייחם לחברי כמוך
	(*kmo at)	(*כמו את)
	I don't relate to my-friends like-you (*like you)	

(2)	...kmo eláyiH	...כמו אליך
	...like to-you	

32.5.2 'As if'

'Hypothetical' manner equivalence, i.e. 'as if', employs (-ש) כאילו
ke'ilu (she-) [14] + finite clause:

hu mitnaheg ke'ilu yesh lo kinim ba-se'ar	הוא מתנהג כאילו יש לו כינים בשיער
PRES	
he's acting as-if he has lice in ⟨his⟩ hair	

eH hirgasht? - hirgáshti ke'ilu	איך הרגשת? - הרגשתי כאילו
(she-)ani nofélet	(ש)אני נופלת
PRES	
how did-you-feel? - I-felt as-if (that) I-am [= was] falling	

Exactly like other כמו *kmo* clauses, כאילו *ke'ilu* clauses have another equivalence meaning, unrelated to manner - see 32.6. But note the present tense, representing the standpoint of the events themselves: unlike כמו *kmo*, or indeed most prepositions, כאילו *ke'ilu* can take not only speaker-oriented ('deictic') but also narrative-oriented ('oblique') tense:

hi rakda ke'ilu hi yeshena/yashna	היא רקדה כאילו היא יְשַנה/יָשנה
OBLIQUE DEICTIC	
she danced as-if she is-asleep/was-asleep	

This is apparently because of kinship to a 'mental act' verb such as 'it seems that' (which takes oblique tense). Another 'mental act' preposition is כדי *kdey* 'in order that'.

32.5.3 'In such a way that...'

Manner + result, i.e. 'in such a way that...', can be expressed by
כך ש... *kaH she*... and באופן ש... *be-ófen she*... (F). אופן *ófen* otherwise means 'manner' and כך *kaH* 'thus'.[15]

ha-ktsinim hitnahagu **be-ófen she**-kulánu	הקצינים התנהגו **באופן ש**כולנו
bikáshnu Hufshat shabat	ביקשנו חופשת שבת
'The officers behaved **in such a way that** we all requested Sabbath leave'	

rov bney-ha-adam mitkonenim **kaH,**	רוב בני-האדם מתכוננים **כך,**
she-si peulatam hu be-reshit ha-yom	**ש**שיא פעולתם הוא בראשית היום
'Most people prepare themselves **in such a way that** their peak of activity is at the start of the day'	

32.6 'General equivalence' clauses

The same prepositions that express *manner* equivalence, כמו, כפי כשם, כאילו *kmo, kfi, keshem, ke'ilu* (and others), can express *general* equivalence, for example:

li yesh ben, kmo she-lo yesh	לי יש בן, כמו שלו יש
to-me is son, like that to-him is	'I have a son, just as he has'

32.6.1 'Real world' equivalence[16]

To express 'real world' general equivalence, Hebrew uses כמו, כפי, כשם *kmo, kfi, keshem*, the same prepositions used in manner equivalence (32.5):

ani mudéget, kfi she-kulHem mudagim   אני מודאגת, כפי שכולכם מודאגים
I'm worried, like that all-of-you worried

        'I'm worried just like all of you are'

But these particular clauses are 'loose' adverbials - they can be preposed, and set off by pause/comma. When preposed, the ensuing main clause often begins with כך *kaH* formally:

keshem she-anashim tsriHim liyot domim,   כשם שאנשים צריכים להיות דומים,
kaH hem tsriHim liyot shonim   **כך** הם צריכים להיות שונים

    'Just as people have to be similar, **so** they have to be different'

However, they do take negative and other focus:

enénu ohavim shigra kfi   איננו אוהבים שיגרה כפי
she-avotéynu ahavúha   שאבותינו אהבוה

    'We don't like routine like our fathers liked it'

Like other such adjunct adverbials (see note 2) this allows structural ambiguity - when the 'like' clause is contracted into a phrase:

enénu ohavim shigra **kmo avotéynu**   איננו אוהבים שיגרה **כמו אבותינו**

    'We don't like routine **like our fathers**'
        (i.e. our fathers like routine)

enénu ohavim shigra, **kmo avotéynu**   איננו אוהבים שיגרה, **כמו אבותינו**

    'We don't like routine, **like our fathers**'
        (i.e. our fathers don't like routine)

Contraction of the כמו *kmo* clause into a suffix is possible, as in manner clauses (32.5) (but without a halfway stage using a ש- *she-*):

ani mitnaged la-kituv kamoH (*kmo she-at)   אני מתנגד לקיטוב כמוך (*כמו שאת)
I oppose polarization like-you (*like that you)

32.6.2 'Hypothetical' equivalence

Another parallel between manner and general equivalence clauses involves כאילו *ke'ilu* 'as if';[17] the hypothetical conditional:

Manner:
ata ro'ed ke'ilu yesh leHa shapáat   אתה רועד כאילו יש לך שפעת

    'You're shivering as if [= in a way that suggests] you have flu'

General:
ata ro'ed. ke'ilu yesh leHa shapáat   אתה רועד, כאילו יש לך שפעת

    'You're shivering, as if [= and the fact suggests] you have flu'

As in 32.6.1, this is a 'loose' adverbial (but not negatable); it generally *follows* the main clause, and with the same tense as כאילו *ke'ilu* in 32.5.[18]

Formal usage also has - כ *ke-*, followed by a present tense verb *phrase* rather than a clause:

hi hibita bi, **ke-**lo mevina et kavanati   היא הביטה בי, **כלא** מבינה את כוונתי
she looked at-me, **as** [= as if] not grasping OM my-meaning

But כאילו *ke'ilu* does not allow such reduction, ruling out:

*hi tsaHaka ke'ilu lo mudéget   *היא צחקה כאילו לא מודאגת
('She laughed as if not worried')

Hypothetical *purpose*, meaning 'as if to', i.e. 'as one would do if one wished to...', involves כאילו ל- *ke'ilu le-* or כמו ל- *kmo le-*:

u-**He'ilu** lehashlim et miHsat ha-kshayim,   ו**כאילו** להשלים את מכסת הקשיים
bnuyot ba-déreH Homot éven   בנויות בדרך חומות אבן
'And **as if** to complete the quota of difficulties,
there are stone walls built on the road'

hu shuv tafaH al rakotav **kmo** lehaanish   הוא שוב טפח על רקותיו **כמו** להעניש
et atsmo al ha-ta'ut she-ta'a   את עצמו על הטעות שטעה
'He again smote his temples **as if** to punish himself
for the error he'd made'

32.6.3 Degree equivalence

For 'the more (she does x), the more (I do y)', i.e. conditional equivalence in degree, Hebrew uses a ככל ש... *ke-Hol she-*... clause (literally 'like all that...') or formally also כל כמה ש... *kol káma she...* ('all as much that...').[19] When *followed* by the main clause (which occasionally precedes), it is often introduced by a correlative adverb: formally כן *ken* or כך *kah*, casually אז *az*. Both clauses commonly have יותר *yoter* 'more'; formal usage need not, particularly in a main clause introduced by כן *ken*, כך *kaH*:

keHol she-ata tiga yoter ba-tinok, (az)   ככל שאתה תגע יותר בתינוק, (אז)
hu yivke yoter   הוא יבכה יותר
like-all that you will-touch more the baby,
(then) he will-cry more
'The more you touch the baby, the more he'll cry'

kol káma she-hu mitmaméa - (kaH)   כל כמה שהוא מתמהמה - (כך)
yaale lo ha-davar beyóker   יעלה לו הדבר ביוקר
all as-much that he delays - (so) will-cost him
the thing dearly
'The more he delays, the more dearly it will cost him'

hakara zo needéret hagshama keHol she-go'im   הכרה זו נעדרת הגשמה ככל שגואים
svivo ha-máyim ha-meayemim lehatbi'o   סביבו המים המאיימים להטביעו
insight this lacks implementation, like-all that rise
around-him the waters that threaten to-drow-him
'The more the waters rising around him threaten to drown him,
the more this insight lacks implementation'

A further possibility is ...{כן/בה במידה} ,...ש במידה *be-mida she* ...,
{*ken/ba be-mida...*} All are disjunct adverbials.

32.6.4 Pseudo-equivalences
Here we are concerned with sentences such as:

hem notsrim, kfi she-amárti	הם נוצרים, כפי שאמרתי
'They are Christians, as I said'	

Section 7.5 describes how numerous verbs or adjectives that ordinarily take a
subject or object clause (ch. 31) can instead take the 'pro-sentence' כך *kaH* :

kaH amárti lo:...	:...כך אמרתי לו
thus I-said to-him...	'I said to him like this...'

kaH kara midey páam	כך קרה מדי פעם
thus happened each time	'It happened like this each time'

It seems that the subject/object above is regarded as denoting some sort of
'equivalence', for כך *kaH* is also used as an adverb of *manner equivalence*:
תלך כך *teleH kaH* 'walk like that'. Moreover, איך *eH* 'how' too can be used in
a non-manner sense to introduce some object clauses:

ra'it/sipárti lo/hizkárti lo **eH**	ראית/סיפרתי לו/הזכרתי לו **איך**
haláHti ba-reHov ve...	הלכתי ברחוב ו...
'You saw/I told him/I mentioned to him **how** I was going down the street and...'	

So it is no surprise that the 'equivalence' prepositions כמו, כפי *kmo, kfi*, etc.
can be extended for use in a similar way[20] - as if subject:

kfi she-ole mi-meHkarénu, dibru ivrit	כפי שעולה ממחקרנו, דיברו עברית
ba-tfutsot [= kmo ma she-ole...]	בתפוצות = כמו מה שעולה...
'As [that] emerges from our research, Hebrew was spoken in the Diaspora [= 'like what emerges...']'	

or as if object:

kulam erim, kmo she-ata yodéa[21]	כולם ערים, כמו שאתה יודע
[= ...kmo ma she-ata yodéa]	=...כמו מה שאתה יודע
'They're all awake, as [that] you know' [= 'like what you know']	

These clauses are disjunctive, and freely preposed.
An 'adjectival' passive participle allows a special contraction (cf.23.3):
כידוע לך מאתמול... *ka-yadúa leHa me-etmol...* 'as known by you from yesterday...', כזכור *ka-zaHur* 'as recalled', כמקווה *ka-mekuve* 'as hoped'.
A different use of the 'equivalence' prepositions is shown by the following:

ha-ets, kfi she-bara oto ha-shem,	העץ, כפי שברא אותו ה',
hu gadol me-ha-adam	הוא גדול מהאדם
'The tree, as God created it, is larger than man'	

Though outwardly similar to the foregoing adverbial clauses, this is actually a predicate or appositional clause - equivalent to an adjective: just as adjectival 'pronouns', איך *eH* 'how' and ככה *káHa* 'thus', outwardly resemble *manner pronouns*, so too there are adjective clauses that resemble manner clauses:[22]

Adjectival clauses

kibálti oto **kmo she-hu**   קיבלתי אותו **כמו שהוא**
I-got it **like that it**   'I got it like it is'

ha-matsav tsariH lehisha'er   המצב צריך להישאר

dome le- $\begin{Bmatrix} \text{kmo} \\ \text{kfi} \\ \text{eH} \end{Bmatrix}$ she-hu   דומה ל $\begin{Bmatrix} \text{כמו} \\ \text{כפי} \\ \text{איך} \end{Bmatrix}$ שהוא

'The situation must remain similar to like [= what] it is'

Pro-adjectives

ze-karúa? kibálti et ze **káHa**   זה קרוע? קיבלתי את זה **ככה**
                                        'It is torn? I got it **like that**'

eH hu, simpáti?   איך הוא, סימפטי?
how he, nice?   'What's he like, nice?'

Appositional clause

mul gzar ha-din omédet ha-hitsamdut   מול גזר-הדין עומדת ההיצמדות
  la-Hayim, kfi she-hi mubáat be-olamam   לחיים, כפי שהיא מובעת בעולמם
  'Opposing the verdict stands the attachment to life,
                      as it is expressed in their world'

32.7 Contrastive clauses: ...בזמן ש *bi-zman she...* 'whereas'

בעוד(ש-) *be'od* (she-), בזמן ש- *bi-zman she-*, (ב)שעה ש- (*be-*)*sha'a she-*, express contrast as well as similarity (see 32.3). These are disjunctive, i.e. they denote 'at the same time it is the case that...'. They are preposable.

shimshon haya shofet, sha'a   שמשון היה שופט, שעה
  she-eliyáhu haya navi   שאליהו היה נביא
                'Samson was a judge, while Elijah was a prophet'

be'od ha-musa mesamen gorem ze, asuya   בעוד המושא מסמן גורם זה, עשויה
  tsurat ha-póal lemamesh gorem aHer   צורת הפועל לממש גורם אחר
        'Whereas the object signifies one element, the form of the verb
                              can realize another element'

32.8 Purpose clauses

Purpose clauses are usually introduced by the prepositions כדי *kdey,* בכדי *biHdey* (mostly official use), בשביל *bishvil* (mostly casual or literary) or על-מנת *al-menat* (F).

As 'purpose' expresses an attitude rather than a fact, it can involve an infinitive - or else a finite clause with future ('modal') tense (just as with a verb of intention, see 30.2):[23]

ma ata tsariH bishvil liHyot? מה אתה צריך בשביל לחיות?

'What do you need so as to live?'

al-menat she-yiHyu be-shalom, tsariH learev על-מנת שיחיו בשלום, צריך לערב

et ha-horim את ההורים

'In order that they should live in peace, one needs to involve the parents'

One occasionally employs the very formal prepositions למען *lemáan* 'so as',
לבל *leval* 'lest'[24] (= in order that not...) or שמא *shéma* 'in case'. These take only
finite clauses, with no conjunction -ש *she-*; the first two require future tense:

vater la, lemáan yiye shlom báyit ותר לה, למען יהיה שלום בית

'Give in to her, so there will be domestic peace'

hu lo hizdaha, leval yifselu oto merosh הוא לא הזדהה, לבל יפסלו אותו מראש

'He didn't identify himself, lest they disqualify him from the outset'

שמא *shéma* does not always strictly denote 'purpose'. It very often denotes
'for fear that...', relating to past, present or future time and taking any tense
appropriate, as in (1,2) below. Sometimes it denotes 'in case', without negative
implications, as in (3):[25]

(1) ani nigash ve-kore et lúaH ha-moda'ot אני ניגש וקורא את לוח המודעות

shéma nitvasef more Hole שמא נתווסף מורה חולה

'I approach and read the notice board, in case a sick teacher
has been added'

(2) kol ha-et haya daruH kmo kfits, shéma כל העת היה דרוך כמו קפיץ, שמא

lo avin éze shinuy hitHolel לא אבין איזה שינוי התחולל

'All the time he was as tense as a spring, lest I would not comprehend
what change had taken place'

(3) yesh lirshom kol Hidush, shéma yavo יש לרשום כל חידוש, שמא יבוא

yomo ve-yishtager ba-shimush יומו וישתגר בשימוש

'One must record every coinage, in case its day comes and it comes
to be regularly used'

Occasionally, *no preposition* is used: a bare infinitive can be used optionally
after motion verbs,[26] occasionally elsewhere, as in (1.2) below. The negative is
שלא ל... *she-lo le...*, not לא ל... *lo le...*, as in (3):

(1) ha-yeladim rátsu la-migrash **lesaHek** הילדים רצו למגרש **לשחק**

'The kids ran to the lot **to play**'

(2) shamáteti yadi me'al ktefo ve-histakálti שמטתי ידי מעל כתפו והסתכלתי

svivi, lir'ot im lo ba míshehu סביבי, לראות אם לא בא מישהו

litpos otánu לתפוס אותנו

'I dropped my hand from his shoulder and looked around,
to see if someone hadn't come to seize us'

(3) hayíti daHuk be-véten ha-sfina, הייתי דחוק בבטן הספינה,

she-lo leorer Hashad **שלא** לעורר חשד

'I was packed in the bowels of the ship, so as not
(*lit.* that not) to arouse suspicion'

A bare finite clause with future tense can be used in very casual or in formal usage (it is disjunctive):

et ha-mapa lo atáfti, she-lo yaHshevu she-zot matana	את המפה לא עטפתי, שלא יחשבו שזאת מתנה

       'I didn't wrap the tablecloth so that (*lit.* that) they won't think
       that it's a gift'

Result clauses also, of various kinds, are introduced by כדי *kdey* etc. (see 32.9). For the infinitive conveying 'illocutionary' purpose, e.g. אם להיות כנה... *im liyot kene...* '['if'] to be honest,...' see 32.11.5.

32.9   Result clauses

       Result clauses are of two main types. They are usually introduced by כך ש... *kaH she...*,[27] which is often preceded by a comma or pause:

meriHim et kol ha-kótej, **kaH** **she**-i-efshar leeHol oto	מריחים את כל הקוטג', **כך** **ש**אי-אפשר לאכול אותו

       '⟨They⟩ smell all the cottage-cheese, **so that** ⟨it's⟩ impossible to eat it'

This is disjunctive, and indeed must *follow* the main clause; even a full stop or new paragraph may intervene, so that this amounts to a *semi*-subordinate clause.

       Following questions or negative clauses ('non-assertives', cf. 29.9), -ש *she*-clauses can convey a *questioned* or *negated* result:[28]

mi ani, im kvar medabrim al ze, **she-lo** uHal lehikanes be-bigdey ténis?	מי אני, אם כבר מדברים על זה, **שלא** אוכל להיכנס בבגדי טניס?

       'Who am I, if we're already talking about this, **that I should not**
       (*lit.* will not) be able to enter in tennis clothes?'

ha'im azávta et ha-histadrut **she-ata** me'iz lehafer haHletotéha	האם עזבת את ההסתדרות **שאתה** **מעיז** להפר החלטותיה?

       'Have you left the Histadrut **that you dare** to flout its decisions?'

kan lo bet-séfer yesodi she-teleH lehitonen lifney ha-more	כאן לא בית-ספר יסודי שתלך להתאונן לפני המורה

       'This is not an elementary school that you should
       (*lit.* will) go to complain to the teacher'

Occasionally, כדי *kdey* and other 'purpose prepositions' (cf. 32.8) express 'result', preceding the main clause and expressing a particularly good or bad result, as in (1,2) below, or using the idiomatic construction אין בו / יש בו כדי ל... *en bo/yesh bo kdey le...* 'it is/is not sufficient to...' (3), or as complement clauses for degree words or quantifiers, as in (4); (see further 20.5):

(1)	kdey laasot et ha-Hayim kalim od yoter, zaHiti hayom be-mifal ha-páyis	כדי לעשות את החיים קלים עוד יותר, זכיתי היום במפעל הפייס

       'To make life even easier, I won the lottery today'

(2) kdey lesabeH od yoter et ha-inyanim,
     toanim ki be-gufénu kayamim káma
     sheonim

כדי לסבך עוד יותר את העניינים,
טוענים כי בגופנו קיימים כמה
שעונים

'To complicate things even more, they claim that in our bodies
there are several clocks'

(3) en bo kdey leshaHnéa otam
     is-not in-it so-as to-convince them

אין בו כדי לשכנע אותם
'It cannot convince them'

(4) ata maspik bari kdey laruts
     you enough healthy so-as to-run

אתה מספיק בריא כדי לרוץ
'You are healthy enough to run'

32.10 Cause clauses: -ש משום *mishum she-* **'because', כי** *ki* **'for'**

Cause clauses are of two chief types. Type (1) are introduced by various prepositions: בגלל *biglal* (non-puristic), משום *nishum*, מפני *mipney*,
(מ)כיוון *(mi)keyvan*, all followed by the conjunction -ש *she-*. Type (2) are introduced by the conjunction כי *ki*, or by the (formal) prepositions היות *heyot*,
מאחר *meaHar*, הואיל *ho'il*, taking the conjunctions -ש/ו- *she-/ve-*.

(1) madúa shaált? - ki ani tsriHa ladáat

מדוע שאלת? - כי אני צריכה לדעת
'Why did you ask? - Because I need to know'

(2) ho'il ve-ha-Hérem husar, en táam lif'ol

הואיל והחרם הוסר, אין טעם לפעול
'Seeing as the boycott has been lifted, there's no reason to act'

All of type (2) are restricted syntactically: (a) כי *ki* only *follows* its main clause,
as if particularly detached from it (like ש כך... *kaH she...* 'so that', 32.9), and
indeed has the facility for expressing the 'reason why one is saying something'
('illocutionary' reason) as well as the actual cause for a situation:

Illocutionary reason:
hu mitHaten, ki hu siper li

הוא מתחתן, כי הוא סיפר לי
'He's getting married, because he told me'

Cause:
hu mitHaten ki yesh la dira

הוא מתחתן כי יש לה דירה
'He's getting married because she has an apartment'

Paradoxically, כי *ki* does undergo negation, questioning and other focusing -
like adjunct clauses:

lo bánu ki Huyávnu lavo éla ki ánu
yedidéha shel yisrael

לא באנו כי חוייבנו לבוא אלא כי אנו
ידידיה של ישראל
'We didn't come because we were made to but [we came] because
we are friends of Israel'

(b) היות, מאחר, הואיל *heyot, meaHar, ho'il* do not readily undergo negation
etc. Yet they precede or follow the main clause, i.e. they are ordinary
disjuncts.

Occasionally 'cause' is expressed by the conjunction -ש *she-*, usually in the
fixed combinations שכן *she-ken*, שהרי *she-harey*, שאמנם *she-omnam*, conveying illocutionary reason:

metsamtsemim et ha-shimush be-antibiótika,   מצמצמים את השימוש באנטיביוטיקה,
she-ken ha-davar pogéa be-tahaliHim   שכן הדבר פוגע בתהליכים
tiviyim   טבעיים

'They are reducing the use of antibiotics, for it affects
natural processes'

It is doubly restricted: it *follows* the main clause, and is beyond the scope of
negation etc. In fact, it can begin a new sentence or paragraph - it is thus only
semi-subordinate.[29]

32.11   Conditional clauses: 'if..., unless..., whoever comes...'

32.11.1   Overview

Hebrew conditionals can express: (a) *conditions*, in the narrow sense
of 'in the event that...':

im titatesh, ani ets'ak   אם תתעטש, אני אצעק
'If you sneeze, I'll scream'

(b) *Concessive ('one-way') conditionals*, i.e. 'even if' or 'even though' or 'whoever,
whatever, etc.' - and the quite distinct use of אם לא *im lo* 'if not' to mean 'or
even':

asig medályat késef **im ki** lo   אשיג מדליית כסף **אם כי** לא
medályat zahav   מדליית זהב
'I'll get a silver medal **even though** not a gold medal'

al kol ma she-lo tishal, ha-maHshev   על כל מה שלא תשאל, המחשב
yaazor leHa   יעזור לך
'Whatever you ask about, the computer will help you'

asig medályat késef **im lo** medályat zahav   אשיג מדליית כסף **אם לא** מדליית זהב
'I'll get a silver medal **if not** a gold medal'

(c) *Suppositions*, i.e. 'if it is the case that...' or 'given that...':

im hitpatHu ha-mata'im,   אם התפתחו המטעים,
ze hodot la-mazkal   זה הודות למזכ"ל
'If the plantations have developed, it is thanks to the General Secretary'

(d) *Illocutionary conditionals*, i.e. 'if..., then I may say...':

im ata sho'el ma daati, harey lo barur li   אם אתה שואל מה דעתי, הרי לא ברור לי
mi ha-anashim ha-éle   לי מי האנשים האלה
'If you're asking my opinion, [then] I'm not clear who
these people are'

32.11.2   Conditions: 'if' words

The 'if' word is usually אם *im* 'if'; also באם *be-im* (officialese),
במקרה ש-/ו- *be-mikre she-/ve-*, במידה ו-/ש- *be-mida ve-*. These introduce both
real-world and (casually) hypothetical conditionals.[30]

Certain other 'if' words introduce *only* hypothetical conditionals: לו, אילו
lu, ilu (F) and negative לולא, אלולא, אלמלא *lule, ilule, ilmale* (literary):

lu hikárti oto, hayíti matsia shiduH   לו הכרתי אותו, הייתי מציע שידוך
if I-knew him, I'd suggest [a] match

im lo hayítem ashirim, hayítem meusharim   אם לא הייתם עשירים, הייתם מאושרים
if not you-were [= if you weren't] rich, you'd-be happy

ilule heyítem ashirim, ki-az   אלולא הייתם עשירים, כי-אז
heyítem meusharim   הייתם מאושרים
if-not you-were [= were you not] rich,
then you'd-be happy

Other 'if' words are: ובלבד ש- *uvilvad she-* 'provided that', as in (1) below;
אלא-אם-כן *éla-im-ken* 'unless' (= 'if not'),[31] which follows a positive or a negative main clause (2), as does the related אלא אם *éla im* 'except if' (which is
less common, see 35.16); and כל עוד, כל זמן ש- *kol od, kol zman she-* 'as long
as' (see 32.3):

(1) ánu muHanim lekableH aHshav, u-vilvad   אנו מוכנים לקבלך עכשיו, ובלבד
she-teshalmi lemafréa   שתשלמי למפרע
'We are prepared to accept you now, provided that you pay
retroactively'

(2) ani avo lishmóa éla-im-ken yered géshem   אני אבוא לשמוע אלא-אם-כן ירד גשם
'I'll come to hear unless it rains'

32.11.3 Other aspects of conditions

The *tense* of 'real-world' conditions reflects 'natural' time (as
explained in 13.12) - see example (1) below. Hypotheticals generally take compound past tense in both conditional and main clauses (it is the *whole* sentence
that is 'real' or 'unreal'). With לו *lu* and the other specialized hypothetical 'if'
words, the simple past is sufficient (as if they were intrinsically hypothetical);
but their 'main clause' always uses compound past - see (2):

(1) *'Real world'*
im ra'it, láma lo amart?   אם ראית, למה לא אמרת?
     SIMPLE   SIMPLE
     PAST   PAST   'If you saw, why didn't you say?'

(2) *Hypothetical*
lu ra'it, hayit mizdazáat   לו ראית, היית מזדעזעת
     SIMPLE COMPOUND
     PAST   PAST   'If you saw, you'd be shocked'

Word order is flexible: conditions precede, follow or even interrupt the 'main
clause', except that 'unless' clauses (see 32.11.2) always follow.

Conditions with no 'if' word ('asyndetics')

In certain registers (notably official instructions, adverts, and very
casual speech), real-world conditions need no 'if' word. Subject noun (if any)
and verb are inverted (except, usually, for subject *pronouns*):

siyem talmid et ha-targil ha-rishon,　　　　　　　סיים תלמיד את התרגיל הראשון,
　　yaHol hu laavor la-sheni　　　　　　　　　　יכול הוא לעבור לשני
has-finished pupil OM the drill the first,
　　can he pass to-the next
　　　　　　'If a pupil has finished the first drill, he can pass to the next'

kanita video - hirváHta　　　　　　　　　　קנית וידיאו - הרווחת
you've-bought video - you've-gained
　　　　　　'If you've bought a video, you've gained'

ha-rofe yekabel tashlum. lo yimtsa Hen　　　הרופא יקבל תשלום. לא ימצא
　　be-enéHa - tuhal lehaHlif rofe　　　　　חן בעיניך - תוכל להחליף רופא
　　midey shana　　　　　　　　　　　　　מדי שנה
the doctor will-receive payment. not will appeal
　　to-you, you-can change doctor every year.
　　　　　　'...If he does not appeal to you, you can change doctor once a year'

make ba-yad shelo - nofel kir shalem　　　מכה ביד שלו - נופל קיר שלם
strikes with his hand - falls wall whole
　　　　　　'If he strikes with his hand, a whole wall falls'

A particular type is the 'whether...or...' clause (actually a concessive, see details in 32.11.4), found without the 'whether' and 'or' words.

Reduction

The main clause is sometimes reduced, notably as מה אם... *ma im...* 'what if...':

ma im eradem?　　　　　　　　　　　מה אם ארדם
What if I-will-fall-asleep　　　　　　　'What if I fall asleep?'

The 'if clause' can be reduced when 'concessive' - see details in 32.2.2. 'If' clauses are sometimes even *omitted*, leaving a hypothetical main clause; the 'if' clause is implicit from the context:

al tegale - ze haya hores ota　　　　　אל תגלה - זה היה הורס אותה
　　MAIN CLAUSE
　　　　　　'Don't let on - it would destroy her'

What appears at first sight to be 'if-clause omission' is not a hypothetical at all but the use of 'hypothetical-type' tense to express mood of 'modest assertion' (see further 13.12.3):

hayíti rotsa lehagid leHa máshehu　　　הייתי רוצה להגיד לך משהו
　　　　　　'I'd like to tell you something'

Conditions without a condition clause

Alternatives to a condition clause often exist, such as:

(kol) mi she-lokéaH antibiótika mear'er et   את (כל) מי שלוקח אנטיביוטיקה מערער את
Hasinuto (= im mishehu lokéaH...)   חסינותו (= אם מישהו לוקח...)
    'Whoever takes antibiotics impairs his immunity'
    (= 'If someones takes...')

and, in officialese, the 'topic dislocation' construction ("ייחוד", see ch. 37):

martse ha-oved be-Hatsi misra, rosh ha-Hug   מרצה העובד בחצי משרה, ראש החוג
   yaHlit im leHadesh et minuyo   יחליט אם לחדש את מינויו
   [a] lecturer who works in [a] half-time post,
   [the] Head of Department shall-decide
   whether to-renew OM his-appointment

32.11.4   Concessive conditionals

The basic construction for concessive conditionals uses אפילו אם
afilu im, גם אם *gam im,* or אפילו *afilu* (F) 'even if':

afilu yiye hesder, tiye metiHut   אפילו יהיה הסדר, תהיה מתיחות
even will-be settlement,   'Even if there's a settlement, there'll
   will-be tension   be tension'

Of the concessive conditionals illustrated in 32.11.1, the 'whatever, whoever...' constructions ('open' conditionals) require elaboration. There are three
types, all disjunctive and able to precede or follow the main clause:
(a)   *Open 'whether' clauses,* with single or double אם *im* or בין אם *beyn*
im:[32]

   im ze milyoner o (**im** ze) asir,   **אם** זה מליונר או (**אם זה**) אסיר,
   ha-ikar she-yiye adam meratek   העיקר שיהיה אדם מרתק
     'Whether it's a millionaire or (**whether**
     it's) a prisoner, the main thing is
     that it should be an exciting person'

(b)   *Open 'wh-word' relative clauses:* Formal usage employs a 'tautologous' relative clause referring to future or generic time. The verb must be future tense
and initial (a 'modal', see 13.9), and the clause begins with ordinary מי ש- *mi*
she- 'who that', איפה ש- *éfo she-* 'where that' and other 'interrogative expressions' or more formal אשר *asher,* ככל *keHol* (for 'extent' or 'degree') and
באשר *baasher* 'wherever':

   yavo mi she-yavo, ha-mesiba tiye   יבוא מי שיבוא, המסיבה תהיה
     meshaamémet   משעממת
   will-come who that will-come, the party   'Whoever comes, the party
     will-be boring   will be boring'

   yikre asher yikre, ánu nisha'er beyáHad   יקרה אשר יקרה, אנו נישאר ביחד
   will-happen that will-happen, we   'Whatever happens, we
     will-stay together   will stay together'

   yaavod keHol she-yaavod, lo yuHal laHsoH   יעבוד ככל שיעבוד, לא יוכל לחסוך
   let-him-work as-much that he'll-work,   'However much he works, he will
     not will-be-able to-save   not be able to save'

yehudi she-Hay be-yisra'el hu yisreeli,   יהודי שחי בישראל הוא ישראלי,
  ve-yikba mekom moshavo aHar-kaH   ויקבע מקום מושבו אחר־כך
  baasher yikba   באשר יקבע
a Jew who lives in Israel is Israeli, and he-will-fix place-of
  his-residence afterwards in-that he-will-fix
[= wherever he afterwards fixes his place of residence]

yiyu ha-matanot yekarot keHol she-yiyu,...   יהיו המתנות יקרות ככל שיהיו,...
will-be the presents expensive   'However expensive the presents,...'
  as-much that will-be,...

All usage allows a negative relative clause with no nucleus (see further 33.4):

mi she-lo yavo, ha-mesiba tiye   מי שלא יבוא, המסיבה תהיה
  meshaamémet   משעממת
who that not will-come [= whoever comes]
  the party will-be boring

ra'iti she-eH she-lo dibárti   ראיתי שאיך שלא דיברתי
  u-ma she-lo amárti,   ומה שלא אמרתי,
  ze galash la-tHum ha-ishi   זה גלש לתחום האישי
I-saw that how that not I-spoke [= however I spoke]
  and what that not I-said [= whatever I said],
  it spilled into the personal sphere

32.11.5   Other conditionals

Supposition conditionals always require the 'if' word אם *im*.

Illocutionary conditionals generally precede the main clause. They usually involve אם *im* 'if' + infinitive with no subject, if the subject would be referring to the *speaker*, i.e. 'if I may...', as in examples (1, 2). Otherwise, אם *im* + finite clause is used, as in (3):

(1) im lishpot lefi ha-matsav be-Heyfa,   אם לשפוט לפי המצב בחיפה,
      yesh mashber   יש משבר
    if to-judge [= if I may judge] by the situation
    in Haifa, there-is [a] crisis

(2) im liyot dúgri,...   אם להיות דוגרי,...
    if to-be frank,...   'To be frank,...'

(3) **im tirtsu**, étsem bikuro shel shamir mehave   אם **תרצו**, עצם ביקורו של שמיר מהווה
      haba'at i-emun   הבעת אי־אמון
           '**If you wish**, the very visit by Shamir constitutes
           an expression of no confidence'

אלא־אם־כן *éla-im-ken* 'unless' too can be used with illocutionary force:

דבר לא נזכר על כך בכתבה, אלא־אם־כן לדוקטור יש מקורות משלו
davar lo nizkar al kaH ba-katava, éla-im-ken la-dóktor yesh mekorot mishelo
'Nothing was said about it in the report, unless
  the doctor has sources of his own'

32.11.6   Miscellaneous details

Wherever a conditional (of any type) *precedes* the main clause, the latter may optionally open with a 'link adverb' - notably (-הרי (ש *harey (she-)*, literary כי־אז *ki-az* or או־אז *o-az*, or casual אז *az*, i.e. 'if...then...'.

אם *im* 'if' clauses are adjuncts, thus allowing focus adverbs: ...רק אם *rak im*... 'only if', ...גם אם *gam im*... 'even if'. But the hypotheticals אילו, לו *ilu, lu* etc. are disjuncts, hence ruling out ...הייתי בא {רק/גם} לו **hayiti ba {rak/gam} lu*... ('I would come {only/even} if...'); so too are the other three types of conditional. Moreover, אם *im*, unlike the other adverbial conjunctions כי *ki* and שמא *shéma*, allows coordination: ...אם...ואם *im...ve-im...* 'if...and if...'.

32.12   Concessive clauses: ...למרות ש *lamrot she*... 'although'

Here we describe *factive* concessives, i.e. 'although, even though' clauses (for 'even if' see 32.11.4). There are two levels of concessive,[33] both of which can precede or follow the main clause:

(a) *Denoting 'even though'*, i.e. 'despite the fact that...' (going against an expected 'cause and effect'), involves למרות ש- *lamrot she-* and more formally אף־על־פי ש-, על אף ש- , אף ש-/כי *af-al-pi she-, al af she-, af she-/ki*. Occasionally אפילו ש- *afílu she-* is also used:[34]

כולם מחרימים את המשחקים,
למרות שטייוואן אינה משתתפת

    kulam maHrimim et ha-misHakim,
    lamrot she-taywan eyna mishtatéfet
                'They're all boycotting the games, despite the
                fact that Taiwan is not participating'

ואפילו שיש תועלת רבה בשימוש,
שוקלת הממשלה לאוסרו

    ve-afilu she-yesh to'élet raba ba-shimush,
    shokélet ha-memshala le-osro
                'And even though there is great benefit in its use,
                the government is considering banning it'

(b) *Illocutionary* 'although I should point out that...' (no cause and effect implied) involves אם כי *im ki* (an idiomatic word with no synchronic relation to כי *ki* 'that'):

כולם מחרימים את המשחקים,
אם כי טייוואן אינה משתתפת

    kulam maHrimim et ha-misHakim,
    im ki taywan eyna mishtatéfet
                'They're all boycotting the games, though (i.e. be it noted that)
                Taiwan is not participating'

כולם מחרימים את המשחקים, אם כי
אינני סבור שזהו מהלך נבון

    kulam maHrimim et ha-misHakim, im ki
    eynéni savur she-zéhu mahalaH navon
                'They're all boycotting the games, though I do not believe that
                this is a judicious step'

32.13 Quasi-negative clauses

Two types of adverbial clause imply a negative: ...במקום *bimkom...*
'instead of...' and ...בלי/מבלי *bli* (or *mibli*)... 'without...':[35]

taazor li bimkom	lehar'ish she-eese hakol levad	להרעיש שאעשה הכל לבד	תעזור לי במקום

help me instead

to-make-noise
[= of making noise]
that I'll do [= of me
doing] everything myself

ozrim li bli	leyalel she-avakesh kol páam	לילל שאבקש כל פעם	עוזרים לי בלי

they help me without

to-wail [= wailing]
that I'll ask [= me asking] each time

They have much in common. Both involve an infinitive (usually harking back
to the main clause subject) or finite clause. The finite verb is usually future.
Since these are 'negatives' expressing a non-fact, this is like a 'modal' use of
future tense; see 13.4. On other 'negative' aspects of these clauses, see 29.12.

FURTHER READING
Azar 1977: ch. 5; Ben-Asher 1972: ch. 7; Glinert 1974, 1982a, b, 1988a, b; Sadka 1981.

33. Relative clauses

33.1 Introduction

Relative clauses 'relate' to nouns, adding information about them in the same way as adjectives and other modifiers, and always tied to the noun phrase. Relative clauses *follow* other modifiers:

tsémaH yafe mi-sin she-higía ata	צמח יפה מסין **שהגיע עתה**
N REL CLAUSE	
plant lovely from China **that arrived just**	'A lovely plant from China **that just arrived**'

Not all clauses qualifying a noun are relative clauses: certain nouns, particularly 'action nouns', can take 'apposed clauses' (see ch.34), generally introduced by the same conjunction (-שׁ *she-*) that introduces relative clauses. Ambiguity sometimes arises:

ha-uvda she-shaHaHt	העובדה ששכחת
the fact that you-forgot	'the fact which you forgot' (REL)
	or 'the fact of your forgetting' (APPOSED)

The 'antecedent' is the noun (or noun phrase) being described by the relative clause; it (and its modifiers) is generally *directly* followed by the clause, and thus cannot be shifted around without the latter.[1]

The relative clause must contain something referring back to the antecedent. Thus in example (1) the 'relative pronoun' הוא *hu* 'he' refers back to מועמד *muamad* 'candidate'. But one sometimes leaves the 'relative pronoun' unsaid, as in (2). Whatever the case, it is useful to regard all relative clauses as having an 'abstract relative noun' referring back to the antecedent.

(1)	muamad she-hu mashak	מועמד שהוא מש"ק
	candidate that he NCO	'a candidate who is an NCO'

(2)	muamad she-ra'íti [ha-muamad]	מועמד שראיתי [המועמד]
	ANTECEDENT UNSAID REL N	
	REL CLAUSE	
	a candidate that I-saw [the candidate]	'a candidate that I saw'

The 'relative noun' varies its pronoun form according to whether it is subject, adverbial etc. of the relative clause, as will be shown, for it is none other than the 'definite pronoun' described in 7.3. See further, 33.3.4.

33.2 General distinctions

Two major semantic distinctions must be drawn, (1) between 'factive' and 'modal' relative clauses and (2) between 'restrictive' and 'non-restrictive' relative clauses. These distinctions have grammatical consequences.

Factive relatives assert or imply a fact; modal relatives convey a possibility or a desire. Contrast:

natáti la máshehu **she-hi tishte**	נתתי לה משהו **שהיא תשתה**
FACTIVE REL	
I-gave her something **that she will-drink**	'I gave her something **that she'll drink**'

natáti la máshehu **lishtot**	נתתי לה משהו **לשתות**
MODAL REL	
I-gave her something **to-drink**	'I gave her something **to drink**'
[= for her to drink, i.e. that she might/should drink]	

Factive relatives are discussed in 33.3-7, and modals in 33.8.

Most of the constructions handled in this chapter allow a fundamental ambiguity, between restrictive and non-restrictive relative clauses. For example, the relative clause in bold type below is ambiguous on paper:

ha-menuyim, **asher mi-siba kólshehi iHru**	המנויים, **אשר מסיבה כלשהי איחרו**
ba-tashlum, shilmu knas	**בתשלום**, שילמו קנס
'The subscribers **who for some reason were late in paying** paid a fine'	

Even with the commas, in the Hebrew it is unclear whether *some* subscribers paid a penalty ('restrictive' relative) or *all* ('non-restrictive' relative). In speech, by contrast, Hebrew like English distinguishes by intonation: the antecedent to a non-restrictive relative has a 'tone-group' to itself (typically הַמֶּנוּיִים *hā-mēnūyīm*) and is thus separated from its relative clause; with restrictive relatives there is no such separation.

Admittedly, in writing too a relative clause with commas is usually non-restrictive, but long clauses tend to have commas even when restrictive - witness this quotation:

séder ze meshane et ha-yáHas ha-pnimi,	סדר זה משנה את היחס הפנימי,
she-beyn ha-tseruf ha-shemani	**שבין הצירוף השימני**
le-kinuy ha-guf	**לכינוי הגוף**
RESTRICTIVE REL	
'This order alters the internal relationship **that there is between the noun phrase and the personal pronoun**'	

Sometimes, indeed, a comma appears after and not before a relative clause:

ha-yisreelim ve-toshavey Hul she-yitgoreru	הישראלים ותושבי חו"ל שיתגוררו
kan, yehanu mi-eHut Hayim meyuHédet	כאן, ייהנו מאיכות חיים מיוחדת
'The Israelis and foreign residents who will be living here will enjoy a special quality of life'	

A grammatical distinction of stylistic, but of no semantic, consequence is the choice between - ש‎ *she-*, אשר‎ *asher*, - ה‎ *ha-*, - ו‎ *ve-* and 'zero' as the conjunction introducing the factive relative clause.[2] - ש‎ *she-* (prefixed to the next word) is the commonest, and can figure in any syntactic context and register. אשר‎ *asher* is particularly formal and slightly constrained syntactically. Such relatives are discussed in 33.3-4. - ה‎ *ha-*, fairly formal, is syntactically limited as to the function of the relative noun in its clause, as are formal - ו‎ *ve-* and 'zero' (i.e. absence of a conjunction). These are discussed in 33.5 and 33.7.

33.3-4 RELATIVE CLAUSES WITH - ש‎ *SHE-* OR אשר‎ *ASHER*

33.3 The relative noun or pronoun

33.3.1 The relative pronoun as subject
Compare the following:

(1) éfo ha-bragim **she-yatsu?**   איפה הברגים שיצאו?‎
    where the screws **that came-out?**   'Where are the screws **that came out?**'

(2) éfo ha-bragim **she-ába hotsi?**   איפה הברגים שאבא הוציא?‎
    where the screws **that Dad**   'Where are the screws **that Dad**
    took-out?   **took out?**'

In (1) above, the subject of the relative clause is unexpressed: it is the 'relative noun' הברגים‎ *ha-bragim* 'the screws'. Hebrew does not usually express the relative noun when subject of the relative clause; thus, the following is ungrammatical whether restrictive (i.e. there is more than one wall) or non-restrictive:[3]

*ha-Homa, she-**hi** hushlema eshtakad,   *החומה, שהיא הושלמה אשתקד,‎
    nehersa kalil   נהרסה כליל‎
the wall, that it [= which] was-completed last-year,
    was-demolished totally

Now it might seen that (1) below indeed contains a 'relative pronoun as subject', but in fact הן‎ *hen* is merely the copula 'be', which is generally obligatory where the predicate is a noun (cf.16.3) as it is below. Replace the second noun by an adjective, and the need for הן‎ *hen* disappears, as in example (2):

(1) éfo ha-kfafot she-**hen** matana?   איפה הכפפות שהן מתנה?‎
        REL CLAUSE
                    'Where are the gloves that **are** a present?'

(2) studéntim she-(hem) adáyin lo pturim   סטודנטים ש(הם) עדיין לא פטורים‎
        ADJ
    students that (are) still not exempt   'students that are still not exempt'

33.3.2 The relative pronoun as direct object
'Relative nouns as direct object' are sometimes left unsaid and sometimes expressed as pronouns, depending on register and sentence structure. For-

mal Hebrew, especially officialese, may use a pronoun, particularly by placing it at the head of relative clauses (even when there is no conjunction, see 33.7):

> lehalan ha-subsídyot she-**otan** kitsátsnu   להלן הסובסידיות **שאותן** קיצצנו
> below [are] the subsidies that **them** we-axed [= that we axed]

Other registers tend to omit the relative pronoun:

> ma im ha-subsídyot **she-kitsátsnu?**   מה עם הסובסידיות **שקיצצנו?**
> what about the subsidies that   'What about the subsidies **that**
> we-axed?   **we axed**?'

For all registers, relative clauses that are long or complex tend to require the pronoun. Formally, as usual, the pronoun can be a suffix (cf.7.3.2):

> ze lo aHad ha-sfarim she-shaálta im   זה לא אחד הספרים ששאלת אם
>   tsariH likro **otam?**   צריך לקרוא **אותם?**
> this not one the books that you-asked if necessary to-read **them**?

> ha'im en ze aHad ha-sfarim she-shaálta   האם אין זה אחד הספרים ששאלת
>   im yesh lekor'am?   אם יש לקוראם?
>   SUFF
> is not this one the books that
>   you-asked if necessary to-read-**them**?
>   'Isn't this one of the books that you asked whether one should read?'

For omission of the whole verb phrase in relative clauses, see 33.3.4.

33.3.3   Relative pronouns in other slots

As indirect object

Such relative pronouns, unlike those acting as direct object, are rarely omitted - this would leave a 'dangling' preposition, as in example (3) below, almost unheard of in Hebrew (see 19.6). Nor can the preposition usually be omitted (4).[4] Thus:

> (1) éle ha-rishumim she-histakalt **bahem**   אלה הרישומים שהסתכלת **בהם**
>   IND OBJ
>   these [are] the prints that you-looked **at-them**

> (2) ze ha-nose she-eemod **alav**   זה הנושא שאעמוד **עליו**
>   IND OBJ
>   this [is] the subject that I'll-go-into **it**

> (3) *éle ha-rishumim she-histakalt be   *אלה הרישומים שהסתכלת ב
>   these the prints that you-looked at

> (4) *éle ha-rishumim she-histakalt   *אלה הרישומים שהסתכלת
>   these the prints that you-looked

As adverbial

Relative pronouns as adverbials mostly look and act exactly like those that are indirect objects:

éle ha-tsrifim she-garnu **bahem**	אלה הצריפים שגרנו **בהם**
ADVERBIAL	
these the huts that we-lived **in-them**	'These are the huts that we lived in'

ha-bóker she-**bo** higáti	הבוקר **שבו** הגעתי
ADVERBIAL	
the morning that **on-it** I-arrived	'the morning **on which** I arrived'

and not:

*ha-tsrifim she-gárnu (be)	*הצריפים שגרנו (ב)
the huts that we-lived (in)	

But the 'pro-adverbs', שם *sham* 'there', אז *az* 'then', כך *kaH* 'thus', can act as relative pronouns (the last two just in non-restrictive relatives):

éfo ha-Hof she-saHínu sham?	איפה החוף ששחינו שם?
where the beach that we-swam there?	'Where is the beach where we swam?'

neHake ad she'ot ha-érev,	נחכה עד שעות הערב,
she-rak **az** hem neorim li-f'ula	שרק **אז** הם ניעורים לפעולה
'Let us wait till evening time, the only time **when** (lit. that only **then**) they stir into action'	

However, the whole adverb (containing the relative noun) is often omitted in restrictive relatives[5] where the antecedent is an 'imprecise' word such as מקום *makom* 'place', שעה *sha'a*, זמן *zman*, תקופה *tkufa* 'time', רגע *réga* 'moment', פעם *páam* 'time', דרך *déreH* 'manner', מצב *matsav* 'situation', סיבה *siba* 'reason', or even a more specific 'time word' such as יום *yom* 'day', ערב *érev* 'evening':[6]

bánu le-makom she-(bo) lo hayu máyim	באנו למקום ש(בו) לא היו מים
we-came to place that (in-it) not were water	'We came to a place in which there was no water'

ze kara ba-yamim she-(bahem) saHíti	זה קרה בימים ש(בהם) שחיתי
it happened on-the days that (on-them) I-swam	'It happened on the days I swam'

ha-siba she-lo kámti ze she-Halíti	הסיבה שלא קמתי זה שחליתי
the reason that not I-got-up is that I-was-ill	'The reason I didn't get up is that I was ill'

Indeed, such omission is a 'must' when one of these 'imprecise' antecedents involves כל *kol* 'every', or when they form part of the 'set phrases' ברגע ש- *be-réga she-* 'the moment when...', במקרה ש- *be-mikre she-* 'in the event that...', במידה ש- *be-mida she-*... 'to the extent that, in the event that...', בזמן ש- *bi-zman she-* 'when'. See also 33.3.4.

kol páam she-nisíti, haya tafus   כל פעם שניסיתי, היה תפוס
'Every time that I tried, it was busy'

33.3.4 General features of the relative pronoun
Relative pronouns and pro-adverbs invariably have the same form as
any 'definite pronouns' (see 7.3). However, זה *ze* (ordinarily 'it') and its inflections are used as relative pronouns in casual usage only, and then only where
the antecedent is not appropriately referred to as הוא *hu* etc. anyway. Thus
example (2) is ungrammatical:

(1) hofánu be-tésha, she-zot ha-sha'a   הופענו בתשע, שזאת השעה
she-ovdim magi'im ba-Hóref   שעובדים מגיעים בחורף
'We arrived at nine, which (*lit.* that it) is the hour that workers arrive in winter'

(2) *ha-tsiyur she-nagat be-**ze** yakar me'od   *הציור שנגעת בזה יקר מאד
the picture that you-touched **it** [is] very expensive

Embedded in a larger structure
The relative pronoun may be deeply embedded in the subject, object
etc. of the relative clause - Hebrew imposes no special limit. But if embedded,
it cannot be omitted.[7] It is particularly common as an embedded 'genitive':

ha-pluga she-ha-mefaked **shela** ze mótke   הפלוגה שהמפקד **שלה** זה מוטקה
    REL
    PRONOUN
the batallion that the commander   'the batallion **whose** commander
of-it is Motke   is Motke'

ha-sofer she-hizkíru et shmo   הסופר שהזכירו את שמו
the author that they-mentioned OM   'the author **whose** name they
name-**his**   mentioned'

Larger-scale 'relative' omission
Even larger-scale omission from the relative clause is possible where
the whole verb phrase is identical with that of the main clause. Then either the
identical preposition + relative noun (1,2) or the whole verb phrase embracing
it (3,4) can drop, often leaving just a noun as indicator of a relative clause:

(1) tishtamesh be-ma she-ani mishtamesh   תשתמש במה שאני משתמש
make-use of what that I make-use   'Use what I'm using'

(2) haláHti étsel mi she-haláHti   הלכתי אצל מי שהלכתי
I-went to who that I-went   'I went to whomever I went to'

(3) yeshnam ke'éle she-efshar lehishtamesh   ישנם כאלה שאפשר להשתמש
bahem ve-yesh ka'éle **she-i-efshar**   בהם ויש כאלה **שאי-אפשר**
'There are some that it's possible to use and there are some **that it's impos-sible** ⟨to use⟩'

(4)   éle she-nisharu, lamrot she-hem margishim   אלה שנשארו, למרות שהם מרגישים
      ma she-anáHnu, Hayavim lehamshiH   מה שאנחנו, חייבים להמשיך
      'Those that remain, although they feel **what we** (feel), have to continue'

33.3.5   Positioning the verb and relative pronoun

The positioning of relative pronouns is frequently a matter of register. As subject or object (direct or indirect), the relative pronoun can, in any register, occupy the normal position of a subject or object, thus:

dirot she-keday lir'ot otan   דירות שכדאי לראות אותן
apartments that worth to-see them   'apartments that it is worth seeing'

ha-báyit she-hityaHásta elav   הבית שהתייחסת אליו
the house that you-referred to-it   'the house that you referred to'

But more formally, the relative pronoun can be preposed:

ha-báyit she-**elav** hityaHásta   הבית שאליו התייחסת
the house that **to-it** you referred   'the house to which you referred'

As adverbial, the relative pronoun may or may not be preposed, in any register:[8]

éfo ha-ratsif she-Hikínu **bo**?   איפה הרציף שחיכינו **בו**?
where the platform that we-waited   'Where's the platform that we were
on-it   waiting on?'

éfo ha-ratsif **she-bo** Hikínu?   איפה הרציף **שבו** חיכינו?
            'Where's the platform on which (*lit.* that on-it) we were waiting?'

But following the 'imprecise antecedents' mentioned in 33.3.3 (as adverbials), any relative pronoun is preposed if it is not omitted:

ba-yom she-**bo** higánu le-Hevron...   ביום ש**בו** הגענו לחברון...
on-the day that **on-it** we-reached   'On the day that we reached
Hebron...   Hebron...'

ha-déreH she-**ba** bits'u zot...   הדרך ש**בה** ביצעו זאת...
the way that **in-it** they-did it...   'The way that they did it...'

The verb in relative clauses commonly precedes its subject in formal usage:[9]

ba-Hagiga she-**arHa** mifléget shas...   בחגיגה ש**ערכה** מפלגת ש"ס...
at-the function that **held** party shas...   'At the function that the Shas party
                                                held...'

33.4   The relative antecedent

The antecedent can be a pronoun rather than a noun. Four types of pronoun are involved: (a) 'personal' pronouns, (b) other 'definite' pronouns, e.g. זה *ze* 'this, it', (c) 'interrogative' words used non-interrogatively, e.g. מה *ma* 'what', איפה *éfo* 'where', (d) 'indefinite' pronouns, e.g. מישהו *míshehu* 'someone' (see ch.7).

33.4.1 Personal pronouns

All personal pronouns, both free-standing and suffixed, can take a relative clause; such cases conform to the rules for relative pronouns set out above:[10]

זה מוזר שאני, שאין לי נסיון, קיבלתי מענק

ze muzar she-**ani**   she-en li nisayon, kibálti maanak

        ANTECEDENT   REL PRONOUN

        'It's strange that I, who don't have (*lit.* that there-isn't to-me) experience, received a grant'

למה רוצים אותך, שלא יודע ולא ראית כלום?

láma rotsim otHa, she-lo yodéa ve-lo ra'íta klum?

        SUFF   v(m.s.)   v(2nd m.s.)

        'Why do they want you, who don't know and didn't see anything?'

Other definite pronouns

Distinguish example (1) below, where the antecedent הוא *hu* 'he' is already identified, from examples (2) and (3), in which the antecedent is identified through the 'restrictive' relative clause (see 33.2). This affects the choice of antecedent. With the non-restrictive clause, one uses the personal pronouns: הוא *hu* and its inflections for people, זה *ze* for things. With the restrictive relative, one uses זה *ze* (and its inflections) or מי *mi* for people, and זה *ze*[11] or מה *ma* for things - in any register[12] (and see 33.4.3):

(1) **hu**, she-himtsi et ha-shita, lo kibel pruta   **הוא,** שהמציא את השיטה, לא קיבל פרוטה

    'He, who (*lit.* that) invented the system, did not receive a penny'

(2) ze. she-Hikíti lo hitakev   זה

    mi   מי

        'The person that I was waiting for was delayed'

(3) ze she-kaníti hu meshumash   זה

    ma   מה

        'The one I bought is second-hand'

        'What

33.4.2 Pseudo-interrogative pronouns

The words מי, מה, מתי, איפה *mi, ma, matay, éfo* etc., described in 26.3 as 'interrogatives' meaning 'who, what, when, where' etc., are in essence just pronouns, pro-adverbs etc. with a meaning ranging over 'someone, whoever, who', 'something, whatever, what' etc. respectively. When antecedent to a relative clause, such a word is non-interrogative, sometimes with a choice of 'specific' or 'non-specific' function:

kaH rak **ma**   she-mat'im   קח רק **מה** שמתאים

        SPECIFIC

take only **what** that fits   'Only take **what** fits'

kaH **ma** she-mat'im	קח **מה** שמתאים
NON-SPECIFIC	
take **what** that fits	'Take **what/whatever** fits'

Which words have both functions depends on the register, as described below.

Specifics

Only מי *mi* 'who' and מה *ma* 'what' are 'specific' in all registers:[13]

mi she-tsiltsel lo masar shem	**מי** שצילצל לא מסר שם
	'**The person** that rang didn't leave a name'

nifgáshnu im **mi** she-haya ha-menahel	נפגשנו עם **מי** שהיה המנהל
	'We met with **the person** who was the director'

ma she-ani ken osek bo ze hége	**מה** שאני כן עוסק בו זה הגה
EMPH	
what that I work on-it is phonology	'**What** I do work on is phonology'

By contrast, איפה *éfo* 'where', לאן *le'an* 'where (to)' are 'specific' in casual speech only:[14]

yashávti **éfo** she-hayínu etmol	ישבתי **איפה** שהיינו אתמול
I-sat **where** that we-were yesterday	'I sat **where** we were yesterday'

lo nasánu **le'an** she-nasánu be-pésaH	לא נסענו **לאן** שנסענו בפסח
not we-went **to-where** that we-went	
on Passover	'We didn't go **where** we went on Passover'

מתי *matay* 'when', איך *eH* 'how', כמה *káma* 'how much' are 'specific' in substandard usage only:[15]

matay she-higáta, yatsáti	**מתי** שהגעת, יצאתי
when that you-arrived, I-left	'**When** you arrived, I left'

shárti **eH** she-sháru ba-séret	שרתי **איך** ששרו בסרט
I-sang **how** that they-sang in-the film	'I sang **the way** they did in the film'

natáti **káma** she-haya li	נתתי **כמה** שהיה לי
I-gave **how-much** that was to-me	'I gave **as much** as I had'

Non-specifics

Any of the 'interrogative words' can be a 'non-specific' - in any register:

nalun **heHan** she-nirtse	נלון **היכן** שנרצה
we-shall-stay **where** that we-shall-wish	'We shall stay over **wherever** we wish'

agid (kol) **ma** she-mitHashek li	אגיד (כל) **מה** שמתחשק לי
I'll-say (all) **what** that appeals to-me	'I'll say **whatever** I fancy'

ruts be-**éze** mehirut she-ata rotse	רוץ **באיזה** מהירות שאתה רוצה
run at **which** speed that you want	'Run at **whatever** speed you want'

Two apparent uses of the non-specific relative are as concessive conditionals, as in (1,2) below, and as 'clefts', as in (3):

(1) le-(kol) mi she-ani lo efne,   לו(כל) מי שאני לא אפנה,
     ani mekabel ota tshuva   אני מקבל אותה תשובה
     to (any) who that I not will-apply,
     I receive same answer

                              'Whoever I apply to, I receive the same answer'

(2) be-Hol shHuna she-lo taavod, yikaH   בכל שכונה שלא תעבוד, יקח
     sha'a lehagia habáyta   שעה להגיע הביתה
     in any area that not you'll-work, it-will-take
     hour to-get home

                     'Whatever area you work in, it will take an hour to get home'

(3) le-mi she-ani pone ze la-mazkal atsmo   למי שאני פונה זה למזכ"ל עצמו
     to who that I am-applying is to-the
     Sec. General himself

                        'It's the Sec. General himself that I'm applying to'

In types (1,2) the non-specific relative is a noun phrase set off at the front of the sentence ('disjunctive'), functioning adverbially as a kind of 'concessive conditional' expressing 'whoever..., whatever...' etc. (see 32.11.4 for concessive adverbials). The antecedent is either a so-called 'interrogative pronoun' (or איזה *éze* 'which' + noun) or כל *kol* 'any' + noun, i.e. something semantically 'open'. The relative clause is usually negative in casual usage, except for purists.[16] No relative pronoun (i.e. אליו *elav* 'to him', בה *ba* 'in-it' for examples (1,2)) is ordinarily inserted. Curiously, in cases where one would expect the verb in the relative clause to be followed by a preposition + object or adverbial, it is in front of the antecedent that one finds the preposition - one might say that a simple clause has been shuffled and a meaningless -ש *she-* and לא *lo* inserted:[17]

         taavod be-Hol shHuna ⇒   תעבוד בכל שכונה⇐
         be-Hol shHuna she-lo taavod   בכל שכונה שלא תעבוד
         you'll-work in any area ⇒ in any area that not you'll-work

Further examples are:

       ידענו מלוח השנה - **למי** שהיה לוח - את התאריך של החג
       yadánu mi-lúaH ha-shana - **le-mi** she-haya lúaH - et ha-taariH shel ha-Hag
       we-knew from the calendar - **to who** that was calendar - OM the date
         of the festival

                 'We knew from the calendar - **whoever** had a calendar - the date
                                   of the festival'

         eH she-lo dibárti, ze histabeH   איך שלא דיברתי, זה הסתבך
         how that not I-spoke, it got-complicated

                         'However I spoke, it got complicated'

Type (3), the cleft, is a way of specifying a noun (see 37.9 for specificationals in general). Here the antecedent is always a so-called 'interrogative pronoun'. It is introduced by whatever preposition (if any) appears following זה *ze* 'is' with the noun (the 'focused noun'). Thus, a simple sentence can be expanded into a 'cleft' to focus on a particular noun:[18]

ába ge'e ba-ktav shelaH⇒   ⇐אבא גאה בכתב שלך

be-ma she-ába ge'e ze ba-ktav shelaH   במה שאבא גאה זה בכתב שלך

Father proud of writing your ⇒

of what that Father proud is of writing your

'Father is proud of your writing' ⇒ 'What Father is proud of

is your writing'

General features of 'interrogative' antecedents

Following מה *ma* and מי *mi* 'what/who(ever)', the relative pronoun conforms to the pattern of 33.3:[19]

kol mi she-dati mekabel yáyin   כל מי שדתי מקבל יין

any who that religious gets wine   'Whoever is religious gets wine'

kol mi she-ani pogesh maskim   כל מי שאני פוגש מסכים

any who that I meet agrees   'Whoever I meet agrees'

ma she-dibárnu alav ze ha-namel   מה שדיברנו עליו זה הנמל

what that we-spoke about-it is the harbour   'What we spoke about was the

harbour'

However, following איפה *éfo* and לאן *le'an* (most typically) the relative pro-adverb *must* be omitted:

yashávti éfo she-yashávta (*sham)   (ישבתי איפה שישבת (*שם

I-sat where that you-sat (*there)   'I sat where you sat'

taamod éfo she-ha-monit (*sham)   (תעמוד איפה שהמונית (*שם

stand where that the taxi (*there)   'Stand where the taxi is'

Furthermore, the relative pronoun cannot be preposed.[20] This holds for definite and indefinite pronoun antecedents too, thus:

*ma she-**alav** dibárnu...   *מה **שעליו** דיברנו

what that **about-it** we-spoke...   ('What we spoke about...')

33.4.3 Indefinite pronouns

The rules spelt out for nouns and their relative pronouns (33.3) hold also for indefinite pronouns, both positive: מישהו *míshehu* 'someone', משהו *máshehu* 'something'; and negative: אף אחד *af eHad* 'no one', כלום/שום דבר *klum/shum davar* 'nothing'. Casually, there is also כאלה ש- *ka'éle she-* 'such people as...' or (with a noun understood) 'some of the type that...'.

míshehu **she-hu** stam rabat lo mat'im   מישהו **שהוא** סתם רב"ט לא מתאים

someone **that is** just corporal not   'Someone **who's** just a corporal isn't

suitable   suitable'

hevéti máshehu **she-bo** tipálti kódem   הבאתי משהו **שבו** טיפלתי קודם
I've-brought something **that with-it**   'I've brought something I
I-dealt before   dealt with before'

33.4.4   A clause as antecedent

Given that Hebrew 'nominalized' phrases, such as פטירתו
הפתאומית *ptirato ha-pitomit* 'his sudden death', can take a relative clause, as
in :

ptirato ha-pitomit, she-ziaz'a et kulánu   פטירתו הפתאומית, שזיעזעה את כולנו
                                                              'his sudden death, which shocked us all'

and given that nominalizations are equivalent to a whole clause, Hebrew clauses
might have been expected to take a relative clause themselves; but that would
be ungrammatical:[21]

*hu niftar pitom, she-ziaza et kulánu   *הוא נפטר פתאום, שזיעזע את כולנו
<u>CLAUSE</u>   ('He died suddenly, which shocked us all')

Instead, formal Hebrew adds a noun like דבר *davar* 'thing' or מה *ma* 'what' in
apposition, while casual Hebrew might insert וזה *ve-ze* 'and this' or suchlike:

	ma she-				מה ש-
hu niftar,	davar she-	ziaza otam		הוא נפטר, דבר ש זיעזע אותם	
	ve-ze				וזה

'He died, {which/and this} shocked them'

33.5   Relative clauses with -ה *ha-* and -ו *ve-*

The conjunction -ה *ha* 'that' is sometimes an alternative to -ש *she-*
in fairly formal usage:

manpikim neyarot ha-nos'im ribit   מנפיקים ניירות הנושאים ריבית
they-issue bonds that bear interest

But -ה *ha-*, unlike אשר *asher* and -ש *she-*, is found only where the relative
noun is understood as *subject* of its clause. Thus contrast:

	ha-				ה
salim	she-	nisgarim		סלים ש נסגרים	
	asher			אשר	

'baskets that close'

	*ha-				*ה
salim	✓she-	kal lisgor otam		סלים ש✓ קל לסגור אותם	
	✓asher	REL N		אשר✓	
		OBJ			

baskets that easy to-close them   'baskets that it is easy to close'

Furthermore, -ה *ha* must directly introduce a *present* tense verb or adjective.
Even the negators לא *lo*, אין *en-* and the present tense 'be' הם , הוא *hu, hem*,
etc. are not considered verbs for this purpose.[22] Thus:

nashim ha-tsamot	נשים הצמות
	'women that fast'

nashim {*ha-/√she-} tsámu	נשים {*ה-/ש-} צמו
	'women that fasted'

nashim ha-ge'ot be-HaH	נשים הגאות בכך
	'women that are proud of it'

nashim {*ha-/√she-} enan tsamot	נשים {*ה-/ש-} אינן צמות
women {that} not fast	'women that do not fast'

This conjunction -ה *ha* is distinct from the definite article -ה *ha-* (though semantically related). The conjunction occurs even after indefinite antedecents - as in the foregoing examples - and introduces verbs, not nouns: צמות *tsamot* 'fast' is not found as a noun.

-ו *ve-* is used as an alternative conjunction, in formal Hebrew, for restrictive clauses with a relative adverbial pronoun placed first. No verb is possible:[23]

hikiru la alman zaken **ve-lo** arba banot   הכירו לה אלמן זקן **ולו** ארבע בנות
'They introduced her to an old widower who had (lit. **and to him)**
four daughters'

33.6   Omitting the antecedent

Intermediate between -ה *ha-* as conjunction and as definite article is -ה *ha* as relative conjunction with no overt antecedent:

ha-bodek et ha-ktiv yimtsa tauyot	**הבודק** את הכתיב ימצא טעויות
that checks OM the spelling	'**Anyone that checks** the spelling
will-find errors	will find errors'

tiskor et **ha-naase** ba-shétaH	תסקור את **הנעשה** בשטח
survey OM **that is-being-done**	'Survey **what is being done**
on-the ground	on the ground'

These examples amount to ...כל מי שבודק *kol mi she-bodek...* 'whoever checks...', ...מה שנעשה... ...*ma she-naase...* '...what is being done...'.[24] The choice between 'human' and 'non-human' interpretation depends on context; but the former is 'non-specific' (33.4.2) and cannot mean, e.g., 'The person who is checking the spelling will find errors' - and it can be plural as well as singular.

The construction requires a verb, not an adjective. Thus, כל מי שעייף *kol mi she-ayef me-ha-tiyul...* cannot be transmuted to *העייף* מהטיול *kol mi she-ayef me-ha-tiyul...* cannot be transmuted to *העייף* ...מהטיול *ha-ayef me-ha-tiyul...* ('anyone tired from the trip...'). Nonetheless, numerous adjectives have a separate existence as fully fledged nouns, e.g. זקנים *zkenim* 'old people', עניים *aniyim* 'poor people' (but not, e.g., יפים* *yafim* for 'good-looking people').[25]

In formal Hebrew, -ש *she-* and אשר *asher* too can occur without antecedents, in a few constructions, notably after the 'direct object marker' את *et*, or when complementing יש / היה *yesh/haya* 'there is/was' or present tense 'be' (cf. ch. 16), or as {אשר/ -ש} כל *kol* {*she-/asher*} 'anything that..., all that...':[26]

tsiyánti et she-/asher bikasht	ציינתי את ^ש אשר ביקשת
I-mentioned OM that you-requested	'I mentioned what you requested'

yesh {she-/asher} mesarvim	יש {ש/אשר} מסרבים
exist that refuse	'There are those that refuse'

hu {she-/asher} hilshin	הוא {ש/אשר} הלשין
he that informed	'He is the person that informed'

33.7 Relative clauses with no conjunction

In formal Hebrew one may forgo the relative conjunction (restrictive or non-restrictive), and instead *prepose* the relative pronoun to mark off the relative clause:[27]

kol eHad yilmad miktso'ot yesod, **otam** yikba ha-váad REL PRONOUN	כל אחד ילמד מקצועות יסוד, **אותם** יקבע הוועד
	'Everyone will study core subjects, which (lit. **them**) the board will determine'

maHar yaazov et bon, **sham** shaha ke-Hódesh	מחר יעזוב את בון, **שם** שהה כחודש
	'Tomorrow he leaves Bonn, where (lit. **there**) he has stayed about a month'

A *subject* relative pronoun will not serve the same purpose, as no departure from normal word order will have come about:

lamádnu dikduk, she-/*hu mehave miktsóa bifney atsmo	למדנו דקדוק, ^ש*הוא מהווה מקצוע בפני עצמו
	'We studied grammar, which (lit. that/*it) constitutes a subject by itself'

33.8 Modal relative clauses

The foregoing relative clauses were 'factive': they asserted or implied a fact. Now we describe 'modal' relatives, which convey a possibility or desire. There is a rich array of modal relatives, in two basic groups: (1) with a noun as antecedent, (2) with no such antecedent, but with a 'pseudo-interrogative' relative pronoun. Both involve an infinitive, not a finite verb. In elevated usage only (2) is generally found:

(1) hayu yeladim   lesaHek itam   היו ילדים לשחק אתם
     ANTECEDENT MODAL REL   'There were children to play with'
     were children to-play with-them

(2) hayu im mi   lesaHek   היו עם מי לשחק
     REL   'There were people to play with'
       PRONOUN
     |_____|
     MODAL REL
     were with who to-play

Modals type 1: noun antecedent

The relative pronoun behaves slightly differently than in 'factive relatives': when a direct object, as in (1) below, it is left unsaid (as always); when an indirect object or adverbial (2, 3), it may be expressed but need not be, unlike 'factives' (see 33.3.3); when a subject (4), it renders the very use of an infinitive ungrammatical - instead, Hebrew uses a finite verb (5):

(1) hine máshehu lilbosh ∧   הנה משהו מעיל ללבוש
        me'il
     (DIR OBJ of *lilbosh* unsaid)
                    'Here's something to wear'
                              a coat

(2) hine tmuna lehistakel (ba)   הנה תמונה להסתכל (בה)
                 IND OBJ   'Here's a picture to look at'
     here's picture to-look (at-it)

(3) hine kise lashévet (alav)   הנה כיסא לשבת (עליו)
              ADVERBIAL   'Here's a chair to sit on'
     here's chair to-sit (on-it)

and not:

(4) *hine káma tmunot ∧ leanyen otaH   *הנה כמה תמונות לעניין אותך
       (SUBJ of *leanyen* unsaid)
     here-are some pictures ∧ to-interest you

but rather:

(5) hine káma tmunot she-yeanyenu otaH   הנה כמה תמונות שיעניינו אותך
             FINITE V   'Here are some pictures that
     here-are some pictures that will-interest you   might interest you'

There are two alternatives to the simple infinitive: (a) כד י *kdey* (ordinarily 'in order to') + infinitive:

     ani tsariH iton kdey likro   אני צריך עיתון כדי לקרוא
     I need newspaper in-order to-read   'I need a paper to read'

     yiye li shulHan ktiva **kdey lashévet leyado**? יהיה לי שולחן כתיבה **כדי לשבת לידו**?
                                   'Will I have a desk to sit at
                                   (lit. **in order to sit at it**)?'

(b) In substandard Hebrew, -ש *she-* + future verb:

אתן לך משהו שתחשוב עליו

eten leHa máshehu she-taHshov alav
I'll-give you something that you-FUT-think
about-it

'I'll give you something to
think about'

Type 1 modals may imply 'necessity' as well as 'possibility':[28]

יש לי עבודה לעשות

yesh li avoda laasot

'I have work to do [= that I can/must do]'

יש לנו תמונות להסתכל בהן

yesh lánu tmunot lehistakel bahen

'We have pictures to look at
[= that we can/should look at]'

Modals type 2: an 'interrogative' relative pronoun

Type 2 is more complex and restricted than type 1. Firstly, the clause containing the relative modal clause must have יש *yesh* 'there is', אין *en* 'there is not' (and their tenses, e.g. היה *haya* 'there was') and similar verbs of existence, e.g. נשאר *nish'ar* 'remain'; thus:[29]

יש עם מי לשחק

yesh ∧ im **mi**   lesaHek
          REL PRONOUN   'There is someone with **whom** to play'
(the antecedent is left unsaid)
there-is with **who** to-play

יהיה לך איפה לגור

yiye laH **éfo**   lagur
          REL   'You'll have **where** to stay'
          PRONOUN
will-be to-you **where** to-stay

The relative noun (labelled REL PRONOUN) in the foregoing examples is adverbial; it can be an object too, but as in type 1 modals, cannot be the understood *subject* of the relative clause. Concerning the antecedent, standard Hebrew rules out an antecendent noun, preferring a type 1 modal:

*אין לי חומר מה לתת לה

*en li **Hómer ma** latet la
isn't to-me **material what** to-give her

אין לי חומר לתת לה

en li Hómer latet la
isn't to-me material to-give her

'I don't have material to give her'

But very casual Hebrew allows at least מקום *makom* 'place' as an antecedent noun:

יש לך מקום (איפה) לגור?

yesh laH makom (éfo) lagur?
is to-you place (where) to-stay?

'Do you have a place to stay?'

Furthermore, in casual registers a quantifier can act as visible antecedent, as in (1) below; but once there is an antecedent, the 'interrogative' pronoun can be dropped altogether (2), making a type 1 modal:

(1)   en harbe   ma   ledaber   אין הרבה מה לדבר
     ANTECEDENT REL   'There isn't much to say'
            PRONOUN
     isn't much what to-say

(2)   en harbe ledaber   אין הרבה לדבר
     isn't much to-say   'There isn't much to say'

FURTHER READING

Berman 1982b; Cole 1976b; Eytan 1953; Givón 1975; Glinert 1976b: 259f; Hayon 1973; Landau 1975; Ornan 1978; Rosén 1977: 8.5.3.; Rubinstein 1971: 2.6; Sadka 1981: ch. 13, 20.3 etc.

34. Apposed clauses

34.1 Introduction

Many nouns express a verbal action or an adjectival state, or the product thereof (see further 30.6):

Verb, Adjective			*Noun*		
isher	'he confirmed'	אישר	ishur	'confirmation'	אישור
batúaH	'certain'	בטוח	bitaHon	'certainty'	בטחון

The main function of apposed clauses is to qualify such verbal or adjectival nouns - by adding the equivalent of an object clause or subject clause:

kibálti ishur **she-ani noséa**   קיבלתי אישור **שאני נוסע**
VERBAL N   APPOSED OBJ CLAUSE
I-received confirmation **that I am-going**
'I received confirmation that I was going'

Compare this with an actual object clause:

ishru she-ani noséa   אישרו שאני נוסע
V   OBJECT CLAUSE   'They confirmed that I was going'

Verbal or adjectival nouns can also be qualified by a further verbal/adjectival noun, as in (1) below, rather than by an apposed clause (2); and in that case the first noun will be genitive, whereas with an apposed clause the introductory noun is not linked in any formal way (construct suffix, של *shel* 'of' or suchlike) to the clause (3):

(1) hakHashat meoravutam ba-hafiHa   הכחשת מעורבותם בהפיכה
     GENITIVE N   ADJECTIVAL N
     denial involvement-their in-the coup
                              'the denial of their involvement in the coup'

(2) ha-hakHasha she-hayu meoravim ba-hafiHa   ההכחשה שהיו מעורבים בהפיכה
     INTRODUCT N   APPOSED CLAUSE
     the denial that they-were involved in-the coup

(3) ha-sheela ha-Hashuva matay lehashkia   השאלה החשובה **מתי להשקיע**
        lo hoalta   לא הועלתה
                              └─────────────┘
                              INF APPOSED CLAUSE
                         'The major question ⟨of⟩ **when to invest** was not raised'

376

34.2 General properties of apposed clauses

Contrast apposed clauses with relative clauses. The former convey 'to the effect that...' while the latter say something *about* the introductory noun:

kulánu shamánu et dvarav shel ya'ári,   כולנו שמענו את דבריו של יערי,
she-hi mishtayéHet le-irgun Hiloni   שהיא משתייכת לאירגון חילוני
kitsoni   קיצוני

    'We've all heard the statement of Yaari ⟨to the effect⟩ that she belongs to an extreme secular organization'

kulánu shamánu et dvarav shel ya'ári,   כולנו שמענו את דבריו של יערי,
she-hiku et ha-kahal be-tadhema   שהיכו את הקהל בתדהמה

    'We've all heard the statement of Yaari that left the audience thunderstruck'

With both apposed and relative clauses, the introductory ('antecedent') noun or noun phrase is treated as nucleus and the clause as modifier; thus the former determines agreement of the main verb. Both types of clause can begin with the conjunction -ש *she-*, and indeed there is occasionally ambiguity between them; but relative clauses can instead use the conjunction אשר *asher* (F), and apposed clauses can use כי *ki* (F) like object clauses (cf.30.2):

ha-shmu'ot ki neherágti **hayu** li le-ezra   **השמועות** כי נהרגתי **היו** לי לעזרה
NUCLEUS (pl.) APPOSED CLAUSE   pl.

    'The rumours that I was killed **were** of help to me'

Several abstract nouns not directly equivalent to a verb or adjective can nevertheless take an apposed clause, e.g. ...ש העובדה *ha-uvda she...* 'the fact that...', ...ש סיכוי אין *eyn sikuy she...* 'there is no chance of...'.

Apposed clauses occasionally amount to a subject clause (for subject clauses see 31.4):

ha-adifut levatséa toHnit zo al-pney   העדיפות לבצע תוכנית זו על-פני
toHnit aHéret...   תוכנית אחרת...
the preferability to-execute plan this
over plan another...

    'the preferability of executing this plan rather than another...'

Compare with a real subject clause:

adif **levatséa toHnit zo...**   ...**עדיף לבצע תוכנית זו**

    '⟨It is⟩ preferable **to execute this plan...**'

Further nouns taking 'subject' apposed clauses are ...ש הכדאיות *ha-kdaiyut she...* 'the usefulness of...', ...ש ההסתברות *ha-histabrut she...* 'the probability that...' However, most adjectives or verbs taking subject clauses simply have no noun equivalent.[1]

Noun + apposed clause is possible in any of the 'slots' in the sentence where one finds nouns, e.g.:

As subject:

ha-shmu'ot she-hu putar lo hukHashu   השמועות שהוא פוטר לא הוכחשו
SUBJ OF WHOLE CLAUSE   'The rumours that he was sacked had not been denied'

As object:

lo hikHishu et **ha-shmu'ot she-hu putar**   לא הכחישו את **השמועות שהוא פוטר**
OBJ OF WHOLE CLAUSE   'They had not denied **the rumours that he was sacked**'

34.3 Types of apposed clause

Like object clauses - to which they closely correspond - apposed clauses can be of various types, depending largely on the meaning of the introductory noun (some verbal nouns, like some verbs, take just interrogative clauses or just infinitives or suchlike), as follows:

(a) Finite apposed clauses, i.e. clauses with a tense, can take the following forms:

(1) *Declarative*, introduced by -ש *she-* or (optionally) by literary-officialese כי *ki*:

ha-shmu'ot she-avo   השמועות שאבוא
FACTUAL   'the rumours that I'll come'

ha-bakasha she-avo   הבקשה שאבוא
SUBJUNCTIVE   'the request that I come'

(2) *Interrogative*:

ha-haHlata {matay/im} avo   ההחלטה {מתי/אם} אבוא
'the decision {when/whether} I'm coming'

(3) *Dubitative* (mostly journalistic), i.e. the speaker casts doubt on an idea, using כאילו *ke'ilu*:[2]

hofiu yedi'ot **ke'ilu** neesru anashim   הופיעו ידיעות **כאילו** נאסרו אנשים
'Reports appeared **that (i.e. alleging that)** people had been detained'

(b) Infinitive apposed clauses express intention, possibility, the mere notion of some situation - rather than facts. (For infinitives in general see 30.4.) These clauses are:

(1) *Declarative*:

en efsharut **laHanot**   אין אפשרות **לחנות**
'There is no way **of parking**'

(2) *Interrogative*:

ha-haHlata {**matay/im**} lehinase   ההחלטה {**מתי/אם**} **להינשא**
'the decision {**when/if**} **to marry**'

34.4-6 TYPES OF INTRODUCTORY NOUN

34.4 Abstract nouns

If a verb (or adjective) that takes an *object clause* has a corresponding 'action or state noun', the latter will generally take an *apposed* clause. Examples:

Verb + object clause:

kiva she...	'hope that'	...ש קיווה
heHlit she...	'decide that'	...ש החליט
batúaH she...	'certain that'	...ש בטוח
ratsa le...	'want to'	...ל רצה
zaHa le...	'be privileged to'	...ל זכה

Noun + apposed clause:

tikva she...	'(a) hope that...'	... ש תקווה
haHlata she...	'decision that...'	...ש החלטה
bitaHon she...	'certainty that...'	...ש בטחון
ratson le...	'wish to...'	...ל רצון
zHut le...	'privilege of...'	...ל זכות

Such verbs and nouns denote mental acts (statements, intentions, etc.) or ability, permission and suchlike. This generally rules out those nouns based on (1) aspectual verbs, e.g. 'stating, continuing, habit': there is no התחלה להילחם* *hatHala lehilaHem* ('a beginning to fight'), המשכה להילחם* *hamshaHa lehilaHem* ('a continuation of fighting'); and on (2) adverbial verbs, e.g. ...ל הרבה *hirba le...* 'do a lot of...', ...ל היטיב *hetiv le...* 'do... well'.[3] Various other verbs such as ...ל למד *lamad le...* 'learn to' have no apposed equivalent, e.g. ...ל לימוד* *limud le...* ('learning to...').

Apposed clauses are also found with most 'product nouns' (denoting the product of a mental action):

ha-sipur she...	'the story that...'	...ש הסיפור
ha-de'a she...	'the view that...'	...ש הדעה
ha-heter le...	'the permit to...'	...ל ההיתר

Many are not directly related to any verb, e.g. ...ש הרעיון *ha-raayon she...* 'the idea that...', ...ש העובדה *ha-uvda she...* 'the fact that...', ...ש הבעיה *ha-baaya she...* 'the problem that...', as in example (1) below. However, 'concrete' nouns (insofar as one can distinguish concrete from abstract) tend not to take apposed clauses, as shown in example (2):

(1) ze naHon be-**muvan ze she**-eyn tauyot   זה נכון **במובן זה שאין** טעויות
'It's correct in **the sense that** there are no errors'

(2) *ha-séfer she-ha-nasi haya soHen Hasha'i   הספר שהנשיא היה סוכן חשאי*
zaHa le-haaratsa raba   זכה להערצה רבה
('The book to the effect that (*lit.* that) the President was a secret agent won great acclaim')

The introductory noun can be definite or indefinite, singular or plural, as meaning may dictate:

(ha)-tikva (ha-)meHudéshet ki...   ...כי (ה)מחודשת (ה)תקווה
'(the) renewed hope that...'

yeshnan de'ot ki...   ...כי דעות ישנן
'There are opinions that...'

A related construction is the 'specificational clause of being' (cf.16.3.7):

ha-tvi'a hi she-nenatsaH   שננצח היא התביעה
'The demand is that we triumph'

ha-tsara (hi) she-hu keréaH   קרח שהוא (היא) הצרה
'The trouble is that he's bald'

But often no such construction is available:

*ha-hakHasha hi she...   ...ש היא *ההכחשה
('the denial is that...')

Many *idiomatic phrases* involve what looks like a noun + apposed clause but which is best regarded as a simple verb:

כבר לפני זמן **הבעתי את דעתי**, בפומבי, שאין לי נחת מהממשלה
kvar lifney zman **hibáti et daati**, be-fumbey, she-eyn li náHat me-ha-memshala
IDIOMATIC
'Some time ago I **expressed the opinion** in public that I have no joy from the government'

34.5 Apposed pronouns

-ש זה *ze she-* and -ש כך *kaH she-* illustrated in the three examples below (and discussed in detail with other pronouns in 7.7) do not correspond to any verb; they are most akin to ...ש העובדה *ha-uvda she-* 'the fact that...', though in fact they do not expressly denote 'the fact that'. The choice between זה *ze*, כך *kaH* and a third pronoun הדבר *ha-davar* depends partly on their position in the clause, the choice of verb etc. (see 7.7). All three need a finite clause, which cannot be interrogative.

ze she-hu meshaker ze lo Hashuv   זה שהוא משקר זה לא חשוב
it [= the fact] **that** he lies isn't important

hitsíu et ze she-nitpasher   הציעו את זה שנתפשר
they-proposed OM it that [= that] we-compromise

dibru al **kaH** she-nitHalef   דיברו על כך שנתחלף
they-talked about **it that** we'll-switch
[= about our switching]

34.6   Positioning and pausing

Apposed clauses must generally follow their introductory noun without pause, although even then a comma is not uncommon:

ha-uvda, ki mo'ed ha-bHina nidHa,   העובדה, כי מועד הבחינה נדחה,
orera Hashadot   עוררה חשדות

'The fact that the date of the exam was put off aroused suspicious'

But the pronouns זה *ze*, זאת *zot* can introduce a specificational apposed clause with a clear pause:

azkir rak zot, she-gam lánu hasagot   אזכיר רק זאת, שגם לנו השגות

'I would mention just this, that we too have reservations'

ha-baaya hi zot, ha'im ha-taktsiv yipaga   הבעיה היא זאת, האם התקציב ייפגע

'The problem is this, whether the budget will be affected'

Apposed clauses, though not set off by pause, can occasionally be separated from their introductory noun by intervening words, particularly following יש *yesh* 'there is', היה *haya* 'there was' and their various inflections (and 'presentative' verbs in general):[4]

hayta **tikva** bekérev ha-maamad ha-benoni,   היתה **תקווה** בקרב המעמד הבינוני,

INTROD N

she-ha-misuy yekutsats   **שהמיסוי יקוצץ**

APPOSED CLAUSE

'There was **hope** among the middle classes **that taxation would be cut**'

FURTHER READING
Dahan 1981; Kogut 1984; Landau 1975; Rubinstein 1968: 101-107; Sadka 1981: 13.2, 37.

35. Coordination

35.1 Introduction

Coordination is a way of stringing together words, phrases or clauses of the same grammatical type, using the following coordinators (or conjunctions as they are sometimes known) or occasionally no coordinator: -ו *ve-* 'and', או *o* 'or', אבל *aval* 'but', אלא *éla* 'but instead' (as in the third example below), and various synonyms of these.

Examples of clause, phrase and word coordination are:

Clause coordination

ani hifsákti ve-hu hitHil   אני הפסקתי והוא התחיל
CLAUSE   CLAUSE   'I stopped and he started'

amárti she-ha délet tipataH aH ha-or yiHbe   אמרתי שהדלת תיפתח אך האור יכבה
OBJ CLAUSE   OBJ CLAUSE
          'I said that the door would open but the light would go out'

Phrase coordination

lo noládeti be-shabat éla be-yom shishi   **לא נולדתי בשבת אלא ביום ששי**
       PREP PHRASE   PREP PHRASE
          'I wasn't born **on Shabbat** but **on Friday**'

hem golelim et ha-tora o meHasim ota   **הם גוללים את התורה או מכסים אותה**
    V PHR   V PHR
          'They **roll the Torah** or **cover it**'

Word coordination[2]

ra'inu harbe yehudim, muslemim, notsrim   **ראינו הרבה יהודים, מוסלמים, נוצרים**
       QUANTIFIED NOUNS
          'We saw many **Jews, Moslems, Christians**'

Coordinated words can be expanded to phrases or whole clauses:[2]

kibásti et ha-garbáyim ve-ha-Hultsot   כיבסתי את הגרביים והחולצות
I-washed OM the socks and the shirts

...et ha... ve-et ha...   ...את ה... ואת ה...
...OM the ... and OM the...

...ve-kibásti et ha-Hultsot   ...וכיבסתי את החולצות
... and I washed OM the shirts

Two other types of structure, 'modification' and 'complementation', are like coordination in that they add one word (or phrase or clause) to another. Modification does so optionally, complementation generally does so obligatorily:

Modification

פנינו להרבה יהודים תושבי עיירות פיתוח

paninu le-harbe yehudim, toshavey ayarot pitúaH

NUCLEUS   APPOSED MODIFIER

'We asked many Jews, inhabitants of development towns'

ani hifsákti   lifney she-hu hitHil   אני הפסקתי לפני שהוא התחיל

NUCLEUS CLAUSE ADVERBIAL MODIFIER   'I stopped before he began'

Complementation

amárta   she-gamárta   אמרת שגמרת

GOVERNING   COMPLEMENT   'You said that you finished'

V   (OBJ CLAUSE)

But, unlike coordinations, these are not strings of the same grammatical type: nucleus and modifier are not the same, nor are governing verb and complement. This distinction should be borne in mind since -ו *ve-* does occasionally introduce a modifier or a complement (35.7).[3]

35.2 'And' in general

35.2.1 Types of -ו *ve-* 'and'

'And' is usually expressed by the coordinator -ו *ve-*. Like other one-letter words, -ו *ve-* is written as a prefix.[4] -ו *ve-* covers several shades of meaning, from simple 'and furthermore' to more complex notions; the following example allows five interpretations of -ו *ve-* 'and':

ani shatáfti kelim ve-baali nigev   אני שטפתי כלים ובעלי ניגב

'I washed the dishes and my husband dried'

More specific paraphrase:

(1) ...ve-yéter-al-ken...   'And furthermore'   ...ויתר-על-כן...
(2) ...u-vo ba-zman...   'And at the same time' ...ובו בזמן...
(3) ...ve-az...   'And then'   ...ואז...
(4) ...az...   'And so' (result)   ...אז...
(5) ...u-ve-Hol zot...   'And yet'   ...ובכל זאת...

Which use of -ו *ve-* is intended is entirely a matter of circumstances, and may not even be clear. By contrast, the paraphrases make one's intentions unambiguous.

A widespread case of 'and then' is -ו *ve-* used following a request. This amounts to 'if..., then...':

A promise:

hakped lidrosh *** ve-hanaatHa tiye shlema! הקפד לדרוש *** והנאתך תהיה שלמה!

'Make sure to ask for *** and your enjoyment will be complete!'

A threat:

tiga bo ve-ani maHnis leHa ba-partsuf   תגע בו ואני מכניס לך בפרצוף
'Touch him and I'll punch your face in'

The following example allows four interpretations of - ו *ve-* 'and':

ani ve-ishti rávnu   אני ואשתי רבנו
'My wife and I were arguing'

More specific paraphrase:

(6) ...rávnu ze im ze   'with one another'   ...רבנו זה עם זה
     (reciprocal)

(7) ...yáHad im...   'together with'   ...יחד עם
     (joint participants)

(8) ...ve-yéter-al-ken...   'and furthermore'   ...ויתר-על-כן
(9) ...u-vo ba-zman...   'and at the same time' ...ובו בזמן

Thus, 'and then', 'and so', 'and yet' always involve coordinated clauses or predicates, as in the example at the beginning of this subsection, never just nouns. Conversely, 'with one another, together with' always involve coordinated nouns (the 'My wife and I were arguing' example above) - אני רבתי ואשתי רבה *ani rávti ve-ishti ráva* 'I was arguing and my wife was arguing' would imply *separate* events, be they simultaneous or otherwise. For details see 35.3–4. Only the meanings 'and furthermore', 'and at the same time' afford a *choice* between clause, predicate and noun phrase coordination.[5]

35.2.2 The place of - ו *ve-* and its punctuation

There can be any number of 'and's: - ו *ve-* can be inserted repeatedly, or (commonly) replaced by a comma or its intonational equivalent, though the last - ו *ve-* usually remains:

saHínu ve-rátsnu ve-galáshnu   שחינו ורצנו וגלשנו
'We swam and ran and skied'

saHínu, rátsnu ve-galáshnu   שחינו, רצנו וגלשנו
'We swam, ran and skied'

To give the effect of an open-ended list, just commas (or separate intonation units) can be used:[6]

katfu tapuzim, shezifim, agasim...   ...קטפו תפוזים, שזיפים, אגסים
'They picked oranges, plums, pears...'

For spacing or emphasis, - ו *ve-* itself can be preceded by a comma or even a full-stop or pause:

leaHar zman hu shatak ve-Hika.   לאחר זמן הוא שתק וחיכה.
ve-shuv diber.   ושוב דיבר.
'After a while he fell silent and waited. And again started talking'

Tagged -ı *ve-* phrases

One or more coordinated phrases (not a verb in mid-sentence) can be delayed to the end of the sentence. -ı *ve-* will be necessary, and usually a support word such as גם *gam* 'too':

ha-bánkim marviHim mi-ze, הבנקים מרוויחים מזה,
ve-ha-yatsranim gám-ken והיצרנים גם-כן
    'The banks do well out of it, and the manufacturers too'

et ha-béduim hu hikir mi-neurav, את הבדוים הוא הכיר מנעוריו,
ve-af heerits ואף העריץ
    'The beduin he knew from his youth, and indeed admired'

But reciprocal and joint coordinations (35.2.1, types 6,7) can never be split up:

heHan réygan nifgash ve-gromíko? היכן רייגן נפגש וגרומיקו?
    ('Where is Reagan meeting and Gromyko?')

35.2.3 Associated phenomena

Repeated words in coordinations

Coordination cuts down on repetition, e.g. rather than be repeated as in example (1), the two identical verbs are ordinarily reduced to one[7] - and the parallel nouns coordinated:

(1) míryam hismíka ve-léa hismíka מרים הסמיקה ולאה הסמיקה
    f.s.   f.s.   'Miriam blushed and Lea blushed'

(2) míryam ve-léa hismíku מרים ולאה הסמיקו
        pl.   'Miriam and Lea blushed'

To avoid repeated nouns, Hebrew may use a pronoun or coordinate:

ido kol ha-yom haya shoHev ba-mita עידו כל היום היה שוכב במיטה
ve-(hu) lo (haya) ose klum ו(הוא) לא (היה) עושה כלום
    'All day Ido would lie in bed and (he would) not do anything'

Prepositions and case prepositions are often repeated, particularly in formal usage:

ten le-shálva u-le-tsívya תן לשלוה ולצביה
    'Give (some) to Shalva and **to** Tsivia'

What can be coordinated with -ı *ve-*

There are some restrictions on coordinating disparate types of word or phrase. In particular, noun+clause, or noun+infinitive or their reverse are awkward:

תבעתי לסלק אותו וכן את פירוק הצוות?
?taváti lesalek oto ve-Hen et peruk ha-tsévet
    INF   N PHR
I-demanded to-sack him and also OM [the] dismemberment [of] the team

But noun, adjective and verb all coordinate with one another, e.g. verb phrase + noun phrase:[8]

> im hi yodáat lashir ve-nagénet tova,...   ‏‏...,אם היא יודעת לשיר ונגנת טובה,‏
> 'If she knows how to sing and ⟨is⟩ a good player,...'

Gapping
'Gapping' omits identical material,[9] leaving a gap in the middle of the coordinated clause:

> ha-eHad haya sar ve-ha-sheni - aluf   ‏האחד היה שר והשני - אלוף‏
> 'One was a minister and the other a general'

A dash often marks the 'gap'. Intonation often uses a marked 'rise-fall' before the gap.

35.3   Joint participants and joint predicates

For actions/events involving *joint* participants, the coordinated subjects or objects take plural agreement, like any other coordinated noun phrases as in (1-3) below. They cannot be moved apart into separate clauses (4), nor moved to the end of the clause (5). Prepositions can be repeated, even though the two objects are conceived as a 'joint' phenomenon (3):[10]

(1)   biálik ve-ravnítski arHu et séfer ha-agada   ‏ביאליק ורבניצקי ערכו את ספר האגדה‏
      pl.
      'Bialik and Ravnitzki edited the Sefer Ha-Agada'

(2)   eliézer ve-éster hem zug neHmad   ‏אליעזר ואסתר הם זוג נחמד‏
      'Eliezer and Esther are a nice couple'

(3)   térner tsiyer et ha-yam ve-(et) ha-shémesh   ‏טרנר צייר את הים ו(את) השמש‏
      Turner painted ᴏᴍ the sea and (ᴏᴍ) the sun

(4)   *biálik araH ve-ravnítski araH   ‏ביאליק ערך ורבניצקי ערך*‏
      et séfer ha-agada   ‏את ספר האגדה‏
      ('Bialik edited and Ravnitski edited the Sefer Ha-Agada')

(5)   *biálik araH...ve-gam ravnítski   ‏ביאליק ערך...וגם רבניצקי*‏
      ('Bialik edited...and so did Ravnitski')

Where a coordinated noun phrase is just an epithet for a single person, e.g. ‏ראש הממשלה ושר החוץ, מר שמיר‏ *rosh ha-memshala ve-sar ha-Huts, mar shamir* 'The Prime Minister and Foreign Minister, Mr Shamir', it is treated as singular (unlike the joint subjects above), and hence there is no preposition repetition (e.g. ‏...ל...ול...‏ *le...ve-le...*):

hu kara le-rosh ha-memshala ve-sar
ha-Huts, mar shamir...   הוא קרא לראש הממשלה ושר
החוץ, מר שמיר...

'He called on the PM and Foreign Minister, Mr. Shamir...'

Coordinated predicates or modifiers (adjectives, verbs and even nouns) of a
plural noun can often be understood either 'respectively' or 'jointly' (circumstances permitting):

kafriyim tseirim u-zkenim   כפריים צעירים וזקנים

'young and old villagers'

is equivalent to:

kafriyim tseirim ve-kafriyim zkenim   כפריים צעירים וכפריים זקנים

'young villagers and old villagers'

as against:

aHayot yafot u-neimot   אחיות יפות ונעימות

'pleasant and attractive nurses' =
'pleasant-and-attractive nurses'

For details on 'adjective stacking', e.g. ספריה איזורית חדשה *sifriya ezorit
Hadasha* 'a new regional library', see chapter 10.4. A notable case where adjectives of the same type are *not* coordinated is colours, e.g. מכונית אדומה-לבנה
meHonit aduma-levana 'a red and white car'.

Doubled verbs, e.g. הוא ניסה וניסה *hu nisa ve-nisa* 'He tried and tried',
convey 'for a long time' (this applies to 'durative verbs', not to אהב *ahav* 'like'
and suchlike).

35.4 Reciprocal 'and'

התנשק *hitnashek* 'kiss' is an inherently reciprocal verb: used with no
object, as below, it denotes that the subjects embraced *one another*. -ו *ve-* here
is thus reciprocal: it signifies not two separate actions but a joint, indeed reciprocal, action.

éli ve-éster
horay   hitnashku shuv   התנשקו שוב   אלי ואסתר
הורי

'Eli and Esther
My parents   kissed again'

התנשק *hitnashek* 'kiss' is even found with an *explicitly reciprocal object*, using
עם *im* 'with':

éli ve-éster
horay   hitnashku ze im ze   התנשקו זה עם זה   אלי ואסתר
הורי

'Eli and Esther
My parents   kissed one another' (lit. this with this)

Alternatively, instead of coordinating two or more nouns, it takes one noun as
subject and the other(s) as object - this too has reciprocal meaning:

éli hitnashek im éster   אלי התנשק עם אסתר
Eli kissed with Esther   'Eli kissed Esther'

Numerous other verbs, adjectives, nouns and other expressions are inherently reciprocal. Their subject (occasionally their object) is either a plural noun or a set of *coordinated nouns*;[11] they are also sometimes found with an explicit reciprocal object (usually with עם *im* 'with'), except for nouns; they also supply a subject+object[12] construction as in the foregoing example (but this is not always reciprocal, see below). Examples are:

(a) *Verbs*: התחבק *hitHabek* 'embrace', התראה *hitra'a* 'see one another', התערבב *hitarbev* 'mingle', נפגש *nifgash* 'meet', נדבר *nidbar* 'talk', נועץ *no'ats* 'confer', הפגיש את *hifgish et* 'introduce'

(b) *Adjectives*: זהה *zehe* 'identical', שווה *shave* 'equal', חופף *Hofef* 'overlapping', מנוגד *menugad* 'contrasting'

(c) *Nouns*: אחים (מיקי ואלי הם) *(míki ve-éli hem) aHim* '(Miki and Eli are) brothers', ידידים *yedidim* 'friends', קרובים *krovim* 'relatives', אויבים *oyvim* 'enemies', שכנים *shHenim* 'neighbours'

Unlike 'joint participant' verbs (35.3), reciprocals do not tolerate the adverb יחד *yáHad* 'together', thus:

éli ve-éster tiyelu yáHad   אלי ואסתר טיילו יחד
           'Eli and Esther were walking together'

but not:

*éli ve-éster nifgeshu yáHad   *אלי ואסתר נפגשו יחד
          ('Eli and Esther met together')

Many verbs etc. used with reciprocal *objects* are, unpredictably, not inherently reciprocal:

éfo nitkáltem eHad ba-sheni?   איפה נתקלתם אחד בשני?
          'Where did you come across one another?'

and not:

*éfo nitkáltem?   *איפה נתקלתם?
          ('Where did you come across?')

Conversely, some words that allow reciprocal coordination are not reciprocal in a subject + object/possessive construction, e.g. יואב הוא אויב של ניר *yóav hu oyev shel nir* 'Yoav is an enemy of Nir', יואב הכיר את שלום *yóav hikir et shálom* 'Yoav knew Shalom', יואב התאהב בחמדה *yóav hitahev be-Hémda* 'Yoav fell in love with Hemda' do not imply the reverse action.

Indeed, where one of the participants is a 'thing', a coordination is normally impossible:

yóram	hitnakesh be hikir	kama psalim	כמה פסלים	יורם התנקש ב הכיר
	'Yoram	collided with knew	several statues'	

but not:

	hitnakshu	התנקשו	*yóram ve-kama psalim
*yóram ve-kama psalim	hikíru	הכירו	יורם וכמה פסלים

'Yoram and several statues   collided'
                               knew each other'

Further, some reciprocal verbs and adjectives are *semi-transitive*, i.e. omit their object if it is non-specific:

hitHatánti (= ...im míshehu)   התחתנתי (= ...עם מישהו)
           'I've got married (= with someone)'

And so plural *hitHatnu* התחתנו can be ambiguous:

אלי ואסתר התחתנו (= זה עם זה/עם מישהו)
éli ve-éster hitHatnu (= ze im ze/im míshehu)
'Eli and Esther got married (= to one another/to someone)'

More semi-transitives are: נאבק *neevak* 'struggle', נלחם *nilHam* 'fight', התאהב *hitahev* 'fall in love', התארס *hitares* 'get engaged', נשוי *nasuy* 'married'.

35.5 Illocutionary 'and'

Statements, questions and commands may be prefaced by אני אומר/שואל/מבקש *ani omer/sho'el/mevakesh* 'I say/ask/request', performing rather than describing what is being said etc., i.e. on a 'higher' ('illocutionary') level of discourse.

Similarly, -ו *ve-* is sometimes illocutionary, meaning 'and I say (*or*: ask, request)', notably in three constructions. A word with apparently nothing to coordinate with, as in:

yesh lehaatik et ha-toHna u-miyad   יש להעתיק את התוכנה ומיד
       'You must copy the software **and immediately**'

can be explained as representing ואני מדגיש: מיד *ve-ani madgish: miyad* 'and I stress: immediately'. This is the 'emphatic -ו *ve-*'. Similarly,

ani, ve-ani levadi, mukar le-Hulam   אני, ואני לבדי, מוכר לכולם
       'I, and I alone, am known to everyone'

Joining a statement with a question or command, as in the following, is equivalent to אני אומר ש... ואני שואל... *ani omer she... va-ani sho'el...* 'I say that... and I ask...' and the like:

	ve-láma hu lovesh svéder?	ולמה הוא לובש סוודר?	
ha-tinok ratuv -	ve-al tagid she-ani menadnédet!	ואל תגיד שאני מנדנדת!	התינוק רטוב -

'The baby's wet -   and why is he wearing a sweater?'
                  and don't say I'm nagging!'

-ו *ve-* also introduces a future tense 'whatever'-type construction (see 32.11.4) such as:

> yehudi she-Hay be-yisra'el hu yisre'eli,　　יהודי שחי בישראל הוא ישראלי,
> ve-yikba mekom moshavo aHar-kaH　　ויקבע מקום מושבו אחר-כך
> ba-asher yikba　　באשר יקבע
>
> 'A Jew living in Israel is an Israeli, and wherever he
> subsequently fixes his place of residence (*lit.* let him
> fix his place of residence subsequently where he will fix)...'

35.6　Coordinated compounds, e.g. משא ומתן *masa u-matan* 'negotiations'

Many constructions can become 'compounds', being felt to refer to a single concept, and thus become more rigid syntactically. For example, construct בן-אדם ~ בני-אדם *ben-adam* ~ (pl.) *bney-adam* 'person(s)' is a compound in casual usage in the way it becomes definite: הבן-אדם *ha-ben-adam* 'the person', rather than בן-האדם *ben ha-adam*.

Coordinated numerals and a few coordinated nouns are *compounds* in all usage. (1) They cannot be split up. (2) -ה *ha-* 'the' is only placed before the whole phrase (-ה *ha-* is elsewhere never omitted: הבנים והבנות *ha-banim ve-ha* banot 'the boys and **the** girls', not *הבנים ובנות* **ha-banim ve-banot* ('the boys and girls'). (3) These coordinated nouns are singular for agreement, whereas all other coordinations of nouns are plural; moreover, the former have no plural:

(1)　esrim ve-shéva shanim　　עשרים ושבע שנים
twenty and seven [= 27] years

*esrim shana ve-shéva shanim[13]　　*עשרים שנה ושבע שנים
twenty years and seven years

(2)　ha-masa u-matan al ha-din ve-Heshbon　　המשא-ומתן על הדין-וחשבון
'the negotiation (*originally*: the taking and giving) about the report (*originally*: the judgement and account)'

(3)　　　　התוהו-ובוהו **האנגלי** במקח-וממכר **הממושך**
ha-tóhu va-vóhu **ha-angli** ba-mékaH u-mimkar **ha-memushaH**
　　　m.s.　　　　　　　　　　m.s.
'the **English** confusion in the **prolonged** haggling'

The compounds דין-וחשבון *din ve-Heshbon*, משא-מתן *masa u-matan* have even been abbreviated to single words: דו"ח (commonly pronounced *dúaH* or *doH*), מו"מ.

The verbs חזר/שב *Hazar / shav* (ordinarily 'return') and הלך *halaH* (ordinarily 'go') form coordinated compounds with many other verbs - with an idiomatic meaning equivalent to the adverbs 'again' and 'gradually', respectively:[14]

be-shuvo ártsa, hu **Hazar ve-kara**   בשובו ארצה, הוא **חזר וקרא**
le-milHama ba-shHitut   למלחמה בשחיתות
    'On returning to Israel, he **again called** for a war on corruption'

ha-medina **holéHet ve-neheféHet**   המדינה **הולכת ונהפכת**
Hevra Hamusha   חברה חמושה
    'The country **is gradually becoming** an armed society'

In these compounds, (1) the coordinated verbs cannot be separated into two clauses (...הוא חזר והוא קרא* *hu Hazar ve-hu kara...*); (2) nor can they be separated by any other word, e.g. עכשיו *aHshav* 'now', לא *lo* 'not'; (3) additional -ו *ve-* 'and' phrases are impossible: ...הוא חזר וקרא והטיף* *hu Hazar ve-kara ve-hetif...* ('he again called and preached...').

35.7   -ו *ve-* as a pseudo-coordinator: -ו יתכן *yitaHen ve-* 'it is possible that'

-ו *ve-* is occasionally not a coordinator but a subordinator ('complementizer') introducing a subordinate clause,[15] (see note 3 on coordinators vs. subordinators). This involves three types of context, described below under (a-c).

(a) After three of the prepositions meaning 'since' ('because'), particularly in technical or journalistic usage, namely -ו הואיל *ho'il ve-*, -ו היות *heyot ve-*, -ו מאחר *meaHar ve-*. However, -ש *she-* is actually more common than -ו *ve-*; and is always used with other 'since' words (בגלל *biglal*, מכיוון *mikevan* etc.).

(b) After certain verbs and expressions of 'limitation'. Notice that these can often be paraphrased with 'may' (in most instances, -ש *she-* is more common):

(1)   *Meaning 'sometimes'*:[16]
      yesh ve-ata megale tauyot   **יש ואתה** מגלה טעויות
      there-is that you find errors   '**Sometimes** you find errors'

      kore u-mi-sibot shonot hem niHshalim   **קורה ומסיבות** שונות הם נכשלים
      happens that for reasons different   '**It happens that** they fail for
         they fail   various reasons'

(2)   *Meaning 'possible, it seems'*:
      yitaHen ve-nivne et ha-toHnit   **יתכן ונבנה** את התוכנית
      it-is-possible that we'll-build OM the programme

      mi meitánu lo Haza ba-toHnit?   מי מאתנו לא חזה בתוכנית?
        dome ve-Hulánu   **דומה וכולנו**
      who of-us has-not seen the programme?   **it-would-seem that** all-of-us [have]

      be-mida ve-yibaHer..../be-mikre ve-yibaHer... במידה וייבחר.../במקרה וייבחר...
      in event that he-will-be-elected   'In the event that he is elected...'

(3) *Meaning 'almost':*
    éfi **kim'at ve-**nafal

אפי כמעט ונפל

                               'Efi **almost [that]** fell'

(4) *Meaning 'soon'* (F) (as -ש *she-* is impossible here, this is perhaps a case of
    'and'):
    od me'at/od réga ve-tofía

עוד מעט/עוד רגע ותופיע

                      'A little longer/another moment and she will appear'

(5) *Meaning 'if only':*
    mi yiten
    halvay   ve-yaskim

מי יתן ויסכים
הלוואי

                                'If only [that] he'd agree'

    (c) Introducing certain clauses that refer back to an item in a previous clause
(formal usage), namely (1) circumstantial clauses (see 32.4), and (2) restrictive
relative clauses (see 33.2):

(1) sára raHva al ha-ofanáyim **ve-hi**
     maHzika be-yada panas

שרה רכבה על האופניים והיא
מחזיקה בידה פנס

     Sara rode on the bicycle **and [= while]** she holds in her-hand [a] flashlight

(2) hikíru la alman zaken **ve-lo** shmona banim

הכירו לה אלמן זקן ולו שמונה בנים

            'They introduced her to an old widower who had (*lit.* **and to him**)
                                eight sons'

35.8 Semantic 'addition' vs. syntactic coordination: 'including, besides' etc.

    Coordination expresses the semantic notion 'addition', but there is
another syntactic structure expressing this same notion in various ways - the
adverbial, including 'preposition + noun phrase':[17]

    kibálti braHot mi-kol ha-morim,
      (be-)nosaf le-Haveray u-krovay
      PREP   N PHR

קיבלתי ברכות מכל המורים,
(ב)נוסף לחברי וקרובי

    I-had greetings from all the teachers, in addition
    to my-friends and my-relations

    katávti le-káma dayarim,
      kolel (et) ha-rav she-mimul
      PREP   N PHR

כתבתי לכמה דיירים,
כולל (את) הרב שממול

    I-wrote to several tenants, including (OM) the rabbi who [is] opposite

More such prepositions are: (1) 'besides': -חוץ מ *Huts mi*,[18] מלבד *milvad* (F);
(2) 'including': על *al* (F), לרבות את *lerabot et* (F), (3) 'excluding', i.e. 'and not...':
-חוץ מ *Huts mi*, להוציא את *lehotsi et* (F), -פרט ל *prat le-* (F).

    Such preposition + noun adverbials differ from coordination. They contain
just a noun phrase and cannot be 'filled out' with repeated prepositions, verbs
or whole clauses, thus ruling out example (1) below; and like many adverbials
they can come first, as in (2):

(1)   *katávti le-káma dayarim,   כתבתי לכמה דיירים,*
       {kolel le-éle/kolel katávti le-éle}   {כולל לאלה / כולל כתבתי לאלה}
       I-wrote to several tenants, {including to these/including I-wrote to these}

(2)   be-nosaf le-Haveray u-krovay,   בנוסף לחברי וקרובי,
       kibálti braHot mi-kol ha-morim   קיבלתי ברכות מכל המורים
       besides my-friends and my-relations, I-had greetings from all the teachers

35.9   'Or' in general

35.9.1   Meanings of או *o* 'or'

'Or' is usually expressed by the coordinator או *o*. Though it does not
have the variety of meanings of -ו *ve-* 'and' (35.2), או *o* 'or' is sometimes ambiguous between an inclusive ('and/or') and an exclusive ('either/or') meaning, notably: (a) in *questions*, such as those in (1,2) below, where the reply could be
simply 'yes' (where the 'or' has been understood as inclusive, i.e. 'and/or') or
specifically 'Israel' or 'Egypt' (where the 'or' has been understood as exclusive);
(b) in contexts where an 'as the case may be' ('distributive') meaning is possible,
as in (3). In speech, the 'exclusive' sense would be marked by a fall in intonation
after או *o* 'or', or more commonly by the use of a 'tagged' phrase as described
in 35.9.2.

(1)   ha'im yisra'el o mitsráyim   האם ישראל או מצרים
       ba-Hatsi ha-gmar?   בחצי-הגמר?
                                                'Are Israel or Egypt in the semi-final?'

(2)   lo barur im yisra'el o mitsráyim   לא ברור אם ישראל או מצרים
       ba-Hatsi ha-gmar   בחצי-הגמר
                                                'It isn't clear whether Israel or Egypt are in the semi-final'

(3)   anashim rabim sholHim et bnehem   אנשים רבים שולחים את בניהם
       o et bnotehem le-kaytana   או את בנותיהם לקייטנה
                                                'Many people send their sons or their daughters to summer camp'
                                                Usual meaning: 'their sons and their daughters' (as the case may be)
                                                Possible meaning: 'either their sons or their daughters'

Elsewhere, או *o* may simply be a less pointed version of 'either... or...', i.e. 'or
perhaps', as in (4), or 'or at least', as in (5):

(4)   ten lo lehikanes, ve-atsía lo kafe o tey   תן לו להיכנס, ואציע לו קפה או תה
                                                'Let him in and I'll offer him coffee or tea'

(5)   ze séret aroH - shalosh va-Hétsi sha'ot,   זה סרט ארוך - שלוש וחצי שעות,
       o shalosh va-réva   או שלוש ורבע
                                                'It's a long film - three and a half hours, or three and a quarter'

Exclusive או *o* 'or' can be made clearer by doubling: ...או ...או *o... o...* 'either..
.or...' (see 35.12). In legal Hebrew (in particular) inclusive או *o* may be
expressed as ו/או *ve/o* 'and/or' with a slash.

When linking numerals, 'or perhaps' needs no 'or' word:[20]

shtáyim shalosh Hovarot	'two or three booklets'	שתיים שלוש חוברות
shéva shmóne peamim	'seven or eight times'	שבע שמונה פעמים

Like -ו *ve-* 'and' (see 35.2.1), או *o* following a request can be conditional - a negative conditional, i.e. a threat:

sa mi-kan o she-ani roshem leHa doH	סע מכאן או שאני רושם לך דו"ח
	'Move off or else I'm writing you a ticket'

bo miyad o al tavo biHlal	בוא מיד או אל תבוא בכלל
	'Come right away or don't come at all'

או *o* can also be 'illocutionary', conveying 'or putting it another way...' (see further 35.13).

35.9.2   Shared features of או *o* and -ו *ve-*

או *o* and -ו *ve-* structures coincide in many ways. Below are brief examples; for a fuller explanation, refer to 35.2. Only *differences* are noted below.

The place of או *o* and its punctuation
Exclusive or inclusive:[21]

efshar lisHot o lashut o letayel	אפשר לשחות או לשוט או לטייל
	'One can swim or sail or walk'

Exclusive only:

efshar lisHot, lashut o letayel	אפשר לשחות, לשוט או לטייל
	'One can swim, sail or walk'

If there is no או *o* at all, and just commas, it means inclusive 'or' or 'and' (not 'either...or'):

efshar lisHot, lashut, letayel	אפשר לשחות, לשוט, לטייל
	'One can swim, sail, walk'

But negative 'or' (see below), amounting to 'and', needs no או *o*:

lo nitan limHot, lehitasef, lehafgin...	לא ניתן למחות, להתאסף, להפגין...
	'One cannot protest, assemble, demonstrate...'

Tagged או *o* phrases

míki yodía laH, o éytan	מיקי יודיע לך, **או איתן**
	'Miki will tell you, **or Eytan** ⟨will⟩'

Repeated words

hu kol ha-yom haya kore o **lo ose klum**	הוא כל היום היה קורא או **לא עושה כלום**
	'All day he would read or **not do anything**'

| im míryam hismíka o at hismakt | אם מרים הסמיקה או את הסמקת |

'If Miriam blushed or you blushed'

more often:

| im míryam o at hismáktem | אם מרים או את הסמקתם |

'If Miriam or you blushed'

Negative 'or', i.e. an 'or' phrase following a negative (such as לא *lo* 'not', ...ל אסור *asur le...* 'one must not...'), cannot be expanded to become a whole clause. Instead, it would need to be turned into a - ו *ve-* 'and' clause:

| lo kibálnu miHtav o tsiltsul | לא קיבלנו מכתב או צילצול |

'We haven't had a letter or a phone call'

| lo kibálnu miHtav ve-gam (*o) | לא קיבלנו מכתב וגם (*או) |
| lo kibálnu tsiltsul | לא קיבלנו צילצול |

'We haven't had a letter and (*or) we also haven't had a phone call'

For what can be coordinated with או *o*, and 'gapping', see - ו *ve-* in 35.2.3.

35.10   Agreement with an או *o* phrase

For subjects with או *o*, agreement is failry complex. With inclusive או *o*, they tend to be treated as plural, as if to emphasize that this is not a case of 'either... or':

| ha'im ánglia o skótland **nitsHu**? | האם אנגליה או סקוטלנד **ניצחו**? |
| ken o lo?   pl. | כן או לא? |

'Did England or Scotland **win**, yes or no?'

| kos tey o uga **yeraanenu** oti | כוס תה או עוגה **ירעננו** אותי |
| pl. |

'A cup of tea or a cake **will refresh** me'

| ve-ata nifne el ha-maazin o ha-maazina | ועתה נפנה אל המאזין או המאזינה |
| ha-**baim** | ה**באים** |
| pl. |

'And now we turn to the **next** [male] listener or [female] listener'

But if one pauses before או *o*, with the meaning 'or at least...', the last noun tends to decide agreement:

| im nátan, o sgano, **yisa** la-halvaya... | אם נתן, או סגנו, **יסע** להלוויה... |
| m.s. |

'If Natan, or his deputy, **goes** to the funeral...'

So too with exclusive 'or', meaning 'either...or':

| ha'im ángliya o skótland **nitsHa**? | האם אנגליה או סקוטלנד **ניצחה**? |
| f.s. |

'Did England or Scotland **win**?'

| o nóomi o sára **titstareH** lavo | או נעמי או שרה **תצטרך** לבוא |
| f.s. |

'Either Naomi or Sara **will have** to come'

35.11 'Or' clauses

'Or' introducing a whole clause can be או ש- *o she-* or simply או *o,* the former more usual for exclusive 'or' and casual usage, particularly where the clause begins with a noun. This - ש *she-* is related to the - ש *she* that introduces subordinate clauses, but is treated as inseparable from או *o.*

In questions

Exclusive:

hu shela o (she-)kanit oto be-Hul?　　　　　　הוא שלה או (ש)קנית אותו בחו"ל?
it hers or (that) you-bought it abroad?　'Is it hers or you bought it abroad?'

Inclusive:

ata holeH le-kontsértim o (she-)yesh lefaHot　אתה הולך לקונצרטים או (ש)יש לפחות
efsharut lishmóa taklitim?　　　　　　　　　אפשרות לשמוע תקליטים?
　　　　　　　　　　　　　'Do you go to concerts or ([that]) is there at least
　　　　　　　　　　　　　　　　　　a chance to listen to records?'

In statements

ha-tayasim ta'u bi-vHirat ha-yáad,　　　　　הטייסים טעו בבחירת היעד, או
o (she-)divHu al dvarim she-lo buts'u　　　　(ש)דיווחו על דברים שלא בוצעו
　　　　　'The pilots erred in selecting the objective, or ([that]) they reported
　　　　　　　　　　　　　　　　things that were not executed'

im yered géshem o (she-)yiye kar miday,...　...,אם ירד גשם או (ש)יהיה קר מדי
　　　　　　　　　　　　　'If it rains or ([that]) it's too cold,...'

After או *o* in questions, formal usage allows the particle שמא *shéma* or האם *ha'im* rather than - ש *she-* :[22]

ha'im　ekashel o shéma yikre nes?　　　　　האם אכשל או שמא יקרה נס?
　　　　　　　　　　'Will I fail or will a miracle happen?'
Q PARTICLE　I'll-fail or *shema* will-happen miracle?

35.12 'Either...or...': ...(ש) או ...(ש) או *o (she)...o (she)...*

'Either...or' (i.e. exclusive 'or') can be expressed (1) by putting או *o* in front of the first coordinate too (or indeed every coordinate),[23] or (2) by putting - ש או *o she-* where this coordinate is a clause. Where - ש או *o she-* is used, it is used with both clauses:

(1)　ashamesh o ke-rav o ke-Hazan o ke-more　אשמש או כרב או כחזן או כמורה
　　　　　　　I-shall-serve **either** as rabbi **or** as cantor **or** as teacher

(2)　o she-ata potéaH o she-ani　　　　　　　או שאתה פותח או שאני
　　kofets déreH ha-Halon!　　　　　　　　קופץ דרך החלון!
　　or that [= either] you open **or** [that]
　　I jump through the window

35.13   Illocutionary 'or'

Like -ו *ve-* (35.5), או *o* is sometimes 'illocutionary', but with the special meaning of 'or putting it another way':[24]

ha-rashlanut **o** (naHon yoter)	הרשלנות **או** (נכון יותר)
ha-i-hitHashvut ba-zulat...	האי-התחשבות בזולת...

'Negligence **or** (more correctly) non-consideration of others...'

ve-ézo efsharut tiye ekvivaléntit? **o** :	ואיזו אפשרות תהיה אקוויוולנטית? **או**:
mahu ha-késher beyn shney ha-dvarim?	מהו הקשר בין שני הדברים?

'And which possibility will be equivalent? **Or** :
what is the link between the two things'

35.14   Various types of 'but'

The following coordinators signify 'but': אבל *aval*, אך *aH*, (ו)אולם (*ve-*)*ulam*, (ש-) אלא *éla* (*she-*), ואילו *ve'ilu*, i.e. they serve to cancel an expectation (be it the other speaker's or a matter of convention etc.). However, there are five kinds of 'but' (detailed in (a)-(e) below), and these words are not always interchangeable.

(a) 'Nevertheless' (i.e. contrary to objective expectations of cause and effect): אבל *aval* and אך *aH* (F) link anything from whole paragraphs down to phrases;[25] אולם *ulam* does not link phrases (for phrasal 'but' see further 35.15):

Linking two sentences:	
maHaneH hu tóar amum. ulam ánu	מחנך הוא תואר עמום. אולם אנו
maaminim be-yeshut zo	מאמינים בישות זו

'Educator is a vague title. But we believe in this entity'

Linking two main clauses:	
hu Hole me'od aval hu lo mitlonen	הוא חולה מאד אבל הוא לא מתלונן

'He's very sick but he doesn't complain'

Linking two phrases:	
harbe Hilonim, aH lo kulam,	הרבה חילונים, אך לא כולם,
yaHHíshu zot	יכחישו זאת

'Many secularists, but not all, will deny this'

(b) 'Except that...' (i.e. speaker departs from what s/he expected, or is expected, to say): אבל *aval*, (ש-) אלא *éla* (*she*),[26] אך *aH* F), אולם *ulam* (F).[27] They link paragraphs, sentences and clauses:

Linking two paragraphs:	
etmol hu azav - éla (she-)ani makdim	אתמול הוא עזב - אלא (ש)אני מקדים
et ha-meuHar, ve-alénu lashuv	את המאוחר, ועלינו לשוב
la-shavúa ha-kodem	לשבוע הקודם

'Yesterday he quit - but I am getting things in the wrong order and
we must return to the previous week'

Linking two clauses:
ze yafe me'od, éla (she-)yesh
le-ze mínus gadol:...   זה יפה מאד, אלא (ש)יש
                                        לזה מינוס גדול:...

'It's very nice, except that it has a big drawback:...'

(c) 'By contrast, whereas' (i.e. contrary to expectation of similarity): אבל *aval*,
אך *aH* (F) and ואילו *ve'ilu* (F).[28] They link sentences or clauses. After ואילו
ve'ilu the contrasting word is usually brought forward:

hi gvoha aval ani namuH   היא גבוהה אבל אני נמוך
                                        'She's tall but I'm short'

hu menagen hetev ve'ilu lashir hu lo yodéa   הוא מנגן היטב ואילו לשיר הוא לא יודע
he plays well but to-sing he doesn't know
[= he doesn't know how to sing]

(d) 'I object' (i.e. denying a statement or its assumptions): אבל *aval*. This can
link two speakers:

tosif mélaH - aval ze kvar malúaH!   תוסיף מלח - אבל זה כבר מלוח!
                                        'Add some salt - But it's already salty!'

(e) 'Anyway' (i.e. dismissing the assumption that one is continuing with the
same topic): אבל *aval*, between speakers, paragraphs, sentences:

nora yafe ba-Huts... aval ma amart   נורא יפה בחוץ... אבל מה אמרת
legabey tinokot?   לגבי תינוקות?
        'It's really beautiful outside... but what were you saying about babies?'

35.15 'But' in general

'But' words link statements or commands (אבל *aval* meaning 'anyway', above, even introduces questions):

shev aval al tishan   שב אבל אל תישן
                                        'Sit down but don't sleep'

Repeated material is avoided, as with ו- *ve-* 'and', או *o* 'or'.
    'But' words do not ordinarily link noun phrases (as against clauses) except to
convey 'x but not y', i.e. a preposed contrastive לא *lo* 'not':[29]

dúdu aval lo áharon lovesh jins   דודו אבל לא אהרן לובש ג'ינס
m.s.
Dudu but not Aaron wears jeans

dúdu lovesh jins aval lo áharon   דודו לובש ג'ינס אבל לא אהרן
Dudu wears jeans but not Aaron

The 'but' word can be omitted in such cases (meaning 'whereas', i.e. contrast):

dúdu, lo áharon, amar et ze   דודו, לא אהרן, אמר את זה
'Dudu, not Aaron, said that'

An alternative is the more general 'reduced' clause with hanging לא *lo*/ כן *ken* (not limited to coordinations). Gapping too is possible (cf. 35.2):

dúdu lovesh jins aval áharon lo	דודו לובש ג'ינס אבל אהרן לא
Dudu wears jeans but Aaron not [= doesn't]	

hem nas'u le-shilo aval anáHnu - le-Hevron	הם נסעו לשילה אבל אנחנו - לחברון
they went to Shilo but we - to Hevron	

A series of 'buts' may be possible, especially of different types. As 'but' operates at various levels in sentences, 'stacking' is possible too:

dror hu neHmad aval atsbani, aval gádi	דרור הוא נחמד אבל עצבני, אבל גדי
neHmad mi-kol ha-bHinot	נחמד מכל הבחינות

         'Dror is nice but irritable, but Gadi's nice in all respects'

Punctuation: a full-stop, a comma or no punctuation is possible before the 'but' word.

35.16   'But instead': אלא *éla,* כי אם *ki im*

אלא *éla* and its synonym כי אם *ki im* (F) introduce positive information (or a command or question) to follow on the heels of negative information etc.[30] Like most other coordinators, they link words, phrases or whole clauses - repetition being avoided usually.[31] Agreement is determined by the positive phrase, so here it is feminine singular:

lo ha-kruv ki im ha-Hasida mevi'a otam   לא הכרוב כי אם החסידה מביאה אותם
     m.s.   f.s.   f.s.
  NEG. PHR   POSITIVE PHR
         'Not the cherub but rather the stork brings them'

                     הוא לא מוכר עגלות אלא רק מתקן אותן?
hu lo moHer agalot éla rak metaken otan?
  NEG PHR   POSITIVE PHR
         'He doesn't sell prams but only mends them?'

                   אין לימודים היום אלא כולם נוסעים לים
en limudim ha-yom éla kulam nos'im la-yam
  NEG CLAUSE   POSITIVE CLAUSE
     'There are no lessons today but rather everyone's going to the sea'

There are two other uses of אלא *éla*, neither of them coordinations; both are akin to אלא (ש-) *éla (she-)* 'except that' (see 35.14). Firstly, ...לא ...אלא *lo... éla...* 'only' (F) (cf. English 'nothing but...'):

lo hevéti **éla** perot	לא הבאתי אלא פרות

         '**I only** brought fruit' (i.e. 'I didn't bring anything but fruit')

This אלא *éla* does not link two parallel phrases like אלא *éla* above; also, it cannot follow אין, לא *lo, en* 'not' directly and thus will not introduce a finite verb:

*hu lo éla tsoHek   *הוא לא אלא צוחק
                                                   ('He only laughs')

Secondly, we find כן-אם-אלא *éla-im-ken*, and (less usual form) אם אלא *éla im* 'unless' (cf. English 'except if'):

avo lishmóa éla im (ken) yered géshem   אבוא לשמוע אלא אם (כן) ירד גשם
                                          'I'll come to listen unless it rains'

These expressions introduce conditional clauses. The preceding clause need not be negative (unlike the 'but instead' constructions above).

FURTHER READING
Azar 1977, 1981; Chayen & Dror 1976; Dascal & Katriel 1977; Ring 1975; Sadka 1981: ch.17; Schwarzwald 1979a.

36. Apposition

36.1 Introduction

Apposition means placing two (sometimes more) words or groups of words side by side (1) usually without such visible links as - ו ve- 'and'[1] or 'possessive' suffixes, sometimes with a comma/pause and sometimes without; and (2) usually signifying either that (a) two phrases are 'referring' to the same thing (i.e. 'co-referent' in that context) or that (b) one of them includes the other. Examples are:

metúla, kfar bi-gvul levanon   מטולה, כפר בגבול לבנון
'Metulla, a village on the Lebanese border'

maHshirim kegon makdeHot   מכשירים כגון מקדחות
'tools such as drills'

Apposition is one type of 'modification': one word or phrase is being optionally added to another, and the two are not equal in function - one (usually the second) being modifier and the other being nucleus. The nucleus determines agreement:

יישוב זה, מושבה קטנה של בני-תימן, עומד על פרשת הדרכים
yishuv ze,   moshava ktana shel bney teyman, omed al parashat ha-draHim
NUCLEUS(m.s.) MODIFIER(f.s.)   v(m.s.)
'This settlement, a small village of Yemenites, stands on the crossroads'

Apposition usually involves noun phrases or clauses, or a combination, occasionally adverbials (36.9) and other phrases (36.6-7) and even pairs of single nouns, verbs etc. (36.13):

חובשים בכל עת כיפה, מנהג שהפך עכשיו לדין
Hovshim be-Hol et kipa, minhag she-hafaH aHshav le-din
     CLAUSE   N PHR IN APPOSITION
'They wear a skullcap at all times,
a custom that has now become a law'

etmol   be-shesh   אתמול בשש
ADVERBIAL ADVERBIAL   'yesterday at six'

mitpáHat kHula-aduma   מטפחת כחולה-אדומה
      ADJ   ADJ
headscarf blue-red   'a blue and red headscarf'

As so often, the syntactic and semantic definitions above do not coincide exactly: (1) a link adverb is sometimes possible or necessary, e.g. בייחוד *beyiHud* 'especially'; (2) the side-by-side construction can also signify 'measurement', e.g. שני מטר סרט *shney méter séret* 'two metres (of) ribbon'.

Furthermore, apposition is not the *only* construction to express 'co-reference' or 'inclusion': 'naming' often involves the construct or של *shel* 'of', e.g. מדינת אורגון *medinat óregon* 'the State of Oregon', and some appositional link adverbs often come with a ו- *ve-* 'and', notably ובפרט *u-vifrat* 'and specifically', ובעיקר *u-ve'ikar* 'and especially'. Conversely, 'coordinative apposition' such as שחקן-מאמן *saHkan-meamen* 'player-coach', where ו- *ve-* 'and' might indeed have been expected, uses the apposition so as to signify a *blend* of properties or persons (as against, e.g., a separate 'player' and 'coach')[2]

36.2-3   PREDICATIVE APPOSITION

Predicative apposition says of a noun or clause that it is such-and-such, i.e. it adds what amounts to a predicate:

| leH le-seadya ha-nagar | לך לסעדיה הנגר |
| APPOSITION | |

    'Go to Seadya the carpenter' [= '...who is the carpenter']

There are two types (with several major limitations): apposition of identity and descriptive apposition.

36.2   Apposition of identity

Apposition of identity adds a definite noun to another noun, supplying a specific identity or reinforcing one:

sha'ul, ha-méleH ha-rishon	שאול, המלך הראשון
APPOSITION	
	'Saul, the first king'

kashish im migbáat, nesi ha-Hevra	קשיש עם מגבעת, נשיא החברה
APPOSITION	
	'an old man in a hat, the company president'

yatsáti gam im máya, ha-mora[3]	יצאתי גם עם מאיה, המורה
APPOSITION	
	'I also went out with Maya, the teacher'

A comma or pause is necessary, except for (1) name plus occupation[4] and (2) contrastive ('restrictive') apposition:

(1)   moshe(,) ha-Hazan   'Moshe(,) the cantor'   משה(,) החזן

(2)   Huseyn ha-*méleH*   '*King* Hussein'   חוסיין המלך

36.3   Descriptive apposition

Descriptive ('attributive') apposition is of two kinds, described in 36.3.1-2.

36.3.1 Two-phrase apposition

Two-phrase apposition adds an indefinite noun phrase, of quite some length and mostly in formal usage:[5]

asher lánu, martsim tseirim bli kvi'ut...   ...אשר לנו, מרצים צעירים בלי קביעות
'As for us, young lecturers without tenure...'

sham nat'u shita, ets midbari she...   ...שם נטעו שיטה, עץ מדברי ש
'There they planted an acacia, a desert tree which...'

hu ba im ishto, yif'at,   הוא בא עם אשתו, יפעת,
studéntit le-mishpatim   סטודנטית למשפטים
'He came with his wife, Yifat, a law student'

To add to a very short phrase, one generally uses a separate clause (but compare 36.3.2):

hu ba im ishto, yif'at, she-hi studéntit   הוא בא עם אשתו, יפעת, שהיא סטודנטית
'He came with his wife, Yifat, who's a student'

hu ba im ishto, yif'at. hi studéntit   הוא בא עם אשתו, יפעת. היא סטודנטית
'He came with his wife, Yifat. She's a student'

A *definite* noun phrase is used (although semantically this is really indefinite, like the preceding examples) in cases such as:

im zélda ha-meshoréret   עם זלדה המשוררת
'with Zelda the poetess'

blums, ha-misada ha-yehudit   בלומס, המסעדה היהודית
'Bloom's, the Jewish restaurant'

where 'the well-known (rather than the one and only!) poetess/Jewish restaurant' is meant. Reverse order is more common, e.g. עם המשוררת זלדה *im ha-meshoréret zélda* 'with the poetess Zelda' (see 36.5), except where contrastive: מנדלסון הפילוסוף *méndelson ha-filosof* 'Mendelssohn the *philosopher*'.

36.3.2 One-phrase apposition

One-phrase apposition adds one phrase to another without comma or pause, typically specifying occupation or status, as in (1,2) below, or adding an 'agent noun+object' (3) - as described further in 6.20, 10.9 and 15.8:

(1) yesh li Haver tov **oreH-din**   יש לי חבר טוב **עורך-דין**
I have friend good **lawyer**   'I have a good lawyer friend'

(2) éyfo ha-talmida **akéret-ha-báyit** she...   ...איפה התלמידה **עקרת-הבית** ש
'Where is the **housewife** student who...'

(3) shlosha asirim **dovrey-ivrit**   שלושה אסירים **דוברי-עברית**
CONSTRUCT
three prisoners **speakers Hebrew**   'three **Hebrew-speaking** prisoners'

A few such noun phrases are construct, e.g. תושב *toshav* 'inhabitant (of)', תוצרת *totséret* 'product (of)', בן/בת *ben/bat* 'aged'[6] (but see 36.12):

kol ha-Hayalim **toshavey** ha-kibutsim
hibíu hitnagdut
    'All the soldiers **resident in** kibbutzim expressed opposition'

כל החיילים **תושבי** הקיבוצים
הביעו התנגדות

teror totséret-báyit
    'home-grown terror'

טרור תוצרת-בית

kol ha-yeladim **bney** ha-Hamesh
mekablim zrika
    'All the children **aged** five (*lit.* consisters-of the five) get an injection'

כל הילדים **בני** החמש
מקבלים זריקה

36.4-9 SPECIFICATIONAL APPOSITION

Specificational apposition is rather like predicative apposition (36.2-3) in reverse - and with a shift in emphasis. Instead of 'someone named x is the y' or '...is a y', it serves to *specify*: 'the y, namely x', or 'a y, namely x'.

    There are various types. Apposition of naming and titles (36.4-5) is one-phrase apposition, with no comma or pause: in הרב פיינשטיין *ha-rav fáynshtayn* 'Rabbi Feinstein', הרב *ha-rav* is not an independent specific entity. Conversely, apposition of detail etc. (36.6-9) is two-phrase apposition, even requiring all prepositions to be repeated.[7]

36.4 Apposition of naming: המלה 'ליכוד' *ha-mila likud* 'the word Likud'

Most naming uses the construct, not apposition (see 6.14): חודש מאי *Hódesh may* 'the month of May', שנת אלף *shnat élef* 'the year 1000', אוניברסיטת קהיר *univérsitat kahir* 'Cairo University', מסעדת פאגודה *misadat pagóda* 'the Pagoda Restaurant', מדבר סהרה *midbar sahára* 'the Sahara desert', הר מרון *har meron* 'Mt Meron'.

But with names of books, pictures and all manner of 'artificial entities', and for referring to words themselves, one uses apposition: המחזה 'מקבת' *ha-maHaze makbet* 'the play Macbeth', התרכיב 'אקאמול' *ha-tarkiv akamol* 'the preparation Akamol', הצוללת 'דקר' *ha-tsolélet dakar* 'the submarine Dakar', המונח 'תוכנה' *ha-munaH toHna* 'the term 'toHna''.

Similarly, apposition is used for names of persons: הפילוסוף מנדלסון *ha-filosof méndelson* 'the philosopher Mendelssohn'; also for עיר *ir* 'city' and sometimes even אי *i* 'island', נחל *náHal* 'wadi'.

    In naming, the name is usually second, taking the stress. There is no comma, The first noun or phrase (the 'nucleus') is definite, in anticipation of being specified - yet occasionally definite *without* -ה *ha-* 'the', i.e. when the naming (or more precisely, the identification) is by number:[8]

Hipásti et dugma shesh   'I was looking for example six'   חיפשתי את דוגמה 6
            (= example number 6)

...et shura yud-gímel   '...row 13'   ...את שורה יג

...et dira esrim   '...apartment 20'   ...את דירה 20

Moreover, in the plural, -ה *ha-* 'the' must appear in all these cases; indeed, the construct too is replaced by apposition with *ha-* (last example below):[9]

ha-dugma'ot Hamesh ve-shesh   הדוגמאות 5 ו-6
'examples five and six'

ha-profesórim rabin ve-morag   הפרופסורים רבין ומורג
'Professors Rabin and Morag'

bemésheH ha-shanim 1982 ve-1983   במשך השנים 1982 ו-1983
'during the years 1982 and 1983'

36.5 Apposition of titles: הרב פיינשטיין *ha-rav fáynshtayn* 'Rabbi Feinstein'

Titles are always in apposition. They *precede* the name,[10] with no comma, and are usually definite[11] (as with descriptive nouns like המחזה 'מקבת' *ha-maHaze makbet* 'the play Macbeth', 36.4); they often occur in direct address ('vocatively'):

ha-shofet Háyim kats	'Judge Hayim Katz'	השופט חיים כ"ץ
ha-aluf david elazar	'Brigadier David Elazar'	האלוף דוד אלעזר
ha-gvéret tátsher	'Mrs Thatcher'	הגברת תאצ'ר
Haver ha-knéset ába éven	'MP Abba Eban'	חבר-הכנסת אבא אבן

For titles with no -ה *ha-* 'the', e.g. סרן משה *séren moshe* 'Captain Moshe' see 5.3.1.

36.6 Apposition of detailing: כלומר... *kelomar...* 'i.e...'

A list of details is often introduced by a colon, or a comma plus 'link adverb' (notably היינו *háynu* 'namely' (F)):

bo musbarim ha-Hagim: pésaH, shavu'ot,   בו מוסברים החגים: פסח, שבועות,
rosh ha-shana, yom kipur, ve-sukot   ראש השנה, יום כיפור, וסוכות
'In it are explained the festivals: Pesach, Shavuot, Rosh Hashana,
    Yom Kipur and Sukot'

A *single* phrase of specification or paraphrase is introduced by a colon or comma, or a comma plus such diverse link adverbs as כלומר *kelomar* 'i.e.', זאת אומרת *zot oméret* 'that is to say', או *o* 'or', (הלא) הוא *(halo) hu* 'none other than' (literary):[12]

hu hitsbía al ma she-gilíti,   הוא הצביע על מה שגיליתי,
   al ha-yáHas beyn ha-enzímim   על היחס בין האנזימים
        'He referred to what I had discovered, to the relation
                 between the enzymes'

az haya aviv shel máyer, halo hu   אז היה אביו של מייר, הלא הוא
   reb dóvid, agent shel ha-turkim   רב דוד, אגנט של התורכים
        'Then Mayer's father, none other than Reb Dovid,
                 was an agent of the Turks'

Clause apposition

For apposition of partial or full details to the foregoing clause, formal usage can allow a 'gapped' clause (i.e. with verb omitted) introduced by a comma:[13]

כל הצופים קיבלו ציוד, הגדולים מכשירי קשר והקטנים כלי בישול

kol ha-tsofim kiblu tsiyud, ha-gdolim maHshirey késher
<u>GAPPED CLAUSE</u>

ve-ha-ktanim kley bishul
GAPPED CLAUSE

'All the scouts received equipment, the older ones walkie-talkies and the younger ones cooking utensils'

The apposed gapped clause can have מהם *mehem* 'of them' (= כמה מהם *káma mehem* 'some of them') as its subject (see also 8.6.2):

alfey bney-nóar she-shahu etslénu zman rav,   אלפי בני-נוער ששהו אצלנו זמן רב,
mehem afilu shanim, hem reaya she...   **מהם** אפילו שנים, הם ראיה ש...

'Thousands of young people who have stayed with us a long while, some of them (*lit.* **of them**) even years, are evidence that...'

But מהם *mehem* 'of them' in apposition, or ביניהם *beynehem*, can also introduce a phrase (in the same way as the preposition כולל *kolel* 'including'):

eshtakad nirshemu matáyim Hiburim,   אשתקד נרשמו מאתיים חיבורים,
mehem shloshim be-anglit   **מהם** שלושים באנגלית
last-year were-registered 200 theses, **of-them** [= including] 30 in English

36.7   Apposition of selection: בעיקר *be-ikar* 'particularly'

'Such as' can be expressed (1) by a colon, parenthesis or suchlike, introducing a list ending in open-ended dots or their equivalent, or (2) by the prepositions כגון *kegon*, כמו *kmo*, -כ *ke-* (F) introducing a noun, or by a link adverb such as למשל *lemashal* 'e.g.' introducing even adverbs or clauses:

ba-medinot ha-metunot,   ke-saudíya u-levanon   כסעודיה ולבנון   במדינות המתונות,
     lemashal be-saudíya   למשל בסעודיה
     ADVERBIAL

'in the moderate states,   like Saudi Arabia and Lebanon'
     e.g. in Saudi Arabia

'Particularly' is expressed by a link adverb such as בייחוד *be-yiHud*, בעיקר *be-ikar*:

ha-shipurim be-shivuk, be-ikar be-pirsómet   השיפורים בשיווק, בעיקר בפרסומת
'the improvements in marketing, especially in advertising'

Addition and exclusion are expressed by focus adverbs such as אפילו *afílu* 'even', גם *gam* 'even', ובין ... בין *beyn...u-veyn* 'both...and...', לא *lo* 'not'. These often introduce an apposed clause:[14]

le-Hol Haveray, afílu le-yóna   לכל חברי, אפילו ליונה
'for all my friends, even for Yona'

kavanati le-baH, lo le-mótsart   כוונתי לבאך, לא למוצארט
                                        'I refer to Bach, not to Mozart'

igudey británya, ha-smolaniyim ve-af   איגודי בריטניה, השמאלניים ואף
   ha-yemaniyim,...   הימניים,...
                'The British unions, the leftist and even the rightist ones,...'

kam ha-katsin ve-azav et ha-emda,   קם הקצין ועזב את העמדה,
   hu u-fkudav   הוא ופקודיו
            'The officer arose and quit the position and so did his men
                                                  (*lit.* he and his men)'

36.8 Partitive apposition
Several 'partitive' words, denoting 'all of them/it etc.', 'each of...',
'some...others...', 'the one...the other...' and the like, can be added in apposition
to the subject or the object:

ha-miflaga **kula** nidhama   המפלגה **כולה** נדהמה
the party **all-it** was-aghast   'The whole party was aghast'

ze **ha-kol** birburim   זה **הכל** ברבורים
it **the-lot** nonsense (c)   'It's all nonsense'

atem **shneyHem** meshuga'im   אתם **שניכם** משוגעים
you **both-you** crazy   'You're both crazy'

móti ve-yáron hitsiu **kol eHad** et pitrono   מוטי וירון הציעו **כל אחד** את פתרונו
Moti and Yaron suggested **each one**
   ᴏᴍ his-solution
                      'Moti and Yaron each suggested his solution'

natáti et ha-tmunot **Helkan** le-aHi   נתתי את התמונות **חלקן** לאחי
I-gave ᴏᴍ the pictures **part-of-them** to my-brother   **וחלקן** לאמי
   ve-**Helkan** le-imi
   and **part-of-them** to my-mother
             'I gave some of the pictures to my brother and some to my mother'

ha-arpadim yashvu **éle** mi-smol ve-**éle**   הערפדים ישבו **אלה** משמאל ואלה
the vampires sat **these** on left and **these**   מימין
   mi-yamin
   on right
             'Some of the vampires sat on the left and some on the right'

The last three examples have 'distributive' partitives (i.e. sharing something out
'respectively'); these must *follow* the verb, as close as possible to the 'distribu-
tee'.

36.9 Apposition of time/place adverbials: אתמול בשש *etmol be-shesh* 'yesterday at six'

Time adverbials can be strung together in multiple apposition, each narrowing down ('specifying') the one before. Commas are sometimes used.

ba-shavúa ha-ba, be-yom sheni, be-sha'a shesh   בשבוע הבא, ביום שני, בשעה שש
       SPECIFYING   SPECIFYING
                            'next week, on Monday, at six o'clock'

Parts of the day, e.g. בבוקר *ba-bóker* 'in the morning', אחה"צ *aHarey ha-tsohoráyim* 'p.m.', come last even if they thereby 'broaden' rather than 'narrow down'. See (2) below (this is called 'predicative order'):

(1) maHar ba-bóker   מחר בבוקר
       SPECIFYING
      tomorrow in-the morning   'tomorrow morning'

(2) be-shesh ba-bóker   בשש בבוקר
       PREDICATIVE
      at six in-the morning

Predicative order is also possible with broader time adverbials, relating to weeks, years etc:

be-yom sheni ba-shavúa ha-ba   ביום שני בשבוע הבא
on Monday in-the week the next   'on Monday next week'

Adverbials of place too allow both orders. 'Narrowing' order requires commas:[15]

gárti bi-bnéy-brak, be-shikun he,   ,גרתי בבני-ברק, בשיכון ה
  bi-reHov tsirelson   ברחוב צירלסון
                I lived in Bney-Brak, in Estate 5, on Tsirelson St'

In 'predicative order', formal Hebrew often inserts a relative conjunction -ש *she-* (see further 11.4); casual Hebrew tends not to:

gárti be-shikun he **she**-bi-bnéy-brak   גרתי בשיכון ה' שבבני-ברק
I-lived in Estate 5 **which** [is] in Bney-Brak

ze haya ba-kiyor ba-ambátya   זה היה בכיור באמבטיה
it was in-the sink in-the bathroom

36.10 Quantity apposition: שני מטר סרט *shney méter séret* 'two metres of ribbon'

Apposition, or the construct genitive, or של *shel* 'of' are used variously in expressing amount and measurement (see also chs 6 and 8).

Measurement by units and containers
של *shel* 'of' is common, but can equally well be omitted:

shney kilo (shel) agasim	'two kilos of pears'	שני קילו (של) אגסים
kapit (shel) sukar	'a spoon of sugar'	כפית (של) סוכר
esrim shana maasar	'20 years' imprisonment'	עשרים שנה מאסר

There is no obvious difference, for most units (being foreignisms and in the singular), between construct and apposition.[16] As for agreement by the verb, it is usually the measurement phrase that determines it:

yardu shney méter shéleg   ירדו שני מטר שלג
v(pl.) MEASUREMENTN(s.)
fell two metre snow   'Two metres of snow fell'

Abstract amount

Abstract amount involves apposition or construct, rather than של *shel* 'of'.[17] Notice that in apposition the agreement depends not on the first phrase of the apposition but on the second;[18] the second is the nucleus:

lo **yiye** laH mi-ze pruta aHat **révaH**   לא **יהיה** לך מזה פרוטה אחת **רווח**
m.s.   f.s.   m.s.
         'You won't **have** from this one penny (*lit.* penny one) **profit**'

haya shalosh shanim hefresh   היה שלוש שנים הפרש
m.s.   f.pl.   m.s.
there-was three years difference

hayta esrim aHuz hishtatfut   היתה עשרים אחוז השתתפות
f.s.   m.pl.   f.s.
there-was 20% participation

36.11   Tagged apposition

Specificational apposition of two distinct phrases (36.6-9) often 'tags' the second phrase to the end of the clause (as long as it is the focus of the clause and no other focus intervenes):

tsayar mefursam haya itam sham, **zaritski**   צייר מפורסם היה אתם שם , **זריצקי**
         'A famous painter was with them there, **Zaritski**'

kulam néged, **afilu sharon**   כולם נגד, **אפילו שרון**
         'All of them are against it, **even Sharon**'

A different sort of 'tagging', of any type of phrase, is obligatory in '*wh-*' questions:

mi amar zot, péres o shamir?   מי אמר זאת, פרס או שמיר?
         'Who said it, Peres or Shamir?'

not:

*mi, péres or shamir, amar zot?   *מי, פרס או שמיר, אמר זאת?

36.12 Pseudo-apposition

In casual usage the noun phrases involving construct תושב *toshav* 'inhabitant' and בן/בת *ben/bat* 'aged',[19] and possibly some others, can (but need not) omit the -ה *ha-* characteristic of 'definite apposition' (as described in 36.3.2). Standing thus between two nouns, these 'nouns' seem to be akin to *prepositions*, as indicated in the translations below:[20]

כל הסטודנטים **תושבי** (ה)קיבוצים הם כאלה

kol ha-studéntim **toshavey** (ha-)kibutsim hem ka'éle

> CONSTRUCT
> APPOSED PHR

all the students **inhabitants** (the) kibbutzim are like-that

'All the students inhabiting [= of] kibbutzim are like that'

ze le-kol ha-banim **bney** (ha-)shesh   זה לכל הבנים **בני** (ה)שש

it's for all the boys **aged** (the) six   'It's for all boys of six'

kvar maHru et kol ha-dirot   כבר מכרו את כל הדירות

bnot shney (ha-)Hadarim   **בנות** שני (ה)חדרים

> CONSTRUCT
> APPOSED PHR

already they-sold OM all the apartments **consisting-of** two (the) rooms[21]

'They've already sold all the apartments of two rooms'

36.13 Coordinative apposition

Hebrew makes much use of a construction midway between a coordination, an apposition and a compound: a compound phrase.

hà-saHkan-bamay-mefik   'the actor-director-producer'   השחקן-במאי-מפיק

There are three main features: (1) It joins words of the same grammatical type (like coordination), but (2) with no link word, just as in apposition; instead it uses a hyphen. (3) Only one -ה *ha-* 'the' is allowed, in both noun and adjective phrases (rather as in compounds, e.g. הרמזור *ha-ramzor* 'the traffic light', see 38.4); and yet any plural, feminine or possessive suffixes present must be placed on each word in the phrase, even on verbs. Rather as with the prefix -ה *ha-* 'the', only one infinitive prefix -ל *le-* 'to' per verbal phrase is allowed; but as *le-* is inseparable from the verb, the very possibility of an infinitive in coordinative apposition is ruled out.

In sum, this construction is akin to such semi-compounds as construct בן-אדם ~ הבני-אדם *ben-adam* ~ *ha-bney-adam* 'person ~ the persons' (38.4).

Nouns in coordinative apposition

These are semi-freely formed in literary/journalistic use, but in general use only in set expressions.[22] Examples are:

ha-tsayéret-zaméret bráHa tsfira   הציירת-זמרת ברכה צפירה
                                            'the painter-singer Bracha Tsfira'

shliHehem-soHnehem radfu aHarav   שליחיהם-סוכניהם רדפו אחריו
messengers-their agents-their pursued him
                                            'Their messenger-agents pursued him'

hu aviha-molida shel ha-toHnit   הוא אביה-מולידה של התוכנית
he father-its begetter-its of the plan   'He is the father-begetter of the plan'

Adjectives

There are two common and freely formed uses: (1) colour combinations, e.g. כחול-לבן *kaHol-lavan* 'blue and white' (not 'blue-white'), and (2) combinations of adjectives (usually noun-based) taking an *-i* suffix, in technical/jounalistic usage:

(1) baaya polítit-kalkalit   בעיה פוליטית-כלכלית
     f.s.   f.s.   f.s.
     problem political-economic   'a politico-economic problem'

(2) ha-siHot ha-siniyot-rusiyot   השיחות הסיניות-רוסיות
     f.pl.   f.pl.   f.pl.
     the talks the Chinese-Russian   'the Sino-Soviet talks'

Though פוליטית וכלכלית *polítit ve-kalkalit* 'political and economic' would have meant the same, the hyphenated construction will often make it plain that the two adjectives are the property of *one* person/thing.[23]

Verbs

There are few common combinations, e.g. אץ-רץ *ats-rats* 'rush-dash'. Literary/journalistic usage is somewhat freer:

ma yetse mi-ze, **kovel-mitmarmer** mar natan,   מה יצא מזה, **קובל-מתמרמר** מר נתן,
nehag monit ben shishim   נהג מונית בן-ששים
               lit. 'What will come of this, **complains-grumbles** Mr. Natan,
                              a 60-year-old cab driver'

Intensification apposition

Adjectives, adverbs and degree words can be reinforced, where appropriate, by repetition, often with a hyphen, in all usage:

Haver tov-tov   חבר טוב-טוב
                                            'a really good (*lit.* good-good) friend'

sanen dak-dak

סנן דק-דק
'Filter very finely (*lit.* fine-fine)'

bedok hetev-hetev

בדוק היטב-היטב
'Check really well (well-well)'

tsariH me'od-me'od le...

צריך מאד מאד ל...
'⟨It's⟩ very very necessary to...'

FURTHER READING
Dahan 1981; Glinert 1978; Ornan 1979a: 4.10; Sadka 1981: ch.14.

37. Topic, focus and word order

37.1 Introduction

This chapter presents two phenomena: prominence, and order of sentence components.

(1) *Prominence of information.* Information can be 'known', e.g. השמן *ha-shémen* 'the oil' has a known identity and may, as such, be given the special prominence of being grammatical *topic* of the sentence:

ha-shémen, hu yashan?	השמן, הוא ישן?
TOPIC	'**The oil**, is it old?'

or it can be 'new' information, which is often given the prominence of being grammatical *focus* of the sentence, as in:

gam **ha-shémen** yakar	גם השמן יקר
FOCUS	'Even **the oil's** expensive'

(2) *Order* of the main sentence components, i.e. subject, verb/adjective, object, predicate noun phrase, adverbials.

Information lay-out is not always conveyed by word order, nor *vice versa*. For example. *stress* can create focus:

ha-*shemen* hityaker	'*Oil's* gone up'	השמן התייקר

and subject-verb inversion can convey *eloquence*:

zoHer ani et yom moto	'I remember his dying day'	זוכר אני את יום מותו

However, information and order have enough in common to be presented in one chapter.

Basic word order

Basic order in all registers is:

Subject + Verb/Adjective + Object
Subject + Predicate Noun Phrase

Most adverbials (if any) precede or follow the object (if any) - see further chapters 21, 22, 24.

37.2-5 THE 'TOPIC'

37.2 Types of topic

A clause often contains some item(s) of information known to speaker and hearer, i.e. something 'known' (37.1). One such item is likely to be marked as the *topic of discussion*. This will be called the 'topic' and the rest of the clause the 'comment', as in:

> My dog ate four bagels
> TOPIC   COMMENT

> the four bagels - my dog ate them
> TOPIC   COMMENT

Definition. The 'topic' of a clause is a word(s) marked out grammatically as topic of discussion.

The 'topic' is most often a *definite noun or pronoun*. (Their identity is 'known' to speaker and hearer).

> **hu** lo marshe li   'He isn't letting me'   הוא לא מרשה לי

> káma olim **ha-Hatsilim**? 'How much are **the egg-plants**?' כמה עולים החצילים?

Even where there is more than one definite noun, just one will be marked as topic. In the following example[1] the topic is the first noun, מר רבין *mar rabin* 'Mr Rabin', uncharacteristically brought forward from normal object position to imply that Mr Rabin is none other than the 'Defence Minister' under discussion; הרמטכ"ל *ha-ramatkal* 'the Chief of Staff', though a known entity, is here part of the 'comment':

> sar ha-bitaHon he-Hadash sakar ha-yom   שר הבטחון החדש סקר היום
> mishmar tsáhal.   משמר צה"ל.
> et mar rabin liva ha-ramatkal   את מר רבין ליווה הרמטכ"ל
> 'The new Defence Minister today inspected an army guard.
> Mr Rabin was accompanied by (*lit.* OM Mr Rabin accompanied)
>   the Chief of Staff'

An *indefinite noun* can be topic, as can a verb, an adverb etc.:

> tish'al shoter - lo,   תשאל שוטר! - לא,
> **shoter eHad** atsar oti ha-yom ve...   שוטר אחד עצר אותי היום ו...
> 'Ask a policeman! - No, **some policeman** stopped me today and...'

> bói lirkod! - **lirkod** ani lo rotsa   בואי לרקוד! - לרקוד אני לא רוצה
> 'Come and dance! - I don't want **to dance**'

> bói be-shesh! - **be-shesh** yesh li tor   בואי בשש! - בשש יש לי תור
> 'Come at six! - At six I have an appointment'

Things being *enumerated, compared* or *contrasted* are paradoxically also frequently the topic - for they must have something in common to be thus compared, e.g. (ˆ indicates rise-fall intonation):

ugiyôt ani ohev, **krâkerim** ani ohev, עוגיׁות אני אוהב, **קׁרקרים** אני אוהב,
vâflim ani lo ohev   **ופלים** אני לא אוהב

'**Cookies** I like, **crackers** I like, **wafers** I don't like'

How is the topic marked?

Hebrew tends to put 'topic' first. This is usually as subject,[2] and so subject topic has no special stress - one's assumption is that the subject is the topic:

éfo ha-tsalaHot? - **ha-tsalaHot** sháma   איפה הצלחות? - **הצלחות** שמה
ba-kiyor!   בכיור!
          TOPIC

'Where are the plates? - **The plates** are there in the sink!'

However, object, verb or adverbial can be 'topicalized' - mostly by coming to the front of the clause, and notably by *topic preposing* or by *topic dislocation* ("ייחוד"), described in 37.3-5 below. As a result, the subject becomes down-graded in topicality.

37.3 Topic preposing

In all usage, objects or adverbials can be 'topic-preposed' to the front of the clause.[3] Casual Hebrew commonly marks such a preposed object by rise-fall intonation (symbol: ˆ). This constitutes secondary stress, the main stress being somewhere in the 'comment'. Adverbials are less often so marked; since they are more mobile anyway (see further, ch. 21), they do not have such a great effect in initial position:

vêlshit ani *lo* lamádeti   ולשית אני לא למדתי
OBJ   Welsh I *didn't* study'

be-shabât ani *lo* lamádeti   בשׁבת אני לא למדתי
ADVERBIAL   MAIN
            STRESS
|_____| |_____|
TOPIC   COMMENT   'On Saturday I *didn't* study'

The object can be an infinitive phrase:

leefot ugâ ani lo maskim   לאפות עוגה אני לא מסכים
TOPIC   'To bake a cake I don't agree'

Casually, predicate nouns or adjectives, as in (1,2) below, and the nucleus noun or verb within such objects (3,4) can be preposed; but finite verbs or verb phrases cannot:[4]

(1) hi bébisiter, aval **ozêret** hi lo!   !היא בייביסיטר, אבל **עוזרת** היא לא
         'She's a babysitter, but **a cleaning lady** she isn't!'

(2) **HaHamâ** hi lo, aval neima hi ken   **חכמה** היא לא, אבל נעימה היא כן
         '**Clever** she isn't, but nice she is'

(3) **ugiôt**, moshe ohev rak agulot   **עוגיׁות**, משה אוהב רק עגולות
     cookies, Moshe likes only round   'Moshe only likes *round* cookies'

(4) **leefôt**, ani muHana rak ugiot   לאפות, אני מוכנה רק עוגיות
     to bake, I'm willing only cookies   'I'm only willing to bake *cookies*'

More formal usage preposes the topic in several circumstances, with no need for rise-fall tone; even finite verbs are preposed. Examples are given below.

Continuation:

medubar afílu al bitúaH Hayim le-Hélek   מדובר אפילו על ביטוח חיים לחלק
min ha-meHablim.   מן המחבלים.
mufalim gam batey-Holim...   מופעלים גם בתי-חולים...
'It is even a case of life assurance for some of the terrorists. Hospitals too are utilized. (*lit.* **are-utilized** also hospitals)'

ha-Hazit ha-amamit konena be-1967.   החזית העממית כוננה ב-1967.
hishtatfu ba shlosha irguney   השתתפו בה שלושה אירגוני
meHablim...   מחבלים...
'The Popular Front was set up in 1967. ⟨There⟩ **participated** in it three terrorist organizations...'

Comparison (this implies a continuation):

Hamur yoter ha-matsav ba-négev   חמור יותר המצב בנגב
'**More serious** ⟨is⟩ the situation in the Negev'

meyuHédet be-mina hi parashat   מיוחדת במינה היא פרשת
ha-hadlafot la-itonut   ההדלפות לעתונות
'**In a class of its own** is the affair of the leaks to the press'

To create a coherent sense of *sequence* (in literary prose):[5]

bánu ve-yashávnu étsel avi.   באנו וישבנו אצל אבי.
sáma ishti et ha-praHim be-agartal   שמה אשתי את הפרחים באגרטל
ve-nashmu bi-rvaHa. sámnu lánu kis'ot   ונשמו ברווחה. שמנו לנו כיסאות
leyad ha-mita ve-heHel avi lesaper al...   ליד המיטה והחל אבי לספר על...
'We came and sat with my father. My wife put (*lit.* put my wife) the blooms in a vase and people breathed freely. We put some chairs by the bed and my father began (*lit.* began my father) to tell of...'

A related use is *preposing of past tense verbs*[6] (as an alternative to אם *im* 'if') in official directives, to create *expectation* of continuity:

lo silek sabal et eglato leaHar   לא סילק סבל את עגלתו לאחר
she-nitstava al kaH,   שנצטווה על כך,
rashay ha-shoter lesalek ota agala   רשאי השוטר לסלק אותה עגלה
'If a porter hs not removed (*lit.* **not has-removed porter**) his cart after being ordered to do so, the policeman may remove said cart'

37.4 Subject-verb inversion

When a topic other than a subject is preposed, formal (and sometimes casual) usage is wont to delay the subject still further by putting the verb (and even verb + object, or verb + adverbial)[7] ahead of the subject. This 'smoothes out' the information contours so that they are not 'top-heavy', by reducing still further the 'topicality' of the subject now that something else has been topicalized:

kmo-Hen meshamesh et rosh ha-memshala   כמו-כן משמש את ראש הממשלה
ha-yo'ets ha-tsva'i she...   היועץ הצבאי ש...
similarly serves OM the Prime Minister the adviser the military who...
                     OBJ   SUBJ
'Similarly the Prime Minister is served by the military adviser who...'

aHshav novHim ha-klavim be-kétsev   עכשיו נובחים הכלבים בקצב
now bark the dogs [= the dogs bark] in rhythm

or:

aHshav ha-klavim novHim be-kétsev   עכשיו הכלבים נובחים בקצב
now the dogs bark in rhythm

Inversion is particularly common for an indefinite subject, as in (1) below, and conversely, uncommon for a definite pronoun, this being intrinsically highly 'topical' (2), except in formal usage (3):

(1) et ha-mafteHot mats'u shney yeladim   את המפתחות מצאו שני ילדים
OM the keys found two children   'The keys were found by two children'

(2) *az etmol ba **hu** le-Han   אז אתמול בא **הוא** לכאן*
so yesterday came **he** here

(3) miyad Hásha **hi** laHazor elav   מיד חשה **היא** לחזור אליו
immediately hastened **she** [= she hastened] to-return to-him

37.5 Topic dislocation (״ייחוד״)

ha-monit ha-zot, mi hizmin ota?   המונית הזאת, מי הזמין אותה?
                                    'That cab, who ordered it?'

A different way of topicalizing a noun phrase (though not an adverbial, infinitive phrase, verb or anything else) is to mention it at the front of the clause,[8] while still leaving it undisturbed in the clause - as a resumptive pronoun. In casual, and occasionally formal, Hebrew such a noun phrase may be detached by pause or comma. This structure is traditionally termed ייחוד *yiHud*; we call it 'topic dislocation'. This functions as a *recall topic*, i.e. not continuing something *just* mentioned or contrasting with it, but recalling a topic mentioned some time ago or just present in the background. Hence there is no rise-fall tone:

az ha-kablan ha-ze, ani ro'e   אז הקבלן הזה, אני רואה
she-hu sider otHa   שהוא סידר אותך
               'So this builder, I see that he ripped you off'

There is no subject-verb inversion (unlike in topic preposing, 37.4), as topic dislocation builds on, rather than upsets, the sentence and its information lay-out. And any noun, however deeply embedded within the sentence, can be 'dislocated', as it retains an easily recognizable pronoun of itself in the sentence:

ha-baHur ha-ze, ata yodéa ma
ha-maskóret **shelo**?

הבחור הזה, אתה יודע מה
המשכורת שלו?

'This guy, you know what **his** salary is?'

Occasionally, officialese begins with a detached topic that it *fails* to 'pick up'
by a pronoun:

ploni ha-roHesh matbéa Huts u-moHer
oto le-bank, ma din ha-hefresh?

פלוני הרוכש מטבע חוץ ומוכר
אותו לבנק, מה דין ההפרש?

'Someone who acquires foreign currency and sells it to a bank, what is the status
of the margin?'

'Dislocation' in reverse

Casual Hebrew also occasionally allows dislocation in reverse: a noun is
first mentioned only in a *pronoun* and not spelt out in full until the end of the
whole sentence:

ma hi osa, efráti shelaH?

מה היא עושה, אפרתי שלך?

'What's she doing, your Efrati?'

This shows that the noun named is particularly 'known' from immediate context, or even that the exact word has escaped one's memory, without too much
ado.[9] But, unlike topic dislocation above, any preposition that preceded the pronoun must be repeated:[10]

ani ge'a **bo** aHshav, **ba**-yéled sheli
            PREP

אני גאה **בו** עכשיו, **בילד** שלי

'I'm proud **of** him now, **of** my little boy'

By contrast, formal Hebrew occasionally uses an 'anticipatory' - ל *le-* as a mark
of *elegance* (with or without comma):

lo iHpat **lahem** la-pkidim halálu
im ata ezraH o tayar

לא אכפת **להם** לפקידים הללו
אם אתה אזרח או תייר

'It matters not to these officials (*lit.* **to them** to officials these) if one is a
citizen or a tourist'

Verb 'dislocation'

Both casual and formal usage occasionally anticipate a *contrastively
topical* verb by using an infinitive - and leave the verb in its full form, for
Hebrew has pronouns but no pro-verbs:[11]

hu hivtíaH she-lishtôt hu yishte ha-kol
he promised that to-drink he
    would-drink everything

הוא הבטיח שלשתות הוא ישתה הכל

'He promised that he'd
drink everything'

37.6-10 THE 'FOCUS'

37.6 Types of focus

The focus of a clause is some item of newsworthy information marked by a strong stress.[12] In 'my *dog* ate the bagels', the topic under discussion is 'the eating of the bagels' and the new information is that it was 'my dog' that ate them. This need not be particularly emphatic.

A Hebrew clause often has such a focus. This is commonly the last word, particularly an adverbial or object (or in their absence, the verb):

ishti metsayéret **reHovot**	אשתי מציירת **רחובות**	'My wife paints **streets**'
FOCUS		

ishti **metsayéret**	אשתי **מציירת**	'My wife **paints**'
FOCUS		

Sometimes, however, there is a particularly newsworthy word(s) being *emphasized*:[13]

taaru laHem, *shóHad* hu natan lahem!   תארו לכם, שוחד הוא נתן להם!
'Imagine, a *bribe* he gave them!'

váflim ani ohev   '*Wafers* I like'   ופלים אני אוהב

This often involves the focus adverbs (see ch. 22) גם *gam* 'also', אפילו *afilu* 'even', רק *rak* 'only' etc.:

hu natan lahem afilu *shóHad*   הוא נתן להם אפילו שוחד
'He even gave them *bribes*'

Although the subject is frequently taken as topic (37.2), it can - by virtue of focus adverbs or just main stress - be taken as focus:[14]

mi natan laH? - ha-*néHed* shèli natan li   מי נתן לך? - הנכד שלי נתן לי
'Who gave you? - My *grandson* gave me'

Indeed, Hebrew does not make a point of delaying a focused subject (except in presentatives, see 37.8, or where there is a topic too):

david diber   '*David* spoke'   דוד דיבר

*diber *david*   *דיבר דוד

Focus can be denoted in various ways other than strong stress: either by (1) preposing to the front of the clause; or conversely, by (2) delaying; or (3) clefting; or (4) anticipation of the verb - all described in 37.7-10 below.

37.7 Focus preposing: וולוו את רוצה? *vólvo at rotsa?* 'A Volvo you want?'

Provided there is no *topicalized* word(s) the *focused* words can be preposed, in all usage. Everything that follows the focus is of equally low informational significance and thus cannot be especially marked as topic:

rak vólvo Hatano rotse / only Volvo his-son-in-law wants — 'His son-in-law only wants a *volvo*'

רק וולו חתנו רוצה

Focus preposing applies to the same kinds of words as topic preposing (37.3), except finite verbs or adjectives:[15]

afilu **lishtot témpo** hi lo hiskíma / even **to-drink Tempo** she didn't agree

אפילו לשתות טמפו היא לא הסכימה

(Casual) rak **garbáyim** ani kibásti levanot / only **socks** I washed white — 'The only white thing I washed was socks'

רק גרביים אני כיבסתי לבנות

but not:

*__mitpashet__ ha-óvesh ha-ze / is-spreading the mould the this — ('This mould is *spreading*')

*מתפשט העובש הזה

However, many adverbials can casually be focused (and topicalized) by preceding the *verb* (see further 21.7.2):

ani **be-shesh** yatsáti — 'I left **at six**'

אני בשש יצאתי

Focus preposing may be used in exclamations:

nevelot kol ha-kablanim ha-éle! / **scum** all the builders the these! — 'Scum, that's what all these builders are!'

נבלות כל הקבלנים האלה!

yafe ha-nof ha-ze! / **beautiful** the view the this! — 'What a beautiful view this is!'

יפה הנוף הזה!

Subject-verb inversion is as for topic-preposing (37.4) - delaying the subject downgrades its inherent 'topicality', and reinforces the focus:

rak aHshav hevi aharon / aharon hevi et ha-kvasim

רק עכשיו הביא אהרן את הכבסים / אהרן הביא

only just brought Aharon / Aharon brought OM the washing

'Aharon only just brought the washing'

37.8 Focus delay

The focus tends naturally to be object or adverbial. But even when subject, it can optionally hold back till after the verb (or become passivized) - in four particular situations, as described below.

(1) The sentence already starts with a previous topic:

ha-trufa ha-zot, hitsía ota dávka **bni** / the medicine the this, suggested it actually **my-son** — 'This medicine, it was actually my son who suggested it'

התרופה הזאת, הציע אותה דווקא בני

(2) There is a particularly strong focus, involving focus adverbs or numerals or מישהו *míshehu* 'someone' or suchlike:

ha-rav amar she-amdu al kaH   הרב אמר שעמדו על כך
shney poskim, deháynu...   **שני פוסקים,** דהיינו...
the rabbi said that dealt with it   'The rabbi said that two authorities dealt
two authorities, namely...   with it, namely...'

(3) The focus is introduced (indeed, created) by a 'presentative' or 'existential'
expression (an extreme case of topic + focus):

Presentative

amad sham   yehudi eHad ve...   עמד שם יהודי אחד ו...
nigash elay   ניגש אלי

stood there   stood there
          some fellow and...   'Some fellow   and...'
came-up to-me   came up to me

mistamnot shalosh megamot Hiyuviot:...   מסתמנות שלוש מגמות חיוביות:...
are-emerging three positive trends:...   'Three positive trends are emerging'

kotev shimon, menahel ha-maHon:...   כותב שמעון, מנהל המכון:...
                        'Writes Shimon, director of the institute:...'

Existential
kayamim mispar zanim, asher...   קיימים מספר זנים, אשר...
                        '(There) exist a number of species, that...'

(4) A subject is *specifying*[16] a predicate:

              ארגון מחבלים פעיל הוא גם **צאעיקה,** מאחוריו עומדת סוריה
<u>irgun meHablim pa'il</u> hu gam **tsáika,** meaHorav omédet súrya
    PREDICATE   FOCUS (SUBJ)
    guerilla organization active is also **Tsaika,** behind-which stands Syria
                  'Another active guerilla organization is Tsaika,
                      behind which stands Syria'

37.9 Focus clefting: אני הוא שפיהקתי *ani hu she-pihákti* **'I** yawned'
      A noun phrase can be made more clearly *focus* (serving to *exclude*)
and the verb made *topic*, by using a variety of 'cleft' constructions - constructions that split the clause into (apparently) *two clauses*, one highlighting the
focus noun:

37.9.1 With a copula, and a pseudo-relative clause for topic (formal usage)

             המובטלים הם שׁ יסבלו = המובטלים יסבלו
                    אשר

ha-*muvtalim* hem she-/asher yisbelu = ha-*muvtalim* yisbelu
           'REL' CLAUSE

the *unemployed* are who will-suffer = 'The *unemployed* will suffer'

ani hu she-pihákti = *ani* pihákti   אני הוא שפיהקתי = אני פיהקתי
I am who I-yawned = '*I* yawned'

Only a subject noun can be 'focused' in this way. The subject is being more strongly focused by having the topic verb 'demoted' into what is at first sight a subordinate, relative clause: שיסבלו *she-yisbelu* 'who will suffer'. The main clause now takes on a new 'copula' verb: הוא, היא *hu, hi* etc. 'is, are'.[17]

37.9.2 זה/אלה *ze/éle* introducing the focus

זה/אלה *ze/éle* can introduce the focus, sometimes with -ש *she-* before the topic:

éle ha-*muvtalim* she-yisbelu	אלה המובטלים שיסבלו
N PHR	
those the *unemployed* who will-suffer	
	'It is the unemployed who will suffer'

ze *ani* she-pihákti	זה אני שפיהקתי
it *I* who yawned (1st s.)	'It is *I* who yawned'

זה היה למען השלום שפתחנו במלחמה

ze haya lemáan ha-shalom she-patáHnu be-milHama

ADVERBIAL

it was for-the-sake-of peace that we-launched a war

In fairly casual or formal (rather than intermediate) usage, any noun phrase or 'loose' adverbial (of time, place, cause etc., see ch. 21) can be focused by introductory זה *ze* 'it' (agreeing with the noun phrase in question, as it does on many occasions, e.g. זאת בעיה *zot baaya* 'it's a problem', - see 18.3.2).

There are in fact two constructions. In the first, זה *ze* 'it' acts to introduce a 'be' clause (any tense is possible, and negation) and the topic becomes a relative clause, except perhaps after an adverbial. 'Be' is not expressed by הוא *hu* etc. in present tense:[18]

זו לא היתה אני {שהשאירה את הדלת פתוחה/שראית בתחנה}

zu lo hayta ani {she-hish'ira et ha-délet ptuHa/she-ra'it ba-taHana}

f.s.   3rd f.s.

'BE' CLAUSE   REL CLAUSE...

it not was I {who left OM the door open/who you-saw at-the stop}

'It wasn't me {that left the door open/that you saw at the stop}'

Formally, the verb 'to be' often comes first:

hayta zo ha-avoda ba-sadot	היתה זו העבודה בשדות
she-ahávti bimyuHad	שאהבתי במיוחד
was it the work in-the fields that I-loved most	
	'It was the work in the fields that I loved most'

In the second, זה *ze* is simply added to the initial focus, if subject or object. The clause remains a simple clause, usually with no -ש *she-* 'who, that'. This is casual.

ze bney-adam tovim o bney-adam ra'im	זה בני-אדם טובים או בני-אדם רעים
rotsim et ze?	רוצים את זה?
it people good or people bad want OM it?	
	'Is it good or bad people that want it?'

ze oti ra'it ba-shuk	זה אותי ראית בשוק
OBJ	
it me you-saw in-the market	'It's me you saw in the market'

37.9.3   Topic precedes focus

In this construction זה *ze* introduces a delayed focus, and topic is introduced by ...ש מי *mi she-*... 'who that...' etc. (C). זה *ze* is glossed here 'it', as in the preceding examples; it could, however, be taken as a copula 'is':

be-mi she-ani ge'e̱ ze **be-yóram**	במי שאני גאה זה **ביורם**
TOPIC FOCUS	
of who that I'm proud it **of Yoram**	'It's Yoram that I'm proud of'

ma she-lo mutsdaḵ ze linzof bo be-galuy̱	מה שלא מוצדק זה לנזוף בו בגלוי
TOPIC FOCUS	
what that not right it to-reprimand him openly	
	'What is not right it to reprimand him openly'

The topic is akin to a blend of an interrogative and a relative clause. (For similar constructions, see 33.4.2.)

37.10   Focus dislocation

The only kind of 'focus dislocation' - and one that does not create a detached phrase - is the 'anticipated verb', also employed as a topic device (details as in 37.5):

gam lishkav shaHávti	גם לשכב שכבתי
also to-lie-down I've-lain-down	'I've also *lain down!*'

37.11-14   REORDERING WITH NO MEANING
Some special word orders have nothing to do with information structure but with purely grammatical considerations. Among them are the positioning of interrogative words and relative pronouns at the head of the sentence; see chapters 26 and 33 respectively. Here we deal with phenomena not discussed in other chapters.

37.11   'Direct quotation' preposing

Hebrew literary narrative may prepose a direct quotation (in main clauses) from the normal object position to the front of the clause. Verb then precedes subject (except for pronouns):[19]

medabrim aléynu, kovéa sason	מדברים עלינו, קובע ששון
they're-talking about-us, states Sason	

37.12   Subject restoration

In any usage, a noun phrase may be 'anticipated' at the front of its clause without pause or comma, with the aim of *creating a kind of subject* for the clause where there is none - a common, though not an essential, ploy.[20] Notable cases are described here:

For a subject-less verb, the oblique noun can be 'copied' forward, as in examples (1)-(5). Alternatively, the whole oblique phrase can often be lifted out and preposed (6):

(1) **tirkóvet zo** yesh la shalosh tHunot   תרכובת זו יש לה שלוש תכונות
        CREATED
        SUBJ
        compound this are to-it three properties
                          'This compound has three properties'

(2) **gam Hole ze** kashe lo linshom   גם חולה זה קשה לו לנשום
        CREATED
        SUBJ
        even patient this hard for-him to-breathe
                          'Even this patient finds it hard to breathe'

(3) **ha-nitba le-din** Hova alav lehishava   הנתבע לדין חובה עליו להישבע
        CREATED SUBJ
        the defendant duty on-him to-swear
                          'The defendant is duty-bound to swear'

(4) tofa'a taHbirit zo nitan lenasHa kaH:...   ...תופעה תחבירית זו ניתן לנסחה כך:
        phenomenon syntactic this it-is-possible to-formulate-it thus:...
                          'This syntactic phenomenon can be formulated thus:'

(5) he-pitgam yesh she-hu menusaH milulit   הפתגם יש שהוא מנוסח מילולית
        ve-yesh she...   ...ויש ש
        the proverb there-are-cases where
        it-is formulated literally and
        there-are-cases where...
                     'The proverb can in some cases be formulated literally and
                                       in some cases...'

(6) le-tirkóvet zo yesh shalosh tHunot   לתרכובת זו יש שלוש תכונות
        to compound this there-are three properties
                          'This compound has three properties'

A related construction is the following:

(7) kol targum o she-hu ekvivalénti o   כל תרגום או שהוא אקוויוולנטי או שהוא
        she-hu lo ekvivalénti   לא-אקוויוולנטי
        every translation either that it is [= is either]
        equivalent or that it is [= or] non-equivalent

For questions (F):

        dikduk generatívi keytsad yesh lenatslo?   ?דקדוק גנרטיבי כיצד יש לנצלו
        grammar generative how can-one use-it?
                       'How can one use generative grammar?'

Rather different is the need sometimes felt to highlight the construct modifier (this is not strictly *subject* restoring):

mekor shem ze bi-shnat 1883 ⇒   ⇐1883 מקור שם זה בשנת
shem ze mekoro bi-shnat 1883   שם זה מקורו בשנת 1883

source name this in year 1883 ⇒ name-this its-source in year 1883
'The source of this name is in the year 1883'

af kri'a zo perusha pshara   אף קריאה זו פירושה פשרה
even call this its-meaning compromise
'Even this call means a compromise'

All such constructions, unlike 'topic dislocation' (37.5), are ordinarily brought just to the front of their own clause (i.e. they are 'bounded'), not to the front of the whole sentence - they serve to promote *structural intelligibility*, not topicalization.[21]

37.13 Subject-verb inversion in subordinate clauses

Subject-verb inversion is common in formal usage for *relative clauses* and those adverbial clauses that can be likened to them, namely time clauses (and not cause or concession clauses):[22]

ha-shétaH she-bo Hanu ha-tsoanim   השטח שבו חנו הצוענים
the area that in-it camped the gypsies
'the area in which the gypsies camped'

ha-shétaH she-azvu ha-tsoanim   השטח שעזבו הצוענים
s.   pl.   pl.
the area that left the gypsies   'the area the gypsies left'

ad she   עד ש
leaHar she   azvu ha-tsoanim,...   לאחר ש   עזבו הצוענים,...
kaasher   כאשר

until CONJ   'until
after CONJ   left the gypsies   'after   the gypsies left'
when   'when

Similarly in comparative clauses:

כמו ש   מעולם לא רבו אנשים
רבו הכנענים   יותר מש

me'olam lo rávu anashim ^{kmo she-} rávu ha-knaanim
                       _{yoter mi-she-}

never not quarrelled people ^{like CONJ} quarrelled the Canaanites
                            _{more than CONJ}
'Never did people quarrel ^{like} the Canaanites quarrelled'
                          _{more than}

Conditional clauses allow inversion even casually, to give an effect of continuity, i.e. that a main clause is coming: 'if..., then...' (see 37.3):

im yelHu ha-tsoanim,...   אם ילכו הצוענים,...
if will-go the gypsies,...   'If the gypsies go,...'

37.14   Reordering for register's sake: גדולה שמחתי *gdola simHati* **'great is my pleasure'**

Multifarious word order requirements are described elsewhere for particular structures, e.g. officialese ...לא ילבש סבל *lo yilbash sabal...* 'a porter should not wear...' with the negative 3rd person command using an *initial* verb. But there are also cases of major reordering for elegance' sake, for example:

Subject pronoun-verb inversion:

zoHer ani adáyin et ha-milim ha-éle   זוכר אני עדיין את המלים האלה
recall I still OM the words the those   'I still recall those words'

Subject-adjective inversion:

gvirotay ve-rabotay, gdola simHati ha-érev   גבירותי ורבותי, גדולה שמחתי הערב
be-vo'i lehartsot bifneyHem   בבואי להרצות בפניכם
'Ladies and Gentlemen, great ⟨is⟩ my pleasure this evening in coming
to lecture to you'

Subject dislocation with inversion:

ezraHéynu tseirim hem   אזרחינו צעירים הם
our-citizens young they   'Our citizens are young'

Formal, rather than elegant, is the inversion of the verb היה *haya* 'be' + adjective where a complement clause follows:[23]

kashe haya lo lehavHin   **קשה היה** לא להבחין
hard was not to-notice   'It was hard not to notice'

dome haya ki...   ...דומה היה כי
apparent was that...   'It appeared that...'

FURTHER READING
Azar 1976; Ben-Horin 1976; Chayen & Dror 1976: ch.4; Friedman 1971; Givón 1976; Ioup 1975; Ornan 1979a: ch.7; Ravid 1977; Rosén 1965, 1982; Sadka 1980, 1981; Schwarzwald 1976a.

38. Noun types

38.1 Introduction

This chapter deals with noun types. For gender and number inflection, see chapter 39; for construct inflection, see chapter 6.

Nouns (and adjectives) are built in one of four ways, described in (1)-(4) below.

(1) With distinctive vowel-patterns and/or affixes, which have meaning; the noun often has distinctive inflectional characteristics too. These are *meaningful noun patterns*. Examples are as set out in the table:

Noun	Pattern	Inflectional characteristics	Meaning of pattern
sapar ספר 'hairdresser'	-a-a-	stem unchanged in plural and construct: saparim ספרים saparey ספרי	Mostly 'someone in a certain job; technical device'
shatkan שתקן 'silent type'	-a--an SUFF	Stem unchanged in plural and construct: shatkanim שתקנים shatkaney שתקני	Mostly 'personality-type'
jóbnik ג'ובניק 'shirker'	-nik SUFF	Stem unchanged in plural and construct: jóbnikim ג'ובניקים	'Someone who belongs to.../ engaged in...'

(2) With other common vowel-patterns and/or affixes, which have no meaning. These are *purely grammatical noun patterns*. An example is:

Noun	Pattern	Characteristics	Meaning of pattern
sadin סדין 'sheet'	-a-i-	Stem in plural and construct: --i- sdinim סדינים	None

(3) Without a particularly common pattern: כפר *kfar* 'village', וילון *vilon* 'curtain', שולחן *shulHan* 'table'.

(4) By compounding two words (sometimes changing their shape): אופנוע *ofnóa* 'motor-bike' (= אופניים *ofnáyim* 'bicycle' + נוע *nóa* 'movement')

427

Affixes can be prefixes or suffixes. The traditional term for a noun's or adjective's vowel pattern (plus any additional affixes) is משקל *mishkal*. A verb's pattern is termed a בניין *binyan*.

38.1.1 Roots and words

To make words, vowel patterns are mounted on a 'skeleton' of consonants, the root, as demonstrated in the table below.

Root	Vowel+affix pattern		Word	
ז.מ.ר z.m.r				
	-a-a-	→	zamar	'singer'	זמר
	-é-e-	→	zémer	'singing'	זמר
	--i-a	→	zmira	'song'	זמירה
	ti--ó-et	→	tizmóret	'orchestra'	תזמורת
ש.מ.ש sh.m.sh				
	-a-a-	→	shamash	'beadle'	שמש
	-é-e-	→	shémesh	'sun'	שמש
	-i--iya	→	shimshiya	'parasol'	שמשיה
	--i-ut	→	shmishut	'usefulness'	שמישות

Certain roots have a sharply defined meaning; usually, however, root meanings are shadowy or non-existent (e.g. one can hardly explain שמש *shémesh* 'sun' and שימש *shimesh* 'to function' synchronically as the sun being a heavenly 'functionary'!). Rather, the root exists to give grammatical form to the word.

The *meaningful* building blocks in word formation are words, not roots - though fairly unpredictably even then:

Word			Derived word with own vowel pattern		
sukar	'sugar'	סוכר →	sakéret	'diabetes'	סכרת
batsal	'onion'	בצל →	betsaltsal	'little onion'	בצלצל
siper	'to cut'	סיפר →	sapar	'hairdresser'	ספר
saval	'to bear'	סבל →	sabal	'porter'	סבל

In addition, many suffixes are simply added to a whole word without imposing a characteristic vowel pattern:

sapar	'hairdresser'	ספר →	saparut	'hairdressing'	ספרות
yevu	'imports'	יבוא →	yevuan	'importer'	יבואן

38.1.2 Formulations

We symbolize roots thus: ז.מ.ר *z.m.r.* We symbolize vowel+affix patterns by using a 'model root': כ.ב.ד *k.b.d.*; thus -a-a- is called the כבד *kabad* pattern (traditionally, the unsatisfactory ק.ט.ל or פ.ע.ל were used). More technically, it is also called the CaCaC pattern (C = any consonant, boldface *C* = a stop consonant).

38.1.3 When pattern affects root and *vice-versa*

The choice of pattern determines the pronunciation of three root letters ב,כ,פ. Whereas they are usually *b,k,p* ('hard', i.e. 'stops') when initial, and *v,H,f* ('soft', i.e. 'spirants') when word-final, their pronunciation *inside* the word depends on the word pattern. For example, the root כ.ב.ס gives מכבסה *maHbesa* 'laundry' in the pattern *maCCeCa* but כביסה *kvisa* 'laundering' in the pattern *CCiCa*: *H* ~ *k* and *b* ~ *v*.

A few root consonants 'interfere' regularly with the vowels of the patterns. For example, ח and ע usually have to have -a- as the preceding vowel, in final or stressed syllables. Thus from the *CoCeC* pattern we have רוקח *rokéaH*, from *CéCeC* we have נחל *náHal*. We shall not regularly list these interferences, but some examples will often be slipped in.

38.2 Meaningful noun patterns, e.g. ספר *sapar* 'hairdresser'

38.2.1 Patterns (1)-(4) Involving internal vowels but no affixes
Patterns (1,2)
These patterns are an abundant source of nouns, and *ongoingly productive.* Indeed, pattern (2) is available almost automatically.

Pattern (1)[1]

(a)	כובד	*koved*	CoCeC
(b)	מכבד	*meHabed*	meCaCeC
(c)	מתכבד	*mitkabed*	mitCaCeC
(d)	מכביד	*maHbid*	maCCiC

Meaning: (1) usually 'human agent' (especially 'in a profession')
　　　　　　(2) occasionally 'device'.
Derivation: Mostly borrowed from active present tense verbs, though many present tense verbs do not yield such nouns.
Examples: (1) רופא *rofe* 'doctor', מחנך *meHaneH* 'educator';
　　　　　　(2) מוצץ *motsets* 'pacifier', מחשב *meHashev* 'computer'.

Pattern (2)
Meaning: Mostly 'action' or 'result (concrete or abstract) of action'.

(a) כבידה *kvida CCiCa*

Derivation: Mostly from *pa'al*-type verbs.

Example: בחינה *bHina* 'examination, exam' (בחן *baHan* 'examine').

(b) היכבדות *hikavdut hiCaCCut*

Derivation: Mostly from *nif'al*-type verbs of the non-passive kind (e.g. נעדר *needar* 'be absent').

Example: הידברות *hidabrut* 'dialogue' (נדבר *nidbar* 'hold dialogue').

(c) כיבוד *kibud CiCuC*

Derivation: Mostly from *pi'el*-type verbs.

Example: טיפול *tipul* 'treatment' (טיפל *tipel* 'treat').

(d) התכבדות *hitkabdut hitCaCCut*

Derivation: Mostly from *hitpa'el*-type verbs.

Example: התבגרות *hitbagrut* 'maturation' (התבגר *hitbager* 'to mature').

(e) הכבדה *haHbada haCCaCa*

Derivation: Mostly from *hif'il*-type verbs.

Example: הגרלה *hagrala* 'raffle' (הגריל *higril* 'to raffle').

Some minor patterns: For (a)   כבודה *kvuda CCuCa*, e.g. קבורה *kvura* 'burial'. For (c)   כבדה *kabada CaCaCa*, e.g. קבלה *kabala* 'receipt'.

Some exceptions: ריקוד *rikud* 'dancing, a dance' (רקד *rakad* 'dance'); הראה *her'a* 'to show' has no noun.

Patterns (3,4)

These involve internal vowels but no affixes. They are abundantly used and productively coined - but only from verbs (*noun*-based derivation today mostly involves affixes; see patterns (5-27)) Note that (3,4) are graphically indistinguishable (with no vowel pointing) - most common patterns today are distinguishable, thanks to affixes.

Pattern (3). כבד *kéved* or כובד *kóved* (*CéCeC* or *CóCeC*). Two-syllable nouns, with penultimate stress and the plural pattern כבדים *kvadim*.[2]

(a) כבד *kéved* (*CéCeC*). Suffixed singular is mostly *kivd-* (*CiCC-*), sometimes *kavd-* (*CaCC-*).

Meaning: (a) Unpredictable, but today (b) occasional verb-based coinages denoting 'action/result of action'.

Examples: (a)   סגן *ségen* 'lieutenant', כבש *kéves* 'sheep'.

(b)   שדר *shéder* 'broadcast' (שידר *shider* 'to broadcast'), כנס *kénes* 'conference' (כינס *kines* 'convene').

(b) כובד *kóved* (*CóCeC*). Suffixed s. *kovd-* (*CoCC-*).

Meaning and derivation: Unpredictable.

Examples: גודל *gódel* 'size', חופש *Hófesh* 'freedom'.

Pattern (4). כבד *kabad* (*CaCaC*) ~ plural כבדים *kabadim* (*CaCaCim*) (sometimes *CaCCaC*).

Meaning: Mostly, and productively, (a) 'someone in a certain job' or (b) 'technical device'.

Derivation: Mostly verb-based; sometimes acronym, e.g. מג"ד *magad* 'company commander' (abbreviation of מפקד גדוד *mefaked gdud*).

Examples: (a) כתב *katav* 'reporter' (כתב *katav* 'write'), כבאי *kabay, kaba'i* 'firefighter' (כיבה *kiba* 'extinguish');

   (b) וסת *vasat* 'regulator' (ויסת *viset* 'regulate').

38.2.2   Patterns (5)-(11) Prefix plus vowel pattern

These involve prefix + vowel pattern (± suffix); they are abundant and ongoingly productive.

Pattern (5). תכביד *taHbid* (*taCCic*).

Meaning: Mostly 'result of action' - increasingly, 'of completed ('perfective') action'.

Derivation: Often nowadays from *hif'il*-type verbs (rather as patterns (1,2) are geared to particular verb types).

Examples: תקליט *taklit* 'disc' (הקליט *hiklit* 'to record'), תסביך *tasbiH* 'complex' (סיבך *sibeH* 'complicate').

Variant: (From ל"ה (-a) verbs): תגלית *taglit* 'discovery' (גילה *gila* 'discover').

Patterns (6,7)

These feminine patterns, with their feminine *suffix*, generally denote something more complex (as does feminine מכבדה *maHbeda* (pattern 11) *vis-à-vis* masculine מכבד *maHbed* (pattern 10)).

Pattern (6). תכבודת *tiHbódet* (*tiCCóCet*); suffixed singular stem: -תכבודת *tiHbodt-*.

Meaning: Mostly 'result of action' - increasingly 'something complex'.
Derivation: Verb-based.
Examples: תסרוקת *tisróket* 'hair-do' (סירק *sirek* 'to comb'), תסמונת *tismónet* 'syndrome' (סימן *simen* 'signify').

Pattern (7). מכבד *miHbad* (*miCCaC*) ~ suffixed plural stem as in מכבדי(כם) *miHbedey* (*Hem*).

Meaning: various - productively (a) 'action or its result', (b) 'location'.
Derivation: Productively verb-based.
Examples: (a) מצעד *mits'ad* 'parade' (צעד *tsa'ad* 'to march'), משדר *mishdar* 'broadcast' (שידר *shider* 'to broadcast'). Much semantic variation arises, e.g. מבחן *mivHan* 'test' (academic or otherwise) vs. בחינה *bHina* 'exam' or '*act* of examining anything'.

   (b) משרד *misrad* 'office', מעגן *maagan* 'anchorage'.

Pattern (8). מכבדה *miHbada* (*miCCaCa*) ~ sometimes a separate stem in the construct: מכבדת *miHbédet* / -מכבדת *miHbadt-*.

Meaning: Various - productively (a) 'location', (b) 'organization'.

Derivation: Mostly verb-based.

Examples: (a)   מדרכה *midraHa* 'pavement' (דרך *daraH* 'to step').

            (b)   מפקדה *mifkada* 'Headquarters' (פיקד *piked* 'to command').

Pattern (9). מכבד *maHbed* (*maCCeC*) (often interchanges, especially colloquially, with (1b) מכבד *meHabed* (*meCaCeC*))

Meaning: Mostly 'device that ...s'.

Derivation: Verb-based.

Example: מפתח *maftéaH* 'key' (פתח *pataH* 'to open').

Pattern (10). מכבדה *maHbeda* (*maCCeCa*).

Meaning: Mostly (a) 'machine', (b) (non-puristic) 'location'.

Derivation: Mostly verb-based.

Examples: (a)   מדגרה *madgera* 'incubator' (דגר *dagar* 'to hatch')

            (b)   מחצבה *maHtseva* 'quarry' (חצב *Hatsav* 'to quarry').

Pattern (11). הכבד *heHbed* (*heCCeC*).

Meaning: 'Result of action'.

Derivation: Mostly from *hif'il*-type verb.

Examples: החזר *heHzer* 'refund' (החזיר *heHzir* 'give back') (contrast החזרה *haHzara* 'act of returning').

38.2.3   Patterns (12)-(15) Vowel pattern plus suffix

These involve vowel pattern + suffix; they are numerous and productive.

Pattern (12). כבדת *kabédet* (*CaCéCet*) ~ plural כבדות *kabadot* ~ suffixed singular stem -כבדת *kabadt-*.

Meaning: Mostly (a) 'illness' or (b) 'group, system'.

Derivation: Verb- /adjective- /noun-based.

Examples: (a)   דלקת *daléket* 'inflammation' (דלק *dalak* 'to burn'), צהבת *tsahévet* 'jaundice' (צהוב *tsahov* 'yellow'), סכרת *sakéret* 'diabetes' (סוכר *sukar* 'sugar');

            (b)   טייסת *tayéset* 'squadron' (טס *tas* 'fly'), ניידת *nayédet* 'patrol' (נייד *nayad* 'mobile'), ניירת *nayéret* 'paperwork' (נייר *niyar* 'paper').

Pattern (13). כבודת *kvódet* (*CCóCet*); the (suffixed singular) stem is -כבודת *kvodt-*.

Meaning: Mostly 'unwanted mass of something'.

Derivation : Mostly from *pa'al*-type verbs.

Examples : פסולת *psólet* 'garbage' (פסל *pasal* 'reject').

Pattern (14). כבדן *kavdan* (*CaCCan*) (ן- -*an* can also be suffixed without affecting the vowel pattern; see pattern (16)). Sometimes *CaCCCan.*

Meaning : Mostly (a) 'personality-type', productively with negative overtones (in literature, very productive);

(b) 'someone engaged in a (voluntary) activity';

(c) 'device';

(d) 'someone in a profession'.

Derivation : Often verb-based, sometimes noun/adjective-based.

Examples : (a) יקרן *yakran* 'overcharger' (יקר *yakar* 'expensive'), גנדרן *gandran* 'dandy' (התגנדר *hitgander* 'to dress up');

(b) שחיין *saHyan* 'swimmer' (שחה *saHa* 'to swim'), קלפן *kalfan* 'card-player' (קלף *klaf* 'card');

(c) לוויין *lavyan* 'satellite' (ליווה *liva* 'accompany'), רעשן *raashan* 'rattle' (רעש *ráash* 'noise');

(d) צנחן *tsanHan* 'paratroop' (notably when pattern (4) is already 'occupied').

Variant : The ת- -*t*- of the *hitpa'el* prefix can be recast as a root consonant: שתלטן *shtaltan* 'domineering person' (השתלט *hishtalet* 'dominate').

Pattern (15). Reduplicative suffixes: כבדבד *kvadvad* (*CCaCCaC*), etc. The last syllable in the source noun is reduplicated, while itself (untypically) changing its vowel to -*a*-, e.g. חזיר *Hazir* → חזרזיר *Hazarzir* (pattern (3) above changes *e-e* to *a-a* before reduplicating, e.g. גבר *géver* → גברבר *gvarvar*).

Meaning : Diminutive (sometimes sarcastically).

Derivation : Based on masculine nouns; there are 10-15 common examples, fairly productive.

Examples : זקנקן *zkankan* 'little beard' (זקן *zakan* 'beard'), חתלתול *Hataltul* 'kitten' (חתול *Hatul* 'cat').

38.2.4 Patterns (16)-(29) Suffix, but no special vowel pattern

Here a suffix is added without affecting the word's shape - except for some standard adjustments. They are numerous, and very productively coined or borrowed.

Patterns (16)-(22) Stressed suffixes

Adjustments to the base word:

(a) Base adjectives mostly use their all-purpose suffixed form, i.e. their plural base: thus גמיש + ות *gamish* + *ut* → גמישות *gmishut* (pl: גמישים *gmishim*), חדישות *Hadishut* (pl: חדישים *Hadishim*).

(b) Base nouns mostly use their suffixed singular base: דוב + ון *dov + on* → דובון *dubon* (דובו *dubo*), גזע + ן + *géza + an* → גזעון *giz'an* (גזעו *giz'o*), כלב + ה *kélev + a* → כלבה *kalba* (כלבו *kalbo*).

But (c) they sometimes drop their feminine genitive ending ת- *-at*: regularly when the suffix is ן- *-an* (תעשיה + ון *taasiya + an* → תעשיין *taasiyan),* אי- *-a'i* (קופה + אי *kupa + a'i* → קופאי *kupa'i*), ונת- *-ónet* (טיפה + ונת *tipa +* ónet → טיפונת *tipónet*), ית- *-it* (מפה + ית *mapa + it* → מפית *mapit-*), יה- *-ia* (חנוכה + יה *Hanuka + ia* → חנוכיה *Hanukia*), and often for ון- *-on* (שעה + ון *sha'a + on* → שעון *sha'on* vs. שפה + ון *safa + on* → שפתון *sfaton*).

Also, (d) they shorten the suffix אי- *-ay/a'i* to א- *-a* when adding ית-, ות- *-it,* *-ut* (בנאי + ות *banay + ut* → בנאות *bana'ut,* קופאי + ית *kupa'i + it* → קופאית *kupa'it*).

Pattern (16). ן- *-an.*

Meaning :   Mostly, and very productively, 'someone with (a) some job/role; (b) 'belief'; (c) 'personality'; or (d) 'an object related to the base noun', often scientific.

Derivation : Mostly noun-based; type (c) in particular is often based on *pa'al/hif'il* present tense verbs. Final base *-a-* of noun usually drops.

Examples :   (a)   כלכלן *kalklan* 'economist' (כלכלה *kalkala* 'economics'), ירקן *yarkan* 'greengrocer' (ירק *yérek* 'vegetables'), יבואן *yevu'an* 'importer' (יבוא *yevu* 'imports');

           (b)   מלוכן *meluHan* 'monarchist' (מלוכה *meluHa* 'monarchy');

           (c)   חוצפן *Hutspan* 'impudent person' (חוצפה *Hutspa* 'impudence');

           (d)   סידן *sidan* 'calcium' (סיד *sid* 'lime'), יומן *yoman* 'diary' (יום *yom* 'day'), פותחן *potHan* 'can-opener' (פותח *potéaH* 'opens').

Pattern (17). אי- *-ay/-a'i.* Tends to be two syllables *-a'i* (especially on a base noun already ending in ה- *-a,* e.g. קופאי *kupa'i*); purists require one syllable (אי- *ay* in כבאי *kabay* and other nouns from ל"ה *-a* verbs is not a suffix - see pattern (4)).

Meaning: 'Someone in a job'.

Derivation: Mostly from nouns, often those ending in a vowel (ה- *-e* and feminine ה- *-a*) or in ן- *-n,* thus generally complementing the suffix ן- *an.*

Examples: ימאי *yama'i* 'sailor' (ים *yam* 'sea'), במאי *bama'i* 'director' (במה *bama* 'stage').

Pattern (18). יה- *-iya.*

Meaning: Mostly (a) 'object for...' (notably: clothing, device, place), (b) 'object generally related to...' (notably: ensemble, flora, (stress: *íya*) place-name).

Derivation: Mostly from nouns or numerals.

Examples: (a) כתפיה *ktefiya* 'cape' (כתף *katef* 'shoulder'), חנוכיה *Hanukiya* 'Hanuka lamp' (חנוכה *Hanuka*), סטייקיה *steykiya* 'steak-house' (סטייק *steyk* 'steak');

       (b) צמחיה *tsimHiya* 'vegetation' (צמח *tsémaH* 'plant'), חמישיה *Hamishiya* 'quintet' (חמש *Hamesh* '5'), שקדיה *shkediya* 'almond-tree' (שקד *shaked* 'almond'), דגניה *dganiya* 'cornflower' (דגן *dagan* 'grain'), נהריה *'Naharia'* (נהר *nahar* 'river').

Pattern (19). ון- *-on.*

Meaning: Mostly (a) 'device for, place for, publication for...', (b) 'publication at...', (c) 'something consisting of...', occasionally (d) 'diminutive/ condescending (often pejorative)'.

Derivation: Mostly based on nouns (masculine for (d)).

Examples: (a) שפתון *sfaton* 'lipstick' (שפה *safa* 'lip'), פעוטון *paoton* 'creche' (פעוט *pa'ot* 'infant'), מחירון *meHiron* 'price-list' (מחיר *meHir* 'price');

       (b) עתון *iton* 'newspaper' (עת *et* 'time'), שנתון *shnaton* 'year-book' (שנה *shana* 'year');

       (c) אזבסטון *azbeston* 'asbestos hut' (אזבסט *azbest* 'asbes-tos');

       (d) סרטון *sirton* 'short film' (סרט *séret* 'film'), פקידון *pkidon* 'petty official' (פקיד *pakid* 'official').

Pattern (20). ה- *-a* (Details are given in chapter 39 'Gender and number in the noun'.)

Meaning: 'Female of...'

Derivation: Near-automatically from nouns denoting humans, and from many animal nouns. But certain noun patterns require the suffix ת- *t* instead (see ch. 39).

Examples: בחורה *baHura* 'girl' (בחור *baHur* 'boy'), פסלת *pasélet* 'sculp-tress' (פסל *pasal* 'sculptor').

Pattern (21). יסט- *-ist.*

Meaning: (a) 'Adherent to an ideology'; (b) casually and semi-productively, 'someone belonging to/engaged in...'.

Derivation: (a) Foreignisms; (b) based on nouns ending (usually) in vowels or *-n* (the counterpart for nouns ending in other consonants is ניק *-nik* (pattern (25)).

Examples: (a) אנרכיסט *anarHist* 'anarchist', פשיסט *fashist* 'fascist';

(b) שמיניסט *shminist* '8th grader' (שמיני *shmini* '8th'),
בלגניסט *balaganist* 'mess-maker' (בלגן *balagan* 'mess').

Pattern (22). ים- *izm.*
Meaning: 'Ideology'.
Derivation: Foreignisms.
Examples: אנרכיזם *anarHizm* 'anarchism', פשיזם *fashizm* 'fascism'.

Patterns (23-25) Stressed-unstressed suffixes

These suffixes are stressed, unless the word-base itself bears pre-final stress (which is, by its very nature, usually fixed). Examples are: שגרירות *shagrirut* (שגריר + ות *shagrir + ut*) vs. ליברליות *liberáliut* (ליברלי + ות *liberáli + ut*).

Pattern (23). ות- *-ut.*
Meaning: Mostly (a) 'abstract quality'; sometimes (b) 'someone's office', or (c) 'political institution'.
Derivation: Based on most adjectives (not אדום *adom CaCoC* type) and on masculine human nouns, even suffixed nouns, e.g. מזרח + נ + ות *mizraH + an + ut* → מזרחנות *mizreHanut.*
Examples: (a) נעימות *neimut* 'pleasantness' (נעים *na'im* 'pleasant'), מציאותיות *metsiutiut* 'realism' (מציאותי *metsiuti* 'realistic'), אזרחות *ezraHut* 'citizenship' (אזרח *ezraH* 'citizen');

(b) גזברות *gizbarut* 'treasurer's office' (גזבר *gizbar* 'treasurer');

(c) קיסרות *keysarut* 'empire' (קיסר *keysar* 'Emperor').

Pattern (24). י- *-i.* (For details see adjectives in י- *-i* in 41.3.4, pattern 11.)
Meaning: 'Someone (usually male) hailing from a certain place'
Derivation: Based on names of most countries and towns.
Examples: ספרדי *sfaradi* 'Spaniard' (ספרד *sfarad* 'Spain'), אמריקאי *amerikái* 'American' (אמריקה *amérika* 'America').

Pattern (25). ית- *it.*
Meaning: (a) 'Female of humans', e.g. סורי ~ סורית *súri ~ súrit* 'Syrian ~ Syrian woman'. It is semi-automatic (details in 39.5.4). Otherwise, mostly and quite productively, (b) 'diminutive/endearingly', (c) 'quasi-diminutive', i.e. smaller but different, (d) 'device for...', notably clothes or vehicles, (e) 'object related to...', notably fauna, vehicles, commercial products.
Derivation: (a) Based on masculine human nouns; (b) mostly based on feminine nouns; (c-e) noun-based.
Examples: (a) See chapter 39;

(b) טיפית *tipit* 'droplet' (טיפה *tipa* 'drop');

(c) מחסנית *maHsanit* 'gun magazine' (מחסן *maHsan* 'store-room');

(d) קרסולית *karsulit* 'garter' (קרסול *karsol* 'ankle'), טיולית *tiyulit* 'makeshift coach' (טיול *tiyul* 'trip');

(e) ורדית *vardit* 'rose-finch' (ורד *véred* 'rose'), מיכלית *meHalit* 'tanker' (מיכל *meHal* 'tank'), פזית *pazit* (brand of cookie, cf. פז *paz* 'gold').

Patterns (26)-(30) Unstressed suffixes
These cause no adjustment in the shape of the base-word.

Pattern (26). ניק- *-nik.*

Meaning: 'Someone belonging to/engaged in...' (mostly in Jewish/Israeli life, notably kibbutz, army, politics, school). It is used in casual speech and is quite productive.

Derivation: Based on nouns ending in a consonant (not *-n*); complements pattern (21).

Examples: קיבוצניק *kibútsnik* 'kibbutz-inhabitant', ג'ובניק *jóbnik* 'shirker' (ג'וב *job* 'job').

Pattern (27). י- *-i.*

Meaning: 'Term of endearment/familiarity'.

Derivation: Based on nouns, notably (and highly productively) on first names - sometimes with shortening of the name.

Examples: חתולי *Hatúli* 'pussycat' (חתול *Hatul* 'cat'), חמודי *Hamúdi* 'darling' (חמוד *Hamud* 'darling'), אסתי *ésti* (אסתר *éster* 'Esther').

Pattern (28). לה- *-le.*

Meaning: 'Term of endearment'.

Derivation: From first names and intimate nouns, ending in a vowel. It is very productive.

Examples: רבקה׳לה *rívkale* (רבקה *rívka*), אבא׳לה *ábale* 'Daddy' (אבא *ába* 'father').

Pattern (29). טור- *-tor.*

Meaning: Mostly 'device'.

Derivation: Foreignism.

Examples: ויברטור *vibrátor* 'vibrátor', טרנספורמטור *transformátor* 'transformer'.

Pattern (30). יזציה- *-izátsya.*

Meaning: 'Imparting of someone's or something's influence'.

Derivation: From proper names; it is very productive.

Examples: בגיניזציה *beginizátsya* 'beginization' (בגין Begin: Israeli Premier).

38.3 Purely grammatical noun patterns (some are also adjective patterns)

These non-meaningful patterns are common enough to be classed as 'distinctive' - although the borderline between them and 'non-distinctive' patterns is fairly arbitrary. Though many are abundantly employed, they are generally no longer *productively* coined, as Hebrew tends to favour 'meaningful' patterns.

The main reason for distinguishing these patterns is that each has its own inflectional habits - there is little relationship to underlying 'roots', for they have scant semantic identity. A great many other patterns, involving handfuls of nouns and in unpredictable ways (sometimes even overlapping with the patterns here), will be disregarded. Note too that 'constructs' (e.g. תנורי, תנורו *tanurey, tanuro* 'ovens-of, his-oven') are mostly restricted to elevated or technical style - and to idiomatic compounds, where they sometimes lose their special form colloquially, e.g. מרק פרות **marak perot** 'fruit soup', rather than **merak perot**.

Patterns will be called after a representative noun (some of these patterns are adjectival too). Inflections are specified only where they involve actual phonetic adjustments (rather than vowel-point adjustments on paper). Any inflections are given in the order singular construct, singular suffixed, plural free ('absolute') and plural construct, but note that one or more of these may not be specified below. Plural is often ות- *-ot* rather than ים- *-im*.

Patterns (1-4). With fixed vowels.

(1)   *CaCuC* תפוז *tapuz.*
Examples: כדור *kadur,* תנור *tanur,* עמוד *amud,* תפוח *tapúaH.*

(2)   *CaCiC* סכין *sakin.*
Examples: פטיש *patish,* לפיד *lapid,* צדיק *tsadik,* שליט *shalit.*

(3)   *CiCoC* גיבור *gibor.*
Examples: צינור *tsinor,* רימון *rimon,* קיפוד *kipod,* כיור *kiyor.*

(4)   *CoC* קול *kol* (contrast with pattern (13)).
Examples: נוף *nof,* דור *dor,* חול *Hol,* עוף *of.*

Patterns (5-8). *-a-* drops.

(5)   *CaCaC* דברי ~ דברים ~ דברו ~ ... דבר ~ דבר *davar ~ dvar... ~ dvaro ~ dvarim ~ divrey...*
Examples: משל *mashal,* מרק *marak,* זקן *zakan,* צבא *tsava.*

(6)   *CCaCa* ...נדבות ~ נדבות ~ נדבתו ~ ... נדבת ~ נדבה *nedava ~ nidvat... ~ nidvato ~ nedavot ~ nidvot...*

Examples: קללה *klala,* פצצה *ptsatsa,* צדקה *tsdaka,* נשמה *neshama.*

(7) *CaCiC* ...סדיני ~ סדינים ~ סדינו ~ סדינו... ~ סדין ~ סדין *sadin ~ sdin...*
~ *sdino ~ sdinim ~ sdiney...*
Examples: שכיר *saHir,* גביע *gavía,* רהיט *rahit,* בציר *batsir.*

(8) *CiCaCon* זכרונות ~ זכרונו ~ ...זכרון ~ זכרון *zikaron ~ ziHron...*
~ *ziHrono ~ ziHronot.*
Examples: נקיון *nikayon,* בטחון *bitaHon,* שטפון *shitafon,* כשלון
kishalon.

Patterns (9-10). *-a-* in plural.

(9) *CiCCa* ...שכבות ~ שכבות ~ ...שכבת ~ שכבה *shiHva ~ shiHvat...~*
shHavot ~ shiHvot...
Examples: ספרה *sifra,* כבשה *kivsa,* שפחה *shifHa,* שמלה *simla.*

(10) *miCCeCet* ...משמרת ~ משמרות ~ משמרתו ~ ...משמרת ~ משמרת
mishméret ~ mishméret... ~ mishmarto ~ mishmarot ~ mishmerot...
Examples: מסגרת *misgéret,* משלחת *mishláHat,* מחברת *maHbéret.*

Pattern (11). *-e-* drops.

(11) *CiCoCet* קידומות ~ קידומתו ~ קידומת *kidómet ~ kidomto ~*
kidomot.
Examples: סיפורת *sipóret,* טינופת *tinófet,* גיורת *giyóret.*

Patterns (12-14). Vowel 'raised'/consonant 'hardened' ('despirantized').

(12) *CeC/CaC* מס ~ מיסו ~ חיכים ~ חיכו ~ חיכו ~ חך *HeH ~ Hiko ~ Hikim,*
~ מיסים *mas ~ miso ~ misim.*
Examples: נץ *nets,* עת *et,* תל *tel,* פת *pat,* גת *gat.*

(13) *CoC* דובים ~ דובו ~ דוב *dov ~ dubo ~ dubim.*
Examples: חוק *Hok,* עול *ol,* תוף *tof,* רוב *rov,* חוד *Hod.*

(14) *CaC* דפים ~ דפו ~ דף *daf ~ dapo ~ dapim.*
Examples: גן *gan,* סל *sal,* אף *af,* גב *gav.*

Patterns (15-17). Suffixes with fixed stress, generally no י- *-ey* construct suffix
- foreignisms, productively borrowed.

(15) נט- *-ent:* סטודנטים ~ סטודנט *student ~ studéntim.*
Examples: ארגומנט *argument,* פרלמנט *parlament,* פטנט *patent.*

(16) ט- -*at* : דמוקרטים ~ דמוקרט *demokrat* ~ *demokrátim*.
Examples :   פורמט *format*, קנדידט *kandidat*, קונגלומרט *konglomerat*.

(17) ציה- -*tsya* (unstressed): אמביציות ~ אמביציה *ambítsya* ~ *ambítsyot*.
Examples :   ריאקציה *reáktsya*, אינפלציה *inflátsya*, אמוציה *emótsya*.

38.4   Compound nouns, e.g. קולנוע *kolnóa* 'cinema'

Compounds are fairly numerous and are semi-productively coined.
They are loosely based on *two existing words*, joined (and sometimes adapted)
to form one word, grammatically and graphically.[3]

38.4.1   Shape

Most compounds are nouns built either of a construct phrase - often
with some shortening - or of verb + noun, the verb radically adjusted so that its
vowels fit a typical 'compound pattern'. Such construct phrases generally
express the same range of semantic relationships as construct phrases in general
(ch.6); verb + noun compounds express 'verb + object'. Examples are given in
the table on page 441.

Exceptions to these constructions are: חידק *Haydak* 'microbe' (noun + adjective: דק + חי *Hay* + *dak* 'life + thin'), אלפבית *alefbet* 'alphabet' (coordinated
nouns); חמשיר *Hamshir* 'limerick' (numeral + noun: שיר + חמש *Hamesh* +
shir '5 + poem').

Trade names are often compounds, e.g. תנועוף *tnu'of* (עוף + תנובה *tnuva*
+ *of* 'Tnuva + fowl'), ריצפז *ritspaz* (פז + רצפה *ritspa* + *paz* 'floor + Paz'),
בנקומט *bankomat* (אוטומט + בנק 'bank + automat'). Except in such trade
names, compound nouns (unlike suffixed nouns) favour 'native' words. A minor
exception are compounds involving a handful of meaningful prefixes that are
not independent words: דו- *du-* 'bi-', פרוטו- *próto-*, etc. Many such prefixes
are not strictly 'native'.

Compounds are kept brief - no more than two base-words, no more than five
consonants, plus drastic shortenings, giving the appearance of a 'native' root.
They also undergo the same derivational processes as native roots: שמרטפת
shmartéfet '(female) babysitter', מרומזר *merumzar* 'with traffic lights'.

38.4.2   Overall grammar

The plural is stressed (unlike foreignisms) and regular, e.g.
רשמקולים *reshamkolim* (contrast קולות ~ קול *kol* ~ *kolot*).
Like any noun, compounds serve as a basis for other words: -ן + אופנוע
ofnóa + *an* → אופנוען *ofnoan* 'cyclist'.

38.5   Acronyms, e.g. רב"ט *rabat* 'corporal'

Acronyms (abbreviations read as words) are fairly numerous and productive, especially in army usage. Most are two-syllabled, with (a) the (canoni-
cal) *a-a* vowel pattern and regular final stress or (b) occasionally, the chief

Examples of compound nouns

Construct phrase	Verb + noun[4]
SIDE BY SIDE	
kadurmáyim 'waterpolo' כדורמים (kadur + máyim 'ball + water' כדור + מים)	madHom 'thermometer' מדחום (madad + Hom 'measure + heat' מדד + חום)
ramkol 'loudspeaker' רמקול (ram + kol 'loud (ADJ) (of) sound (N)' רם + קול)	
CONFLATED CONSONANTS	
kadurégel 'football' כדורגל (kadur + régel 'ball + foot' כדור + רגל)	daHpor 'bulldozer' דחפור (daHaf (v) + Hafar (v) 'push + dig' דחף + חפר)
maHazémer 'musical' מחזמר (maHaze + zémer 'play + music' מחזה + זמר)	
DROPPED CONSONANTS	
migdalor 'lighthouse' מגדלור (migdal + 'or 'tower + light' מגדל + אור)	zarkor 'spotlight' זרקור (zarak + 'or 'throw + light' זרק + אור)
karnaf 'rhinoceros' קרנף (keren + 'af 'horn + nose' קרן + אף)	ramzor 'traffic light' רמזור (ramaz + 'or 'wink + light' רמז + אור)
DROPPED SYLLABLES	
rakével 'cablecar' רכבל (rakévet + kével 'train + cable' רכבת + כבל)	madHan 'parking meter' מדחן (madad + Hanaya 'measure + parking' מדד + חניה)
midraHov 'pedestrian precinct' מדרחוב (midraHa + reHov 'pavement + street' מדרחה + רחוב)	

'segolate' pattern *é-e* (or *á-a*), or (c) an *o* or *u* vowel when the letter *vav* is being represented. A double apostrophe precedes the final letter.

Examples are (a) תנ"ך *tanaH* 'Bible' (תורה-נביאים-כתובים *tora-nevi'im-ktuvim* 'Torah-prophets-writings'), רב"ט *rabat* 'corporal' (רב-טוראי *rav-turay*); (b) צה"ל *tsáhal* 'Israel Defence Forces' (צבא הגנה לישראל *tsva hagana leyisra'el*), אש"ל *éshel* 'board and lodging expenses' (אכילה-שתיה-לינה *aHila-shtiya-lina*); (c) חו"ל *Hul* 'outside of Israel' (חוץ לארץ *Huts la-árets*), מו"ל *mol* 'publisher' (מוציא לאור *motsi la-or*).

Many abbreviations, however, are read only as full words, e.g. ארה"ב = ארצות הברית *artsot ha-brit* 'USA', סה"כ = סך הכל *saH hakol* 'total'.

38.6   Which syllable is stressed?

Most nouns take stress on their final syllable - and this shifts onto any added suffix:

tapil + im   טפיל + ים   →   tapilim 'parasites' טפילים

However, a large class of nouns, of the כבד *CéCeC*, כובד *CóCeC* type (and their variants of the נעל *náal*, פרח *péraH*, נוהל *nóhal* types) and nouns ending in ת- -*et* (e.g. the כתובת *któvet*, משמרת *mishméret*, סכרת *sakéret* types, i.e. segolates) take stress on the *pre*-final syllable,[5] though stress does shift onto any added suffix, e.g. כתובתו *ktovtó*.

Notwithstanding, many nouns of כובד *CoCeC* and כבד *CaCaC* vowel patterns *are* final-stressed, i.e. patterns (1a), (4) - שומר *shomer*, טייס *tayas*, etc.

Foreignisms mostly have fixed stress, which does not shift to an added suffix. Where it falls depends on the particular suffix, but usually roughly as set out in (1)-(3) below.

(1) Foreignisms ending in a double consonant have final stress, e.g. -*ent*: סטודנט *student*; -*izm*: מרקסיזם *marksizm*; -*ekt*: פריוקט *proyekt*.

(2) Others have final or, preponderantly, non-final stress, e.g. -*op*: טלסקופ *teleskop*; -*us*: פרימוס *primus*; -*tor*: רפלקטור *refléktor*; -*a*: ויזה *víza*.

(3) Some exceptional types are: -*ika*: פוליטיקה *polítika*; -*on*: מיקרופון *mikrofón* vs. טלפון *télefon*.

Similarly, some emotive words (e.g. some first names/children's words), and initials, do not shift stress, e.g. גולה ~ יעקב ~ יעקבים *yáakov* ~ *yáakovim*, ~ גולות *gúla* ~ *gúlot* 'marbles', סבתא ~ סבתות *sávta* ~ *sávtot* 'grandmas', מ"ם-כ"ף ~ מ"ם-כ"פים *mem-kaf* ~ *mem-káfim* 'platoon commanders'.

FURTHER READING
Ben-Hayyim 1971; Bolozky 1972, 1980; Di-nur 1979; Masson 1976; Netzer 1976; Nir 1979; Rabin 1985; Rosén 1955, 1977, 1979.

39. Gender and number in the noun

39.1 What is gender?

All Hebrew nouns have a gender, either masculine or feminine (the conventional terms). There are two types - intrinsic gender and inflectional gender.

Intrinsic gender

For most nouns, gender has nothing to do with male or female or even masculinity and femininity - not even to the extent of causing any sexual loading on asexual words - but rather with two purely grammatical phenomena: agreement and the noun's own form.

	Gender	Characteristic
Primary phenomenon: *Agreement* (details in chs 12, 18)	Masculine noun	Adjectives qualifying such a noun add no suffix (are 'unmarked') in the singular.
	Feminine noun	Adjectives qualifying such a noun add ת-/ה- -*a* / -*t* in the singular.
Secondary phenomenon: *The noun's own form*	Masculine noun	Usually these are 'unmarked', i.e. have no special suffix in the singular.
	Feminine noun	Usually these end in ת / ה -*a* / -*t* in the singular.

Examples are: השק נשבר *ha-sak nishbar* 'The sack has broken' (m.); השקית נשברה *ha-sakit nishbera* 'The bag has broken' (f.).

Such nouns do not offer a 'choice' of gender - it is *intrinsic* (and is the same for singular as for plural); thus תקלה *takala* 'mishap' (f.) has no תקל* **takal* as a masculine counterpart. See further in 39.2-3.

Inflectional gender

Most nouns denoting humans (and often animals) have two versions: feminine for females, masculine for males, the feminine usually adding a predictable suffix to the masculine base - this is *inflectional* gender; see further in 39.4-5. ('Number', too, is inflectional; see 39.6).

39.2-3 INTRINSIC GENDER AND ITS FORM

39.2 Meaning-based gender

Several semantic domains might appear to have a preferred gender, thanks to the meaningfulness of particular noun patterns, e.g. ailments, being largely of the כבדת *kabédet* pattern, are mostly feminine as a result. Such things aside, only a handful of domains have a clearly preferred gender - mostly feminine:

39.2.1 Names

Countries and towns are feminine singular (note feminine מדינה *medina* 'country', ארץ *érets* 'country', עיר *ir* 'town'), though they need not be feminine singular in *form*: ארצות הברית *artsot habrit* 'the United States', ישראל *yisra'el* 'Israel', לבנון *levanon* 'Lebanon', הונגריה *hungárya* 'Hungary', דניה *dénya* 'Denmark', תל אביב *tel aviv*, חדרה *Hadéra*, רחובות *reHóvot*, חיפה *Háyfa / Heyfá* 'Haifa'.

Villages are often of both genders (note masculine מקום *makom* 'place', כפר *kfar* 'village'):

shilo dey	meruHak (m.) meruHéket (f.)	מרוחק שילה די מרוחקת
		'Shilo is rather far'

Regions, islands, mountains, rivers are generally masculine (איזור *ezor* 'region', אי *i* 'island', הר *har* 'mountain', נהר *nahar* 'river' are masculine.) However, feminine-looking cases are often treated as feminine:

ha-témza dey	amok amuka	po	פה	עמוק התמזה די עמוקה
				'The Thames is quite deep here'

First ('given') names follow the sex of the bearer. Many names for females end in ה-, ת- *-a, -t*; most names for males have no suffix.[1] This holds particularly for newer names. Examples are: females: גילה *gíla*, שרית *sarit*, מירב *merav*; males: גיל *gil*, אביב *aviv*.

Companies are 'personified' according to the form of the name (even though אסם מייצר... חברת אסם *Hevrat ósem* 'The Osem **Company**' is feminine); *ósem meyatser...* 'Osem produces...', תנובה/ויטה מייצרת... *tnúva / vita meyatséret...* 'Tnuva / Vita produces...'. Exceptions include אל-על *el-al* (f.). Names of products are masculine: אמה התייקר *áma hityaker* 'Ama has gone up in price'.

Festivals are masculine (חג *Hag* 'festival' is masculine): מתי מתחיל חנוכה/סוכות? *matay matHil Hanuka / sukot?* 'When does Hanuka / Sukot begin?', פורים שמח *purim saméaH* 'Happy Purim'. So too are books and newspapers (ספר *séfer* 'book', עיתון *iton* 'newspaper' are masculine).

Letters of the alphabet are feminine (אות *ot* 'letter' is feminine) and numbers masculine (as is מספר *mispar* 'number'): אל"ף גדולה *álef gdola* 'a big alef', איי אדומה *ay aduma* 'a red I'. But אלף-בית *alefbet* 'alphabet' and איקס *iks* 'x' are concepts in themselves and are masculine.

39.2.2 Other nouns

Words for *paired or multiple limbs* are mostly feminine - but mostly unsuffixed: אוזן *ózen* 'ear', שן *shen* 'tooth, קרן *kéren* 'horn', שפה *safa* 'lip', גבה *gaba* 'eyebrow', כתף *katef* 'shoulder', יד *yad* 'arm, hand', אצבע *étsba* 'finger', עצם *étsem* 'bone', כנף *kanaf* 'wing'.

Words for *intrinsically paired* objects,[2] used in the 'dual plural' (the suffix is ים-- *-áyim*, see 39.11) and not in the singular, tend to allow either gender, with a preference for feminine, influenced perhaps by paired-limb words (above). Purists, however, regard them as masculine: מכנסיים *miHnasáyim* 'pants', משקפיים *mishkafáyim* 'glasses', אופניים *ofnáyim* 'bicycle', מספריים *misparáyim* 'scissors', מאזניים *moznáyim* 'scales'.

Words for paired objects[3] *other than limbs*, used in both the singular and the dual, do not act as a group as regards gender. Thus: יום ~ יומיים *yom* ~ *yomáyim* 'day', חודש ~ חודשיים *Hódesh* ~ *Hodsháyim* 'month', מגף ~ מגפיים *magaf* ~ *magafáyim* 'boot', קב ~ קביים *kav* ~ *kabáyim* 'stilt, crutch' are all masculine, but שנה ~ שנתיים *shana* ~ *shnatáyim* 'year', נעל ~ נעליים *náal* ~ *naaláyim* 'shoe' are feminine.

39.3 Non-meaning-based gender

Nouns with the suffixes ה- ,ת- *-a*,[4] *-t*[5] are virtually all feminine, e.g. מלה *mila* 'word', וילה *víla* 'villa', גלות *galut* 'exile', תווית *tavit* 'label', מחתרת *maHtéret* 'underground'.

Other nouns are mostly masculine, e.g. בורג *bóreg* 'screw', תכשיט *taHshit* 'jewel', שגעון *shiga'on* 'lunacy'.

There are a few feminine words (besides those in 39.2) among unsuffixed nouns, including many segolates (*é-e*, *á-a* nouns), but not in a productive way. Notable examples are: ארץ *érets* 'land', קרקע *karka* 'ground', תבל *tevel* 'World'; רוח *rúaH* 'wind, spirit', אש *esh* 'fire', שמש *shémesh* 'sun', תהום *tehom* 'abyss'; אבן *éven* 'stone', באר *be'er* 'well', גדר *gader* 'fence', חצר *Hatser* 'yard', גורן *góren* 'barn', דרך *déreH* 'way, road', כיכר *kikar* 'square, loaf', עיר *ir* 'town'; ציפור *tsipor* 'bird', נפש *néfesh* 'soul'; בטן *béten* 'stomach', לשון *lashon* 'tongue'; גפן *géfen* 'vine'; נעל *náal* 'shoe', מחט *máHat* 'needle', כוס *kos* 'glass', (casually) עט *et* 'pen', חרב *Hérev* 'sword'; פעם *páam* 'time'; אמת *emét* 'truth'; קשת *késhet* 'bow' and most segolates with ת- *-t*.

A handful possess both genders, notably: סכין *sakin* 'knife' (but סכין גילוח *sakin gilúaH* 'razor' is masculine), דיו *dyo* 'ink', יתד *yated* 'peg', פנים *panim* 'face'.

39.4-5 INFLECTIONAL (MALE ~ FEMALE) GENDER AND ITS FORM

39.4 When is there inflection?

39.4.1 Denoting people

Virtually all nouns that ordinarily denote people have a masculine and a feminine form:[6]

tabaH ~ tabaHit	טבח ~ טבחית
	'male cook ~ female cook'
more ~ mora	מורה ~ מורה
	'male teacher ~woman teacher'
sgan menahel ~ sganit menahel	סגן מנהל ~ סגנית מנהל
	'male deputy manager ~ female deputy manager'

The feminine form is even used, as predicate, for *countries* (which are them-selves feminine: 39.2.1), as in:

brit ha-moatsot doréshet, ke-**sapakit** neft,...   ברה"מ דורשת, **כספקית** נפט,...
                    f.
              UNDERLYING PRED
                                'The USSR insists, as an oil **supplier**,...'

39.4.2 Exceptions to 39.4.1

A few nouns denoting people do not inflect but are nevertheless both masculine and feminine in terms of agreement; they include:

(a) The titles פרופסור *profesor*, דוקטור *dóktor*, some (puristically, all) military ranks, e.g. סגן *ségen* 'Lieutenant', סרן *séren* 'Captain'.

(b) ראש *rosh* 'head' in such expressions as:

Denoting a woman

rosh ha-memshala ha-	noHeHi (m.) noHeHit (f.)	maamina...		נוכחי מאמינה... ראש הממשלה ה
		f.		נוכחית

Denoting a man
...noHeHi...maamin...   ...ראש הממשלה הנוכחי מאמין
   m.   m.

                                    Both: 'The present Prime Minister believes...'

(c) The feminine of שר *sar* 'minister' can be either שר *sar* or שרה *sara*.

(d) A few miscellaneous items, e.g. מותק *mótek* 'darling', קולגה *koléga* 'col-league':

ata kaze mótek!	אתה כזה מותק!
m. m.	'You're such a darling!' (to male)
at kazot mótek!	את כזאת מותק!
f. f.	'You're such a darling!' (to female)

39.4.3   No gender distinction

אדם *adam* and בן-אדם *ben-adam* 'person' lack a feminine form, but can be used of females as well as males when acting as predicate. However, as such they are clearly masculine nouns in their own right, (unlike מותק *mótek* - see 39.4.2), as is shown by their agreement:[7]

hi lo (ben-)adam aHra'i (*not* *aHra'it)	היא לא (בן-)אדם אחראי (*אחראית)
m. f.	
she not person responsible	'She isn't a responsible person'

39.4.4   Animals

Animal terms in which 'male vs. female' has some significance usually have a masculine and feminine form:

avaz ~ avaza	'goose'	אווז ~ אווזה
táyish ~ iza	'goat'	תיש ~ עיזה
kélev ~ kalba	'dog'	כלב ~ כלבה

However, one of the two forms is used as a generic term, usually the masculine, e.g. כלב *kélev* 'dog', אווז *avaz* 'duck', but occasionally the feminine,[8] e.g. פרה *para* 'cow', כבשה *kivsa* 'sheep'.[9]

Where only one form exists, 'male vs. female' can be achieved by נקבת הנשר *nekevat ha-nésher* 'female of the eagle' etc., but usually the noun is simply used in whatever gender it has with no respect for sex:

m.: שועל *shu'al* 'fox', נחש *naHash* 'snake', עורב *orev* 'crow'
f.: ציפור *tsipor* 'bird', ארנבת *arnévet* 'hare', נמלה *nemala* 'ant'

39.5   The form of the inflection

39.5.1   Suffixes

The form of the feminine depends near-automatically on the form of the masculine (mostly morphophonologically but in 39.5.2 sometimes phonologically) - as set out in 39.5.2-4. We are concerned here with the suffixes, not with internal adjustments such as those in דוב ~ דובה *dov ~ duba* 'bear ~ she-bear'.

Sections 39.5.2-3 mainly involve *native, unsuffixed* nouns ('core nouns'), while 39.5.4 involves mainly *suffixed* nouns, or foreignisms. For a general outline of noun patterns, suffixes and internal adjustments, see chapter 38.

The inflection of nouns vs. verbs and adjectives

The rules in 39.5.2-4 also apply largely to adjectives and verbs (see chs. 40, 41), where these exist in the relevant patterns. For example, the inflection of *-e-* words (39.5.3) creates שופט ~ שופטת *shofet~shofétet* both as a noun (meaning 'judge') and as a verb ('is judging'). Similarly, the feminine of loan words involves ית- *-it* both for nouns (39.5.4), e.g. ברבר~ברברית

barbar~barbárit 'barbarian', and for adjectives, e.g. זיפת ~ זיפתית *zift~zíftit* 'rotten'.

The *plural* suffix, by contrast, often differs for nouns and adjectives (see 39.8), e.g. שולחנות עגולים *shulHanot agulim* 'round tables'. Furthermore, the *internal* adjustments caused by feminine suffixes on nouns and adjectives are often quite unlike those found in verbs:

| N: | gamal~gmala | 'camel~she-camel' | גמל~גמלה |
| V: | gamal~gamla | 'bestowed (m.)~bestowed (f.)' | גמל~גמלה |

39.5.2 Taking the stressed suffix ה- *-á*
The following take the suffix ה- *-á* (stressed):[10]

(a) One-syllable nouns, e.g. אל ~ אלה *el~ela* 'god~goddess'. Similarly, שר *sar* 'minister', צבי *tsvi* 'deer', and others.

(b) Nouns whose last stem-vowel is *-i-* or *-u-* ('high vowels') or *-o-*; e.g. (1) *-i-* תלמיד ~ תלמידה *talmid~talmida* 'student'; similarly מנהיג *manhig* 'leader', עני *ani* 'pauper' etc. (2) *-u-* בחור ~ בחורה *baHur~baHura* 'boy~girl'; similarly חלוץ *Haluts* 'pioneer', פצוע *patsúa* 'casualty' etc. (3) *-o-* יתום ~ יתומה *yatom~yetoma* 'orphan'; similarly לקוח *lakóaH* 'customer', חמור *Hamor* 'donkey' etc.

(c) Nouns whose last stem-vowel is *-e-* or *-a-*, provided they belong to a pattern with a 'fluctuating' first vowel (for those with a 'fixed' first vowel, see 39.5.3), e.g. (1) כבד *kaved* pattern: שכן ~ שכנה *shaHen~shHena* 'neighbour'; (2) כבד *kavad* pattern: גמל ~ גמלה *gamal~gmala* 'camel'; (3) כבד *kéved* pattern (and variants, see ch. 38): ילד ~ ילדה *yéled~yalda* 'boy~girl', כבש ~ כבשה *kéves~kivsa* 'sheep'.

(d) Nouns ending in ה- *-e*, e.g. מורה ~ מורה *more~mora* 'teacher'. Similarly, מרצה *martse* 'lecturer', שוטה *shote* 'lunatic', and others

(e) Ethnicity nouns ('gentilics') ending in the *stressed* suffix י- *-i* (38.2 pattern (24)), most of which are apparently those European/Middle Eastern groups perceived as prominent around 1900, e.g. צרפתי ~ צרפתיה *tsarfatí~tsarfatiá* 'Frenchman~Frenchwoman';[11] and similarly, אנגלי *anglí* 'Englishman', גרמני *germaní* 'German', הונגרי *hungarí* 'Hungarian', תורכי *turkí* 'Turk', ערבי *araví* 'Arab', אשכנזי *ashkenazí* 'Ashkenazi', יהודי *yehudí* 'Jew', נוצרי *notsrí* 'Christian', נכרי *noHrí* 'foreigner', צועני *tsoaní* 'Gypsy', כפרי *kafrí* 'peasant', דתי *datí* 'religious person'.

Examples of gentilics with unstressed י- *-i* plus feminine suffix ת- *-t* are בלגי ~ בלגית *bélgi~bélgit* 'Belgian', הודי ~ הודית *hódi~hódit* 'Indian' etc.

39.5.3 Taking the unstressed suffix ת- *-et* (or its variant ת- *-at*)
This involves nouns whose last stem-vowel is *-e-* or *-a-* (cf. 39.5.2) but with a 'fixed' first vowel:[12] (1) *-e-* גיבן ~ גיבנת *giben~gibénet* 'hunchback'; similarly מודד *moded* 'surveyor', מחנך *meHaneH* 'educator'. (2) *-a-* כוכב ~ כוכבת *koHav~koHévet* 'star (performer)'; similarly גנן *ganan* 'nursery

teacher', חייל *Hayal* 'soldier', סרטט *sartat* 'draughtsman', שמרטף *shmartaf* 'babysitter'. Verb-shaped nouns with *-a-*: נאשם *neesham* 'defendant', משומד *meshumad* 'apostate', מועמד *muamad* 'candidate'.

It also involves the few nouns with diminutive ון- *-on*, e.g. טיפשון~טיפשונת *tipshon~tipshónet* 'little fool'.

39.5.4 Taking the suffix ית- *-it* (commonest of the three suffixes)

(a) Nouns with a suffix ן- *-an* (see 38.2): (1) כבד+ן *kavd+an* pattern' מרדן~מרדנית *mardan~mardanit* 'rebel': also בכיין *baHyan* 'crybaby', דקדקן *dakdekan* 'pedant' etc. (2) ן- *-an* pattern: ליצן~ליצנית *letsan~letsanit* 'clown'; also מדען *mad'an* 'scientist', סולן *solan* 'soloist' etc.

(b) Nouns with suffix אי- *ay, -a'i* : חקלאי~חקלאית *Haklay~Hakla'it* 'farmer'; also כבאי *kabay* 'fireman', עתונאי *itona'i* 'journalist' (-*y, -i* drop before -*it* is added - also before plural -*im*, see note 17).

(c) Ethnicity nouns ending in unstressed י- *-i*: יפני~יפנית *yapáni~yapánit* 'Japanese' (-*i* drops before -*it* is added).

(d) Some כבד (*kabad*)-type nouns, notably (1) those with ן- *-an*, appearing as if ן- *-an* were a suffix rather than part of the stem; (2) uncommon words, treated as foreignisms, like those below; (3) sundry (for various reasons):

(1) זבן~זבנית *zaban~zabanit* 'salesperson'; also נגן *nagan* 'musician', גנן ~ גננית *ganan~gananit* 'gardener' (but גננת *ganénet* 'nursery teacher', 39.5.3).

(2) דווד~דוודית *davad~davadit* 'kettle-maker', קשט *kashat* 'decorator' etc.

(3) כנר~כנרית *kanar~kanarit* 'violinist'; also ספר *sapar* 'hairdresser', טבח *tabaH* 'cook' etc.

(e) The few nouns with four-consonant stems, e.g. אזרח~אזרחית *ezraH~ezraHit* 'citizen'; also גזבר *gizbar* 'treasurer', אפרוח *efróaH* 'chick' etc. (except כבד *CaCCaC* type, e.g. סרטט, see 39.5.3).

(f) 'Marginal' words - unstressed ית- *-it*, e.g. (1) foreignisms: שוויצר~שוויצרית *shvítser~shvítserit* 'show-off'; also סטודנט *student*, דיפלומט *diplomat*, צ'ליסט *tshelist* 'cellist' etc. (2) Acronyms: סג"מ~סג"מית *sagam~sagámit* '2nd Lieutenant', רב"ט *rabat* 'Corporal' etc.

39.6-13 NUMBER IN THE NOUN

39.6 What is number?

Every occurrence of a Hebrew noun has 'number', singular or plural; many but by no means all nouns can occur with either. 'Number' is a matter of meaning (for most nouns) and of grammar.

39.6.1 Meaning

Note first that nouns are either 'countable' or 'non-countable' (some are both, depending on their meaning):

	Singular			Counted Plural	
COUNTABLE:					
	kéves	'a sheep'	כבש	shlosha kvasim	שלושה כבשים
					'three sheep (pl.)'
NON-COUNTABLE:					
Collective:	tson	'sheep'	צאן	*but not:*	
Stuff:	kéraH	'ice'	קרח	*shlosha	
				{tson/tsonim}	*שלושה {צאן/צאנים}
Abstract:	kor	'cold'	קור	('three sheep (s.)/(pl.)') etc.	
Proper name:	yaakov		יעקב		

For nearly all 'countable' nouns: *Singular* denotes *one*: אוניה *oniya* 'a ship'; *Plural* denotes more than one: אוניות *oniyot* 'ships'. 'Non-countable' nouns lack number contrast - nearly all are only singular, and a few only plural (thus, singular is 'unmarked'); see further 39.7.

ONLY SINGULAR:	óHel	'food'	אוכל
ONLY PLURAL:	Hadashot	'news'	חדשות

39.6.2 Grammar

The noun's own form: singular has no special ending: plural usually ends in ים- *-im* or ות- *-ot*.

Agreement: words agreeing with a singular noun add no special ending for number; words agreeing with a plural noun add ים- *-im* (m.) or ות- *-ot* (f.). Examples are:

Hatulim Humim	חתולים חומים	Hatul Hum	חתול חום
pl. pl.		s. s.	
cats brown	'brown cats'	cat brown	'brown cat'

Dual

Though traditional grammars talk of three-way number, i.e. singular, plural and (for a few nouns ending in ים-*-áyim*) dual, dual is mostly none other than a particular form of the plural used with certain words, as in:

shloshim shináyim	'thirty teeth'	שלושים שיניים
arba ragláyim	'four legs'	ארבע רגליים

This is discussed under the heading 'Pseudo-dual' in 39.11. By contrast, a few nouns have a real dual suffix, equivalent to adding the numeral '2' (see 39.11), e.g. יומיים *yomáyim* 'two days'.

39.7 Countable and non-countable: בגד *béged* 'garment' vs. ביגוד *bigud* 'clothing'

39.7.1 Countability

Commonly, nouns for individual objects or events are countable (מכונית *meHonit* 'car', תאונה *teuna* 'accident') while those denoting stuff (אש *esh* 'fire', זהב *zahav* 'gold'), quality (יופי *yófi* 'beauty', חום *Hom* 'heat'), proper names (יעקב *yaakov* 'Jacob') and many abstract nouns (סיוע *siyúa* 'help', שכר *saHar* 'pay', שלום *shalom* 'peace') are non-countable.

Often, however, something can be viewed as both countable and non-countable, in four ways:

Countable			Non-countable		

(1) Using the same word for both (especially if a 'stuff' can commonly be had in units)

zHuHit	'a pane of glass'	זכוכית	zHuHit	'glass'	זכוכית
léHem	'a loaf'	לחם	léHem	'bread'	לחם
dag	'a fish'	דג	dag	'fish'	דג
sukar	'a piece of sugar'	סוכר	sukar	'sugar'	סוכר
gir	'a piece of chalk'	גיר	gir	'chalk'	גיר
ets	'a piece of wood'	עץ	ets	'wood'	עץ
niyar	'a sheet of paper' (C)	נייר	niyar	'paper'	נייר

This is the general rule for vegetables, but not for fruit:

sheu'it	'a bean'	שעועית	sheu'it	'beans'	שעועית
afuna	'a pea'	אפונה	afuna	'peas'	אפונה

and חסה *Hása* 'lettuce', גזר *gézer* 'carrot', סלק *sélek* 'beetroot', בצל *batsal* 'onion', חיטה *Hita* 'wheat(-ear)' etc. (but עדשה *adasha* 'lentil' is only countable) - as against תפוח *tapúaH* 'an apple', ענב *enav* 'a grape', עגבניה *agvaniya* 'a tomato' etc.

(2) But often, one noun can hereby have two distinct meanings (a 'doublet'):

of	'a bird'	עוף	of	'chicken'	עוף
mazal	'a sign (of Zodiac)'	מזל	mazal	'luck'	מזל
barzel	'a wire, railing'	ברזל	barzel	'iron'	ברזל

(3) Occasionally the basic meaning distinction between countable and non-countable can be achieved by using two different nouns:

para	'a cow'	פרה	bakar	'beef'	בקר
béged	'a garment'	בגד	bigud	'clothing'	ביגוד
seara	'a hair'	שערה	se'ar	'hair'	שיער
srefa	'a fire'	שרפה	esh	'fire'	אש
medura		מדורה			
maase rétsaH	'an act of murder'	מעשה רצח	rétsaH	'murder'	רצח

(4) But sometimes, surprisingly, a concrete object is non-countable - usually an inherent plural or dual, e.g. מגורים *megurim* 'residence'. See further in 39.7.2.

Further countable non-countables

Proper names can regularly be used as countable common nouns - in two ways (details in 39.10.):

'100 people called Einstein'	mea áynshtayn(im)	מאה איינשטיין(ים)
'100 Einsteins'	mea áynshtaynim	מאה איינשטיינים
(Einstein-like people)		

But 'three kinds of sugar, bread', etc. is usually expressed as שלושה מיני סוכר, לחם *shlosha miney sukar, léHem* 'three kinds of...', not שלושה סוכרים,* לחמים *shlosha sukárim, leHamim* ('three sugars, breads'); an exception is יינות *yenot* 'wines'.

39.7.2   The plural with non-countables[13]

A good few non-countables *require* the plural: דברים *dvarim* 'words' (דבר *davar* 'a thing'), חיים *Hayim* 'life', כבסים *kvasim* 'laundry', כלולות *klulot* 'wedding', מגורים *megurim* 'residence', מיים *máyim* 'water', עשרות *asarot* 'tens (of...)', אירוסים *erusim* 'engagement'. *Dualia tantum*: אופניים *ofanáyim* 'bicycle', מכנסיים *miHnasáyim* 'pants', משקפיים *mishkafáyim* 'glasses'.[14] This is a productive phenomenon.

39.8   Singular and plural

39.8.1   When is there singular or plural?

Virtually all countable nouns allow the distinction: singular 'one' vs. plural 'more than one'. Even when singular nouns are collective, denoting people or things viewed as one unit (ועד *váad* 'commitee', סט *set* 'set' etc.), they are *singular* in form and agreement:[15]

ha-váad hitpater (*hitpatru)   הוועד התפטר (*התפטרו)
the committee has- (*have-)resigned

Occasionally, a plural noun is employed as a name - and then has the number (as well as the gender, see 39.2.1.) of the person/thing named: *a person*: חיים *Háyim*, רחמים *ráHamim* (contrast *Hayím* (final stress) meaning 'life'); *a place*: ארצות הברית *artsot ha-brit* 'USA', רחובות *reHóvot*, עלומים *alumím*.

No plural

A few countables rely on paraphrase ('suppletion') for their plural, e.g. מכולת ~ חנויות מכולת *makólet ~ Hanuyot makólet* 'grocery store ~s', אדם ~ בני-אדם *adam ~ bney-adam* 'person~s'.
The pronouns מי *mi* 'who?', מישהו *míshehu* 'someone' have no plural (though they have gender):

| mi
míshehu | ba (*ba'im) | מי
מישהו | בא (*באים) |

who
someone   is (*are) coming

Several countables with no plural *suffix* can in fact be plural ('zero plural'), e.g. שני יעקב *shney yáakov* 'two Yaakovs', שני אבוקדו *shney avokádo* 'two avocados'; see further 39.10.

No singular

A few countables rely on paraphrase for their singular:

shlosha Hévre	~ adam eHad	שלושה חברה ~ אדם אחד
shlosha anashim		שלושה אנשים
		'three people ~ one person'

shlosha bney-nóar ~ náar eHad	שלושה בני-נוער ~ נער אחד
	'three youths ~ one youth'

Most plurals with no singular are in fact *non*-countables (see 39.7.2).

A handful of non-countable plural nouns with no singular are re-employed (casually) as countables (as if like חבר'ה *Hévre* 'people'), e.g. פנים~שני פנים *panim* ~ *shney panim* 'face ~ two faces', מאזניים ~ שני מאזניים *moznáyim* ~ *shney moznáyim* 'scales ~ two scales' (but often זוג *zug* 'pair' is used: מספריים ~ שני זוגות מספריים *misparáyim* ~ *shney zugot misparáyim* 'scissors ~ two pairs of scissors'; see 39.7.2).

39.8.2 The placement of the plural suffix

The plural 'morpheme' always comes at the *end* of the noun. But how to define this 'end' is a matter of some complexity.

There are four degrees of noun combination (see 38.4) as set out in the table here; notice the position of ה- *ha-* 'the'. The *plural suffix* is in fact the ultimate key to 'surface' word-division.[16]

Placement of plural suffix in the four types of noun combination

Combination type	Example		Plural placement	
Compound	ha-ramzor 'the traffic-light'	הרמזור	ha-ramzorim (End of noun)	הרמזורים
Semi-compound (C)	ha-ben-adam 'the person'	הבן-אדם	ha-bney-adam (End of first noun)	הבני-אדם
Tight construct phrase	bet-ha-séfer 'the school'	בית-הספר	batey-ha-séfer (End of first noun)	בתי-הספר
Loose construct phrase	maftéaH ha-séfer '⟨the⟩ index-of the book'	מפתח הספר	mafteHot ha-séfer '⟨the⟩ indices-of the book' (End of first noun)	מפתחות הספר

39.9 -10 FORM OF THE PLURAL

Plural is virtually always expressed by a *suffix*, occasionally by 'nothing' ('zero'). The suffix often entails internal adjustments to the word - briefly described in 38.2 together with other suffix adjustments.

39.9 Plural suffixes

39.9.1 General outline

The masculine plural suffix is ים- *-im* in the *'absolute* (free) state' and י- *-ey* in the *'construct* state', e.g. the plural of ארגז *argaz* 'crate' is:

Absolute plural:	argazim	'crates'	ארגזים
Construct plural:	argazey (tapuzim)	'crates-of (oranges)'	ארגזי (תפוזים)

There are numerous exceptions, described in 39.9.2.

The feminine plural suffix is ות- *-ot* in both absolute and construct state, e.g. the plural of תקרה *tikra* 'ceiling' is:

Absolute plural:	tikrot	'ceilings'	תקרות
Construct plural:	tikrot (ets)	'ceilings-of (wood)'	תקרות (עץ)

There are occasional exceptions.[17]

39.9.2 Masculine nouns with exceptional plurals

Plural ות- *-ot* (non-productive)

At least eighty masculine nouns take ות- *-ot*. Of these over half have *-o-* as their last stem-vowel. The main types are as follows:

(a) Most nouns with ון- *-on* (whether clearly a suffix or not),[18] e.g. ארמון *armon* 'palace', וילון *vilon* 'curtain', יתרון *yitron* 'advantage'.

(b) Most other nouns with *-o-* (or *-óa-*) as last vowel,[19] especially: one-syllable: אור *or* 'light', כוח *kóaH* 'force', בור *bor* 'pit'; two-syllable: חלום *Halom* 'dream', יסוד *yesod* 'basis', לקוח *lakóaH* 'customer'; *m-* prefix: מבוא *mavo* 'preface', מחול *maHol* 'dance', מקצוע *miktsóa* 'profession'.

(c) Most nouns in ה-ֶ *-e*, e.g. מחזה *maHaze* 'play', מחנה *maHane* 'camp', מקווה *mikve* 'ritual bath' (מקוואות~ *mikva'ot*), משקה *mashke* 'drink' (משקאות~ *mashka'ot*), שדה *sade* 'field' (some exceptions: מבנה *mivne* 'structure', מקרה *mikre* 'instance').

(d) Sundry, e.g. זוג *zug* 'pair', לוח *lúaH* 'blackboard', אב *av* 'father', אוצר *otsar* 'treasury', אילן *ilan* 'tree', מפתח *maftéaH* 'key', מזלג *mazleg* 'fork', יער *yáar* 'forest', נהר *nahar* 'river', לילה *láyla* (*~lelot*) 'night'.

39.9.3 Feminine nouns with exceptional plurals

Most ות-, ית- *-it, -ut* nouns drop ת- *-t* and then add יות- *-yot* (not ות- *-ot*),[20] e.g. כפית~כפיות *kapit~kapiyot* 'spoon', כמות~כמויות *kamut~kamuyot* 'quantity'.

Plural ים- *im* (non-productive)

Some thirty feminine nouns take -*im*, including about half of the feminine nouns lacking a feminine suffix, e.g. אבן ~ אבנים *éven~avanim* 'stone', עיר ~ ערים *ir~arim* 'town'. The group includes some dozen plants, fruits etc., e.g. אפונה ~ אפונים *afuna~afunim* 'pea', בוטנה *botna* 'peanut', שושנה *shoshana* 'lily'; some fauna, e.g. יונה *yona* 'pigeon', דבורה *dvora* 'bee', כינה *kina* 'louse', נמלה *nemala* 'ant'. It also includes sundry items, e.g. ביצה *betsa* 'egg', גחלת *gaHélet* 'coal', אשה ~ נשים *isha~nashim* (construct נשי/נשות *neshey* or *neshot*) 'woman', שנה ~ שנים *shana~shanim* (construct שנות *shnot*) 'year'.

39.10 'Zero plural', e.g. שני אבוקדו *shney avokádo* 'two avocados'

Proper names in the plural and a small phonological class of nouns can express plural without using a suffix, i.e. 'zero plural'.

Proper names have three supplementary roles, in which they can be plural: These are described in (a)-(c) below.

(a) Family names can be used to denote *all the family* - in the plural: either with ה... -ים *ha* (DEF)-*im* (pl.) (i.e. in all respects a common noun) or with neither (i.e. a kind of proper noun):

ha-grínbergim ba'im grinberg	הגרינברגים באים גרינברג
	'The Greenbergs are coming'
aHron ha-kénedim	אחרון הקנדים
	'the last of the Kennedys'

(b) Family names 'commonized' to denote 'people called...' can take ים- -*im* or zero:

góldberg eHad u-shlosha grínberg(im)	גולדברג אחד ושלושה גרינברג(ים)
	'one Goldberg and three Greenbergs'

Other names take 'zero':[21]

shney yáakov ve-shalosh miHal	שני יעקב ושלוש מיכל
	'two Yaakovs and three Michals'

(c) A name denoting a 'type' is generally suffixed, like any plural common noun:

hayu fróydim ve-yiyu fróydim	היו פרוידים ויהיו פרוידים
	'There have been Freuds and there will be Freuds'

A phonological class are nouns ending in the vowels ו ;ו- -*o, -u*. They tend to take zero plural. (To avoid the same problem of vowel + suffix, י-, ה ֶ , -*e, -i* as final vowels, and often -*a*, drop before a suffix.) Examples are:

shney avokádo, rádyo, kenguru, tábu   שני אבוקדו, רדיו, קנגורו, טאבו
                                        'Two avocados, radios, kangaroos, taboos'

Items with uncertain plural are: אוטו *óto* 'car', קונצ'רטו *kontshérto* 'concerto',
סולו *sólo* 'solo'.

39.11 Dual (יומיים *yomáyim* 'two days') and pseudo-dual (רגליים *ragláyim* 'legs')

There are two types of 'duality'.

Real dual - an 'allomorph' of שתיים *shtáyim* (see further 8.11)

With time units, the number 'two' is expressed not by שתיים
shtáyim but by the dual suffix -ַיים *-áyim,* usurping the plural suffix:[22]

shaatáyim	'two hours'	שעתיים
shvu'áyim	'two weeks'	שבועיים
(not necessarily 'two consecutive weeks' etc.)		

Pseudo-dual: a type of plural

At least thirty nouns form their *plural* in -ַיים *-áyim* instead of in
-ִים, -וֹת *-im, -ot.* Like other plural (and singular) suffixes, this has a construct
form, -ֵי *-éy,* and agreeing verbs etc. have the usual plural form:

ragley	ha-yeladim	'the legs of the children'	רגלי הילדים
CONSTRUCT			

ha-yadáyim koavot	'My arms hurt'	הידיים כואבות
pl.		

There are four types of pseudo dual, set out in (a)-(d) below.

(a) Most paired external limbs (they may in practice be more than two - hence
the heading '*pseudo*-dual': רגליים *ragláyim* is 'two legs' in pragmatic usage):[23]

shtey/shalosh oznáyim, sfatáyim,	שתי/שלוש אוזניים, שפתיים,
shináyim, tsipornáyim	שיניים, ציפורניים
	'two/three ears, lips, teeth, nails'

(b) A few other typically-paired objects, e.g. שתי/שלוש נעליים, גרביים, קביים
shtey/shalosh naaláyim, garbáyim, kabáyim 'two/three shoes, socks, stilts'.

(c) A few intrinsically-paired objects (mostly non-countable), e.g. מלקחיים
melkaHáyim 'pliers', משקפיים *mishkafáyim* 'glasses', ריחיים *reHáyim* 'mill-
stone'.

(d) A few non-paired objects, e.g. מים *máyim* 'water', צהריים *tsohoráyim*
'lunchtime', כיריים *kiráyim* 'stove'.

However, a few such nouns also have a non-paired sense and a non-dual plural,
e.g. שפה ~ שפות *safa~safot* 'language'.

39.12-13 'PLURAL-LOSS' (שלושים יום *SHLOSHIM YOM* **'THIRTY DAYS')**
Certain plural nouns - plural in meaning and agreement - are superficially singular *in form* when combined with certain numerals:

shloshim yom avru (*...yamim...)   (...ימים...*) שלושים יום עברו
30 day passed (*...days...)
Two alternative processes are at work: 'plural-loss' and 'super-plural-loss'.

39.12 'Plural-loss'
Time units[24] with ים- -*im* may revert to their singular form when combined with *numerals over 10* ('non-digitals')[25]:

(1) aHad-asar yom/yamim   אחד-עשר יום/ימים
     11 day/days

(2) esrim réga   עשרים רגע
     20 minute

(3) esrim u-shlosha Hódesh/Hodashim   עשרים ושלושה חודש/חודשים
     23 month/months

(4) shva-me'ot shana   שבע-מאות שנה
     700 year

Plural-loss is obligatory when the numeral itself ends in a plural suffix, as in examples (2,4) - thus avoiding two consecutive plural suffixes - and optional elsewhere.[26]

Some other, disparate nouns, notably חבר *Haver* 'member', ילד *yéled* 'child', נפש *néfesh* 'person', תלמיד *talmid* 'pupil', פעם *páam* 'time', מנה *mana* 'portion', עמוד *amud* 'page', also undergo plural loss - optionally.

39.13 'Super-plural-loss'
This process goes further: amount terms, and certain 'group terms', with ים- -*im* revert to singular form when combined with *any* numeral[27] (except puristically):

hayu shmonim dólar/ish   היו שמונים דולר/איש
there-were eighty dollar/person

Amount terms are of four types: (1) currencies: מארק *mark,* גרוש *grush,* פונט *funt* etc.; (2) measurements: מטר *méter* 'metre', קילו *kílo,* ואט *vat* 'watt', קשר *késher* 'knot' etc.; (3) numerals: מליון *milyon,* מליארד *milyard* 'billion', תריסר *tresar* 'dozen' etc.; (4) אחוז *aHuz* 'per cent'. Group terms are: חייל *Hayal* 'soldier', ראש *rosh* 'head (of livestock)', איש *ish* 'person'.

FURTHER READING
Blau 1967; Cohen & Zafrani 1968; Glinert 1976a, 1977a; Grosu 1969; Guiora *et al.* 1980; Ornan 1979a; Podolsky 1981; Rosén 1955, 1977; Schwarzwald 1982b.

40. Verb types and their inflections

40.1 Introduction: what is a verb?

Verbs usually denote an *action*, but this is only a rough guide: צדק *tsadak* 'be right', טעה *ta'a* 'be wrong', אהב *ahav* 'love' and many others arguably denote *state*, just like adjectives.

Verbs are distinct in shape from adjectives or nouns, in that they alone have past and future tense inflections, and imperative and infinitive forms:[1]

Past :	daráHti	'I stepped'	דרכתי
Future :	edroH	'I'll step	אדרוך
Imperative :	droH	'Step!'	דרוך
Infinitive:	lidroH	'to step'	לדרוך

However, the present tense form (and inflection) of verbs is not exclusive to verbs; it is used for many nouns and adjectives too, especially 'present participle' adjectives and nouns (derived from many verbs):

Present verb :	noded	'migrate'	נודד	mealef	'train'	מאלף
Noun :	noded	'wanderer'	נודד	mealef	'trainer'	מאלף
Adjective :	noded	'migratory'	נודד	mealef	'instructive'	מאלף

Yet all verbs, even present tense, are distinct *syntactically* from adjectives and nouns. (1) They always directly complement their subject, with no intervening copula (הוא *hu*, היא *hi*, etc., see 16.2):

Hatulim (*hem) megargerim	'Cats (*are) purr'	חתולים (*הם) מגרגרים
gam nemerim (*hem) yeHolim	'Even tigers (*are) can'	גם נמרים (*הם) יכולים

(2) For several other *negative* distinctions, see 41.2.

40.2-9 VERB TYPES

In 40.2-9 are described the various types of root and verb pattern. The rest of the chapter deals with inflection of such patterns, for tense, gender, number and person.

All Hebrew verbs[2] consist of (a) some vowel pattern or prefix + vowel pattern (traditional term: *binyan*, pl. *binyanim*, i.e. 'structure'), slotted into (b) a skeleton of consonants (the 'root').[3] The pattern and root do not occur independently but only in combination. For a given root, up to seven patterns may be available:

Root	Vowel pattern		Verb		
מ.ס.ר m.s.r.	-a-a-	⇒	masar	'hand'	מסר

458

Prefix + vowel
pattern

ni--a-	⇒	nimsar	'be handed'	נמסר
hit-a-e-	⇒	hitmaser	'devote oneself'	התמסר

40.2 Roots

Roots will be represented as letters and dots, e.g. *m.s.r.*

40.2.1 Meaning

Many roots have a well-defined meaning, elaborated in certain well-defined ways by way of the various *binyanim* :

ר.ט.ב.	nirtav	'get wet'	נרטב
r.t.v.	hirtiv	'make wet'	הרטיב
	hurtav	'be made wet'	הורטב
	hitratev	'get wet'	התרטב

Indeed, an awareness of a 'root meaning' is apparent from the way that roots are currently coined or extended across the *binyanim* (see 40.3).

On the other hand, in many roots there is nothing approaching a general root meaning. One meaning may obtain in one or two of the *binyanim*, while in the others a quite different meaning (or meanings) may obtain, as in (1) below; or else some related but unpredictable meaning, as in (2). The root here is a *grammatical*, not a semantic, entity (so too the relationship between the *binyanim* on the different lines below), rather as the English verbal prefixes *de-*, *ex-*, *sub-* etc. are grammatical, but scarcely meaningful, entities:[4]

(1) ז.מ.ר. z.m.r.

zamar 'prune' זמר   zimer 'sing'   זימר

(2) ב.ש.ל. b.sh.l.

bashel 'ripe' בשל	hivshil 'ripen' הבשיל	hitbashel 'mature'	התבשל
bishel 'cook' בישל	bushal 'be cooked' בושל	hitbashel 'become cooked'	התבשל

40.2.2 Form

Most roots have three or four, a few two or even five consonants, capable of slotting into a prefix + vowel pattern to make a one- or two-syllable verb:[5]

Root			Verb (for example)		
2 consonants	g.r.	ג.ר.	gar	'reside'	גר
3	k.l.l.	כ.ל.ל.	hiHlil	'generalize'	הכליל
4	m.H.sh.v	מ.ח.ש.ב.	miHshev	'computerize'	מיחשב
5	f.l.r.t.t.	פ.ל.ר.ט.ט.	flirtet	'flirt'	פלירטט

Out of a noun built from a verb or verbal root by adding a prefix (shown in bold type in this example) or suffix, Hebrew in turn frequently creates a further, *secondary* root. Example:

asa עשה   ⇒   taasiya **ת**עשיה
'make'   'industry'

⇓

Secondary root: t.'.s. .ת.ע.ש
                          ⇓   ⇓
              ti'es תיעש   ti'us תיעוש
            'to industrialize' 'industrialization'

yasad יסד   ⇒   mosad **מ**וסד
'to institute'   'institution'

⇓

Secondary root: m.s.d. .מ.ס.ד
                          ⇓   ⇓
              mised מיסד   mimsad ממסד
            'to institutionalize' 'Establishment'

Another method is to reduplicate the final root consonant of a verb or noun,[6] e.g.:

kadur	'ball'	כדור	→	kidrer	'to dribble'	כידרר
erev	'to involve'	עירב	→	irbev	'to mix'	עירבב
toHnit	'programme'	תוכנית	→	tiHnen	'to plan'	תיכנן
af	'to fly'	עף	→	ofef	'to fly'[7]	עופף

Noun-based roots as a whole are productively coined today.

40.3   Verb patterns (*binyanim*) and their general meaning

40.3.1   Form

There are seven *binyanim*. On the left we list their 'basic' prefix + vowel pattern (i.e. the 3rd masculine singular past tense form traditionally considered the 'basic' unaffixed reference form). The dashes are for root consonants to be inserted. On the right are their traditional names, which make use of a 'model root' .פ.ע.ל *p.'.l.*[8]

1	-a-a-	פעל	*pa'al* (also called *kal*)[9]
2	ni--a-	נפעל	*nif'al*
3	hi--i-	הפעיל	*hif'il*
4	hu--a-	הופעל	*huf'al*
5	-i-e-	פיעל	*pi'el*
6	-u-a-	פועל	*pu'al*
7	hit-a-e-	התפעל	*hitpa'el*

These basic forms can vary according to tense, person etc. (see 40.11-15) or because of the shape of the root (40.17-23).

In patterns 5-7, most roots with identical 2nd and 3rd consonant have *-o-e-*, *-o-a-* and *hit-o-e-*. These are treated not as separate patterns but as an effect of the root; see 40.23.

A few verbs are formed in patterns 5-7 by prefixing - ש *sh-* (often creating or reinforcing some sense of a 'repeated action'), - ת *t-* and arguably even - א *'-* (neither has a distinct meaning) to certain roots. These processes are too unproductive and too indistinct in meaning to be rated as further *binyanim*. These are all simply individual new roots, for example:

katav	'write'	כתב	~	shiHtev	'rewrite'	שיכתב
kafal	'double'	כפל	~	shiHpel	'duplicate'	שיכפל
Hazar	'return'	חזר	~	shiHzer	'reconstruct'	שיחזר
délek	'fuel'	דלק	~	tidlek	'refuel'	תידלק
HaHam	'clever'	חכם	~	metuHkam	'sophisticated'	מתוחכם
maHsan	'storehouse'	מחסן	~	iHsen	'to store'	איחסן

Similarly, new roots formed by reduplication (see 40.2.2) do not represent an additional *binyan*.

Root insertion

Pa'al and *nif'al* use only one consonant per consonant slot, e.g., קלט, נקלט *kalat, niklat*, i.e. *three*-consonant roots.

Of *binyanim* 3-7, *hif'il* and *huf'al* usually have one consonant per slot, e.g. הקליט, הוקלט *hiklit, huklat*; whereas *pi'el, pu'al, hitpa'el* often use *two* consonants in their middle slot (one per syllable, as they all have an open syllable to exploit, in all tenses), e.g. עידן, עידכן *iden, idken*; התעדן, התעדכן *hitaden, hitadken*.[10]

40.3.2 Meaning

Binyanim are meaningful in a restricted way. They are used with a considerable number of verbs to express a limited number of general '*grammatical*' notions, or more strictly 'relationships' between verbs. The root is used in more than one *binyan* to create various *systems*, notably those set out in the following table:[11]

System	Example		
1. Active vs. passive	lakaH vs. nilkaH	'take' 'be taken'	לקח נלקח
2. Intransitive vs. transitive	hityabesh vs. yibesh	'become dry' 'to dry'	התייבש ייבש
3. Transitive vs.causative of transitive	lavash vs. hilbish	'wear' 'dress (someone)'	לבש הלביש
4. Non-reflexive vs. reflexive	hilbish vs. hitlabesh	'dress (someone)' 'dress oneself'	הלביש התלבש
5. Non-reciprocal vs. reciprocal	nishek vs. hitnashek	'kiss' 'kiss one another'	נישק התנשק
6. Stative vs. inchoative ('becoming')	yashav vs. hityashev	'sit' 'sit down'	ישב התיישב

Sometimes they relate synchronically to an adjective or noun; noun-based coinages are very productive:

> Inchoative: shamen 'fat'   שמן ~ hishmin 'become fatter' השמין

> Do something typical of something:
>   klipa   'a peel' קליפה ~ kilef   'to peel'   קילף

Rarely, they express other notions such as diminutive, intensive, repeated, repetitive, prolonged.

However, not all *binyanim* are strictly associated with a particular meaning. For example, whereas *pu'al* and *huf'al* act only as passive (and only of *pi'el* and *pu'al* respectively), *hif'il* verbs are only *sometimes* causative, sometimes for *pa'al*, e.g. אכל *aHal* 'eat' ~ האכיל *heeHil* 'feed', sometimes for *nif'al*, e.g. נזהר *nizhar* 'be careful' ~ הזהיר *hizhir* 'warn', and sometimes for no current word at all, in which case they will not be deemed causative, e.g. השמיד *hishmid* 'destroy'.

Conversely, none of these 'grammatical notions' has one specific *binyan* : for example, reciprocal (system 5 above) is sometimes *hitpa'el* (e.g. חיבר *Hiber* 'attach' vs. התחבר *hitHaber* 'get attached') and sometimes *nif'al* (e.g. פגש

pagash 'meet (someone)' vs. נפגש *nifgash* 'meet one another').[12] Similarly, intransitive (system 2) is sometimes *pa'al* (e.g. קטן *katan* 'become smaller' vs. הקטין *hiktin* 'reduce') and sometimes *hitpa'el* (e.g. התמעט *hitma'et* 'become less' vs. מיעט *mi'et* 'lessen').

A general rule is that use of the *binyanim* with prefixes (*nif'al*,[13] *hif'il*, *hitpa'el*) often adds something to the meaning of verbs in the bare, unprefixed *binyanim pa'al* and *pi'el*: an extra participant in the action, i.e. reciprocity, reflexiveness, causativeness, or an extra aspect of the action: 'begin to...'. By contrast, *pi'el* rarely adds anything to *pa'al* (except occasionally causative); nor can *pu'al* and *huf'al*, the passive counterparts of *pi'el* and *hif'il*, from which they differ by a mere change of vowel, be said to *add* anything to these.

However, *binyanim* frequently add no such general meaning: they may signal (1) a mere synonym, e.g. כפל *kafal* and הכפיל *hiHpil* both mean 'double'; or (2) a particular twist of meaning, e.g. ברח *baraH* 'flee' vs. הבריח *hivriaH* 'smuggle',[14] סרק *sarak* 'comb' (= search) vs. סירק *sirek* 'comb (hair)'; or (3) an apparently unrelated idea, e.g. לווה *lava* 'borrow' vs. ליווה *liva* 'accompany', בצר *batsar* 'harvest' vs. ביצר *bitser* 'fortify', ספר *safar* 'count' vs. סיפר *siper* 'cut (hair)',[15] or (4) they may simply be unavailable for a given root: דיבר *diber* 'speak' but no *דבר* *davar*, התאפק *hitapek* 'restrain oneself' but nothing else with א.פ.ק. '*.p.k.*, גמר *gamar* 'finish' but no *הגמיר* *higmir*.

There are two contributory factors, one phonological and one semantic. First, when coining verbs from nouns with initial consonant clusters, Hebrew favours the *hif'il* pattern, which alone can preserve such clusters (vowels may be altered, e.g. טלפון *telefon* 'phone' → טילפן *tilfen* 'to phone', but not consonants): שוויץ *shvits* → השוויץ *hishvits* 'brag'.

Second, Hebrew chooses another *binyan* if the expected *binyan* is occupied: מתון *matun* 'moderate' (ADJ) → מיתן *miten* 'to moderate' (המתין *himtin* = 'wait'), פשוט *pashut* 'simple' → פישט *pishet* 'simplify' (הפשיט *hifshit* = 'undress').

Statistics on just how meaningful a *binyan* is depend, *inter alia*, on whether one counts all verbs or the commonest, or indeed gives weight to frequency. Thus, taking 100-200 dictionary verbs at random, only one in five *pa'al* verbs have a *hif'il* causative or a *pi'el* causative or intensive; and indeed, of *pa'al* and *pi'el* verbs, only about half have a *hitpa'el* at all (Ornan 1979b). But in frequent verbs, *binyanim* are much more meaningful; and coinages and word-coining tests suggest that *binyanim* are felt to have meaning (Bolozky 1978a; Schwarzwald 1981b).

Binyanim are thus *partly meaningful*. Unlike inflection patterns (tense, gender, etc), which are consistent in meaning and almost automatically available, *binyan* patterns are unpredictable in meaning and frequently unavailable in a particular root. But they have frequent enough meaning, especially in common roots, and are currently productive enough to be deemed 'partly meaningful', rather like noun patterns (see ch. 38).

40.4   Uses of each *binyan*: an overview

The *binyanim* with regular meaning are:

(1)   *Huf'al*: Passive of *hif'il*
(2)   *Pu'al*: Passive of *pi'el*

The *binyanim* with statistically preponderant meaning are:[16]

(3)   *Nif'al*: Passive of *pa'al*
(4)   *Hif'il*: Causative of *pa'al, nif'al,* adjectives
(5)   *Pi'el*: Action using or involving a noun
        or
        No distinctive meaning
(6)   *Hitpa'el*: Intransitive of transitive *pi'el*;
        Inchoative of verbs etc. of state; reflexive

No distinctive meaning can be ascribed to:

(7)   *Pa'al*

Examples are:

1. huzkar	'be reminded'	הוזכר	(hizkir	'remind'	הזכיר)
2. gubash	'be crystallized'	גובש	(gibesh	'crystallize'	גיבש)
3. nizkar	'be remembered'	נזכר	(zaHar	'remember'	זכר)
4. hizkir	'remind'	הזכיר	(zaHar	'remember'	זכר)
5. gibesh	'crystallize'	גיבש	(gavish	'crystal'	גביש)
6. hitgabesh	'become crystallized'	התגבש	(see 2.)		
7. zaHar	'remember'	זכר			

40.5   *Pa'al* (i.e. kal)

Pa'al has no overall meaning. Nor is it productively coined today, partly because it cannot accommodate four-letter roots and is already 'occupied' in the case of many three-letter roots.

Pa'al provides a broad range of intransitive and transitive verbs, e.g., intransitive ישב *yashav* 'sit', עצר *atsar* 'stop', רזה *raza* 'become slimmer'; transitive לבש *lavash* 'wear', נתן *natan* 'give', עצר *atsar* 'stop'. However, *pa'al* transitives are hardly ever causatives of existing intransitive verbs or adjectives, thus נתן *natan* 'give' is not based on any existing verb meaning 'receive'. Nor does *pa'al* generally provide inchoatives, perfectives, reciprocals, reflexives or passives for other verbs.[17] It is *morphosemantically basic*.

40.6   *Nif'al*

Nif'al mostly serves to build verbs from verbs of other *binyanim*. It is thus 'derivative'. Uses 1-3 involve transitivity, and use (4) involves aspect. (1) The passive for many transitive *pa'al*[18] verbs (and still semi-productively coined):

nir'e	'be seen'	נראה
niHtav	'be written'	נכתב
nisgar	'be closed'[19]	נסגר

(2) The 'middle' (i.e. expressing an autonomous action not caused by anyone) for quite a few transitive *pa'al* verbs, and still semi-productively coined:

ra'a	'see'	נראה → ra'a	nir'e	'appear'	נראה
mana	'prevent'	מנע → mana	nimna	'refrain'	נמנע
sagar	'close'	סגר → sagar	nisgar	'close (intrans.)'	נסגר

(3) The reciprocal for a few *pa'al* verbs:

| pagash | 'meet (someone)' | פגש → pagash | nifgeshu | 'meet one another' | נפגשו |
| nasa | 'wed (someone)' | נשא → nasa | nis'u | 'be wed' | נישאו |

(4) The inchoative (i.e. 'enter a state of...') for a few *pa'al* verbs:

haya	'be'	היה → haya	niya	'become'	נהיה
amad	'stand'	עמד → amad	neemad	'come to a stop'	נעמד
shaHav	'be lying'	שכב → shaHav	nishkav	'lie down'	נשכב

(5) The *nif'al* also supplies many 'basic' verbs', though not productively:

niHna 'surrender' נכנע   niHnas 'enter' נכנס   nilHam 'fight' נלחם[20]

These may be transitive, but never take a direct object (...את *et*...)

40.7 *Hif'il* and *Huf'al*

Hif'il

Hif'il too is largely *derivative* - but, unlike *nif'al*, it is mainly transitive, taking a direct object (...את *et*...). It commonly and semi-productively supplies:

(1) Causatives for (a) *pa'al* and (b) sometimes *nif'al*: (a) הלביש *hilbish* 'dress', האכיל *heeHil* 'feed', החתים *heHtim* 'sign (someone) up', התרים *hitrim* 'raise contributions', העזיב *heeziv* 'make (someone) quit'; (b) הרדים *hirdim* 'put to sleep', הכניע *hiHnía* 'subdue', השאיר *hish'ir* 'leave over', הכניס *hiHnis* 'bring in'.

(2) Causative inchoatives for adjectives, e.g. החליש *heHlish* 'weaken', המתיק *himtik* 'sweeten', הכעיר *hiHír* 'uglify', התפיל *hitpil* 'desalinate'.

(3) Intransitive inchoatives for colour and other physical properties (other inchoatives use *hitpa'el*), e.g. הלבין *hilbin* 'become whiter', הבריא *hivri* 'recover', הבשיל *hivshil* 'ripen', החמיץ *heHmits* 'become sour'.

(4) *Hif'il* also supplies some 'basic' verbs, though not productively, e.g. החליט *heHlit* 'decide', הגזים *higzim* 'exaggerate'.

Synthetic vs. analytic causatives

Instead of a synthetic form such as the *hif'il*, Hebrew often uses 'analytic' *phrases*, of such kinds as:

garam li lehikanes	'cause me to enter'	גרם לי להיכנס
asa et ze kal yoter	'make it easier'	עשה את זה קל יותר
naasa/niya/hafaH adom	'become red'	נעשה/נהיה/הפך אדום

but with frequent idiosyncratic differences, such as those between the following pairs:

hevi matana	'bring a gift'	הביא מתנה
garam le-matana lavo	'cause a gift to come'	גרם למתנה לבוא
hishmin me'od	'become very much fatter'	השמין מאד
nasa shamen me'od	'become very fat'	נעשה שמן מאד

Huf'al

Huf'al is the near-automatic passive for the transitive *hif'il*[21], e.g. הולבש *hulbash* 'be dressed', הוקל *hukal* 'be made easier'.

The present tense form is also used automatically as a 'perfective' adjective (denoting a completed action), e.g. מורכב *murkav* 'composite', מופנם *mufnam* 'internalized'.

40.8 *Pi'el* and *pu'al*

Pi'el

Pi'el verbs, like *hif'il* verbs, are mostly transitive and tend to take a direct object (i.e. ...את *et*...). But unlike *hif'il*, *pi'el* are frequently (1) '*basic*' or (2) *based on nouns* (or occasionally (3) on adjectives). Examples are given below.

(1) Basic: היגר *higer* 'migrate', טיפל *tipel* 'treat', קיבל *kibel* 'receive', בישל *bishel* 'cook'.

(2) Noun-based (productive):[22]

(a) 'Put something in...', e.g. ביים *biyem* 'to stage', תייק *tiyek* 'to file', שיווק *shivek* 'to market', מיקד *miked* 'to focus', מיקם *mikem* 'to place'.
(b) 'Use...', e.g. גישר *gisher* 'to bridge', מיכן *miken* 'to mechanize', ויסת *viset* 'to regulate', מימן *mimen* 'to finance', מיקש *mikesh* 'to mine', טילפן *tilfen* 'to phone'.
(c) Sundry: ניווט *nivet* 'to navigate', שרש *sheresh* 'to uproot', קילף *kilef* 'to peel',[23] ייבא *yibe* 'to import', סימל *simel* 'to symbolize', כיכב *kiHev* 'to star', תיפקד *tifked* 'to function'.

(3) Inchoative causative ('cause to become') for adjectives: חימם *Himem* 'warm up', קיצר *kitser* 'shorten', חיזק *Hizek* 'strengthen', וידא *vide* 'verify'.
(4) *Pi'el* is also sometimes casuative for *pa'al* verbs, e.g. טיבע *tiba* 'drown', שימח *simaH* 'make happy', לימד *limed* 'teach'.

Pu'al

Pu'al is rather like *huf'al* (see 40.7): (1) it is a near-automatic passive of *pi'el*, e.g. חוסל *Husal* 'be liquidated', בויים *buyam* 'be staged'; (2) the participle acts automatically as a perfective adjective, e.g. מחוסל *meHusal* 'liquidated', משוכנע *meshuHna* 'convinced'. Moreover, many such adjectives are formed directly from nouns - no *pi'el* verb exists (see 41.3.1): משופם *mesufam* 'moustached', משומש *meshumash* 'used', ממושקף *memushkaf* 'bespectacled', etc.

40.9 Hitpa'el

Hitpa'el, like *nif'al* and the passive *binyanim*, is often based on another *binyan*. It is typically 'dynamic' (i.e. denoting action rather than state) but this action is often intransitive and where it does involve an object this is invariably an indirect object.[24] *Hitpa'el* has three main roles, described below. Most productively and commonly, *hitpa'el* provides:

(1) 'Middles' (i.e. actions with no implied agent) for dynamic transitive *pi'el*:

    Pi'el   sovávti oto 'I revolved it' סובבתי אותו—
    Hitpa'el   hu histovev 'it revolved' הוא הסתובב

Further examples are התפרק *hitparek* 'fall apart', התקרר *hitkarer* 'become cool', התבשל *hitbashel* 'cook' (i.e. get cooked).

(2) Inchoatives (transitive or intransitive) for verbs of state, adjectives and nouns, except those of colour or of a physical nature:[25]

(a) shatak 'be silent' שתק → hishtatek 'fall silent' השתתק
      ahav 'love' אהב → hitahev 'fall in love' התאהב

(b) ayef 'tired' עייף → hitayef 'get tired' התעייף
      atsuv 'sad' עצוב → hitatsev 'be saddened' התעצב

(c) yadid 'friend' ידיד → hityaded 'become friendly' התידד
      ezraH 'citizen' אזרח → hitazréaH 'be naturalized' התאזרח

Semi-productively, *hitpa'el* provides:

(3) Reflexives:[26]

    mataH 'stretch' מתח → hitmatéaH 'stretch oneself' התמתח
    hilbish 'dress' הלביש → hitlabesh 'get dressed' התלבש
    zikef 'erect' זיקף → hizdakef 'straighten oneself' הזדקף

Most of these denote bodily action.[27]

    Occasional uses of *hitpa'el*:

(4) Passive of *pi'el*, e.g. התקבל *hitkabel* 'be accepted', התבקש *hitbakesh* 'be asked', התגלה *hitgala* 'be discovered' (ch. 19).

(5) Reciprocity:

    egrof 'fist' אגרוף → hitagref 'box' התאגרף
    katav 'write' כתב → hitkatev 'correspond' התכתב
    tsiltsel 'ring' צילצל → hitstaltsel 'ring one another' הצטלצל

(6) Pretence (negative connotation):

> HaHam 'clever' חכם → hitHakem 'act clever' התחכם
> Hala 'be ill' חלה → hitHala 'act ill' התחלה

(7) Repetition:

> rats 'run' רץ → hitrotsets 'run around' התרוצץ
> halaH 'walk' הלך → hithaleH 'walk around' התהלך

Sometimes it is used as:

(8) Basic: התבונן *hitbonen* 'stare', התחרט *hitHaret* 'regret', התפלל *hitpalel* 'pray', השתרע *histaréa* 'extend'.

Summary of currently productive coinage in *binyanim* (after Bolozky 1978a)

Transitive:

Causative:	*hif'il*	hitpil	'desalinate'	התפיל
		himHish	'concretize'	המחיש
Otherwise:	*pi'el*	mikem	'position'	מיקם
		gisher	'bridge'	גישר

Intransitive:

Colour, physical inchoative:

	hif'il	hivrid	'become pink'	הווריד
		hirza	'slim'	הרזה

Other inchoatives, reciprocal, reflexive, middle (of *pi'el*):

	hitpa'el	hitparek	'fall apart'	התפרק
		hitnashek	'kiss one another'	התנשק
Otherwise:	*pi'el*	kiHev	'star'	כיכב
		bilef	'bluff'	בילף

40.10-24   VERB INFLECTION
Rules for regular and semi-regular inflection are productive for all verbs (including foreignisms), save those beginning with י- ,נ- *n-* and *y-* (40.22-23). As a result, the verb has more such rules than the noun - and most of these are *specific* to the verb.

40.10   Verb inflection: general rules

Basic forms

A verb has five sets of forms: past tense, present tense (historically also called participle), future tense, and (except in the passive *binyanim*, i.e. *huf'al* and *pu'al*) imperative and infinitive forms.

The imperative is formal except in a handful of verbs - see chapter 28. A further form, the so-called infinitive absolute, is restricted to literature and some idioms.

The past tense has just suffixes - for person, gender and number.

The present tense has suffixes for gender and number, and a prefix to mark present tense in *binyanim* 3-7.

The future tense has prefixes for person and 3rd person gender; and suffixes for gender and number.

The imperative has suffixes for gender and number, identical to future suffixes.

The infinitive has the prefix -ל *l-*, or occasionally (formally) an adverbial preposition such as -ב *be-* or עד *ad* introducing it (in which case it is called a gerund: see 30.5.1.).

The inflectional affixes are summarized in the table on page 470.

Feminine present suffixes

The present tense has two alternative feminine singular suffixes, depending mostly on the shape of the verb and partly on its grammatical function. The suffix -ת *-et* is used with verbs whose last vowel is *e* or *a*, i.e. present tense of all *binyanim* save *hif'il*.

The suffix -ה *-a* is used with verbs whose last vowel is *i* (i.e. *hif'il*) or which end in *-e* (e.g. קורה *kore* 'happen', מחכה *meHake* 'wait'); it is also used with one-syllable verbs (e.g. קם *kam* 'arise'), and with a handful of others, e.g. יכול *yaHol* 'can', מקל *mekel* 'make easy'.[28]

Vowel loss

Vowel loss, and stress (see below), is different for present tense than for other tenses - and altogether different from that in nouns, adjectives, etc.

In the present tense, *e* in the last syllable drops when a stressed suffix is added (-ה, -ים, -ות *-a, -im, -ot*): הולך~הולכות *holeH~holHot* 'go', מדבר~מדברים *medaber~medabrim* 'speak', קונה~קונה *kone~kona* 'buy'. This contrasts with forms with *a* or *i* (i.e. *hif'il* and some *nif'al, huf'al* and *pu'al* forms) which have, e.g. נבגד~נבגדות *nivgad~nivgadot* 'betrayed', מדביר~מדבירים *madbir~madbirim* 'control', מפונק~מפונקים *mefunak~mefunakim* 'pampered'.

In other tenses, *any* vowel in the last syllable drops, except in *hif'il* and one-syllable verbs: these keep the stress on the stem (e.g. הדבירו *hidbíru*, הגנה *hegéna*, קמה *káma*, קומי *kúmi*) and hence הלך~הלכו *halaH~halHu* 'went', דיבר~דיברה *diber~dibra* 'spoke', יפקוד~יפקדו *yifkod~yifkedu* 'will order'.

Verb stress

For present tense the stress is on the last syllable (except -ת *-et*): מפסיקה *mafsiká* 'stop', כותבים *kotvím* 'write', קמות *kamót* 'arise'.

For other tenses stress is on the last syllable *before* the suffix, when (a) the former has a high vowel (*i* or *u*), e.g. תריבי *tarívi* 'argue', הפסיקה *hifsíka* 'stopped', תפסיקו *tafsíku* 'stop', הקימה *hekíma* 'set up', יקומו *yakúmu* 'will arise'; or (b) the latter begins with a consonant (i.e. they are 1st or 2nd person past suffixes): דיברתי *dibárti* 'I spoke', קנינו *kanínu* 'we bought', הפסקתם *hifsáktem* 'you stopped'.

Inflectional affixes (using a pi'el verb: קִיפֵּל kipel 'fold')

	PRESENT	PAST	FUTURE	IMPERATIVE
		Singular		
1st, 2nd, 3rd m.	mekapel מקפל			
1st		kipálti קיפלתי	akapel[e] אקפל	
2nd m.		kipálta קיפלת	tekapel תקפל	kapel קפל
f.		kipalt קיפלת	tekapli תקפלי	kapli קפלי
1st, 2nd, 3rd f.	mekapélet[b] מקפלת			
3rd m.		kipél קיפל	yekapel יקפל	
f.		kipla קיפלה	tekapel תקפל	
		Plural		
1st		kipálnu קיפלנו	nekapel נקפל	
1st, 2nd, 3rd m.	mekaplim מקפלים			
2nd m.		kipáltem קיפלתם	tekaplu תקפלו	kaplu קפלו
f.		kipalten[d] קיפלתן	(tekapélna)[f] (תקפלנה)	(kapélna)[f] (קפלנה)
1st, 2nd, 3rd f.	mekaplot מקפלות			
3rd m.		kiplu קיפלו	yekaplu יקפלו	
f.		kiplu קיפלו	(tekapélna)[f] (תקפלנה)	

Explanations: (a) There is no -מ m- prefix in *pa'al* or *nif'al*. (b) On feminine present suffixes, see relevant paragraph in the text. (c) Formally, the biconsonantal suffixes תֶן- -*ten*, תֶם- -*tem* are stressed. (d) Formal. (e) While the *consonants* in the present and future prefixes are standard for every verb, the *vowel* varies according to *binyan* and root type: see 40.11-15. (f) Formal and optional.

Otherwise,[29] i.e. in future, imperative and most 3rd person usage, the stress is on the last syllable: כתב *katáv* 'wrote', כתבה *katvá* 'wrote', תקפלי *tekaplí* 'fold', נסגרו *nisgerú* 'were shut'.

40.11-15 REGULAR INFLECTIONS, *BINYAN* BY *BINYAN*

Besides the general affixes and vowel changes described in 40.10, there are vowel changes distinguishing the *tenses* (some or all), in the stem of each *binyan*.

40.11 *Pa'al*

Most *pa'al* verbs inflect their vowels for tense. Arguably, no one tense is 'basic'. The prefix vowel is -*i*- (1st singular future has *e*-, and casually sometimes *i*-):[30]

PAST	gadar	'enclose'	גדר
PRES	goder		גודר
FUT	yigdor		יגדור
IMP	gdor		גדור
INF	ligdor[31]		לגדור

40.12 *Nif'al*

Nif'al has two stems: --*a*- for past and present, -*a-e*- for the rest. There is a '*binyan* marker': - נ *n*- for past and present, - ה *h*- for imperative and infinitive. The prefix vowel is -*i*- (1st singular future has *e*-, and casually even *i*-), but note that in the infinitive it is the *second* prefix vowel which is -*i*-:

PAST	nigdar	'be enclosed'	נגדר
PRES	nigdar		נגדר
FUT	yigader		ייגדר
IMP	higader		היגדר
INF	lehigader		להיגדר

40.13-15 *HIF'IL, HUF'AL, PI'EL, PU'AL* AND *HITPA'EL*: COMMON CHARACTERISTICS

These five *binyanim* have much in common. Firstly, they have just one basic stem - though *i* or *e* vowels in the stem become *a* in certain well-defined circumstances - where preceded or followed by a person, tense or infinitive affix (i.e. by exclusively *verbal* affixes, as against the gender or number affixes -*a*, -*t*, -*im*, -*ot*, -*i*, -*u*).[32] Examples are:

hifsik~hifsáknu   'He/we stopped'   הפסיק~הפסקנו

pihek~yefahek   'He yawned/will yawn'   פיהק~יפהק

The *binyan* prefix (*h-*, and *h* in *hit-*) is not used where there is already a tense prefix (future or present prefix, thus מתגדר *mitgader*) but infinitive and *binyan* prefixes do co-exist: להתגדר *lehitgader.*

40.13   *Hif'il* and *huf'al*

The basic stem is *i--i-*, to which is prefixed the *binyan* marker - ה *h-* in past, imperative and infinitive. The pattern is set out in the table below, for the verb הגדיר *higdir* 'define'.

PAST	higdir		הגדיר
	(higdárti...higdíra[33]...higdíru)		(הגדרתי...הגדירה...הגדירו)
PRES	magdir		מגדיר
	(magdira, magdirim, magdirot)		(מגדירה, מגדירים, מגדירות)
FUT	yagdir		יגדיר
	(agdir...tagdíri...yagdíru)		(אגדיר...תגדירי...יגדירו)
IMP	hagder[34]		הגדר
	(hagdíri, hagdíru)		(הגדירי, הגדירו)
INF	lehagdir		להגדיר

Huf'al

The stem is *u--a-* throughout (akin to *-u-a-* of the other passive *binyan*, *pu'al*), to which is prefixed the *binyan* marker - ה *h-* in past tense.

There is no imperative or infinitive (nor in *pu'al*), save by way of the helper verb היה *haya*: היה מוגדר, להיות מוגדר *heye mugdar, liyot mugdar.*

PAST	hugdar	'be defined'	הוגדר
PRES	mugdar		מוגדר
FUT	yugdar		יוגדר

40.14   *Pi'el* and *pu'al*

These have no *binyan* marker. If the middle consonant is ב, כ, פ it is often *b, k, p* (see 40.17). The prefix vowel is short *e* (for 1st s. future it is *a*).

Pi'el

The basic stem is *-i-e-*, with *i* and *e* becoming *a* by the rule in the preamble to 40.13. The pattern is set out in the table below, using the verb גידר *gider* 'fence in'.

PAST	gider	גידר
	(gidárti...gidra...gidru)	(גידרתי...גידרה...גידרו)
PRES	megader	מגדר
	(megadéret, megadrim, megadrot)	(מגדרת, מגדרים, מגדרות)
FUT	yegader	יגדר
	(agader...tegadri...yegadru)	(אגדר...תגדרי...יגדרו)
IMP	gader	גדר
	(gadri, gadru)	(גדרי, גדרו)
INF	legader	לגדר

Pu'al

The stem is *-u-a-* throughout. There is no imperative or infinitive, save by way of היה מגודר, להיות מגודר *heye megudar, liyot megudar.*

PAST	gudar	'be fenced in'	גודר
PRES	megudar		מגודר
FUT	yegudar		יגודר

40.15 *Hitpa'el*

The basic stem is *-a-e-*,[35] with *e* becoming *a* by the rule in the preamble to 15.13. The *binyan* marker is הת *ht*, the *h* dropping when present or future prefixes are added. Formally, the *binyan* marker can be נת *nt* (נתפעל *nitpa'el*) in the past tense. The prefix vowel is *i* (for the 1st person future it is *e*, casually sometimes *i*). The pattern is set out in the table below, using the verb התגדר *hitgader* 'excel'.

PAST	hitgader	התגדר
	(hitgadárti...hitgadru)	(התגדרתי...התגדרו)
PRES	mitgader	מתגדר
	(mitgadéret...mitgadrot)	(מתגדרת...מתגדרות)
FUT	yitgader	יתגדר
	(etgader...titgadri...)	(אתגדר...תתגדרי...)
IMP	hitgader	התגדר
	(hitgadri, hitgadru)	(התגדרי, התגדרו)
INF	lehitgader	להתגדר

40.16 Verbs with missing inflections ('inflection suppletion')

At least twenty verbs are 'defective': they lack the regular form for some tense or tenses, or occasionally for the 3rd person of one tense. Sometimes this gap is covered by an existing verb from another *binyan* or even another root, and sometimes by forming a compound of היה *haya* 'be' + present. Where this other verb exists *solely* as a 'filler-in', e.g. יש *yesh* 'there is' as present tense of היה *haya* 'there was', this is called 'suppletion'.[36] Usually there is no phonological necessity for the deficiency.

Perhaps half of all defective verbs lack an infinitive of the expected kind, and very often a future tense too (these are closely related). For example יכול *yaHol* 'can': covered in some uses by להיות מסוגל *liyot mesugal* 'to be capable';[37] צדק *tsadak* 'be right': suppleted by יהיה/להיות צודק *yiye/liyot tsodek*; הלך *halaH* 'go': suppleted by י.ל.ך. *y.l.H.*; ניגש *nigash* 'approach': suppleted by *pa'al*; נהיה *niya* 'become': covered by להיות/יהיה *liyot/yiye*; נדהם *nidham* 'be shocked'.

Many others lack present tense. Some lack present alone, e.g. הצטרך *hitstareH* 'must': covered by צריך *tsariH*;[38] היה *haya* 'be': suppleted by יש *yesh* (see ch. 16), הוא, היא, הם *hu, hi* etc. or zero. Others lack present *and* another tense, e.g. חיה *Haya* 'live': suppleted by חי *Hay* in present and in past 3rd person masculine singular (casually in 3rd person feminine singular too)[39] and 3rd person plural; הגיד *higid* 'say': covered by אמר *amar* in present and past; החל *heHel* 'commence': covered by התחיל *hitHil* in present and infinitive.

Past is occasionally the only tense lacking, e.g. the past of פיחד *piHed* 'be afraid' is covered in formal usage by פחד *paHad*. Past 3rd person masculine singular lacks for יכול *yaHol* 'can', suppleted by היה יכול *haya yaHol* or very casual יכל *yaHal*, and for נחשב *neHshav* 'be considered', suppleted by היה נחשב *haya neHshav* when ambiguous between past and present. Past 3rd masculine singular and 3rd plural lack in one verb: חיה *Haya*.

Often verbs have just one tense, e.g. past: הרה *hara* 'conceive',[40] יעץ *yaats* 'advise';[41] future: יתכן *yitaHen* 'be possible', ייפלא *yipale* 'be amazing'; present: צריך *tsariH* 'need/it is necessary',[42] יש(נו) *yesh(no)* 'there is', ישנו *yeshno* 'is present',[43]

40.17 Roots with spirantization (ב, כ, פ)

While the consonants of a root are generally constant, whatever *binyan* or inflection is being used, this is not usually the case when the root contains any of the three *variable letters* ב, כ, פ. These have either a 'hard' (plosive) or a 'soft' (spirant) pronunciation, depending partly on their whereabouts in the word and partly on the type of word: *b, k, p* vs. *v, H, f* respectively. Thus compare initial and final ב, כ in these two pairs of words:

bar	'pure'	בר	rav	'rabbi'	רב
kar	'pillow'	כר	raH	'soft'	רך

This 'spirantization' affects all types of words and is still broadly productive. As it is particularly complex for verbs, it is dealt with in this chapter.

Note first that three of these sounds (*k, v, H*) also represent other letters (ק, ו, ח) that do not alternate - as in קר *kar* 'cold', רק *rak* 'only'. This has led to many coinages bending these rules, for the sake of semantic clarity, e.g. מכֹכב *mekaHev* 'starring' from כֹוכב *koHav* 'a star'; and indeed to other colloquial over-extensions of 'spirantization', e.g. כיבה *Hiba* 'extinguish'. Moreover, hosts of foreignisms ignore this alternation, e.g. פופ *pop* 'pop'.

General rules

(1) Word-initially, ב, כ, פ are usually *hard*, and word-finally *soft*:

patar	'exempt'	פטר	~	asaf	'gather'	אסף
kizev	'mislead'	כיזב	~	bereH	'bless'	בירך

(2) Within the word, the tendency for *verbs* is that ב, כ, פ are soft after a vowel and otherwise hard:[44]

Soft (v):	gavar	'prevailed'	גבר	gover	'prevail'	גובר
	hivshil	'ripened'	הבשיל	mavshil	'ripen'	מבשיל
Hard (b):	yigbar	'will prevail'	יגבר	yagbir	'will augment'	יגביר

Bending the rules

In most usage, rule (2) above is flouted by verbs echoing their source noun, notably in *pi'el, pu'al, hitpa'el*:

Hard:	mekaHev	'starring'	מככב	(koHav	'a star'	(כֹוכב
	sibsed	'subsidize'	סיבסד	(subsidya	'subsidy'	(סובסידיה
	tekafter	'button up!'	תכפתר	(kaftor	'a button'	(כפתור
Soft:	makaHev	'starring'	מככב	(koHav	'a star'	(כֹוכב
	yive	'imported'	ייבא	(yevu	'an import'	(יבוא
	mesufam	'moustachoed'	משופם	(safam	'moustache'	(שפם
	hishtavets	'have a stroke'	השתבץ	(shavats	'stroke'	(שבץ

Casually, in reduplicating roots, the hard 3rd root consonant influences the 1st: הבזבז *tebazbez* 'waste', מבולבל *mebulbal* 'confused'.

Casually, within verb inflections, the more common stem form often replaces the less common, if this means extending, not reducing, spirantization - notably (i) in *pi'el* מכבס, יכבס, לכבס *meHabes, yeHabes, leHabes* 'washes, will wash, to wash' triggers כיבס *Hibes* 'washed' (whereas פתח, פותח *potéaH, pataH* 'opens, opened' does not trigger *יפתח *yiptah* (for 'will open'); (ii) in *pa'al, nif'al* תפס, תופס *tofes, tafas*, 'catch, caught' triggers נתפס, יתפוס *yitfos, nitfas* 'will catch, is caught'.

Foreignisms too (mostly casual) generally flout the rules of (1), e.g. פילוסוף *filosof* 'philosopher', ג'יפ *jip* 'jeep', ג'וב *job* 'job' (exceptions include מפוסטר *mefustar* 'pasteurized').

40.18-23 ANOMALOUS ROOT TYPES

A number of consonants, when found in a certain position in the root - or indeed roots with just two consonants - create upsets in the basic *inflection rules* outlined in 40.10-16, usually in a predictable, sometimes even in a productive, way. Any given root is quite likely to have one such consonant. In nouns and adjectives, by contrast, many such root types have no productive effect - and so are not discussed there.

As these root types are fully set out in tables (of formal or literary usage) by most Hebrew grammars, we shall merely sketch out the underlying *rules*, noting any colloquial or productive features.

40.18 Two-consonant roots (ע"ו) : קם *kam* 'arise'

Two-consonant roots have a stem of one syllable. Although מת *met* 'die' is associated with a three-consonant noun מוות *mávet* 'death', חב *Hav* 'owe' with חייב *Hayav* 'owe', and בול *bul* 'stamp' with the new verb בייל *biyel* 'to stamp' and so on, these are too sporadic for two-consonant verbs to be considered as basically having an extra *v* or *y* as middle consonant.

They exist in a special *binyan* with similarities to *pa'al*, and in the three *binyanim* with outwardly one-syllable stems: *nif'al* (rarely), *hif'il*, *huf'al*; examples are given here:

Pa'al	zan	'feed'	זן
Nif'al	nizon		נזון
	nazon		
Hif'il	hezin		הזין
Huf'al	huzan		הוזן

The stem vowels are:

> *Pa'al*: Past, present *a*; otherwise *u* (with some exceptions in *i*, *o*), e.g. זנו *zánu* 'fed', זנים *zanim* 'feed', יזונו *yazúnu* 'will feed' לזון *lazun* 'to feed'.
>
> *Nif'al*: *o*, e.g. נזון *nazon* 'is fed', נזונה *nazóna* 'is fed'.
>
> *Hif'il, huf'al*: As with regular roots, e.g. יזין *yazin* 'will nourish', יוזן *yuzan* 'will be nourished'.

The prefix vowel throughout is *a*, except that *hif'il* past and present use *e* (a unique vowel alternation) and *huf'al* is regular, e.g. יזון *yazun* (future), הזין *hezin* (past), מזין *mezin* (present), יוזן *yuzan* (future).[46]

40.19 Roots with an 'underlying guttural'

א, ה, ע, ח were all once guttural (ʔ, ʕ, h, ḥ) and are still pronounced so by some Israelis. But a majority pronounce ע (and often ה) as א, or simply omit all three; and ח as כ (H), a non-guttural. Thus for them א, ע, ה are still potentially guttural-sounding, but not ח. However, all four are 'underlying gutturals', for they still cause 'lowering' of adjacent vowels (i.e. a shift away from *i* towards *e* or *a*, making gutturals easier to pronounce), though א, ח less so (ר too occasionally acts as if guttural). Some such changes apply to all words (i.e. they are phonological), others just to verbs.

א, ע, ה, ח are generally no problem *when a full vowel follows* (enabling them to be clearly sounded), e.g. חידש *Hidesh*, עיקם *ikem*.[47] But (a)-(c) below set out what happens where this is not the case.

(a) Where ע, ה, ח *end* a word, the foregoing vowel must be *a*. This usually means inserting an *a* (without adding a letter), e.g. יודע *yodéa* 'know'; מתמיה *matmia* 'puzzling'; משכנע, ישכנע, לשכנע *meshaHnéa, yeshaHnéa, leshaHnéa* 'convince'; התגלח, מתגלח, יתגלח, להתגלח *hitgaléaH, mitgaléaH, yitgaléaH, lehitgaléaH* 'shave'; and nouns etc., e.g. שליח *shaliaH* 'messenger'.

(b) Sometimes *a* will *replace* the vowel, notably (i) in *pa'al* future, imperative, e.g. ישלח *yishlaH* 'will send' (even for א: יקרא *yikra* 'will call' etc.); (ii) in most *nif'al* future, imperative, infinitive, e.g. יישמע *yishama* 'will be heard', להיפתח *lehipataH* 'to be opened'; (iii) formally, in *pi'el* past, and future with ח, e.g. ניצח *nitsaH* 'won', שיכנע *shiHna* 'convinced', ינצח *yenatsaH* 'will win'. (Final א is never pronounced, so does not have this effect.)

(c) Where א, ע, ה, ח are directly followed by a further consonant (or just a short vowel), there are three possibilities:

  (1) Following a *prefix*: the vowel preceding the 'guttural' changes to *a* or *e* (depending partly on which guttural), and for further support the selfsame vowel is sometimes inserted *after* the guttural, e.g. אחשוב *eHshov* 'I'll think', אעבוד *eevod* 'I'll work', אארוז *eeroz* 'I'll pack', תחשוב *taHshov* 'think', תעבוד *taavod* 'work', תארוז *teeroz* 'pack', נחשב *neHshav* 'is thought', החליט *heHlit* 'decide' (and nouns, e.g. מערב *maarav* 'west').[48]

  (2) Where ע, ח precede a *suffix*: with the feminine singular suffix ת- *-et*, the preceding vowel and that in *-et* become *a-* as *-et* has a *short* vowel: יודעת *yodá'at* 'know', מגלחת *megaláHat* 'shave' (and in nouns). Preceding the consonant suffixes, ת-, תי-, *-ti, -ta* etc., the vowel is *a* anyway: טיפחתי *tipáHti* 'I nurtured'.[49]

  (3) Elsewere, *a* is inserted *between* the guttural and the next consonant (casually, ח *H* in mid-word needs no such support): עבור *avor* 'pass', גואלים *goalim* 'redeem', בוחרים *boH(a)rim* 'elect', שיחקו *siH(a)ku* 'played' (and in nouns).

40.20   Roots beginning with a sibilant: metathesis, e.g. הסתדר *histader* 'manage'

In *hitpa'el*, when the first root consonant is a sibilant (*s, sh, ts, z*, i.e. ס, ש, צ, ז), it automatically leapfrogs in front of the ת- *-t-* of the prefix in all tenses:

  hit + sader → histader 'manage'   הת + סדר ← הסתדר

  hit + shaper → hishtaper 'improve'   הת + שפר ← השתפר

With צ *ts*, the *t* of the prefix will be written as ט. *With* ז *z*, this *t* actually changes (regressive voice assimilation, widespread in Hebrew as a *semi*-assimilation of voice) to ד *d*:

| hit + tsamtsem | → | hitstamtsem | 'diminish' | הצטמצם — צמצם +התּ |
| hit + zaken | → | hizdaken | 'grow old' | הזדקן — זקן +התּ |

This also occurs in *hitpa'el*-based nouns (e.g. הסתדרות *histadrut* 'organization'). It does *not* occur elsewhere in the verb, thus יתסוס *yitsos* 'will effervesce', התשיש *hitshish* 'weaken'.

Further, *d* and *t* as 1st root consonants swallow the *t* of *hit*, sometimes in spelling too (note substitute י): הידרדר *hidarder* 'decline', הידפק *hidapek* 'keep knocking'.

40.21 Roots ending in a zero consonant (ל"ה roots): קנה *kana* 'bought'

Many roots have no third consonant - but behave as if they did by maintaining a second vowel, i.e. they have a notional (i.e. 'zero') 3rd consonant (symbol: ø):

Root: k-n-ø ק.נ.ø
Example: In *binyan pa'al*: kana 'bought' קנה

The second vowel alternates in a special way: (1) unsuffixed, it is usually -*a* in past, -*e* in present, future, imperative; and in infinitive -*o*- but with added תּ- -*t*. Taking *hif'il* as an example:

PAST	hikna	'impart'	הקנה
PRES	makne		מקנה
FUT	yakne		יקנה
IMP	hakne		הקנה
INF	lehaknot		להקנות

But casually, past and present can vary: many speakers prefer -*a* for the present *nif'al*, e.g. נבנה *nivna* 'is built'; and some form their past *hitpa'el* with -*e* (e.g. התפנה *hitpane* 'was cleared'), for complex reasons.
(2) With 1st and 2nd person (consonant-initial) suffixes, this *a* becomes *i* in *pa'al* and *pi'el* but otherwise *a* → *e*:

| paniti | 'I turned' | פניתי | piniti | 'I cleared' | פיניתי |
| hitpanéti | 'I had free time' | התפניתי | | | |

The past 3rd feminine singular suffix is unusually תה- -*ta*, e.g. קנתה *kanta* 'bought'.

40.22 Roots beginning with נ- *n-*: נ.פ.ל. *n.f.l.*

When נ- *n-* as first root consonant would directly precede another consonant, i.e. in future, imperative, infinitive of *pa'al* and in past and present of *nif'al*, it often *drops*:[50]

	Pa'al			*Nif'al*		
PAST	nasa	'travel'	נסע	nitsal (*nintsal)	'be saved'	ניצל (*ננצל)
PRES	noséa		נוסע	nitsal (*nintsal)		ניצל (*ננצל)
FUT	yisa (*yinsa)	יסע (*ינסע)	yinatsel		יינצל
IMP	sa (*nesa)	סע (*נסע)	hinatsel		היגצל
INF	li(n)sóa	לי(נ)סוע	lehinatsel		להינצל

However, not all such tenses or verbs drop נ- *n-* equally. *Pa'al* imperatives and infinitives may do so *optionally*: (נ)פול (*ne*)*fol* 'fall', (נ)צור (*ne*)*tsor* 'guard', לי(נ)טול *li(n)tol* 'to take', לי(נ)זול *li(n)zol* 'to flow'.[51]

In *pa'al* future, *n-* drops for *a-* vowel verbs (e.g. יסע *yisa* 'travel', יגע *yiga* 'touch') and for יפול *yipol* 'fall'; sometimes for יטול *yitol* 'take', יזול *yizol* 'flow'; and formally for יצור *yitzor* 'guard', יקום *yikom* 'avenge', ישור *yishor* 'drop out', ישוך *yishoH* 'bite'. But it remains in most verbs, e.g. ינבוט *yinbot* 'sprout', ינגוס *yingos* 'bite', ינשוק *yinshok* 'kiss', and particularly before 'gutturals' e.g. ינחל *yinHal* 'inherit'.

Nif'al loses *n-* for, e.g. ניבט *nibat* 'gaze', ניתן *nitan* 'be given', but only sometimes for ניקם *nikam* 'be avenged', ניטש *nitash* 'be abandoned' and most others.

Moreover, *n-* clearly drops in a few *hif'il* verbs, notably הפיל *hipil* 'drop' (נפל *nafal* 'fall'), הסיע *hisia* 'drive (someone)'; but it does not drop in most, e.g. הנמיך *hinmiH* 'lower', הנציח *hintsiaH* 'perpetuate', הנביט *hinbit* 'germinate' etc. Meanwhile, הביט *hibit* 'look', הכיר *hikir* 'know', התיר *hitir* 'permit' etc. with no related verb such as נבט *navat* are best considered two-consonantal *hif'il* verbs (cf. 40.18), rather than *n-* verbs.

40.23 Maverick verbs: נתן *natan*, יכול *yaHol*, חנן *Hanan* etc.

A few *pa'al* verbs are irregular, each in its own way, notably the verbs listed below.

לקח *lakaH* 'take': In the future, imperative and infinitive there is no *l*, e.g. יקח *yikaH*, קח *kaH*, לקחת *lakáHat*.

נתן *natan* 'give': In the past and infinitive the second *n* is assimilated, e.g. נתתי *natáti*, לתת *latet*.

יכול *yaHol* 'can': In the future, אוכל, תוכל *uHal, tuHal* etc. In the past, יכולתי, יכולת *yaHólti, yaHólta* etc. (and see 40.16).

אכל, אמר, אבד, אהב *aHal, amar, avad, ahav* 'eat, say, perish, love': In the future tense, אוכל, תאכל *oHal, toHal* etc.

Among *y-* roots is a small, unproductive but much-used group that changes vowels and drops *y-* (or converts it to *v-*, *o*) in certain forms:[52]

י.ד.ע. *y.d.'.*, י.ל.ד. *y.l.d.*, י.צ.א. *y.ts.'.*, י.ר.ד. *y.r.d.*, י.ש.ב. *y.sh.v.* have *e* rather than ...אי *ey...*, ...תי *tiy...* etc., in *pa'al* future, imperative and infinitive, and convert their other vowels to *e*:

FUT	ye-e-	yered	'descend'	ירד
IMP	-e-	red		רד
INF	la-é-et	larédet		לרדת

For *nif'al*, *hif'il* and *huf'al* the *y-* again drops, in these and most other *y-*roots[53] (including those that have no actualized existence with *y-* in *pa'al*, e.g. הושיט *hoshit* 'extend (hand)'). In *nif'al* future, imperative and infinitive *y-* becomes *v* before vowels; in other *nif'al* forms and in *hif'il* it becomes *o* and in *huf'al u*:

yalad ילד ~	nolad נולד ~	yivaled יוולד ~	holid הוליד
pa'al PAST	*nif'al* PAST	*nif'al* FUT	*hif'il* PAST
'bore'	'was born'	'will be born'	'fathered'

notar נותר ~	yivater יוותר ~	hotir הותיר
'remained'	'will remain'	'left over'

40.24 Roots with an identical second and third consonant

Most roots with an identical second and third consonant ('doubled' roots) are regular. In formal usage, however, a few of them drop one such consonant in some inflections of *pa'al* and/or *nif'al*, with unusual effects on adjacent sounds and stress. (Some of these forms cause doubt; learned usage allows even more, cf. traditional grammars.) ס.ב.ב *s.v.v.*, ח.ג.ג *H.g.g.* and ח.נ.ן *H.n.n.* are three such roots. Thus:

Pa'al	FUT	aHon...yaHónu 'pardon'	אחון... יחונו
	INF	laHon	לחון

Nif'al	PAST	naHon 'was pardoned'/nasav 'went round'/	נחון/נסב/
		names 'melted'/neyHan 'was blessed'	נמס/ניחן...
		... naHónu/nasábu etc.	נחונו/נסבו
	PRES	naHon/nasav/names/neyHan... neHonim etc.	נחון/נסב/נמס/ניחן... נחונים
	FUT	yimas[54]	ימס

For *pi'el*, *pu'al* and *hitpa'el* most 'doubled' roots have an *-o-* as first stem vowel, i.e. *-o-e*, *-o-a-*, *hit-o-e-* respectively, e.g.[55] דובב *dovev* 'chat up', כונן *konen* 'set up' ~ כונן *konan* 'be set up' ~ התכונן *hitkonen* 'get ready'.

Hif'il verbs traditionally associated with such 'identical consonant' roots, e.g. הצר *hetser* 'grieve', הסב *hesev* 'recline', are best considered unrelated. See note 46.

FURTHER READING
Ariel 1972; Barkaï 1975, 1978; Ben-Asher 1972; Berman 1975a,b, 1978, 1979a; Blanc 1965; Bolozky 1978a, b, 1980; Donag-Kinnarot 1978; Fischler 1975, 1976; Ornan 1979b; Rabin 1985; Rosén 1955, 1976; Schwarzwald 1975, 1977b, 1980, 1981a,b, 1982b, 1984; Yannai 1974.

41. Adjective types and their inflection

41.1 Adjective types: introduction

Adjectives, somewhat like nouns (see ch. 38), are built in one of four ways.

(1) Using distinctive vowel patterns and/or suffixes, to create *grammatical-semantic* adjective types like those in the following table (for details see 41.3).

Example	Pattern	Grammatical type	Meaning type
shavir 'breakable' שביר	-a-i-	Suffixed form: --i- e.g. shvirim שבירים	'able' as in 'breakable, washable' etc.
salHani 'forgiving' סלחני	-a-- + ani SUFF	Suffixed form: unchanged	Mostly 'which does (something), who tends to do (something)'
sifruti 'literary' ספרותי	+ i SUFF	Suffixed form: unchanged	Mostly 'pertaining to a...'

The main such adjective types are listed below, with examples:

1. 'Present tense' ('participle') patterns, e.g.

		meratek	'gripping'	מרתק
		mag'il	'disgusting'	מגעיל
2.	*CaCuC*	shavur	'broken'	שבור
3.	*CaCiC*	kavis	'washable'	כביס
4.	*CaCoC*	varod	'pink'	ורוד
5.	*CiCeC*	giben	'hunchbacked'	גיבן
6.	*CaCCan*	baHyan	'crybabyish'	בכיין
7.	*CaCCani*	savlani	'patient'	סבלני
8.	*CCaCCaC*	ktantan	'tiny'	קטנטן
9.	*-ani*	kolani	'vociferous'	קולני
10.	*-i*	yami	'marine'	ימי
11.	*-a'i*	parisa'i	'Parisian'	פריסאי
12.	*-iáni*	froydiáni	'Freudian'	פרוידיאני

(2) Using distinctive vowel patterns or suffixes, to create purely *grammatical* adjective types, with no general meaning (for details see 41.4):

Example	Pattern	Grammatical type
kabir 'mighty' כביר	-a-i-	Suffixed form: unchanged e.g. kabirim כבירים

The main such types are exemplified by:

yatsiv	'stable'	יציב
katsar	'short'	קצר
zaken	'old'	זקן
gadol	'big'	גדול
raH	'soft'	רך
na'ívi	'naive'	נאיבי
liberáli	'liberal'	ליברלי
prákti	'practical'	פרקטי

(3) With no particularly distinctive vowel pattern or suffix (as with nouns, 'distinctive' is purely a matter of degree). Examples: נוקשה *nukshe* 'rigid', חום *Hum*, 'brown', פייר *fer* 'fair', אומלל *umlal* 'wretched', עליון *elyon* 'upper', שכול *shakul* 'bereaved'.

(4) By adjoining two words (usually a special prefix + noun) and adding י- *-i*, to create a *composite* ('phrase-based') *adjective*, e.g. דו-פרצופי *du-partsufi* 'two-faced' (for details see 41.5).

Roots and words

As with nouns (38.1.1), these vowel patterns (if any) are mounted on a root; alternatively, many suffixes are simply added to a whole word without inducing a characteristic vowel pattern of their own, e.g. ספרות+י←ספרותי *sifrut+i→sifruti* 'literary'. The description uses the 'model root' כ.ב.ד. *k.b.d.*, and the linguistic formula ccc, as with nouns (see 38.1.3).

41.2 What is an adjective: syntax vs. shape

The shape of a Hebrew word is a good indication of whether it is noun, verb or adjective. In particular, adjectives do not have past and future tense inflections (unlike verbs), nor possessive suffixes (unlike nouns, e.g. בחורינו *baHurénu* 'our' boys'). But they do frequently coincide with present tense verbs, and with nouns in general - all three share comparable plural and feminine inflections. Examples are:[1]

Verb:	nodedim	'are wandering' (m.pl.)	נודדים
Noun:	nodedim	'wanderers'	נודדים
Adjective:	nodedim	'migratory' (m.pl.)	נודדים

And ultimately, it is syntax - interaction with other words - that gives Hebrew users the sense of what is adjective, as against verb or noun.

Some syntactic traits of Hebrew adjectives (ADJ = adjective(s), v = verb(s), N = noun(s)):

(1) *Involving 'be...' (ch.16)*

(a) ADJ (and N, but not V) are used with *all* forms of the verb 'to be', thus:

haya		היה
yiye	muHraH/mesugal ADJ	ADJ מוכרח/מסוגל יהיה
liyot		להיות

was		'had to.../was able to...'
will-be	forced/able	'will have to.../will be able to...'
to-be		'to have to.../to be able to..'

as against:

haya		היה
*liyot	tsariH/yaHol V	V צריך/יכול
		*להיות

was		'had to.../could...'
to-be	needing/able	('to have to.../to be able to...')

(b) ADJ (and N, but not V) as predicates are often introduced by הוא *hu* 'is' and its various forms:

avazim hem ksherim	אווזים הם כשרים
ducks are kosher	
*Hatulim hem megargerim	*חתולים הם מגרגרים
cats [are] purr	

(c) Predicative ADJ (unlike N) can always do without this הוא *hu* 'is' etc.[2]:

avazim ksherim	אווזים כשרים
ducks kosher	'Ducks are kosher'
Hatulim megargerim	חתולים מגרגרים
cats purr	'Cats purr'
*avazim tsiporim	*אווזים ציפורים
ducks birds	('Ducks are birds')

(2) ADJ are not found unqualified as subject or object (nor is V) - save when some noun is implied:

éfo ha-Hadashim?	איפה החדשים?
where the new (m.pl.)?	'Where are the new (ones)?'

Even then, ADJ do not take a possessive suffix: זקנינו *zkenéynu* 'our **old**' is a *noun*.

(3) ADJ (and V) as predicates can have an 'impersonal' subject (see 17.3), i.e. no subject:

ani ro'e she-{ayefim/mitayefim}	{אני רואה ש{עייפים/מתעייפים
I see that {tired/tiring}	'I see that **people** are {tired/tiring}'

(4) ADJ are less amenable than V to expressing the basic subject-object relation. Thus:

(a) They normally take indirect, not direct, objects[3] (for this distinction see ch.15); v take either.

(b) They rarely take עַל-יְדֵי *al-yedey...* 'by...';[4] v can:

*ze shavur al-yedey ha-yéled

   ADJ

it's [in a state of] broken by the boy   ‏*זה שבור על-ידי הילד‎

ze nishbar al-yedey ha-yéled

   V

it was-broken by the boy   ‏זה נשבר על-ידי הילד‎

(5) ADJ can qualify a noun. Few N do, and v do only in restricted contexts (see ch.10):

	Haverim adukim	‏חברים אדוקים‎
sha'álti	Haverim rabanim	‏חברים רבנים‎ שאלתי
	*Haverim yod'im	‏*חברים יודעים‎

	friends religious		religious friends'
I-asked	friends rabbis	'I asked	some rabbi friends'
	friends knowing		(knowing friends)

(6) Many ADJ (and v) can take degree words (ch.20); N do so in a very limited way.

ani atsbani **me'od**   ‏אני עצבני מאד‎
I'm **very** uptight

hitatsbánti **me'od**   ‏התעצבנתי מאד‎
I-got-uptight **very**

Some implications of these criteria

Most words of the ‏מכובד‎ *meCuCaC* pattern will be counted as verbs, e.g. ‏מפונק‎ *mefunak* 'spoilt'; all of them as adjectives too; and some even as nouns, e.g. ‏מקובל‎ *mekubal* 'kabbalist'.

Similarly, ‏חכם‎ *HaHam* 'wise' is both an adjective and a fully-fledged noun ('sage'), whereas ‏בשל‎ *bashel* 'mature' is just an adjective.

Conversely, ‏צריך‎ *tsariH* 'must' - even in ‏היה צריך‎ *haya tsariH* 'had to' - is not an adjective but a verb, for there is no ‏*להיות צריך‎ **liyot tsariH* 'to have to'. Thus this verb is one of many with *defective inflection* (see 40.16):

PAST	PRES	FUT	INF
hitstareH ‏הצטרך‎	tsariH ‏צריך‎	yitstareH ‏יצטרך‎	lehitstareH ‏להצטרך‎
haya tsariH ‏היה צריך‎		yiye tsariH ‏יהיה צריך‎	

41.3 Grammatical-semantic adjective patterns

41.3.1 Pattern (1) Verb-shaped adjectives ('participles')

Shape:	These share the same patterns as present tense verbs (ch.40) - with slight variations in inflection (see 41.7).[5]
Derivation:	Mostly based on present tense verbs, except (f) below, and much of (d).
Meaning:	Often closely related to the matching verb.[6]

Active verb Patterns	Present tense verb		Adjective		
Meaning:	state/ongoing action		In a state/capable of action (often intransitively) - fairly productively		
(1a) *Pa'al*	to'em	'is compatible with' תואם	to'em[7]	'compatible'	תואם
(1b) *Pi'el*	meratek	'grips' מרתק	meratek	'gripping'	מרתק
(1c) *Hif'il*	mafli	'amazes' מפליא	mafli	'amazing'	מפליא

Passive verb patterns	Present tense verb		Adjective		
Meaning:	ongoing action[8]		In a state of completed action ('past participle') - near automatically		
(1d) *Pu'al*	meHubar 'is being connected' מחובר		meHubar	'connected'	מחובר
(1e) *Huf'al*	mukaf	'is being surrounded' מוקף	mukaf	'surrounded'	מוקף

(1f) *Nif'al* usually supplies a special adjective pattern (see (2) below), rather than using its verb pattern adjectivally: thus נפתח *niftaH* 'is opened' has a semi-automatic adjective פתוח *patúaH* 'open'. However, the *hitpa'el* pattern is rarely adjectival.[9] There is no מתפלא ,מתבייש ,להיות מתווכח *liyot mitvakéaH, mitbayesh, mitpale* for 'to be argumentative, in a state of shame, surprised', etc. Instead, other adjectives or verb forms (in these last three examples להתפלא ,להיות מבוייש ,להיות וכחן *liyot vakHan, liyot mevuyash, lehitpale* etc.) typically fill the gap.

Further examples[10] - and additional meanings of this pattern:

(1a) כובד *koved CoCeC.*

Meaning:	(i) as in the foregoing table; or occasionally (ii) varied (not directly geared to a verb).
Examples:	(i) צודק *tsodek* 'correct', נוכח *noHéaH* 'present', תוסס *toses* 'effervescent'.

(ii) בודד *boded* 'lonely', שונה *shone* 'different', קופא *kofe* 'freezing' (e.g. day).

(1b) מכבד *meHabed meCaCeC.*

Meaning: as in table.

Examples: מדכא *medake* 'depressing', משגע *'meshagéa* 'maddening', מסנוור *mesanver* 'blinding'.

(1c) מכביד *maHbid maCCiC.*

Meaning: as in table.

Examples: מקפיד *makpid* 'fussy', מסריח *masríaH* 'stinking', מגעיל *mag'il* 'disgusting', מביך *meviH* 'embarrassing'.

(1d) מכובד *meHubad meCuCaC.*[11]

Meaning: Mostly (i) as in table; (ii) 'having an abstract quality'; (iii) 'wearing/ featuring' (often 'full of') a garment/physical feature - human or non-human; (iv) 'having...(a disease)'; occasionally (v) miscellaneous. Ambiguity is often possible: מסופק *mesupak* 'supplied, doubtful' (meaning i or ii).

Derivation: (i) are from *pu'al* verbs, near-automatically; (ii-iv) are mostly based on a noun or a *hitpa'el* verb (even with four consonants), and are numerous and productive; (v) have no regular source, and are not numerous.

Examples: (i) מפותח *mefutaH* 'developed', מקולקל *mekulkal* 'ruined', מדוכא *meduke* 'depressed'.

(ii) מטופש *metupash* 'foolish' (טיפש *tipesh* 'fool'), ממושך *memushaH* 'prolonged' (התמשך *hitmasheH* 'go on'), מתורבת *meturbat* 'cultured' (תרבות *tarbut* 'culture'), מצוברח *metsuvraH* 'in a mood' (מצב-רוח *matsav-rúaH* 'mood').

(iii) מסונדל *mesundal* 'in sandals' (סנדל *sandal*), ממושקף *memushkaf* 'bespectacled' (משקפיים *mishkafáyim* 'spectacles'), משופם *mesufam* 'moustached' (שפם *safam* 'moustache'), מתולתל *metultal* 'curly' (תלתל *taltal* 'curl'), מכוכב *mekuHav*[12] 'starry' (כוכב *koHav* 'star'), משונן *meshunan* 'toothed' (שן *shen* 'tooth'), מחומש *meHumash* 'five-sided' (חמש *Hamesh* 'five').

(iv) מקורר *mekorar* 'with a chill' (התקרר *hitkarer* 'to catch a chill'), משופע *meshupa* 'flu-stricken' (שפעת *shapáat* 'flu').

(v) מיותר *meyutar* 'unnecessary', משונה *meshune* 'odd'.

(1e) מוכבד *muHbad muCCaC.*

Meaning: (i) as in table; (ii) occasionally, varied - no regular source.

Examples: (i)   מושלם *mushlam* 'perfect', מוגזם *mugzam* 'exaggerated', מותר *mutar* 'permitted';

(ii)   מובחר *muvHar* 'choice', מופלא *mufla* 'wondrous'[13]

(1f) נכבד *niHbad niCCaC.*

Meaning: Occasionally (i) 'in a state of completed action'; usually (ii) varied.

Derivation: (i) *nif'al*-based; (ii) no regular source.

Examples: (i)   נפרד *nifrad* 'separate', נוסף *nosaf* 'added', בלתי-נראה *bilti-nir'e* 'invisible';

(ii)   נמרץ *nimrats* 'vigorous', נחמד *neHmad* 'nice', ניתן *nitan* 'possible'.[14]

41.3.2 Patterns (2-5) Involving internal vowels but no affixes[15]

(2) כבוד *kavud CaCuC* ~suffixed form (כבוד(ים *kvud(im) CCuC(im).*

Meaning: (a) 'in a state of completed action' (i.e. 'past participle'); (b) occasionally 'in ongoing state'; (c) various.

Derivation: (a) from *nif'al* verb, semi-automatic; (b) from *pa'al*; (c) no regular source.

Examples: (a)   שבור *shavur* 'broken', ידוע *yadúa* 'known', רצוי *ratsuy* 'desired, desirable';

(b)   לבוש... *lavush...* 'wearing...', רכון *raHun* 'leaning', רכוב *raHuv* 'riding (on...)';

(c)   ברור *barur* 'clear', דגול *dagul* 'outstanding', רטוב *ratuv*[16] 'wet'.

(3) כביד *kavid CaCiC* ~suffixed form (כביד(ים *kvid(im) CCiC(im).*

Meaning: (a) 'capable of being (broken, etc.)';[17] occasionally, (b) 'capable of, tending to (deviate, etc.)'; (c) various.

Derivation: (a) mostly from *pa'al* verbs (not ל'ה *-a* / ע'ו *-u-* verbs); occasionally from *pi'el*, *hif'il*; moderately productive; (b) mostly from *pa'al* verbs; (c) no regular source.

Examples: (a)   קריא *kari* 'legible', (קרא *kara*), חדיר *Hadir* 'permeable' (חדר *Hadar*), כביס *kavis* 'washable' (כיבס *kibes*), קביל *kavil* 'acceptable' (קיבל *kibel*),[18] אמין *amin* 'credible' (האמין *he'emin*), זחיח *zaHíaH* 'sliding' (הזיח *hezíaH*);

(b)   סביל *savil* 'passive' (סבל *saval*), חריג *Harig* 'deviant' (חרג *Harag*);

(c)   ישיש *yashish* 'elderly', סדיר *sadir* 'regular', טרי *tari* 'fresh'.

(4) כבוד *kavod CaCoC* ~suffixed form (כבוד(ים *kvud(im) CCuC(im)*.[19]
Of all the affix-less patterns among adjectives and nouns, patterns (4) and (5) alone are *semantically* distinct yet not verb-based.

Meaning: (a) most colours;[20] (b) various (mostly beginning with 'gutturals').

Derivation: (ai) no regular source; (aii) based on nouns; (b) no regular source.

Examples: (ai) אדום *adom* 'red', ירוק *yarok* 'green', צהוב *tsahov* 'yellow';
(aii) ורוד *varod* 'pink', זהוב *zahov* 'golden';
(b) איום *ayom* 'awful', ארוך *aroH* 'long', עגול *agol* 'round', מתוק *matok* 'sweet'.

(5) כיבד *kibed CiCeC* ~suffixed form (כיבד(ים *kibd(im) CiCC(im)* (often as a noun too).

Meaning: mostly 'having a (human) defect'.[21]

Derivation: no regular source; neither numerous nor productively coined.

Examples: עיוור *iver* 'blind', גיבן *giben* 'hunchbacked', חרש *Heresh* 'deaf', איטר *iter* 'lefthanded'.

41.3.3   Patterns (6-8)   Vowel pattern plus suffix

Unlike nouns and verbs, adjectives do not take characteristic prefixes (41.5 describes quasi-prefixes[22] such as -דו *du-*, -אנטי *ánti-*).

(6) כבדן *kavdan CaCCan*.[23]

Meaning: 'having personality-type' - used of persons, as in ילד עקשן *yéled akshan*[24] 'stubborn child'.

Derivation: Mostly verb-based; very productive.

Examples: בכיין *baHyan* 'crybabyish' (בכה *baHa*), פטפטן *patpetan* 'talkative' (פיטפט *pitpet*), קפדן *kapdan* 'fussy' (הקפיד *hikpid*), סתגלן *staglan* 'opportunistic' (הסתגל *histagel*).

(7) כבדני *kavdani CaCCani*.[25]

Meaning: (a) 'having a certain personality or emotion' (mostly mirroring the related verb, like pattern (1)); (b) 'having a certain effect' (with emotive connotations).

Derivation: (a) mostly verb-based (i.e. no *CaCCan* to act as base); not numerous; (b) verb-based; fairly productive in literature.

Examples: (a) סבלני *savlani* 'patient' (סבל *saval*), עצבני *atsbani* 'uptight';
(b) לטפני *latfani* 'caressing' (ליטף *litef*), פלשני *palshani* 'intrusive' (פלש *palash*).

(8) Reduplicative suffix כבדבד *kvadvad CCaCCaC*.
The last syllable of the base word is repeated, changing its vowel to *-a-* (unlike reduplicative nouns, cf. 38.2, pattern (15)).

Meaning: mostly (a) 'diminutive'; (b) 'very ...' (occasionally).

Derivation: mostly from unsuffixed adjectives (C-C-C); not numerous but fairly productive.

Examples: (a) עגלגל *agalgal* 'roundish', ורדרד *vradrad* 'pinkish', לבנבן *levanvan* 'whitish', חמצמץ *Hamatsmats* 'sourish';

(b) קטנטן *ktantan* 'tiny', חלקלק *Halaklak* 'slippery' (חלק *Halak* 'smooth'), הפכפך *hafaHfaH* 'fickle' (הפך *hafaH* 'to change').

41.3.4 Patterns (9-12) Suffix, but no special vowel pattern

Here a suffix is added but no special vowel pattern (the base-word keeps its own), except for a few standard adjustments. Adjustments to the base word (akin to 38.2 (16-22)) are as set out below.

Most often, base nouns (i) use their suffixed genitive ('construct') base, giving e.g. ביתי *beyti* 'domestic' (cf. ביתו *beyto*), כספי *kaspi* 'monetary' (cf. כספו *kaspo*), חורפי *Horpi* 'wintry' (cf. חורפו *Horpo*), פרחוני *pirHoni* 'flowery' (cf. פרחו *pirHo*), קדחתני *kadaHtani* 'feverish' (cf. קדחתו *kadaHto*).

However, (ii) a few nouns ending in ה- *-a* maintain their 'free' ('absolute') base, e.g. אוניברסיטאי *universita'i* 'university' (אוניברסיטה *univérsita*), אגודאי *aguda'i* 'pertaining to the Aguda Party' (אגודה *agúda*), אמריקאי *amerikái* 'American' (אמריקה *amérika*).

Also (iii) some nouns drop ('apocopate') their feminine ending ת- *-at*, e.g. רפואי *refu'i* 'medical' (cf. רפואתו *refuato*), יומרני *yomrani* 'pretentious' (יומרתו *yomrato*).[26] Some nouns drop the *-iya/-ya* of names of countries, e.g. אנגלי *angli* 'English' (אנגליה *ángliya*), *ostráli* 'Australian' (אוסטרליה *ostrálya*).[27]

Stressed suffix
(9) ני- *-ani*.[28]

Meaning: mostly 'having certain human (a) external features, (b) personality/emotions, (c) outlook'; (d) 'having a certain effect' (often with emotive connotations), like (7b) and often literary.

Derivation: from nouns or present tense *pa'al* verbs; fairly numerous and productive.

Examples: (a) קולני *kolani* 'vociferous' (קול *kol* 'voice'), לסתני *listani* 'big-jawed' (לסת *léset* 'jaw');

(b) יומרני *yomrani* 'pretentious' (יומרה *yomra* 'pretence'), סובלני *sovlani* 'tolerant' (סובל *sovel* 'suffers'), חולמני *Holmani* 'dreamy' (חולם *Holem* 'dream (v)');

(c) שמאלני *smolani* 'leftist' (שמאל *smol* 'left'), לאומני *leumani* 'nationalistic' (לאום *le'om* 'nation'), רוחני *ruHani* 'spiritual' (רוח *rúaH* 'spirit');

(d) זוחלני *zoHlani* 'creeping' (זוחל *zoHel* 'creeps'), דוקרני *dokrani* 'spiky' (דוקר *doker* 'pricks').

(10) אי- - *a'i.*

Meaning: 'pertaining to/hailing from a certain place'
Derivation: mostly from names of cities;[29] neither numerous nor productive.
Examples: פריסאי *parisa'i* 'Parisian', ברלינאי *berlina'i* 'of Berlin', חלמאי *Helma'i* 'of Chelm'.

Stressed or unstressed suffix

(11) י- - *-i.*[30]

This suffix is by far the commonest way of converting nouns into adjectives. These denote 'pertaining to...' in various ways. This is a 'semantic' pattern in the loosest sense.

י- - *-i* is stressed when added:

(a) to *native* words, e.g. ימי *yami* 'marine', מיידי *miyadi* 'immediate';

(b) to *names of most countries* in the 'Jewish realm' around 1900, e.g. רוסי *rusi* 'Russian', תורכי *turki* 'Turkish', תימני *teymani* 'Yemenite', פרסי *parsi* 'Persian', צרפתי *tsarfati* 'French', אנגלי *angli* 'English' - vs. דני *déni* 'Danish', פורטוגזי *portugézi* 'Portuguese', צ׳כי *tshéHi* 'Czech', לבנוני *levanóni* 'Lebanese', הודי *hódi*[31] 'Indian'.

It is unstressed when added:

(c) to most *foreign* nouns,[32] e.g. דמוקרטי *demokráti* 'democratic', אנרכיסטי *anarHísti* 'anarchistic', דני *déni* 'Danish', ניו-יורקי *nyu yórki* 'of New York';

(d) to most *names of towns* (in the region of Israel): תל-אביבי *tel avívi* 'of Tel Aviv', רחובותי *reHovóti* 'of Rehovot', ירושלמי *yerushálmi* 'of Jerusalem', חדרתי *Haderáti* 'of Hadera', בגדדי *bagdádi* 'of Baghdad'.[33]

Derivation: mostly from nouns; very numerous and productive (highly so in technical usage); almost automatic with names of countries.
Examples: כלכלי *kalkali* 'economic' (כלכלה *kalkala* 'economics'), תזונתי *tzunati* 'nutritional' (תזונה *tzuna* 'nutrition'), נשי *nashi* 'feminine' (נשים *nashim* 'women'), אישי *ishi* 'personal' (איש *ish* 'person'), אנושי *enoshi* 'human' (אנוש *enosh* 'Man'), אידיוטי *idyóti* 'idiotic' (אידיוט *idyot* 'idiot').

Unstressed suffix

(12) יאני- - *-iáni.*

Meaning: 'pertaining to...
Derivation: from names of famous persons; fairly common and productive.
Examples: פרוידיאני *froydiáni* 'Freudian', ג׳ויסיאני *joysiáni* 'Joycean'.[34]

41.4 Purely grammatical adjective patterns

Below are given the relatively distinctive grammatical patterns. They are no longer productive, though (15, 18-20) are numerous. The introductory remarks in 38.3 apply here too.

Firm vowels

(13) *CaCiC*³⁶ יציבי ~ יציבים ~ יציב *yatsiv* ~ *yatsivim* ~ *yatsivey.*
Examples: צדיק *tsadik* 'righteous', יקיר *yakir* 'darling', קליל *kalil* 'very light', כביר *kabir* 'mighty', אמיץ *amits* 'brave'.

(14-16) *-a- drops*

(14) *CaCaC*³⁷ קצרי ~ קצרים ~ קצר *katsar* ~ *ktsarim* ~ *kitsrey.*
Examples: לבן *lavan* 'white', ישן *yashan* 'old'.

(15) *CaCeC*³⁸ זקני ~ זקנים ~ זקן *zaken* ~ *zkenim* ~ *zikney.*
Examples: טפל *tafel* 'secondary', שלם *shalem* 'whole', יבש *yavesh* 'dry'.

(16) *CaCoC.* גדולי ~ גדולים ~ גדול *gadol* ~ *gdolim* ~ *gdoley.*
Examples: טהור *tahor* 'pure', קרוב *karov* 'near', נכון *naHon* 'correct', נפוץ *nafots* 'widespread', מנוח *manóaH* 'deceased'.

Consonant 'hardened'

(17) *CaC* רכי ~ רכים ~ רך *raH* ~ *rakim* ~ *rakey.*
Examples: חד *Had* 'sharp', דק *dak* 'thin', קל *kal* 'light', זך *zaH* 'pure', מר *mar* 'bitter'.

(18-20) *Suffixes with pre-final stress*
These are foreign adjectives. The ending is borrowed intact with the word.

(18) יבי- *-ívi.*
Examples: נאיבי *na'ívi* 'naive', פסיבי *pasívi* 'passive', פרימיטיבי *primitívi* 'primitive' (see also note 34).

(19) לי- *-áli.*
Examples: ריאלי *re'áli* 'real', ליברלי *liberáli* 'liberal', קלריקלי *klerikáli* 'clerical'.

(20) י- *-i.*
Examples: פרקטי *prákti* 'practical', דבילי *debíli* 'foolish', אנונימי *anoními* 'anonymous', דוגרי *dúgri* 'frank'.

41.5 Phrasal adjectives

41.5.1 Phrase-based adjectives: רבגוני *ravgoni* 'multi-coloured'
Like ימי *yami*-type adjectives (11), these are formed by adding *-i*, but to a compound noun phrase, not to a single word. There are two basic types (the (a) set are not numerous, the (b) set are very numerous).

(a) *Noun phrase base*   *Example of adjective with -i*
An already existing compound
phrase, e.g.
tat-hakara 'sub-conscious' תת-הכרה   tat-hakarati 'sub-conscious' תת-הכרתי
(38.4)

(b) A compound phrase with no
function except as basis for an
adjective, e.g.
du-partsuf 'two-face' דו-פרצוף   du-partsufi 'two-faced' דו-פרצופי
QUANT + N

The suffix י- *-i* requires the same adjustments to the 'second word' as it does
in (9-11), listed in section 41.3 - e.g. רחם *réHem* 'uterus', חוץ-רחמי *Huts-raHmi* 'extra-uterine'. Often, this resulting 'second word' never otherwise exists:
there is no פרצופי* *partsufi* (though there exists רחמי *raHmi* 'uterine'). This
underscores the fact that the phrase *in toto* is an adjective, not the second word
in it.

The noun phrase base usually involves a meaningful, though semi-fixed prefix.[39] Close on twenty prepositions and quantifiers can be prefixed to nouns -
for use particularly in type (b) phrase-based adjectives. These are all one-syllable
prefixes (except אנטי- *ánti-*), thanks to the use of specially adapted or foreign
prepositions and quantifiers - which are also more technical-sounding. They are
mostly hyphenated (see note 39). The noun itself is generally 'native'; foreign
nouns come with their own prefix.

Type (a). There are two sub-types, both very limited:

(i) [Prefix + noun] + i tat-hakarati   'subconscious'   תת-הכרתי
almoti   'immortal'   אלמותי

(ii) [Point-of-compass drom-afrikái   'South African'   דרום-אפריקאי
noun + noun] + i ; (cf. drom-áfrika 'South Africa'   (דרום-אפריקה
productive[41]   merkaz-eropéi   'Central European'[40] מרכז-אירופאי
tsfon-maaravi   'North Western'   צפון-מערבי

Type (b). Very productive use of nouns (semi-automatic in technical Hebrew):

[Prefix + noun] + i

(i) [Preposition   al-koli   'supersonic'   על-קולי
+ noun] + i   tat-karka'i   'subterranean'   תת-קרקעי
(i.e. 'exocentric')   kdam-tsva'i   'pre-Army'   קדם-צבאי
trom-histór   'prehistoric'   טרום-הסטורי
batar-mikra'i   'post-Biblical'   בתר-מקראי
beyn-koHavi   'interstellar'   בין-כוכבי
Huts-raHmi   'extrauterine'   חוץ-רחמי
pnim-yabashti   'inland'   פנים-יבשתי
toH-vridi   'intravenous'   תוך-ורידי
pro/ánti-milHamti   'pro/antiwar'   פרו/אנטי-מלחמתי

(ii) [Quantifier +   Had-/du-/tlat-tsedadi 'uni-/bi-/tri-lateral' חד-/דו-/תלת-צדדי
     noun] + *i*   rav-erki   'polyvalent'   רב-ערכי
     (i.e. 'endocentric') kol-/klal-afrikái   'Pan-African'   כל-/כלל-אפריקאי

Overall grammar

Though phrase-based, these expressions act as single words - hence
ה- *ha-* 'the' can only be placed at the beginning and the plural suffix just at the
end:[42]

     ha-revadim ha-tat-hakaratiyim   הרבדים התת-הכרתיים
     the layers the sub conscious   'the subconscious layers'

Like any adjective, these serve as bases for other words:

     du-partsufiut   'two-facedness'   דו-פרצופיות

41.5.2 Compound adjectives, e.g. אינפרא-אדום *infra-adom* 'infra-red'

Several meaningful prefixes (and occasionally some of those above)
can be attached to *pre-existing* adjectives (of any sort, i.e. not only to -*i* type
adjectives), making *compound adjectives*. These act as one word:

     ha-karnáyim **ha**-infra-adumot   הקרניים האינפרא-אדומות
     the rays **the** infra red   'the infra-red rays'

There is generally a semi-productive choice of nouns to go with these prefixes.
Examples of the prefixes are:[43]

me'en-otomáti	'quasi-automatic'	מעין-אוטומטי
pséudo-klási	'pseudo-Classical'	פסבדו-קלאסי
próto-shémi	'proto-Semitic'	פרוטו-שמי
néo-fashísti	'neo-fascist'	ניאו-פאשיסטי
ínfra-adom	'infra-red'	אינפרא-אדום
últra-modérni	'ultra-modern'	אולטרא-מודרני
bilti-muvan[44]	'incomprehensible'	בלתי-מובן
al-enoshi[45]	'non-human'	אל-אנושי
tat-muda[46]	'subconscious'	תת-מודע

41.5.3 Apposed adjectives

     ha-siHot ha-siniot-sovyétiot   השיחות הסיניות-סובייטיות
     the talks the Chinese-Soviet   'the Sino-Soviet talks'

These 'compound *phrases*' (they are not single words) are discussed in chapter
36 with other apposition phrases like הצייר-זמר *ha-tsayar-zamar* 'the painter-
singer', אצו-רצו *átsu-rátsu* 'they rushed-dashed'.

41.6-10 ADJECTIVE INFLECTION: A BRIEF SURVEY

Here are described the inflectional endings - for the feminine, plural and construct.
In certain adjective patterns, the body of the word changes too when inflected; see
individual patterns (41.3-4).

41.6 Overview: feminine and plural

For general syntactic questions (e.g. where can there be adjective agreement) see chapters 12 and 18.

All adjectives can take the following endings,[47] except a handful that do not inflect at all.

f.s. [48]	-a	ה-	-t	ת-	-it	ית-	*untressed*: -et/-at ת-
m.pl.	-im	ים-					
f.pl.	-ot	ות-					

Some 31% of dictionary-listed adjectives take *-a*, 38% *-t*, 3% *-it*, 27% *-et/-at* (Schwarzwald 1982b).

41.7 Verb-shaped adjectives (pattern (1) in 41.3)

Inflection is mostly as in the matching verb (ch. 40), even where the particular adjective is not based on one:[49]

(a) tsodek, tsodéket, tsodkim, tsodkot   צודק, צודקת, צודקים, צודקות
'correct'

(b) meratek, meratéket, meratkim, meratkot   מרתק, מרתקת, מרתקים, מרתקות
'gripping'

(c) makpid, makpida, makpidim, makpidot   מקפיד, מקפידה, מקפידים, מקפידות
'fussy'

(d) mekuHav, mekuHévet, mekuHavim, mekuHavot   מכוכב, מכוכבת, מכוכבים, מכוכבות
'starry'

(e) muvHar, muvHéret, muvHarim, muvHarot   מובחר, מובחרת, מובחרים, מובחרות
'choice'

(f) nimrats, nimrétset, nimratsim, nimratsot   נמרץ, נמרצת, נמרצים, נמרצות
'vigorous'

41.8 Unsuffixed adjectives (notably patterns (2)-(5), (8), (13)-(17))[50]

(a) Inflection mostly ות- ,ים- ,ה- *-a, -im, -ot* (except pattern (5))[51]. Examples are:

shavur, shvura, shvurim, shvurot   שבור, שבורה, שבורים, שבורות
'broken'

adom, aduma, adumim, adumot   אדום, אדומה, אדומים, אדומות
'red'

raH, raka, rakim, rakot   רך, רכה, רכים, רכות
'soft'

kHalHal, kHalHala, kHalHalim, kHalHalot   כחלחל, כחלחלה, כחלחלים, כחלחלות
'bluish'

giben, gibénet, gibnim, gibnot   גיבן, גיבנת, גיבנים, גיבנות
                                                                    'hunched'

(b) It is among these unsuffixed adjectives that the few uninflecting adjectives
are found:

ha-simla ha-**bezh** u-shney svéderim **bórdo**   השמלה הבז' ושני סוודרים **בורדו**
the dress the **beige** and two sweaters **maroon**   'the beige dress and two maroon
                                                                        sweaters'

Similarly: תורקיז *turkiz* 'turquoise', הנ"ל *ha-nal* 'the above-mentioned',[52]
פרווה *párve* 'parev' (religious term: neither meaty nor dairy); generally with
masculine singular and feminine singular nouns respectively: אלף-בית *alef-bet*
'superb' (army slang), רבתי *rabati* 'almighty'.

41.9 Suffixed adjectives (notably patterns (6)-(7), (9)-(11), (18)-(20))
Inflection by steps:

Add *-i* to word (where there is none)   ⇒   ⇐   י +
Then add *-t, -im, -ot*   ⇒   ⇐   ת, ים, ות +
Result: *-it, -i(y)im, -i(y)ot*   ית, יים, יות

For example:

kapdan + *i* ⇒   ⇐   קפדנ+י
kapdan+*i*+t, kapdan+*i*+m ⇒   ⇐   קפדנ+י+ת, קפדנ+י+ים
kapdanit, kapdaniyim, kapdaniyot   קפדנית, קפדניים, קפדניות

More examples ('irritable', 'idiotic', 'Syrian'):

atsbani, atsbanit, atsbaniyim, atsbaniyot   עצבני, עצבנית, עצבניים, עצבניות
debíli, debílit, debíliyim, debíliyot   דבילי, דבילית, דביליים, דביליות
súri, súrit, súriyim, súriyot   סורי, סורית, סוריים, סוריות

However, those nationality adjectives ('gentilics') with stressed י- *-i* (pattern
(11)) can take ה- *-a* for feminine - in reference to persons.[53] They then look like
the corresponding noun:

zaméret anglit/angliya   'an English *chanteuse*'   זמרת אנגלית/אנגליה

ir anglit   'an English town'   עיר אנגלית

But in the masculine plural the adjectives and nouns are generally distinct:

Nouns
anglim, germanim   'Englishmen, Germans'   אנגלים, גרמנים

Adjectives
angliyim, germaniyim   'English, German'   אנגליים, גרמניים

The few diminutive adjectives with ון- *-on* take ות- ,ים- ,ת- *-et, -im, -ot*:
טיפשונת *tipshónet* 'soppy'.

Other adjectives in ון- *-on* take ות- ,ים- ,ה- *-a, -im, -ot*. They are few, unproductive and probably not perceived as suffixed, e.g. תחתון *taHton* 'bottom',
ראשון *rishon* 'first'.

The few in אי- *-ay* act like nouns of the אי- *-ay* type (בנאי *banay* 'builder'): *-y* becomes *-i*; then add *-t*, (surprisingly) *-m, -ot*:

rashay, rasha'it, rasha'im, rasha'iot   'entitled'   רשאי, רשאית, רשאים, רשאיות

41.10 'Construct' adjectives

For the general syntax of where construct adjectives occur, see 6.19. All but suffixed adjectives (41.9) can occur in construct structures:[54]

gvina dalat-shuman	גבינה דלת-שומן
CONSTRUCT	
cheese low fat	'low-fat cheese'
ets me'ukam-géza	עץ מעוקם-גזע
CONSTRUCT	
tree gnarled trunk	'a tree with a gnarled trunk'

not:

*géver **anaki**-koma	*גבר ענקי-קומה
SUFF	
ADJ	
man giant size	(a '**giant**-sized' man)

The endings are invariably as follows (using דל *dal* 'low, poor' as an example):

f.s.	dalat	דלת	(free form	dala	דלה)[55]
m.pl.	daley	דלי			
f.pl.	dalot	דלות			

For certain patterns, the word changes internally too - see 41.3-4 for common changes.

FURTHER READING
Ben-Hayyim 1971; Berman 1980a; Blanc 1957a; Blau 1952; Bolozky 1972, 1980; Di-nur 1979; Kaddari 1965; Masson 1976; Mirkin 1968; Netzer 1976; Podolski 1981; Rosén 1955, 1956, 1966b, 1977; Schwarzwald 1982b; Werner 1981.

42. Prepositions: form and inflection

42.1 Form of the preposition

Hebrew prepositions are a distinct word class syntactically (see ch.19), but, unlike verbs and nouns, have no characteristic patterns or affixes to render them distinct. Rather, for historical reasons, a few prepositions look like verbs (e.g. הואיל *ho'il* 'since', כעבור *kaavor* 'after') and many look like nouns (e.g. בשביל *bishvil* 'for', מפני *mipney* 'because'); and most take a suffixed pronoun of the same kind as nouns (see ch.6) - while not at all 'noun-like' syntactically.

Four prepositions are written as a single letter, and so, like other such words (e.g. -ה *ha-* 'the'), are prefixed to the next word: -ב *be-* 'in',[1] -כ *ke-* 'as', -ל *le-* 'to', -מ *mi-* 'from', e.g. בישראל *be-yisra'el* 'in Israel'.

42.2 Inflection of the preposition

42.2.1 Suffixation

A preposition governing a personal pronoun must suffix it,[2] e.g.

bishvil + hu → bishvilo   'for him'   בשביל + הוא ← בשבילו

But several prepositions taking nouns do not, idiosyncratically, take personal pronouns at all, notably:[3] אגב *agav* 'in the course of', במשך *bemésheH* 'during', בשל *beshel* 'owing to', בתור *betor* 'as (= qua)', -כ *ke-* 'as', כגון *kegon* 'such as', לאור *le'or* 'in view of', לאחר *leaHar* 'after', ללא *lelo* 'without', למרות *lamrot* 'despite', על-אף *al-af* 'despite', מאז *me'az* 'since', מחמת *maHmat* 'owing to', משום *mishum* 'because of', תוך-כדי *toH-kdey* 'in the course of'.

Most prepositions (a) take the same suffix as *singular nouns*, and (b) undergo the same internal adjustment, if any, as nouns of their shape; but some of the commonest display some irregularities.

Several prepositions take the same suffix as *plural nouns*, particularly if they already have the 'plural-like' ending -י *-ey* or -ות *-ot*. A handful take a mixture of 'singular' and 'plural' suffixes.

42.2.2 The most common suffixes
Most prepositions take the following suffixes:

i	'me'	י
Ha	'you' (m.s.)	ך
eH	'you' (f.s.)	ך
o	'him'	ו
a	'her'	ה
énu	'us'	נו
Hem	'you' (m.pl.)	כם
Hen	'you' (f.pl.) (F)	כן
am	'them' (m.)	ם
an	'them' (f.) (F)	ן

Examples are:[4]

bishvil: bishvili, bishvilHa, bishvileH,[5]
  bishvilo, bishvila, bisvilénu,
  bishvilHem, bishvilam

בשביל: בשבילי, בשבילך, בשבילך
בשבילו, בשבילה, בשבילנו
בשבילכם, בשבילם
'for: for me, for you...'

déreH: darki, darkeHa, darkeH, darko,
  darka, darkénu, darkeHem, darkam

דרך: דרכי, דרכך, דרכך, דרכו
דרכה, דרכנו, דרככם, דרכם
'through: through me, through you...'

Further examples of prepositions that change their vowel(s) when inflected (rather like 'segolate' nouns, cf. 38.2, pattern (3)):

bekérev: bekirbi etc.	'among'	בקרב: בקרבי...
le'óreH: le'orki etc.	'along'	לאורך: לאורכי...
néged: negdi etc.	'against'	נגד: נגדי...

Exceptions are:
(a)

  (i) with *-aHem*, *-ahem* in 2nd, 3rd pl.
    be 'in' -ב
    bi, beHa, baH, bo, ba, bánu, baHem, bahem[6]   בי, בך, בך, בו, בה, בנו, בכם, בהם

    le 'to' -ל
    li, leHa, laH, lo, la, lánu, laHem, lahem   לי, לך, לך, לו, לה, לנו, לכם, להם

    im 'with' (F) עם
    imi, imHa, imaH, imo, ima, imánu,
      imaHem, imahem

עמי, עמך, עמך, עמו, עמה, עמנו,
עמכם, עמהם

  (ii) With *-Hem*, *-am* in 2nd, 3rd pl.
    im[7] 'with' עם
    iti, itHa, itaH, ito, ita, itánu, itHem,
      itam

אתי, אתך, אתך, אתו, אתה, אתנו, אתכם,
אתם

et (OM) את

oti, otHa, otaH,[8] oto, ota, otánu,   אותי, אותך, אותך, אותו, אותה, אותנו,
etHem,[9] otam   אתכם, אותם

(b)

kmo 'like' כמו
kamóni, kamóHa, kamoH, kamóhu,   כמוני, כמוך, כמוך, כמוהו,
   kamóha, kamónu, kmoHem,[10] kmohem[11]   כמוה, כמונו, כמוכם, כמוהם

(c)

min[15] 'from' מן
miméni, mimHa, mimeH, miménu,[12]   ממני, ממך, ממך, ממנו
   miména, miménu,[13] mikem,[14] mehem   ממנה, ממנו, מכם, מהם

(d) Composite מעל ל- *me'al le-* 'over', מתחת ל- *mi-taHat le-* 'under',
מסביב ל- *mi-saviv le-* 'around' lose ל- *le-* when inflected, e.g., מעלינו,
מתחתינו, מסביבנו *mealénu, mitaHténu, misvivénu* etc.

For מעבר ל- *me'éver le-* and other prepositions involving ל- *le-*, see 42.2.3
(exceptions) below.

42.2.3 Other common suffixes
Several prepositions take the following suffixes:

-ay	'me'	י-
-éHa	'you' (m.s.)	יך-
-áyiH	'you' (f.s.)	יך-
-av	'him'	יו-
-éha	'her'	יה-
-énu (or -éynu)	'us'	ינו-
-eHem	'you' (m.pl.)	יכם-
-eHen	'you' (f.pl.) (F)	יכן-
-ehem	'them' (m.pl.)	יהם-
-ehen	'them' (f.pl.) (F)	יהן-

Examples are:[4]

aHarey 'after' אחרי
aHaray, aHaréHa, aHaráyiH, aHarav,   אחרי, אחריך, אחריך, אחריו,
   aHaréha, aHarénu, aHareHem,   אחריה, אחרינו, אחריכם,
   aHarehem   אחריהם

odot 'concernig' אודות
odotay, odotéHa, odotáyiH, odotav,   אודותי, אודותיך, אודותיו,
   odotéha, odoténu, odoteHem,   אודותיה, אודותינו, אודותיכם,
   odotehem   אודותיהם

The same applies to the following:

lifney: lefanay,..., lifnehem	'before'	לפני: לפני,..., לפניהם
mipney: mipanay,..., mipnehem	'of'[16]	מפני: מפני,..., מפניהם
bidey: beyaday,..., bidehem	'by'	בידי: בידי,..., בידיהם

and similarly to:

meaHorey	'behind'	מאחורי	el[17]	'to'	אל
me'al	'above'	מעל	klapey	'towards'	כלפי
al	'on'	על	legabey	'concerning'	לגבי
al-gabey	'upon'	על-גבי			

Exceptions are:

(a) bli 'without' בלי

The suffixes are regular, but the stem becomes בלעד- *bilad-*:

biladay, biladéHa, biladáyiH, biladav,   בלעדי, בלעדיך, בלעדיו,
biladéha, biladénu, biladeHem,   בלעדיה, בלעדינו, בלעדיכם,
biladehem   בלעדיהם

(b) ל- *le-* expressing 'movement' is replaced by אל- *el-* when inflected:

elay, eléHa etc.   'to me, to you etc.'   ...אלי, אליך

This also affects ל- *le-* used with words of 'communicating' and 'referring', e.g.
התקשר *hitkasher* 'contact', התייחס *hityaHes* 'refer (to), relate (to)', פנה *pana*
'turn (to)', and with words denoting 'concerning', e.g., בנוגע ל- *benogéa le-*,
בקשר ל- *bekésher le-*, באשר ל- *baasher le-* (cf. 15.6).

42.2.4 Mixing plural and singular suffixes

These prepositions mix singular and plural-type endings in various
ways:

(a) בין *ben* 'between' has plural-type suffixes in the plural:[18]

beni, benHa, beneH, beno, bena,   ביני, בינך, בינך, בינו, בינה,
benéynu/benénu, beneHem, benehem   בינינו/ביננו, ביניכם, ביניהם

(b) (מ)תחת *(mi-)taHat* 'under' has plural-type suffixes, or alternatively in 3rd
person, (מ)תחתו *(mi-)taHto* and especially (מ)תחתם *(mi-)taHtam*.

(c) על-ידי *al-yedey* 'by (passive)' generally takes singular-type suffixes despite
its *-ey*, but some speakers prefer על-ידיו, על-ידיה *al-yadav, al-yadéha*.
Thus there is ambiguity in inflection with על-יד *al-yad* 'next to' (here
לידו, לידה *leyado, leyada* is sometimes preferred in 3rd person).

FURTHER READING
Blau 1967: vol. 2, 97 ff; Peretz 1972: 227; Rosén 1955: 210, 1966a: ch. 3.

Notes to chapters

Chapter 5

1. Purists pronounce -ה as *ha-* before certain types of word beginning with ה, ח, ע *ha-, Ha-, a-*.

2. An entirely different *ha-* denotes 'who, which' in some present tense relative clauses, e.g. נכים הנוהגים *naHim ha-nohagim* 'invalids who drive'.

3. את *et* is discussed more fully in 15.5; it is a 'governed' preposition introducing the *direct* object, e.g. שמעו את דוד *sham'u et david* 'they heard David' vs. indirect object שמעו לדוד *sham'u le-david* 'they listened to David'.

4. 'One morning' is בוקר אחד *bóker eHad* (morning one), not בבוקר **be-boker* (in a morning). 'In the morning (i.e. in general)' too is בבוקר *ba-boker* 'in the morning'; see 5.4. Words for days of the week do not have -ה *ha-* 'the'; they are usually 'proper names', thus ביום שני *be-yom sheni* (*lit.* on second day) is used for both 'on a Monday' and 'on (this) Monday'; see 5.3.2 and 5.5. Similarly, the names for festivals are usually proper names, e.g. פסח *pésaH* 'Passover'.
Re. -ב *ba-* meaning 'in the': see 5.6, under 'conflation of *ha-*'.

5. Contrast בבית-ספר *be-bet séfer* 'in school', which involves an indefinite, quasi-proper noun. The same holds for certain other institutions - see 5.4.

6. There are exceptions. Instead of האב, האם *ha-av, ha-em* 'the father, the mother', possessive suffixes are employed, as in אביו, אמך *aviv, imeH* 'his-father, your-mother', or (casually) אבא שלו, אמא שלך *ába shelo, íma shelaH* etc. אבא, אמא *ába, íma* are intrinsically definite in such cases, hence, in most usage, we do not have האבא שלו **ha-ába shelo* '**the** father his'. Indeed, one intimately employs אבא, אמא *ába, íma* as proper nouns, e.g. איפה אמא? *éfo íma?* 'Where's Mom? [= my/our/your Mom]'.

   'Grandfather, grandmother' too require possessive sufixes (and are *not* always intrinsically definite): (ה)סבא שלו, (ה)סבתא שלך *(ha-) sába shelo, (ha-) sávta shelaH* 'his grandfather, your grandmother'. They too have a separate use as proper nouns: איפה סבתא? *éfo sávta?* 'Where's Grandma?'

7. There are exceptions. Among proper nouns requiring -ה *ha-* are (a) names of rivers, e.g. הדנובה *ha-danúba* 'the Danube', התמזה *ha-témza* 'the Thames'; (b) certain other places, e.g. החרמון *ha-Hermon* 'Mt Hermon', הכרמל *ha-karmel* 'Mt Carmel', הגולן *ha-golan* 'the Golan', הנגב *ha-négev* 'the Negev'; (c) 'proper nouns' deriving from a 'common noun' with -ה *ha-*, e.g. קראתי את הארץ *karáti et ha-árets* 'I read ⟨the paper⟩ Haarets', נכנסתי להזורע *niHnásti le-ha-zoréa* 'I went into ⟨the shop⟩ Hazorea'; (d) most abbreviations of Rabbis' names, e.g. הריטב"א *ha-ritva* 'Ritva', המהר"ל *ha-maharal* 'Maharal' (a few *optionally* take -ה *ha-*, e.g. (ה)רד"ק *(ha)radak* 'Radak'; and רש"י *ráshi* 'Rashi' disallows it). Mountains, lakes, seas etc. are usually introduced by הר... *har...* 'Mt...', אגם... *agam...* 'Lake...' etc; see 6.14.

8. However, ראיתי ציור של פיקאסו *ra'íti tsiyur shel pikáso* 'I saw a painting of Picasso', not ראיתי פיקאסו **ra'íti pikáso* 'I saw a Picasso'.

501

9. An exception is שבת *shabat* 'The Sabbath, Saturday', which is generally a common noun except that with -ב *be-* 'on' it is a proper noun too:

Common noun:

matay niHnéset ha-shabat?

מתי נכנסת השבת?

'When does the Sabbath begin?'

heevárti sham et ha-shabat

העברתי שם את השבת

'I spent the Sabbath there' (general or particular)

heevárti sham shabat

העברתי שם שבת

'I spent a Sabbath there'

Proper noun:

hayíti sham be-shabat

הייתי שם בשבת

'I was there on ⟨the⟩ Sabbath'

10. In ההוא, ההיא *hahu, hahi* etc. 'that' and הללו *halálu* 'these', -ה *ha-* is an inseparable part of the word.

11. It is as if מי *mi* 'who?' were underlyingly intrinsically partitive, denoting מ... *mi mi...* 'who of (people in general)'. It is not coincidental that the inanimate מה *ma* 'what?' and משהו *máshehu* 'something' are indefinite and strictly incapable of taking a partitive: *מה מהם* *ma mehem 'which of them'; see further, 8.6.

12. However, with days of the week and special days 'this...' (i.e. 'the coming...') is usually הזה *ha-ze*: ביום שני הזה *be-yom sheni ha-ze* 'this Monday'.

13. Where an intensifier precedes the adjective, -ה *ha-* will precede the whole phrase: הילד המאד פרוע *ha-yéled ha-me'od parúa* 'the very wild child'.

14. Exceptionally, noun + adjective can be a semi-compound (see 10.8), thus הבן-יחיד *ha-ben yaHid* 'the only child'.

15. Where -ה *ha-* seems to introduce a verb, it is not the 'definite article' but a (formal) variant of -ש *she-* 'that'; thus the preceding noun need not even be 'definite' (see 33.5):

martsim ha-mevakshim haala'a   מרצים המבקשים העלאה

meaymim be-shvita   מאיימים בשביתה

'Lecturers that are seeking a rise are threatening a strike'

16. Thus one cannot add a further -ה *ha-* as definite article:

*ha-léHem **ha-**haHi tov

*הלחם ההכי טוב

the bread **the** most good   'The best bread'

Chapter 6

1. The traditional terms are נסמך and סומך or 'construct' and 'construent'.

2. Thus *endocentric* phrases are ruled out.

3. Construct phrases are ṉ(X NP), X being a single word and ṉ a category that ranks between N and NP, such that a whole construct phrase usually ranks too large to function as X itself.

4. Exceptions are few, e.g. שנים ~ שנות *shanim ~shnot* 'years'.

5. These are morphological rather than phonological rules. Indeed, many speakers lacking a command of formal Hebrew may lack many of these rules and just make these variations lexically for particular set expressions.

6. Penultimate in the underlying 'free' form, e.g. מוצר, מוצרים *mutsar, mutsarim*. But vowels are retained for most suffixes of the plural noun, thus מוצרי ~ מוצריו *mutsrey ~mutsarav*.

7. Although with indefinite nouns there is no direct syntactic evidence that these are construct phrases at all (rather than appositions), the use of the construct form with שניים *shnáyim* is indirect evidence. The numeral אחד *eHad* follows its noun and is akin to an adjective.

8. Thus only words that constitute the whole component A can have construct form.

9. This is not a morphological constraint, as no construct ending need be involved in many instances; and names used as common nouns can indeed take regular *plural* endings (39.10): כולם איינשטיינים *kulam áynshtaynim* 'they're all Einsteins'. Possibly, just as the most highly 'definite' nouns (pronouns, names) are most typically 'possessors', so too they may be least typically 'possessed' or amenable to this most direct possessive construction.

10. If חיל אוויר שבדיה *Heyl avir shvédya* were possible as a simple chain of constructs, it would have to mean 'the force of Sweden's air'; and חיל אווירנו *Heyl avirénu* would mean 'the force of our air'. There are, however, exceptions, e.g. שיוויון נפשנו *shivyon nafshénu* 'our equanimity', בא כוחו *ba koHo* 'his proxy'.

11. זה *ze* 'it', itself a personal pronoun (7.3), is never suffixed; indeed, for 'its' one tends to prefer שלו *shelo* (i.e. של + הוא *shel + hu* 'of it' m.s.):

al titen li et ze, ki ze ratuv ve-ani   אל תתן לי את זה, כי **זה** רטוב ואני
lo ohev et ha-tséva **shelo**   לא אוהב את הצבע **שלו**

'Don't give me this, because **it**'s wet and I don't like **its** colour'

12. As elaborated in 6.8.3, a 'definite' component B usually entails a 'definite' component A.

13. An exception: חלק מ- *Hélek mi-* 'some of', yet חלקם *Helkam* 'some of them' etc. Construct suffixes are impossible with adjectives, hence הארצות עשירות הנפט *ha-aratsot ashirot ha-neft* 'the oil-rich countries' but not *הארצות עשירותיו *ha-aratsot ashirotav* 'the its-rich countries'.

14. This creates the most 'open' of genitive phrases. At the other extreme are set phrases, to all intents and purposes a single word, where an adjective will *not* qualify the second word.

15. Sometimes the noun + name phrase is nevertheless felt to be a set phrase: סיפורי עגנון האחרים *sipurey agnon ha-aHerim* 'the other Agnon stories', פרוורי תל-אביב החדשים *parverey tel aviv ha-Hadashim* 'the new Tel Aviv suburbs'.

16. Determiners are structurally tighter to the noun than are adjectives; indeed they are not commonly free-standing; see chapter 9.

17. Very formally also הצעתך זאת *hatsaatHa zot* (proposal-your this).

18. חברי בעלה *Havrey baala* 'her husband's friends' is itself not a chain of construct *nouns*, for the second construct involves just a pronoun *suffix* ה- *-a*.

19. A similar (formal) emphatic construction forgoes של *shel*: דירתו הוא *dirato hu* (apartment-his he) '*his* apartment', מולדתנו אנו *moladeténu ánu* (homeland-our we) '*our* homeland'.

20. Casually, the masculine plural is used instead.

21. The general grammatical exceptions have been outlined in 6.7. There are also lexical exceptions of various kinds, listed here in (1)-(5).

   (1) Certain nouns *must* be construct to another noun, i.e. they do not take של *shel*, nor are they ever free-standing. They include several nouns denoting a space or time relationship: פני *pney* 'surface', ראש *rosh* 'top', רחבי *raHavey* 'length and breadth', גמר *gmar* 'end', משך *mésheH* 'duration'; also some nouns of membership, e.g. בן (הכפר, אותו מעמד,...) *ben (ha-kfar, oto maamad,...)* 'one of (the village, the same class,...)', איש (הליכוד, האופוזיציה,...) *ish (ha-likud, ha-opozitsya,...)* 'a member of (the Likud, the Opposition,...)'. However, not all relational nouns are like this, thus התחתית של... *ha-taHtit shel...* 'the bottom of...', דרומה של יוון *droma shel yavan* 'the South of Greece'.

(2) Certain relational nouns require the construct *if* possessive, e.g. ימין (התמונה) *yemin (ha-tmuna)* 'the right of (the picture)', קצה (המגש) *ktse (ha-magash)* 'the edge of (the tray)', and סוף *sof* 'end', מועד *mo'ed* 'date', יליד *yelid* 'native'.

(3) A few nouns require single or double construct, e.g. בעל *báal* 'owner', תולדות *toldot* 'history', and a few require double construct, e.g. בעלה של *baala shel* 'the husband of', אשתו של *ishto shel* 'the wife of', דעתו של *daato shel* 'the opinion of' (very casually also הבעל של *ha-báal shel*, האשה של *ha-isha shel*).

(4) Certain nouns are similarly restricted when followed by a particular type of noun, i.e. they are semi-fixed expressions. Those requiring a construct include שנות (הששים, השבעים,...) *shnot (ha-shishim, ha-shivim,...)* 'the sixties, seventies,...', גיל (ששים, שבעים,...) *gil shishim, shivim,...)* 'the age of (sixty, seventy,...)', כאב (בטן, גרון,...) *ke'ev (béten, garon,...)* '(stomach, throat,...) ache'; those requiring a single or double construct include שלום *shlom* 'welfare'.

(5) The pronoun suffix, otherwise usually a mark of formality, is always possible or even required with kinship terms. It is generally preferred to של *shel* 'of' for אשה *isha* 'wife' (אשתי, אשתך *ishti, ishteHa* 'my wife, your wife' etc.), בעל *báal* 'husband', אב *av* 'father', אם *em* 'mother', חם *Ham* 'father-in-law', חמות *Hamot* 'mother-in-law', דוד *dod* 'uncle', דודה *dóda* 'aunt'; however, casual usage has (ה)אבא שלי *(ha-)ába sheli*, 'my dad', (ה)אמא שלי *(ha-)íma sheli* 'my mum', דוד שלי *dod sheli* 'my uncle', דודה שלי *dóda sheli* 'my auntie' (and שלך... *...shelHa* 'your...' etc.). The pronoun suffix is an *alternative* to של *shel* 'of' for הורים *horim* 'parents', בן *ben* 'son', בת *bat* 'daughter', אח *aH* 'brother', אחות *aHot* 'sister' and the terms for 'brother/sister-in-law, cousin, nephew, niece'. סבא *sába* 'grandfather' and סבתא *sávta* 'grandmother' take של *shel* and not the pronoun suffixes.

22. Exceptionally, there is a *definite* משל *mishel* phrase when 'my own...' denotes 'my own respective...', as in יש לי את הצרות משלי *yesh li et ha-tsarot misheli* 'I have my own troubles.' משל *mishel* is used (formally) with nouns or non-reflexively in *partitives*: היום קראתי שני מאמרים {של/משל} ויטגנשטיין ואחד {שלך/משלך} *hayom karáti shney maamarim {shel / mishel} vitgenshtayn ve-eHad {shelHa / mishelHa}* 'Today I've read two articles of Wittgenstein and one of yours'.

23. There is also a formal idiom לא לו *lo lo* 'not his', לא להם *lo lahem* 'not theirs' etc.: במלים לא לה *be-milim lo la* 'in words that were not hers'.

24. By contrast, noun *compounds* inflect as single words: רמזור~ רמזורים *ramzor ~ramzorim* 'traffic light (~ lights)'.

25. So too adjective + noun constructs, e.g. התותח ארוך הטווח, התותח הארוך-טווח *ha-totaH aroH ha-tvaH, ha-totaH ha-aroH tvaH* (the cannon long the range, the cannon the long range) 'the long-range cannon'.

26. But then the pronoun suffix (חבריו *Haverav* 'its members') is impossible.

27. Where both the subject and the direct object are to be mentioned, the *object* tends to be expressed through the genitive (this position, directly following the 'action word', being normal for an object), whereas the *subject* is couched in an על-ידי *al-yedey* or בידי *bidey* 'by' phrase: פינוי הילדים בידי חיילים *pinuy ha-yeladim bidey Hayalim* 'the evacuation of the children by troops'.

28. Among the few exceptions are מתן *matan* 'giving' (only construct, and the following noun must be an 'object') as in מתן אוטונומיה *matan otonómya* 'giving of autonomy', הולדת *hulédet* 'birth', מלאת *mlot* 'passing (of years)'; מות *mávet* 'death', צאת *tset* 'departure', בוא *bo* 'arrival' (construct or double genitive).

29. Casual Hebrew prefers such all-purpose constructions as אלה שנותנים *éle she-notnim* or מי שנותן *mi she-noten* 'someone who gives'.

30. Whereas the verb or adjective taking an *indirect* object (with the prepositions ל-,-ל, עם *le-*, *im* etc.) simply requires the same preposition for its corresponding 'action or state noun', e.g. השפעה על ילדים *hashpa'a al yeladim* 'influence on children' (ch. 30), the agent noun cannot take a preposition - it is a case of either the genitive or nothing: **mashpi'im al yeladim* משפיעים על ילדים* 'influencers of children'. Indeed, action or state nouns need no object noun at all: ההשפעה מורגשת *ha-hashpa'a murgéshet* 'the influence is felt'. Exceptions include idiomatic uses of certain verbs taking adverbials, e.g. באי (הקונגרס,...) *ba'ey* (*ha-kongres,...*) 'those attending (the congress,...)', יושבי (הבקעה,...) *yoshvey* (*ha-bik'a,...*) 'those living in (the valley,...)', יוצאי (פולין,...) *yots'ey* (*polin,...*) 'emigrants from (Poland,...)', and a few set phrases such as הולכי רגל *holHey régel* 'pedestrians', מיטיבי לכת *meytivey léHet* 'good walkers'.

31. The adjective proves that these are nouns: נועלי סנדלים צעירים *noaley sandalim tseirim* 'young wearers of sandals'.

32. Except in certain set phrases.

33. However, with brand names the construct with ה- *ha-* 'the' is avoided: הכוס של טמפו *ha-kos shel témpo* 'the glass of Tempo' rather than **kos ha-tempo* כוס הטמפו*. Moreover, as the construct component B is in general not *intrinsically* definite, it will not generally be a pronoun: בקבוק היין *bakbuk ha-yáyin* 'the bottle of wine' but not **bakbuko* בקבוקו* 'its bottle'. The same is true for purpose and identification genitives.

34. With נמל-תעופה *nemal teufa* 'airport' and similar construct nouns, formal Hebrew prefers *apposition* of the name: נמל-התעופה קנדי *nemal ha-teufa kénedi* 'Kennedy airport'. Casually the construct is used, but without changing the form of תעופה *teufa* etc.: נמל-תעופה קנדי *nemal teufa* (COMPONENT A) *kénedi* (COMPONENT B), בית-חולים הדסה *bet Holim hadása* 'The Hadasa Hospital' etc.

35. In coordination, dates require apposition, e.g. החודשים יוני ויולי *ha-Hodashim yúni ve-yúli* 'the months June and July'.

36. Or (more technical) by apposition: הנחל ירקון *ha-náHal yarkon*.

37. And for this reason, perhaps, קיבוץ דגניה *kibuts degánya*, קבוצת דגניה *kvutsat degánya* 'Kibbutz Deganya'.

38. In apposition (36.4), ה- *ha-* 'the' is prefixed to the *whole* phrase: העיר חיפה *ha-ir Heyfa* 'the City of Haifa'.

39. עץ *ets* 'tree' is thus used as a 'classifier', but not פרח *péraH* 'flower', צמח *tsémaH* 'plant', ציפור *tsipor* 'bird' and other such terms.

40. This applies only when the name is itself used as a 'common noun', e.g. יש לי פיאט *yesh li fiat* 'I have a Fiat'. With other names one needs של *shel* 'of' (indeed, של *shel* can always be used): הריבה של אוסם *ha-riba shel ósem* 'The Osem jam'. Apposition is impossible.

41. Unlike adjectives, they always require this head noun. As with the foregoing construct types, no pronoun suffixes are possible.

42. של *shel* is not used, nor a pronoun (**toveyhem* טוביהם* 'their best'), even when not generic.

43. Much varied use is made of בעל (חי, בית, שמחה,...) *báal* (*Hay, báyit, simHa,...*) 'animal, landlord, host,...', בן (אדם, זוג, תורה,...) *ben* (*adam, zug, tora,...*) 'person, spouse, learned Jew,...', בית (ספר, קיבול, שימוש,...) *bet* (*séfer, kibul, shimush,...*) 'school, receptacle, toilet,...'. The regular meaning of בעל *báal* is 'possessing'; בן *ben* is 'son, member, comprising' and בית *bet* is 'house'.

44. *Adjective* phrases such as דו-לשוני *du-leshoni* 'bilingual', רב-צדדי *rav-tsdadi* 'multilateral' are not construct, for in all constructs component B is a noun. Hence ה- *ha-* 'the' can only precede the whole phrase, as in הילד הדו-לשוני *ha-yéled ha-du-leshoni* 'the bilingual child' (see 41.5). Unlike אי- *i-* 'non-', חוסר *Hóser* 'non-' is a true noun.

45. In addition, certain determiners are genitive in form, e.g. **כל מיני**
בעיות *kol miney baayot* 'all kinds of problems', עיקר הפתרון *ikar ha-pitaron* 'the basic
solution'. See chapter 9.

46. Type (1) is exocentric and type (2) endocentric.

47. This definiteness is not 'inherent' in the noun; whereas המבצרים
מוקפי האויבים *ha-mivtsarim mukafey ha-oyvim* 'the forts surrounded by enemies' is
acceptable, a change to אויבינו *oyvéynu* 'our enemies' (inherently definite) makes it
unacceptable.

48. A degree word may be added, e.g. כבד-גוף כלשהו *kvad-guf kólshehu* 'somewhat
heavy of build'.

49. Thus they are simultaneously free and fixed expressions.

50. As adjectives, בעל *báal* and בן *ben* occur *only* in such contexts. They are thus akin
to the derivational suffix -י *-i* '-ous'.

51. In addition, בעל *báal* is a noun meaning 'owner' and a noun in certain idioms, e.g.
בעל אמצעים *báal emtsa'im* 'man of means', but otherwise it is an adjective (i.e. it usually requires a head noun). חסר *Haser* 'lacking' is also a regular adjective, in two senses
which are really synonymous:

Haser la éreH musari	חסר לה ערך מוסרי
lacks to-her value moral	

hi Hasera éreH musari	היא חסרה ערך מוסרי
she lacks value moral	'She lacks moral value'

בן *ben* and its feminine בת *bat* require a numeral, ruling out *בית בן חדרים
אדירים* *báyit ben Hadarim adirim* 'house consisting of huge rooms'. By contrast,
בן/בת *ben / bat* denoting 'aged...' are nouns, witness המוסד מקבל בני ארבע
ha-mosad mekabel bney arba 'The institution accepts four-year-olds'. Like certain other
nouns, these are commonly in apposition: ילדים בני ארבע *yeladim bney arba* 'four-
year-old children' (see 36.12).

52. The similarity extends to the type of verb involved: *ילדים שרי שירי
עם* *yeladim sharey shirey am* 'children **singing** folksongs'. This is a 'generic' construction, i.e. the noun of component B is generally indefinite, thus contrast acceptable
מקבלי הטיפול הזה *mekabley ha-tipul ha-ze* 'recipients of this treatment' (agent genitive) with *החולים מקבלי הטיפול הזה* *ha-Holim mekabley ha-tipul ha-ze* 'patients
receiving this treatment' (verbal participle genitive). The only definite noun possible is
one really belonging to the whole phrase: העיתונים רודפי-הסנסציות *ha-itonim
rodfey-ha-sensátsyot* 'the sensation-seeking papers'.

Chapter 7

1. Pronoun prefixes and suffixes are just 'agreement formatives', even though the pronoun they agree with is often omitted. Unlike possessive suffixes, they cannot be contrastively stressed (and they are grammatically obligatory):

séfer~sifrénu	'book~*our* book'	ספר~ספרנו

as opposed to:

ra'a~*ra'ínu	'*he* saw (3rd pers.)~*we* saw (1st pers.)'	ראה~*ראינו

Further, a suffix such as נו- *-nu* '1st pl.' sometimes reflects not a subject pronoun אנחנו
anáHnu 'we' but rather a combination of nouns: אני והשוער ראינו *ani ve-ha-sho'er
ra'ínu* 'The doorman and I saw'. However, in a few formal idioms the subject pronoun
itself is suffixed, e.g. זכורני *zHuráni / zaHúrni* 'I recall', כמדומני *kimedumáni*
'methinks'.

2. Significantly, 3rd person inflection only marks gender and number. Person is zero-
marked.

3. All mention of זאת *zot* and אלה *éle* henceforth is meant to include their variants (זו *zu, zo* and אלו *élu* respectively). Formal הללו *halálu* is only a definite pronoun 'these ones' and a determiner 'these (people, things)'.

4. This 'dummy' *ze* is not related to the antecedent זה ש- *ze she-* above (by means of extraposition) as the infinitive creates זה קשה לדעת *ze kashe ladáat* (it is hard to know) but not *זה לדעת קשה* *ze ladáat kashe* (it to-know [is] hard). Neither 'dummy זה *ze*' nor 'antecedent *ze*' are ordinary nouns, for they do not allow one to refer back to them using אותו, הוא *hu, oto* etc.; nor, interestingly, do clauses themselves:

*ze lo matsdik et **atsmo** lehashkía sham	*זה לא מצדיק את **עצמו** להשקיע שם
	('It does not justify **itself** to invest there')

*ze she-hu mefursam **hu** lo mashpía alay	*זה שהוא מפורסם **הוא** לא משפיע עלי
it that he's famous **it** not influences me	('The fact he's famous doesn't influence me')

5. Formal usage does have an option of using זה *ze* in past or future tense *inversions*:

haya (ze) barur she...	...היה (זה) ברור ש
was (it) plain that...	'It was plain that...'

6. איזה *éze* 'which' supplies איזהשהו *ézeshehu* 'some or other', and כל *kol* 'any' supplies כלשהו *kólshehu* 'any' (9.2). Although מי *mi* 'who?' is strictly masculine, מישהו *míshehu* 'someone' has a feminine form מישהי *míshehi*, and מי ש... *mi she...* 'the one who...' can act as feminine with feminine agreement.

7. Thus אחד ש... *eHad she...* and זה ש... *ze she...* are both restricted to *people* ('someone who..., the person who...'), except when referring back to a particular noun ('one which..., the one which...').

Chapter 8

1. A few quantifiers are also ordinary nouns (with normal plurals), notably חצי *Hétsi* 'half', מחצית *maHatsit* 'half', רוב *rov* 'majority', מיעוט *mi'ut* 'minority', טיפה *tipa* 'drop', חלק *Hélek* 'part', מספר *mispar* 'number', המון *hamon* 'mass', מבול *mabul* 'flood', אחוז *aHuz* 'percentage'. Some are also adjectives: מעט *me'at* 'few', כפול *kaful* 'double'; degree words: מעט *me'at* 'a bit', קצת *ktsat* 'a bit', טיפה *tipa* 'a tiny bit', כפליים *kifláyim* 'double as', פי... *pi...* 'x times as', יותר *yoter* 'more', פחות *paHot* 'less', יותר מדי *yoter miday* 'too', כמה שיותר... *káma she-yoter...* 'as much... as possible', מספיק *maspik* 'enough', די *day* (with adjective) 'quite', (as a quantifier) 'enough', כמה *káma* 'how'.

2. Theoretically, 'amount' too amounts to 'portion' (i.e. of the indefinite): five sheets = five of the totality of sheets.

3. However, הרבה *harbe* as subject (i.e. with a clearly plural verb or suchlike) = 'many people' as well as 'a lot (of things)'.

Further exceptions are: (1) open-ended הכל *ha-kol* 'everything' (as against 'specific' הכל *ha-kol* 'all of it') is indefinite, like הרבה *harbe* 'a lot' or similar, i.e. it does not take את *et*; (2) הכל *ha-kol* is also 'everyone', particularly as subject, in formal usage; casual usage, however, prefers כולם *kulam* (also = 'all of them'), but not when qualified: 'everyone who came' is not *כולם שבאו* *kulam she-báu* but כל מי שבא *kol mi she-ba* (all who that came), and similarly 'like everyone else' is כמו כלאחד אחר *kmo kol eHad aHer* (like each one else) or similar.

4. 'Imprecise' numerals are indeed open-ended (see 8.5.3), e.g. מליונים יתנגדו *milyónim yitnagdu* 'millions will object'.

5. An exception is המעט (שנשאר) *ha-me'at* (*she-nish'ar*) 'the little (that remains)'.

6. However, מחצית *maHatsit* 'half' (formal) is usually construct to a definite noun and thus syntactically definite, e.g. מחצית היום *maHatsit ha-yom* 'half the day'. Occasionally one also finds החצי *ha-Hétsi*, e.g. ריססתי את החצי *risásti et ha-Hétsi* 'I sprayed half'. Moreover, all fractions can be definite when qualified: העשירית האחרונה *ha-asirit ha-aHarona* 'the last tenth', etc.

7. However, the fractions ending in ית- *-it*, i.e. מחצית *maHatsit* 'half' and those for '1/5, 1/6' onwards, require a definite noun, e.g. עשירית (השנייה, הליטר,...) *asirit (ha-shniya, ha-liter,...)* 'a tenth of (a second, a litre,...)'.

One cannot generally form a partitive at all with amount quantifiers that express a more complex notion than simple amount, e.g. יותר *yoter* 'more', מספיק *maspik* 'enough' (as against שש *shesh* 'six', הרבה *harbe* 'much'): מספיק מהם* **maspik mehem* ('enough of them'), עוד מהלחם* **od me-ha-leHem* ('more of the bread'). A rather different use is היה לי מספיק מהם *haya li maspik mehem* 'I've had enough of them'.

8. Casual usage has irregular singular שני שליש *shney shlish* '2/3' (formal: שני שלישים *shney shlishim*); and שלושת רבעי *shlóshet rivey* '3/4' using the construct form even when the fraction is used in isolation (formal: שלושה רבעים *shlosha reva'im*).

9. Exceptions are the following. (1) Two constructions with רוב *rov* 'most' require the 'double genitive' (sec 6.1): רוב רובם של..., רובם המכריע של... *rov rubam shel..., rubam ha-maHria shel...* 'the vast majority of'; (2) יתר, שאר *yéter, she'ar* 'the rest' + noun are sometimes indefinite (formal): מחשבים ויתר מוצרים בני-קיימא *meHashvim ve-yéter mutsarim bney-kyama* 'computers and other durables'.

10. In formal usage the following can take the various construct ('possessive') suffixes instead: חצי *Hétsi* 'half' (e.g. חציכם *HetsyeHem* 'half of you'), חלק *Hélek* 'some', קצת *ktsat* 'a few', מקצת *miktsat* 'a few'. Moreover, מחצית *maHatsit* 'half' tends to require the construct: מחצית המועמדים *maHatsit ha-muamadim* 'half the candidates'. When it means 'a large part of' rather than precisely 'half', חצי *Hétsi* too uses the construct: חצי העיר נפגעה *Hatsi ha-ir nifge'a* 'half the city was affected', חצי זמנו *Hatsi zmano* 'half his time'.

11. Similarly, formal מקצת *miktsat* 'some'.

12. Curiously, when the following noun lacks ה- *ha-* 'the', מ- *mi-* is required for אחד *eHad* or אחת *aHat* :

eHad mi-Hadrey ha-shena	אחד מחדרי השינה
one of rooms-of the sleep	'one of the bedrooms'
eHad mi-doday	אחד מדודי
one of uncles-my	'one of my uncles'

13. When qualified, they require של *shel* 'of', e.g. מאות רבות של *me'ot rabot shel* 'many hundreds of', מספר גדול של *mispar gadol shel* 'a large number of'.

14. Numeral + fraction is treated as a single numeral: casually, שש וחצי שעות *shesh va-Hétsi sha'ot* 'six and a half hours'; formally, שש שעות וחצי *shesh sha'ot va-Hétsi* 'six hours and a half'.

15. עוד *od* 'more' is exceptional in following the 'question words' which it qualifies, e.g. מי עוד *mi od* 'who else?', איפה עוד *éfo od* 'where else?', כמה עוד חולצות *káma od Hultsot* or כמה חולצות עוד *káma Hultsot od* 'how many more shirts?' (Similarly איזה עוד *éze od* or עוד איזה *od éze* 'which other...?'). In this role, עוד *od* is akin to a quantifier qualifying another quantifier, as in עוד קצת *od ktsat* 'a little **more**' (8.13).

16. The construct is occasionally found, e.g. (witness the position of ה- *ha-* 'the'):

kilo ha-batsal	קילו הבצל
kilo the onions	'the kilo of onions'

However, plural units that are singular in shape, e.g. מטר *méter* 'metre', as in ששה מטר *shisha méter* 'six metres', are never construct.

17. The partitive + collective is not felt to be so 'cohesive' a construction, hence the impossibility of construct אחד *eHad* 'one of': *אחד (*אחד מ-) הכיתה *aHad (√eHad me-) ha-kita* 'one of the class' and even of *אחד ממנה *eHad mimena* 'one of it'. Equally impossible is the common 'definitization' of אחד *eHad* 'one' by contamination with the following definite noun: *...את אחד מהכיתה *...et eHad me-ha kita* ('DEF OM one of the class').

18. מעט *me'at* is not used in the masculine singular except as a quantifier preceding its noun: מעט סבלנות *me'at savlanut* 'a little patience'.

19. The following quantifiers can also act as nouns, with their own inherent gender: חלק *Hélek* 'part, some', הרוב *ha-rov* 'the majority', אחוז אחד *aHuz eHad* (etc.) 'one per cent (etc.)', e.g. חלק ישן *Hélek yashen* 'A portion is [i.e. are] asleep'.

20. Occasionally this is true of quantifier + של *shel* 'of', e.g.

miutan shel ha-reshatot **meshamshot**		מיעוטן של הרשתות משמשות
m.s.	f.pl.	f.pl.
atuda reduma		תעודה רדומה

'A **minority** of the networks **constitute** a dormant reserve'

21. חציים *Hetsyam* 'half-of-them', חלקם *Helkam* 'part-of-them', חלק מהם *Hélek mehem* 'part of-them' also count as ordinary nouns: חציים נרדם *Hetsyam **nirdam*** 'half of them **dozed off** (m.s.)'

Adjectives qualifying the *quantifier* agree with it as with an ordinary noun: הרוב **המכריע** מ... *ha-rov **ha-maHria** mi...* 'the **overwhelming** majority of...'.

22. In casual usage, masculine אחד *eHad* 'one' often supplants feminine אחת *aHat* 'one' in page, telephone, bus numbers, etc.

23. The construct of אחד *eHad* 'one' means 'one of...', not 'the one...'. For the latter one uses הגל האחד *ha-gal ha-eHad* (the wave the one, i.e. 'the one wave'), with אחד *eHad* agreeing in definiteness just like an adjective. The plural adjective אחדים/אחדות *aHadim / aHadot* means 'a few' or 'singles', not 'ones'.

An indication that a singular noun is in itself felt to have an implicit אחד *eHad* 'an, one' is the coordinated construction of the type שאלה או שתיים *sheela o shtáyim* 'a question or two'.

24. These are semi-compounds. On the one hand, like other semi-compounds, they have no construct form: עשרים ושניים (*ושני) שחקנים *esrim u-shnáyim* (*u-shney) *saHkanim* '22 players', עשרים ושלושה (*ושלושת) השחקנים *esrim u-shlosha* (*u-shlóshet) *ha-saHkanim* 'the 23 players'. Nor is ordinary coordination-reduction possible: *עשרים ושש או שבע **esrim ve-shesh o sheva* '26 or ⟨twenty-⟩seven'. On the other hand, asyndetic coordination is possible: עשרים ושש-שבע *esrim ve-shesh-shéva* '26-7 (players)'.

25. However, for numbering years one has מאה וששים שנה *mea ve-shishim shana* '160 years'.

26. אחד *eHad* 'one', coming after the noun, does not itself coordinate with שניים *shnáyim* 'two' - it is the noun that does so, but without או *o* 'or' dropping (and אחד *eHad* 'one' itself can be omitted):

Haki daka (aHat) o shtáyim	חכי דקה (אחת) או שתיים
wait minute (one) or two	'Wait a minute or two'

27. Purists prefer שני חדרים וחצי *shney Hadarim va-Hétsi* 'two rooms and a half'. Generally אחד *eHad* 'one' is not expressed, e.g. שעה וחצי *sha'a va-Hétsi* '⟨an⟩ hour and ⟨a⟩ half' and:

gàrti be-Héder va-Hétsi	'I lived in ⟨a⟩ room and ⟨a⟩ half'	גרתי בחדר וחצי

28. Unlike numerals, they do not yield ordinals ('for the *100's-th* time') or multiples ('*tens of times* more accurate'); they are in fact 'quasi-numerals'.

29. These numerals have no inherent gender.

30. Substandardly we sometimes find העשרים ושלישי *ha-esrim u-shlishi* (the twenty and third). Standard Hebrew is altogether averse to thus adding an adjectival suffix to a phrase.

31. Even an *implied* definite noun (as in 'I failed the 19th time but passed the 20th') is not sufficient.

32. 'Two minutes / moments' is שתי דקות / שני רגעים *shtey dakot / shney rega'im*. But 'twice' is פעמיים *paamáyim* or שתי פעמים *shtey peamim*.

33. However, these qualifiers precede בן *ben* 'aged' in the construction הוא כבן ארבעים *hu ke-ven arba'im* 'He's about [aged] 40.'

34. However, where preceding כל *kol* 'all, every', אותו *oto* 'the same' or any partitive quantifier. כמעט *kim'at* 'almost' must be kept ahead of any preposition: כמעט בכל תחום *kim'at be-Hol tHum* 'almost in every area'.

35. Thus הרבה *harbe* 'many', מעט *me'at* 'a few'. קצת *ktsat* 'a few', not being adjectival, are impossible here.

36. מעט *me'at* has a separate function as a *quantifier*, e.g. מעט גשם *me'at géshem* 'a little rain', מועט *muat* has another feminine form מועטת *muétet*.

37. *yoter harbe* יותר הרבה* 'more much' and *yoter me'at* יותר מעט* 'more few' are impossible.

38. Adjectives too require a 'head noun' to be explicit when it is a mass noun:
*ha-óHel kar, tavi **yoter Ham** beHayéHa!   *האוכל קר, תביא **יותר חם** בחייך!
('The food's cold, bring **warmer**, will you!')

39. Another adjectival trait is the ability to coordinate with adjectives, e.g.
be-irgunim **rabim** ve-shonim   באירגונים **רבים** ושונים
'In **many** [and] different organizations'

Chapter 9

1. See also type (d).

2. Substandard usage also employs זאתי *zóti*.

3. הלה *hala* is occasionally used as 'this (here, just mentioned)' of a person (singular). דנן *denan* denotes 'foregoing' thing(s) or person(s). Both are formal.

4. Although historically equivalent to כ + זה *ke* + *ze* 'like + this', they do not act as such: whereas modern כמו זה *kmo ze* 'like this' allows זה *ze* to agree with whatever it is referring to, e.g. מיטה כמו אלה *mita kmo éle* 'a bed like **these**', the determiner כזה *kaze* 'such' *must* agree with the noun it qualifies: מיטה כזאת *mita kazot* (both words f.s.) 'such a bed'. See also (f).

5. איזה *éze* also acts as a qualifier of numerals (see 8.13): e.g. איזה מאה פועלים *éze méa poalim* 'some 100 workers'.

6. The formal forms assume איזה *éze* to be a compound of אי + זה *e* + *ze*.

7. שהוא *shehu*, שהיא *shehi* etc. can be related historically to a relative clause: ש + הוא *she* + *hu* 'that it ⟨may be⟩'.

8. This has a further meaning: 'any...whatsoever', see (i). The 'split construction' כל...שהוא *kol...shehu* - see (i) - has only the latter meaning.

9. מין *min* and its synonym סוג *sug* are both nouns, meaning 'sort', and determiners. As determiners they both occur in plural expressions of the kind 'all sorts of, three sorts of' - see types (j,k).

10. כזה *kaze* can co-occur with both איזה *éze* and מין *min*.

11. כמו *kmo* is also an adverb: עזרא **כמו** התנער לפתע *ézra **kmo** hitna'er leféta* 'Ezra **as it were** shook himself suddenly'.

12. משום *mishum* has no connection with משום *mishum* 'because' or with any word denoting 'something'.

13. As nouns, גדר *gader* and בחינה *bHina* denote 'definition, limit' and 'aspect' respectively.

14. This is also a noun ('bone') and a pronoun ('myself, yourself' etc.).

15. This is also a masculine noun, e.g.: עיקרי הדת *ikrey ha-dat* 'the fundamentals of the religion'.

16. For איזה...שהוא *éze...shehu*, the best gloss is 'some... or other'. See also type (d).

17. The expression is syntactically idiomatic, in that כל *kol* 'all' would ordinarily require a *definite* plural noun - and of course agreement is not governed by כל מיני *kol miney* but by the next noun.

18. When the noun is singular, as in שני סוגי **כתיבה** *shney sugey **ktiva*** 'two kinds of **writing**', סוגי *sugey* 'kinds of' will be taken as the nucleus rather than as the determiner - and this determines agreement. Note that such a singular noun is generally a mass noun; for count nouns, one requires שני סוגי **פרות** *shney sugey **parot*** 'two sort of **cows**', not פרה...* * *...para* '...cow'.

19. Literary usage also employs מה *ma* for 'what...?'

20. Furthermore, יופי *yófi* etc. admit no qualification themselves:

yófi lo ragil shel...	'incredible beauty of...'	...יופי לא רגיל של*
kaze yófi shel...	'such beauty of...'	...כזה יופי של*

21. Contrast מיטב הגברים *meytav ha-gvarim* 'the best of the men' (= the best men) with מיטב האומה *meytav ha-uma* 'the best of the nation' (≠ 'the best nation'), hence:

meytav ha-uma	**aHuz** yir'a		מיטב האומה **אחוז** יראה
m.s.	f.s.	m.s.	'The best of the nation **is gripped** by fear'

22. מבחר *mivHar* can be a noun, e.g. מבחר גדול של *mivHar gadol shel* 'a large **choice** of'.

23. However, as can be seen from זה *ze* 'this, that' and some other determiners, the noun can sometimes be *indefinite* syntactically even though its referent and determiner suggest that it is definite semantically.

24. Though הללו *halálu* and ההוא *hahu* (and their inflections) feature the definite article -ה *ha-* (thus האיש ההוא *ha-ish ha-hu* 'that man' (the man the he), not איש ההוא* **ish ha-hu* (man the he)), it otherwise acts as an integral part of the determiner - thus not obeying the ב ← ה + ב *be + ha → ba* rule:

le-hahu (*la-hu)	'to that guy'	(להוא (*להוא
be-halálu (*ba-lálu)	'in these'	(בהללו (*בללו

25. משום *mishum* 'something of' can take a definite noun phrase as long as the first word does not begin with -ה *ha-* 'the'.

26. איזה *éze* can take a definite noun, using -מ *mi-*: איזה מהעטים *éze mi-ha-etim* 'which **of** the pens'. But such a partitive phrase, usually associated with quantifiers and pronouns, is possible only because איזה *éze* can behave like a free-standing pronoun, as in איזה רצית? *éze ratsit* '**Which** did you want?' (see 9.5).

27. The indefinite form is mostly confined to formal usage. This does not affect the range of meanings of זה *ze*.

28. דנן *denan* 'foregoing' is an exception. See also note 24.

29. This might seem to be because את *et* here is *directly followed* by an intrinsically definite determiner. However, paradoxically, את *et* occurs directly with such non-definites as מי *mi* 'who?', מישהו *míshehu* 'someone', אחד מה... *eHad me-ha...* 'one of the...' (see 5.3.3):

shaláHnu et míshehu	'We've sent someone'	שלחנו את מישהו

30. However, formal usage allows רישומי זה *rishumi ze* (drawing-my this). Unlike the common construction רישום זה *rishum ze* (drawing this) 'this drawing', the former accepts the 'definite object maker' את *et*:

kabel et rishumi ze	'Accept my drawing'	קבל את רישומי זה

Here זה *ze* seems very much like a regular adjective, except that one would then expect

הזה **ha-ze**; compare רישומי האחרון *rishumi* **ha-aHaron** 'my last drawing'.

31. This phrase is normal as the 'idiomatic construct' in the sense 'these kibbutz-members'. As a whole, this constraint on noun + possessive reflects the special definiteness of possessive pronouns *vis-à-vis* common or proper nouns.

32. Literary usage allows (...,הנער) זה ה *ze* **ha-**(*náar*,...) 'this (lad,...)'.

33. This reflects greater 'noun-ness': adjectives and quantifiers can occur by themselves, like nouns, whereas determiners, and even more peripheral items such as preposition phrases and relative clauses, rarely can.

34. Determiners do not ordinarily act as pronouns in their own right. Even without a noun, a determiner like איזה *éze* 'which?' is felt to be qualifying a particular noun, inferred from context. Thus where a quantifier accompanies a determiner, the former acts as 'nucleus' - a pronoun - whereas the latter is a mere qualifier: שניים כאלה *shnáyim ka'éle* 'two such', not שני כאלה* **shney ka'éle* 'two (CONSTRUCT) such', and השניים ההם *ha-shnáyim hahem* 'those two', not שני ההם* *shney hahem.

35. Furthermore, unlike determiners (see note 34), pronoun זה *ze* can act as *nucleus* of a phrase, hence:

shney	éle	שני אלה	ha-shnáyim ha-éle	השניים האלה
CONSTRUCT	NUCLEUS		NUCLEUS	
two	these	'these two'	the two the these	'these two'

36. Such clauses are less likely to be conflated than other comparative clauses, which rules out:

**al timraH riba be-oto sakin kmo*   אל תמרח ריבה באותו סכין כמו*
   (she-)Hem'a   (ש\חמאה)

         don't spread jam with [the] same knife like (CONJ) butter

Chapter 10

1. Predicative adjectives (and nouns) are sometimes apposed to a noun - generally with a comma or pause (details in ch. 36):

     ve-ha-yam meraHok, afluli kólshehu,   וחים מרחוק, אפלולי כלשהו,
     mezuham, nohem, nasog min ha-ir   מזוהם, נוהם, נסוג מן העיר
         'And the sea far away, somewhat darkish, polluted, rumbling, retreated
                                          from the city'

2. Notable exceptions are a few 'profession terms', e.g. חבר עורך-דין *Haver oreH-din* 'a lawyer friend', and some technical usages. Even quasi-adjectives such as those in examples (1,2) below do not occur attributively (examples (3,4)):

     (1) hu me'od **géver**   הוא מאד גבר
         he['s] very **man** [= masculine]

     (2) hi kol-kaH **idishemáme**   היא כל-כך אידישעמאמע
         she['s] so **Jewish-mother**

     (3) *dóda idishemáme   דודה אידישעמאמע*
         [an] aunt Jewish-mother

     (4) *martse ben-adam   מרצה בן-אדם*
         [a] lecturer nice-guy

We say 'quasi' because the degree word is unwontedly restricted in its positioning, thus contrast:

hu rashlan me'od	'He's very negligent'	הוא רשלן מאד
ADJ DEGREE		

*hu géver me'od	('He's very masculine	הוא גבר מאד*
QUASI-ADJ DEGREE	(*lit.* man'))	

3. For general agreement within the noun phrase, see chapter 12.

4. There are a few exceptions. A few foreign adjectives take no suffix but do take ‏-ה‏ *ha-*, as in:

aruHa párve	'a pareve (neither meat nor dairy) meal'	‏ארוחה פרווה‏
simla bórdo	'a maroon dress'	‏שמלה בורדו‏
ha-smalot ha-bórdo	'the maroon dresses'	‏השמלות הבורדו‏

Apposed adjective phrases, as in (1) below, and semi-compounds, as in (2), involve inflectional suffixes on each word but only a single ‏-ה‏ *ha-* 'the' prefix (see further, 36.13 and 10.8 respectively):

(1) ha-mitpáHat ha-yeruka-levana   ‏המטפחת הירוקה-לבנה‏
the kerchief the green-white   'the green-and-white kerchief'

(2) ha-shanot-tovot   ‏השנות-טובות‏
the years good   'the New Year ⟨cards⟩'

Casual ‏מותק של (ילד)‏ *mótek shel* (*yéled*) 'darling (boy)' etc. (10.2 above) do not inflect.

5. It is as if each adjective were a relative clause qualifying the preceding noun phrase; stacking is therefore impossible for predicative adjectives - they have no noun phrase to qualify:

*ha-mita ktana smuHa le-mitati   ‏*המיטה קטנה סמוכה למיטתי‏
the bed [is] small close to my-bed

6. Coordination would create a different meaning:

tnu'a avirit u-pnimit   ‏תנועה אווירית ופנימית‏
traffic aerial and internal   'air traffic and internal trafic'

7. Quite generally, words 're-used' by casual speech for its own ends are distinguished by penult stress, e.g. ‏רחל‏ *ráHel* 'Rachel' (first name), ‏גולות‏ *gúlot* 'marbles' (children's game). Some noun+noun combinations too are semi-compounds casually: for example, ‏בן-אדם‏ *ben-adam* 'person' (casually also ‏בנאדם‏ *benadam*) has the casual definite form ‏הבן-אדם‏ *ha-ben-adam* and plural ‏הבני-אדם‏ *ha-bney-adam* rather than ‏בן-האדם‏ *ben-ha-adam* etc (see 38.4 for details).

8. Denoting members of the National Religious movement.

9. The second example involves a comparative phrase.

10. These examples are acceptable once a relative conjunction is added, turning the adjective phrase into a full relative clause:

...**she**-nasuy le...   '...**who** ⟨is⟩ married to...'   ‏...שנשוי ל‏...

A notable exception are objects of ‏דומה‏ *dome* 'similar', ‏שונה‏ *shone* 'different', ‏זהה‏ *zehe* 'identical' - these being akin to comparatives (see note 9); for example:

hayta aliya shel mea aHuz, shi'ur   ‏היתה עליה של מאה אחוז, שיעור‏
kim'at zehe la-aliyat ha-madad la-tsarHan   ‏כמעט זהה לעלית המדד לצרכן‏
     'There was a rise of 100%, a rate almost identical to the rise of the Consumer Price Index'

11. Notable exceptions, especially in speech, are disjunct adverbials (ch.23), e.g.:

ze matsav **beétsem** dey tov   ‏זה מצב בעצם די טוב‏
it situation **actually** quite good   'It's actually quite a good situation'

sham matsáti nitúaH zol, **ledaati**,   ‏שם מצאתי ניתוח זול, לדעתי,‏
  mipiv shel...   ‏מפיו של‏...
there I-found analysis cheap, **to-my-mind**,
  given by...
     'There I found a cheap analysis, to my mind, given by...'

12. 'Specificational' past participles and adjectives (15.8), when attributive to a noun, prefer the tighter construct rather than the looser object:

atsru shney nearim	neuley magafáyim	עצרו שני נערים }נעולי מגפיים/
N	CONSTRUCT PHR	*נעולים מגפיים{
	*neulim magafáyim	
	OBJ	

shney bakbukim mele'ey spirt	שני בקבוקים **מלאי ספירט**
N CONSTRUCT PHR	'two bottles **full of spirit**'

13. The adjective can, as in (2), be accompanied by a degree word; this, after all, belongs to the adjective phrase. But an added שלך *shelHa* 'your', which belongs to the noun phrase as a whole, would be awkward (similarly an added numeral אחד *eHad* 'one'), except with ordinals and superlatives:

*al tilbash et ha-Hadasha **shelHa**	*אל תלבש את החדשה **שלך**
*don't wear OM the new **your**	('Don't wear your new ⟨one⟩')

ze ha-shlishi shela!	זה השלישי שלה!
this the third her	'This is her third!'

14. Nor can they coordinate with reference to a single person: example (1) with its *explicit* noun is normal, but (2) is not (except in a case of bigamy):

(1) hi nesu'a le-**adam** kashish ve-ashir	היא נשואה ל**אדם** קשיש ועשיר
she married to **man** elderly and wealthy	'She's married to an elderly and wealthy **man**'

(2) hi nesu'a le-kashish ve-ashir	היא נשואה לקשיש ועשיר
she married to elderly and wealthy	'She's married to an elderly man and a wealthy man'

Chapter 11

1. This is quite apart from their use as adverbs (ch.21) or objects (ch.15):

Adverb: limádeti lemáta	לימדתי למטה
	'I taught downstairs'

Object: limádeti al iyov	לימדתי על איוב
	'I taught about Job'

2. את *et* is not an independent meaningful preposition and is in many further respects a 'weak' preposition.

3. This despite the fact that agent nouns are usually identical in form with the present tense of the verb.

4. Unlike ordinary instances of preposition phrases modifying a noun, examples like (1) below cannot be paraphrased by means of a *predicative* preposition phrase as in (2):

(1) maaminim be-datot	מאמינים בדתות
	'believers in religions'

(2) *ha-maaminim she-hem be-datot	*המאמינים שהם בדתות
	('the believers that are in religions')

5. In all but example (4), של *shel* can be a predicate, as in:

ha-mitriya hi shelánu	'The umbrella's ours'	המטריה היא שלנו

6. Thus the following is ambiguous:

malka kmo elízabet	'a queen like Elizabeth'	מלכה כמו אליזבט
(= ...כגון *kegon...* 'such as...' or שהיא כמו... *she-hi kmo...* 'who is like...')		

An entirely different construction is the 'partitive' (see 8.5), for example:

Hélek me-ha-tsiporim   'some of the birds'   חלק מהציפורים

כזה *kaze* 'such' is a determiner (see ch.9), although its form might suggest that in (1) it is an adverbial meaning 'like that'. As it must agree with its nucleus noun (2), it is quite distinct from כמו זה *kmo ze* 'like that', illustrated in (3):

(1) adam **kaze**	'such ⟨a⟩ guy'	אדם **כזה**
(2) mitot **ka'éle**	'such beds'	מיטות **כאלה**
f.pl. pl.		
(3) mitot kmo **zot**	'beds like **this**'	מיטות כמו **זאת**
f.pl. f.s.		

7. Where the adverbial involves a pronoun, -ש *she-* is common and even obligatory:

af ki ha-taviyot **she-alav** dey Hazakot...   ...אף כי התוויות **שעליו** די חזקות

'Although the labels **which ⟨are⟩ on it** are quite strong...'

-ש *she-* is also common with בין *beyn* 'between':

ha-siHsuH she-beynéynu leveynam   הסכסוך שבינינו לבינם

'the dispute between us and them'

Chapter 12

1. There are a number of adjectives that express quantity and behave like other adjectives (see 8.15) for gender-number-definiteness agreement, e.g. הכוהנים הרבים *ha-kohanim ha-rabim* 'the many priests', התיקיה האחת *ha-tikiya ha-aHat* 'the one filing-cabinet'.

2. שתיים *shtáyim* 'two' is particularly likely to be used as both masculine and feminine.

3. Ordinals for 11, 12,... have the further peculiarity of only occurring with 'definite' nouns.

Other exceptional adjectives include: uninflectible foreign colour terms such as בורדו *bórdo* 'wine', בז' *bezh* 'beige' (השמלה הבורדו *ha-simla ha-bórdo* 'the wine dress'), although most foreignisms do inflect; פרווה *párve* 'neither meaty nor dairy', which not only does not inflect but also tends not to agree in definiteness (הסיר(ים) פרווה *ha-sir (im) párve* 'the "parve" pan(s)', or even (in the singular) סיר הפרווה *sir ha-párve* 'the "parve" pan'; and the uninflectible idiom שחור-לבן *shaHor-lavan* 'black and white' in טלביזיה שחור-לבן *televízya shaHor-lavan* 'black and white television' (the TV, set itself may be red).

4. This use of just one -ה *ha-* 'the' is reminiscent of construct phrases; see 6.2.

5. Formal usage occasionally has הישראליות-המצריות... *ha-yisreeliyot-**ha**-mitsriyot* etc.

Chapter 13

1. In the negative, the past tense is generally used, as the event in itself is not conceived as durative.

2. Ambiguity may arise at times, thus this example could mean 'How long do you (habitually) teach?', 'How long are you teaching for?'.

3. These, and several other 'aspectual', 'modal' and 'adverbial' verbs such as המשיך *himshiH* 'continue', צריך *tsariH* 'must' and מיהר *miher* 'be quick to', are in many respects not verbs governing an object clause but rather take a *subject* clause; see 31.3 for details.

4. An occasional casual use is as a rhetorical question of encouragement, e.g. ‏זָזנו‏? *záznu* ? 'Shall we get moving?'

5. By contrast, the future form (13.4) cannot express 'future-in-the-past' or 'future continuous' time, i.e. 'I will have finished' and '(When you come) we will be eating'. In this and in certain other ways, the past and future tense are asymmetric.

6. Unlike other aspectual markers, e.g. ‏נעשה‏ *naasa* 'become', ‏נהג‏ *nahag* 'be accustomed', ‏היה‏ *haya* is best considered a special 'auxiliary' verb rather than a syntactically regular verb; see 31.3.

7. Purists require ‏גרה‏ *gará* in the present and ‏גרה‏ *gára* in the past.

8. In the negative, the order ‏לא יכול היה‏ *lo yaHol haya* is particularly common; see further 13.13.

9. However, the compound past requires actions that are repeatable, i.e. true habituals, thus ruling out statives: ‏הייתי מאמין‏ *hayíti maamin ('I used to believe') etc.

10. Even where the main clause has present or future tense, the adverbial clause will have past tense wherever it refers to past time, as in:

ha-shana **timasheH** Hasifat ha-Homa, ‏השנה **תימשך** חשיפת החומה,‏
   leaHar she-ad ko **neHsefu** ‏לאחר שעד כה **נחשפו**‏
   shishim méter miména ‏ששים מטר ממנה‏
       'This year the uncovering of the wall **will proceed**, after sixty metres of it **have** so far **been uncovered**'

11. However, ‏עד‏ *ad* is occasionally treated as if it were a verb of 'waiting' with its own 'contemplator' distinct from the speaker. The tense is then as in object clauses (13.11):

rak ha-télefon notar ba-dira ha-reka, ‏רק הטלפון נותר בדירה הריקה,‏
   ad she-yavóu ha-teHna'im lehasir gam oto ‏עד **שיבואו** הטכנאים‏
   FUT ‏להסיר גם אותו‏
       'Only the telephone remained in the empty flat, until the technicians **could come** to remove it too'

12. ‏-כש‏ *kshe-* and ‏כאשר‏ *kaasher* can also denote 'after', as in this example, strictly speaking. In addition, the casual ‏איך ש‏- *eH she-* 'just when' occurs just in sense (1). 'As long as' is expressed by ‏כל עוד‏ *kol od* or ‏-כל זמן ש‏ *kol zman she-*, using the 'tense and time rule'.

13. An alternative in formal usage, denoting a momentary event while another event is happening, employs a *present* tense clause introduced by ‏עוד‏ *od* 'still' plus a clause in 'natural' tense introduced by coordinative ‏והנה‏ *ve-hine*:

odéni mashve et yaldey ha-dor ha-yashan ‏**עודני משווה** את ילדי הדור הישן‏
   le-sára ha-ktana, ve-hine tsiltsel ‏לשרה הקטנה, והנה צילצל‏
   ha-paamon... ‏הפעמון...‏
       '**While I was comparing** the children of old times to little Sara, the bell rang...'

14. Naturally, any clause withhin the purpose clause will gear its tense to this vantage point:

kdey she-yir'u kshe-yavóu ‏כדי שיראו כשיבואו‏
   FUT   FUT
       'in order that they might see when they came'

‏שמא‏ *shéma* 'in case' often has a meaning akin to 'so that...not' and often implies a 'fear' on someone's part, hence the future tense:

heHlátnu lo leHakot, shéma **yegalu** ‏החלטנו לא לחכות, שמא **יגלו**‏
   et ha-minhara ‏את המנהרה‏
       'We decided not to wait, in case **they discovered** the tunnel'

15. Future tense tends to be favoured where the main clause is negative:

אף פעם לא נתתי לה סוכריה

af páam lo natáti la sukariya

    bli she-hem yavHínu   בלי שהם יבחינו

    FUT

                'I've never given her a sweet without them seeing'

16. With a *future* tense in the main clause, לפני *lifney* 'before' sometimes takes future tense:

bétaH she-hu yikaH oto lifney she-egmor   בטח שהוא יקח אותו לפני שאגמור

              FUT   'Sure he'll take it before I finish'

But statives (except היה *haya* 'be') require the present tense:

hu kibel rishyon lifney she-hu   הוא קיבל רשיון לפני שהוא

    yodéa linhog!   יודע לנהוג!

    PRES

               'He's received a licence before he **knows** how to drive!'

17. Furthermore, any adverbial or other clause *within* a subordinate clause will follow that same contemplator's vantage point, thus:

לא הסכמת שאלך לביקור אלא-אם-כן יתלוו אלי

lo hiskamt she-**eleH** levikur éla-im-ken **yitlavu** elay

     FUT | FUT

                         ADVERBIAL CLAUSE

|_____|

        OBJ CLAUSE

            'You didn't agree that **I should go** on a visit unless they **accompanied** me'

18. An apparent exception are the 'present tense' clauses governed by verbs of perception as in:

ra'íti ota **tsoHéket**   'I saw her **laughing**'   ראיתי אותה צוחקת

        PRES

These are in fact non-finite clauses with a *fixed 'participle verb'* and no subject, akin to infinitival clauses (See 30.3):

ilátsti ota litsHok   'I forced her to laugh'   אילצתי אותה לצחוק

19. Present tense is required in relative clauses (formal usage) expressing 'who/which has (in it, under it, etc.)', introduced by a relative conjunction plus anaphoric adverbial, with the verb 'to be' implied:

Hilku le-Hol eHad tarmil,   חילקו לכל אחד תרמיל

    she-bo   שבו

           kol ha-darush la-déreH   כל הדרוש לדרך

    u-VO   ובו

    CONJ ADV

          'They gave everyone a rucksack, in which ⟨was⟩ everything needed for the journey'

20. However, future tense does express the quasi-negative (see 13.10).

21. The verb היה *haya* 'be' lacks a compound past form and instead uses its simple past form, with possible ambiguity:

im hayit kan, hayit shikora   אם היית כאן, היית שיכורה

    PAST   PAST   'If you were here, you'd be drunk' (*Hypothetical*),

          or

             'If you were here, you were drunk' (*Real*)

22. An exception is יכול *yaHol* 'can', possible formally in the simple past.

23. כאילו *ke'ilu* has a separate rhetorical sense, using the 'tense and time rule':

ke'ilu **iHpat li** ma hu shar!   כאילו איכפת לי מה הוא שר!

    PRES   'As if **I cared** what he sings!'

ke'ilu hevánti!   כאילו הבנתי!

PAST   'As if I understood!'

24. With צריך *tsariH*, the future tense tends to be יצטרך *yitstareH* etc. (except when subject-less).

25. צריך *tsariH*, חייב *Hayav* and מוכרח *muHraH* all denote factive necessity ('is having to') and non-factive necessity (subjective 'ought to' and objective 'has to'); also in the past, factive 'had to' and non-factive 'should have' - but not past-from-the-present epistemic 'must have'.

26. So too, (אי-)אפשר היה (*i-)efshar haya* 'it was (im)possible', אמור היה *amur haya* 'was meant to', אסור היה *asur haya* 'one shouldn't have/couldn't't'. With 'mental' adjectives in general (e.g. ברור *barur* 'obvious', חשוב *Hashuv* 'important') inversion of conditional or past tense היה *haya* is quite common, but not with other adjectives or with verbs.

Chapter 14

1. An argument against 'deriving' passives from actives is their use in the 3rd person impersonal, illustrated below. The impersonal has an unsaid subject, which has no *overt* manifestation in any construction in Hebrew: nothing can even refer back to it. As there is no construction with an impersonal object, there is no active from which this passive example can be derived:

nitpasim kol páam bidey shotrim   נתפסים כל פעם בידי שוטרים

IMPERSONAL   '⟨One⟩ **is caught** each time by police'

2. 'Middle' verbs, e.g. התבשל *hitbashel* 'cooked', התבייש *hitbayesh* 'was ashamed', נפתח *niftaH* 'opened (by itself)', imply that there is no agent at all (מעצמו *me-atsmo* 'by itself'), or else a non-human one, amounting to the same. They are fairly distinctive by their *binyan* ('pattern').

3. Hebrew evidently does not seek to maintain an initial subject at any cost, if it means disturbing the basic grammatical relations. Thus it is almost devoid of subject-subject and object-subject raising or '*there*-insertion'. However, dummy זה *ze* 'it' is productive, in casual speech especially - probably because this does not upset grammatical relations.

4. Several *nif'al* verbs are not even derivable from another verb, e.g. נשבע *nishba* 'swore'.

5. *Nitpa'el* is a less common and very formal past tense alternative to *hitpa'el* for passive and occasionally for non-passive use:

aHiv **nitmana** le-shalit yehuda   אחיו נתמנה לשליט יהודה

'His brother **was appointed** as ruler of Judea'

6. Exceptions are: (1) random gaps, e.g. אסוף* *asuf* ('gathered'), בחור* *baHur* ('elected'), לווי* *lavuy* ('borrowed'); (2) *pa'ul* denoting '*currently* being done', e.g. תפוס (בידי...) *tafus (bidey...)* 'occupied (by...)', נהוג (בידי...) *nahug (bidey...)* 'driven (by...)', ידוע (ל...) *yadúa (le...)* 'known (to...)', זכור (ל...) *zaHur (le...)* 'remembered (by...)' (some are derived from *statal* verbs); (3) non-passive meanings of *pa'ul*, e.g. שעון על *sha'un al* 'leaning on' - see 41.3.

7. The case preposition cannot 'dangle' without a following noun, though certain adverbial prepositions can 'dangle' casually, e.g. ?אם או בלי *im o bli?* 'with or without?'.

8. However, certain verbs with a *clause* instead of a noun as direct object do allow their indirect object to be promoted to subject of passive:

ani neesárti   אני נאסרתי
ani nidráshti lehitgaléaH   אני נדרשתי להתגלח

I-was-forbidden
I-was-required   to-shave

9. עלל-ידי... ....*al-yedey* 'deliberately influenced by'.

10. עלל-ידי... ....*al-yedey* 'surprised by (thieves etc.)'.

11. Another instance is the stative as against the dynamic use of כלל *kalal* 'include' in (1) and (2) respectively:

(1)   אסיה כוללת את ישראל ⇐ ישראל נכללת באסיה

        ásya kolélet et yisra'el ⇒ *yisra'el niHlélet be-ásya*

        STATIVE

        Asia includes OM Israel ⇒ Israel is-included in Asia

(2)   הם כוללים את ישראל ⇐ ישראל נכללת על-ידיהם

        hem kolelim et yisra'el⇒ *yisra'el niHlélet al-yedeyhem*

        they are-including OM Israel ⇒ Israel is-being-included by-them

12. This unique combination of active object and passive complement may tie in with the difficulty of having clause-like 'subject first' structure in what is after all a noun phrase - instead of coming forward to subject position, the active object stays as it is.

13. That the subordinate clauses are not subjects is shown by the questionableness of dummy - ש זה סוכם *ze sukam she...* 'it was decided that...' etc. The subject cannot even be easily expressed by an על-ידי *al-yedey* 'by' phrase.

Chapter 15

1. The object noun is often introduced by a preposition (a 'case marker'). Semantically speaking, this belongs to the verb; but in terms of syntactic movement and prosody it belongs with the object noun phrase, so the whole construction will sometimes be referred to as the 'object'.

2. Verbal and adjectival *nouns* ('action/state nouns') themselves govern something amounting (semantically) to an object:

    ha-ashma ba-avera   'the guilt for the offence'   האשמה בעבירה

    ha-ratson lehavin   'the wish to understand'   הרצון להבין

But these objects are best regarded, in 'surface terms', as modifiers of the noun and as apposed clauses respectively; see chapter 30.

3. Besides these three 'coding properties', there are two 'behaviour properties' by which casual *and* formal Hebrew treat such nouns as object: indefinite object deletion and use of - ה *ha-* as relative marker (this requiring a *subject* as relative noun):

    li yesh taanot ve-gam laH yesh   לי יש טענות וגם לך יש

                                'I have complaints and you too have'

    *ha-anashim ha-yesh (✓she-yesh) kan   האנשים היש (✓שיש) כאן

                                  'the people that there are here'

Thus formal Hebrew treats these nouns as object, but not to the extent of 'coding' them unambiguously as such. (See also 'gerunds', in section 30.5, which require a subject noun.)

4. Many adverbials which could be 'set off' are not, for complex reasons.

5. Casually, איפה, מתי *éfo, matay* can be *object* pronouns, i.e. 'which place, time' as against '*at* which place, time':

    le-éfo (*even* le'an) hitkavant?   {לאיפה/לאן} התכוונת?

                                  'Where were you referring to?'

    al matay dibart?   על מתי דיברת?

                                    'When were you talking about?'

6. Definite objects cannot be thus deleted:

hivtáHti laasot et ha-avoda,   הבטחתי לעשות את העבודה,
  ve-asíti **ota**   ועשיתי **אותה**

'I promised to do the job, and I did **it**'

Even 'obligatory adverbials' (see below) can be deleted:

hivtáHti she-nitgorer be-pénthaus,   הבטחתי שנתגורר בפנטהאוס,
  ve-**hitgorárnu**   ו**התגוררנו**

'I promised that we'd live in a penthouse, and we **lived** ⟨in one⟩'

7. Motion verbs, being in close cohesion with motion adverbials (15.3.5.), can quite generally be considered transitive (weakly):

báti (le-paris)   'I came (to Paris)'   באתי (לפריס)

8. For exceptions, see 15.6.7. and 15.8.

9. את *et* is also omitted before הכל *ha-kol* 'everything' when used in its broadest sense, as in (1), and optionally before reflexive pronouns in formal usage, as in (2):

	ha-kol		
(1) hu mevin	et ha-kol	הכל	הוא מבין
		את הכל	

	the all		everything '(general)
he understands	OM the all	'He understands	the lot' (specific)

(2) hu hit'a atsmo   'He deceived himself'   הוא הטעה עצמו

10. A few examples must suffice:

kib**lam** be-simHa   קיבל**ם** בשמחה
'He received **them** joyfully'

ha-séfer melamd**éni** al...   הספר מלמד**ני** על...
'The book teaches **me** about...'

mi yed'**éna**   מי ידע**נה**?
'Who would know **it**?'

11. The *hitpa'el* pattern rarely, and the *nif'al* never, take את *et*. As transitive verbs, these are often 'non-ergative', i.e. the action is semantically passive - which may have affected their general behaviour.

liva et	ליווה את	*but*	hitlava el	התלווה אל
'accompany'			'accompany'	
ahav et	אהב את		hitahev be	התאהב ב-
'love'			'fall in love with'	
pagash et	פגש את		nifgash im	נפגש עם
'meet' (by chance)			'have a meeting with'	
zaHar et	זכר את		nizkar be	נזכר ב-
'remember'			'recall'	

12. The preposition governed by each verb is listed in Even-Shoshan's Hebrew-Hebrew dictionary but not in most Hebrew-English-Hebrew dictionaries.

13. By contrast, relativization, dislocation (ייחוד), topicalization and other processes act identically on all the various indirect objects.

14. -ל *le-* of ...יש ל *yesh le...* 'have' displays the same word order although it is not an 'experiencer' (see ch. 16). The same is true casually of ברור לי *barur li* 'it's clear to me', כדאי לי *keday li* 'it's worth my while' and several others.

15. And with some miscellaneous verbs: הפסיק *hifsik* 'stop', היטיב *hetiv* 'be good to', החמיר *heHmir* 'be severe on' etc.

16. And with some miscellaneous verbs, e.g. ביקש *bikesh* 'ask', דרש *darash* 'require (of someone)'.

17. This is distinct from כמו *kmo*, which means 'like' and very occasionally adopts the form -כ *ke-* in formal usage.

-כ *ke-* phrases are on the borderline of adverbials. See 21.9 ('as' adjuncts), especially the כעל ...הכריז על *hiHriz al...ke-al* construction.

18. In word order, in undergoing indefinite object deletion (see 15.4), and in sometimes taking a case preposition.

19. These complements can be considered reduced object clauses or whole predicates, rather like the participial predicates following verbs of perception in 30.3:

tishma otam **mezamzemim**	'Hear them **humming**'	תשמע אותם מזמזמים

20. Where a verb governs -ב *be-*, the addition of a -ל *le-* of movement compels one to change -ב *be-* to את *et*:

| baat ba-kadur | 'kick the ball' | בעט בכדור |
| baat et ha-kadur le... | 'kick the ball to...' | ...בעט את הכדור ל |

Many two-object verbs are causatives based *approximately* on verbs taking את *et*, e.g. הראה ~ ראה *ra'a ~ her'a* 'see ~ show (cause x to see y)'. The first object ('x') usually has -ל *le-*.

21. Exceptions: -ל *le-* objects precede את *et* objects when denoting 'recipient' or 'person being caused to...', e.g. הסגיר, הראה *hisgir, her'a*, 'show, hand over' above - perhaps because these two indirect object types are the most typically 'human' and thus on a par with the direct object. Similarly, for שאל, לימד *sha'al, limed* 'ask, teach', the 'human' את *et* object precedes the 'non-human' (all else being equal):

| limádeti banot shira | 'I taught girls poetry' | לימדתי בנות שירה |

22. Verbs taking ...ל ...את *et... le...*, illustrated above, where -ל *le-* does not denote 'recipient', use אלי, אליך *elay, eléHa* etc. as pronouns, not לי, לך *li, leHa* etc.: הרגילו *elay, eléHa* אותו אליו *hirgílu oto elav*, not לו ...*אותו לו/אותו *...lo oto / *oto lo* 'they got him used to it' - although such verbs otherwise do *not* accept אל *el*. This serves to keep this type of -ל *le-* object after the את *et* object.

23. (-ב) לבוש *lavush (be)* 'dressed in', (ב-) ספוג *safug (be)* 'soaked in' and a few others are (unlike מוקף *mukaf* 'ringed' in (2)) *active* adjectives, corresponding to לובש *lovesh* 'wearing', סופג *sofeg* 'soaking up'. Thus their subject is not a 'quasi-subject', though their object is an irregular object.

Chapter 16

1. היה *haya* supplies the past, future, infinitive and imperative forms for 'be'. הוא *hu* and זה *ze*, unlike היה *haya*, will not undergo 'focusing processes' such as negation and emphasis:

dan lo	haya *hu	kan		דן לא	היה *הוא	כאן

Dan not	was *is	here		'Dan	was *is	not here'

dan ken	haya *hu	rav		דן כן	היה *הוא	רב

Dan EMPH WORD	was *is	rabbi		'Dan	*was *is*	a rabbi'

In this, they resemble agreement affixes such as past tense endings; but unlike affixes, they are not bound to some other word.

2. However, material can intervene between subject and copula or between copula and predicate:

ha-gil, agav, hu markiv Hashuv ba-matsav   הגיל, אגב, הוא מרכיב חשוב במצב
'The age, incidentally, is a major element in the situation'

ha-gil hu beheHlet Hashuv   הגיל הוא בהחלט חשוב
'The age is certainly important'

3. Furthermore, אין *en* in very formal usage can immediately *precede* the subject; see 29.6.

4. The exception is that הנ- *hin-*, and negative אין *en*, do not tolerate inversion of subject and predicate:

ma hi   ha-alternatíva?   מה היא האלטרנטיבה?
    *hina   *הינה

'What is the alternative?'

5. Unlike 'leftward copying' (see 37.5), the copula construction has no 'topicalizing' effect. Moreover, it can occur within any other 'copying' or 'movement' context, such as questions, and can co-occur with 'leftward copying' itself.

6. זהו *zéhu* and זוהי *zóhi* are written as one word, unlike זאת היא *zot hi* and אלה הם *éle hem*. This reflects the fact that this particular use of the copula is different from its normal function of helping towards the 'balance' of clauses whose predicate is as definite or more definite than their subject. See further, 16.3.9.

7. The predicate already identifiable in advance is akin to the 'specificational' construction (16.3.7), in which the copula is obligatory - suggesting a further scale of 'copula likelihood'.

8. Here even the negator לא *lo* can count as a sufficient 'link word':

orit lo shminístit tipusit   אורית לא שמיניסטית טיפוסית
Orit not eighth-grader typical   'Orit isn't a typical eighth-grader'

9. With a *pronoun* subject, by contrast (see 16.3.2), a definite predicate does not of itself make a copula necessary. Pronouns are more 'definite' than proper nouns.

10. זה *ze* can arguably be regarded as a special 'clefting pronoun' rather than a copula, as in clefts such as זה אני (ש)צעקתי *ze ani (she-)tsaákti* 'It's me (that) shouted' (see 37.3). The reason is that זה *ze* co-occurs with היה *haya* 'be':

mi she-haya aHara'i po **ze haya** eHad   מי שהיה אחראי פה **זה היה** אחד
    me-ha-moshav sheli   מהמושב שלי
who that was in-charge here **it was**   'The person who was in charge here was
    someone from the moshav my   someone from my moshav'

11. Even where the predicate is an adjective rather than a noun (see 16.5), the copula זה *ze* is obligatory. It is also optional, casually, where the predicate is a *verb* (this is not really a copula - see 31.5):

linsóa káHa **ze** lo bari   לנסוע ככה **זה** לא בריא
'To travel in such a way **is** not healthy'

laléHet lisHot (**ze**) lo yazik   ללכת לשחות (**זה**) לא יזיק
'To go swimming won't hurt'

12. Subordinate clauses are so indefinite that one cannot refer back to them by a definite or reflexive pronoun; see 7.5.

13. זה *ze* (uninflected) sometimes occurs casually even with adjectival or verbal predicates, when the subject is generic or expresses 'the notion of...':

hoda'a shel yom **ze** meHubad me'od   הודעה של יום **זה** מכובד מאד
'A day's notice **is** very respectable'

14. Similarly, pronoun + adjective constructions never allow a copula (except -הנ *hin-*, negative אין *en* and their inflections, which are even used in front of verbs - see 16.2):

| *ata hu akshan | *אתה הוא עקשן | *zéhu maksim | *זהו מקסים |
| you are stubborn | | this is gorgeous | |

15. The same factor is at work in noun + noun clauses; recall 16.3.5.

16. Instead, Hebrew either uses the special verb of 'existence' and 'having', יש *yesh* (and its opposite, uninflected אין *en*), as described in 16.9-10; or, in formal usage, it can invert the subject+adverbial order - while still not using a copula (see the last two examples):

yesh kélev ba-salon   יש כלב בסלון
there-is dog in-the lounge   'There's a dog in the lounge'

la-séfer yesh atifa na'a   לספר יש עטיפה נאה
to-the book there-is cover nice   'The book has a nice cover'

ba-salon kélev aHzari   בסלון כלב אכזרי
in-the lounge dog fierce   'There's a fierce dog in the lounge'

la-séfer atifa na'a   לספר עטיפה נאה
to-the book cover nice   'The book has a nice cover'

17. Where an idea is being defined, it is treated as a 'proper noun'.

18. מיהו, מהו *míhu, máhu*, etc. can be written as one word.

19. In this type of example, הוא *hu* and its inflections are rather formal, casual usage favouring (uninflected) זה *ze*.

20. This contrasts with the corresponding 'be' clause:

ha-nemalim ha-éle hen ba-árets   הנמלים האלה הן בארץ
the ants the these are in Israel   'These ants are in Israel'

The existential implies that only some such ants are found in Israel, i.e. it is a partitive.

21. This is the main construction. There are other existential terms, e.g. the adjective קיים *kayam* 'existing'.

22. However, in a less demonstrative way even formal usage treats it as object, by allowing 'indefinite object or predicate deletion' to apply to it. Just as object and predicate are omitted in examples (1,2), so is the existential noun in example (3) (subjects cannot be):

(1) im ata lokéaH sal, gam ani **lokéaH**   אם אתה לוקח סל, גם אני **לוקח**
                                                       'If you're taking a basket,
                                                        I'm also **taking**'

(2) im at tiyi kena, gam ani **eye**   אם את תהיי כנה, גם אני **אהיה**
                                                       'If you'll be honest, I'll also **be**'

(3) kaH et, im yesh   קח עט, אם יש
                                                       'Take a pen, if there is ⟨one⟩'

23. Circumstantial and relative clauses provide for special existential clauses of this type (see 13.8.3 and ch. 13, n.19): place adverbial+noun, with no verb even where past or future היה *haya* 'be' might have been expected:

ha-merkaz kalal migdal ben esrim komot   המרכז כלל מגדל בן עשרים קומות
u-vo dirot ve-pénthauzim   ובו דירות ופנטהאוזים
‾‾‾‾‾‾‾‾‾‾‾‾‾‾‾‾‾‾‾‾‾‾
REL CLAUSE

'The centre included a 20 storey tower in which were
(*lit.* and in-it) flats and penthouses'

24. Except for contrast, as in:

etsa yesh li עצה יש לי

idea exists to-me 'I do have an idea'

The 'possessor' cannot be omitted to save repetition; this distinguishes adverbials from possessor phrases:

le-arad yesh sherut aval rakévet en לעָרַד יש שירות אבל רכבת אין

to Arad exists cab but train not-exists 'There's a cab **to Arad** but there isn't a train'

***le-dov** yesh shvédi aval patish en *לדוב יש שבדי אבל פטיש אין

to Dov exists spanner but ('**Dov has** a spanner but has
hammer not-exists no hammer')

25. What was said in note 3 applies here too.

26. Even agreement with the noun does not make the latter the 'subject' - copulas and subject pronouns agree with their *predicate* (see 18.2.3), and the 'have' verb may simply be agreeing with the 'object' as the only noun available.

Chapter 17

1. Repetition of a qualified noun can also be avoided, leaving a residual adjective: גדול *gadol* 'a big one'; see 10.10.

2. One can alternatively use an indefinite pronoun (7.8), e.g אחד *eHad*, כאלה *ka'éle*. No 'indefinite ellipsis' is possible for *subject* nouns.

3. Many adjectives, referring only to persons, not situations, cannot function in this way: אני עייף *ani ayef* 'I'm tired', not *עייף לי **ayef li* (*lit.* 'it is tired to me'), similarly for רעב *ra'ev* 'hungry'.

4. Most verbs and adjectives, even of feeling and reaction, do require a subject, be it a noun (including זה *ze* 'it') or a clause (see also 31.4-5), thus example (3) is unacceptable:

(1) ani omer laH she-**ze** maftía oti אני אומר לך שזה מפתיע אותי

'I tell you that **it** surprises me'

(2) maftía (oti) **she-hitgarasht** מפתיע (אותי) **שהתגרשת**

surprises (me) **that you-got-divorced**

SUBJ CLAUSE

'It surprises me / is surprising that you got divorced'

(3) *ani omer laH she-maftía (oti) *אני אומר לך שמפתיע (אותי)

I tell you that surprises (me) ('I tell you that it surprises me') / is surprising')

More examples: מטריד *matrid* 'bothers, bothersome', מצחיק *matsHik* 'amuses, amusing', מעצבן *meatsben* 'annoys, annoying', מוזר *muzar* 'strange', טוב *tov* 'good', עדיף *adif* 'better', חשוב *Hashuv* 'important', ברור *barur* 'plain'.

5. This unsaid subject is neither אנשים *anashim* 'people' nor הם *hem* 'they', nor any actual word - for it is unique in not allowing any pronoun to refer back to it, thus ruling out:

*rotsim leherashem, aval enéni *רוצים להירשם, אבל אינני

makir **otam** מכיר **אותם**

PRONOUN

('⟨They⟩ want to enrol, but I don't know **them**')

*barur she mashlim et **atsmam**   **עצמם** את שמשלים ברור*
PRONOUN

('It's plain ⟨they⟩ are deluding **themselves**')

Instead, Hebrew prefers:

anashim rotsim leherashem, aval   אבל להירשם, רוצים **אנשים**
enéni makir otam   אותם מכיר איננו

'**People** want to enrol, but I don't know them'

However, implied reference is possible:

...aH enéni marshe le-**af eHad**   **אחד לאף** מרשה אינני אך...

'...but I do not permit **anyone**'

6. By contrast, a few verbs allow a generic *or* a non-generic interpretation of their infinitive object:

ani mevakesh **lishon**   **לישון** מבקש אני

'I'm attempting **to sleep**'
'I ask (you/people) **to sleep**'

Chapter 18

1. A few minor exceptions are mentioned in note 3 to chapter 12.

Although verbs, especially past and future forms, are frequently used without an overt subject pronoun, e.g. תפלי *tipli* 'you (f.s.) will fall', they should still be regarded as agreeing with an implied subject - for one has to account for the agreement of plural inflections with *combinations* of subject pronouns, e.g. נפול והוא אני *ani ve-hu nipol* 'I and he will fall (1st pl.)'; see 18.6.3.

2. The quite distinct use of אין *en* as a negative copula, as in בקיא **איננו** הוא *hu eno baki* 'He **is not** an expert', or as a negator as in נוהג **איננו** הוא *hu eno noheg* 'He **doesn't** drive', is discussed in chapter 29.

3. By contrast, אין *en* as a negator or copula (note 2) has an alternative form אינו *eno* (m.s.), אינה *ena* (f.s.).

4. When the predicate is plural, זה *ze* remains uninflected.

5. Sometimes זה *ze* (uninflected) occurs even with an adjectival or verbal predicate, when the subject is generic or expresses 'the notion of...':

hoda'a shel yom **ze** meHubad me'od   מאד מכובד **זה** יום של הודעה

'A day's notice **is** very respectable'

6. Where the predicate is a plural *pronoun*, agreement is unlikely:

ha-baaya ze   anáHnu   אנחנו זה הבעיה
f.s. m.s. 1st pl.   'The problem is us'

Formal usage prefers היא *hi*, agreeing with the subject.

7. Similarly, for asking the price of something:

káma ze ha-tapuHim?   התפוחים? זה כמה

'How much are the apples?'

8. אין *en* is also the existential verb 'there is/are not' - see 18.2.2. לא *lo* too means 'not', but differs syntactically.

9. -הנ *hin-* is related to הנה *hine* 'here is'. Introducing a noun or adjective, it can be rendered 'be'; before a verb, it has no English equivalent.

10. Similarly in formal usage, if the subject is bulky or in cases where the more usual order 'given element + stressed new element' is reversed so that main stress falls on the first noun:

ha-*giyus*	hu / hi	ha-	baaya		הבעיה	הוא / היא	הגיוס ה
m.s.	{m.s./f.s.}		f.s.				

'The *call-up* is the problem'

Where the stressed 'new element' is a personal pronoun, it controls agreement in the singular only (which suggests that it is the 'predicate'):

ata hu ha-baaya
m.s.m.s.   f.s.
אתה הוא הבעיה
'*You* are the problem'

anáHnu hi ha-baaya
pl.   f.s.   f.s.
אנחנו היא הבעיה
'*We* are the problem'

11. This is not a copula, as the other forms of the verb היה *haya* 'be' are unacceptable here.

12. The copula הם *hem* too is used with masculine or feminine subjects in casual usage:

ha-oniyot hem oniyot krav
f.pl.   f.pl.
האוניות הם אוניות קרב
'The ships are warships'

Similarly, מי *mi* as a non-interrogative pronoun can be masculine (which is also neutral) or specifically feminine:

kóva ose dvarim le-**mi** she-Hovéshet oto
                 f.s.   f.s.
כובע עושה דברים **למי**
שחובשת אותו
'A hat does things to **whoever wears it**'

13. But very casually the pronoun seems to be 'contaminated' by the subject זה *ze*, and resumes 3rd person:

ze ata she-**siken** otánu
        3rd m.s.
זה אתה **שסיכן** אותנו
'It's you that **endangered** us'

ze lo ani she-**amar** káHa
          3rd m.s.
זה לא אני **שאמר** ככה
'It's not me that **said** it'

14. Hebrew ordinarily strives to make morphological distinction between male and female nouns, e.g. פסל *pasal* 'sculptor' ~ פסלת *pasélet* 'sculptress'.

Chapter 19

1. Here it is appropriate to mention subtle but clear *syntactic* differences between preposition and noun. They are unlike construct nouns in the following ways: (a) Prepositions introduce clauses, e.g. ...על מנת ל *al menat le..* 'in order to...', ...על-ידי ש *al yedey she...* 'by...ing'; (b) They can govern the clause pronouns כן *ken*, כך *kaH* or ככה *káHa*, e.g. לאחר-מכן *leaHár-miken* 'after this', as against the unacceptable אישור כן* *ishur ken* 'confirmation of this' (which one might have actually expected, given the acceptability of the corresponding אישרו כן *ishru ken* 'They confirmed this'); (c) They can govern reflexive pronouns, e.g. ראיתי מפלצת בתוך עצמי *ra'íti miflétset betoH atsmi* 'I saw a monster within myself'. (d) When the 'focusing adverbs' -עצמ *atsm-* '-self' and -לבד *levad-* 'alone' are appended to a 'preposition + suffix', the former agree with the *suffix* as if it were a noun in its own right, e.g. בשבילנו עצמנו *bishvilénu* **atsménu** 'for us **ourselves**', whereas after 'noun + suffix' agreement is with the noun rather than the suffix: דרכנו עצמה *darkénu* **atsma** 'our way **itself**' rather than דרכנו עצמנו* *darkénu atsménu* 'our way ourselves (i.e. our own way)', מינויה לבדו *minuya levado* 'her appointment alone' rather than מינויה לבדה* *minuya levada* ('the appointment of her alone'). Phonologically too, certain prepositions differ from corresponding construct nouns (in casual usage at any rate), e.g. בשביל *bishvil* 'for' vs. בשביל *be-shvil* 'in the path of'.

2. A few verbs of location, movement etc. take a direct object, i.e. they need no preposition to express such a semantic relationship. Contrast ...יצא מ *yatsa mi...* and עזב *azav* 'leave'.

3. Synonymous with -ל *le-* but suffixed to its noun is the unstressed 'ה- *-a* of destination', found with a handful of nouns, e.g. העירה *ha-íra* 'to town'. (See 21.8.).

4. The same holds for verbs and adjectives.

5. However, -ב *be-* is used with the gerund היות *heyot* 'being'.

6. This is distinct from אם *im* 'if'.

7. A few adverbs are identical to prepositions, notably קודם *kódem* 'before/beforehand', אגב *agav* 'while/by the way', מאז *me'az* 'since/since then'.

8. But some verbs take an object *clause* but no object noun, so in אילץ לנהוג *ilets linhog* 'compel to drive', שיכנע לצאת *shiHnéa latset* 'persuade to leave', for example, no preposition can be said to be 'missing'; see 31.1.

9. A minor exception are business names, where it means 'and': כהן את לוי *kohen et levi* 'Cohen & Levi'.

Chapter 20

1. Some 'nouns' act as adjectives casually, thus היא כל-כך תינוקת *hi kol-kaH tinóket* 'She's so [= such] a baby', הוא נורא גבר *hu nora géver* 'He's very ⟨much⟩ a man'. A few noun phrases too behave this way, e.g. זה מאד עניין של מזל *ze me'od inyan shel mazal* 'It's very ⟨much⟩ a matter of luck'.

2. An apparent exception is the use of the comparatives, e.g. יותר *yoter* 'more' and פחות *paHot* 'less', as 'detached comparatives'; see 20.4.

3. However, some degree words, notably מאד *me'od* 'very', form a phrase with לא *lo* 'not', e.g. הוא מאד לא מוצא חן בעיני *hu me'od lo motse Hen be-eynay* 'He **very much** doesn't appeal to me', זה היה מאד לא ברור *ze haya me'od lo barur* 'It was **very unclear**'. See also note 2.

4. There is also the common idiom מה טוב *ma tov* 'how much the better', as in 'If you can come, how much the better'.

5. To express interrogative 'how', one often uses כמה *káma*, and particularly עד כמה *ad káma*, as an adverbial, i.e. unlike degree words it can usually stand some way ahead of the adjective or verb:

ad káma ha-ramatkal gamish?	עד כמה הרמטכ"ל גמיש?
till how the Chief-of-Staff flexible?	'How flexible is the Chief of Staff?'

ad káma ata mud'ag?	עד כמה אתה מודאג?
till how you worried?	'How worried are you?'

But casual usage often prefers a different strategy altogether:

ata me'od mud'ag? 'Are you very worried?'	אתה מאד מודאג?

Not being a degree word, interrogative כמה *káma* cannot provide an attributive construction:

*toHnit kama gmisha drusha?	*תוכנית כמה גמישה דרושה?
plan how flexible required?	('How flexible a plan is required?')

6. This is presumably a quasi-morphological rule to avoid a repeated -ה *ha-*. The same holds for הללו *halálu* 'these' and ההם *hahem* 'those'; see 9.3.1. Nor can this -ה *ha-* in הכי *haHi* be conflated so that ב+ה- *be+ha* → ב- *ba*, hence בהכי יפה *be-haHi yafe*, '**in** the most beautiful (house, etc.)'.

7. This is because הכי מהר *haHi maher* is felt to be degree word+adverb, whereas המהיר ביותר *ha-mahir beyoter* is definite article+*adjective*+degree word.

8. הכי פחות *haHi paHot* is peculiar in that פחות *paHot* itself means 'less', yet הכי פחות *haHi paHot* means not 'the most less' but 'the most little', i.e. 'the least'. But its counterpart יותר *yoter* 'more' does not supply *הכי יותר* *haHi yoter* for 'the most';

instead one uses הכי הרבה *haHi harbe* (i.e. the most much) for quantification, or just הכי *haHi* for 'degree':

tsarfat savla haHi harbe	'France suffered the most'	צרפת סבלה הכי הרבה
ze lakaH haHi harbe zman	'This took the most time'	זה לקח הכי הרבה זמן
ze haHi kasher	'This is the most kosher'	זה הכי כשר

9. Similarly יותר *yoter* 'more' may be omitted in formal usage when the other term in the comparison is mentioned: יפה מכל אחיו *yafe mi-kol eHav* '(more) handsome than all his brothers'.

10. These conjunctions all incorporate the preposition -מ *mi-* 'from' which is the basic 'case marker' of all comparatives. -מכפי ש *mi-kfi she-* idiomatically relates to כפי *kfi* 'like', while -ממה ש *mi-ma she-* is literally 'than what that'.

11. The direct object here requires את *et*, hence the simplest form of comparative (ממני *miméni* 'than me') is not usual here. In relative clauses, however, direct object pronouns are treated just like subject pronouns; see 33.3.

12. Derived, i.e. verb-based or noun-based, adjectives such as מקופח *mekupaH* 'deprived' and דתי *dati* 'religious' are also unable to act as construct adjectives.

13. Adjectives and participles in such a construction can be converted into a kind of noun with -ה *ha-* 'the':

kar (yoter) min	ha-tsafuy ha-ragil	קר (יותר) מן הצפוי הרגיל

cold (more) than	the expected the usual	'It is colder than expected' usual

14. A particular case of this is 'sarcastic כמו *kmo*':

hu mevin yídish kmo she-ani méleH
románya   הוא מבין יידיש כמו שאני מלך
רומניה

'He understands Yiddish like I'm the king of Roumania'
(i.e. he doesn't understand Yiddish)

15. Historically -מ *mi* 'from, than' plus כדי *kdey* 'for, so that, sufficiently that'.

16. Otherwise meaning 'for, in order (to)'.

17. The finite clause is usually only found when the subject is different from the main clause subject.

18. This construction somewhat resembles the comparative גבוה מיעקב *gavóa mi-yáakov* 'tall⟨er⟩ than Yaakov' (20.4).

19. The unsaid subject of such infinitivals need not be identified with the subject of the main clause; it can be impersonal 'one':

ha-ktav maspik barur kdey lehavin oto   הכתב מספיק ברור כדי להבין אותו
the writing enough clear so-as   'The writing's clear enough for one to
to-understand it   understand it'

20. יותר *yoter* 'more', when qualified, cannot be omitted in the way described in 20.4, ruling out:

*hu ktsat gavóa mi-david   *הוא קצת גבוה מדוד
he slightly tall than David   'He is slightly taller than David'

קצת *ktsat* and its synonym מעט *me'at* can *precede* the adjective even when יותר *yoter* follows it.

21. It can be treated either as the normal יותר *yoter* 'more' or added following the whole phrase, e.g. ...פי עשר אנשים יותר מאשר *pi éser anashim* **yoter** *measher...* (ten times people **more** than...). The latter position is required with כמה *káma* 'how many':

káma anashim yesh yoter   כמה אנשים יש יותר

    mi-she-ba-paam ha-kodémet?   משבפעם הקודמת?

how-many people are-there more

[= how many more people...] than last time?

22. The exception is adjectives being used adverbially:

hem nimtsa'im shiva mayl **raHok** mi-po   הם נמצאים שבעה מייל **רחוק** מפה

they are-situated seven miles **distant** from here

and where the measure phrase is a fraction, e.g. רבע מלא *réva maley* '(a) **quarter** full',

גמור חצי *Hétsi gamur* '**half** complete'.

Chapter 21

1. Also known as 'adjuncts' or 'VP adverbials'. Like subject, verb and object, they are a 'core component' of the sentence.

2. Furthermore, they can be 'focused on', i.e. negated, questioned and contrastively emphasized:

lo **báti** biglal ha-Hag (éla...)   (...לא באתי בגלל החג (אלא

     ADJUNCT   'I didn't come because of the festival (but rather...)'

ze po'el **yeshirot** o **ba-akifin**?   זה פועל ישירות או בעקיפין?

     ADJUNCT   ADJUNCT   'Does it act directly or indirectly?'

lo, lo be-*Elat* ani gar!   לא לא, באילת אני גר!

     ADJUNCT   'No no, I live in *Elat*!'

3. Examples like (2) themselves are often equivalent to a predicate adjunct:

ha-séret she-mi-yapan lo ra   הסרט שמיפן לא רע

                       'The film that ⟨is⟩ from Japan isn't bad'

Adjuncts of manner and extent (21.3-4) can qualify a verb but not a noun. Instead, the corresponding adjective or quantifier, respectively, is used, e.g. the uninflected adjunct קשה *kashe* 'hard' vs. the inflected adjective הקשה *ha-kasha* 'hard':

avádti **kashe** ha-shana imahem   עבדתי **קשה** השנה עמהם

   ADJUNCT ADJUNCT   ADJUNCT   'I worked **hard** this year with

                                  them...'

avodati **ha-kasha** ha-shana imahem...   ...עבודתי **הקשה** השנה עמהם

     ADJECTIVE   ADJUNCT   ADJUNCT

my-work **the hard** this year with-them...   'my **hard** work this year with

                                  them...'

4. Degree words do however go with such qualifiers, and all adverbials go with a *passive participle* qualifying something (as if it were a full relative clause in its own right):

tinok atsbani me'od   תינוק עצבני מאד

baby tetchy very   'a very tetchy baby'

batsal mekulaf hetev   בצל מקולף היטב

onion peeled well   'a well peeled onion'

5. By contrast, a measure phrase qualifying a non-adverbial *follows* it. In this example, רחוק *raHok* 'distant' is the *predicate*:

hi reHoka **méa méter**   היא רחוקה **מאה מטר**

   PRED   MEASURE PHR   'It is **100 metres** distant'

6. With ו- הלך *halaH ve-* '...gradually' and the 'extent verbs', the infinitive is in some ways unlike an object clause subordinate to the verb (for the distinction between 'raised

subject clauses' and 'object clauses' in general, see 31.3); for instance, these verbs permit (and ו- הלך *halaH ve-* requires) a 'non-intentional' subject, and thus allow the passive, as in:

matslemot marbot lehitkalkel u-lehiganev   מצלמות מרבות להתקלקל ולהיגנב
cameras do-a-lot to-go-wrong and   'Cameras go wrong and get
  to-be-stolen   stolen a lot'

Other adverbial verbs, conversely, cannot express a non-intentional subject as in 'I quickly understood, the drug quickly combines, it combines well, he was seized again'.

7. Further examples are ...ל איחר *iHer le...* '...late' and ...ו חזר *Hazar ve...* '... again'.

8. Similarly לדבר מיעט *mi'et ledaber* 'spoke little', although the adverb מעט *me'at* means both 'little' and 'a little'.

9. An 'absolute infinitive' is possible in a few idioms, e.g. לכת הרחיק *hirHik léHet* 'went far', קום השכים *hishkim kum* 'rose early', והדגש חזור הדגיש *hidgish Hazor ve-hadgesh* 'stressed repeatedly'.

10. Distinguish extent from frequency (21.7.1), which also employs quantifiers, e.g. הרבה *harbe* 'often'; and from simple nouns:

ra'íti harbe   'I saw a lot'   ראיתי הרבה

11. Adjectives of the מכובד *meHubad* and מוכבד *muHbad* patterns tend to be exclusively animate. Instead, one can use an abstract noun, for example, 'surprisedly' could be rendered by בהפתעה *be-hafta'a* 'with surprise'.

12. And sometimes, unpredictably, these structures may express other things:

be-ófen rishmi, sagur   באופן רשמי, סגור
in way official, closed   'Officially, it's closed'

13. The echo phrases usually count positionally etc. as manner adverbials. Though they require the (unmarked) 'object marker' את *et* when definite, no preposition is possible with adjectives; nor can such pseudo-objects suffer passivization, pronominalization or the presence of a real direct object. Indeed, the verb can be intransitive as in examples (2,5) or passive, as in example (3). The noun is formed by the usual rules for nominalization (38.2).

Some verbs take echo nouns as *true objects*. Here no manner adjective is needed and one can pronominalize and usually passivize:

she'al oti sheela   'Ask me a question'   שאל אותי שאלה
hitsáti hatsa'a   'I proposed [= made] a proposal'   הצעתי הצעה

14. Also (very casually) certain nouns, for example:

hi shára {yófi/shiga'on/zva'a}   {זוועה / שיגעון / יופי} שרה היא
she sang {beauty/craze/horror}   'She sang {beautifully/incredibly/horribly}'

Related to this are casual *clauses* (using any suitable noun) of the type:

hu {mitnaheg/meHo'ar} she-ze zva'a   זוועה שזה {מכוער / מתנהג} הוא
he {behaves/ugly} that it's a horror   'He behaves horribly'
                                        'He's horribly ugly'

These are not result clauses but indeed manner clauses, being suited to verbs that require manner adverbials (e.g. התנהג *hitnaheg* 'behave').

15. For qualifying all other adjectives or adverbials, manner adverbials are mostly eschewed - save (1) the צורה / באופן *be-ófen/tsura* type (21.4.1), (2) the very casual noun-centred constructions of the לא-רגיל משהו *máshehu lo-ragil* and זוועה *zva'a* type (21.4.1 and n. 14), and (3) the להפליא *lehafli* type (21.4.3), which is more like a degree word:

séfer gizani {lehadhim/be-tsura tsínit} book racist {to-frighten/in way cynical}	ספר גזעני {להדהים/בצורה צינית} 'a frighteningly racist book' cynically

hi raza {máshehu meyuHad/lehafli} she thin {something special/to-amaze}	היא רזה {משהו מיוחד/להפליא} 'She is amazingly thin'

ani néged ze be-ófen yesodi I'm against it in way fundamental	אני נגד זה באופן יסודי 'I'm fundamentally against it'

and not:

*séfer gizani be-tsiniyut	book racist with cynicism	*ספר גזעני בציניות
*hi raza nifla	she thin amazing	*היא רזה נפלא

16. An apparent exception is ...כמו *kmo...* 'like...' (which often acts as a manner adverbial, see 21.4.4):

hi kmo sus	'She ⟨is⟩ like ⟨a⟩ horse' היא כמו סוס

An idiomatic exception is בסדר *beséder* 'OK', commonly treated as one word [pséder] rather than as ב+סדר *be+séder*.

17. Manner, degree and extent correspond to *adjectives*, which Hebrew tends to coordinate, not stack. But even coordination is impossible for diverse adverbs.

18. An apparent combination of manner adverbials is probably a case of 'manner + means':

otomáti	אוטומטי
adam lo mitnaheg yafe be-ófen spontáni	אדם לא מתנהג יפה באופן ספונטני
tiv'i	טבעי
automatically'	
'A person doesn't behave nicely spontaneously'	
naturally'	

19. One-word adverbs too often take degree words, e.g. מהר מאד *maher me'od* 'very quickly'; an exception is היטב *hetev* 'well'.

20. Contrast with a means adverbial (involving a definite noun):

dibárnu ba-yadáyim	דיברנו בידיים
we-spoke with-the hands	'We spoke with our hands'

21. This is not a normal clause, in that (1) the copula, e.g. הוא *hu* 'is' and אינו *eno* 'is not', is impossible; (2) the subject can be indefinite; and (3) subject cannot be a personal pronoun such as הוא *hu* 'it' as it would have to be affixed to עם *im* 'with' as אתו *ito* 'with it'. Hence the term 'quasi-clause':

   (1) *yats'u im ha-se'ar eno mesurak yafe   *יצאו עם השיער אינו מסורק יפה
       they-went-out with the hair is-not combed nicely

   (2) hu yashen im ragláyim ba-avir   הוא ישן עם רגליים באוויר
       he sleeps with feet in-the air

   (3) bat im ha-me'il patúaH? *lo,   באת עם המעיל פתוח? *לא,
       báti **ito** sagur   באתי **אתו** סגור
       you-came with the coat open? No, I-came **with-it** closed

22. חיים *Hayim* 'alive' tends to be used without agreement in idioms like אכל/תפס חיים *aHal/tafas Hayim* 'eat/catch alive'.

23. With or without comma, this is an adjunct and can be negated etc.

   In casual usage such predicates can be more akin to 'because' than to circumstantial 'while' (and are then in fact disjuncts, not adjuncts):

ani mefaHed bishvila, **omédet sham káHa**   אני מפחד בשבילה, **עומדת שם ככה**
m.s.   f.s.f.s.

I am-afraid for-her, **stands** [= standing] **there like-that**

Another, widespread, use of predicates is as object clauses for verbs of 'noticing, finding' etc;
see 30.3.

24. The adverb עוד *od* 'still' can behave in formal usage like a curious combination of
adverb + positive copula הנני, הנך *hineni, hinHa* etc. (see 16.2): in the present tense it
can take suffixes agreeing with its subject (but not in the negative):

sára | od / odéna | zoHéret   עוד / עודנה זוכרת שרה

Sara | still / still + COP | remembers   'Sara still remembers'

25. But partitive אחד *eHad* 'one' needs ב- *be*-: באחד מימי האביב *be-eHad mi-ymey
ha-aviv* 'on one spring day'. So too determiner זה *ze* 'this': ברגע זה *be-réga ze* 'at this
moment'.

26. So too with phrases of the type ערב-ערב *érev-érev* 'every evening'.

27. With certain actions, the quantifiers express duration, not frequency, for both the
verb and its related action noun:

káma yashant, sha'a?   כמה ישנת, שעה?
                                        'How much did you sleep, 1 hour?'

leaHar harbe shena...   לאחר הרבה שינה...
                                        'after much sleep...'

but not:

*káma Hikit/shahit po?   *כמה חיכית/שהית פה?
how much did you wait/stay here?

*leaHar harbe hamtana/shehut   *לאחר הרבה המתנה/שהות...
after much waiting/stay...

28. תכף *téHef* meaning 'right away' (with past tense) can follow the verb too.

29. These may be further qualified by degree or measure phrases, e.g. יותר למעלה
yoter lemáala 'further up'. With certain adjuncts a clause can be incorporated - this is a
relative clause (details in 33.4.2); for example:

atsárnu éfo she-hitpalelu   עצרנו איפה שהתפללו
we-halted where that they-were-praying   'We halted where they were praying'

30. Formal usage also employs אל *el*, except with place names. The suffixed forms are
אלי, אליך *elay, eléHa* etc., whereas ל- *le*- as an 'object preposition' usually has the suffixed forms לי, לך *li, leHa* etc.

31. Formal usage also employs מן *min*, before ה- *ha*- 'the'.

32. There are exceptions. (1) The adjectives קרוב/רחוק *karov/raHok* 'near/far' must
agree (are not adverbs) when predicates. (2) (ב)חזרה *(be-)Hazara* 'back' needs qualifying
when predicate: הוא (ב)חזרה בצמרת *hu (be-)Hazara ba-tsaméret* 'He's back at the top'.

33. Exceptions are verbs of intent, as in example (1) below, commands implying verbs
of command as in (2) and motion adverbials qualified by a measure phrase, as in examples (3,4):

(1) le'an ata rotse? ani tsariH le-áza   לאן אתה רוצה? אני צריך לעזה
    to-where you want? I need   'Where do you want to go? I need
    to Gaza   Gaza'

(2) hála   'Further!'   הלאה!
     ha-Hútsa   'Out!'   החוצה!

(3) hi nimtset me'ot kilométrim mi-kan   היא נמצאת מאות קילומטרים מכאן
     MEASURE PHR   MOTION ADV
     she is hundreds [of] kilometres from here

(4) éser dakot la-siyum heHmátsnu   עשר דקות לסיום החמצנו
     od hizdamnut   עוד הזדמנות
     ten minutes to-the end we-missed another chance

34. A 'loose' locative adverbial, or several tiers of them, is always possible too:
ba-árets, garim be-dirot gam **ba-parvarim**   **בארץ,** גרים בדירות גם **בפרברים**
'**In Israel**, ⟨they⟩ live in apartments even **in the suburbs**'

35. -כ *ke-*, but not בתור *betor*, allows the insertion of a second אל *el* or על *al* (rarely
-ב *be-* or any other preposition), echoing the אל *el* or על *al* in the foregoing object - a
curious construction as these -כ *ke-* phrases are not abbreviated versions of a full clause
with אל *el* or על *al*:

     hityaHasu **la**-mifrats ke-**el** shétaH riboni   התייחסו למפרץ כאל שטח ריבוני
     they-referred **to**-the gulf as **to**   'They referred to the gulf as
     territory sovereign   sovereign territory'

36. This interchange of prepositions betokens an object rather than an adverbial, as does
the ability to 'extract' material out of a -כ *ke-* 'as' verb phrase (adverbial clauses do not
permit 'extraction'):

     éze maHalot ha-glulot zuhu ke-mon'ot?   איזה מחלות הגלולות זוהו כמונעות?
                                                                'Which diseases ⟨were⟩ the pills identified
                                                                               as preventing?'

However, the ...כאל *ke-el...*, כעל *ke-al...* phrases suggest the opposite.

37. This can include a 'malefactee', as against a 'benefactee' for whom there is a particular construction.

     Unlike *object* datives (e.g. -הקשיב ל *hikshiv le-...* 'listen to...'), affectee datives com-
monly express the reflexive by לי, לך *li, leHa* etc. rather than by the reflexive pronouns
לעצמי, לעצמך *le-atsmi, le-atsmeHa* etc.:

     oy, shavárti li od zug mishkafáyim!   אוי, שברתי לי עוד זוג משקפים!
     oh, I've-broken to-me another pair   'Oh, I've broken another pair
     glasses!   of glasses!'

38. For reflexive, both the reflexive and the ordinary 'adverbial-type' pronoun are
employed:

     hayíta yaHol lakáHat leHa levad   היית יכול לקחת לך לבד
     you-were able to-take for-you alone   'You could have taken for yourself alone'

39. Indeed, in constructions such as example (1) below, the verb + dative tend to come
before the subject to give this effect. The reflexive is the general reflexive pronoun, as
for objects (2):

     (1) ko'ev li ha-rosh   כואב לי הראש
          hurts to-me the head   'My head hurts'

     (2) hu nisa lehorid le-atsmo ózen   הוא ניסה להוריד לעצמו אוזן
          he tried to-remove to himself ear   'He tried to remove an ear'

40. Not with verbal nouns, however.

Chapter 22

1. Another set of adverbs, 'link adverbs', expresses this kind of relationship just between clauses - and is generally clause-initial (ch.24):

    kmo-Hen, ra'ínu atsmot pilim   **כמו-כן,** ראינו עצמות פילים

                                   '**Similarly**, we saw elephant bones'

Focus on individual words can be added by routine intonation or reordering.

2. רק *rak* (not בלבד *bilvad* etc.) is also 'no earlier than' - preceding the verb:

    ani **rak** noséa be-purim   אני **רק** נוסע בפורים

                  'I'm **only** going on Purim' (= 'at the earliest' or 'just')

    ani noséa **rak** be-purim   אני נוסע **רק** בפורים

                                  'I'm going **just** on Purim'

3. This is also a manner adverb 'by oneself' (= unaided) - generally anywhere after the verb:

    patárti oto {levad/levadi}   פתרתי אותו {לבד/לבדי}

    I-solved it by-myself

4. במיוחד *bimyuHad*, but not בייחוד *beyiHud*, has two other roles, (1) as a manner adverb, and (2) as a degree word:

    (1) bánu **bimyuHad**   באנו **במיוחד**

                                  'We came **especially**'

    (2) nekuda regisha **bimyuHad**   נקודה רגישה **במיוחד**

                          'An **especially** sensitive point'

5. This is also (1) a link adverb and (2) a manner adverb, לאו דווקא *lav dávka* 'not necessarily' is a disjunct (3):

    (1) hu dávka mash'ir et ha-óHel   הוא דווקא משאיר את האוכל

                          'On the contrary, he leaves his food'

    (2) hu mash'ir et ha-óHel dávka   הוא משאיר את האוכל דווקא

              'He leaves his food {out of spite/in spite of everything}'

    (3) ze lav dávka ason   זה לאו דווקא אסון

                          'It's not necessarily a disaster'

6. This is also a manner adverb 'by oneself' (= unaided), as in note 3 above.

7. These are the personal pronouns, attached by hyphen to a noun with the corresponding possessive suffix (but 'our own' is אנו- *-ánu* rather than אנחנו- *-anáHnu*).

8. This is a focus adverb in just a few respects (see 22.4.3.). It is described fully in chapter 29.

9. The focus on prepositional suffixes reflects the adverbial status of focus adverbs - modifiers of the noun, e.g. determiners, cannot modify a suffix.

10. Other focus adverbs do not focus on such suffixes, thus ruling out:

    *mishpaHti {levadi/atsmi} yodáat   *משפחתי {לבדי/עצמי} יודעת

    my-family {alone-me/self-me} [= alone/myself] knows

'Own' can instead be expressed by a שלי, שלך *sheli, shelHa* 'my, your' etc. phrase, added to an already existing possessive suffix:

    mishpaHto shelo   משפחתו שלו

    family-his of-him   'his own family'

11. But focus adverbs cannot operate from in front of the subject noun - except to focus on the latter:

    rak *miHal* kibla kaved   **רק** מיכל קיבלה כבד

    only *Michal* got liver

    ***rak** miHal kibla *kaved*   *רק** מיכל קיבלה כבד

    ***only** Michal got *liver*

ani **gam** esh'al et *Hotanti*   אני **גם** אשאל את חותנתי
I'll **also** ask OM my-*mother-in-law*

*****gam** ani esh'al et *Hotanti*   ***גם** אני אשאל את חותנתי
*****also** I'll ask OM my-*mother-in-law*

This 'regulative' effect of the subject noun ties in with its 'unextractability' from its clause (ch.37).

12. An exception is sometimes made for 'noun + possessive phrase', e.g.

hu mevi shemot rak shel balshanim   הוא מביא שמות רק של בלשנים
he mentions names only of linguists

Only apparently exceptional are 'nominalized' noun phrases; being akin to self-contained sentences, they *can* have their own focus adverbs:

toH hitbasesut **gam** al peilut polítit   תוך התבססות **גם** על פעילות פוליטית
with reliance **also** on political activity

13. גם *gam* 'also', רק *rak* 'only', עצמו *atsmo* 'oneself' cannot focus on *wh*-words (גם*
מה *****gam ma* 'what too?' as against מה במיוחד *ma bimyuHad* 'what especially?') but do appear *in* questions.

14. Evidence of this is its impossibility *inside* noun or preposition phrases (recall 22.4.3):

*shvi im o...o...   *שבי עם או... או...
sit with either ...or...

15. These ש *she* do not signal a subordinate clause (as if it were 'only it is a fact that...'), witness their inseparability: ...וש ...ש רק* *****rak she...ve-she...* ('only that...and that...'). Similarly ...או ש *o she...* 'either' (contrast ...וש...ש ברור *barur she...ve-she...* '⟨It is⟩ clear that... and that...') Hence the analyses must be ˢ[FOCUS ADV + S].

16. לא רק ש, לא זו בלבד ש *lo rak she, lo zo bilvad she* can turn up *between* subject and negated verb - to focus on parts of sentences (a curious use of ש *she* also found where לא *lo* 'not' lacks a finite verb; see 23.2):

hu lo rak she-**lo makir** ota éla...   ...**הוא** לא רק ש**לא מכיר** אותה אלא
SUBJ   NEG V   'He not only **doesn't know** her but...'

17. Idiomatically composed of לא *lo* 'not' plus זו *zo* 'it' plus בלבד *bilvad* 'only'.

18. אך *aH*, a formal word for 'only', does introduce sentences without needing -ש *she-*, but it is a coordinator (like אבל *aval* 'but'; see ch. 35) and thus allows 'coordination reduction':

ani memaher **aH** meaHer   אני ממהר **אך** מאחר
I hurry **but** come-late

19. או *o* requires -ש *she-* even when as a mere coordinator it begins clause B of a coordination:

hu lo mistakel o she-hu shikor   הוא לא מסתכל או שהוא שיכור
he not looks or that he drunk   'He's not looking or he's drunk'

20. -ש *she-* here is separable and repeatable (...וש ...ש אפילו *afilu she...ve-she...* 'even though...and though...') as in object or complement clauses.

Chapter 23

1. כמובן *kamuvan* 'of course', כנראה *kanir'e* 'apparently' have a meaning that cannot 'exactly' be analysed as כ + מובן *ka* + *muvan* 'as is understood', כ + נראה *ka-nir'e* 'as appears'. However, comment disjuncts are regularly formed in this way (see 23.3), e.g. כמתוכנן *ka-metuHnan* 'as planned'. Furthermore, ...ש מובן *muvan she...* and ...ש נראה *nir'e she...* do denote 'it is self-evident that..., it appears that...', respectively.

2. Distinguish the adjective ודאי *vada'i* 'definite' from the disjunct ודאי *vaday* 'definitely, probably'.

3. שמא *shéma* generally introduces the second part of an 'either...or' question, as in the last example in the list of examples of truth disjuncts, so is best rendered 'or else'.

4. כן *ken* parallels the negator לא *lo* (see ch.29); indeed the two cannot co-occur: הם כן יודעים *hem ken yod'im* 'They do know'.

5. Mid-sentence -ש *she-* otherwise occurs, unrelatedly, in -לא זו בלבד ש *lo zo bilvad she-* 'not only' and לא רק שלא *lo rak she-lo* 'not only...not', as in (1) below, and optionally before negated adverbials and negated infinitives, as in (2,3):

> (1) ata lo rak **she**-lo ozer éla...
>   you not only **that** not help but...
>
>   אתה לא רק שלא עוזר אלא...
>   'You not only don't help but...'

> (2) hi neetsra **she**-lo be-tsédek
>   she was-detained **that** not justly
>
>   היא נעצרה שלא בצדק
>   'She was detained unjustly'

> (3) heedáfti **she**-lo lariv
>   I-preferred **that** not to-quarrel
>
>   העדפתי שלא לריב
>   'I preferred not to quarrel'

-ש *she-* in כמובן ש *kamuvan she-* 'of course' etc. stems at first sight from a blend with the 'predicate + clause' construction מובן ש... *muvan she*... '(it is) self-evident that...' (see 31.5). But closer analysis reveals: (a) several such disjuncts with *no* 'predicate + clause' equivalent; (b) a number of genuine 'predicate + clause' traits in these disjuncts, e.g. the -ש *she-* is separable (example (1)) and no subject-verb inversion of the type found after adverbials is possible (example (2)); and conversely (c) the construction is restricted to main clauses, *unlike* the 'predicate + clause' construction:

> (1) kenir'e gam she...
>
>   כנראה גם ש...
>   'apparently also [that]...'

> (2) *kenir'e she-maskimim kulam
>   apparently that agree all
>
>   *כנראה שמסכימים כולם
>   ('Apparently all agree')

6. Thus these, for example, are unlikely:

?le-Haasi	'to my annoyance'	?לכעסי
?le-marbe ha-daavon	'regrettably'	?למרבה הדאבון
?be-ófen maftía	'surprisingly'	?באופן מפתיע

7. מרבה *marbe* and מרבית *marbit* are idiomatic nouns.

8. אופן *ófen* and אורח *óraH* both denote 'manner' in manner adverbials (21.4), e.g. 'in an unexpected manner'. The other manner noun, צורה *tsura*, is not used.

9. Some adjectives too are used, e.g. כרגיל *ka-ragil* 'as usual'.

10. All these three patterns can be adverbials of manner too:

> yisra'el to tif'al {tsava'it/be-ófen tsva'i}
>
> ישראל לא תפעל {צבאית/באופן צבאי}
> 'Israel will not act militarily'

> dibárti birtsinut
>
> דיברתי ברצינות
> 'I was talking seriously'

11. With a negator, נא *na* follows this negator: אל נא נהסס *al na nehases* 'Let us not hesitate'.

12. Condemned by purists.

13. Despite the common confusion between 'except' and 'besides', little real ambiguity arises.

14. בטוח *batúaH* 'definitely' can be negated, questioned etc:

> ata nish'ar? - lo batúaH
>
> אתה נשאר? - לא בטוח
> 'You staying? - Not definitely'

sha'álti im at batúaH titremi   שאלתי אם את בטוח תתרמי
'I asked if you're definitely giving'

15. An exception: פשוט *pashut* 'simply' resists inversion.

Chapter 24

1. Rather than by an adverb linking two independent sentences, a logical connection can often be expressed by a preposition creating a subordinate clause, which can even precede the other clause with which it is connecting. Thus, instead of y ואולם, x *x, ve-ulam y* 'x, and nevertheless y' one can use x, y - ש למרות *lamrot she-y, x* 'Although y, x'.

As for the differences between link adverbials and coordinators, such as -ו *ve-* 'and' or אך *aH* 'but', see chapter 35. A clause containing a link adverbial may in any case begin with such a coordinator.

2. These are strictly clause-initial, except כל-קודם *kódem-kol* 'first of all'.

3. Many of these are clause-initial, but casual עוד *od* 'what's more' is not found initially:

aval ha-ben-adam dati od!   אבל הבן-אדם דתי עוד!
'But the fellow's religious, what's more!'

and formal עוד *od* 'likewise' is not found finally and typically accompanies verbs of information:

od moser katavénu ki...   **עוד** מוסר כתבנו כי...
'Our correspondent **further** reports that...'

Those not restricted positionally are מזה חוץ *Huts mi-ze*, לכך (ב)נוסף *(be-)nosaf le-HaH*, זה מלבד *milvad ze* 'furthermore', כן גם *gam ken* 'likewise', בעצם *beétsem* 'in actual fact', למעשה *lemaase* 'as a matter of fact', אכן *aHen*, אמנם *omnam* 'indeed', and אמנם *omnam* 'admittedly'.

4. After כן *ken*, the predicate usually precedes the subject:

ken hizkir ha-meHaber...   'The author **also** mentioned...'   ...**כן** הזכיר המחבר

5. These are only initial, except ובכן *uvHen* 'well' and אגב (דרך) *(déreH) ágav* 'incidentally', which also occur within the clause.

6. ...באשר ל *baasher le*..., unlike ...אשר ל *asher le*..., can also introduce an adjunct, i.e. an adverbial that can be stressed and generally focused (see 21.1):

ha-sheela kayémet baasher la-aHaronim   השאלה קיימת באשר לאחרונים
'The question exists with regard to the latter'

7. These mostly take any position.

8. These are clause-initial or phrase-initial.

9. Except for clause-initial כך למשל *kaH lemashal*, these are not restricted positionally.

10. These differ greatly in their positioning.

11. These are mostly clause-initial.

12. Nor can אז *az* or כן אם *im ken* 'so' be so used.

13. An exception is that inversion is *required* after כן *ken* 'likewise':

ken hizkir ha-rav, ki...   ...**כן** הזכיר הרב, כי
likewise mentioned the rabbi that...   'The rabbi **likewise** mentioned that...'

14. Unlike coordinators (e.g. -ו *ve-* 'and', ואילו *veílu* 'whereas'), conjuncts do not entertain clause reduction.

15. ועכשיו *ve-aHshav*, ואז *ve-az* do occur in the more 'temporal' sense 'and now, and then'.

16. There are exceptions. Link adverbials meaning 'namely/in other words' do not allow
-ו *ve-* 'and':

..., (*ve-)kelomar,...   '..., (*and) in other words'   ...,כלומר (ו*)...,

..., (*ve-)háynu...   '..., (*and) namely'   ...היינו (ו*)...,

A few require more than a comma, notably:

...; zot va-od:...   '...; furthermore...'   ...: זאת ועוד ;...

Conversely, a few do not allow -ו *ve-* 'and' because they are felt to 'run on' from the
preceding (see 24.3):

...; az...   '...; so...'   ... אז ;...

17. However, a clause of 'saying' and suchlike can intervene (arrows show link to previous clause):

...; ata svurim ki le-yarden, **nosaf le-Hah,**   **לכך, נוסף** לירדן כי סבורים עתה ;...

    tafkid estratégi Hashuv ⟵┘   חשוב אסטרטגי תפקיד ⟵┘

                '...; now it is thought that Jordan, **additionally**,
                has an important strategic role'

18. But not: ...לכן, ,...ו *היות** *heyot ve...,* *laHen...* ('Since..., therefore...').

Chapter 26

1. האם *ha'im* is historically the question particle ה *ha* + אם *im* 'if, whether'.

2. Formal הלא *halo* is a clause-initial adverb meaning 'surely', not a question particle
ה *ha* + negator לא *lo*:

halo yashnu   'Surely they were asleep'   ישנו הלא

3. More literary terms are אנה *ána* 'whither', מנין *mináyin* 'whence', and אימתי
eymatay 'when'.

4. In formal usage the feminine is איזו *ézo* and the plural optionally אילו *éylu.*

5. Hebrew often prefers a construction like example (1) below, or, with measurements,
a construct noun as in example (2):

    (1) hu **me'od** Hazak?   חזק? **מאד** הוא
                                                 'Is he **very** strong?'

    (2) ma haya óreH ha-kéresh?   הקרש? אורך היה מה
         what was length the plank?   'What was the length of the plank?'

6. Thus the following is impossible:

    *mi at nosáat im?   עם? נוסעת את *מי
    who you are-going with?   ('Who are you going with?')

7. Such 'extraction of material' also happens in 'relative pronoun movement' (ch. 33)
and 'topic and focus movement' (ch.37). Roughly, they all permit 'extraction' from subordinate questions, object clauses and relative clauses (even involving '*wh-* word crossing',
and 'double dislocation' of two interrogative words out of a single clause). But extraction
is not possible out of a factive clause or one headed by a complex noun phrase; nor may
priority relations between subjects, the various objects and adverbials be infringed.

8. 'Some' with a singular noun is קצת *ktsat* or the like, or is even unexpressed:

    tavi li (ktsat) dvash   'Give me some honey'   דבש (קצת) לי תביא

An exceptional use of כמה *káma* with a *singular* noun is כמה זמן *káma zman* 'some
time': לפני כמה זמן *lifney káma zman* 'some time ago'.

9. As אם *im* also means 'if' (= 'in the event that'), ambiguity may arise:

    todía li im taazov   תעזוב אם לי תודיע
                                                 'Tell me whether you're leaving'
                                                 or:
                                                 'Tell me in the event that you leave'

10. This is akin to ...ש העובדה *ha-uvda she...* 'the fact that...'

11. The same distinction exists in non-question infinitives (see 28.9). Following most verbs, the infinitive denotes an 'action' by the *subject* of the verb (i.e. by the subject of the main clause), but with some verbs of request, it relates automatically to their *object*:

ציוויתי לעצור, אז עצרו

tsivíti laatsor, az atsru

I-ordered to-stop, so they-stopped

'I ordered ⟨them⟩ to stop, so they did'

12. Truncation deletes what *follows* 'wh-' words; thus prepositions preceding them are not deleted. Compare Hebrew with English:

רבנו עם מישהו, אך

rávnu im míshehu, aH enéni

אינני יודע **עם** מי

yodéa **im** mi

we-quarrelled with someone, but I-don't

know **with** who

'We quarrelled with someone, but I don't know who (we quarrelled with)'

13. Certain other pronouns are used strictly in negatives, e.g. אף אחד *af eHad* 'no one, anyone' (see 29.11).

Chapter 27

1. The noun may be singular or plural, mass or countable.

2. מה *ma* is a literary alternative to כמה *káma*.

3. That these are indeed simple 'question-shaped' clauses, not 'noun + relative clause', emerges from a comparison with actual 'relative clause' exclamations in 27.3; there the 'question word' איזה *éze* 'what' is impossible, significantly (see note 6).

4. Instead one can employ the negative (see 27.3):

איפה היא לא היתה!

éfo hi lo hayta!

where she not has-been!

5. They cannot be cut back to a single word:

*eze!   ('what!')   *איזה!   *káma!   ('how!')   *כמה!

6. This construction is not a form of question clause but a headless relative clause, for איזה *éze* + noun as in the example below is impossible, just as one allows 'the man who..., the place where...' but not '*the man which man...'. See a similar 'concessive conditional' construction in 33.4.2.

*איזה תירוצים שהוא לא ממציא!

*éze terutsim she-hu lo mamtsi!

*what excuses that he not invents!

('What excuses he only invents!')

Chapter 28

1. Note that the imperative form is just one of several ways of conveying a command. For the shape of verb forms, see chapter 40.

2. The present tense can occasionally convey a sharp request, in any person; see 28.8.

3. Formal styles of request, in all persons, may add the particle נא *na* 'please' to soften the request. It follows the verb, optionally with a hyphen; but in the negative it directly follows אל *al*:

אל נא תטעו

al na tit'u

not please you-will-err

'Please do not err'

4. The terms 'past, present, future' used of tense are a considerable oversimplification anyway; see chapter 13.

5. In the feminine and plural, such 'prefix omission' commonly yields סגרי, סגרו *sgeri, sgeru* 'Close' and the like, rather than the normative imperative forms סגרי, סגרו *sigri, sigru*. Similarly, with the ('spirantizing') ב, כ, פ letters, one commonly finds, e.g. תשפוך ← שפוך *tishpoH → shpoH* 'Pour out' rather than normative שפוך *shfoH*. A further indication that casual Hebrew is 'shortening' its future tense form rather than simply using the traditional imperative form is the common use of half-shortened forms such as תלמד *tlamed* 'Teach'.

6. The reason may be that the 'please' word preceding an infinitive is a different construction, like a verb+infinitive meaning 'I ask you to stand up' etc.

7. A further, occasional use of the infinitive in all persons, in formal usage, is the negator אל *al* + ...ל *le*... + infinitive:

al	leHa le-morim	lismoH al nisim		אל לך למורים לסמוך על נסים
not	for-you for teachers	to-rely on miracles	‹ Do not Let teachers not	rely on miracles'

8. With the infinitive they are impossible:

leharim ata et ha-sfarim *להרים אתה את הספרים

to-pick-up you OM the books ('Pick up the books')

9. If the understood subject is 'you' coordinated with another noun, 'you' must be mentioned overtly:

tavóu ata ve-dov תבואו אתה ודב

come you and Dov 'You and Dov come'

10. Alternatively, there are such paraphrases as ...הוא צריך ל *hu tsariH le*... 'He must...'

11. 'Future time' sometimes borders on a request:

neleH ve-day 'We'll go and that's it' נלך ודי

12. Infinitives in *non*-questions convey a remote request by the speaker (28.4): לענות *laanot* 'Answer'. But as a questioner (in unmarked situations) would ask about *another's* request, ?לענות *laanot*? naturally means 'Do *you* request that I answer?'

13. Further, the 'governing' verb itself need not have a stated object; the object can be deduced from context:

amárti lo lekashkesh I-said not to-scribble אמרתי לא לקשקש

(= that you/they/one shouldn't scribble)

With a few verbs, too, the infinitive can be understood either as a request or as an *attempt* on one's own behalf:

hitsáti bikáshti	lisrog		הצעתי ביקשתי לסרוג

as a request : 'I suggested 'I asked (to you/people) to knit'

as a non-request : 'I suggested 'I tried knitting (myself)'

Chapter 29

1. The gerund (30.5), in many ways more verbal than nominal, cannot however be negated. The negator לא *lo* is basically pre-verbal, and no pre-verbal elements are found with gerunds:

*al-af **lo** sayemam kurs ze... ...על-אף **לא** סיימם קורס זה*

despite **not** finishing-their course this... 'Despite their **not** finishing this course...'

2. This is not a hard and fast distinction. It may sometimes simply serve to create variety:

hi **ena** zkuka li-ksamim, hi **lo** zkuka
le-rakdaniyot mefazezot, ve-hi
enéna tsriHa tafura

היא **אינה** זקוקה לקסמים, היא **לא** זקוקה
לרקדניות מפזזות, והיא
איננה צריכה תפאורה

'She does **not** need charms, she does **not** need prancing dancers,
and she does **not** require decor'

3. But the particles for present tense 'be' (הוא *hu*, זה *ze* etc; ch.16) do not count as verbs, so the negator directly precedes the noun, adjective etc. that *follow* them:

gad hu lo ga'on

גד הוא לא גאון

'Gad is not ⟨a⟩ genius'

ha-meltaHa ze lo po?

המלתחה זה לא פה?

'The cloakroom is not over here?'

4. There is some parallel between לא *lo and* כן *ken* 'yes': the latter doubles, casually, as a pre-verbal positive particle of affirmation, as in (1) below. But, unlike לא *lo*, it is only a 'sentence-operator', not a 'constituent-operator' (2):

(1)   hu *ken* mevashel   'He *does* cook'   הוא כן מבשל

(2)   *ken *Dan* mevashel   ('*Dan* cooks')   *כן דן מבשל

5. Casual usage prefers simple לא *lo*, or a combination of a 'be' particle (e.g. הוא *hu*) plus לא *lo*:

dov hu lo av   'Dov is not ⟨a⟩ father'   דב הוא לא אב

6. Formal Hebrew also has a positive particle הנה *hine*, almost the exact counterpart of this אין *en*. It means 'be' or simply precedes the verb as a 'dummy verb' (with no emphasis). Like אין *en* it inflects; but it cannot precede the subject:

dov hino   maskim   דב הנו מסכים
Dov DUMMY v agrees

7. These constraints are so severe that inflected אין *en* cannot be placed ahead of its subject, even by virtue of the ordinary process of subject-verb inversion (cf. ch.37):

*be-áko eno yored shéleg   *בעכו אינו יורד שלג
in Ako not + SUFF falls snow   ('In Acre snow does not fall')

8. By contrast, אין *en* is normal within an unstated impersonal 'they' (ch.17):

yodim o en yodim?   יודעים או אין יודעים?
m.pl.   m.pl.
know or not know?   'Do they or don't they know?'

9. In this respect אין *en* behaves not like a verb but like 'be' particles (see example (1) below) by contrast with verbs (2). Even לא *lo* 'not' and כן *ken* (affirmative particle) do not need anything following them in casual usage:

(1) *...aH ha-aronot hem   *...אך הארונות **הם**
                                          ('...but the cupboards are')

(2) ...aH ha-aronot lo hayu   ...אך הארונות לא היו
                                          '...but the cupboards were not'

10. For more indications that אין *en* in this role is transitive and has no subject, see 15.2.

11. Its counterpart יש *yesh* 'there is/are' can inflect, however; see 16.9.

12. The 3rd singular forms אינו *eno* and אינה *ena* are possible only where אין *en* means 'not, is not' (29.6).

13. Like most determiners (see 9.5.), these all *need* a noun or some other word to modify, ruling out:

*Hipásnu et, aH lo matsánu af   *חיפשנו עט, אך לא מצאנו אף
(✓ lo matsánu)   (✓ ...לא מצאנו)
we-looked-for pen but not we-found a-single
(✓ not we-found)

14. אף *af* can co-occur with אחד *eHad* 'one':

en af méteg eHad   אין אף מתג אחד

there-isn't any switch one   'There isn't one single switch'

שום *shum* always means 'not at all', rather than 'not a single':

en li shum isha   אין לי שום אשה

'I haven't a wife at all'

(*not*: 'I haven't a single wife')

15. With 'concrete' mass nouns, e.g. חלב *Halav* 'milk', Hebrew tends to use no word at all for 'any' (just as, in the positive, 'some milk' is usually just חלב *Halav*).

16. Specifically feminine 'no one' is אף אחת *af aHat*. The word also serves to refer to nouns already mentioned, i.e. 'none':

hayu Halukim, aval **af eHad** lo hitim   היו חלוקים, אבל **אף אחד** לא התאים

'There were bathrobes, but **not one** fitted'

17. איש *ish*, besides meaning 'person, man', also means 'anyone' in questions and conditionals:

im tesaper le-ish...   'If you tell anyone...'   ...אם תספר לאיש

18. There is also a formal expression ולא כלום *velo Hlum*, only following the verb directly:

lo kara **velo Hlum**   '**Nothing** happened'   לא קרה **ולא כלום**

19. דבר *davar*, besides meaning 'thing' ('something' is generally משהו *máshehu*), also means 'anything' in questions and conditionals (cf. note 17).

20. *af páam* comprises אף + פעם *af* + *páam* 'no + time'.

21. לעולם *leolam* also means 'forever' in formal usage. לתמיד *le-tamid* or לנצח *la-nétsaH* are commoner terms for 'forever'.

22. The 'negative words' are not, it seems, a case of intrinsically negative items co-occurring with a negator as 'double negation', for (a) the negator never drops in full sentences, unlike French; (b) even the one clear case of double negation, 'strings of 'nots''' (29.8), is impossible where the 'neither..nor' comes first; (c) some (elevated) 'negative words' do not stand free.

23. The complex negators all amount to 'have/be/must not' or 'so that not'.

24. The range of indefinite שהו- *-shehu* words (משהו *máshehu* 'something', כלשהו *kólshehu* 'some... or other' etc.), though they can have a 'non-specific' sense ('anything, any' etc.) under negation and quasi-negation, are not negated backwards. Nor can they be stressed when 'non-specific'.

25. By contrast, עוד לא *od lo* means 'still not', not 'not again' as in:

lo shaalu od   'They did not ask again'   לא שאלו עוד

26. Negators do not reach into adverbial clauses, but can 'scope' them - with the notable exception of those introduced by כי *ki* 'because' and כך ש- *kaH she-* 'with the result that'.

Chapter 30

1. Complementizers sister a whole clause ^{S}[COMP S[NP VP]] which is thereby open to coordination.

They are not themselves head nouns, denoting 'the notion that, the fact that...', for they are used with relative clauses.

For coordination, either the whole ש- *she-* (or other complementizer) plus clause, or just the clause, can be repeated. (Prepositions are usually inseparable from their ש- *she-*, thus ruling out: ...*לפני או אחרי ש* **lifney o aHarey she...* 'before or after...'; ש- *she-* must be repeated with each preposition.)

2. Finite and other subordinate clauses and phrases in this chapter are not (with the exception of 'action/state' phrases) functionally noun phrases - their ultimate node is S. Thus, for example, they do not undergo 'pied-piping' (as defined in Ross 1967) *en bloc*.

3. Participle phrases are surface VP, embracing the negator לא *lo* but not the 'copular' negative אינו *eno*, nor preposed matter (this being 'daughter of S') except when this is preposed into the matrix S. (The same holds for infinitives - see 30.4.) Thus:

tafásti oto lo makshiv	תפסתי אותו לא מקשיב
I-caught him not listening	'I caught him not listening'

and not:

*tafásti oto alay medaber	*תפסתי אותו עלי מדבר
I-caught him about-me speaking	('I caught him speaking about me')

4. A quite unrelated structure is שמע ש... *shama she...* 'he heard that...', מצא ש... *matsa she...* 'he found that...'

5. With התחיל, החל *hitHil, heHel* 'begin', the participle implies 'deliberate action', i.e. does not allow 'raising' (rather as with 'adverbial verbs' like היטיב *hetiv* 'do well' - see 21.2.4); thus ruling out:

*yisrael hitHíla nitpeset ke...	*ישראל התחילה נתפסת כ....
(✓ lihitapes ke...)	(✓ להיתפס כ...)
Israel began being-regarded as...	
(✓ to-be-regarded as...)	

6. Like finite and infinitival object clauses, participle phrases can undergo 'extraction', of an interrogative word for example, to the front of the sentence:

ma tafast otam osim?	**מה** תפסת אותם עושים?
	'**What** did you catch them doing?'

Another difference from circumstantials is that these can even involve adjectives or nouns, whereas object participles must be verbs, and specifically 'dynamic' verbs; 'statal' verbs such as נמצא *nimtsa* 'be', ידע *yada* 'know' are excluded. Thus:

Object participle phrase

ra'iti oto **omed** al ha-sulam	ראיתי אותו **עומד** על הסולם
	'I saw him **standing** on the ladder'

Circumstantial participle phrase

zéhu, hi amra, **yodáat** she-ani...	זהו, היא אמרה, **יודעת** שאני...
	'That's it, she said, **knowing** that I...'

7. An outwardly similar verb form, the gerund, has no such fixed prefix and very different functions; see 30.5.

8. Infinitive phrases are 'surface VP' for the same reason as participle phrases (note 3).

9. Formal Hebrew occasionally adds a meaningless -ש *she-*, apparently identical with the conjunction -ש *she-*, in front of a negated infinitive. This is possible even following verbs for which -ש *she-* plus finite clause is ordinarily inappropriate:

yaHólnu (she-)lo leheanot	יכולנו (ש)לא להיענות
	'We were able not to respond'

10. Neutral word order can be changed without affecting the underlying rule:

levater ani lo muHan	לוותר אני לא מוכן
	'To give up I'm not willing'

11. Intention that *someone else* do something is mostly expressed by a finite clause; but some verbs, e.g אמר *amar* 'tell', אסר *asar* 'forbid', do it via the infinitive too.

12. Aspectual and modal infinitives can be regarded 'underlyingly' as subject clauses whose subject has been 'raised'; see 31.3

13. The prepositions ('object markers'), save ‎-מ‎ *mi-*, are omitted - except very casually:

הוא עסוק **בלאכול**

hu asuk **be-leeHol**

'He's busy **with** eating'

14. A slightly different form, the 'absolute infinitive', is limited to a few idioms involving adverbials and not subordination; see 21, note 9.

15. The second root consonant is 'soft'. In the infinitive, it is hard: ‎לכבוש‎ *liHbosh*, ‎לספור‎ *lispor* (vs. ‎כבוש‎ *kvosh*, ‎ספור‎ *sfor*).

Pa'al verbs with a weak first consonant tend to adopt the regular gerund shape, as against their irregular infinitive, when suffixed:

yashav	‎ישב‎ :	lashévet ~ be-yoshvo	לשבת ~ בישבו
natan	‎נתן‎ :	latet ~ be-notno	לתת ~ בנותנו
but yatsa	‎יצא‎ :	latset ~ be-tseto	לצאת ~ בצאתו

Huf'al and *pu'al* patterns have neither infinitive nor gerund. Instead we find ‎להיות/בהיות מפונה‎ *liyot/bi-yot mefune* 'to be evacuated, on being evacuated', with an auxiliary verb ‎היה‎ *haya* 'be'.

16. Finite verbs need *no* subject in the impersonal 3rd-person plural; but gerunds (and action nouns) have no such option. Note, however, the idiomatic ‎ב... בהתחשב‎ *be-hitHashev be...* 'taking...into consideration'.

17. The reason is that the whole 'clause' functions externally rather like a noun phrase, which generally has the order nucleus + modifier. See action/state phrases (30.6) too.

18. Action nouns, by contrast, do put their negator first:

i-hadgasha   '**non**-emphasis'   אי-הדגשה

19. Though gerunds thus seem to be dominated by NP, they are like finite S (and unlike action NP) in not becoming pronominalized as pro-nouns:

*לפני התרסק המטוס וגם לאחריו (√לאחר מכן)

*lifney hitrasek ha-matos ve-gam leaHarav (√leaHar mi-Ken)

                    PRO-N   PRO-S

                    'Before the crashing of the plane and even after **it**

                                        (√afterwards)'

Gerunds are not inherently factive, e.g. ‎לשם היבחרו‎ *leshem hibaHaro* 'in order to be elected'.

20. Three signs of true action nouns are: an ‎על-ידי...‎ *al-yedey* 'by...' phrase, an ‎את‎ *et* 'accusative marker' phrase (if directly transitive), ‎אי-‎ *i* 'non-' (the latter also with state nouns).

21. By contrast, in *clauses* the adverb may precede its verb:

etmol gila ha-ikar...   ...אתמול גילה האיכר

                    'Yesterday the peasant discovered...'

22. Unlike genitives with ordinary nouns, these genitives can be shifted away from the nucleus, just as subjects or objects can move away from their verb:

ha-zrima el ha-miflaga shel hamoney olim   הזרימה אל מהפלגה של המוני עולים

NUCLEUS N   'SUBJ' GENITIVE

                    'the inflow to the party of masses ⟨of⟩ immigrants'

23. Nor with 'static' action nouns, e.g. ‎רצון‎ *ratson* 'wish'.

24. The 'object' cannot also be in construct relationship once the action noun + 'subject' have already created a construct phrase. Nor is ‎של‎ *shel* 'of' possible. This is a general constraint on 'possessive' genitives (see 6.8).

Construction (6) with ‎את‎ *et* is an occasional formal usage. Note also the occasional use of ‎את‎ *et* with no 'subject' after such nouns as ‎ידיעה, תפיסה‎ *yedi'a, tfisa* 'knowledge of, conception of':

mitoH yedi'a yesodit et ha-naase sham...　　　　　...מתוך ידיעה יסודית את הנעשה שם

from knowledge thorough OM

the goings-on there　　　　　　　　　'...a thorough knowledge of...'

25. Degree and manner adverbs are structurally intimate to the verb; the 'outer' adverbials are possible with verbs *and* nouns, as in example (1). Action/state nouns also allow a (formal) 'echo manner phrase' ('internal object' - see 21.4.2).

haHsharat　　ha-karka haHshara yesodit　　　　הכשרת הקרקע הכשרה יסודית

CONSTRUCT N　　　　　ECHO PHR

preparation the ground preparation thorough

'thorough preparation of the ground'

26. Examples (1,2) have a parallel using ...ש זה *ze she...* 'it that..., the fact that...' (see 7.7.3).

Chapter 31

1. Participial clauses are·only occasionally encountered.

2. Subjunctives (also called 'modals') are dealt with fully as part of the system of 'requests' and 'commands' in chapter 28. For interrogatives, see chapter 26.

3. This is because זה *ze* is altogether a less 'specific' pronoun - thus it is less common as a relative pronoun too: הוא *hu* etc. is generally preferred (cf. 33.3). זה *ze*, and not הוא *hu*, also acts as a 'boundary marker' marking the end of subject clauses; see 31.5.

4. But none of these are possible unless the verb can take a noun phrase anyway, thus these 'pro-sentences' themselves behave like nouns; so there is *no* 'pro-form' for referring back to object clauses like those illustrated at the start of this subsection (except occasionally preposed כך *kaH* - see 7.5):

kaH　　　　　　　　　　　　　　　　　　　　כך

natáti lo　et ze　　　　('I allowed him this')　　נתתי לו　את זה

zot·　　　　　　　　　　　　　　　　　　[הרשיתי =] זאת

5. Complement clauses undergo focus, negation and other sentence processes:

margiz oti **gam** she-hu lo yodéa　　　　מרגיז אותי **גם** שהוא לא יודע

lehistarek　　　　　　　　　　　　　　　　להסתרק

annoys me **also** that he doesn't know

to-comb-his-hair

6. This is provided the pronoun is not *subject* of this clause.

7. Factive verbs in general, e.g. הצטער *hitsta'er* 'regret', prevent extraction, but this is no proof that 'underlying' ש - זה *ze she-* 'it that' is at the head of their object clause. For ש - זה *ze she-* also denotes 'the *notion* that...', as in הציע (את זה) שתבוא *hitsía (et ze) she-tavo* 'suggest that you come', and yet ...הציע ש *hitsía she...* 'suggest that...' does not prevent extraction.

8. This use of כך *kaH* (which is also a manner adverb: 'like this') is akin to the use of כפי ש-, כמו ש- *kfi she-, kmo she* 'as...' clauses, which are themselves also manner clauses (32.5), except that 'as' clauses imply a fact:

efshar leaHer, kfi she-amart　　　　　　אפשר לאחר, כפי שאמרת

'One can be late, as you said'

9. The whole structure is traditionally called an 'extended predicator'; a current technical term is 'subject raising'.

10. Subject-less ...צריך ל *tsariH le...* 'it is necessary to...' is not 'raised'.

11. Exceptions: verbs of 'beginning' and נשאר *nish'ar* 'remain' also allow a participle clause, and verbs of 'repetition' and 'continuation' also allow a (pseudo) coordinated clause using ו - *ve-* 'and':

hitHálti tsoHéket　　　　　　　　　　　התחלתי צוחקת

I-began laughing

bi-zmano, hu mosif u-mesaper,   בזמנו, הוא מוסיף ומספר,
  haya shalom   היה שלום
in his-time, he continues and relates [= to relate],
  there-was peace.

12. This does not extend, however, to other 'adverbial' verbs such as מיהר *miher* 'be quick' and היטיב *hetiv* '...well'. See further 21.2.4. This analysis also explains the use of 'raising' verbs with *subject-less* structures such as:

haya li kar   היה לי קר
was to-me cold   'I was cold'

haya et kol ze   היה את כל זה
was OM all this   'There was all this'

After 'raising':

matHil liyot li kar   מתחיל להיות לי קר
starts to-be to-me cold   'I'm starting to be cold'

alul liyot et kol ze sham   עלול להיות את כל זה שם
likely to-be OM all this there   'There's likely to be all this there'

13. A few such verbs evidently also take a *true* object clause, witness the permissibility of a pro-sentence: התחיל בכך *hitHil be-HaH* 'begin it', הרבה בכך *hirba be-HaH* 'do a lot of it'. צריך *tsariH* is more complicated: meaning 'I need to...', it allows a pro-sentence (אני צריך את זה *ani tsariH et ze*), but not meaning 'I'm bound to'.

14. The action noun is thus formed with reference to 'abstract structure'.

15. היה *haya*, too, never omits its participle in this role.

16. Subject (unlike object) clauses cannot be participial, as the object participial clause (see 30.3) cannot be made into the subject by passivization.

17. Hebrew is here finding perceptual difficulty in having a clause that itself begins with a subordinate clause - except where the subordinate clause is detached from the main body of the clause by intonation or pause (as in adverbial clauses). Indeed, a declarative finite subject clause can come first *only* if it is factive or modal (as in 31.4.1), hence:

yitaHen **she-hu yire**   יתכן **שהוא יראה**
      SUBJ CLAUSE   '⟨It⟩ is possible **that he will see**'

but not:

*she-hu yire yitaHen   *שהוא יראה יתכן
      ('That he will see is possible')

Other examples are נדמה לי ש... *nidme li she...* 'it seems to me that...' and עלול לקרות ש... *alul likrot she...* 'it is liable to happen that...'.

  Moreover, 'extraction' (see 31.1.2) is also impossible for 'subject clauses'.

18. In 'surface' terms, this subject clause fills the 'object' clause slot: once 'postposed', the subject clause cannot co-occur with a 'real' object clause - thus the sentence:

she-hu noshem moHíaH she-hu Hay   שהוא נושם מוכיח שהוא חי
      'That he is breathing proves that he is alive'

cannot be transformed to:

*(ze) moHíaH she-hu Hay she-hu noshem   *(זה) מוכיח שהוא חי שהוא נושם
      ('(it) proves that he is alive that he is breathing')

זה *ze* blocks 'extraction'. Given that extraction from subject clauses is also blocked (see n.17), it may be that זה *ze* is felt to be a nucleus of a subject clause.

*ma ze naHuts she-eese?   *מה זה נחוץ שאעשה?
what it necessary that I'll-do?   ('What is it necessary that I do?')

זה *ze* is dubious with passive הוחלט ל... *huHlat le...* 'was decided to...', נאמר ש...

neemar she... 'was said that...' etc., as the complement clause is apparently *object* (see 14.8). Some predicates are averse to זה *ze*, suggesting that they too are taking object rather than subject clauses, e.g. (possibly a semantic class) ...נכון ש.../ל *naHon she...* / *le...* 'correct that.../to...', מותר *mutar* 'permissible', אסור *asur* 'forbidden'.

19. Unlike copular זה *ze* 'is' (see ch.16), this is also used with a verb.

20. The clause cannot begin with זה ש... *ze she...*, even when factive. Unlike specificational *nouns*, these clauses cannot be preposed, even using זה *ze* as copula rather than הוא *hu*:

*she-hu *yafe* zo ha-baaya   שהוא יפה זו הבעיה*

('that he's *handsome* is the problem')

21. Firstly, unlike predicate clauses, these subordinate clauses cannot generally be introduced by a copula (...סימן הוא ש *siman hu she...* 'a sign is that...'), nor by היה *haya* 'was' etc. in the past tense. Second, מזל *mazal* 'luck' can casually take זה *ze*: ...ש זה (היה) מזל *ze (haya) mazal she...* 'it (was) lucky that...', just as happens with many subject clauses (31.5). Third, זכותי, זכותך *zHuti, zHutHa* 'my right, your right' etc. can casually stand alone, as a complete sentence, like אפשר *efshar* 'it is possible', חבל *Haval* 'it's a pity':

im at lo merutsa, zHuteH   אם את לא מרוצה, זכותך

if you not satisfied, your-right

[= it's your right]

So its complement clause is arguably an object rather than a subject clause.

Chapter 32

1. Strictly speaking, where the adverbial involves a preposition or conjunction introducing a clause, as in the two examples following, the clause is just one part of the adverbial. We shall, however, refer to the whole adverbial as an 'adverbial, adjunct or disjunct clause'.

2. Like adjuncts in general, many of these clauses can be left *outside* the 'scope' of such focusing - sometimes with markedly different meaning:

hu lo make ba, biglal she-hu ohev ota   הוא לא מכה בה, בגלל שהוא אוהב אותה

'He doesn't hit her, because he loves her'

lo dibru aHarey she-yatsáti   לא דיברו אחרי שיצאתי

'They didn't talk [i.e. they were silent] after I left'

When set off by comma or pause, or ordinarily when preceding the main clause, such adjuncts will clearly be outside the scope of negation etc. However, when manner and time clauses complement a verb of manner or time, they constitute a 'tight' (rather than a 'loose') adjunct, akin to an object (cf. 21.4, 21.7):

al titnaheg kmo she-kulam mitnahagim   אל תתנהג כמו שכולם מתנהגים

'Don't behave like they're all behaving'

3. Instead, one might employ the adjunct ...לא משום... אלא משום *lo mishum...éla mishum...* 'not because...but because...'.

4. Traditionally מאז ש- *me'az she-* 'since', במקום ש- *bimkom she-* 'instead of' and the like are classed as 'subordinating conjunctions', despite the substantial use of the same 'prepositions' for introducing both nouns *and* clauses, and despite certain specific properties of these so-called 'subordinating conjunctions':

(a) Many prepositions take either a clause or a noun phrase, e.g. בשביל *bishvil* 'for', בגלל *biglal* 'because', על-אף *al-af* 'despite'; many take just the latter, e.g. עבור *avur* 'for', עקב *ékev* 'as a result of', חרף *Héref* 'despite'; a few take just the former, e.g. על-מנת *al-menat* 'in order to', היות *heyot* 'because', הגם *hagam* 'although'. There is no overall semantic reason; see chapter 19.

(b) Although one cannot shift the clause away from its preposition, as is possible with verb + clause, it appears that following most prepositions (and verbs) the conjunction -שׁ *she-* is treated as a separate word. So in coordination one can optionally have a repeated -שׁ *she-*:

ad **she**-yiye HósheH ve-**she**-kulam yishnu	עד **שׁ**יהיה חושך ו**שׁ**כולם יישנו
till **that** will-be dark and **that** everyone will-sleep	'till it's dark and everyone's asleep'

But words meaning 'because' and אף כי ,-שׁ אף *af she-*, *af ki* 'although' treat their conjunction as inseparable:

mishum she-yiye HósheH ve-	משׁום שׁיהיה חושך
(mishum she-) kulam yishnu	ו (משׁום שׁ) כולם יישנו
because that it'll-be dark and (*optional*: because that) everyone will-be-asleep	

5. Although, on the surface, infinitive 'clauses' are just verb phrases with no subject, both infinitive and finite clauses are best held to belong to a sentence node - see 30.4 for reasons. Gerund clauses too (found in formal usage) can be regarded as adverbial clauses in function; however, by internal structure they are like noun phrases and are only found with prepositions that can take a noun. Since they are a subordinate clause-type all of their own, gerunds are described in 30.5. An example:

be- hilakaH mehem rabam,...	בהילקח מהם רבם,...
PREP GERUND	
with being-taken from-them their rabbi,...	'When their rabbi was taken from them,...'

6. This is strictly a 'sentence pronoun' ('pro-clause'). See 7.5.

7. Exception: כיוון שׁכך *keyvan she-kaH* 'because of that' retains the conjunction -שׁ *she-*.

8. Unstressed אם כן *im ken* means 'in that case' or 'thus'. The same structures occur in object clauses and very casually in relative clauses and main clauses:

mi amar she-lo?	מי אמר שׁלא?
who said that not?	'Who said to the contrary?'

rubam lo yodim, éle **she-ken**, shotkim	רובם לא יודעים. אלה **שׁכן**, שׁותקים
	'Most don't know. Those **that do**, keep quiet'

at lo báa? - ani ken!	את לא באה? - אני כן!
	'You aren't coming? - I **am**!'

9. Apposition reduction behaves similarly (cf. ch. 36):

shaálti aHadim, lo et kulam	שׁאלתי אחדים, לא את כולם
	'I asked some, not all'

10. By 'preposition' we also mean words introducing a clause rather than a noun, e.g. -כשׁ *kshe-*, -עת שׁ *et she-*, -איך שׁ *eH she-*. These are arguably one-word items, i.e. conjunctions of time in their own right rather than preposition + conjunction, as their -שׁ *she-* does not act independently in any sense.

11. כל עוד ,-כל זמן שׁ *kol zman she-*, *kol od* 'as long as' are a blend of time and conditional (32.11): 'if and for as long as it continues to be the case':

kol od (tiye) kayémet ha-shita ha-zot, ze yimasheH	כל עוד (תהיה) קיימת השׁיטה הזאת, זה יימשׁך
	'As long as this system exists, it'll go on'

12. This is distinct from -ו *ve-* meaning 'and' or the -ו *ve-* equivalent to a restrictive or non-restrictive 'who/which' (see 33.5). It is immune to the 'coordinate structure constraint' of Ross (1967).

13. Even a double constituent with 'gapping' is possible (as in: כמו אתה לחבריך *kmo ata le-HavereHa* like you to your-friends), clear evidence of a reduction.

By contrast, comparative -מ *mi-* 'than' phrases (see 20.4) such as מנסה יותר ממך *menase yoter **mimeH*** 'tries more **than you**' are underlyingly both clause and phrase.

14. -ש *she-* here is casual.

כאילו *ke'ilu* 'as if' can usefully be understood as its component parts: -כ *ke-* 'like' + אילו *ilu* 'if', e.g. 'He's acting like ⟨he would act⟩ if he had lice in his hair'. But it is in most respects a *frozen expression*: regular אילו *ilu* 'if' (a) does not take -ש *she-* whereas כאילו *ke'ilu* can, just like a preposition; (b) requires hypothetical (past) tense, whereas כאילו *ke'ilu* takes 'real-world' tense (see 13.12.3). Further, (c) -כ *ke-* does not combine with other hypothetical 'if' words, nor can כמו *kmo* 'like' be used instead of -כ *ke-*.

כמו *kmo* can itself mean 'as if' in literary usage, without -ש *she-*, i.e. as a conjunction itself. (See note 18 for another כמו *kmo*.)

15. For simple result: ...כך ש... *...kaH she...* '...so that...':

hayíti sham kol ha-káyits, kaH (*be-ófen)	הייתי שם כל הקייץ, כך (*באופן)
she-higáti le-shney ha-knasim	שהגעתי לשני הכנסים
	'I was there all the summer, so (*in such a way) that I got to both congresses'

16. This can express 'sardonic equivalence':

yesh leHa tóar dóktor kmo she-yesh li rishyon tisa!	יש לך תואר דוקטור כמו שיש לי רשיון טיסה!
	'You have a doctoral degree like I have a flying licence!'

כמו *kmo* clauses and phrases are also used as complements of the determiner אותו *oto* 'same' (see 9.6):

li yesh oto et kmo she-yesh leHa	לי יש אותו עט כמו שיש לך
I have same pen as that have you	'I have the same pen as you have'

17. Formal and casual usage also employ כמו *kmo* and -כאילו ש *ke'ilu she-* respectively. This construction also expresses sarcasm, even with no main clause, as in example (2):

(1) hu yoshev kadíma (ke'ilu hu meunyan!)	הוא יושב קדימה, (כאילו הוא מעוניין!)
	'He's sitting up front (as if he were (*lit.* is) interested!)'

(2) ke'ilu iHpat li	'As if I cared (*lit.* care)!' כאילו איכפת לי!

18. כאילו, כמו *ke'ilu, kmo* also act as disjunct adverbs (like כביכול *kivyaHol* 'as it were'), cf. 23.2; כמו *kmo* directly precedes the verb phrase:

yatsárti et ha-pésel yesh me-áyin, **ke'ílu**	יצרתי את הפסל יש מאין, **כאילו**
	'I created the statue *ex nihilo*, **as it were**'

ba-maHatsit ha-shniya **kmo** nirata	במחצית השנייה **כמו** נראתה
ba-migrash rak kvutsa aHat	במגרש רק קבוצה אחת
	'In the second half we saw **as it were** (*lit.* as it were was seen) only one team on the field'

19. ככל *keHol* is also used as a 'pronoun' of degree in '-ever' clauses (cf. 32.11). כמה *káma* too is a pronoun (cf. ch.25).

20. In fact, in כפי שעולה *kefi she-ole* 'as emerges', the equivalence is being stated in reverse *vis-à-vis* כך עולה *kaH ole* 'emerges like this'.

21. Although ידע *yada* 'know' does not allow כך ידעת* **kaH yadáta* ('thus you knew'), it does allow כמו שידעת *kmo she-yadáta* 'as you knew'.

22. כפי *kefi* similarly alternates with -מה ש *ma she-* and אשר *asher*, both of them pronouns and complementizers, in introducing comparative clauses:

hu lomed yoter mi-kfi she-Hashávti   הוא לומד יותר מכפי שחשבתי

he studies more than like (*or perhaps*:
'what') that I-thought

23. The only other adverbial clauses with infinitives or 'modal' tense are 'instead' and 'without' clauses, i.e. quasi-negative adverbials (32.13).

24. לבל *leval* is intrinsically negative: it does not allow לא *lo* 'not'. It strictly denotes 'in order that...not'.

25. For שמא *shéma* as a conjunction in פחד שמא *paHad shéma...* 'be afraid in case...', see 30.2.

26. Where the motion verb has no motion adverb (רצתי לקנות פיצה *rátsti liknot pítsa* 'I ran to buy a pizza'), the infinitive is an object clause, not an adverbial, witness 'extraction':

ma ratst liknot?   מה רצת לקנות?

'What did you run to buy?'

27. כך *kaH* is also the manner pro-adverb 'thus, so'. By contrast, clauses like the following are handled in 20.5 as complements of the degree words כל-כך *kol-kaH* or כה *ko* 'so':

haya kol-kaH muzar she-lo yashánti   היה כל-כך מוזר שלא ישנתי

'It was so weird that I didn't sleep'

28. These are adjunct clauses - the negation or question reaches into the result clause (challenging the *causality* and not necessarily the *fact*, cf. the second example).

29. Both this and type (2) clauses defy coordination, i.e. only one is used per sentence, as an 'umbrella' structure: ...וכי... ...כי...* *...ki ...ve-ki...* '...because ...and because...', ...לא כי... אלא כי...** *...lo ki ...éla ki...* 'not because... but because...'

A further, literary, cause construction (semi-subordinate) is illustrated by:

Hashávti ki od me'at taazov et ha-Héder,   חשבתי כי עוד מעט תעזוב את החדר,

kol-kaH hayu panéha mabi'ot tsáar u-He'ev   **כל-כך היו פניה מביעות צער וכאב**

'I thought that soon she would leave the room, **so much did her face express her anguish and pain**'

30. אם *im* 'if' can interchange with -כש *kshe-* 'when' (or its synonyms) when the meaning is, e.g. 'if on some particular occasion it's raining in London':

im/kshe-yored géshem be-lóndon, rov   {אם/כש} יורד גשם בלונדון, רוב

ha-anashim nos'im mitriya   האנשים נושאים מטריה

'If it rains in London, most people carry umbrellas'

אם *im* (which is also the interrogative complementizer 'whether') and the hypothetical 'if' words rarely take the complementizer -ש *she-*.

31. It is not found in hypotheticals.

32. The 'whether' words can be omitted: ...,מליונר או אסיר *milyoner o asir,...* 'Millionaire or prisoner,...'.

33. They differ in that the first allows a double clause: ...ולמרות ש ...למרות ש *lamrot she... ve-lamrot she...*, whereas the second, being illocutionary, allows only one כי אם *im ki* 'although' per sentence (as with the illocutionary 'because' word כי *ki* in note 29). Further, the second type can be contracted to a phrase; see 32.2.2.

34. אפילו אם *afílu im* denotes 'even *if*'; see 32.11.4.

35. בלא *belo* too denotes 'without'; it only takes *finite* clauses.

Chapter 33

1. Similarly, where there is both an object noun and an object clause, the latter follows. Existential nouns with a numeral can sometimes be detached from their relative clause:

shney gormim yesh she...
שני גורמים יש ש...

two factors there-are that...
'There are two factors that...'

2. Substandard Hebrew can also use - ש מה *ma she-* as a conjunction; despite apparently being related to inanimate מה *ma* 'what?' and to the construction מה ש... *ma she-...* 'that which, whatever...' (see 33.4.3), it occurs with both inanimate and animate antecedents:

ve-ézra ha-zaken, **ma she-ohev** et ha-ben
shelo, shotek
ועזרא הזקן, **מה שאוהב** את
הבן שלו, שותק

'And old Ezra, **who loves** his son, keeps quiet'

kol láyla mistovev sham ha-shed **ma
she-yesh lo** shalosh ragláyim
כל לילה מסתובב שם השד **מה
שיש לו** שלוש רגליים

'Going around there every night is the demon with (*lit.* what has got) three legs'

A construction akin to a relative clause is the following, in which the כמו *kmo* 'like' clause acts as complement to the determiner אותו *oto* 'same', on which it depends (see 9.6 for details):

tikne oto séfer kmo she-hu kana
buy same book like CONJ he bought
תקנה אותו ספר כמו שהוא קנה

'Buy the same book as he bought'

Similarly, a - ש *she-* clause complementing the determiner כזה *kaze* 'such' can be considered an adverbial result clause, for no relative pronoun is necessary (1) and indeed even the determiner can be omitted, creating a blend between a relative and a result clause (2):

(1) ze bet-séfer **kaze she-**kol ha-kitot
     hen kita aHat gdola
זה בית-ספר **כזה ש**כל הכיתות
הן כיתה אחת גדולה

'It is a school **such that** all the classes are one large class'

(2) yesh patifónim **she-**lo tsariH lahafoH
     et ha-taklit
יש פטיפונים **שלא** צריך להפוך
את התקליט

'There are record players such that (*lit.* **that**) you don't need to turn the record over'

3. The 'relative pronoun as subject' is actually obligatory when 'coordinated' with some other word. (In English, however, the very construction is impossible.) Thus:

ole **she-hu ve-horav** mitgorerim beyáHad...
עולה **שהוא והוריו** מתגוררים ביחד...

[an] immigrant that **he and his-parents** live together...

The conjunctions - ש *she-*, and אשר *asher*, - ה *ha-* etc., are clearly not relative pronouns themselves: - ש *she-* and הוא, היא *hu, hi* etc. are often in the same relative clause. So the closest English equivalent to - ש *she-* is 'that' ('which, who' are themselves relative pronouns).

An apparent relative clause is the 'superlative' ש ב... *she-be...* (see 20.2.2); only present tense is possible, and no other conjunction can replace - ש *she-*. Another deceptive construction is the determiner שהוא *shehu* 'whatsoever' (historically 'that it be'), cf. 9.2:

ha-gdolim she-ba-malHinim
the great that among-the composers
הגדולים שבמלחינים

'the greatest composers'

kol maHshev she-hu
כל מחשב שהוא

'any computer whatsoever'

4. For omission of the whole preposition + relative noun, or even the whole verb phrase containing them, see 33.3.4.

5. Non-restrictives are different, thus:

ad ha-daka ha-shishim, she-ba huvka   עד הדקה הששים, שבה הובקע
ha-sháar ha-rishon,...   השער הראשון,...

'Until the sixtieth minute, when (*lit.* that in it)
the first goal was scored,...'

6. These 'imprecise' antecedents need not themselves be part of an adverbial, hence:

yavo zman she-ha-adam...   יבוא זמן שהאדם...
will-come time that the man...   'A time will come when Man...'

However, the relative adverbial itself must be the 'unmarked' one, involving - ב *be-* 'at' (and בגלל *biglal* with סיבה *siba* 'reason').

7. An exception is the 'imprecise antecedent'; see 33.3.3.

8. When preposing the adverb שם *sham* 'there, where', one tends to avoid the combination ששם *she-sham*; instead (in formal Hebrew):

higánu le-arad, sham huHlat lanúaH me'at   הגענו לערד, שם הוחלט לנוח מעט
'We reached Arad, where (*lit.* there) a decision was taken
to rest a while'

9. For an explanation, see 37.13 on subject-verb inversions in general.

10. To express 'I, who am a/the (dean)', one cannot say, on the model of אני (הוא) הדיקן *ani* (*hu*) *ha-dikan* 'I am the dean':

*ani, she-dikan,...   *אני, שדיקן,...
I, who dean,...

*ani, she-hu ha-dikan,...   *אני, שהוא הדיקן,...
I, who COPULA the dean,...

Instead, one may (casually) *repeat* the antecedent as a relative pronoun, or use another construction:

ani, she-ani (ha-)dikan,...   אני, שאני (ה)דיקן,...
I, that I (the) dean,...   'I, who am a/the dean,...'

ani ke-dikan...   אני כדיקן...
                                            'I as ⟨a⟩ dean...'

11. זה *ze* referring to a thing implies that it has been named, i.e. 'the one that...'.

12. The relative pronoun harking back to such pronouns cannot be preposed, thus:

zot she-panit eléha   זאת שפנית **אליה**
                                            'the person that you applied **to [her]**'

ma she-iyánti bo   מה שעיינתי **בו**
                                            'what I looked **at [it]**'

13. This construction is distinct from casual indirect questions of the type (see 26.7):

ata batúaH **ma she-**tsariH lakáHat?   אתה בטוח **מה שצריך** לקחת?
you sure **what that** necessary to-take?   'You sure **what** we're supposed to take?'

The - ש *she-* conjunction here is optional and pleonastic.

14. Formal usage prefers במקום ש- *ba-makom she-* 'in the place that', למקום ש- *la-makom she-* 'to the place that'. A rather formal form condemned by purists is היכן ש- *heHan she-* 'where' (היכן *heHan* ? = 'where?').

15. Casual איך ש- *eH she-* also denotes 'just when', as does כמו ש- *kmo she-* (ordinarily 'just like').

16. See 13.10 for the tense here.

17. This would be 'nominalization of a clause', but for the preposition introducing it in examples (1,2). Where there is כל *kol* 'any', a second version of this construction is possible, with no preposition at the beginning and with a relative pronoun; this is just an ordinary noun phrase set apart:

kol mi she-ani lo efne elav, ani   כל מי שאני לא אפנה אליו, אני
  mekabel ota tshuva   מקבל אותה תשובה

any who that I not will-apply to-him,
  I receive same answer

'Whoever I apply to, I receive the same answer'

18. Were it not for the *non*-'interrogative' nouns used in the foregoing construction, one might have taken both constructions as *blends* of an indirect question and a relative clause.

19. However, where a noun is predicate (see 33.3.1) ...ש מי *mi she-...* 'someone who is...' needs no copula, unlike ...ש מה *ma she-...* 'the thing that is...'.

20. This is only to prevent it closely following the antecedent pronoun, not to rule out:

ke-mi she-al ktefav...   ...כמי שעל כתפיו

'As someone on whose (*lit.* that on his) shoulders...'

21. Even a clause introduced by ש- זה *ze she-* 'the fact that' is considered a bare clause rather than a noun phrase, so cannot take a relative clause.

22. Another restriction: following the pseudo-interrogative pronouns or זה *ze* (and its inflections) 'he who...' (cf. 33.4.1), only ש- *she-* is used as a conjunction:

ze/mi she-mevin ne'elav   זה/מי שמבין נעלב

he/who that understands takes-offence   'Whoever understands takes offence'

23. ו- *ve-* also introduces another type of clause, circumstantial adverbials, provided that they too have an anaphor (see 35.7). Both are immune to the 'coordinate structure constraint'. Hence the ו- *ve-* clause under discussion is indeed a relative clause (cf. ch.35, note 3).

24. A particular use of this is with *ka-* to introduce adverbial clauses of the type (see 23.3):

ka-mudgam le'el   'as (*lit.* like that) is   כמודגם לעיל
  exemplified above'

25. Although this construction is a relative clause - in our examples בודק *bodek* takes an object and is thus not a noun, and נעשה *naase* has no independent existence as a noun - the ה- *ha* does act like a 'definite article' by conflating ב + ה ← ב *be + ha → ba-* etc.:

tityaHes la-naase sham   תתייחס לנעשה שם

refer to-that is-being-done there   'Refer to what is being done there'

26. Another construction is the positive noun + contrasting negative relative:

makpidim shotim mits ve-**she-enam**   מקפידים שותים מיץ **ושאינם**
  makpidim shotim máyim   מקפידים שותים מים

'Sticklers drink juice and non-sticklers
(*lit.* that are not sticklers) drink water'

27. Rather similarly, 'pseudo-interrogative' pronouns act as relative pronouns, with no conjunction (see 33.8):

en **ma**   lehagid   אין **מה** להגיד
  REL PRONOUN
is-not **what** to-say   'There isn't **anything** to say'

28. In the 'necessity' sense the relative pronoun for indirect objects or adverbials is obligatory, and כדי *kdey* + infinitive is impossible. Thus the following example denotes just 'possibility':

yesh lánu tmunot lehistakel   יש לנו תמונות להסתכל
'We have pictures we can look at'

29. Evidence that these are indeed relative clauses rather than indirect questions is the inadmissibility of עוד מי *od mi* 'who else', עוד איפה *od éfo* 'where else' etc.

Chapter 34

1. Apposed clauses do not fulfil the same function towards their nucleus noun as do apposed *phrases* (ch.36). They cannot always be said to *specify* the noun as כהן *kóhen* specifies רב *rav* 'rabbi' in הרב כהן *ha-rav kóhen* 'Rabbi Cohen' ('a rabbi, namely Cohen'). Nor are they otherwise 'predicative': although העובדה, הסיכויים ש... *ha-uvda, ha-sikuyim she...* 'the fact, the chances that...' can be paraphrased as predicatives (העובדה היא ש... *ha-uvda hi she...* 'the fact is that...' etc.), this is not so for ההכחשה ש... *ha-hakHasha she...'* 'the denial that...', זה ש... *ze she...* 'the fact/ notion that...'.

2. כאילו *ke'ílu* is otherwise the adverb 'as it were' or the conjunction 'as if' (ch.32.5.2).

3. Some such exceptions can be explained as cases of 'subject-to-subject raising' (see 31.3).

4. The same is true of relative clauses. In general, however, modifiers cannot be 'set adrift' from their introductory noun.

Chapter 35

1. This is an example where no coordinator is used.

2. With the exception of reciprocal or joint actions such as:

ani ve-at nifgáshnu sham páam אני ואת נפגשנו שם פעם

'You and I met there once'

3. A basic characteristic of coordination is that a simple coordinated constituent or its parts will not undergo 'extraction', e.g. WH-fronting, relative deletion, focus/topic preposing:

haláHta   ve-asáfta et mi? הלכת ואספת את מי?

COORDINATE 1   COORDINATE 2

you-went and you-collected OM whom?

does not yield:

*et mi haláHta ve-asáfta? *את מי הלכת ואספת?

OM whom you-went and you-collected?   'Whom did you go and collect?'

Absence of such a constraint is evidence that - ו *ve-* is sometimes a *subordinating* conjunction instead (see 35.7).

4. Puristically, and in certain set phrases, it becomes ו *u-* before *b, m, f, v* (i.e. labials) or any consonant pointed with 'shva':

u-moshe	'and Moshe'	ומשה
u-glida	'and ice-cream'	וגלידה
u-lefi ze	'and according to this'	ולפי זה

5. In such cases, coordinated NPs are often analysed as transforms of coordinated clauses.

6. With the focus adverbs אף *af* 'even' and גם... גם... *gam... gam...* 'both... and...', - ו *ve-* can be omitted in formal usage:

aH lo yisra'el **af** lo áshaf lo naanu אך לא ישראל **אף** לא אש״ף לא נענו
be-Hiyuv בחיוב

'But neither Israel nor (*lit.* **even** not) the PLO responded positively'

gam mi-bHina polítit **gam** mi-bHina **גם** מבחינה פוליטית **גם** מבחינה
musarit,... מוסרית,...

'**Both** politically and (*lit.* **both**) morally,...'

The same happens commonly and obligatorily with או... או... *o...o...* 'either... or...' as focus adverbs; see 35.12.

7. Only with semantically complex uses of -ו *ve-*, 'and then, and so, and yet', is such repetition of the verb phrase essential - unless one resorts to a 'tag' (cf. 35.2.2):

míryam hismíka ve-az léa   מרים הסמיקה ואז לאה
                        'Miriam blushed and then Lea'

8. Complement clauses coordinate well, e.g. ...ש...ש אמר *amar she...ve-she...* 'he said that...and that...', ...וכי...כי ברור *barur ki...ve-Hi...* 'it is plain that...and that...'; but in adverbials, ...ש...ש משום *mishum she...ve-she...* 'because [that] ...and [that]...' and the like are unacceptable, as the -ש *she-* is felt to be an inseparable part of -ש משום *mishum she-* etc.

9. The missing material need not be a constituent, but it must be a 'daughter' of S or VP:

ani natáti lahem matana ve-le-aHoti késef   אני נתתי להם מתנה ולאחותי כסף
                        'I gave them a present and my sister money'

10. This repetition of prepositions in what is *not* the residue of a separate full clause arises by a 'copying rule' that is also found with coordinated relative antecedents. Note that the verb in the relative clause is plural, hence this is true noun coordination:

Hashávti **al** ha-géshem ve-**al** ha-shéleg   חשבתי **על** הגשם ו**על** השלג
  she-yordim sham   שיורדים שם
I-thought **about** the rain and **about** the snow
that are-falling there

11. A collective noun is not used (cf. 39.8):

*ha-tsévet hitHabka (zo im zo)   *הצוות התחבקה (זו עם זו)
                    ('The team embraced (one another)')

12. With nouns, this must be a subject + *possessive*:

míki hu aHiv shel éli   מיקי הוא אחיו של אלי
                      'Miki is the brother of Eli'

13. This is of course acceptable for, say, 'They last twenty years and seven years respectively'.

14. With הלך *halaH*, the reverse order is possible in formal usage, as in (1) below - except where an object follows, showing that הלך. *halaH* is not functionally just an adverb:

(1) ha-hafsakot nitkatsru **ve-halHu**   ההפסקות נתקצרו **והלכו**
    the breaks shortened **and went**   'The breaks **gradually** shortened'
(2) *ha-ananim meshanim ve-holHim   *העננים משנים והולכים
    et tsuratam   את צורתם
    the clouds change and go [= gradually change] their-form

15. In all cases -ו *ve-* is more limited than -ש *she-* in its inability to combine with a true coordinator -ו *ve-*: (...ש...√) ...וו...ו *הלוואי *halvay ve...u-ve...(√...ve-she...)* 'if only that...and that...'.

16. By contrast, in ?איך קורה שנכשלים *eH kore she-niHshalim*? 'how does it happen that they fail?', -ש קורה *kore she-* does not imply 'it may happen that' (it is factive), hence no -ו *ve-*.

17. Such clauses are not constrained by the coordinate structure constraint against 'extraction' (cf. note 3):

ma asit be-nosaf le-ze?   ?מה עשית בנוסף לזה
                      'What did you do besides that?'

18. -מ חוץ *Huts mi-* can be expanded into a full comparative construction (cf. English 'other than'):

hayu be-Hol Héder, Huts measher   היו בכל חדר, חוץ מאשר
  ba-ambátya   באמבטיה
    'They were in every room, except [than] in the bathroom'

19. כולל *kolel* 'including' need not have the object marker את *et* and is thus felt to be akin to both preposition and verb.

20. This is also possible with a 'true dual' noun, e.g. שלוש פעמיים *paamáyim shalosh* 'two or three times', יומיים שלושה *yomáyim shlosha* 'two or three days'.

21. The fact that each inclusive 'or' needs repetition of או *o* reflects its affinity to illocutionary 'or', which itself requires או *o* for each 'or' (see 35.13).

22. שמא *shéma* is a complementizer (cf. ...שמא פחד *paHad shéma...* 'be afraid lest...'), acting here as a question word and akin to the S-initial adverb שמא *shéma* meaning 'perhaps'.

23. או...או... *o...o* cannot directly precede the noun when prepositions are present as in example (1), which suggests that it is a (correlative) focus adverb, like ובין...בין *beyn... uveyn* (see 22.6), replacing the coordinator (cf. note 6) — as if one should have expected...ואו...או *o...ve-o...* 'either... and or...'.

24. Neither או ש- *o she-* nor ...או...או *o...o...* are used in illocutionaries.

25. אבל *aval* etc. cannot link clauses introduced by ש- *she-* (see examples (1,2) below); the second ש- *she-* must be omitted. But the combination אך ה- *aH ha-* 'but who/which' is possible linking relative clauses. There is no such limitation on ו- *ve-* 'and' or או *o* 'or':

(1) amárti she-ani ayef aval (*she-)avo   אמרתי שאני עייף אבל (*ש)אבוא
     beHol-zot   בכל-זאת

'I said that I was tired but (that) I'd come anyway'

(2) anashim she-yod'im tov anglit aH   אנשים שיודעים טוב אנגלית אך
     (*she-)kor'im rak ivrit   (*ש)קוראים רק עברית

'People who know English well but (who) read only Hebrew'

26. The other, and more basic, use of אלא *éla* is as 'but instead', following a negation, e.g. לא זה אלא זה *lo ze éla ze* 'not this but that' (discussed fully in 35.16). In the present case, there need not have been a negation but there is an implied cancellation of an expectation, i.e. 'things are not as you would expect but instead...'. In the example in the text: 'You might have thought things were in this order, but instead I'm getting things in the wrong order...' Compare also אלא-אם-כן *éla-im-ken* 'unless, except if' in 35.16.

27. אולם *ulam* can be followed by a comma, and is thus also a link adverb meaning 'however' (ch.24).

28. ואילו *ve'ílu* is not a combination of ו- *ve-* 'and' plus אילו *ílu* 'if' synchronically.

29. Ordinarily, לא *lo* would precede the *verb*.

30. By contrast, אבל *aval* and the other 'but' words serve to *negate* an implied expectation (see 35.14).

31. As always, the second coordinate (כי אם החסידה *ki im ha-Hasida*) can be tagged to the end.

Chapter 36

1. Unlike coordination (ch.35), apposition allows extraction, e.g. WH-fronting, relative pronoun deletion and focus fronting, as in:

gam et dáfna zaHárti, kfar katan   גם את דפנה זכרתי, כפר קטן
be-toH ha-émek...   בתוך העמק...

'Dafna too I remembered, a tiny village in the valley...'

2. For constructs and coordination, see chapters 6 and 35 respectively.

3. There may be more than one teacher, so המורה *ha-mora* signifies 'the teacher we both know about'.

4. Titles like מלך *méleH* 'king', נשיא *nasi* 'president' are not usually treated as 'occu-

pations': they either take a comma or (more often) actually come first: המלך חוסיין
ha-méleH Huseyn 'King Hussein'; see further, 36.5.

5. Multiple ('stacked') apposition is possible for both predicatives and   (36.4-9)
specificationals; see the third example.

6. By contrast, בן/בת *ben / bat* meaning 'consisting of' is not a noun but an adjective,
for it requires a 'head noun', e.g. בתים *batim* 'houses' in example (2) here; see further,
6.19.

    (1) bney shesh   בני שש
                'six-year-olds' (*lit.* having six)

    (2) **batim** bney shesh komot   **בתים** בני שש קומות
        houses consisting-of six storeys

7. Two-phrase apposition is derivable from an underlying apposed clause. There are
no underlying apposed *phrases*.

8. By contrast, הדוגמה שש *ha-dugma shesh* would signify that '6' itself is a דוגמה
dugma 'example'. Of course numerals do themselves tend to become 'proper names'
(תגיד לשש לבוא) *tagid le-shesh lavo* 'tell 6 to come') but are essentially more like adjectives: 6 דוגמה *dugma shesh* 'example 6' is equivalent to הדוגמה השישית *ha-dugma
ha-shishit* 'the sixth example'. A different kind of definite apposition without *ha-* 'the'
is in apposition of titles: פרופסור בובר *profésor búber* 'Professor Buber' (36.5).

9. Names used as *common* nouns use the construct and not apposition: מטוסי מיג
metosey mig 'Mig planes', עצי אקליפטוס *atsey ekalíptus* 'Eucalyptus trees'.

10. Compare this with 36.2.

11. Some 'titles' are intrinsically definite if there is only one holder of them, e.g. ראש
העיר *rosh ha-ir* 'the Mayor', הנשיא *ha-nasi* 'the President', and thus can also permit
identity apposition (note the comma): ראש העיר, מר קולק *rosh ha-ir, mar kólek* 'the
Mayor, Mr Kollek'.

12. Most such link adverbs also introduce verbs or any other phrases or clauses (see
ch.24). Another method of clause apposition is:

      ha-baaya hi zo: ma yiye im...   ...הבעיה היא זו: מה יהיה אם
                          'The problem is this: what will be if...'

13. This resembles a coordinated clause (see 35.2.2), except that the apposed comma
cannot have -ו *ve-* 'and' and the verb must be omitted.

14. נוסף ל- *nosaf le-* 'in addition to', כולל (את) *kolel (et)* 'including', and their synonyms, are prepositions. The structures they introduce are adverbials and capable of
manoeuvering around the sentence, not appositions.

15. The 'widest' adverbial(s) is often placed at the front of the sentence, with the meaning 'when in...':

      bi-bnéy-brak, gárti be-shikun he   בבני-ברק, גרתי בשיכון ה'
      [when I was] in Bney-Brak, I-lived in Estate 5

16. However, the very use of the 'de-pluralized' singular form שנה *shana* 'year' is a sign
that this is apposition. For the construct requires the *plural* form: עשרים שנות (*שנת)
מאסר *esrim shnot* (not: **shnat*) *maasar* '20 years-of (not: year-of) gaol'. Conversely the
expected appositional structures קילו אחד אגסים *kílo eHad agasim* 'one kilo of (*lit.*
kilo one) pears', הקילו אגסים *ha-kílo agasim* 'the kilo pears' are awkward in the singular.

17. But when the amount comes *after* the noun, של *shel* is required (see 8.5.4):

      hefresh shel shalosh shanim   הפרש של שלוש שנים
      difference of three years   'three years' difference'

18. It is as if שלוש שנים הפרש *shalosh shanim hefresh* were underlyingly הפרש של
שלוש שנים *hefresh shel shalosh shanim* 'a difference of three years' (cf. note 17).

19. This also applies to the construct adjective בן/בת *ben / bat* 'consisting of' (cf.note
6). בן *ben* otherwise means 'son, member of'.

20. When not between two nouns, 'the six-year-olds' is בני השש *bney ha-shesh*, not בני שש *bney shesh*.

21. More common everyday usage: של שני חדרים *shel shney Hadarim* 'of two rooms'.

22. -ו *ve-* 'and' is sometimes preferred:

rosh ha-memshala ve-sar ha-bitaHon,   ראש הממשלה ושר הבטחון,
     mar ben-guryon   מר בן-גוריון

         'the Prime Minister and Defence Minister Mr Ben-Gurion'

23. Examples like (2) amount to combining two nouns (סין ורוסיה) *sin ve-rúsya* 'China and Russia'), indeed these adjectives cannot be used predicatively of these nouns:

*ha-siHot hen síniyot   *השיחות הן סיניות

         ('The talks are Chinese')

Chapter 37

1. The example is based on Rosén 1982.

2. Indeed, a 'topical' object can be converted into subject by passivization; cf. 14.2.

3. But the (intra-clausal) need to keep subject and object distinct prevails over the (supra-clausal) need to topicalize: כלבים אוהבים ילדים *klavim ohavim yeladim* generally means 'dogs love children' and not the reverse.

4. Adverbs and noun phrases, but not verbs or verb phrases, have pronoun forms - probably no coincidence.

     Non-constituents can be preposed:

lirkôd im ha-talmidim ani muHan   לרקוד עם התלמידים אני מוכן
     afílu hóra   אפילו הורה

     to-dance with the students I'm willing even a hora

A word within a subordinate clause can be preposed to the front of *this* clause or the *whole* sentence ('unboundedness'):

leefôt íma amra she-hi muHana   **לאפות** אמא אמרה שהיא מוכנה
     rak ugiyot   רק עוגיות

     to-bake Mom said that she's willing
     only cookies.

5. This example is from Amihai, cited by Rosén 1982.

6. לא יסלק *lo yesalek* (future tense) generally denotes, in officialese, 'he shall not remove', i.e. an order; see 28.6.

7. However, predicative adjectives and nouns do not precede their subject (save in formal usage, for other reasons; see 37.14).

8. Unlike 'topic preposing', this generally brings the topic to the front of the *whole* sentence, disqualifying:

*ani ro'e she-ha-monit ha-zot,   *אני רואה שהמונית הזאת,
     ata hizmánta ota   אתה הזמנת אותה

         ('I see that this cab, you ordered it')

9. Two idiomatic constructions are:

     (1) eyn davar kaze, levater al molédet   אין דבר כזה, לוותר על מולדת

         'There isn't such a thing ⟨as⟩ to forgo a homeland'

     (2) Where זאת אומרת *zot oméret* 'this means' is equivalent to copular זה *ze* 'is' (see 16.7):

ma zot oméret láyla?   מה זאת אומרת לילה?
what this means night?   'What does night mean?'

ma ze láyla? מה זה לילה?

what is night?

10. Similarly, once a preposition joins a suffixed pronoun, any conjoined noun must repeat the preposition:

alav ve-al yaakov   'about him and about Yaakov'   עליו ועל יעקב

11. Simultaneously, the *object* of the verb can be preposed without leaving a pronoun 'trace':

lirkod hora ani ken erkod ita   לרקוד הורה אני כן ארקוד אתה

V   N   V

to-dance hora I *will* dance with-her   'I *will* dance a hora with her'

12. The 'topic' has, at best, secondary stress. Particularly strong stress is put on an 'emphatic' and on a 'contrastive' focus; see below.

13. This emphasis is *exclusive*, whereas 'topic' in ופלים אני אוהב *vâflim ani ohev* 'wafers, I like' has contrastive but not all-exclusive force ('I also like cookies...').

14. Where a 'topic' has *already* been mentioned, a 'focus' can ensue:

banânot rak *Shálva* ohévet   בננות רק שלוה אוהבת

TOPIC   FOCUS   'Bananas only *Shalva* likes!'

But *following* a 'focus', everything else is of equally low informational significance, so there will be no special 'topic'; instead of example (1), example (2) is preferred:

(1) *móshe shata et ha-bîra aval   *משה שתה את הבירה אבל

     Yéntl shateta et ha-víski   ינטל שתתה את הוויסקי

     FOCUS   TOPIC

                      ('Moshe drank the beer but *Yentl* drank the whiskey')

(2) ...aval et ha-víski shateta *Yéntl*   ...אבל את הוויסקי שתתה ינטל

     TOPIC   FOCUS   '...but the whiskey *Yentl* drank'

15. But a non-constituent or an 'unbounded' preposing of focus is rare.

16. For 'specificational clauses' in general see 16.3.7.

17. This is not a true copula, nor a relative clause. (1) No other form is possible in this 'copula': neither ...ש הם יהיו* *hem yiyu she...* (they will be who...) nor אני אינני* ...ש *ani enéni she...* (I am-not who...); rather: ...ש לא אני הוא *lo ani hu she...* (not I am who...). (2) The verb must agree with the *main* subject, hence אני הוא שדיבר* *ani hu she-**diber** I am who **spoke-3rd s.**, אני הוא שדיברת אלי* *ani hu she-**dibárta** elay* I am who **you-spoke** to-me. So both the copula and the conjunction ש-/אשר *she-/asher* are just pleonastic. Nor is an adjective possible. (3) Alternatively, Hebrew allows a 'pseudo-copula' but a true relative clause:

ani hu **ze** she-diber   אני הוא זה שדיבר

                 'I am **the one** who spoke'

ani hu **ze** she-dibárta elav   אני הוא זה שדיברת אליו

I am **he** that you-spoke to-him   'I am the one who you spoke to'

18. As for the agreement of the verb in these 'relative clauses', as in שהשאירה *she-hish'íra* (3rd person) vs. שהשארתי *she-hish'árti* (1st person), see 18.6.4.

19. A related use is inversion in television credits and the like:

katav yoel armon, ibda shúli aHituv   כתב יואל ערמון, עיבדה שולי אחיטוב

wrote yoel armon, adapted shuli achituv

                   'written by Yoel Armon, adapted by Shuli Achituv'

20. This is not topic dislocation - the noun concerned can readily have a focus adverb, i.e. it can be focus, or simply neutral.

21. The copula (see 16.2), being הוא, היא *hu, hi* etc. (identical with the personal pronouns 'he, she, they'), looks like a case of topic dislocation:

hértsl hu sémel   הרצל הוא סמל

Herzl COPULA symbol   'Herzl is a symbol'

But such copulas between two nouns are usually *obligatory* and thus quite unlike the constructions described.

22. What these have in common is the 'underlying' existence of a preposed noun or comparative word - triggering an inversion. For the position of the relative pronoun, see 33.3.3.

Purists may decry inversion of *present* tense verbs. For other reasons, the verb in the *main* clause too inverts - the whole of the preceding subordinate clause constitutes an adverbial and topic for this main clause.

23. A different reordering, serving the same end of register distinction, is:

haya ze kashe le...   היה זה קשה ל...

was it difficult to...   'It was difficult to...'

Chapter 38

1. Some exceptions are שוטר *shoter* 'policeman' (no corresponding verb) and מורה *more* 'teacher' (corresponding verb means 'give instructions').

There are many variants, just as in the present tense (see ch.40), and notably with *two* middle consonants in patterns (1b, c), e.g. מערבל *mearbel* 'concrete mixer'. Patterns (2), (4), (14) too have many variants, e.g. ניטרול *nitrul* 'neutralization'.

2. These, and three-syllable nouns similar in stress and plural pattern, are traditionally called 'segolates'. See 38.6 on stress. (3b), though a non-meaningful pattern, is grouped with (3a). Generally, *-é-e-* and *-é-a-* patterns take penultimate stress; *-o-e-* can be *-ó-e-* (3b) or *-o-é-* (1a), and *-a-a-* is generally *-á-a-* (3a) or *-a-á-* (4).

3. Some items are on the borderline, e.g. בן-אדם *ben-adam* 'person' is grammatically like two words (witness בני-אדם *bney-adam* 'persons'), but also rather like one word (witness הבן-אדם *ha-ben-adam* 'the person'), and graphically one word in some casual usage: בנאדם *benadam*.

4. The verbs in compounds are compressed to one syllable with an *-a-* vowel (the 'canonic' vowel also favoured in acronyms, e.g. מנכ"ל *mankal* - see 38.5), save where this would create three successive consonants (hence רשמקול *reshamkol*, not רשמיקול **rashmikol*).

5. An abstract analysis of segolates as *CiCC*, *CCoCt*, etc - a shape they often have with construct suffixes - means that they do have (abstract) final stress, but it has the difficulty that this construct form is literary and unproductive, except when used as a basis for derivational suffixes.

Chapter 39

1. Endearment terms use *-i* or *-le* for *either* sex, e.g. יהודה'לה *yehúdale*, רבקה'לה *rívkale*. Occasionally, females are named after a masculine noun, e.g. תמר *tamar* 'palm'; and, rarely, males use a feminine noun: יונה *yona*, שמחה *simHa* ('dove, joy').

2. Exceptions include נחיר *neHir* 'nostril', שד *shad* 'breast', קרסול *karsol* 'ankle', מותן *móten* 'hip'.

3. Some ים-- *-áyim* words are not paired objects, e.g. צהריים *tsohoráyim* 'lunchtime', שמיים *shamáyim* 'sky' (both are masculine).

4. The few ending in unstressed א- *-a* go according to their meaning as human nouns (39.1): אבא *ába* 'father', סבא *sába* 'grandfather', אמא *íma* 'mother', סבתא *sávta* 'grandmother'.

5. Where ת- *-t* is clearly part of the *root*, nouns are mostly masculine, e.g. שרות *sherut* 'service' (שרת *sheret* 'to serve'), זית *záyit* 'olive' (pl. זיתים *zetim*), קשת *kashat* 'archer' (pl. קשתים *kashatim*). But most segolates with ת- *-t* are feminine - see 39.3.2. לילה *láyla* 'night' is masculine.

6. A few notable cases of feminine forms quite unrelated ('suppletive') to the masculine form are: אם ~ אב *av* ~ *em* 'father ~ mother', אשה ~ גבר *géver* ~ *isha* 'man ~ woman', גברת ~ אדון/מר *adon* / *mar* ~ *gvéret* 'Mr ~ Mrs', כלה ~ חתן *Hatan* ~ *kala* 'bridegroom/son-in-law ~ bride/daugher-in-law', פרה ~ פר/שור *par* / *shor* ~ *para* 'bull ~ cow', אתון/חמורה ~ חמור *Hamor* ~ *aton/Hamora* 'jackass ~ she-ass', לביאה ~ אריה *arye* ~ *levia* 'lion ~ lioness'.

7. But in all other functions, e.g. as subject or object (i.e. involving a 'presupposition' rather than an 'assertion' of their femininity), they cannot denote females at all - in the following example, for instance, with 'person' referring to 'Sara':

hine sára - *ata makir et   הנה שרה - *אתה מכיר את
ha-ben-adam haze?   **הבן-אדם** הזה

'Here's Sara - do you know this **person**?'

8. An entirely different word is occasionally used, e.g. עז *ez* 'goat' (generic), which happens to be feminine.

9. The generic *plural* for 'sheep' is masculine: כבשים *kvasim.*

10. Some exceptions: (a) גיורת ~ גר *ger* ~ *giyóret* 'convert', דודה ~ דוד *dod* ~ *doda* 'uncle ~ aunt' (casually, the *stem* can be stressed); (b) טירונית ~ טירון *tiron* ~ *tironit* 'recruit', תינוקת ~ תינוק *tinok* ~ *tinóket* 'baby', אפרוחית ~ אפרוח *efróaH* ~ *efroHit* 'chick' (39.5.4.); (c) מומחית ~ מומחה *mumHe* ~ *mumHit* 'expert'; (d) stressed *-i* but feminine suffix *-t*: ישראלי *yisreelí* 'Israeli', מוסלמי *muslemí* 'Moslem', ליטאי *lita'í* 'Lithuanian'.

11. The suffix יה- *-ia* keeps nouns distinct from adjectives (צרפתית *tsarfatit* 'French' etc.), as does the masculine plural suffix (צרפתים *tsarfatim* 'Frenchmen' vs. צרפתיים *tsarfatiim* 'French', see 39.9.1). No such distinction is made when the feminine gentilic has ית- *-it*, thus *súrit* is both 'Syrian woman' and the adjective 'Syrian (f.)'.

12. Some exceptions: (1) Some 20 per cent of כבד *kabad*-type 'occupation nouns' take ית- *-it* for various reasons, see 39.5.4; (2) The few nouns with four-consonant stems take ית- *-it* (except *CaCCaC*), e.g. מלצר *meltsar* 'waiter' - see 39.5.4; (3) Sundry, e.g. רופאה ~ רופא *rofe* ~ *rof'a* 'doctor', איכרה ~ איכר *ikar* ~ *ikara* 'farmer', ~ שובב שובבה *shovav* ~ *shoveva* 'naughty child'.

13. Simply by virtue of generally being just singular, non-countables in a few cases use their plural to express something akin to 'a lot of...':

ráam	'thunder'	רעם	reamim	'thunder'	רעמים
géshem	'rain'	גשם	gshamim	'rains'	גשמים
Hol	'sand'	חול	Holot	'sands, dunes'	חולות
adama	'earth'	אדמה	adamot	'lands'	אדמות
késef	'money'	כסף	ksafim	'funds'	כספים

Some non-countables are really a separate category, 'non-numerable': they do take *non*-exact counting, e.g. מאות *me'ot* 'hundreds of', כמה *káma* 'some': מאות הכנות *me'ot haHanot* 'hundreds of preparations' (and not מאות מים* **me'ot mayim* 'hundreds of waters').

14. Countably: שני זוגות אופניים *shney zugot ofanáyim* = 'two *pairs* of bicycles' etc, but also simply הרבה אופניים *harbe ofanáyim* 'lots of bicycles' etc.

15. Exception: the few nouns used *partitively* with plurals or collectives can have plural agreement, though singular in form: חלק מה{מפגינים/יחידה} מתפזרים *Hélek me-ha-{mafginim* / *yeHida} mitpazrim* 'a portion of the {protestors/unit} are dispersing'. See 8.5.

16. Exception: בן-דוד *ben-dod* 'cousin' ('son-of uncle'), though not בן-אח *ben-aH* 'nephew' ('son-of brother'), is casually a semi-compound with *double* number-gender

markings (agreeing with each other): בני-דודים *bney-dodim* 'male cousins', בת-דודה
bat-dóda 'female cousin', בנות-דודות *bnot-dodot* 'female cousins'.

17. These suffixes are stressed, except in foreignisms (see 38.2).

Any existing suffix ‎י- *-i*, ה‎ֶ *-e*, ת- *-(e)t* or ה‎ָ *-a* is first dropped and then the plural
suffix is added, e.g.

yehudi ~ yehudim ~ yehudey	'Jew'		יהודי ~ יהודים ~ יהודי
mivne ~ mivnim ~ mivney	'structure'		מבנה ~ מבנים ~ מבני
Hayétet ~ Hayatot ~ Hayatot	'tailor'		חייטת ~ חייטות ~ חייטות

18. Among exceptions: diminutive ‎ון- *-on*, e.g. ילדון ~ ילדונים *yaldon ~ yaldonim*
'little child'; recent coinages, e.g. אווירון *aviron* 'aeroplane', ביטאון *bita'on* 'organ',
חניון *Henyon* 'parking lot'.

19. Among exceptions: recent coinages, e.g. מטוס *matos* 'aeroplane', מסוף *masof* 'ter-
minal', מסוק *masok* 'helicopter' - but דו"ח ~ דו"חות *doH / dúaH ~ doHot* 'report'.
A handful of plural-only nouns, with legal associations, take ‎ין- *-in* as a free variant of
‎ים- *-im*, e.g. ארוסין/ארוסים *erusin/erusim* 'engagement'; also קידושין *kidushin*
'marriage', גירושין *gerushin* 'divorce', נזיקין *nezikin* 'tort', פיטורין *piturin* 'dismissal'
etc. (but תפילין *tefilin* 'phylacteries', not *תפילים *tefilim*).

Aberrant plurals include: איש~אנשים *ish~anashim* 'person', אישיות~אישים
ishiyut~ishim 'celebrity'.

20. Some exceptions: (i) טליתות *talitot* 'prayer shawls', חניתות *Hanitot* 'spears'; (ii)
‎יות- *-iut* (e.g. מדיניות *mediniut* 'policy', אישיות *ishiut* 'personality') allows no such
plural.

Occasionally, ‎ה-, ת- *-t, -a* are treated as part of the stem, so do not drop, e.g.
דלת~דלתות *délet~dlatot* 'door', רשת *réshet* 'net', שבת *shabat* 'sabbath';
דוגמה~דוגמאות *dugma~dugma'ot* 'example' (‎!-אות), פתקה *pitka* 'note',
אוניברסיטה *univérsita* 'university', סיסמה *sisma* 'slogan'.

Aberrant internal changes include אם~אמהות *em~imahot* 'mother', אשה~נשים
isha~nashim 'woman', בת~בנות *bat~banot* 'daughter'.

21. Substandard usage even has:

shney yáakovim ve-shalosh miHáliot	שני יעקבים ושלוש מיכליות

22. Dual is a numeral, not a part of a singular-dual-plural system, thus: (1) agreeing
verbs and adjectives have the usual plural suffix (יומיים חולפים *yomáyim Holfim* 'two
days pass'); (2) שלושה ימים *shlosha yamim* 'three days' but not *שני יומיים *shney
yomáyim* 'two days-two' (simply יומיים *yomáyim*); (3) unlike singular and plural, dual
has no construct form.

23. Some exceptions: גבות *gabot* 'eyebrows', מרפקים *marpekim* 'elbows', בוהנים
bohanim 'thumbs'.

24. The numeral/noun אלף *élef* '1000' too obeys the rule, e.g. עשרת אלפים *aséret
alafim* '10,000' vs. אחד-עשר אלף *aHad-asar élef* '11,000'.

25. 'Non-digitals' are further special by having no genitive ('construct') or ordinal form
(both are 'marked' categories, like '+ plural' itself).

26. *Modified* nouns prefer the plural: עשרים ימי מאסר *esrim yemey maasar* 'twenty
days of detention', עשרים ימים סוערים *esrim yamim soarim* 'twenty stormy days',
עשרים הימים *esrim ha-yamim* 'the twenty days'.

27. And when combined with the 'pro-numeral' כמה *káma* 'how many?'.

Chapter 40

1. A few verbs lack some or all of these inflections, and often fill in with other roots
or patterns (see suppletives, 40.16). Some may even make use of the verb for 'be' (היה
haya) as a 'helper' verb in its past or future tense for constructing their past or future

tense, just like adjectives. But as long as they cannot use this 'helper' verb in the infinitive too (להיות *liyot*), they must still be regarded as verbs rather than adjectives:

PRES	tsariH	'needs'	צריך	yaHol	'can'	יכול
PAST	hitstareH haya tsariH	'needed'	הצטרך היה צריך	haya yaHol	'could'	היה יכול
INF	lehitstareH *but not*: *liyot tsariH	'to need'	להצטרך *להיות צריך	*none, and not*: *liyot yaHol		*להיות יכול 'to be able'

See also further on in this subsection.

2. By contrast, many nouns and adjectives (chs 38,41) have no pattern or root, e.g. בנק *bank* 'bank', פורמלי *formáli* 'formal'.

3. Certain roots have a 'zero' consonant in certain forms or patterns; see 40.21 and subsequent sections.

4. Strictly speaking, root 'meaningfulness' is a matter of degree, but hard to quantify; it depends on how one defines polysemy, and on the number of *binyanim* in which a meaning appears.

5. Where exactly consonant *clusters* (as in *flirtet*) occur in such patterns is explained in 40.3.1.

There are several families of defective roots, which occasionally omit a consonant; details are given in 40.21-23.

6. These roots are used for verbs and derived nouns of patterns 5-7 (see 40.3).

7. Several two-consonant roots (see 40.18) are of this type.

8. פ is sometimes 'hard' *p* and sometimes 'soft' *f*; ע is represented by ', though often silent.

9. As the vowel pattern of this *binyan* is occasionally -*a-e*- or rarely -*a-o*-, the term '*kal*' has its advantages.

10. Some foreignisms go one better: they can have a consonant+consonant cluster in the middle slot in *pi'el*, *pu'al*, *hitpa'el* as in (1) below, and two consonants in the middle slot of *hif'il* and *huf'al* (2); rarely, the first slot has a cluster (3):

(1)	-i-e-	Hintresh	'talk rubbish'	חינטרש
(2)	hi--i-	hishprits	'spray'	השפריץ
(3)	-i-e-	flirtet	'flirt'	פלירטט

11. Even as such, there are often differences in meaning and use between the one-word *binyan* and the analytical alternatives: המית *hemit* 'put to death' signifies direct causation, unlike גרם למות *garam lamut* 'cause to die'; nor can it apply to, say, trees. התראה *hitra'a* signifies a particular kind of 'seeing one another' - not, for example, 'see one another in the newspaper'.

12. Also 'have a meeting (with someone)'.

13. In the case of *nif'al*, less frequently.

14. Also 'cause to flee'.

15. Also 'tell, recount'.

16. These *binyanim* have other, less common meanings, e.g. *hif'il* can denote 'becoming': הווריד *hivrid* 'become pink'. Some *binyanim* overlap, e.g. *pi'el* can be causative like *hif'il*.

17. Exceptions include עצר *atsar* 'stop' (transitive and intransitive), inchoative רזה *raza* 'to slim' (cf. the adjective רזה *raze* 'slim') and the perfectives ישב *yashav* 'sit down' (cf. ישב *yashav* 'be sitting'), שכב *shaHav* 'lie down' (also 'be lying down') and לבש *lavash* 'put on' (also 'wear').

18. Occasionally passive for other *binyanim*, e.g. האשים *heeshim* 'blame' → נאשם *neesham* 'be blamed'; אילץ *ilets* 'compel' → נאלץ *neelats* 'be compelled'.

19. See also use (2).

20. לחם *laHam* too means 'fight'.

21. Casual usage is sparing in its use of passives in general (see ch. 14). Thus its main use of *huf'al*, *pu'al* and passive *nif'al* is as adjectival participles (see immediately below), so that מורכב *murkav* will mean 'composite' more often than 'is being put together' (its meaning as a present tense verb).

22. The exact semantics of each verb is largely determined by the noun involved.

23. This is one of a subgroup of verbs of 'removal'.

24. Even השתכר *histaker* 'earn', which does exceptionally take a direct object, takes an indefinite one so that no את *et* shows up.

25. Though type (a) involves a change in transitivity and type (b) a change in aspect, both yield a 'dynamic' verb and both emphasize autonomy of action. Among stative exceptions: גאה *ge'e* 'proud' → התגאה *hitga'e* 'take pride in', ביֵיש *biyesh* 'shame' → התבייש *hitbayesh* 'be ashamed'.

26. The verbs on which these are based may be of various *binyanim*; they all take direct objects.

27. Exceptions include: התבטא *hitbate* 'express oneself', התכונן *hitkonen* 'ready oneself', הצטדק *hitstadek* 'justify oneself', התמסר *hitmaser* 'devote oneself'. Occasionally, reflexives are *causative*-reflexive, e.g. הצטלם *hitstalem* 'have oneself photographed'.

28. Exceptions: *-e* verbs of *nif'al* and *muf'al* (*CVCCe*) take *-t*. (These and *pu'al* and *hitpa'el*, e.g. מושווה *mushve* 'compared', מפונה *mefune* 'cleared', משתנה *mishtane* 'change', can vacillate casually between *-a* and *-t*.)

29. However, two-consonant verbs (see 40.18) stress the syllable *preceding* the suffix in the past tense and, in casual usage, in present tense feminine singular, e.g. קמה *káma* 'arose', קמו *kámu* 'arose (pl.)', and קמה *káma* 'arises'(c) vs. קמה *kamá* 'arises' (F).

30. Several verbs, of no particular form or semantic type, have *a* instead of *o*: in (3)-(5), e.g. שכב *shaHav* 'lie'; or in (2)-(4), e.g. גדל *gadal* 'grow', חסר *Hasar* 'lack'; or in (3)-(4), e.g. למד *lamad* 'study'.

31. With suffix: גודרנ(ו) *godr (o)* etc.

32. Exception: imperatives usually have the same vowels as future tense, even though they have no prefix.

33. For stress, see 40.10.

34. This vowel is exceptional.

35. Or perhaps *-i-e-*, like *pi'el*, with *i* → *a* through proximity to the *ht* prefix.

36. Often a 'missing' tense does exist in some literary or substandard usage, not dealt with here.

We do not consider missing imperatives, as these are quite generally *specialized* (ch.28).

37. יכול *yaHol* arguably draws its future tense too from a different *binyan*, namely *huf'al*. The usual paradigm of יכול *yaHol* is:

PAST	YaHólti, yaHólta, yaHolt, (usually)	יכולתי, יכולת, יכולת,
	haya yaHol, yaHla, yaHólnu,	היה יכול, יכלה, יכולנו,
	yaHóltem, yaHlu	יכולתם, יכלו
PRES	yaHol, yeHola, yeHolim, yeHolot	יכול, יכולה, יכולים, יכולות
FUT	uHal, tuHal etc	אוכל, תוכל...

38. The combined paradigm is generally as follows (note that הצטרך *hitstareH* is not used in any tense for 'it is necessary to'):

PAST	hitstareH	הצטרך *or* haya tsariH היה צריך (and their inflections)
PRES	tsariH...	צריך...
FUT	yitstareH...	יצטרך...
INF	lehitstareH	להצטרך

39. The usual paradigm is thus:

PAST	Hayíti, Hayíta, Hayit, Hay,	חייתי, חיית, חיית, חי,
	Hayta/Háya,	חיתה/חיה,
	Hayínu, Hayítem, Háyu	חיינו, חייתם, חיו
PRES	Hay, Háya, Hayim, Hayot	חי, חיה, חיים, חיות
FUT	eHye etc.	אחיה...
INF	liHyot	לחיות

40. Except in literary usage.
41. Suppleted by the *pi'el* verb ייעץ *yiets*.
42. For the meaning 'need', see note 38. For the meaning 'it is necessary', the helper verb היה *haya* is added in other tenses.
43. Suppleted by the verb היה *haya*.
44. There are three major types of exception for certain patterns and inflections:

   (1) In *pi'el*, *pu'al* and *hitpa'el*, ב, כ, פ as the middle root consonant are usually hard, e.g. חיבר *Hiber* 'join', חובר *Hubar* 'be joined'.

   (2) In one particular *binyan*, *nif'al*, ב, כ, פ as first root consonant are hard in future, imperative and infinitive (these three forms are altogether very similar in *nif'al*, cf. 40.12), e.g. ייבחן *yibaHen* 'will be tested', להיבחן *lehibaHen* 'to be tested'. Additionally, in *hif'il* and *huf'al* ב, כ, פ as first root consonant are hard throughout a few two-consonant verbs (cf. 40.18), e.g. הכיר *hikir* 'know', הביע *hibía* 'express', as against הפיג *hefig* 'relieve'.

   (3) In any *binyan*, ב, כ, פ as last root consonant are *soft* in almost every case, e.g. נושבים *noshvim* 'blow', מנשבים *menashvim* 'blow'.
Many nouns and adjectives are exceptional in this way, and only some for evident morphological reasons, e.g. חיבור *Hibur* 'joint'. In particular, after an initial consonant, 'soft' is the rule: כפר *kfar* 'village', שבורים *shvurim* 'broken'.
45. Thus contrast התחבר *hitHaber* 'be joined' with התחבר *hitHaver* 'befriend' (cf. חבר *Haver* 'friend').
46. Certain *hif'il* verbs, e.g. הכיר *hikir* 'know', הגיע *higía* 'arrive', הגיד *higid* 'tell', though traditionally classed as *n*- initial roots because of their *i* prefix vowel (and 'hard' ב, כ, פ), are today best considered as deriving from exceptional two-consonant roots (casually, they often have the *-e-* prefix vowel typical of two-consonant *hif'il* verbs, e.g. מכיר, מגיע *mekir, megía* etc.) So too some twenty *hif'il* verbs, e.g. הגן *hegen* 'defend', המס *hemes* 'melt', הקל *hekel* 'lighten', traditionally classed as 'doubled consonant' roots (ג.נ.נ. *g.n.n*, מ.ס.ס. *m.s.s.* etc.). Few have a clearly related verb etc. with such a doubled consonant. Actually, a few verbs that are indeed traditionally classed as having a two-consonant root do have a related verb (in *pi'el* and /or *hitpa'el*) with a doubled consonant: קם *kam* 'arise' → קומם *komem* 'arouse', עף *af* 'fly' → עופף *ofef* 'fly', while a few yield a *pi'el* or *hitpa'el* that has an added *-y-* or *-v-* for middle root consonant, e.g. קיים *kiyem* 'maintain', התדיין *hitdayen* 'litigate'.

As regards inflection, the second vowel is *e*, not *i* - except that before present, and 1st, 2nd person past suffixes, the vowel becomes regular: הגנתי...הגנו, מגן...מגינות, יגן *hegánti...hegénu, megen...meginot, yagen* 'defend'.

47. In two particular verb types, even gutturals followed by a *full* vowel cause upsets:

(1) For many, especially in formal usage: before א, ר as a middle root letter in *pi'el* or in *pu'al*, the high vowels *i, u* become *e, o* respectively, e.g. צירף *tseref* 'combine', מפואר *mefo'ar* 'luxurious' (and always in related nouns: צירוף *tseruf* 'combination'). Similarly, *i → e* in FUT, IMP, INF of *nif'al*, before א, ע, ה, ח, ר, e.g. תיאלץ *tealets* 'will be forced', יירדם *yeradem* 'will fall asleep', להיחתם *leheHatem* 'to be signed'.

(2) After gutturals as middle root letters in FUT of *pa'al*, *o → a*, e.g. ינאם *yin'am* 'will speak', יבחן *yivHan* 'will test' (optional casually for ח).

48. Casually (1) there is no vowel-copying after ח *H*; (2) there need be no *i → e* in *hif'il* before ח *H*, e.g. החליט *hiHlit*.

49. א, which has 'guttural' effects *within* the word and occasionally (cf. above) at the end, has exceptional effects before suffixes beginning with a consonant or short vowel: (a) In 1st, 2nd past tense forms, *a → e*: נקראתי *nikréti* 'I was called', רופאת *rupéta* 'you were cured' etc. Exception: *pa'al* קראתי *karáti* 'I called' etc.; (b) Present feminine singular suffix *et → t*: קוראת *koret* 'call', נקראת *nikret* 'am called' etc.

50. In other phonologically identical (but morphologically different) cases, *n*- cannot drop: ניגנתי *nigánti* 'I played', not *ניגתי *nigáti*.

51. An exception is ליפול *lipol* 'to fall'.

52. A few other *y*- roots do not change their vowels to *e*, and they maintain the *y*- on paper at least - though it is not pronounced in the forms in question. Hence, e.g.:

yizom	'will initiate'	ייזום
yinok/yinak	'will suckle'	יינוק/יינק
yishan	'will sleep'	יישן

However, יצק *yatsak* 'pour' and ירש *yarash* 'inherit' are maverick in the infinitive: לצקת *latséket*, לרשת *laréshet*.

53. This process is no longer productive, hence the *nif'al* of ייזם *yazam* 'initiate' is ניזם *nizam*.

54. Casually יינמס *yinames*, infinitive even more generally להינמס *lehinames* (as if *n.m.s.*).

55. A few relate to two-consonant verbs, e.g. גר *gar* 'live' ~ התגורר *hitgorer* 'stay' (see 40.18).

Chapter 41

1. Adjectives can sometimes function like nouns while not intrinsically nouns themselves: גבוה *gavóa* 'tall' can mean 'a tall one' provided a specific noun is implied; otherwise it has none of the qualities of a noun as listed below, and is quite different from words such as מבוגר *mevugar* 'adult, an adult', קדוש *kadosh* 'sacred, a saint' which are adjectives *and* nouns.

2. The circumstances in which nouns too do without הוא *hu* 'is' are complex; see 16.3.

3. There are a handful of exceptions, e.g. מלא *male* 'full (of)', שווה *shave* 'worth'; see 15.5.2.

4. An exception is תפוס *tafus* 'occupied'.

Thus examples like the following involve a present tense *pu'al* verb, not a past participle (which would indeed be adjectival):

anáHnu muzmanim al-yedey ha-iriya	אנחנו מוזמנים על-ידי העירייה
we are-invited by the municipality	

5. Apparent exceptions: מפואר *mefo'ar* 'luxurious', מפורט *meforat* 'detailed' and a few others (with middle א or ר) are often distinct from מפואר *mefo'ar* 'embellished' (c: *mefu'ar*) and מפורט *meforat* 'specified' (c: *mefurat*) etc. The latter are truly verb-based, the former no longer.

6. Like many adjectives, these can relate both to persons and to 'looks, behaviour' and the like: מבט כועס *mabat ko'es* 'an angry look'.

7. The past tense of all these adjectives is היה (תואם) *haya (to'em)* 'was (compatible)' etc.

8. Unless context suggests otherwise, (d), (e) are taken as adjectives. For 'ongoing action', not the passive but the active verb (including *hitpa'el*) is preferred.

9. Exceptions include מיטלטל *mitaltel* 'portable' and מידבק *midabek* 'contagious'.

10. These examples also illustrate the variations in the vowels or consonants caused by 'anomalous root types' involving gutturals etc. (see 40.18-23).

11. This has soft or hard ב, כ, פ, depending on whether they are soft or hard in the noun 'base'.

12. Also: 'asterisked'.

13. The active *hifil* verb here happens to mean 'cause wonder'.

14. These are *indirectly* related to *nif'al* verbs meaning 'be desired' and 'it is possible (+ infinitive)'.

15. Patterns (1) and (2), where verb-based, are close enough to verbs to take adjectival adverbs (other verb-based patterns do not):

    shatuf/menugav **yafe**   'washed/dried **nicely**'   שטוף/מנוגב יפה

16. Formal pronunciation: *ratov* (pattern (4)).

17. Occasional use is also made of phrases with the particle בר *bar* (f.s. בת *bat*, m.pl. בני *bney*) + action noun, e.g. בר-ביצוע *bar-bitsúa* 'achievable', בר-הוכחה *bar-hoHaHa* 'provable'. By contrast, בר-אכילה *bar-aHila* and בר-חילוף *bar-Hiluf* are not commonly used for 'edible, exchangeable'.

18. קביל *kavil* is also 'open to complaint', based on *pa'al* קבל *kaval* 'complain'.

19. However, (שחורים) *shHor(im)* 'black', (אפורים) *afor(im)* 'grey'. This pattern often overlaps with (2). For כבוד ~ כבודים *CaCoC ~ CCoCim*, see (16).

20. Some exceptions: לבן *lavan* 'white', חום *Hum* 'brown', בז' *bezh* 'beige'.

21. Arguably exceptions: חיוור *Hiver* 'pale', עיקש *ikesh* 'stubborn'.

22. Syntactic reasons will be given for not regarding these as prefixes in the full sense of the word.

23. These are also used as 'personality' *nouns*; see 38.2, pattern (14).

24. By contrast, parallel forms with י- *-i* are used of 'things' (see pattern (11)):

    nisayon akshani   'a stubborn attempt'   ניסיון עקשני
    be-ófen akshani   'in stubborn fashion'   באופן עקשני

25. This often looks identical to pattern (11) of the *CaCCan + i* kind, *e.g.* עקשני *akshani* 'stubborn'.

26. Contrast תעשייתי *taasiyati* 'industrial' (תעשייתו *taasiyato*), קדחתני *kadaHtani* 'feverish' (קדחתו *kadaHto*), חדרתי *Haderáti* 'from Hadera' (חדרה *Hadéra*).

27. Rarely, ־ות *-ut* of nouns ending in ־אות *-a'ut* is dropped before adding י- *-i*, e.g. עתונאי *itona'i* 'journalistic' (עתונאות *itona'ut* 'journalism'), בנקai *banka'i* 'bank...' (בנקאות *banka'ut* 'banking'). But some אי- *-ai* endings belong to (ii) above, and some to the אי- *-a'i* suffix in (10) below.

    Some exceptions to the whole adjustment rule: עממי *amami* 'popular' (עם *am*), שמימי *shmeymi* 'heavenly' (שמיים *shamáyim*), איטלקי *italki* 'Italian' (איטליה *itálya*).

28. This sometimes looks identical to the לטפני *latfani* or עקשני *akshani* patterns (7,11).

29. From countries: תוניסאי *tunisái* 'Tunisian' (תוניס *tunis* 'Tunisia'), מרוקאי *marokái* 'Moroccan' (מרוקו *maróko*). Note the stress.

30. Do not confuse with יבי- *-ívi*, לי- *-áli* and other one-piece suffixes (18-19).

31. However, even אמריקאי *amerikái* 'American', הולנדי *holándi* 'Dutch', מרוקאי *marokái* 'Moroccan' and a few others in this 'Jewish realm' fail to stress their י- *-i* (sometimes shifting the stress within the stem).

32. י- *-i* on *all* foreignisms might best be seen as integral to the word. Thus דמוקרטי *demokráti* is stressed as an *-áti* adjective, without reference to דמוקרט *demokrat* - and could be listed in 41.4 alongside פרקטי *prákti* 'practical' etc. (18).

33. An exception is חיפאי *Heyfa'i* 'of Haifa' (חיפה *Heyfa*).

34. But, e.g. שקספירי *shekspirí* 'Shakespearian'. In addition, certain other 'relational' suffixes are used with some foreignisms (and not just borrowed along with them), e.g.

| *-ívi* | יבי- : | sportívi | 'sporting' | ספורטיבי |
| *-iáli* | יאלי- : | studentiáli | 'of students' | סטודנטיאלי |

36. Contrast pattern (3).

37. Belonging to this pattern but with variations due to gutturals: רחב *raHav* 'wide'.

38. This is occasionally a present tense verb pattern (15).

Belonging to this pattern but with variations due to gutturals is חסר *Haser* 'missing'.

39. Unlike other derivational prefixes and suffixes, such as in תחפושת *taHpóset* 'fancy dress' and עצבני *atsbani* 'uptight', these can be detached from the 'base' in coordination:

    reHov Had- o du-sitri   רחוב חד- או דו-סטרי

                         'a one- or two-way street'

They are thus semi- (or 'quasi-') prefixes. This is even more evident when they are prefixed to nouns, e.g. דו-המשמעות *du-ha-mashma'ut* 'the ambiguity'. (See note 42).

40. Or *eropi*.

41. Exceptionally, a point-of-compass noun + *adjective* is used as a base:

    mizraH tiHon   מזרח תיכון   mizraH-tiHoni   מזרח-תיכוני

    N   ADJ   'Middle East'   'Middle Eastern'

Similarly, ים-תיכוני *yam-tiHoni* 'mediterranean'.

42. By contrast, ה- *ha-* in the underlying noun phrase can come *between* prefix and noun (see 38.4):

    ha-tat-hakara/tat-ha-hakara   התת-הכרה/תת-ההכרה

    the sub conscious/sub the conscious   'the subconscious'

43. A similar suffix is לחמצה *lemeHtsa* :

    mevudad lemeHtsa   'semi-insulated'   מבודד למחצה

44. See also negatives (29.8).

45. אל- *al-* (as opposed to על- *al-* 'super-') is rare.

46. תת *tat* is far more prevalent with phrase-based adjectives (41.5.1).

47. By contrast, many nouns - though masculine - have *-ot* in the plural; and some feminine nouns have *-im* (see ch.39). This does not affect adjectives: they respond to the *gender* of their noun, not to its endings, hence אבות חדשים *avot Hadashim* 'new fathers'.

48. The choice of ending depends on the adjective pattern.

49. The feminine is exceptional in a few arbitrary adjectives, not directly verb-based, notably:

    Sub-type

    (a): בודדה *bodeda* 'lonely', שוממה /שוממת *shomema* / *shomémet* 'waste';

    (b): מתמדת *matmédet* 'steady (increase...)', ממארת *mam'éret* 'malignant', מספקת *maspéket* 'sufficient';

(e): מופלאה *mufla'a* 'wondrous', מוכרחה *muHraHa* 'must', מוזרה *muzara* 'odd',
מוכנה *muHana* 'ready', מוצקה *mutsaka* 'solid';

(f): נכבדה *niHbada* 'respectable', נפלאה *nifla'a* 'wonderful', נחמדה *neHmada*
'nice', נאמנה *neemana* 'loyal', נוראה *nora'a* 'awful' (also casually
נוראי ~ נוראית *nora'i* ~ *nora'it*).

50. This includes reduplicative pattern (8): its suffix, having fixed vowels, need not be
considered a suffix.

51. Minor exceptions: (i) foreignisms take ית-, ים-, ות- *-it*, *-im*, *-ot*, e.g. מבסוט
mabsut 'happy', זיפת *zift* 'bad', פייר *fer* 'fair'; (ii) מת ~ מתה, חי ~ חיה *met* ~ *méta*
'dead', *Hay* ~ *Háya* 'alive', where stress is as in matching verb; (iii) sundry:
אכזר ~ אכזרית, מועטה/מועטת ~ מועט *muat* ~ *mu'ata* /sometimes *mu'étet* 'little', טיפש
aHzar ~ *aHzarit* 'cruel', נייד ~ ניידת *nayad* ~ *nayédet* 'mobile', pattern (5) טיפש
tipesh ~ *tipsha* 'foolish', פיקח ~ פיקחית *pikéaH* ~ *pikHit* 'clever', pattern
(8) (with human associations) קטנטונת *ktantónet* 'tiny', שמנמונת *shmanmónet*
'plump', שחרחורת *shHarHóret* 'swarthy'.

52. Abbreviation of הנאמר למעלה *ha-neemar lemáala.*

53. יהודי *yehudi* 'Jewish' obligatorily takes ה- *-a* for feminine.

54. Suffixed adjectives do not act as *adverbs* either: דבר איטי* *daber iti* ('speak slow').
Apparently, being 'derived' adjectives (usually), they are 'protected' against these 'marginal' adjectival roles.

55. Where the feminine singular adjective already ends in ת- *-t*, its ending is unchanged
in the 'construct': שורצת *shorétset* 'swarming' (free or construct).

Chapter 42

1. These and certain other prepositions have a wide range of meanings and functions,
so the gloss is selective.

2. By contrast, verbs governing a direct object usually have an intervening preposition
את *et* when the direct object is a suffix, e.g. ראו אתכם *ra'u etHem* 'they saw you' (occasionally ראוכם *reuHem*, but never an unsuffixed object pronoun: ראו אתם* *ra'u
atem*); and most *nouns* have the choice (register etc. permitting) between direct suffix
and intervening של *shel* + suffix: חברכם/החבר שלכם *HaverHem / he-Haver shelaHem*
'your friend' (but never unsuffixed חבר אתם* *Haver atem*).

3. לולא/אלמלא *lule / ilmale* 'were it not for' falls in between being a preposition and
a conjunction. Like the former it introduces nouns; like the latter (e.g. אם *im* 'if') it
introduces clauses without an introductory -ש *she-*; but unlike both, it introduces pronouns without converting them to suffixes, e.g.:

    lule hu　　　　　　　　　'were it not for him'　　　　　　　לולא הוא

4. The feminine plural forms have been omitted.

5. Casually also *bishvilaH, bishvilánu, bishvilaHem, bishvilahem* by analogy with -ל *le-*
below.

6. Literary usage also allows בם *bam.*

7. Thus עם *im* 'with' has two paradigms, one strictly formal and the other for any
usage.

8. Substandard alternative: *oteH.*

9. Casual alternative: אותכם *otHem*. The feminine plural, being inherently formal, is
אתכן *etHen.*

10. Thus the 2nd plural ending is exceptional in taking the stress. The same is true of
2nd plural תם- *-tem* in verbs, in formal usage.

11. Casual alternative: *kamóhem.*

12. Casual alternative: *miméno*, making it distinct from *miménu* 'from us'.

13. Formally also מאתנו *meitánu* (cf. literary מאת *me'et* 'from, by') as distinct from ממנו *miménu* 'from *him*'.

14. Casual alternative: ממכם *mimHem*.

15. Formally either מן *min* (before -ה *ha-* 'the') or מ- *mi-*, otherwise only מ- *mi-*. Inflection turns מן *min* to ממ- *mim-*.

16. Used with verbs of 'fear (of)' and the like.

17. The 2nd and 3rd plural is pronounced *aleHem, alehem* puristically (making it identical to עליהם, עליכם *aleHem, alehem*), and otherwise *eleHem, elehem*.

18. בינם *benam* is used for 3rd plural in the idiom בינם לבין עצמם *benam leven atsmam* 'among themselves'.

Bibliography

The transcription system used for this Bibliography is the conventional academic one, and not the simplified system used in the main text.

Agmon-Fruchtman, M. 1980. *Bi-netivey ha-taxbir.* Tel Aviv: University Publishing Projects.

1981. Al ha-yidua ve-al implikacyot signoniyot. *Hebrew Computational Linguistics* 18:5-18.

1982. *Ha-yadua ve-ha-satum.* Tel Aviv: Papyrus Publishing House.

1984. Ha-teurim 'lefeta' ve-'bimhirut': hearot axadot beikvot maamaro šel eliezer rubinštayn. *Hebrew Computational Linguistics* 21:5-8.

Altbauer, M. 1964. New negation constructions in Modern Hebrew. In *For Max Weinreich on his seventieth birthday: studies in Jewish languages, literature and society,* eds L.S. Dawidowicz *et al.* The Hague: Mouton.

Amit, M. 1976. Seder ha-teurim ba-mišpat. *Lešonenu* 41:44-7.

Ariel, S. 1972. The functions of the conjugations in colloquial Israeli Hebrew. *Bulletin of SOAS* 35:514-30.

Avineri, Y. 1962. Toar ha-poal be-ivrit. *Lešonenu La-am* 13:97-123.

Azar, M. 1972. Simaney hacraxa, milot hadraxa ve-ha-yexidot ha-miloniyot šel ha-poal: iyun taxbiri ve-semanti bi-fealim baaley mašlimim. *Lešonenu* 36:220-7, 282-6.

1976. The emphatic sentence in Modern Hebrew. In *Studies in Modern Hebrew syntax and semantics,* ed. P. Cole. Amsterdam: North-Holland.

1977. *Šetax ve-omek be-taxbir.* Haifa: Haifa University Press.

1978. Kama hearot le-mišpetey ha-baalut ve-ha-šayaxut. *Hebrew Computational Linguistics* 13:5-12.

1981. Aval, ela ve-ela še ba-ivrit šel yameynu. *Lešonenu* 44: 133-48.

1985. Miyun ha-smixuyot. In *Hora'a akademit šel ha-ivrit bat-zmanenu,* ed. R. Nir. Jerusalem: International Center for University Teaching of Jewish Civilization.

Bachi, R. & Schmelz, U.O. 1974. Hebrew as everyday language of the Jews in Israel - statistical appraisal. In *Salo Wittmayer Baron Jubilee Volume : On the occasion of his eightieth birthday,* vol. 2, ed. S. Liebermann. New York: American Academy for Jewish Research.

Bahat, Y. & Ron, M. 1960. *Vedayek.* Jerusalem: Hakibbutz Hameuchad.

Bar-Adon, A. 1966. New imperative and jussive formation in contemporary Hebrew. *Journal of the American Oriental Society* 86:410-13.

1975. *The rise and decline of a dialect.* The Hague: Mouton.

Barkaï, M. 1975. On phonological representations, rules and opacity. *Lingua* 37:363-76.

1978. Phonological opacity vs. semantic transparency: two cases from Israeli Hebrew. *Lingua* 44:363-78.

Barri, N. 1978. Šem-toar muacam ve-šem-ecem mut'ar be-ivrit xadaša diburit. *Lešonenu* 42:252-70.

Ben-Asher, M. 1969. *Hitgabšut ha-dikduk ha-normativi.* Haifa: Hakibbutz Hameuchad.

1972. *Iyunim be-taxbir ha-ivrit ha-xadaša.* Tel Aviv: Hakibbutz Hameuchad.

1974. Al milot-ha-yaxas ba-ivrit ha-xadaša. *Lesonenu* 38:285-94.

1976. Šimušey ha-makor ve-šem ha-peula bi-lešon ha-mikra leumat lešon yameynu. In *Rabin Jubilee Volume*, eds B-Z. Fischler & R. Nir. Jerusalem: Council on the Teaching of Hebrew.

1977. Mašlim ha-toar ke-xelek mišpat nifrad. *Ha-ḥinnukh* 49:229-33.

Bendavid, A. 1956. Šem ha-peula u-mašmeuyotav. *Lešonenu La-am* 6, fascicles 4,6,8; and 7, fascicles 1,3,4.

Ben-Hayyim, Z. 1971. Morphology. In *Encyclopedia Judaica*, vol. 8: 103-18.

Ben-Horin, G. 1976. Aspects of syntactic preposing in Spoken Hebrew. In *Studies in Modern Hebrew syntax and semantics*, ed. P. Cole. Amsterdam: North-Holland.

Bentolila, Y. 1983. The sociophonology of Hebrew as spoken in a rural settlement of Moroccan Jews in the Negev. Hebrew University Ph.D. dissertation.

Ben-Zadok, E. & Goldberg, G. 1984. Voting patterns of Oriental Jews in development towns. *The Jerusalem Quarterly* 32:16-27.

Berman, R.A. 1974. Haca'ot le-nisuax klaley het'em ba-ivrit ha-xadaša. *Hebrew Computational Linguistics* 8:1-17.

1975a. Mimušam ha-morfologi šel tahalixim taxbiriyim be-maarexet ha-binyanim. *Hebrew Computational Linguistics* 9:25-39.

1975b. Rišumam ha-miloni šel pealim - šorašim u-vinyanim. In *Rosén Memorial Volume*, ed. U. Ornan & B-Z. Fischler. Jerusalem: Council on the Teaching of Hebrew.

1976. On derived and deriving nominals in Modern Hebrew. In *Studies in Modern Hebrew syntax and semantics*, ed. P. Cole. Amsterdam: North-Holland.

1978. *Modern Hebrew structure*. Tel Aviv: University Publishing Projects.

1979a. Lexical decomposition and lexical unity in the expression of derived verbal categories in Modern Hebrew. *Afroasiatic Linguistics* 6,3:1-25.

1979b. Form and function: impersonals, passives, and middles in Modern Hebrew. *Berkeley Linguistic Society* 5:1-27.

1980a. On the category of auxiliary in Modern Hebrew. *Hebrew Annual review* 4:15-37.

1980b. The case of an (S)VO language: subjctless constructions in Modern Hebrew. *Language* 56:759-76.

1982a. Dative marking of the affectee role: data from Modern Hebrew. *Hebrew Annual Review* 6;35-59.

1982b. On the nature of 'oblique' in bitransitive constructions. *Lingua* 56:387-411.

Bin-Nun, Y. 1979. Al ha-mišpat ha-stami. *Lešonenu La-am* 30,8:225-39.

Blanc, H. 1957a. Hebrew in Israel: trends and problems. *Middle East Journal* 11:397-409.

1957b. Keta šel dibur ivri-yisreeli. *Lešonenu* 21:33-9.

1964. Israeli Hebrew texts. In *Studies in egyptology and linguistics in honour of H.J. Polotsky*, ed. H.B. Rosén. Jerusalem: Israel Exploration Society.

1965. Some Yiddish influences in Israeli Hebrew. in *The field of Yiddish*, 2nd. collection, ed. U. Weinreich. The Hague: Mouton.

1968. The Israeli koine as an emergent national standard. In *Language problems of developing nations*, ed. J.A. Fishman *et al.* New York: Wiley and Sons.

Blau, Y. 1952. Benoni pa'ul be-hora'a aktivit. *Lešonenu* 18:67-81.

1957. Toar ha-poal ke-nos'im ve-xi-nesu'im hegyoniyim ve-dikdukiyim be-ivrit. *Lešonenu* 20:30-40.

1966. *Yesodot ha-taxbir.* Jerusalem: Hamachon Hayisraeli Lehaskala Bichtav.

1967. *Dikduk ivri šitati.* Jerusalem: Hamachon Hayisraeli Lehaskala Bichtav.

1973. Keycad lehavxin ba-hora'a beyn musa akif le-te'ur. *Lešonenu* 37:202-4.

1977a. Le-rik'a šel tofa'a axat be-taxbir ha-ivrit ha-xadaša. *Lešonenu La-am* 28:175-6.

1977b. An adverbial construction in Hebrew and Arabic: sentence adverbials in frontal position separated from the rest of the sentence. *Proceedings of the Israel Academy of Sciences and Humanities* 6,1.

Bolozky, S. 1972. Categorial limitations on rules in the phonology of Modern Hebrew. Univ. of Illinois Ph.D. dissertation.

1977. Fast speech as a function of tempo in natural generative phonology. *Journal of Linguistics* 13:217-38.

1978a. Word formation strategies in the Hebrew verb system: denominative verbs. *Afroasiatic Linguistics* 5,3:111-36.

1978b. Some aspects of Modern Hebrew phonology. In *Modern Hebrew structure,* R.A. Berman. Tel Aviv: University Publishing Projects.

1979. On the new imperative in colloquial Hebrew. *Hebrew Annual Review* 3:17-23.

1980. Paradigm coherence: evidence from Modern Hebrew. *Afroasiatic Linguistics* 7,4:103-26.

1981. Note on frequency in phonetic change. *Hebrew Annual Review* 5:15-19.

1982. Remarks on rhythmic stress in Modern Hebrew. *Journal of Linguistics* 18:275-89.

Forthcoming. Subsidiary stress in Modern Hebrew. *Glossa.*

Borer, H. 1984. *Parametric syntax: case studies in Semitic and Romance languages.* Dordrecht: Foris.

Chayen, M.J. 1973. *The phonetics of Modern Hebrew.* The Hague: Mouton.

Chayen & Dror, Z.1976. *Introduction to Hebrew transformational grammar.* Tel Aviv: University Publishing Projects.

Cohen. D. & Zafrani, H. 1968. *Grammaire de l'hébreu vivant.* Paris.

Cole, P. 1976a. A causative construction in Modern Hebrew: theoretical implications. In *Studies in Modern Hebrew syntax and semantics,* ed. P. Cole. Amsterdam: North-Holland.

1976b. An apparent asymmetry in the formation of relative clauses in Modern Hebrew. In *Studies in Modern Hebrew syntax and semantics,* ed. P. Cole. Amsterdam: North-Holland.

Cole, P., Harbert, W., Sridhar, S., Hashimoto, S., Nelson, C. & Smietana, D. 1977. Noun phrase accessibility and island constraints. In *Syntax and Semantics,* vol. 8, ed. P. Cole & J. M. Sadock. New York: Academic Press.

Cooper, R.L. 1984. A framework for the description of language spread: the case of Modern Hebrew. *International Social Science Journal* 36:87-112.

Dahan, H. 1980. Ha-refleksiviyut. *Lešonenu* 44:219-23.

1981. Štey hearot be-taxbir. *Lešonenu La-am* 32:15-20.

Dascal, M. & Katriel, T. 1977. Between semantics and pragmatics: the two types of 'but' - Hebrew 'aval' and 'ela'. *Theoretical Linguistics* 4:143-72.

Devens, M. 1978. The phonetics of Israeli Hebrew: 'Oriental' versus 'General' Hebrew. UCLA Ph.D. dissertation.

1980. Oriental Israeli Hebrew: a study in phonetics. *Afroasiatic Linguistics* 7:127-42.

1981. Misconceptions about accent and national origin among native Israeli Hebrew speakers: a preliminary report. *Hebrew Annual Review* 5:21-36.

Di-nur, M. 1979. Ha-kešer beyn mašma'ut le-cura bi-tecurot baalot siyomet -an ve-ani. In *Kodesh Jubilee Volume*, ed. C. Rabin & B-Z. Fischler. Jerusalem: Council on the Teaching of Hebrew.

Donag-Kinnarot, R. 1978. Lešon ha-talmidim ba-arec. Hebrew University Ph.D. dissertation.

Enoch, P. & Kaplan, G. 1969. Ha-mahut ha-fisikalit šel ha-hatama ba-ivrit ha-yisreelit. *Lešonenu* 33:208-22.

Eytan, E. 1953. Al šimuš ha-levay u-mišpat ha-zika. *Lešonenu La-am* 4,2:3-8.

Fellman, J. 1973. *The revival of a classical tongue* : *Eliezer Ben-Yehuda and the modern Hebrew language*. The Hague: Mouton.

Fischler, B-Z. 1975. Bet, kaf, pe degušot u-refuyot šelo kadin ba-ivrit ha-yisreelit. In *Rosén Memorial Volume*, eds U. Ornan & B-Z. Fischler. Jerusalem: Council on the Teaching of Hebrew.

      1976. Ha-suplecya u-mekoma be-hora'at safa nosefet. In *Rabin Jubilee Volume*, eds B-Z. Fischler & R. Nir. Jerusalem: Council on the Teaching of Hebrew.

Fishman, J.A. & Fisherman, H. 1975. The 'official languages' of Israel: their status in law and police attitudes and knowledge concerning them. In *Multilingual political systems* : *problems and solutions*, eds J.G. Savard and R. Vigneault. Quebec: Laval University Press.

Friedman, S.Y. 1971. Kol ha-kacar kodem. *Lešonenu* 35:117-29.

Gil, D. 1982. Case marking, phonological size, and linear order. In *Syntax and semantics*, vol. 15, ed. P.J. Hopper & S.A. Thompson. New York: Academic Press.

Givón, T. 1973. Complex NP's, word order and resumptive pronouns in Hebrew. In *You take the high node. I'll take the low node*, eds C. Corum, T.C. Smith-Stark & A. Weiser. University of Chicago, Ill.: Chicago Linguistic Society.

      1975. On the role of perceptual clues in Hebrew relativization. *Afroasiatic Linguistics* 2,8:131-47.

      1976. On the VS word order in Israeli Hebrew: pragmatics and typological change. In *Studies in Modern Hebrew syntax and semantics*, ed. P. Cole. Amsterdam: North-Holland.

      1978. Negation in language: pragmatics, function, ontology. In *Syntax and semantics*, vol. 9, ed. P. Cole. New York: Academic Press.

      1979. From discourse to syntax: grammar as a processing strategy. In *Syntax and semantics*, vol. 12, ed. T. Givón. New York: Academic Press.

Glinert, L.H. 1974. A generative study of peripheral categories in Modern Hebrew. University of London Ph.D. dissertation.

      1976a. Ha-sofit -ayim: dugma be-homonimiyut taxbirit leksikalit. *Hebrew Computational Linguistics* 10:1-16.

      1976b. How *od* : a study of a Modern Hebrew pseudo-quantifier. In *Studies in Modern Hebrew syntax and semantics*, ed. P. Cole. Amsterdam: North-Holland.

      1977a. Number-switch: a singular feature-change rule of Modern Hebrew. *Afroasiatic Linguistics* 4,2:1-38.

      1977b. Kamatim ve-taviyot ivriyim be-hora'at safa šniya. *Oraxot* 10:36-46.

      1978. Cerufey šem 'clalim' ba-ivrit ha-meduberet. *Hebrew Computational Linguistics* 13:28-69.

      1982a. Negative and non-assertive in contemporary Hebrew. *Bulletin of SOAS* 45:434-70.

      1982b. The preposition in Biblical and Modern Hebrew: towards a redefinition. *Hebrew Studies* 23:115-25.

      1983. The recovery of Hebrew. *Times Literary Supplement* 17 June 1983.

1987. Toar ha-poal ha-mekašer. *Am Va-sefer* 4:68-79.

1988a. A unified framework for identity and similarity structures: Israeli Hebrew *kmo.* In *Studia linguistica et Orientalia Memoriae Haim Blanc dedicata,* ed. P. Wexler, A. Bjorg & S. Somekh. Wiesbaden: Otto Harrassowitz.

1988b. Adverbial clauses and clauses as adverbials. *Fucus: A Semitic/Afroasiatic gathering in remembrance of Albert Ehrman,* ed. Y. Arbeitman. Amsterdam: Benjamins.

Gordon, A. 1982. The development of the participle in Biblical, Mishnaic and Modern Hebrew. *Afroasiatic Linguistics* 8,3:121-66.

Goshen-Gottstein, M.H. 1969. *Introduction to the lexicography of Modern Hebrew.* Jerusalem: Schocken.

Greenbaum, S. 1984. Corpus analysis and elicitation tests. In *Corpus linguistics,* ed. J. Aarts & W. Meijs. Amsterdam: Rodopi.

Grosu, A. 1969. The isomorphism of semantic and syntactic categories as illustrated by a study of sex and gender, numerosity and number in English and Hebrew. *Hebrew Computational Linguistics* 1:35-50.

Guiora, A.Z., Beit-Hallahmi, B. & Sagi, A. 1980. A cross-cultural study of symbolic meaning. *Balshanut Shimushit* 2: xxvii-xl.

Hayon, Y. 1971. Relative clauses with nonverbal predicates. *Hebrew Computational Linguistics* 4:7-68.

1972. Having and being in Modern Hebrew. *Hebrew Computational Linguistics* 5:10-23.

1973. *Relativization in Hebrew.* The Hague: Mouton.

Hofman, J.E. & Fisherman, H. 1972. Language shift and maintenance in Israel. In *Advances in the sociology of language,* ed. J.A. Fishman, vol. 2. The Hague: Mouton.

Horn, L.R. 1978. Remarks on neg-raising. In *Syntax and semantics,* vol. 9, ed. P. Cole. New York: Academic Press.

Ioup, G. 1975. Some universals for quantifier scope. In *Syntax and semantics,* vol. 4, ed. J.P. Kimball. New York: Academic Press.

Kaddari, M.Z. 1965. Al herkevey šem-toar ba-ivrit šel yameynu. *Lešonenu La-am* 16:195-206.

1977. Hitnahaguta ha-taxbirit šel milat ha-tafkid *vaday. Hebrew Computational Linguistics* 11:47-60.

1982. Axad ha-xidušim be-taxbir ha-ivrit ha-modernit (ceruf ha-yaxas *kekaze*). *Hebrew Computational Linguistics* 19:44-6.

1985. Toar ha-poal ba-ivrit ha-modernit. In *Hora'a akademit šel ha-ivrit bat-zmanenu,* ed. R. Nir. Jerusalem: International Center for University Teaching of Jewish Civilization.

Kogut, S. 1984. *Psukey ha-toxen, tivam u-mivneyhem.* Jerusalem: Akademon.

Kopelovich, Z. 1982. Modality in Modern Hebrew. Univ. of Michigan Ph.D. dissertation.

Landau, J.M. 1970. Language study in Israel. In *Current trends in linguistics,* vol. 6, ed. T.A. Sebeok. The Hague: Mouton.

Landau, R. 1975. Mišpat ha-zika u-mišpat levay ha-toxen le-sugav ba-ivrit šel yameynu. *Bikoret U-faršanut* 7-8:132-6.

1985. Mišlav he-hagut ke-emca'i le-haba'at méser xevrati-politi. In *Uma ve-lašon* (Arieh Tartakover Memorial Volume), ed. M. Zohari *et al.* Jerusalem: Brit Ivrit Olamit.

Laufer, A. 1974. *Hangana šel ivrit meduberet.* Jerusalem: Akademon.

1976. Te'ur foneti šel tnu'ot. *Lešonenu* 41:117-43.

Lerner, Y. 1976. Iyun mexudaš bi-šeelat ha-havxana beyn musa le-te'ur. *Lešonenu* 40:148-51.

Levenston, E.A. 1970. *English for Israelis*. Tel Aviv: Israel Universities Press.

1976. Likrat stilistika hašvaatit šel ha-anglit ve-ha-ivrit. In *Ki-lešon Amo*, ed. R. Nir & B-Z. Fischler, Jerusalem: Council on the Teaching of Hebrew.

Levi, J.N. 1976. A semantic analysis of Hebrew compound nominals. In *Studies in Modern Hebrew syntax and semantics*, ed. P. Cole. Amsterdam: North-Holland.

Mackenzie, J.L. 1978. Ablative-locative transfers and their relevance for the theory of case-grammar. *Journal of Linguistics* 14:129-56.

Malisdorf, Z. 1979. Love through death in Israeli Hebrew. *Afroasiatic Linguistics* 7,2:1-16.

Masson, M. 1976. *Les mots nouveaux en hébreu moderne*. Paris: Publications Orientalistes de France.

Mirkin, R. 1962. I u-šemot ha-peula ba-ivrit ha-sifrutit ha-xadaša. *Lešonenu* 26:217-19.

1968. Miškal mefu'al. *Lešonenu* 32:140-52.

Morag, S. 1973. Hearot axadot le-teura šel maarexet ha-tnu'ot šel ha-ivrit ha-meduberet be-yisra'el. *Lešonenu* 37:205-14.

Nadel, E. & Fishman, J.A. 1975. English in Israel: a sociolinguistic study. In *The spread of English: the sociology of English as an additional language*, ed. J.A. Fishman *et al*. Rowley, Mass.: Newbury House.

Nahir, M. 1978. Normativism and educated speech in Modern Hebrew. *International Journal of the Sociology of Language* 18:49-67.

Netzer, N. 1976. *Ha-nikud halaxa le-maase*. Tel Aviv: Massada.

Nir, R. 1979. Ha-mivne ha-semanti šel šemot ha-ecem ha-murkavim ba-ivrit ha-xadaša. *Hebrew Computational Linguistics* 15:5-18.

1981. Ma beyn šimuš normativi leveyn šimuš kavil ba-ivrit ha-xadaša. In *Iyunim be-valšanut u-ve-semiotika*, ed. L. Davis *et al*. Haifa; Haifa University Press.

Ornan, U. 1968. *Kaze* ve-*kazot*. *Lešonenu* 32:46-52.

1973. Bicueyhem šel crorot fonemiyim. In *Mikra'a le-torat ha-hege*, ed. U. Ornan. Jerusalem: Akademon.

1978. Ha-yidua u-mišpat ha-zika. *Hebrew Computational Linguistics* 14:5-7.

1979a. *Ha-mišpat ha-pašut*. Jerusalem: Akademon.

1979b. Od al hora'ot ha-binyanim. In *Kodesh Jubilee Volume*, ed. C. Rabin & B-Z Fischler. Jerusalem: Council on the Teaching of Hebrew.

Peretz, Y. 1972. *Ivrit ka-halaxa*. Tel Aviv: Sreberk.

Podolski, B. 1981. Ha-taam ke-gorem morfologi ba-ivrit ha-xadaša. *Lešonenu* 45:155-6.

Rabin, C. 1940 (republished 1973). Hašmatat ha-pocec ha-sidki ba-ivrit ha-meduberet ve-hitgabšut kvucat tnu'ot xadaša. In *Mikra'a le-torat ha-hege*, ed. U. Ornan. Jerusalem: Akademon.

1958. Le-xeker ha-ivrit ha-sifrutit ha-xadaša. *Lešonenu* 22:246-57.

1974a. *A short history of the Hebrew language*. Jerusalem: Jewish Agency.

1974b.*Taxbir lešon ha-mikra*. Jerusalem: Akademon.

1977. Anaxnu ve-ha-lašon. In *Maasaf Yerušalayim*, vol. 11-12. Jerusalem.

1978. Xoker ha-normativiyut ha-lešonit. In *Xoker ha-normativiyut: Kovec le-zexer mordexay ben-ašer*. Haifa: Haifa University Press.

1983. The sociology of normativism in Israeli Hebrew. *International Journal of the Sociology of Language* 41:41-56.

1985. Miškeley ha-šem. In *Sefer Avraham Even-Shoshan*, ed. B. Luria. Jerusalem: Kiryat-Sefer.

Ravid, D. 1977. Mispar hebetim šel baayat seder ha-markivim be-ivrit yisreelit modernit. *Hebrew Computational Linguistics* 11:1-45.

Reif, J.A. 1968. Construct state nominalization in Modern Hebrew. Univ. of Pennsylvania Ph.D. dissertation.

Ring, Y. 1971. La-havxana beyn musa akif ve-te'ur ha-poal. *Maalot* 2,6:13-18.

    1975. Pealim baaley hacraxa šel nose mexubar. *Hebrew Computational Linguistics* 9:17-24.

Rosén, H.B. 1955. *Ha-ivrit šelanu.* Tel Aviv: Am-Oved.

    1956. Mefu'al ba-ivrit ha-yisreelit. *Lešonenu* 20:139-48.

    1962. Some possible systemic changes in a Semitic system of language. In *Proceedings of the ninth international congress of linguistics*, ed. H.G. Lunt. The Hague: Mouton.

    1965. Quelques phénomenes d'absence et de présence de l'accord dans la structure de la phrase en hébreu. *Comptes-Rendus du Groupe Linguistique d'Études Chamito-Sémitiques* 10:78-86.

    1966a. *Ivrit tova.* Jerusalem: Kiryat-Sefer.

    1966b. Composition adjectivale et adjectifs composés en hébreu israëlien. *Comptes-Rendus du Groupe Linguistique d'Études Chamito-Sémitiques* 10:126-35.

    1976. Haknayat netiyat ha-poal ha-ivri ha-regulari - bsisey moca u-maavarim sdurim. *Rabin Jubilee Volume*, ed. B-Z. Fischler & R. Nir. Jerusalem: Council on the Teaching of Hebrew.

    1977. *Contemporary Hebrew.* The Hague: Mouton.

    1979. Klalim sdurim u-musag ha-sdirut. *Lešonenu La-am* 30,3:67-96.

    1982. Aspektim be-xeker seder xelkey ha-mišpat ba-ivrit ha-yisreelit ha-ktuva. In *Proceedings of the eighth world congress of Jewish studies.* Jerusalem: World Union of Jewish Studies.

Ross, J.R. 1967. Constraints on variables in syntax. M.I.T. Ph.D. dissertation.

Rubinstein, E. 1968. *Ha-mišpat ha-šemani.* Tel Aviv: Hakibbutz Hameuchad.

    1970. Te'ur ha-nesu ve-te'ur ha-mišpat u-maamadam ha-taxbiri. *Lešonenu* 35:61-74.

    1971. *Ha-ceruf ha-pooli.* Tel Aviv: Hakibbutz Hameuchad.

    1973. *Kax, axeret* ve-*ex* be-maamad šel mašlim šeni. *Lešonenu La-am*, 24,10:292-6.

    1975. Tezuzot kategorialiyot be-cerufey šem ha-toar ba-lašon ha-meduberet. In *Rosen Memorial Volume*, ed. U. Ornan & B-Z. Fischler. Jerusalem: Council on the Teaching of Hebrew.

Sadka, Y. 1977. Hu katav al ha-xol al ha-xol al ha-xol. *Hebrew Computational Linguistics* 11:61-112.

    1978. *Taxbir ha-mišpat.* Jerusalem: Akademon.

    1980. Mišpat yixud ha-nose ve-ha-kinuy ḥu. *Lešonenu* 44:224-39.

    1981. *Taxbir ha-ivrit be-yameynu.* Jerusalem: Kiryat-Sefer.

Schmelz, U.O. 1984. New immigrants' progress in Hebrew - statistical data from Israel. In *Contemporary Jewry - Studies in honor of Moshe Davis*, ed. G. Wigoder. Jerusalem: Institute of Contemporary Jewry.

    1987. The population of Jerusalem. In *American Jewish Year Book.*

Schwarzwald, O.R. 1972. Tnu'ot be-ivrit u-ve-anglit: Mexkar spektrografi. *Hebrew Computational Linguistics* 6:1-11.

    1975. Od be-inyan yaxasey šoreš ve-degem ba-milon ha-ivri. *Hebrew Computational Linguistics* 9:47-59.

    1976a. Li-šeelat takinutam ve-hivacrutam šel mišpetey ha-yixud. *Bar Ilan Annual* 18.

1976b. Al hora'at ha-nasu ha-murxav: Ha-nasu ha-murxav ve-ha-oged. *Haḥinnukh* 3,4:246-52.

1977a. Hora'at ha-nasu ha-murxav: Nivim, musa'im, toarey poal u-nesu'im kolelim. *Hahinnukh* 49:365-72.

1977b. Yicugam ha-leksikali šel ha-pealim ha-alulim. *Hebrew Computational Linguistics* 12:25-36.

1979a. Ha-brera: Iyun bi-šeela taxbirit, logit u-morfologit. *Lešonenu* 43:112-20.

1979b. Ma beyn ha-mišpat he-xaser la-mišpat ha-stami? *Lešonenu La-am* 30,1:15-21.

1979c. Klaley het'em be-min u-ve-mispar ve-universalim lešoniyim. *Bikoret U-faršanut* 13-14:251-63.

1980. Me-alilut ha-poal he-alul. *Balšanut Šimušit* 2:63-76.

1981a. *Dikduk u-meci'ut ba-poal ha-ivri*. Ramat Gan: Bar Ilan University.

1981b. Frequency factors as determinants in the binyanim meanings. *Hebrew Studies* 22:131-7.

1982a. Hearot axadot al netivot *yeš* ve-*en* kiyumiyot ba-ivrit ha-meduberet. *Hebrew Computational Linguistics* 19:59-70.

1982b. Feminine formation in Modern Hebrew. *Hebrew Annual Review* 6:153-78.

1984. Analogy and regularization in morphophonemic changes: the case of the weak verbs in postbiblical and colloquial Modern Hebrew. *Afroasiatic Linguistics* 9,2:87-100.

Seikevics, C. 1979. The possessive construction in Modern Hebrew: a sociolinguistic approach. Georgetown Univ. Ph.D. dissertation.

Semiloff-Zelasko, H. 1973. Vowel-reduction and loss in Modern Hebrew fast speech. *Hebrew Computational Linguistics* 7:53-72.

Sivan, R. 1974. *Leksikon le-šipur ha-lašon*. Jerusalem: Karni.

Statistical abstracts of Israel. 1984. Jerusalem: Israel Central Bureau of Statistics.

Stern, N. 1977. Ha-poal ba-ivrit ha-yisreelit. Tel Aviv Univ. Ph.D. dissertation.

1979. Poaley *et* ba-ivrit ha-yisreelit. *Hebrew Computational Linguistics* 15:28-57.

1981. Pealim tlat-atriyim ha-mexilim mašlim *et* ve-axerim. *Hebrew Computational Linguistics* 17:46-61.

1983. Xasrey guf u-mispar u-dmuy poal + šem-poal ba-ivrit ha-yisreelit. *Lešonenu* 47:248-63.

Svartvik, J. 1968. Plotting divided usage with dare and need. *Studiana Neophilologica* 40:130-40.

Tēnē, D. 1962. Ha-mešex ha-nimdad šel ha-tnu'ot be-ivrit. *Lešonenu* 26:220-68.

Turkel, R. 1976. Mišpatim šemaniyim u-mišpetey *yeš* be-rusit u-ve-ivrit xadaša. *Hebrew Computational Linguistics* 10:17-26.

Werner, F. 1981. Die Wortbildung der hebräischen Adjektiva. University of Vienna Ph.D. dissertation.

Yannai, Y. 1974. Pealim merubey-icurim ba-lašon ha-ivrit. *Lešonenu* 38:118-30, 183-94.

Zilkha, A. 1970. Negation in Hebrew. Univ. of Texas Ph.D. dissertation.

Ziv, Y. 1976. On the reanalysis of grammatical terms in Hebrew possessive constructions. In *Studies in Modern Hebrew syntax and semantics*, ed. P. Cole. Amsterdam: North-Holland.

Index